From Protracted Conflict to Sustainable Peace?

From Protracted Conflict to Sustainable Peace?

The Humanitarian-Development-Peace Nexus and International Law

Edited by
HEIKE KRIEGER
Professor of Public Law and International Law, Freie Universität Berlin, Germany

GIEDRE JOKUBAUSKAITE
Senior Lecturer in International Law, University of Glasgow, UK

ASLI OZCELIK
Senior Lecturer in International Law, University of Glasgow, UK

ANDREAS BUSER
Senior Research Associate, Freie Universität Berlin, Germany

OXFORD
UNIVERSITY PRESS

OXFORD
UNIVERSITY PRESS

Great Clarendon Street, Oxford, OX2 6DP,
United Kingdom

Oxford University Press is a department of the University of Oxford.
It furthers the University's objective of excellence in research, scholarship,
and education by publishing worldwide. Oxford is a registered trade mark of
Oxford University Press in the UK and in certain other countries.

Published in the United States of America by Oxford University Press
198 Madison Avenue, New York, NY 10016, United States of America

British Library Cataloguing in Publication Data

Data available

Library of Congress Control Number: 2026931293

ISBN 9780198967378

DOI: 10.1093/9780198967385.001.0001

Printed and bound by
CPI Group (UK) Ltd., Croydon, CR0 4YY

MIX
Paper | Supporting
responsible forestry
FSC® C013604

The manufacturer's authorized representative in the EU for product safety is
Oxford University Press España S.A. of Parque Empresarial San Fernando de Henares,
Avenida de Castilla, 2 – 28830 Madrid (www.oup.es/en or product.safety@oup.com).
OUP España S.A. also acts as importer into Spain of products made by the manufacturer.

Preface

In late summer of 2025, efforts to end the Russian aggression against Ukraine peacefully have intensified. However, the plurality of interests involved, the bad faith of the aggressor, the power asymmetries between the aggressor and the victim state, and the apparent disregard for the international legal framework, among other factors, render a sustainable peace unlikely.

The war against Ukraine is by no means the only example of the phenomenon of protracted armed conflicts yet it is a particularly prominent one. Many other cases, such as the simultaneously evolving civil war in Sudan, receive lesser international attention but underscore the sobering insight: Existing (legal) governance regimes are ill-equipped to address the far-reaching consequences of protracted conflicts or bring about their resolution. Humanitarian and development needs remain vast and unrelenting, while the political will to address these needs, to constrain civilian harm in conflict, and to support efforts to achieve sustainable peace often falters.

During the last decade, international institutions have aimed to respond to these challenges by establishing the policy of the humanitarian-development-peace (HDP) nexus (so-called triple nexus). The approach seeks to combine immediate relief with longer-term development assistance and peacebuilding, aiming to provide a more holistic response to protracted conflicts worldwide. Yet, it is not only subject to multiple critiques but also further weakened by ongoing geopolitical developments.

Recent years have not seen a strengthening of international cooperation to resolve protracted conflicts—rather the opposite. Humanitarian and development assistance in conflict-affected environments faces severe and growing setbacks in light of budget cuts and restructuring processes. Support budgets have been constrained by shifting political priorities and fiscal pressures, whereas military budgets have been ramped up, particularly in Europe, to respond to Russia's unlawful war against Ukraine and rising geopolitical tensions. The global policy climate has further shifted with the United States' announced direction on development aid under the second Trump administration, signalling a reorientation towards narrowly defined national interests and away from multilateral approaches.

Within the aid sector, these cuts have deepened two parallel but interconnected conversations and proposals on how to move forward. One focuses on immediate needs—forced by shrinking budgets—prioritising life-saving humanitarian programmes and (potentially) letting go of activities in the development and peace domains, as well as broader social service provision. The other looks further ahead and reframes the current crisis as an opportunity to fundamentally rethink power structures, the political economy of the aid sector, and the ethical frameworks that underpin humanitarianism. From this perspective, the crisis only re-emphasises the need for transformation—reimagining humanitarian aid as a sustained response to the needs generated by protracted crises which differ from sudden-onset emergencies. Whether these shifts will reinvigorate the HDP nexus or push for its replacement by other policy concepts remains an open question. This book offers a diversity of perspectives and empirical evidence that promise to inform these conversations.

While the HDP nexus has emerged as a policy of global governance in relation to how international institutions respond to protracted conflict, taken literally it can also be understood as a holistic approach to the drivers and consequences of protracted conflict. This approach emphasizes that protracted conflicts harm virtually all aspects of civilian life, infrastructure and environment, inflicting far-reaching, long-term harm on affected societies. The holistic approach also acknowledges that protracted conflicts cannot be understood or resolved by disregarding their root causes, which often have local and global dimensions, such as exclusion, poverty and exploitation. It is this broader understanding of the HDP nexus that this book adopts in its examination of how international law responds to the challenge of protracted conflict.

The aim of this book is to provide researchers, policymakers and practitioners with new conceptual, interpretive, institutional and empirical knowledge and approaches, in order to better understand the relationship between protracted armed conflicts and the HDP nexus. For this purpose, the contributions to this book investigate a range of relevant questions: Can international law address and mitigate the self-perpetuating and interconnected drivers and consequences of protracted conflicts sufficiently and holistically? Is there a need for tailoring international legal responses when conflict is protracted? What are the implications of seeing protracted conflict through critical legal, critical space, political economy, or gender lenses for international responses to protracted conflict? How do protracted conflicts challenge the siloed approach in international law and its institutional landscape to humanitarian, development, and peace fields? Does international law offer normative bases, avenues, and tools for anchoring an integrated and accountable approach to humanitarian, development, and peace objectives in protracted conflict and in pursuit of sustainable peace? In this respect, is there a particular role for human rights-based approaches?

To address these questions, we invited a group of academics and practitioners from diverse geographical and disciplinary backgrounds to provide their reflections on the subject of this book. Our authors include critical scholars as well as officials working for international organisations, lawyers alongside political scientists, researchers from conflict-affected regions as well as analysts from countries primarily engaged in providing assistance to such regions.

Bringing this book about was enabled by the collaborative research project: 'The Law of Protracted Conflict: Overcoming the Humanitarian-Development Divide'. The project was jointly funded by the UK Arts and Humanities Research Council (AHRC) and the German Research Foundation (Deutsche Forschungsgemeinschaft, DFG, project number 428994051) under the UK-German Funding Initiative in the Humanities between 2020 and 2024. We gratefully acknowledge their generous support, which, inter alia, allowed us to convene an in-person workshop in Berlin in summer 2022 and a series of panel discussions that brought together scholars, practitioners, and policymakers from across sectors and regions. Another key event was a multi-stakeholder workshop on human rights approaches to protracted conflicts, held in Glasgow in 2023, with active participation from government agencies, international organisations, and civil society.

We thank all contributors to these workshops and the book for their expertise, candour, and willingness to engage in constructive debates, which have greatly enriched the reflections presented in this book. We are particularly grateful to our project partners at the University of Rosario (Colombia) and the Pan African Institute Cardinal Martino at the Catholic University of Congo (DRC) for their contribution to the intellectual development of this book, including the workshops that they organised in Bogota, Kinshasa and Bukavu, the outcomes of which have enriched our discussions and contributions. A special thank you goes to Johanna Cortes Nieto and Pascal Sundi who coordinated the work of the project in their respective institutions.

In addition to the overall funding for our research project by the DFG and AHRC, the open-access publication of this volume was made possible by additional financial support from the open-access publication fund established by Freie Universität Berlin. We thank the University of Glasgow School of Law for additional financial support for research assistance.

We also want to express our thanks to Robin Geiss, who was initially a principal investigator of our research project but subsequently assumed the role of Director of the United Nations Institute for Disarmament Research (UNIDIR).

Finally, we are deeply grateful to all research assistants and student assistants involved in the editing process, including Georg Fritz, Héloïse Guichardaz, Charlotte Droese, Mia Hanebeck, and Jack Jones.

Andreas Buser, Heike Krieger, Asli Ozcelik, Giedre Jokubauskaite

Contents

Abbreviations

AU	African Union
CBD	Convention on Biological Diversity
CofEU	Council of the European Union
DAC	Development Assistance Committee
DDR	disarmament, demobilization and reintegration
DFS	Department of Field Support
DNH	do no harm
DPF	development policy financing
DRC	Democratic Republic of the Congo
ESCR	economic, social, and cultural rights
EAC	East African Community
ECGLC	Economic Community of the Great Lakes Countries
FCV	fragility, conflict, and violence
HDP nexus	humanitarian-development-peace nexus
HRBA	human rights-based approach
HRH	human right to health
HRP	Humanitarian Response Plan
ICC	International Criminal Court
ICCPR	International Covenant on Civil and Political Rights
ICGLR	International Conference on the Great Lakes Region
ICJ	International Court of Justice
ICRC	International Committee of the Red Cross
IDP	Internally Displaced Person
IFC	International Finance Corporation
IFMA	Integrated Forestry Management Agreement
IHL	international humanitarian law
IHRL	international human rights law
INCAF	International Network on Conflict and Fragility
IO	international organization
IOIA	International Organizations Immunities Act
IOM	International Organization for Migration
IR	international relations
ISSSS	International and Security and Stabilisation Support Strategy
JNIM	Jama'at Nasr al-Islam wal Muslimin
MEA	multilateral environmental agreement
NSDP	National Strategic Development Plan
OCHA	United Nations Office for the Coordination of Humanitarian Affairs
OECD	Organisation for Economic Cooperation and Development

PBF	United Nations Peacebuilding Fund
PLO	Palestine Liberation Organization
RTD	right to development
SADC	Southern African Development Community
SDG	Sustainable Development Goals
TWAIL	Third World Approaches to International Law
UCDP	Uppsala Conflict Data Program
UN	United Nations
UNCT	United Nations Country Team
UNGA	United Nations General Assembly
UNGPs	United Nations Guiding Principles
UNHCR	United Nations High Commissioner for Refugees
UNOCD	United Nations Office on Drugs and Crime
UNRWA	United Nations Relief and Works Agency for Palestine Refugees in the Near East
UNSDCF	UN Sustainable Development Cooperation Framework
WB	World Bank

Contributors

Jinan Bastaki is Associate Professor of Legal Studies at New York University, Abu Dhabi, and has held research posts at the University of Oxford. She specializes in public international law, forced displacement, refugee law, and citizenship. Her work has appeared in major publications, including the *Journal of Refugee Studies, Citizenship Studies, Refugee Survey Quarterly*, and others.

Armi Beatriz E. Bayot was legal counsel to the Republic of the Philippines government peace panel in talks with the Moro Islamic Liberation Front (MILF) from 2010 to 2016. She has worked at the Office of the Solicitor General, where her fields of practice included indigenous peoples' rights law, and the Commission on Human Rights, where she served as the Deputy Coordinator of the National Task Force Against Extrajudicial Killings and as the founding Head of the Analysis Unit. She is pursuing a Doctor of Philosophy in Law degree at the University of Oxford, where she is undertaking research on the human rights implications of intrastate peace agreements. She is a contributing editor at CIL Dialogues, the blog of the Centre for International Law (CIL) of the National University of Singapore (NUS).

Andreas Buser is Senior Research Associate at Freie Universität Berlin and was Co-Investigator of the AHRC-DFG funded project on 'The Law of Protracted Conflicts'. He obtained fellowships with the Berlin Potsdam Research Group 'The International Rule of Law—Rise or Decline?' (funded by the German Research Foundation) and the New York University's Jean Monnet Center (Emile Noël fellowship). His research expertise lies predominantly in the fields of international economic law, international environmental law, international humanitarian law and human rights, and German constitutional law.

Amanda Cahill-Ripley is Senior Lecturer in Law at the School of Law and Social Justice, University of Liverpool, UK. She is also Visiting Researcher at Lancaster University Law School, UK. In 2023 she was awarded the prestigious Glasgow Law Fellowship at the University of Glasgow, UK. Dr Cahill-Ripley is an expert in international human rights law, with a specialization in economic, social, and cultural rights. Her recent monograph *Socio-Economic Rights in Times of Crisis and Normality—Article 4 Limitations under the International Covenant on Economic, Social and Cultural Rights* (2025) is published by Bristol University Press. She is currently working on her third monograph, *Economic, Social and Cultural Rights and Peacebuilding*, for Cambridge University Press. Dr Cahill-Ripley is also working with the UN Committee on Economic, Social and Cultural Rights on drafting a new General Comment on the Application of the International Covenant on Economic, Social and Cultural Rights in times of Armed Conflict.

Antonio Coco is Associate Professor (Senior Lecturer) at Essex Law School, University of Essex. His research focuses on general international law, the application of international law to new technologies, and international criminal law. He is the author of *The Defence of Mistake of Law in International Criminal Law: A Study on Ignorance and Blame* (Oxford University Press, 2022). He holds a PhD in Law from the University of Geneva and is admitted to practice in Italy.

Johanna del Pilar Cortes-Nieto is Associate Professor at the Faculty of Law, Universidad del Rosario, Bogotá. She was also recently appointed Governmental Expert to the Working Group on the Additional Protocol to the American Convention on Human Rights in the area of Economic, Social, and Cultural Rights (Protocol of San Salvador) of the Organization of American States. Her research focuses on constitutional law, law and development, and economic, social, cultural, and environmental rights.

Daniëlla Dam-de Jong is Professor of International Sustainable Development Law at the Grotius Centre for International Legal Studies at Leiden University. She is a member of the Dutch Advisory Committee on Public International Law (CAVV), Deputy Chair of the IUCN WCEL Specialist Group on Environmental Security and Conflict Law, and one of the Editors-in-Chief of the *Netherlands Yearbook of International Law*. Her publications include a monograph on *International Law and Governance of Natural Resources in Conflict and Post-Conflict Situations* (CUP 2015), and the *Research Handbook on International Law and Environmental Peacebuilding*, co-edited with Britta Sjöstedt from Lund University (Edward Elgar 2023).

Marc DuBois is an independent humanitarian analyst/consultant, member of Médecins sans Frontières's International Board, Senior Fellow at SOAS University of London, and Senior Lecturer at the Geneva Centre of Humanitarian Studies. His work typically explores the 'big picture'—the principles, culture, architecture, and politics of humanitarian action. Key publications include research on humanitarian ethics, breaking away from siloed humanitarianism though nexus thinking, and a call for a more back-to-basics approach to humanitarian aid. Prior to consulting, Marc spent fifteen years at Médecins sans Frontières, and he is the former Executive Director of MSF-UK/IE.

Andrés Gómez Rey is Associate Professor at the Faculty of Law at Universidad del Rosario, Bogotá. His research focuses on environmental law, public utilities, and mining law. These subjects are addressed with law-focused perspectives as well as with insights from law and anthropology, legal sociology, and critical science studies.

Kathryn Greenman is Senior Lecturer in the Faculty of Law at the University of Technology Sydney. Kathryn has published widely on state responsibility, international investment law, and international humanitarian and human rights law. Her monograph *State Responsibility and Rebels: The History and Legacy of Protecting Investment Against Revolution* was published with Cambridge University Press in 2021.

Héloïse Guichardaz is a PhD graduate from the University of Glasgow. Her research focuses on the United Nation's de facto absolute immunity. She has a Bachelor's in Public Law and a Masters in Public International Law, both from the Université Jean Moulin Lyon III, Lyon. She was a research assistant for the AHRC-DFG funded project on 'The Law of Protracted Conflicts' as well as a graduate teaching assistant in public international law and European law. She has recently published an article titled 'A Human Rights-based Challenge: The Key to Unlocking the UN's Immunity Problem?' in the *Brazilian Journal of International Law*. She currently works as a PA-X Peace Agreement Analyst at the University of Edinburgh.

Giedre Jokubauskaite is Senior Lecturer in International Law at the University of Glasgow. Previously she was Visiting Research Fellow at the University of Rosario (Bogota, Colombia), Research Fellow at the Centre for International Sustainable Development Law at the University of Cambridge, and Post-Doctoral Research Associate at the Durham Law School. She was a guest editor of the special issue on the Environmental and Social Framework (ESF) of the World Bank published by *Leiden Journal of International Law*. She has conducted research on the case studies of development projects in Colombia, Georgia, Kazakhstan, Cameroon, and the DRC.

Olga Jurasz is Professor of Law at the Open University. She specializes in legal responses to violence against women and international law. Her research focuses on gender and post-conflict situations, transitional justice, international criminal law, and international human rights law. She co-edited *Gender and War: International and Transitional Justice Perspectives* (Intersentia 2019) together with Solange Mouthaan.

Pablo Kalmanovitz is Professor in the Department of International Studies at the Instituto Tecnológico Autónomo de México, Mexico City. He has published widely on normative aspects of collective violence, particularly on the international regulation of armed force. Since 2022, he is coeditor of the *Yearbook of International Humanitarian Law* and his book *The Laws of War in International Thought* was published by Oxford University Press in 2020.

Patience Kabamba holds university degrees in Mathematics from the University of Kikwit, Development Studies from Durban University of Technology, and Philosophy from the Jesuit School of Philosophy, Paris and the Catholic University of Leuven, and a PhD in Cultural Anthropology from Columbia University, New York. After directing the Anthropology Programme at Utah Valley University, Orem, Utah, Dr Kabamba was recently appointed Professor of Anthropology at the National Pedagogical University (UPN) in Kinshasa. He is also an international consultant on community forestry and the protection and preservation of biodiversity in the Congo Basin forests. He has extensively published on his experiences as an anthropologist in the Nande community of Butembo, in Grand Nord Kivu, and on his twenty years as a student and university professor in the US.

Heike Krieger is Professor of Public Law and International Law at Freie Universität Berlin. She was Chair of the DFG-funded research group 'The International Rule of Law—Rise or Decline?' and Principal Investigator of the AHRC-DFG funded project on 'The Law of Protracted Conflict'. She has been Visiting Professor at the Centre for Transnational Legal Studies, London, and the Universities of Macerata and Paris 1 Panthéon-Sorbonne. Heike Krieger is the president of the German Society of International Law and a member of the DFG Senate. Her research focuses on general international law, international humanitarian law, and human rights protection.

Amrei Müller is currently Lecturer/Assistant Professor at Sutherland School of Law, University College Dublin. Her research is situated in human rights law and international humanitarian law (IHL). She is particularly interested in international, European, and comparative human rights law, (democratic) institutional dimensions of human rights law, the human rights to health and science, and IHL and its interplay with human rights law.

Ansgar Münichsdorfer is Research Fellow and PhD candidate at the Chair for Public Law and International Law (Professor Heike Krieger) at Freie Universität Berlin, where he worked on the AHRC-DFG funded project on 'The Law of Protracted Conflict'. His research focuses on the law of international organizations, particularly the World Bank, as well as international humanitarian law.

Asli Ozcelik is Senior Lecturer in International Law at the University of Glasgow, where she directs the Erasmus Mundus Joint Master in International Law of Global Security, Peace and Development and was co-investigator of the AHRC-DFG funded project on 'The Law of Protracted Conflicts'. Previously, she was Postdoctoral Researcher and Academic Coordinator of the Glasgow Centre for International Law and Security. Her research expertise and published work are concerned with international peace and security, with a focus on armed conflicts and peacemaking.

Moa Peldán is a doctoral researcher in War Studies at the Swedish Defence University. Her research is on United Nations peacekeeping and how we can theoretically and historically understand how ideas of war and peace are re/conceptualized and re/negotiated in relation to liberal interventionism. Her research interests also include militarized narratives in popular culture and archives as political and aesthetic sites. Previously, she worked at the Stockholm International Peace Research Institute (SIPRI) and with peacekeeping training at the Swedish Armed Forces.

Janosch Prinz is Associate Professor of Social and Political Philosophy at Maastricht University. His research aims to connect normative and empirical approaches to studying politics. An example of this aim is the co-development of the radical form of realism in political theory. His current work focuses on theorizing democracy that can withstand the threat posed by oligarchic power (www.antioligarchy.net).

Mutaz M. Qafisheh is Professor of International Law and the founding and former dean, Hebron University College of Law and Political Science, Palestine. He holds a PhD from the Graduate Institute, Geneva, and is a practising lawyer, pleading before the International Criminal Court. He chairs the board of trustees of Law for Palestine Organization, UK. He advises the UN, PLO, NGOs, and companies. He supervises PhDs in Europe and the Middle East. Qafisheh worked as Human Rights Officer at the UN Human Rights Office in Geneva, Beirut and Ramallah and as Legal Advisor for the Palestinian Parliament, and co-founded the Human Rights Programme of Al-Quds-Bard Honors College, NY. He has authored six books and seventy peer-reviewed articles and is a member of twenty global foundations.

Abhisekh Rodricks is a lawyer specializing in international and European law and currently serves as an Operational Risk Manager at UBS Investment Bank. He has been a panelist at the UN, World Bank, and Commonwealth forums, and has consulted for the

Border Security Force under India's Ministry of Home Affairs. Passionate about access to justice, he has advised the UN and governments including Afghanistan and Somaliland on conflict, peace, and security, while also leading research projects with universities and institutions worldwide. He has published twenty-six research papers, authored one book and edited six, and delivered lectures at the State University of New York and WBNUJS.

Andrés Rodríguez Morales is a PhD candidate at Universidad de los Andes, Bogotá. His research focuses on human rights, particularly the rights of workers and people excluded from the social security system. His latest articles, 'Espacializando a Galanter: Hacia un Derecho Procesal Situado' and 'What Happens after the Ruling? Everyday Impacts in Colombia', were published in *ACME: An International Journal for Critical Geographies* and *Oñati Socio-legal Studies*, respectively.

Ben Saul is Challis Chair of International Law at the University of Sydney, Associate Fellow of the International Centre for Counter-Terrorism in The Hague, and elected Fellow of the Australian Academy of Social Sciences. He has published twenty books and taught at Oxford, Harvard, The Hague, and Xiamen Academies of International Law, and specializes in international counter-terrorism law.

Conrad Schetter is Director of the Bonn International Centre for Conflict Studies (BICC) and Professor for Peace and Conflict Studies at the University of Bonn. His research focuses on violent conflicts, livelihood, and humanitarian interventions in Afghanistan and East Africa.

Britta Sjöstedt is Senior Lecturer at the Faculty of Law of Lund University, researching and teaching environmental law and public international law. She is currently conducting research focusing on the environment, armed conflict, peacebuilding, and corporate responsibility. She recently co-edited the *Research Handbook on International Law and Environmental Peacebuilding* (Edward Elgar 2023) together with Daniëlla Dam-de Jong. She is also one of the founding board directors of the Environmental Peacebuilding Association (EnPax).

Pascal Sundi Mbambi is Associate Professor at the *Université Pédagogique Nationale* (Kinshasa, DRC) and Academic Secretary General of the *Institut Supérieur Pédagogique de Mbanza-Ngungu*. He holds a PhD in Political Science from the University of Antwerp, where his research examined capacity development through the DRC–UNICEF 'Healthy Village' programme. His work focuses on governance, development policy, and human rights in sub-Saharan Africa, with emphasis on water, sanitation, and health. He is affiliated with Antwerp's Law and Development Research Group and has published in leading journals, including *The International Journal of Human Rights* and *Anthropologie & développement*.

Rafael Tamayo-Álvarez is Professor and Member of the research group on international law at Universidad del Rosario, Bogotá. His research combines the analysis of international economic law and political economy.

Sofie-Marie Terrey is a PhD candidate in international law at Freie Universität Berlin where she worked on the AHRC-DFG funded project on 'The Law of Protracted Conflict'.

Her research focuses on the intersection of international human rights law and international private sector development finance. She has also published in the areas of global security and counterterrorism.

Sâ Benjamin Traoré is Associate Professor at the African Institute for Research in Economics and Social Sciences, Faculty of Governance, Economics and Social Sciences, Mohammed VI Polytechnic University, Rabat and an Extraordinary Lecturer at the Faculty of Law of the University of Pretoria. He holds a PhD from the University of Neuchâtel and an LLM from the Geneva Academy of International Humanitarian Law and Human Rights. His research covers various fundamental issues in international law. He is the author of a book on *The Interpretation of United Nations Security Council Resolutions* (*L'interprétation des resolutions du Conseil de sécurité*, Helbing, 2020).

Leena Vastapuu is Academy Research Fellow at the Tampere Peace Research Institute, University of Tampere, and Visiting Researcher at the University of Turku, Finland. She leads the HomeFront project (2025–2029), which examines everyday militarization in Finland through a gender lens. Currently on leave from her role as Senior Lecturer at the Swedish Defence University, Vastapuu has published extensively on gender, peace, and security in war and its aftermath, with a particular focus on marginalized groups such as child and female soldiers. She is the author of *Liberia's Women Veterans: War, Roles and Reintegration* (Zed Books, 2018).

Martin Wählisch is Associate Professor of Transformative Technologies, Innovation and Global Affairs, School of Government, University of Birmingham. He holds a JD in Public International Law and an MA in Mediation. His current research focuses on new methods and practices for conflict analysis, peacebuilding, and diplomacy, including the use of emerging technologies and behavioural science.

1

Conceptualizing Protracted Conflicts and International Law

Andreas Buser, Giedre Jokubauskaite, Heike Krieger, and Asli Ozcelik

A. Overview

Currently, there is a widespread perception that contemporary protracted armed conflicts raise a range of unprecedented challenges across legal, institutional, humanitarian, developmental, environmental, and (geo-)political dimensions that require their protractedness to be brought into the spotlight. In Afghanistan, Colombia, the Democratic Republic of the Congo (DRC), Iraq, Palestine, Sudan, Ukraine, Yemen, and other parts of the world, populations have been affected by conflict for years on end, and in some instances for decades. Such conflicts are causing immense human suffering at enormous social and economic cost, while international responses seem unable to substantially ameliorate the situation. Against this background, policy agendas repeatedly point towards the need to facilitate the so-called triple nexus between humanitarian, development, and peace objectives to address the far-reaching consequences of protracted conflicts in a complementary and sustainable manner.[1] However, overcoming the divide between these three fields remains a serious challenge in the absence of a better understanding of the legal drivers, characteristics, relations, and mechanisms that shape humanitarian, developmental, and peace interventions in protracted armed conflicts. This book aims to address this gap by offering an analysis of how international law can be rethought to account for the compounded nature of physical, social, economic, and environmental issues facing societies entrapped in protracted conflicts in substantive and institutional international legal responses.

[1] United Nations General Assembly (UNGA), 'Review of the United Nations Peacebuilding Architecture' 70th sess, (27 April 2016) UN Doc A/RES/70/262; United Nations Security Council (UNSC) Res 2282 (27 April 2016) UN Doc S/Res/2282; UNGA, 'One Humanity: Shared Responsibility' UN GAOR 70th sess, Agenda Item 73(a) (2 February 2016) UN Doc A/70/709 ('*Agenda for Humanity*'); World Bank and others, 'The Grand Bargain' (Inter-Agency Standing Committee 2017) <https://interagencystandingcommittee.org/grand-bargain/grand-bargain-shared-commitment-better-serve-people-need-2016> accessed 27 March 2024 ('*Grand Bargain*'); General Secretariat of the Council of the European Union, 'Council Conclusions: Operationalising the Humanitarian-Development Nexus' (19 May 2017) Doc No 9383/17; World Bank and United Nations, *Pathways for Peace: Inclusive Approaches to Preventing Violent Conflict* (World Bank 2018) ('*Pathways for Peace*'); Development Assistance Committee (DAC) of the Organisation for Economic Co-Operation and Development (OECD), 'Recommendation on the Humanitarian-Development-Peace Nexus' (2019) Doc No OECD/LEGAL/5019 ('*OECD DAC Recommendation*').

Andreas Buser, Giedre Jokubauskaite, Heike Krieger, and Asli Ozcelik, *Conceptualizing Protracted Conflicts and International Law* In: *From Protracted Conflict to Sustainable Peace?* Edited by: Heike Krieger, Giedre Jokubauskaite, Asli Ozcelik, and Andreas Buser, Oxford University Press. © Andreas Buser, Giedre Jokubauskaite, Heike Krieger, and Asli Ozcelik 2026. DOI: 10.1093/9780198967385.003.0001

To enable such an analysis, this introduction offers a conceptual, legal, and critical framework on the notion of protracted armed conflict from an international law perspective. In Section B, we discuss the concept of 'protracted conflict', focusing on its policy origins, features, and legal relevance. In Section C, we highlight some of the potential pitfalls of employing 'protractedness' as a lens of analysis. In Section D, we outline the legal challenges that protracted conflicts present, and in Section E, we introduce and critically engage with the concept of the 'triple nexus'. Section F explains the research design and the structure of the book, the contributions of the individual chapters, and our major findings.

B. Conceptualizing 'Protracted Conflict'

Attempts to pin down a specific definition of 'protracted conflict' are bound to run into difficulties. Neither international humanitarian law (IHL) in particular nor international law in general currently include a legal notion of 'protracted conflict' to which specific legal consequences are attached. Indeed, the exercise of defining 'protractedness' can be particularly taxing. First, factually drawing a temporal boundary between non-protracted and protracted situations naturally comes with a high degree of arbitrariness. Given that 'protractedness' simultaneously refers to an abstract timeframe (a long duration) and an indeterminate process (an ongoing conflict which could not be stopped), it is difficult to draw a clear-cut line between 'protracted' and 'normal' conflict situations.

Second, in legal terms, that an armed conflict is protracted is already accepted to be a requirement for the classification of a situation as a non-international armed conflict.[2] Although the term is absent from the treaties of international humanitarian law, the requirement of 'protractedness' was authoritatively spelled out in international jurisdiction and later incorporated into the Rome Statute.[3] For the purposes of conflict classification, this requirement is not associated with the duration of a conflict, but rather with the intensity of conflict.[4] Even a conflict of short duration but a high level of violence can arguably amount to a non-international armed conflict.[5] In any case, the requirement of protractedness in the classification of non-international armed conflict leads to the question of how a further distinction between non-international

[2] Prosecutor v Tadic (Jurisdiction) IT-94-1-A (2 October 1995) para 70; Rome Statute of the International Criminal Court (adopted 17 July 1998, entered into force 1 July 2002) 2187 UNTS 90 (Rome Statute) art 8(2)(f); ICRC, 'How Is the Term "Armed Conflict" Defined in International Humanitarian Law?' (ICRC 2008).

[3] Rome Statute, art 8(2)(f).

[4] Prosecutor v Fatmir Limaj (Judgment) IT-03-66-T (30 November 2005) paras 84, 90; Prosecutor v Ramush Haradinaj (Judgment) IT-04-84-T (3 April 2008) para 49.

[5] Dapo Akande, 'Classification of Armed Conflicts: Relevant Legal Concepts' in Elizabeth Wilmshurst (ed), *International Law and the Classification of Conflicts* (OUP 2012) 32, 53; Marco Sassòli and Julia Grignon, 'Les Limites du Droit International Pénal et de la Justice Pénale Internationale dans la Mise en Œuvre du Droit International Humanitaire' in Abdelwahab Biad and Paul Tavernier (eds), *Le Droit International Humanitaire Face aux Défis du XXIe Siécle* (Bruylant 2012) 145 (criticizing the subjective nature of construing protractedness in terms of duration).

armed conflict per se and 'protracted' non-international armed conflict can be viably introduced as a matter of legal categorization.

Mindful of these factual and legal challenges, we nonetheless maintain that there is value in developing the notion of 'protractedness' as a lens of analysis. To do so, we do not approach 'protracted armed conflict' as a separate legal category of conflict. Nor do we propose a clear-cut temporal criterion in identifying 'protractedness'. Instead, we treat protracted armed conflicts as phenomena with shared, compounded, and marked features that have implications for the application of the relevant substantive and institutional legal frameworks. Developing such shared understandings of core concepts—legal or analytical—can facilitate rigorous analysis and coherent academic discussion.

1. Protracted Conflicts in Policy, Legal, and Academic Debate

Most of the definitions of 'protracted conflict' to date were developed for the purposes of policy documents. The result is that such definitions often highlight—usually only in a cursory manner—those characteristics of protracted conflicts that are specifically relevant to the policy goals in question.

One of the first reports which focused on the protractedness of conflicts as a distinct phenomenon in humanitarian work is the 2016 International Committee of the Red Cross (ICRC) report 'Protracted Conflict and Humanitarian Action: Some Recent ICRC Experiences'.[6] The report introduces its subject matter by way of giving examples, and the examples are chosen according to the conceptual needs of the ICRC, such as fragmentation in view of a rise of armed groups, challenges of humanitarian action in urban settings, or internationalization in view of party status.[7] Yet, the challenges of 'protracted conflicts' highlighted in that particular report are ICRC-specific and mostly focused on viability and future directions for humanitarian action. Understandably, the report engages neither with a diversity of development approaches, nor with international responses to protracted conflict by the United Nations (UN) and other international and regional institutions with a peace and security mandate.

On the one hand, policy documents on protracted conflicts such as the one by the ICRC emphasize the significance of the 'protractedness' prism in practice, and, as such, they render the category relevant in legal terms. Indeed, it can be argued that without wide acceptance by international institutions, 'protractedness' would not have become a salient analytical category, as it arguably is at present. On the other hand, policy reports such as the one by the ICRC provide only limited guidance on the meaning of 'protractedness' in general terms. They allow us to ascertain the content that has been prescribed to 'protracted conflict' by each individual institution, but not so much what it means in international law or global policy more generally. On the whole, policy reports are a good starting point to understand what 'protracted

[6] ICRC, 'Protracted Conflict and Humanitarian Action: Some Recent ICRC Experiences' (ICRC 2016).
[7] ibid 9–11.

conflicts' mean in institutional practice and policy discourses, but they are insufficient to provide a conceptual basis for the analysis in this book.

In legal scholarship, the notion of 'protracted conflict' has attracted attention predominantly in the context of conflict classification. More precisely, the enquiry has related to two issues: the factors that indicate the intensity of violence that meets the threshold of non-international armed conflict[8] and, connectedly, whether the Rome Statute has introduced a new category of conflict by explicitly referring to 'protracted armed conflict'.[9] The scholarship (and jurisprudence) surrounding the former, that is, intensity of violence, is concerned with distinguishing non-international armed conflicts from 'situations of internal disturbances and tensions, such as riots, isolated and sporadic acts of violence and other acts of a similar nature', which are not governed by IHL.[10] The concept of 'protracted armed conflict' as laid down in article 8(2)(f) of the Rome Statute also fulfils a similar purpose in that it offers a standard for identifying when internal upheavals reach the level of a non-international armed conflict, thus establishing the jurisdiction of the Court.[11]

This scholarship is of some but ultimately limited relevance to our understanding of protracted conflict. By regulating the application of IHL, conflict classification determines which kinds of conflicts are legally relevant for analysing protracted conflicts, while also reinforcing the very 'siloes' that the triple nexus aims to overcome. It builds legal hurdles to understand the relevance of grey areas as a challenge created by protracted conflicts, such as in cases of protracted criminal violence. However, in its limitation to a discussion of temporal duration of conflict, or intensity of physical violence, it cannot grasp the compounded nature of such conflicts.

Another strand of legal scholarship that is worth noting is that on 'prolonged occupation'. Under international law, occupation is traditionally understood as a temporary situation.[12] Therefore, situations of prolonged occupation have prompted enquiry as to whether they necessitate changes to the applicable legal framework.[13] Some scholars put forward a precise temporal criterion, such as prolonged occupations of 'more than five years'[14] or semi-prolonged occupations of 'more than three years'.[15] Others, on the other hand, advise against such criteria and the treatment of

[8] nn 1, 2, 3; Miloš Hrnjaz and Janja Simentić Popović, 'Protracted Armed Violence as a Criterion for the Existence of Non-international Armed Conflict: International Humanitarian Law, International Criminal Law and Beyond' (2020) 25 Journal of Conflict and Security Law 473.

[9] Eg Martha Bradley, 'The "Intensity" Threshold in art 8(2)(f) of the Rome Statute: The Conundrum Created by the Term "Protracted Armed Conflict" and the Possibility of a New Category of Non-International Armed Conflict' (2017) 42 South African Yearbook of International Law 42.

[10] Protocol Additional to the Geneva Conventions of 12 August 1949, and relating to the Protection of Victims of Non-International Armed Conflicts (adopted 8 June 1977, entered into force 7 December 1978) 1125 UNTS 609 (Protocol II), art 1(2).

[11] Michel Cottier, 'Art 8 Rome Statute' in Kai Ambos (ed), *Rome Statue of the International Criminal Court, Article-by-Article Commentary* (4th edn, Beck/Hart/Nomos 2022) paras 870 and 993.

[12] Jean Pictet (ed), *The Geneva Conventions of 12 August 1949: Commentary—IV Geneva Convention Relative to the Protection of Civilian Persons in Time of War* (ICRC 1958) 275.

[13] Eg Adam Roberts, 'Prolonged Military Occupation: The Israeli-Occupied Territories Since 1967' (1990) 84 The American Journal of International Law 44. On the legal consequences of Israel's prolonged occupation of the Occupied Palestinian Territory, see *Legal Consequences Arising from the Policies and Practices of Israel in the Occupied Palestinian Territory, including East Jerusalem* (ICJ Advisory Opinion of 19 July 2024).

[14] Roberts (n 13) 47.

[15] Yoram Dinstein, *The International Law of Belligerent Occupation* (CUP 2009) 116.

'prolonged occupation' as a separate legal category. For example, Koutroulis states that '[t]he adjective "prolonged" is descriptive' and suggests focusing on 'whether and to what extent the duration of an occupation affects the interpretation and application of . . . [the applicable] rules'.[16] In its focus on establishing clear-cut temporal categories the 'prolonged occupation' discussion suffers from the same limitations as the debate on 'protracted armed conflicts' as a conflict category for understanding the characteristics of 'protracted conflict'. Yet, the underlying questions of whether 'prolonged occupation' constitutes a distinct legal category or should rather be treated as a phenomenon that is of relevance to the interpretation and application of the law are similar to those of our analysis.

Looking outside of law, most academic observers credit the notion of 'protracted conflict' to the work of the political scientist Edward Azar.[17] As early as 1986, Azar together with Chung In Moon raised the criticism that interventionism by superpowers—be it through military force or economic aid—'has been ineffectual in resolving conflict situations in the Third World'.[18] As a reason for this failure, they identified the specific nature of most of these conflicts, which they described as 'protracted social conflicts'. According to Azar and Moon, protracted social conflicts consist of

> a pattern of hostile interactions among individuals and groups within a nation state, or with those of neighbouring countries. [Their] origin . . . is mainly attributable not to clashes of national interest, but rather to conflicting socio-cultural-ethnic relationships amidst chronic underdevelopment . . . [They] are endemic to a given society and are characterized by (1) temporal protractedness, (2) fluctuations in intensity and frequency, (3) conflict spillover from one realm to the other, (4) a tendency towards partial equilibrium, (5) absence of an explicit termination, and (6) blurred demarcation between internal and external sources of conflict.[19]

As one of the root causes of such conflicts, they highlighted structural inequality and victimization producing imbalanced development policies and preferring nominal growth over distributive justice.[20]

Nearly forty years later, Azar's and Moon's definition still provides an important starting point for identifying essential characteristics of 'protracted conflict'. In line with Azar's approach, we propose to understand protracted conflicts as real-life phenomena with shared characteristics across different conflict situations. As further explained in section B.2, the similarities relate to the type of hostilities, far-reaching

[16] Vaios Koutroulis, 'The Application of International Humanitarian Law and International Human Rights Law in Situation of Prolonged Occupation: Only a Matter of Time?' (2012) 94 International Review of the Red Cross 165, 169.

[17] Ellen Policinski and Jovana Kuzmanovic, 'Editorial: The Enduring Legacy of Endless War' (2019) 101 International Review of the Red Cross 965, 966; Mona Rishmawi, 'Protecting the Right to Life in Protracted Conflicts' (2019) 101 International Review of the Red Cross 1149, 1152–54; ICRC (n 6) 9.

[18] Edward Azar and Chung In Moon, 'Managing Protracted Social Conflicts in the Third World' (1986) 15 Millenium—Journal of International Studies 393, 393; Edward Azar, *The Management of Protracted Social Conflicts* (Dartmouth 1990).

[19] Azar and Moon (n 18) 394–95.

[20] ibid 396.

and compound consequences for affected populations, systemic root causes, resistance to conflict resolution, and dependence on international interventions. Focusing on commonalities that underpin situations of protracted conflict expands the lens of analysis that currently prevails in international law from categorization of conflict to include causes, consequences, and timeline of conflict. Understood in this way, 'protracted conflict' is not a category that leads to legal consequences per se, but it helps to highlight the legal relevance of facts that previously would have been excluded from legal analysis. It also allows to critically assess grey areas that legal categorization ignores. This, in turn, opens up a possibility for the authors in this book to address such core questions in conflict dynamics as the fulfilment of socio-economic rights, social exclusion, poverty, and distributive (in)justice—all of which traditionally have not been part of conflict analysis under international law.

2. Protracted Conflict as a Phenomenon: Particular Features of Protractedness

The wording of 'protracted conflict' implies that a core distinguishing feature of such conflicts is their longevity, as indeed was argued by various authors, beginning with Azar, and by policy reports such as that by the ICRC. Nonetheless, whether a conflict is 'protracted' or not is difficult to understand merely by looking at its duration. Most conflicts around the world have been ongoing for a long time, and whether their duration is long enough to be 'protracted' can be relative to the circumstances; and as conflicts mutate, or when they are interrupted by relatively long periods of ceasefire, they might no longer be viewed as a single conflict. Indeed, the ICRC suggests that many protracted conflicts nowadays are in fact a series of geographically related yet distinct conflicts, which are continued by different parties and for different reasons than those that were relevant at the start of the conflict, as for instance is the case in the DRC.[21] Together, this implies that focusing on conflict duration alone might be a useful indicator of 'protractedness' of a given conflict, but it is insufficient to understand the distinctive features of protracted conflicts and to give it meaningful substance.

We suggest that 'protracted conflicts' as real-life phenomena are characterized by (i) a certain *type of hostilities*, which are of a fluid nature over time and space; (ii) *root causes* such as social inequality, group discrimination, and structural violence; (iii) far-reaching socio-economic and compounded *consequences*; (iv) resistance to *conflict resolution*; and (v) vulnerability to and dependence on *international intervention*.

Type of hostilities: Protracted conflicts are characterized by their fluid nature over time and space. Their intensity and frequency but also their geographical scope fluctuates. Such conflicts are not necessarily manifested in fully fledged active combat among military forces but are often characterized by low-level violence. They may create areas of limited statehood, which can co-exist in parallel to governmental claims of authority. Such areas, which are sometimes limited to remote rural areas but can also be located in urban centres, create a governance challenge, and often diverse

[21] On fragmentation and mutation: ICRC (n 6) 10.

actors—other than the state—may step in and provide governance functions.[22] Hostilities in these conflicts are intermittent and periods of relative normality alternate with periods of intense fighting and disruption while fragility and tensions prevail throughout. As a result, systemic violence is normalized.

Root causes. As mentioned previously, Azar and Moon trace the root causes of protracted social conflict to structural inequality, victimization, and 'ideological domination by one social group over another'.[23] In their argument, colonial legacy and integration of developing states into the international (economic) system play a key role in staging these social cleavages and discriminative practices, as they 'concentrate political and economic power in the hands of specific forces that use state machinery and hegemonic ideology as instruments of domination'.[24] Accordingly, while there might exist a variety of distinct triggers that set off armed conflict and perpetuate conflict dynamics, at the heart of such conflicts lie systemic disrespect for human rights, socio-economic deprivation, and structural violence. These root causes are likely to be exacerbated during conflict, and they may lay dormant in a society even if the manifestations of armed conflict are addressed through means of conflict resolution.

Consequences. 'Protractedness' as a phenomenon is not limited only to the specific manifestation of this type of hostilities, such as its fluidity over time, but is also associated with far-reaching and compound consequences beyond that of damage inflicted as a direct result of military hostilities. 'Protracted conflicts' corrode basic services, life chances, and livelihoods, and in the long run lead to a notable surge in 'war poor' populations, 'lost generations' of children, and prolonged displacement.[25] The migration of hostilities into urban spaces exacerbates these adverse socio-economic consequences,[26] which in turn aggravate and prolongate the conflict. As conflict continues, the state is unable to ensure basic service provision without external funding.[27] International borrowing and aid become a key source of public income, thus creating unsustainable levels of debt and leading to economic dependency. This often opens doors to aggressive exploitation of natural resources, which further depletes the natural environment for local populations and exposes them to poor working conditions in the absence of effective labour protection, contributing to more inequality and underlying conflict in a society.[28] Overall, what appears to characterize 'protracted conflicts' are their far-reaching and interconnected consequences for education, health, food and water security, livelihoods, displacement, and the natural environment, among others.

[22] Tanja Börzel and Thomas Risse, *Effective Governance under Anarchy: Institutions, Legitimacy, and Social Trust in Areas of Limited Statehood* (CUP 2021) 34–44, 176–80.

[23] Azar and Moon (n 18) 396.

[24] ibid.

[25] On the related notion of 'cumulative impact': ICRC (n 6) 5, 10.

[26] *Pathways for Peace* (n 1).

[27] Börzel and Risse (n 22) 216–28.

[28] Tata Precillia Ijang and Cleto Ndikumagenge, 'Dependency on Natural Resources: Post-Conflict Challenges for Livelihoods Security and Environmental Sustainability in Goma, The Democratic Republic of Congo' (2013) 23 Development in Practice 372; Irene Costantini, 'Statebuilding and Foreign Direct Investment: The Case of Post-2003 Iraq' (2013) 20 International Peacekeeping, 263; Leo Zulu and Sigismond Wilson, 'Whose Minerals, Whose Development? Rhetoric and Reality in Post-Conflict Sierra Leone' (2012) 43 Development and Change 1103.

Resistance to conflict resolution: 'Protracted conflicts' are by definition conflicts that appear to be impossible to end either through military victory or by negotiated settlement. The conflicts in the DRC, Libya, Palestine, Ukraine, and Yemen, in light of the failed negotiated settlement attempts, are cases in point. The resistance of such conflicts to conflict resolution has been associated with various reasons. The joint UN/World Bank study *Pathways for Peace* warns that internationalized, geographically diffuse, and fragmented contemporary armed conflicts have challenged the efficacy of traditional methods of conflict resolution and negotiated political solutions.[29] The 'new wars' theory further suggests that these conflicts are characterized by a 'logic of persistence' as '[b]oth for political reasons—the need to underpin extremist identity politics—and for economic reasons—the need to maintain access to resources—the various warring parties acquire a vested interest in continued violence'.[30]

Vulnerability to and dependence on international intervention: 'Protracted conflicts' are subject to international interventions of multiple types, ranging from military intervention to peacekeeping and peace enforcement, and from humanitarian aid to foreign investment and development grants.[31] Justifications span the severity of conflict and the resulting humanitarian consequences; the threat to regional and international peace and security, including the claim to fight root causes of international terrorism; the (presumed) need for political and economic reform; or simply the invitation of the territorial state.

It could be argued that these highlighted features pertain to most contemporary armed conflicts. Nonetheless, the systemic causes and consequences of conflict discussed here, leading to vicious cycles of violence, insecurity, deprivation, and distrust, are arguably more pronounced in some contexts, thus indicating a higher degree of protractedness.

C. Problematizing 'Protractedness' as a Lens of Analysis

Protractedness offers a distinct lens of understanding, analysing, and approaching conflict, as well as international responses to sustain peace. However, it also has limitations and blind spots, some of which are worth highlighting before discussing how this lens will be used in the current book.

First, a shallow understanding of 'protracted conflict' can appear apologetic: it can be seen as an attempt to justify 'business as usual', whereby unsuccessful international attempts to address humanitarian needs and resolve conflicts are glossed over, despite vast resources and institutional efforts that are spent on such attempts. Put otherwise, this lens can be seen as a normalization of institutional failure; an attempt to revamp existing ideologies of peacebuilding and post-conflict development with a squandering legitimacy. Indeed, this 'apologetic' stance is a risk, especially in policy terms.

[29] *Pathways for Peace* (n 1) 6; Christina Buchhold, Jonathan Harlander, Sabrina Quamber, and Øyvind Ege, 'The End of the Big Peace? Opportunities for Mediation' (Oslo Forum 2018 Meeting Report, The Centre for Humanitarian Dialogue 2018).

[30] Christine Chinkin and Mary Kaldor, *International Law and New Wars* (CUP 2017) 18–19.

[31] Börzel and Risse (n 22) 103–23.

However, in this book we invoke the category critically, and in a way that invites a re-thinking of established ways to address conflict through international law.

Second, if used as a relevant category under international law, the notion of protracted conflict risks creating further justification for international interventions into conflict situations. If some conflicts are seen as 'protracted'—and thus fundamentally more difficult to resolve—then more long-term planning (and adequate resources) becomes essential to address them, thus justifying further presence of international actors. In addition, the notion of protracted conflict points towards multiple *internal* tensions within conflict-affected societies, thus potentially making structural inequality, socio-economic deprivation, and political violence internationally (more) relevant. While this might be a desirable consequence from the perspective of human rights law and other fields of international law concerned with the protection of individuals and the environment, this could also become a 'Trojan horse' that justifies more interventionist international approaches to internal conflict, including those under Chapter VII of the UN Charter. While this indeed might cause issues for international law and policy in the long run, in this book we use 'protracted conflict' as a descriptive category, without attaching pre-determined normative consequences or policy responses to it.

Third, and more critically, a focus on 'protracted conflict' could be seen as a way of misdiagnosing the problem for which international institutions such as the ICRC, World Bank, or UN are looking for solutions. Examined through a lens of protractedness, conflicts appear to be mostly features of specific (fragile) states and their societies. Structural conditions such as exploitative and unequal global economy, neo-colonial practices and patriarchy, hegemony, and domination by some states over others are treated as contextual features against which (protracted) conflicts are unfolding, rather than their essential root causes. In this sense, focus on 'protracted conflict' is a continuation of the standard approach in international law, whereby conflict is seen as an anomaly that affects certain (dysfunctional) societies in an otherwise orderly, consent-based functioning of international society. While this concern about incorrect characterization of the problem is valid, the strength of analysis of protracted conflict is that it explicitly opens up a conventional understanding of conflict under international law to new perspectives. It takes the structural causes of conflict seriously, and as such it calls for a systemic rethinking of international legal approaches, while also keeping in sight the specific situation of each society in conflict.

Fourth, at a deeper level, focusing on 'protracted conflict' risks perpetuating the top-down patterns of knowledge creation that rely on a neutral observer (eg an international policymaker, a donor, a scholar) proposing solutions to the problems 'out there' in the Third World.[32] 'Protractedness' offers a way of expanding the sphere of knowledge relevant to conflict, thus further reinforcing a role of expert advice in

[32] The term 'Third World' here is not used as a geographically defined space that marks a group of states that emerged from the process of decolonization, as was originally understood when the term had first emerged during the Cold War. Rather, we refer to the 'Third World' to underline the continuous relevance of the centre–periphery dynamic that exists between the western states and other major geopolitical powers that are 'at the centre' of international policy making and debate, and the rest of the world (which is often described in the literature as 'the Third World'), and which are subject to the policy prescriptions by those at the 'centre'.

conflict resolution. At the same time, it further entrenches the characterization of the Third World as a space of (endless) conflict, violence, and poverty. Such an act of observation, physically and psychologically removed from the experiences of the conflict itself, is not only an expression of technocratic decision-making, or epistemic domination. It can also become a source of suffering for conflict-affected populations, because it is able to justify the top-down international responses to conflict that are based on 'neutral' data that is often incomplete, biased, and possibly skewed.[33] The issue of powerful western entities observing processes in a Third World and qualifying them as something that needs to be fixed from an Outside is a long-standing problem in development studies.[34] 'Protractedness' as a lens, if employed critically, must not perpetuate such neo-colonial projects. However, given the policy origins and current uses of the term, an idea of 'protracted conflict' does risk expanding and thus entrenching the top-down analytical frameworks and policy approaches in the area of conflict resolution.

Finally, from a different perspective, a protractedness lens for analysing conflict can appear over-inclusive and therefore too ambitious. For instance, from a perspective of distinct regimes of international law (IHL, ICL, human rights, etc), a protractedness lens could be opening legal analysis of armed conflict too much, potentially undermining its coherence and value in practice. In particular, in terms of IHL, a broad concept of protracted conflicts may go against the idea of seeing IHL as a 'single normative system of protection' and 'might weaken that system's claims to universality, coherence and discernibility'.[35] As the rest of this introduction and the chapters in this book will illustrate, we propose that examining international law through a lens of protracted conflict in fact leads to a rich discussion, which sometimes challenges but also expands the traditional frames that currently prevail in international law.

D. Legal Challenges Arising from Protracted Conflicts

Protracted conflicts raise several challenges to the applicable laws. For the purposes of our study, we classify these as substantive and institutional legal challenges. By substantive challenges, we refer to conceptual or thematic challenges that arise from protracted conflict situations to the application and interpretation of the various legal frameworks at play. As to institutional challenges, our focus is on the extent to which the institutional legal frameworks within which humanitarian, peace, and development actors operate require adjustments, or should be preserved, in protracted conflict settings. The following provides a rough sketch of these challenges, which are further explored in the chapters of this book.

[33] In more depth Ch 23.

[34] Arturo Escobar, *Encountering Development: The Making and Unmaking of the Third World* (Princeton University Press 1995).

[35] Dustin Lewis, 'The Notion of "Protracted Armed Conflict" in the Rome Statute and the Termination of Armed Conflicts under International Law: An Analysis of Select Issues' (2019) 101 International Review of the Red Cross 1091, 1112–13.

1. Substantive Challenges

Protracted armed conflicts implicate a number of legal frameworks, including international humanitarian law, international development law, international economic law, international refugee/internally displaced persons (IDP) law, international human rights law, international environmental law, international criminal law, and the law applicable to peacebuilding. This is markedly so in the case of protracted conflicts due to their long duration, far-reaching consequences, and complex nature, often with the involvement of multiple non-state armed groups and international actors in military, humanitarian, development, and peace roles.

The phenomenon of protracted conflict presents challenges to the application and interpretation of the individual legal regimes due to their particular features highlighted in section B.2. In terms of application, it collides with different aspects of conflict categorization in international humanitarian law. International and non-international armed conflicts as well as high-level protracted criminal violence or internal upheavals may be part and parcel of protracted conflicts. This raises the question as to whether international humanitarian law should include specific rules for this type of conflict, or should formulate any kind of presumption that in such cases the applicability of IHL should be suspended in favour of international human rights norms.[36] A related concern applies to the conflict/post-conflict distinction,[37] which is put under pressure because the specific characteristics of protracted conflicts place social tensions and armed conflict on a continuum of dispossession and violence. Are traditional categories therefore outdated, or does blurring the categorical lines between the phases 'armed conflict' and 'post-conflict' settings lead to an extended application of IHL and thus, maybe unintendedly, reduce the level of protection for the civilian population?[38]

In terms of interpretation, the type of hostilities that characterizes protracted armed conflicts—that is, low-level, simmering, intermittent, and diffuse armed violence—often has an impact on the interpretation of the existing rules of IHL in relation to, inter alia, targeting, proportionality, and precautions. For example, in the case of norms that give room to certain balancing processes or unspecific standards of care (due diligence obligations), the element of time may weigh inand concretize legal obligations. Examples include due diligence duties under common article 1 Geneva Conventions I–IV[39] and human rights law.[40] In addition, even though many situations of protracted hostilities may formally qualify as situations of armed conflict, their socio-economic and societal impacts over time far exceed IHL's traditionally limited

[36] ibid 1092.

[37] On the notion of a 'ius post bellum': Jennifer S. Easterday, Jens Iverson, and Carsten Stahn, 'Exploring the Normative Foundations of Jus Post Bellum: An Introduction' in Carsten Stahn, Jens Iverson, and Jennifer S. Easterday (eds), *Jus Post Bellum: Mapping the Normative Foundations* (OUP 2014).

[38] Dustin Lewis, 'The Notion of "Protracted Armed Conflict" in the Rome Statute and the Termination of Armed Conflicts under International Law: An Analysis of Select Issues' (2019) 101 International Review of the Red Cross 1091, 1112–3.

[39] Geneva Conventions (adopted 12 August 1949, entered into force 21 October 1959) 75 UNTS 31, 85, 135, 287 (Geneva Conventions I-IV); ICRC, *Commentary on the Third Geneva Convention: Convention (III) relative to the Treatment of Prisoners of War* (CUP 2021) paras 197–206.

[40] In more depth, see Ch 19.

protective ambit. A case in point is the traditional debate about the extent to which the reverberating or indirect effects of an attack have to be taken into account in the proportionality assessment.[41] Here, the phenomenon of 'protracted conflict' militates in favour of an interpretation of the principle of proportionality according to which these effects on the civilian population, in particular long-term damage to the civilian infrastructure, need to be taken seriously in the balancing exercise.[42] These considerations raise the question of whether IHL is in need of reform to respond to the particular features of protracted armed conflict.

Similar challenges affect the other applicable regimes. For example, in the field of human rights, challenges relating to the temporal aspect of protracted conflict and the interrelated and cumulative nature of multiple human rights violations add up to a particular severity of human rights impacts in protracted conflicts and may need to be taken into account in legal interpretation. A conceptualization of conflicts as deeply rooted in socio-economic inequalities also brings up the question of whether human rights can be interpreted to guide national and international responses to protracted conflicts in the spheres of humanitarian, peace, and development cooperation.[43] Further examples from other legal regimes are highlighted by the contributions to this book.[44]

More generally, protracted armed conflicts require a systemic rethinking of the applicability of, and interactions between, the relevant legal regimes. This goes beyond the traditional debate on the interplay between IHL and international human rights law.[45] For example, protracted conflicts additionally raise questions of conflict between the law of development cooperation, IHL, and the UN Charter, for example when economic sanctions authorized by the Security Council restrain humanitarian and development actors to provide assistance in settings of protracted conflicts.[46] The underexplored interplay between IHL and international environmental law is another pertinent example among others that are emphasized in the contributions to this book.[47]

[41] Marco Sassoli, *International Humanitarian Law* (Edward Elgar 2019) 8.321–8.326.

[42] Michael Talhami and Mark Zeitoun, 'The Impact of Attacks on Urban Services II: Reverberating Effects of Damage to Water and Wastewater Systems on Infectious Disease' (2020) 102 International Review of the Red Cross 1293; International Law Association Study Group on the Conduct of Hostilities in the 21st Century, 'The Conduct of Hostilities and International Humanitarian Law: Challenges of 21st Century Warfare—Final Report' in 'International Law Association Report of the Seventy-Seventh Conference' (Johannesburg 2016) (International Law Association, London 2016) 24–25.

[43] See in more depth Ch 18.

[44] See below Section F.

[45] Among the plethora of contributions, see the overview by Norman Weiß and Andreas Zimmermann, 'Remarks on the Relationship between International Human Rights Law and International Humanitarian Law' in Norman Weiß and Andreas Zimmermann (eds), *Human Rights and International Humanitarian Law: Challenges Ahead* (Edward Elgar 2022) 1–11.

[46] Ansgar Münichsdorfer and Sofie-Marie Terrey, 'Humanitarian Exemptions: Illusive Progress in Safeguarding Humanitarian Assistance in the International Counterterrorism Architecture?' (2024) 29 Journal of Conflict and Security Law 249–272; Nathalie Weizmann, 'Respecting International Humanitarian Law and Safeguarding Humanitarian Action in Counterterrorism Measures: United Nations Security Council Resolutions 2462 and 2482 Point the Way' (2021) 103 International Review of the Red Cross 325, 336.

[47] Section F.

2. Institutional Challenges

Protracted armed conflicts see extensive international intervention, not least across the humanitarian, development, and peace fields. When protracted conflict is not only associated with the presence of physical hostilities over a longer period of time, but understood holistically with its socio-economic and environmental dimensions, the traditional divides between the humanitarian, development, and peace fields have been considered to be untenable. The dichotomous conceptualization of humanitarian assistance as short-term relief during ongoing crises and development assistance as long-term socio-economic programming for the post-conflict phase has proven unfeasible to address the needs of affected communities. First, the conceptual distinction increasingly becomes blurred in practice because humanitarians find themselves having to address development needs, while development actors increasingly work under and respond to conflict situations and are faced with humanitarian needs. Second, the ever-increasing need for humanitarian aid and the pressure this creates for the aid system make long-term solutions all the more important. Furthermore, the need to cooperate with the peace sector arises, as humanitarian and development aid should not exacerbate the root causes and consequences of conflict, and humanitarian and development considerations need to be incorporated into conflict-resolution efforts.

However logical the need for cooperation and coordination across the three fields—that is, the need for a triple nexus—appears, translating it into practice is not without significant institutional legal challenges and pitfalls. These relate to the mandates, foundational principles, immunities, and accountability frameworks that constitute and shape the operation of the actors from the three fields. For example, for humanitarians, the need to address developmental needs in protracted conflicts and taking part in triple nexus projects raises concerns as to compatibility with the humanitarian principles of neutrality, impartiality, and independence,[48] which are firmly rooted in international (humanitarian) law in situations of armed conflict[49] and statutes of humanitarian actors[50] in general.

Similar mandate-related challenges persist in the development field. Development actors have traditionally refrained from engaging in ongoing conflicts as development is largely considered as a post-conflict objective. Within international economic law, including the law of development cooperation, conflicts are perceived as anomalies and as risks to political stability that threaten the predictability of economic

[48] See Ch 13.

[49] *Military and Paramilitary Activities in and against Nicaragua (Nicaragua v United States of America)* (Merits) ICJ Rep 14, paras 242–244; Protocol Additional to the Geneva Conventions of 12 August 1949 relating to the Protection of Victims of International Armed Conflicts (adopted 8 June 1977, entered into force 7 December 1978) 1125 UNTS 3 (Protocol I) art 70; Protocol Additional to the Geneva Conventions of 12 August 1949, and relating to the Protection of Victims of Non-International Armed Conflicts (adopted 8 June 1977, entered into force December 1978) 1125 UNTS 609 (Protocol II), art 18.

[50] Eg Statutes of the International Committee of the Red Cross (adopted on 21 December 2017, entered into force on 1 January 2018) <https://www.icrc.org/en/document/statutes-international-committee-red-cross-0> accessed 21 June 2023, art 4.

transactions.[51] Hence, researchers have largely focused on post-conflict situations in examining economic, financial, and development issues.[52] This approach has undergone some change in institutional legal and policy frameworks, yet development remains predominantly state-centric and driven by economic aims.[53] Although the linkage between peace and development is acknowledged, particularly with the adoption of the Sustainable Development Goals,[54] the extent to which the field of development can accommodate and support humanitarian and conflict-sensitive approaches remains to be explored. There are only very few studies[55] that accept that fragility and ongoing conflict as a widespread phenomenon can co-exist with economic development for many decades, and that economic interventions are part of the self-perpetuating dynamic of protracted conflict. Overall, the extension of humanitarian assistance into the development sphere, and vice versa, requires a re-thinking of how and with whom the institutions in the two sectors form legal relations, and what the legal limitations to their engagement with different actors are, such as those stemming from their mandates or the existence of a sanctions regime.

Finally, the relationship between peacemaking and peacebuilding with humanitarian and development assistance has not been studied to date from an international legal perspective. The question remains open as to whether peacemaking and peacebuilding, which are essentially political in nature, are amenable to integrating humanitarian and development objectives.

E. The Nexus Approach: Rethinking Current Approaches to Protracted Conflict

The increasingly evident linkages between the drivers and consequences of protracted conflict, ranging from climate change to mass displacement and from food scarcity to organized crime, point to the need for comprehensive and integrated approaches in international legal and institutional responses to protracted conflict.

In terms of institutional responses, since the middle of the last decade, international agendas focus on the need to deliver the so-called triple-nexus approach between humanitarian, development, and peace (HDP) objectives.[56] A clear definition of what

[51] One example is Peace and Security Clauses in investment agreements, in more depth on the relationship between investment law and the law of armed conflict: Katia Fach Gómez, Anastasios Gourgourinis and Catharine Titi (eds), *International Investment Law and the Law of Armed Conflict* (Springer 2019).

[52] Paul R Williams and Milena Sterio (eds), *Research Handbook on Post-Conflict State Building* (Edward Elgar 2020).

[53] For more details, see Ch 14.

[54] Goal 16: Promote just, peaceful, and inclusive societies.

[55] Marie von Engelhardt, *International Development Organizations and Fragile States* (Palgrave Macmillan 2018); Annamaria Viterbo, 'The Role of the International Financial Institutions in Fragile and Conflict-Affected Countries' in Giovanni Cellamare and Ivan Ingravallo (eds), *Peace Maintenance in Africa—Open Legal Issues* (Springer 2018).

[56] United Nations General Assembly (UNGA), 'Review of the United Nations Peacebuilding Architecture' 70th sess (27 April 2016) UN Doc A/RES/70/262; (UNSC) Res 2282 (27 April 2016) UN Doc S/Res/2282; Agenda for Humanity (n 1); Grand Bargain (n 1); General Secretariat of the Council of the European Union, 'Council Conclusions: Operationalising the Humanitarian-Development Nexus' (19 May 2017) Doc No 9383/17 (n 1); Pathways for Peace (n 1); OECD DAC Recommendation (n 1); UN/WB 2021 (n 1).

the triple-nexus approach stands for seems to be lacking. The academic literature on the topic is limited, and most policy papers engage with obstacles to its practical application instead of providing any kind of conceptual clarification. One attempt of a definition offered describes the nexus as

> [t]he stronger integration and coordination across the Humanitarian–Development–Peacebuilding spectrum [as] one of the frameworks through which donors, the United Nations (UN) and civil society are working towards achieving the Sustainable Development Goals (SDG) by 2030.[57]

The triple-nexus approach builds on earlier policy concepts in the development field. The concepts of linking relief, rehabilitation, and development (RRD), early recovery, connectedness, and the 'whole-of-government' approach developed in the literature aimed to facilitate institutional, operational, and policy linkages between humanitarian and development assistance at national and international levels.[58] The linear conceptualization of the timing of humanitarian and development assistance as a 'continuum' has also been replaced with the 'contiguum' perspective, which indicates the continuous and simultaneous need for both types of assistance in complex crises.[59]

Following these earlier debates on the RRD and other holistic responses, international cooperation has witnessed a growing visibility and acceptance of the so-called triple-nexus agenda. This agenda emphasizes the need to examine the humanitarian, development, and peace aspects of protracted conflict in an integrated manner, both institutionally and 'on the ground',[60] and often portrays the turn to the triple nexus as a significant shift.[61] Yet, how this policy approach works on the ground and to what extent it really offers a new take on the challenges of protracted conflict is still far from clear.[62] This is partly due to the indeterminate nature of the concept, which policy papers highlighted early on. Is the term about the interaction of the challenges involved?

[57] Eric Sanchez Garcia, 'Unpacking the Peace Pillar of the Triple Nexus' (2022) 33 Development in Practice 328, 328.

[58] Alexander Kocks, Ruben Wedel, Hanne Roggeman, and Helge Roxin, *Building Bridges Between International Humanitarian and Development Responses to Forced Migration* (Swedish Expert Group for Aid Studies (EBA) and German Institute for Development Evaluation (DEval) 2018).

[59] Margie Buchanan-Smith and Paola Fabbri, 'Linking between Relief, Rehabilitation and Development in the Tsunami Response: A Review of the Debate' (Evaluation Report, Tsunami Evaluation Coalition 2005).

[60] ICRC 2015; UNGA, 'Outcome of the World Humanitarian Summit: Report of the Secretary General' (23 August 2016) UN Doc A/71/353; Emma Fanning and Jessica Fullwood-Thomas, *The Humanitarian-Development-Peace Nexus: What does it mean for multi-mandated organizations?* (Oxfam 2019); Marc Dubois, 'Threat or Opportunity for the Humanitarian Principles?' (Centre for Humanitarian Action 2020).

[61] Hugo Slim, 'Keynote Address to the World Food Programme (WFP) Annual Partnership Consultations' (2017) <https://www.icrc.org/en/document/nexus-thinking-humanitarian-policy-how-does-everything-fit-together-ground> accessed 15 June 2023.

[62] Merry Fitzpatrick and others, 'Making the Nexus Real: Moving from Theory to Practice' (Report, Feinstein International Center 2021); FAO, DI and NRC, *Development Actors at the Nexus: Lessons from Crises in Bangladesh, Cameroon and Somalia, Synthesis Report* (FAO, DI and NRC 2021); Sultan Barakat and Sansom Milton, 'Localisation across the Humanitarian-Development-Peace Nexus' (2020) 15 Journal of Peacebuilding & Development 147.

Does the term describe a policy imperative, or an operational imperative? Is it simply a conundrum, or do we have to understand it as a whole-of-system approach?[63]

The indeterminacy and the lack of a proper definition of the triple nexus are characteristic of the notion's function as a 'buzzword' in humanitarian and development policies. Such buzzwords serve to 'frame problems by distinguishing some aspects of a situation from others—and in so doing, define paths of action'.[64] Thereby, buzzwords create legitimacy for certain policy agendas and allow different development actors to relate their specific policy goals to such a buzzword. Since buzzwords are often historically contingent, analysing their shifting meanings and practical implications allows one to trace how—or whether at all—policy priorities change over time or to what extent buzzwords may simply hide hegemonic goals of the actors involved.[65] Thus, while buzzwords may on the one hand help to improve and legitimize new policy approaches,[66] they may at the same time imply hegemonic continuities.[67] These concerns about certain practices based on policy concepts, such as the triple nexus, mirror the arguments voiced in section C against the analytical lens of protracted conflicts.[68] The oft-hidden epistemic effects of analytical approaches or policy concepts require the disclosure of their implications in each and every case, in order to allow for critical engagement.

In the case of the triple nexus, hegemonic continuities may lie in certain types of top-down global governance. Interventionism in war-torn states by international organizations and Western states is heavily criticized for its conceptual fallacies and its hidden imperialistic and neo-colonial nature.[69] International relations research on governance in areas of limited statehood has highlighted the 'in-built Western bias' in policy agendas and parts of the academic discourse when development goals are based on the model of Western democracies.[70] Likewise, critical scholars in international law have been vocal about the destructive impacts of international economic law and development policies on the local populations.[71] Some observers describe the policies of 'humanitarian exceptionalism' even as a driver of protracted conflict, since the focus on humanitarian emergencies seems to turn them into a constant of the international order which calls for 'permanent intervention'.[72] As a consequence,

[63] Inter-Agency Standing Committee and UN Working Group on Transitions Workshop, 'Background paper on Humanitarian-Development-Peace Nexus' (Prepared by Inter-Agency Standing Committee and UN Working Group on Transitions, 2016).

[64] Kaja Borgrevink and Kristin Bergtora Sanvik, 'The Afterlife of Buzzwords: The Journey of Rights-Based Approaches through the Humanitarian Sector' (2022) 26 The International Journal of Human Rights 285, 285.

[65] Allison Schnable and others, 'International Development Buzzwords: Understanding Their Use Among Donors, NGOs, and Academics' (2021) 57 The Journal of Development Studies 26, 27.

[66] ibid 28.

[67] For further discussion on this point, see Ch 2.

[68] Section C.

[69] Most notably: Anthony Anghie, *Imperialism, Sovereignty and the Making of International Law* (CUP 2004) chapter 6.

[70] Tanja Börzel and Thomas Risse, *Effective Governance under Anarchy: Institutions, Legitimacy, and Social Trust in Areas of Limited Statehood* (CUP 2021) 14-17.

[71] Eg Luis Eslava, *Local Space, Global Life: The Everyday Operation of International Law and Development* (CUP 2015); Sundhya Pahuja, *Decolonising International Law: Development, Economic Growth and the Politics of Universality* (CUP 2011).

[72] Philip Cunliffe, *Cosmopolitan Dystopia: International Interventions and the Failure of the West* (Manchester University Press 2020).

these interventions become a primary focus in and characteristic of the work of international institutions.[73]

Can the triple nexus disrupt such continuities and offer viable alternatives to top-down global governance modes, or does it only present a new label for interventionist practices of international organizations? Both could be the case, if we understand the triple nexus not as a concrete policy proposal but as an 'empty signifier' that means different things to different actors.[74] Thus, the interpretation of the triple nexus is not fixed to the limited meaning currently given to it by policy documents. Based on this insight, it would be too simplistic to discard the nexus as old wine in new bottles.[75] Taking the nexus seriously could provide for a progressive agenda to argue against siloed thinking and demand genuine coordination and cross-fertilization across sectors. Moreover, the fundamental idea behind the triple nexus—that the consequences of protracted conflict should be addressed in a holistic way and that humanitarian, development, and peace objectives should not undermine each other—can be the basis for a genuine rethinking of international legal and institutional responses to protracted conflicts.

F. Research Design and Content of the Book

The book starts from two assumptions. First, we hypothesize that the 'protractedness' of armed conflicts is not only relevant in policy terms but also affects the application of pertinent legal regimes. Second, we question the functions and purposes of the triple-nexus approach. These two points determine both our methodological approaches and the structure of the book.

We assume that the phenomenon of protracted conflict requires the questioning, problematizing, and rethinking of some of the essential conceptual distinctions and applicable rules that currently characterize and organize various debates in international legal regimes pertaining to conflict situations. These conflict situations are difficult to accommodate within binary categories, such as peace/war, conflict/post-conflict, potential/ongoing (conflict), or armed conflict/violence. This questioning of settled categorizations and paradigms on which international law is still largely premised opens up new possibilities to re-examine some core principles (eg neutrality, impartiality),[76] rights (eg human right to water),[77] and institutional mandates and immunities,[78] which otherwise might appear to have a clearly determined meaning and scope in international law.

In order to substantiate our hypothesis in terms of methodology, the book relies on holistic and inclusive approaches. It does so by bringing together authors from different backgrounds for a comprehensive, interdisciplinary, and cross-sectoral exchange across: (i) relevant sub-fields of international law, including international

[73] ibid.
[74] On the concept of empty signifiers: Ernesto Laclau, *Emancipation(s)* (Verso 1996) 34.
[75] Sonja Hövelmann, 'Triple Nexus to Go' (Centre for Humanitarian Action 2020) 3.
[76] See Ch 13.
[77] See Ch 18.
[78] See Ch 14 (mandates) and Ch 15 (immunities).

humanitarian law, international development law, international economic law, international human rights law, international environmental law, international criminal law, and the law applicable to peacebuilding; (ii) relevant disciplines, including international law, international relations, political science, philosophy, geography, and anthropology; and (iii) communities of scholarship and practice.

The book approaches the concepts of protracted conflict and the triple nexus through various perspectives, deconstructing traditional narratives and critically questioning the related legal and policy concepts. We contrast theoretical perspectives with empirical case studies. On the theoretical side, approaches include historical, critical legal, critical spatial, gender, geopolitical, and political economy perspectives. The case studies focus on states and regions which are particularly affected by protracted conflict, including Central America, Colombia, the DRC, Palestine, the Philippines, and the Sahel. In light of these considerations, the book is structured in four parts, consisting of the following chapters.

Part I: Protracted Conflicts and the Triple Nexus in Perspective: Deconstructing Established Narratives

Part I deals with the conceptual challenges identified in the introduction that are created by the analytical lens of 'protracted conflicts' and the policy approach of the triple nexus. Does the lens of protractedness serve as a normalization of institutional failures in the global architecture of security, humanitarian, and development actors? Does it revive established narratives that depict conflicts as anomalies characteristic of certain dysfunctional states, thereby masking highly problematic structures of the international order, such as neocolonial and hegemonic practices? Are the notions of 'protractedness' and the 'triple nexus' just buzzwords that are turned into justification for continuing international interventions, despite their failures on the ground? Do they contribute to further processes of securitization by de-categorizing the distinction between peace and war? Do these notions entrench biased top-down expert-based frameworks, but ignore in fact the needs of the affected populations? In addressing these questions in more detail, Part I offers the interdisciplinary conceptual and theoretical groundwork for the book, with which the analyses in Parts II–IV critically engage in their examination of the core legal concepts and principles applicable to protracted conflicts.

In her chapter, *Kathryn Greenman* argues that the triple-nexus approach intends to justify the increasing influence and engagement of international financial institutions in situations of protracted conflict by shifting the discourse on armed conflicts from the political sphere to technical risk management. Likewise, from a perspective of critical space theory, *Conrad Schetter* and *Janosch Prinz* warn against the possibility that the triple nexus might turn humanitarian relief into a means for furthering security interests of international actors—a development that they call a 'humanitarian aid-development-war nexus'. Adopting a feminist perspective, *Olga Jurasz*, *Moa Peldán*, and *Leena Vastapuu* critically examine how a gendered understanding of the triple nexus might contribute to feminist peace. These more abstract observations are further spelled out by two case studies. *Pablo Kalmanovitz* investigates the specific obstacles international institutions have to confront in providing aid under the conditions of protracted criminal violence in Northern Central America. Offering a differentiated analysis of the merits and obstacles of extending the humanitarian-development nexus to the activities of the World Bank and the ICRC in these situations, he sees some potential for the nexus to restrict securitization efforts of state actors. The hegemonic nature of the pertinent concepts is stressed in the chapter by *Johanna del Pilar Cortés-Nieto, Andrés Gómez-Rey, Rafael Alberto Tamayo-Álvarez,* and *Andrés Rodríguez-Morales.* They analyse USAID discourses on peacebuilding and development in post-conflict Colombia and deconstruct liberal discourses ('liberal peace') as hegemonic means to shape domestic policies.

Thus, Part I demonstrates the risks that arise from taking international policy concepts at face value. The contributions demask hidden motives and interests of international actors, and they warn against the negative implications of such policies for the affected societies. Not all of the contributions utterly reject the triple-nexus approach as a means to address protracted armed conflicts, but they all call for deeper structural ways to reimagine the relationship between humanitarian aid, development approaches, and peace.

Part II: Drivers, Consequences, and Interdependencies of Protracted Conflicts

Part II examines five key phenomena: food crisis and starvation; healthcare; forced migration and displacement; climate change and environmental degradation; and (counter-)terrorism. These phenomena have a multi-layered relationship with protracted conflict: (i) they play a role in the eruption and prolongation of armed conflicts; and/or (ii) protracted armed conflict creates adverse consequences for these phenomena; and (iii) addressing the challenges associated with these phenomena is a prerequisite for sustainable peace. Acknowledging such interdependencies, this part offers reflections on the following fundamental questions: Does international humanitarian law provide an adequate framework for dealing with the complexity and compounded consequences of protracted conflicts for affected populations and environments? What is the promise of other international legal regimes, such as human rights law or environmental law, in providing complementary protection? How can international legal responses to protracted conflict be rethought for a holistic approach to drivers and consequences at play?

Antonio Coco demonstrates how hunger and protracted conflict fuel each other, and the role of international law, particularly international humanitarian law and international human rights law, in tackling conflict-related food insecurity. He proposes preventive and responsive measures that international and local actors should take to address the root causes of food insecurity and conflict, to break the vicious cycle between the two phenomena. Similarly, analysing international human rights law and international humanitarian law, *Amrei Müller* develops a comprehensive approach to the right to health in protracted conflict that encompasses the duties to develop an accessible (primary) health care system and to promote broad participation in, and even local democratic control over, this health system. By examining the International

Law Commission's draft principles on the protection of the environment in relation to armed conflict, and the ICRC's updated guidelines on the protection of the natural environment in armed conflict, *Britta Sjöstedt* explores the role of international law in hampering the adverse effects of environmental emergency in exacerbating conflicts and conflict-prone situations, as well as in preventing environmental degradation as a result of protracted conflict. Finally, starting from a premise that terrorism, underdevelopment, and unresolved prolonged conflict feed each other, *Ben Saul* explores how counterterrorism measures adopted in such situations may prove counterproductive and undermine humanitarian, development, and peace efforts. He emphasizes the promise of mainstreaming human rights in mitigating the excesses of counterterrorism and, as a result, enhancing effective humanitarian, development, and peace action. *Mutaz M. Qafisheh* and *Jinan Bastaki* turn to the issue of long-term displacement that has increasingly become a dire consequence of protracted conflict, focusing in particular on the legal regime that determines and protects the rights of four generations of Palestinian refugees. On conflict-related displacement, *Sâ Benjamin Traoré* shifts the attention to the Sahel region and IDPs, reflecting on the structural, political, and economic drivers that the most pertinent (international) legal regimes are not designed to address.

Taken together, the chapters in this part demonstrate the need to recognize the complexity of the relationship between protracted conflict and the conflict-related phenomena. It follows from this analysis that treating these phenomena as a consequence of conflict, and addressing the conduct of conflict parties, is not sufficient for effective responses. Instead, the role of social, economic, and environmental factors in triggering or exacerbating conflict, as well as in transitioning to sustainable peace, need to be borne in mind. This then reveals the need for cross-regime analysis, systemic interpretation, and thinking beyond the role of states in international law, as the chapters in this part have done.

Part III: Creating the Divide? (In)compatible Institutional Frameworks

The third part of the book interrogates the international legal framework in which institutional reform for triple nexus is taking place. Is international law perpetuating institutional siloes, or does it hold the key to more effective inter-institutional cooperation? What scope is there to reinterpret and revise the existing rules of international law, to enable more institutional convergences and better international interventions? Does international law prevent expansion of institutional mandates that might facilitate the triple nexus, or does it provide a justification for expanding the authority of the most powerful actors into new areas of international activity? Given the changing nature of conflict and conflict interventions, to what extent can international law hold international actors intervening in protracted conflict to account? Chapters in this part are concerned with the role of international law in creating, but also bridging, the distinct institutional approaches in the HDP sectors.

Since principles of international humanitarian law are often portrayed as a hurdle for operational convergence among the HDP sectors, *Marc DuBois* questions whether such an understanding of IHL principles is justified. He argues instead that principles of humanity and impartiality in particular, given their roots in human dignity, can become valuable guideposts for all three sectors and foster closer cooperation. Focusing on legal constraints in the development sector, *Ansgar Münichsdorfer* argues that a particular kind of legal interpretation allowed the World Bank to expand its institutional mandate, enabling interventions in situations of active (protracted) conflict while maintaining some conceptual boundaries around the notion of 'development', thus allowing the Bank to disengage from difficult conflict situations when risks become too high. The issue of expanding institutional mandates is further interrogated by *Héloïse Guichardaz*, who contrasts different immunities of the UN and other international institutions, arguing that the UN being the only organization enjoying *de facto* absolute immunity from domestic jurisdiction can become an obstacle to closer inter-institutional cooperation, and can hamper accountability towards people affected by conflict. Given the organization's key role in facilitating peaceful settlement of protracted conflict, *Martin Waehlisch* finally examines the UN's responses to protractedness, including the expanding remit of peacekeeping, and a shift to conflict prevention that enables the UN's engagement with the triple-nexus agenda.

Together, the chapters in this part demonstrate that as a framework of international cooperation, international law does contribute to upholding sectoral differences and siloes. Yet, this 'stabilizing' function emanates not necessarily from legal provisions in treaty law, but rather from settled legal interpretations of institutional mandates, immunities, and powers. Since such interpretations are constructed by legal thinking, and since they tend to be upheld by settled sectoral commitments, cultures, and practices rather than by law, they are open to revision. As a promising way forward, some concepts that originate in specific sectors, such as 'humanity', 'do no harm', or 'root causes', could be integrated across all three sectors, thus facilitating synergies, trust, and more coordinated exercise of international authority. However, the chapters also highlight that such potential institutional convergence across sectors comes with significant risks. For instance, there is a real risk that the most powerful institutions with the best access to resources, such as the World Bank, could use the triple nexus and related policy frameworks to further expand their authority and contested economic agendas—not only geographically, but also across the international institutional terrain. Similarly, given the pressure by donors to ensure accountability for aid spending, weak and ineffective accountability mechanisms risk becoming the norm across the three sectors, representing a 'minimum common denominator' of accountability, rather than providing an effective remedy for affected populations.

Part IV: Bridging the Divide: A Key Role for Human Rights?

Part IV concludes the book with reflections on possible transitions from protracted conflict to sustainable peace. It puts a spotlight on the role of human rights law and related policy approaches pursued by institutional actors under the label of human rights-based approaches in protracted conflicts.[79] In this respect, the book

[79] On the relationship between human rights law and human right-based approaches: Giedre Jokubauskaite, Andreas Buser, and Sofie-Marie Terrey, 'Human Rights-Based Approaches to Protracted

pays particular attention to the promise of human rights as an alternative—or rather complementary—approach to the current triple nexus policies. Chapters raise several interrelated questions: what is the role of human rights law and human rights-based approaches as a potentially unifying dimension across the humanitarian-development-peace divide? How can peace agreements be formulated to facilitate the transformation of conflicts sustainably? Is a rights-based approach the way forward because it provides a common 'language' and guidance towards better links and more coordination among various institutional responses? How does a human rights 'lens' on poverty and conflict help to overcome protractedness?

The chapter by *Andreas Buser* critically analyses promises and challenges of human rights as a common legal language for integrating humanitarian, development, and peace concerns along the nexus, and their potential to increase accountability of international actors active in each field. Whether human rights can fulfil such an integrative task and increase the protection of affected communities is further investigated by other chapters. Drawing on the right to water, *Sofie Terrey* analyses how the extended duration of protracted conflicts and varying degrees of intensity play out in the assessment of states' human rights obligations and develops several proposals to strengthen the human right to water in practice. *Daniëlla Dam-de Jong* identifies land disputes as one root cause of triggering armed conflicts, and critically assesses the role of land rights in resolving such conflicts sustainably.

The part continues with chapters analysing peace processes and, in particular, the role of peace agreements, which are, at least in theory, crucial for transitioning from protracted conflict to sustainable peace. *Armi Beatriz Bayot* examines the tension between the pursuit of negative peace and the achievement of a post-conflict political order that respects and promotes human rights, with a focus on indigenous rights, through a case study of the Bangsamoro peace processes in the Philippines. *Amanda Cahill-Ripley* scrutinizes the extent to which peace agreements address humanitarian and development assistance, exploring also the presence of relevant rights-based perspectives. Finally, *Pascal Sundi*, *Patience Kabamba*, and *Abhisekh Rodricks* explore the lessons learned from rolling out the triple nexus in peace processes in the DRC. Building on extensive fieldwork, put into the context of critical postcolonial literature, they identify numerous inadequacies with nexus policies in the DRC, and advocate moving from the current 'aid paradigm', which continues to dominate the triple nexus, to a 'paradigm of rights', which should develop in tandem with a right to development.

These contributions highlight the importance of human rights, while at the same time cautioning about limitations and ambivalences of human rights-related policy concepts. The ambiguities surrounding the application of human rights in settings of armed conflict and their universalist or liberal assumptions leave reliance on human rights open to criticism. Concerns also remain about the practice of some international organizations and donor states to develop their own social and environmental standards instead of accepting legal human rights accountability or engaging in more fundamental reform. Nonetheless, most contributions to this book positively evaluate the possibility to meaningfully apply human rights in settings of protracted

Conflicts' (Policy brief, Endless Conflicts 2023) <https://gcils.org/wp-content/uploads/2026/02/2023-Policy-Brief-HRBA-Endless-Conflicts-1.pdf>

conflicts and their contribution to address challenges and root causes of protracted conflicts. Human rights retain a critical potential to be used by those seeking reform of international responses to protracted conflict. Although human rights law has limits in protracted conflicts (eg regarding the disputed application to armed groups, NGOs, and private companies), further specifying hard and soft-law duties and responsibilities, and especially the need to cooperate in order to realize human rights protection in situations of protractedness, has the potential to bring opposing actors together and build trust. As several chapters highlight, economic and social rights are well positioned to address the compounded effects of protracted conflicts on populations and individuals.

*

Having outlined the central themes and highlighted the focus of each contribution, the volume now turns to the chapters themselves. The summaries provided above could only sketch the contours of the discussions to come. What follows allows the reader to engage more fully with the arguments as they unfold and intersect. In doing so, the chapters give concrete elaboration to the broader questions raised in the introduction, and in particular on how international law can be genuinely rethought to provide a more holistic framework to respond to the compounded nature of present-day protracted conflicts. Our final conclusion reflects on common themes, current challenges, and provides thoughts on protracted conflict as a lens for (further) research, and on rethinking international law through a holistic approach to protracted conflict.

PART I
PROTRACTED CONFLICTS AND THE 'TRIPLE NEXUS' IN PERSPECTIVE
Deconstructing Established Narratives

2

The 'Triple Nexus' and the Risk Management of Conflict

Kathryn Greenman

A. Introduction

The idea that a 'triple nexus' of humanitarianism, development, and peace is necessary to respond to contemporary armed conflict is increasingly influential in international policy and practice. This idea is often traced to a series of mid-2010s policy documents published by international organizations such as the United Nations (UN), the World Bank, the Organisation for Economic Co-operation and Development (OECD), and the Council of the European Union (CofEU).[1] These policy documents argue that the international architecture for peace and security needs to adapt to address the challenges posed by today's 'increasingly protracted and transnational' conflicts.[2] According to the UN Secretary General, 'the international aid architecture . . . is seen as outdated and resistant to change, fragmented and uncommitted to working collaboratively'.[3] Humanitarian, peace, and development actors thus need to 'move beyond traditional silos, and work across mandates, sectors and institutional boundaries' to overcome the global crisis of widespread and protracted conflict.[4]

Critical international law scholars of various persuasions—including Third World Approaches to International Law (TWAIL), feminist, Marxist, and Critical Legal Studies—have already analysed humanitarianism, development, and peacebuilding separately as continuations of and guises for imperialism and intervention.[5] The

[1] United Nations General Assembly (UNGA), 'One Humanity: Shared Responsibility' UN GAOR 70th sess, Agenda Item 73(a) (2 February 2016) UN Doc A/70/709 ('*Agenda for Humanity*'); General Secretariat of the Council of the European Union, 'Council Conclusions: Operationalising the Humanitarian-Development Nexus' (19 May 2017) Doc No 9383/17 ('*EU Council Conclusions*'); World Bank Group and United Nations, *Pathways for Peace: Inclusive Approaches to Preventing Violent Conflict* (World Bank 2018) ('*Pathways for Peace*'); Organisation for Economic Co-operation and Development, 'Development Assistance Committee (DAC) Recommendation on the Humanitarian-Development-Peace Nexus' (2022) OECD/LEGAL/5019 ('*OECD DAC Recommendation*').

[2] *Pathways for Peace* (n 1) 231–32.

[3] *Agenda for Humanity* (n 1) 12.

[4] ibid 109, 126.

[5] Eg, David Kennedy, *The Dark Sides of Virtue: Reassessing International Humanitarianism* (Princeton University Press 2005); Sundhya Pahuja, *Decolonising International Law: Development, Economic Growth and the Politics of Universality* (Cambridge University Press 2011); Luis Eslava, *Local Space, Global Life: The Everyday Operation of International Law and Development* (Cambridge University Press 2015); Maj Grasten and Ntina Tzouvala, 'The Political Economy of International Transitional Administration: Regulating Food and Farming in Kosovo and Iraq' (2018) 24 Contemporary Politics 588; Karen Engle, *The Grip of Sexual Violence in Conflict: Feminist Interventions in International Law* (Stanford University Press 2020).

Kathryn Greenman, *The 'Triple Nexus' and the Risk Management of Conflict* In: *From Protracted Conflict to Sustainable Peace?*
Edited by: Heike Krieger, Giedre Jokubauskaite, Asli Ozcelik, and Andreas Buser, Oxford University Press.
 DOI: 10.1093/9780198967385.003.0003

establishment of a triple nexus of all three seems as likely to recreate and even to reinforce the dark sides of its constituent parts as to overcome them. This assumption is borne out by empirical research on the triple nexus in practice. For example, after a case study in Mali, Tronc and others concluded:

> Without improving upon each of the nexus' three prongs individually, inter-linking these prongs will actually have little utility for the local actors on the ground that the 'triple nexus' ultimately aims to serve . . . [Where] each of the three prongs of the 'triple nexus' plays some role in aggravating the country's fragility and limiting an independent development future as a state or a nation—forging linkages between humanitarian, development, and peacebuilding initiatives appears far from worthy as a policy priority.[6]

In this chapter, however, I will argue that the triple nexus is more than just an interlinking of humanitarianism, peace, and development. Rather, it reflects a radical revision of the international legal order based on a logic of prevention, risk management, and resilience. Through an analysis of the relevant international policy documents, I will first show how the triple nexus fundamentally reframes armed conflict as an ahistorical and technical risk to be managed, and attempt to think through the potential implications of this project. Drawing on Obiora Okafor's work on asserting newness as a political practice that seeks to justify (otherwise untenable) international legal reform,[7] this chapter will argue that claims that the nature of contemporary protracted conflicts is unprecedented are in effect normative rather than descriptive. It will argue that the project that such claims found is one that proposes a profound expansion of the role and authority of international, especially financial, institutions and promotes market-friendly solutions to conflict that extend the role of private corporations and management experts in the Global South.

In the second section of the chapter, I will discuss the relationship between the triple nexus in policy and in practice. There are two possible approaches to this question. One is to consider the extent to which the triple nexus has been operationalized in practice and whether that practice reflects policy. The other approach is to consider, following Anne Orford's work on the responsibility to protect, whether the triple nexus is serving to systematize already existing practice.[8] These two approaches are not necessarily mutually exclusive. Here I will argue that, while the extent to which the triple nexus has been operationalized is contested,[9] there is evidence that the situation on the ground does reflect the policy, albeit unevenly. At the same time, it may well be

[6] Emmanuel Tronc, Rob Grace, and Anaïde Nahikian, 'Realities and Myths of the "Triple Nexus": Local Perspectives on Peacebuilding, Development, and Humanitarian Action in Mali' (Harvard Humanitarian Initiative 2019) 29–31.

[7] Obiora Chinedu Okafor, 'Newness, Imperialism, and International Legal Reform in Our Time: A TWAIL Perspective' (2005) 43 Osgoode Hall Law Journal 171.

[8] Anne Orford, *International Authority and the Responsibility to Protect* (Cambridge University Press 2012) 2.

[9] Summer Brown and Rodrigo Mena, 'A Review of the Triple Nexus Approach in Discourse and Practice' (Islamic Relief Worldwide 2021) 6.

that the most significant impact of the triple nexus is to legitimize the pre-existing expansion of the role of international financial institutions (IFIs) in conflict.

B. Newness Claims in International Law

It is commonly claimed in international policy and scholarship that there is something new about contemporary wars that makes them uniquely difficult to resolve. In their joint study *Pathways for Peace*, the UN and the World Bank argue that 'violence has become increasingly . . . protracted and intractable', while the UN Secretary General's report *Agenda for Humanity* claims that 'negotiating peace agreements has become more difficult'.[10] Chinkin and Kaldor argue that contemporary 'new wars', which have a different logic to the wars of the past, tend towards longevity.[11]

Scholarship and policy documents identify several novel features of contemporary protracted conflicts that, such documents argue, account for their stubborn duration: more states are involved, including 'middle-income states'; they involve increasing numbers of non-state armed actors; they involve greater levels of violence, terrorism, human rights violations against civilians, and displacement; they are financed by organized crime or other illegal activities; they are trans-nationalized and internationalized; and they are urbanized.[12] None of these features, however, are entirely new. Many have their antecedents going back to the end of the Cold War and beyond. For example, scholars have been expressing concern about the proliferation of non-state armed groups and the link between urbanization and conflict for decades.[13] Armed groups have been associated with getting funds through illicit activities since the 1980s.[14] Reports about the increasing impact of conflict on civilians date back to at least the early 1990s.[15] While the number of conflicts decreased globally in the 1990s and 2000s, during the Cold War and peak decolonization period, third-state intervention in conflicts in middle-income countries was common. This is not to say that nothing is ever new, but rather that it is a choice or an interpretation to emphasize the relative discontinuities over the continuities.

[10] *Pathways for Peace* (n 1) 2; *Agenda for Humanity* (n 1) 24.

[11] Christine Chinkin and Mary Kaldor, *International Law and New Wars* (Cambridge University Press 2017) 7, 18.

[12] Eg, *Pathways for Peace* (n 1) 11–20; *Agenda for Humanity* (n 1) 23.

[13] On the proliferation of armed groups, see eg, Ron Dudai, 'Closing the Gap: Symbolic Reparations and Armed Groups' (2011) 93 International Review of the Red Cross 783, 783: 'The influence of armed groups has been rising exponentially in the last two decades.' On the urbanization of conflict, see eg, Jennifer Morrison Taw and Bruce Hoffman, 'The Urbanisation of Insurgency: The Potential Challenge to US Army Operations' (1995) 6 Small Wars and Insurgencies 68.

[14] Eg, Subcommittee on Terrorism, Narcotics and International Operations of the Committee on Foreign Relations United States Senate, 'Drugs, Law Enforcement and Foreign Policy (United States Government Publishing Office 1989) 36–61; Ricardo Vargas, 'The Revolutionary Armed Forces of Colombia (FARC) and the Illicit Drug Trade' (Transnational Institute Policy Briefing, 1999); John Horgan and Max Taylor, 'Playing the "Green Card": Financing the Provisional IRA: Part 1' (1999) 11 Terrorism and Political Violence 1.

[15] Eg, Christer Ahlstrom and Kjell-Ake Nordquist, *Casualties of Conflict: Report for the World Campaign for the Protection of Victims of War* (Department of Peace and Conflict Research, Uppsala University, Sweden, 1991).

So what to make of these newness claims about contemporary protracted conflicts? Writing in the context of 9/11's impact on the international legal order, Obiora Okafor has argued:

> [T]he newness claim is best understood as a deeply political practice. The very process of asserting newness is . . . a key political manoeuvre that allows proponents of radical international reform . . . to justify, more successfully than was previously possible, many of their pre-existing imperial ambitions . . . [N]ewness claims are deployed in order to render otherwise untenable reforms of the international legal order seemingly necessary and even imperative.[16]

In this chapter, taking up Okafor's call to unpack the myth of newness,[17] I want to see what is revealed by approaching claims that protracted conflicts are new as a normative practice rather than as a descriptive one. The political nature of such claims can seem closer to the surface than that of similar claims about 9/11. Claims about the newness of protracted conflicts do not always seem to convince even those who make them. Chinkin and Kaldor, for example, concede that new wars are not '*empirically* new'.[18] At the same time, the political project that such claims further is perhaps more obscure in comparison to the War on Terror. In the next section, I will attempt to understand the work that newness claims about protracted conflicts are doing through an analysis of the relevant policy documents. In doing so, I will follow those scholars who have understood policy documents as 'highly political texts', produced by 'social relations in institutions and expert communities'.[19]

C. The Project of the Triple-Nexus Policy

In this section, I will argue that the foundational triple-nexus policy documents propose a radical revision of the international legal order based on a logic of prevention, risk management, and resilience. My argument is that the triple-nexus policy signals a new approach to conflict centred on early and sustained engagement, managing the risk of potential future conflicts rather than responding to actual conflicts, and building the resilience of vulnerable communities. This move to managing conflict through the lens of risk mirrors a broader trend that scholars have been observing and analysing across various fields since the 1980s.[20] This scholarship has sought to

[16] Okafor (n 7) 172–73.

[17] ibid 190.

[18] Chinkin and Kaldor (n 11) 6 (emphasis added). They go on to explain that rather than being new, new wars are instead 'different from an idealised conception of "old wars"'.

[19] Susanne Soederberg, 'Risk Management in Global Capitalism' in Susanne Soederberg (ed), *Risking Capitalism* (Research in Political Economy vol 31, Emerald Books 2016) 11; David Mosse, *Adventures in Aidland: The Anthropology of Professionals in International Development* (Berghahn Books 2011) 3.

[20] Eg, Ulrich Beck, *Risk Society: Towards a New Modernity* (first published 1986, Mark Ritter tr, Sage 1992); François Ewald, 'Insurance and Risk' in Graham Burchell, Colin Gordon, and Peter Miller (eds), *The Foucault Effect: Studies in Governmentality with Two Lectures by and an Interview with Michel Foucault* (University of Chicago Press 1991); Anthony Giddens, 'Risk and Responsibility' (1999) 62 Modern Law Review 1; Michael Power, *The Risk Management of Everything: Rethinking the Politics of Uncertainty* (Demos 2004).

understand the significance of the rise of risk as a way of thinking about and managing uncertainty in many diverse parts of life.

1. Theorizing Risk

A number of scholars have traced the origins of the predominance of risk in contemporary governance to the environmental politics of the 1970s.[21] They argue that it was in the context of the environment that risks, such as nuclear accidents and pollution, were first understood as global, diffuse, radically uncertain, and potentially catastrophic.[22] Thus, a 'precautionary' approach to risk—which 'creates a specific relation to the future', requiring monitoring, controlling, and avoiding the future's potentially harmful effects; which necessitates quick action in the face of uncertainty, marking a shift from legal to administrative decision making; which deploys technologies of profiling and surveillance across entire populations; and which empowers risk managers over democratic politics—emerged in response and then spread to other areas of governance from there.[23]

This origin story is certainly consistent with the fact that international environmental law is one area of international law where we see risk at work early on via the precautionary principle.[24] Cultural theorists and political economists, however, offer an alternative account of the development of precautionary risk. Randy Martin notes with interest that 'the literature on risk emerges at the same time as the phenomenon of financialization'.[25] For Martin, financialization is not only the increasing predominance of financial markets, motives, institutions, and elites in the economy, but also the spread of the logic of finance as a means to manage other areas of life, including the home and foreign policy.[26] Martin understands finance:

> not just simply as a form of capital but as a set of protocols for organizing daily life. The intricate acrobatics of high finance that occur somewhere in the stratosphere have all manner of parallel expression in dances on the ground. Designs for living brought to us by imperial agencies trace their blueprints to the realm of finance.[27]

[21] Eg, Claudia Aradau and Rens van Munster, 'Governing Terrorism through Risk: Taking Precautions, (Un)Knowing the Future' (2007) 13 European Journal of International Relations 89, 101.

[22] Beck (n 20) 21–22.

[23] Aradau and van Munster (n 21) 91: 'What is new is not so much the advent of a risk society as the emergence of a "precautionary" element that has given birth to new configurations of risk that require that the catastrophic prospects of the future be avoided at all costs.'

[24] Monika Ambrus, Rosemary Rayfuse, and Wouter Werner (eds), *Risk and the Regulation of Uncertainty in International Law* (Oxford University Press 2017) 5, arguing that the 'underlying logic [of the precautionary principle] is beginning to figure prominently in other areas of international law'.

[25] Randy Martin, 'America as Risk/Securitizing the Other' (2004) 6 Interventions 351, 352 fn 2. Martin, at 358, traces the lineage of risk management in security to Ronald Reagan's Strategic Defense Initiative, or Star Wars.

[26] Randy Martin, *The Financialization of Everyday Life* (Temple University Press 2002); Randy Martin, *An Empire of Indifference: American War and the Financial Logic of Risk Management* (Duke University Press 2015).

[27] Martin, *An Empire of Indifference* (n 26) 3.

Central to these protocols, argues Martin, are self-management and pre-emption. Self-management is the 'watchword of personal finance', as financialization reframes individuals from consumers to investors—'the ideal kind of beings, who manage their affairs and take care of their own future' through their portfolios, credit, and debt.[28] The world is divided into the self-managed, who embrace risk, and the unmanageable, who cannot and are thus at risk—of exclusion, incarceration, or dispossession; lines of exclusion and inclusion are risk-based rather than geographical.[29] Pre-emption, on the other hand, or the 'bringing of the future into the present', is at the heart of fiscal policy, as governments use interest rate increases to try to manage inflation.[30] Along these lines, financialization thus creates a new form of imperialism where enemies are anticipated and pre-empted, future threats are turned into present conflicts, and war has no spatial or temporal limits.[31] This financialized imperialism is also leaner, since its subjects are supposed to manage themselves.[32]

Susanne Soederberg also links the rise of risk with financial capitalism. Soederberg argues that, driven by the World Bank, the World Economic Forum (WEF), and management consultants such as McKinsey, risk management has emerged as a new form of global governance that has sought to 'depoliticize the structural violence inherent to the nature and continued expansion of financial capitalism'.[33]

> By rebranding structural violence as an apolitical process of adjusting to seemingly objective global risks, and by recasting relationships of exploitation as 'opportunities' or 'value creation', the global risk management trope serves to erase the historical social relations of class power and wider capital accumulation processes from our gaze . . . At the same time, global risk management also facilitates the necessary expansion of credit-led accumulation and its inherent structural violence.[34]

Risk management as promoted by the World Bank and the WEF uses 'management techniques that emphasize the use of markets and market-type mechanisms, competition and choice, devolution of authority, cost-benefit analysis and programme budgeting'.[35] It reorganizes global governance 'along corporate lines of efficiency, innovation and cost effectiveness' and envisions a leading role therein for corporate actors and private finance.[36] International organizations in both the humanitarian

[28] ibid 3, 5, 8–9.
[29] ibid 8, 14, 58.
[30] ibid 3–4.
[31] ibid 3.
[32] ibid 5. Martin, at 14, argues: 'Compared to earlier imperial forms, the empire of indifference stands as a massive flight from commitment, urging an embrace of risk and self-management to others as it would to its own domestic subjects, then ignoring, incarcerating, or dispossessing those who cannot make the grade.'
[33] Soederberg (n 19) 5. Soederberg, at 4, traces the emergence of risk management as a response to the corporate scandals of the 1990s such as the collapse of Barings Bank. For more on this, see Power (n 20) 11, 29–30. On risk and management consultants, see Louise Amoore, *The Politics of Possibility: Risk and Security Beyond Probability* (Duke University Press 2013); Sarah Sharma and Susanne Soederberg, 'Redesigning the Business of Development: The Case of the World Economic Forum and Global Risk Management' (2020) 27 Review of International Political Economy 828, 846–48.
[34] Soederberg (n 19) 10–11.
[35] Sharma and Soederberg (n 33) 829.
[36] ibid 830.

and development sectors have already started to embrace these techniques of market-based risk management.[37]

As well as its impact on international organizations, scholars have shown how risk and its associated management techniques can be disruptive and corrosive to existing international law categories, procedures, and protections.[38] For example, in the counterterrorism context, Kessler and Werner have shown how the shift to a pre-emptive risk-based approach has vastly expanded the number of individuals against whom action, such as targeted killings or sanctions, can be taken—from just those who pose an actual threat (even if of varying levels of immediacy) to include those who are simply perceived as a risk.[39] For Kessler and Werner, foundational distinctions, such as war/peace and combatant/civilian, are blurred and as a result, action such as targeted killings becomes 'a deformalized form of risk management' beyond regulation by rules and not subject to existing accountability mechanisms.[40] In the refugee context, Daria Davitti has argued that the financialization of refugee assistance and the move to market-led solutions to displacement has undermined refugee protection in international human rights and refugee law, accelerating policies of non-entry, deterrence, and containment, and 'depoliticiz[ing] refugee lives and experiences'.[41] Drawing on this scholarship, in the next sub-section I will argue that the triple nexus marks the spread of the protocols of finance to manage peace, development, and humanitarianism, and legitimizes the marketization and corporatization of these fields and the corrosion of existing international law protections, procedures, and categories.

2. Risk and the Logic of the Triple Nexus

Leading international policy documents envision the triple nexus as founded on principles of pre-emption and self-management—the central tenets of financial logic. The triple nexus thus homogenizes peace, development, and humanitarianism along these future-oriented risk-focused lines. Documents such as the UN Secretary General's report *Agenda for Humanity* and the UN and World Bank's joint study *Pathways for Peace* emphasize the pressing need to move to a preventive approach to conflict. *Pathways for Peace* begins with the claim that 'the attention of the international community needs to be urgently refocused on prevention', while for *Agenda for Humanity* 'a shift from perpetual crisis management towards effectively managing prevention

[37] Eg, ibid 830–31; Daria Davitti, 'Refugee Finance: External(ized) Protection and Investments for Refugees' (2022) 65 Quaderni della Facoltà di Giurisprudenza Università di Trento 83.

[38] Aradau and van Munster (n 21) 106: 'The inclusion of "indefinite detention", "house arrest" as instruments in the UK fight against terrorism, the creation of "legal limbos" like Guantanamo captures the inadequacy of law to deal with situations of precautionary risk. What counts is a coherent scenario of catastrophic risk and imaginary description of the future. The other's actions are no longer relevant.'

[39] Oliver Kessler and Wouter Werner, 'Extrajudicial Killing as Risk Management' (2008) 39 Security Dialogue 289. See also, in the context of the use of force and maritime security, Nicholas Tsagourias, 'Risk and the Use of Force' in Monika Ambrus, Rosemary Rayfuse, and Wouter Werner (eds), *Risk and the Regulation of Uncertainty in International Law* (Oxford University Press 2017); Douglas Guilfoyle, 'Maritime Security' in Monika Ambrus, Rosemary Rayfuse, and Wouter Werner (eds), *Risk and the Regulation of Uncertainty in International Law* (Oxford University Press 2017).

[40] Kesser and Werner(n 39) 305.

[41] Davitti (n 37) 90–91, 97, 99.

and early action is urgently needed'.[42] The triple nexus is not just about ending or even preventing a particular conflict, but about reducing the risk of conflict more broadly.[43] The OECD's *Development Assistance Committee (DAC) Recommendation on the Humanitarian-Development-Peace Nexus* ('*OECD DAC Recommendation*'), for example, notes that the triple-nexus approach aims to 'strengthen risk management capacities' and urges that 'joined-up development, peace and humanitarian programming is risk-focused'.[44]

Under this precautionary risk-based approach, conflict no longer has temporal or geographical limits. It is not an event that happens at a particular time and place but a risk to be managed. This new approach requires international involvement over a much longer period, both '*long before* crisis situations deteriorate or serious violations of human rights and humanitarian law are committed' and *after* any actual conflict.[45] As well as at any time, international involvement can also be necessary *anywhere* since, in the words of *Pathways for Peace*, 'violent conflict can potentially affect every society'.[46] This move vastly expands the scope of the international authority and what is understood as the legitimate concern of international organizations. These include the Security Council and its coercive powers. In *Agenda for Humanity*, the UN Secretary General explicitly envisages a significantly larger role for the Security Council, one which arguably goes beyond its mandated authority. According to *Agenda for Humanity*, the Security Council 'must overcome its divisions and move from being a predominantly conflict management body to one that is actively engaged in conflict prevention . . . The Council should embrace risk analysis earlier'.[47] The triple nexus potentially undermines the need for a threat to international peace and security in order for the Security Council to exercise its coercive powers in favour of a new standard—a *risk* to international peace and security.

A preventive, precautionary approach to conflict means that quick and decisive action in the face of uncertainty is required.[48] According to *Agenda for Humanity*, '[w]hile there may be different interpretations of a particular context, there needs to be greater resolve to work more quickly towards unity and to ensure that initiatives to address tensions and de-escalate violence are closely aligned'.[49] Once a potential risk has been identified, there is no room or time for dissent. Although the triple-nexus policy is ultimately vague about which actors have the final say here, presumably it is international ones since according to the UN Secretary General, '[n]ational leaders need to be more willing to *accept* information and analysis'.[50] Just as in the War on Terror, then, the introduction of risk into international law's approach to conflict through the

[42] *Pathways for Peace* (n 1) 1; *Agenda for Humanity* (n 1) 29.

[43] The policy documents repeatedly cite reducing risk as an aim. Eg, *Pathways for Peace* (n 1) 5, 7, 18; *Agenda for Humanity* (n 1) 5, 103, 140; *OECD DAC Recommendation* (n 1) 3, 5, 6–7.

[44] *OECD DAC Recommendation* (n 1) 6, 9; *EU Council Conclusions* (n 1) 4, including among its aims promoting 'local and national capacities to address risks and vulnerabilities' and 'developing prevention measures'.

[45] *Agenda for Humanity* (n 1) 42 (emphasis added).

[46] *Pathways for Peace* (n 1) 5.

[47] *Agenda for Humanity* (n 1) 37, 67.

[48] Eg, ibid 31–34, stressing the need for timely and decisively political leadership and early action.

[49] ibid 36.

[50] ibid 34 (emphasis added).

triple nexus has disrupted existing categories and distinctions, and empowered international executive authority without any resulting increase in accountability.

As well as pre-emption, self-management is a key feature of the triple nexus. In *Pathways for Peace*, for example, the UN and World Bank make a telling analogy between preventing conflict and healthcare—just as the 'most effective prescription' is to convince people to adopt a healthy lifestyle, becoming resilient is a society's best way to prevent conflict.[51] Resilience or self-reliance often tie together the three components of the triple nexus, since they are broad or vague enough goals to contain any contradictions or tensions between the triple nexus's constituent parts.[52] *Agenda for Humanity*, for example, defines success for the triple nexus as 'the achievement of measurable reductions in people's risk and vulnerability and their ability to become more self-reliant'.[53] The *OECD DAC Recommendation* also has 'fostering self-reliance and resilience' as one of the triple nexus's ultimate goals.[54]

The triple nexus thus divides the world into those societies that are *at risk* of conflict and those that can appropriately embrace risk and transform it to opportunity. *Pathways for Peace* describes the triple nexus as a framework for creating societies that can 'navigate the risks of violence and harness opportunities for peace'.[55] In this way, societies are modelled after investors—they should manage their own risk in order to, in *Agenda for Humanity*'s words, 'seek a more prosperous future'.[56] It is not only societies but also peace, development, and humanitarian actors that must take risks. The *OECD DAC Recommendation* advises that 'peacebuilding and development efforts should be risk tolerant'.[57] *Agenda for Humanity* identifies a 'lack of risk tolerance' as a barrier to international engagement in countries at risk—risk aversion is part of the problem, something that needs to be overcome to solve protracted conflicts.[58]

Those societies at risk, who fail to self-manage, can now be subject to all sorts of outside management in order to pre-empt the materialization of those risks. It is not only peace, development, and humanitarian actors that need to take timely and decisive action in response to risk, states at risk must also 'be more willing to . . . act before situations deteriorate' and accept 'early assistance from bilateral, regional and international partners'.[59] This is not the imperialism of military interventions and occupation. It is Martin's *leaner* imperialism, as its subjects are urged to embrace risk and manage themselves. Since it is less spectacular, it might seem more benign, but its pre-emptive logic means it can spread everywhere. The assistance that those societies at risk must accept takes the form of the spread of markets, corporations, and private

[51] ibid xviii, 5. On the World Bank's turn to resilience in addressing violence and conflict, see Dimitri Van Den Meerssche and Geoff Gordon, '"A New Normative Architecture": Risk and Resilience as Routines of Un-Governance' (2020) 11 Transnational Legal Theory 267, 286–93.

[52] Brown and Mena (n 9) 18. On the rise of resilience and its broad range of meanings and uses in different contexts, see David Chandler, *Resilience: The Governance of Complexity* (Routledge 2014) 5–9; Jeremy Walker and Melinda Cooper, 'Genealogies of Resilience: From Systems Ecology to the Political Economy of Crisis Adaptation' (2011) 42 Security Dialogue 143.

[53] *Agenda for Humanity* (n 1) 103.

[54] *OECD DAC Recommendation* (n 1) 10; *EU Council Conclusions* (n 1) 4.

[55] *Pathways for Peace* (n 1) 6.

[56] *Agenda for Humanity* (n 1) 109, 148.

[57] *OECD DAC Recommendation* (n 1) 9.

[58] *Agenda for Humanity* (n 1) 28.

[59] ibid 34.

finance into and through peace, humanitarianism, and development activities. This has already been seen in the post-conflict reconstruction context.[60] The significance of the triple nexus, I argue, is to legitimize both the expansion of these practices and the form they take. There will no longer be any need to wait until after a conflict to justify reconstructing a society—a precautionary approach requires such reconstructions for states *at risk* of conflict.

Just as the War on Terror 'displays an insatiable quest for knowledge',[61] an approach to conflict based on precautionary risk authorizes new techniques for conflict prevention already in use in the context of counterterrorism—beginning with monitoring, data collection, and analysis. The triple nexus envisions increasingly massive and continuous surveillance.[62] Describing data and analysis as the 'bedrock of our action', the UN Secretary General counsels that

> National Governments and subregional, regional, and international actors need to dedicate significant financial and human resource capacity towards collecting data and monitoring and analysing risk before, during and after crises, particularly in the most risk-prone countries and areas.[63]

Information and communications technology (ICT) is given a crucial role to play here. To detect 'risk and patterns of conflict and violence', the UN and World Bank identify geographic information systems, crisis mapping, crowdsourcing, and 'crowdseeding' as useful tools for collecting data, and advise the development of '[g]reater capacity to mine and manage big data'.[64] For *Agenda for Humanity*, '[r]isk analysis and capacity mapping should be the primary basis for determining the type and level of international engagement'.[65]

The policy documents thus portray being 'at risk' as an objective designation from which certain interventions necessarily flow as a matter of technicality. Conflict is a technical, ahistorical risk, which will be identified through seemingly neutral processes of data collection and analysis, as will the appropriate responses to such risk. Yet such processes are not neutral and they lack transparency and accountability, empowering experts, managers, and algorithms. The power to decide who is at risk of conflict and subject to international management is a matter not of political debate and contestation but of opaque technique. The opening up of societies to markets,

[60] Eg, Kristen E Boon, '"Open for Business": International Financial Institutions, Post-Conflict Economic Reform, and the Rule of Law' (2007) 39 Journal of International Law and Politics 513; Ntina Tzouvala, 'Food for the Global Market: The Neoliberal Reconstruction of Agriculture in Occupied Iraq (2003–2004) and the Role of International Law' (2017) 17 Global Jurist 1.

[61] Aradau and van Munster (n 21) 91.

[62] On the shift to the centrality of data in humanitarian and development work, see Fleur Johns, 'From Planning to Prototypes: New Ways of Seeing Like a State' (2019) 82 Modern Language Review 833; Fleur Johns, *#Help: Digital Humanitarianism and the Remaking of International Order* (Oxford University Press 2023); Van Den Meerssche and Gordon (n 51) 292.

[63] *Agenda for Humanity* (n 1) 137; *Pathways for Peace* (n 1) 277–78, on monitoring as the first step of prevention.

[64] *Pathways for Peace* (n 1) 59, 278; *Agenda for Humanity* (n 1) 109, arguing that international assistance needs to 'embrace the opportunities of the twenty-first century', including technology and communications; *OECD DAC Recommendation* (n 1) 10, encouraging 'innovative approaches in data collection'.

[65] *Agenda for Humanity* (n 1) 122.

corporations, and private finance is now, in Soederberg's words, 'rebrand[ed] . . . as an apolitical process of adjusting to seemingly objective global risks'.[66] In this way, the triple nexus disguises the structural causes of violence and conflict, even as it proposes to solve them.

Just as Soederberg identified, the risk management of conflict sees the translation of private sector corporate management models—bringing with them for example a focus on outcomes and efficiency, the expansion of managerial roles, the use of auditing and benchmarks, a preference for private sector financial tools, and the resulting reduction of the public sector—to the peace, development, and humanitarianism sectors. Thus, under the triple-nexus policy, data collection and analysis is aimed at achieving 'a common understanding of risks, needs, gaps and existing capacities' and on that basis, the identification of 'collective outcomes that are strategic, clear, quantifiable and measurable'.[67] There must be 'clear performance benchmarks . . . to monitor and measure progress towards the collective outcomes'.[68] Achieving such collective outcomes will require 'collaboration among diverse groups of stakeholders . . . based on comparative advantage' (that is to say, based on lowest opportunity cost).[69]

By bringing in risk management as the solution to protracted conflicts, the triple nexus envisages the takeover of the peace, development, and humanitarian sectors by managers and management consultants, whose expertise now suddenly becomes necessary. It requires a parallel industry of education and training in the type of management consultant jargon—'navigating risks', 'harnessing opportunities', 'securing buy-in from stakeholders', 'diversifying resource bases'—and diagrams in which the triple-nexus policy is expressed (see Figure 2.1).[70]

Central to the risk management of conflict is a significant role for private actors, such as corporations, at all stages of the process. The UN Secretary General states:

> [P]rivate sector leaders and business councils are not only providers of goods or logistics. They also have interests in stable economic markets, in healthy and secure consumers who can purchase their products and services and in good governance and strong institutions. I encourage business leaders to use their knowledge, technology and individual influence and leverage to promote sustainable solutions that bring stability and dignity to people's lives . . . They should invest in and create new markets and infrastructure that connect us even further. We cannot confront the challenges of our time successfully . . . without them.[71]

In particular, the private sector has an essential role to play in financing. According to *Pathways for Peace*, it is 'critical to prioritize private sector solutions . . . and to use

[66] Soederberg (n 19).

[67] *Agenda for Humanity* (n 1) 127, 130.

[68] ibid 139.

[69] ibid 134. Other policy documents also use the language of comparative advantage: *Pathways for Peace* (n 1) xviii, xxiv, xxvi; *EU Council Conclusions* (n 1) 4; *OECD DAC Recommendation* (n 1) 3, 6, 7.

[70] Eg, *Pathways for Peace* (n 1) 6, 185; *Agenda for Humanity* (n 1) 164.

[71] *Agenda for Humanity* (n 1) 45, 175; *Pathways for Peace* (n 1) 288: 'The private sector, including small- and medium-size enterprises and international investors, can play an important role in preventing violent conflict.'

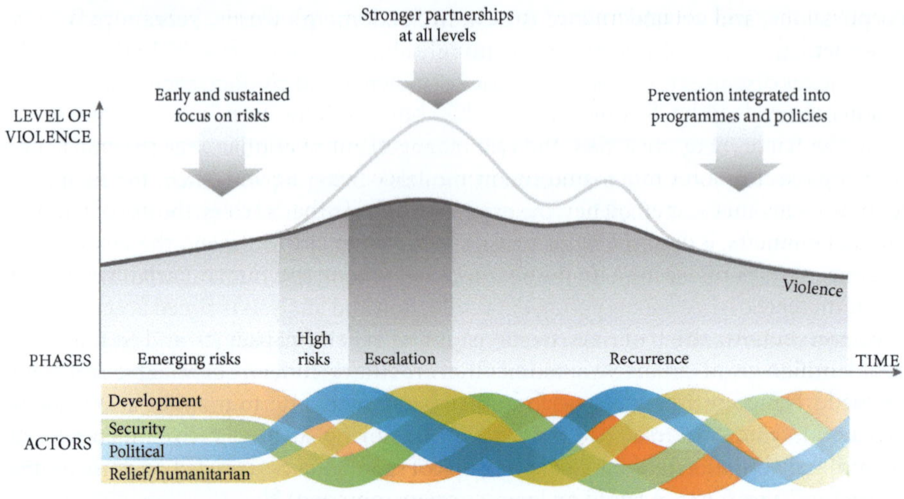

Figure 2.1 Sustained Approach to Prevention

Source: Figure 8.2, Sustained Approach to Prevent. © 2018 United Nations and World Bank. From Pathways for Peace: Inclusive Approaches to Preventing Violent Conflict. Washington, DC: World Bank. Licensed under Creative Commons Attribution 3.0 IGO (CC BY 3.0 IGO). https://unsdg.un.org/sites/default/files/2021-02/Pathways-for-peace_web.pdf

scarce public finance where it is most needed'.[72] Indeed, an important context for the triple nexus policy is a 'dramatic increase in funding requirements' for humanitarian action—from \$3.4 billion to \$19.5 billion between 2004 and 2019, leading to a \$9.3 billion deficit.[73] To meet this shortfall, the triple nexus demands a shift to greater *investment* in prevention and risk reduction, since this can 'reap the greatest rewards' and is 'more cost effective'.[74] The UN Secretary General describes this move to investing in prevention as 'the most critical shift we must agree upon'.[75] It requires, however, reform to the current funding models for peace, humanitarian, and development programmes in order to 'invest more based on risk', with greater involvement of the private sector.[76] The UN Secretary General explains:

> Public-private partnerships should promote risk-based investment. They can expand access to open, transparent risk-modelling methods. They can also build the capacity of Governments in low-income countries to improve the quality of risk analysis to inform decisionmaking. The insurance industry's experience in risk identification, risk regulation and pricing can provide crucial support for a shift from managing crises to managing risks. I encourage the insurance industry to integrate risk considerations into their asset investments. This can ensure not only that capital returns are real,

[72] *Pathways for Peace* (n 1) 288.
[73] *Agenda for Humanity* (n 1) 8, 147.
[74] ibid 145, 151; *Pathways for Peace* (n 1) 2, describing prevention as 'rational and cost-effective'.
[75] *Agenda for Humanity* (n 1) 143, 151.
[76] ibid 146.

but that they will not undermine future growth or place people and infrastructure in danger.[77]

Financing needs to be 'flexible' and 'nimble', but also 'long-term' and 'predictable'.[78] Since the triple nexus vastly extends the scope of international engagement, it necessarily requires a lot more funding over a longer time period. *Pathways for Peace* acknowledges that it may be hard to convince donors that such costs are worth it.[79] Current financing is described as too 'risk averse', whereas investment embraces risk.[80] Investment requires taking a long-term view and staying the course, even if results are not immediate.

Fundamentally, the triple nexus envisions a transformation from 'funding projects' through grants in the style of the public sector to 'financing outcomes' through a broader range of financing tools including 'risk-pooling and transfer tools, impact bonds, micro-levies, loans and guarantees' in the style of the private sector.[81] Accordingly, the resource base must be diversified and cost efficiency must be increased.[82] To this end, *Agenda for Humanity* recommends that the UN and IFIs co-host an international financing platform 'catering to the wide array of constituencies involved in delivering collective outcomes, each based on their comparative advantage' and offering non-traditional finance instruments.[83] *Pathways to Peace* suggests something based on the World Bank's Pandemic Emergency Financing Facility, which 'funds coverage through financial markets and a complementary cash window'.[84] To access the facility, 'countries could be required to have a risk management plan in place . . . as well as a risk-monitoring platform with regional actors'.[85]

In sum, the triple-nexus policy represents the financialization of peace, humanitarianism, and development and, together with the War on Terror, can be understood as part of a new mode of empire based on pre-emption and self-management. The triple nexus also serves as a vector of risk management as a form of governance based on corporate management techniques that use markets and market-type mechanisms. In this way, it legitimates the role of private corporations in all sorts of projects—ranging from data collection and ICT to utilities and infrastructure—in the Global South and empowers a professional class of managers and management consultants.

D. The Triple Nexus in Practice

So far, this chapter has focused on the policy documents that set out the triple nexus. While these policy documents are significant in themselves as political texts, this does

[77] ibid 151(b).
[78] ibid 157; *OECD DAC Recommendation* (n 1) 10–11; *EU Council Conclusions* (n 1) 10.
[79] *Pathways for Peace* (n 1) 5.
[80] ibid 287.
[81] *Agenda for Humanity* (n 1) 156, 159; *Pathways for Peace* (n 1) 281, 287–88.
[82] *Agenda for Humanity* (n 1) 163–68.
[83] ibid 161.
[84] *Pathways for Peace* (n 1) 288. On the significant criticisms of this facility, see Davitti (n 37) 96.
[85] *Pathways for Peace* (n 1) 288.

nevertheless raise questions about the situation on the ground. The first question asks whether the triple nexus as envisioned by the policy documents has been operationalized in practice. To what extent have the ideas in the policy documents travelled and what sort of effects have they had? The second question, drawing on Anne Orford's work on the responsibility to protect, focuses on the extent to which the triple nexus systematizes or legitimatizes *already existing* practice.[86]

Taking each question in turn, I will first argue that there is evidence that the situation on the ground does reflect the policy, albeit unevenly. Although research suggests that professionals working in peace, humanitarianism, and development still widely view the triple nexus as 'more theoretical than operational', there have been a number of projects taking a triple-nexus approach or implementing aspects of the triple nexus.[87] Daria Davitti, writing in the context of refugee assistance, has argued that *Agenda for Humanity* and associated policy documents 'spear-headed a series of reforms that not only irreversibly changed the nature of emergency funding, but also consolidated the international community's intention to see through this shift "from funding to financing"'.[88] These have included new financial instruments, partnerships with the private sector, market-led solutions, and a focus on refugee resilience and self-reliance.[89]

For example, the Kalobeyei settlement project in Kenya aims to promote self-reliance for refugees fleeing conflict in South Sudan.[90] While the project is not framed in terms of risk as the triple-nexus policy is, it shows some of the key hallmarks of financialization and market-based risk management techniques. Betts and others, in their three-year study of Kalobeyei, describe the EU-funded settlement as 'market-based', with the formation of new markets as one of its explicit goals.[91] It was designed to offer 'market-based opportunities' both to refugees and local communities.[92] For example, refugees are given cash to build their own shelter, not only to give them greater choice but also so that they can 'attempt to reduce the costs of the construction in order to save money for further investments' and contribute to the local economy.[93] Similarly, they are given cash for food so that they can 'suit their preferences while supporting the growth of local markets'.[94] Refugees are given 'specific training to support

[86] Orford (n 8).

[87] Brown and Mena (n 9) 18. The EU, for example, has 'piloted' the implementation of the triple nexus in six countries since 2017. See Pauline Veron and Volker Hauck, 'Connecting the Pieces of the Puzzle: The EU's Implementation of the Humanitarian-Development-Peace Nexus' (Discussion Paper 301, ECDPM 2021); Inter-Agency Standing Committee (IASC) Results Group 4, 'Mapping Good Practice in the Implementation of Humanitarian-Development-Peace Nexus Approaches: Synthesis Report' (September 2021); Center on International Cooperation, 'The Triple Nexus in Practice: Toward a New Way of Working in Protracted and Repeated Crises' (December 2019) ('The Triple Nexus in Practice').

[88] Davitti (n 37) 89.

[89] ibid.

[90] UNHCR, 'KISEDP Kalobeyei Integrated Socio and Economic Development Programme in Turkana West' (2018). The project is framed in terms of the humanitarian-development nexus rather than the triple nexus.

[91] Alexander Betts and others, 'The Kalobeyei Model: Towards Self-Reliance for Refugees?' (Oxford Refugee Studies Centre, 2019) 6, 7. Betts and others, at 19, explain that '[m]arket-based approaches to service delivery are at the core of the Kalobeyei settlement model'.

[92] ibid 4.

[93] ibid 30.

[94] ibid 6.

the[ir] entrepreneurial potential' and the project aims to foster small business.[95] Angelina Abbaticchio concludes that the Kalobeyei settlement project frames self-reliance 'in Western neo-liberal terms to suit the interests of states [and] as a result, . . . has to do with making refugees less dependent on aid rather than finding solutions for refugees'.[96] Indeed, Betts and others' study reveals that the project has not been very successful even on its own terms.[97]

Another example comes from the triple-nexus projects of international non-governmental organization of Islamic Relief. Aimed at strengthening resilience to conflict, they include activities such as '[t]rainings on savings and loan schemes to adopt a culture of savings as collateral for loans to expand economic activities' and the '[e]stablishment of business co-operatives, such as mushroom farming and baking'.[98] Repeatedly stressing the complexity of nexus projects, Brown and Mena's report on Islamic Relief's triple-nexus programme also demonstrates the additional managerial roles that the triple nexus creates and the economy around training and education that it produces.[99] The report notes that a triple-nexus approach requires 'full-time technical specialists in each element' as well as the overall project leader.[100] It also requires staff to be 'retrained and upskilled'.[101] Indeed, in 2022, the UN Development Programme, together with the OECD's Development Assistance Committee among others, launched the so-called Nexus Academy, which provides training and technical support to peace, humanitarian, and development professionals, producing 'experts fluent in the trilingual humanitarian-development-peace nexus'.[102] Thus, I argue that key aspects of the triple-nexus policy—the promotion of market-friendly solutions that expand the role of private corporations and management experts in the Global South (and the vast majority of triple-nexus projects are in practice being implemented in the Global South)—are reflected on the ground too.[103]

Turning to the second question, I argue that, regardless of any operationalization of the triple nexus, it may well be that its most significant impact is to give authority to the pre-existing expansion of the role of IFIs—and with them private corporations and other financial institutions—in conflict. Since the early 1990s, the IFIs have steadily increased their involvement, particularly in post-conflict reconstruction

[95] ibid 6, 7.

[96] Angelina Abbaticchio, 'Is the Humanitarian-Development Nexus Leading to Solutions for Refugees? Self-Reliance, Donor Interests, and the Kalobeyei Integrated Socio-Economic Development Programme in Kenya' (Local Engagement Refugee Research Network Paper No. 9, 2020) 6.

[97] Betts and others (n 91) 31, describing their research as presenting a 'slightly grim picture'.

[98] Brown and Mena (n 9) 25, 26.

[99] ibid 30.

[100] ibid 32; 'The Triple Nexus in Practice' (n 87) 4, 10, noting the urgent need for more dedicated 'nexus advisers' who can support implementation and coordination of the triple nexus approach.

[101] Brown and Mena (n 9) 20, 21, 29, 31.

[102] Nexus Academy, 'The New Humanitarian nods to 150+ nexus champions' (Twitter, 5 January 2023) <https://twitter.com/NexusAcademyHDP/status/1610651479546957826> accessed 19 May 2023.

[103] Regarding the location of most triple nexus projects in the Global South, see the map produced by the IASC. IASC Results Group 4, 'Mapping good practices in the implementation of Humanitarian-Development-Peace Nexus approaches' (IASC Inter Agency Standing Committee) <https://interagencystandingcommittee.org/mapping-good-practices-implementation-humanitarian-development-peace-nexus-approaches> accessed 19 May 2023.

but also more broadly in so-called fragile or conflict-affected countries.[104] Their role in high-profile post-conflict economic reconstructions, for example in Iraq, is relatively well known.[105] However, there has also been expansion into prevention, risk reduction, and resilience work.[106] For example, in 2007, the World Bank expanded its Operational Policy on Rapid Response to Crises and Emergencies to enable lending to assist with risk reduction (including through studies and analysis) and to 'mitigate or avert the potential effects of imminent emergencies or future emergencies or crises in countries at high risk'.[107] One of the objectives of the World Bank's State and Peace Building Fund, which was established in 2008, is to 'boost resilience' in countries affected by fragility, conflict, and violence.[108]

The IFIs have been careful not to exceed their mandates and step on the toes of, for example, the UN with this expansion of their work.[109] Indeed, there is nothing in the founding documents to authorize these practices on the part of the IFIs. Kristen Boon has argued that they have been enabled by 'interpretive leaps' when it comes to the IFIs' articles of agreement and by Security Council Chapter VII resolutions, while Van Den Meerssche and Gordon posit that internally the World Bank shifted to a deformalized, risk-based approach to interpreting its mandate.[110] Over time, the division between the peace and security mandate of the Security Council and the economic mandate of the IFIs has blurred.[111] The triple-nexus policy, in which the World Bank has played a central role, can be understood, I argue, as systematizing and rationalizing the broadening role of the IFIs in preventing and managing conflict in the absence of more formal authorization.

E. Conclusion

In this chapter, I have argued that claims that protracted conflicts are a new phenomenon are in effect normative rather than descriptive. They justify a project of otherwise untenable reform, the triple nexus, which, through reframing conflict as a technical and ahistorical risk to be managed, proposes a profound expansion of the role and authority of international, especially financial, institutions and promotes

[104] For a detailed overview of the institutional developments, see Annamaria Viterbo, 'The Role of the International Financial Institutions in Fragile and Conflict-Affected Countries' in Giovanni Cellamare and Ivan Ingravallo (eds) *Peace Maintenance in Africa* (Springer 2018).

[105] Eg, Boon (n 60).

[106] Van Den Meerssche and Gordon (n 51) 286–93.

[107] World Bank, 'Operational Policy 8.00: Rapid Response to Crises and Emergencies' (World Bank Operational Manual Operational Policies, 1 July 2014) [4(f)–(g)]; World Bank, 'Operational Policy 2.30: Development Cooperation and Conflict' (World Bank Operational Manual Operational Policies, June 2005) [2(a)], which provides that 'in countries that the Bank determines are vulnerable to conflict: [the objective of the Bank's work in relation to conflict is] to use its usual instruments to promote economic growth and poverty reduction through development assistance that minimizes potential causes of conflict'.

[108] World Bank, 'State and Peacebuilding Fund 2021 Annual Report' (2022) 7; World Bank, 'World Bank Group Strategy for Fragility, Conflict, and Violence 2020–2025' (2020) 2, 16, 21.

[109] Viterbo (n 104) 113.

[110] Boon (n 60) 515, 538–43; Van Den Meerssche and Gordon (n 51).

[111] ibid 553–5.

market-friendly solutions to conflict that expand the role of private corporations and management experts in the Global South. This project does not just exist in policy documents, but has also begun to be implemented in practice, albeit in partial and uneven ways. Nevertheless, its most significant impact may be to give authority to the *pre-existing* expansion of the role of IFIs in conflict.

3

Peace or War?

On the Logic of the 'Triple Nexus' from the Humanitarian Aid Perspective

Conrad Schetter and Janosch Prinz

A. Introduction

The rise of the humanitarian-development-peace (HDP) nexus poses the question of how humanitarian aid, development, and peace can be brought together under one conceptual umbrella. Since the term was introduced in 2017, technocratic considerations of donors and practitioners have dominated the debate.[1] In their arguments in support of it, donors and practitioners stress that the HDP nexus, as a holistic approach, can achieve synergies and efficiencies between budget lines and practical implementation, which have previously been separate and conflicting. However, such technocratic approaches underestimate the conceptual difficulties of bringing together the three strands that make up the HDP nexus, as well as the problem of instrumentalizing them for political interests. The academic and practical approaches behind the three strands—humanitarian, development, and peace—emerged in specific historical contexts and are shaped by distinctive combinations of normative and conceptual elements, which are often contested even within one of these strands. In this chapter, we will focus on the concept and practices of humanitarian aid to illustrate these difficulties involved in creating the HDP nexus.

The implementation of humanitarian aid appears to be the normatively required minimum to enable the 'bare survival' of people in violent conflicts. If one attempts to locate humanitarian aid between war and peace, humanitarian aid appears at first glance to be a civil intervention belonging to the realm of peace, which comes into play during war. However, as our short inquiry into the conceptual history will show, humanitarian aid emerged not from the logic of peace but from the logic of war. Reviewing these origins and the paths to which they have led offers insights about how humanitarian aid has responded to the systemic changes that war has undergone in

[1] For example, Anan Kittaneh and Antoinette Stolk, 'Doing Nexus Differently: How Can Humanitarian and Development Actors Link or Integrate Humanitarian Action, Development, and Peace?' (Care Research Paper 2018) <https://resourcecentre.savethechildren.net/pdf/humanitarian_development_peace_nexus_research_2018.pdf/> accessed 11 July 2023; Paul Howe, 'The Triple Nexus: A Potential Approach to Supporting the Achievement of the Sustainable Development Goals?' (2019) 124 World Development 104629; Manisha Thomas, 'NGO Perspectives on the EU's Humanitarian-Development-Peace Nexus Approach: Exploring the Challenges and Opportunities' (Voice Report 2019) <https://voiceeu.org/publications/ngos-perspectives-on-the-eu-s-humanitarian-development-peace-nexus.pdf> accessed 11 July 2023.

Conrad Schetter and Janosch Prinz, *Peace or War?* In: *From Protracted Conflict to Sustainable Peace?* Edited by: Heike Krieger, Giedre Jokubauskaite, Asli Ozcelik, and Andreas Buser, Oxford University Press.
 DOI: 10.1093/9780198967385.003.0004

the twentieth and early twenty-first centuries—for these changes have fundamentally called into question the nature of humanitarian aid and have posed dilemmas for the humanitarian idea over the past three decades.

Drawing a line between humanitarian aid and development cooperation is becoming similarly difficult. The HDP nexus seems to be the latest of a variety of technocratic approaches, such as the linking relief, rehabilitation, and development (LRRD) continuum or contiguum, which have attempted to bridge such difficulties at the level. However, as this chapter will argue, the conceptual hurdles to bringing together humanitarian aid, development cooperation, and peace remain formidable. What is needed, therefore, is a fundamental reconceptualization of humanitarian aid that must break with the prevailing paradigms. If this does not happen, there is a danger that the HDP nexus will pave the way for the further instrumentalization of humanitarian aid by security and military interests of donors. To put it provocatively: without a close consideration of the complex conceptual and practical history of humanitarian aid, the HDP nexus could develop into a HDW nexus (humanitarian aid-development-war nexus), in which the logic of war is the binding link and the guiding force.

To support our argument, we will: (a) trace the conceptual link between humanitarian aid and war; (b) show how the limits of war have been eroded, leading to a crisis of humanitarianism; and (c) show how, in response to these developments, attempts have been made in various ways to institutionally undermine the uniqueness of humanitarian aid. In the concluding chapter, we then consider the challenges this poses for the HDP nexus from the perspective of the logic of humanitarianism and the extent to which peace rather than war, stability, or security could become the focal point of an approach seeking to integrate humanitarian, development, and peace strands.

B. Humanitarianism and the Laws of War

Humanitarian aid is the application of the idea of humanitarianism to situations teetering between war and peace. The concept of humanitarian aid is thus normatively laden. On the one hand, the ethos of humanitarianism is based on Christian thought, including charity, the protection of life, and the spiritual significance of suffering.[2] Particularly in a (post-) Christian context, the idea of a common humanity has a long tradition associated with the demand for moral rights for every human being since the early modern period. On the other hand, the notion of a global humanity at the heart of humanitarianism is rooted in the individualist, universalist, and Eurocentric thought of the Renaissance and Enlightenment.[3] In humanitarianism, 'humanity'

[2] Craig Calhoun, 'The Idea of Emergency: Humanitarian Action and Global (Dis)order' in Fassin Didier and Pandolfi Mariella (eds), *Contemporary States of Emergency: The Politics of Military and Humanitarian Interventions* (Zone Book 2010) 29–58; Didier Fassin, *Humanitarian Reason: A Moral History of the Present* (University of California Press 2012).

[3] Bruce Mazlish, *The Idea of Humanity in a Global Era* (Palgrave Macmillan 2009); John Hobson, *The Eurocentric Conception of World Politics: Western International Theory 1760–2010* (CUP 2012).

is prioritized in prescriptions for action and a general moral obligation to help is postulated.[4]

In theory, humanitarian aid is fundamentally different from forms of intervention such as development cooperation or military operations. Based on the core principles of humanity, impartiality, and neutrality, humanitarian organizations are committed to providing assistance to anyone in need, without profit motive and regardless of political, cultural, or social affiliation.[5] The imperative to physically rescue people who find themselves in an emergency situation, for example caused by natural disasters or wars, is the linchpin of humanitarianism.[6] The International Committee of the Red Cross (ICRC) most fully embodies this idea of humanitarian aid, while other humanitarian aid organizations—such as Médecins Sans Frontières (MSF)—claim to deviate from these normative guidelines in individual aspects, for example by taking political positions.

The Battle of Solferino (1859) marked the birth of humanitarian aid. Inadequate medical care for the wounded on the battlefield prompted Henry Dunant to found the International Red Cross (1864) to provide neutral and impartial assistance to injured combatants of all warring parties. This basic principle of humanitarian aid has found its way into international law and is enshrined in the Geneva Conventions.[7] For example, Common Article 3 of the Geneva Conventions foreshadowed humanity and impartiality as principles of humanitarian aid in international law, which, together with neutrality, were affirmed in UN General Assembly Resolution 46/182 of 1991. The ICRC and many other humanitarian organizations further insist on their independence from governments and other authorities that are not parties to a war.

Historically speaking, humanitarian aid emerged as a corrective to the wars waged by states in the nineteenth century and not as peace intervention. In this sense, humanitarian aid is intimately linked to the nature of war. The wars between nation states during the nineteenth century, in the course of which humanitarian aid emerged, were highly formalized displays of violence that had very specific boundaries which can be—as an ideal type—captured by the following aspects.

First, wars were fought between clearly identifiable actors, namely states. Aspiring states were legitimized or delegitimized as equal enemies by the laws of war (eg Italian wars of liberation). Thus, there were clearly identifiable actors who decided on war and peace and who, *second*, maintained a symmetrical relationship with each other in the sense that they recognized each other as enemies. *Third*, because states had the sovereignty to declare war and to end it, wars were limited to a well-defined period of time. *Fourth*, wars were often limited in space. The battlefield and trenches were concrete places where troops challenged each other. *Fifth*, the distinction between

[4] Jürgen Lieser, 'Was ist humanitäre Hilfe?' in Jürgen Lieser and Dennis Dijkzeul (eds), *Handbuch Humanitäre Hilfe* (Springer 2013) 9–28.

[5] Didier Fassin, 'Inequality of Lives, Hierarchies of Humanity: Moral Commitments and Ethical Dilemmas of Humanitarianism' in Ilana Feldmann and Miriam Iris Tickti (eds), *In the Name of Humanity. The Government of Threat and Care* (Duke University Press 2010) 238–55; Peter Redfield, 'The Impossible Problem of Neutrality' in Peter Redfield and Erica Bornstein (eds), *Forces of Compassion: Humanitarism between Ethics and Politics* (School for Advanced Research Press 2010) 53–70.

[6] Michael Barnett, 'Humanitarian Governance' (2013) 16(1) Annual Review of Political Science 379–98.

[7] Geneva Conventions (adopted 12 August 1949, entered into force 21 October 1959) 75 UNTS 31, 85, 135, 287 (Geneva Conventions I–IV).

civilians and combatants was essential. The latter were supposed to wear uniforms for identification, lived in barracks, followed a chain of command, and so on. The war was focused on the mutual exchange of information but—at least in the ideal case—civilians were not part of the equation. Nevertheless, even combatants were not 'fair game'; their status had been precisely defined since the beginning of the twentieth century by the laws of war in the Geneva Conventions (1949) and the Hague Convention respecting the Laws and Customs of War on Land (1899/1907).[8] Many other rules of war have found their way into international law and show that war was not seen as an untamed, chaotic clash of wild hordes but as an act fraught with codes and norms, a prerogative of the noblest men of a country. In this context, humanitarian aid appears as just one more—arguably the most moral—element contributing to the 'ennoblement' of the laws of war. It could be said that the introduction of humanitarianism into the laws of war provided the final impetus to civilize war and maintain it as a violent expression of divergent interests. In other words, from a perspective of peace promotion, one criticism of humanitarian aid is that it was originally not directed against war per se, but rather enabled a morally legitimate continuation of war. These origins continue to haunt humanitarian aid to this day.[9]

However, war and humanitarian aid have undergone drastic changes—especially since the end of the twentieth century. From the perspective of the *longue durée*, the highly ordered warfare that developed in Europe in modern times was probably more of a temporal and regional exception in world history. The emergence of a world divided into nation states at the end of the nineteenth century was accompanied by an order of war that was specific to Europe and did not necessarily reflect the ideas about war in other parts of the world and in other periods. This becomes clear even when one compares it to warfare in early modern Europe, which was characterized by quite different logics based primarily on the fact that there was no clear demarcation between war and peace, between military and civilian, and so on, as Herfried Münckler has argued.[10] A similar blurring was characteristic of most wars outside Europe and still is today.

Against this background, it is important to realize that the laws of war, as enshrined in international law, sought to generalize the peculiarly regulated case of nineteenth-century European state wars on a global scale. A side effect of this generalization was that wars that did not conform to the European order of warfare appeared as barbaric and 'inhumane'. It was no coincidence, then, that in the era of colonialism and imperialism, the arguments for the 'superiority' of European civilization over 'barbarians' and 'savages' were partly based on the claim that the laws of warfare drew a clear line between the civilized and the uncivilized.[11] From today's perspective, it hardly needs

[8] Hague Convention II with Respect to the Laws and Customs of War on Land and its Annex (adopted 29 July 1899, entered into force 4 September 1900) 13 Stat 1803; Hague Convention IV respecting the Laws and Customs of War on Land and its Annex (adopted 18 October 1907, entered into force 26 January 1910) 36 Stat 2277.

[9] Conrad Schetter, 'Krieg' in Ferdinand Bitz and Masnfred Speck (eds), *Helden des Helfens: Die deutsche Katastrophenhilfe im internationalen Einsatz* (Lau Verlag 2018) 221–24.

[10] Herfried Münkler, *Neue Kriege* (Rowohlt 2002).

[11] Patrick Porter, *Military Orientalism: Eastern War through Western Eyes* (Hurst 2009).

to be mentioned that this view completely ignored the monstrous acts of violence committed by colonial and imperial armies during these periods.[12]

The centrality of the idea of humanitarianism for colonial politics can hardly be overstated, especially whenever colonialism was interpreted as the implementation of the idea of universal humanity, which included a mandate for a *mission civilisatrice*.[13] If we follow Talal Asad,[14] the idea of universal humanity has prepared the ground for defining the human rights agenda in the post-colonial phase.[15] This universalist approach may reject political or social or biological division. However, the distinction between those who provide humanitarian aid and those who receive it still creates an important inequality that delimits the scope of agency of providers and recipients and establishes a hierarchy.[16] Critical scholars therefore see humanitarian aid, in the context of a new humanitarian interventionism, as the 'nice face of a new colonialism'[17] or as 'the left hand of Empire'.[18]

This brief overview of the origins and development of the idea of humanitarian aid shows that the link with the Western order of warfare is not limited to its origins. In the following chapter, we will take a closer look at how the dissolution of the boundaries of war has affected humanitarian aid (and its connection to the Western order of warfare).

C. The End of Highly Regulated Warfare and the Dilemmas of Humanitarian Aid

It was not until the 1990s that the public became aware that highly regulated warfare and the role played in it by humanitarian aid was an exception rather than the rule. The previous, Cold War era was geared towards reordering the many political and social changes that two world wars had brought about (including decolonization and a bipolar world order). The colonial wars of liberation, wars of secession, and proxy wars of the superpowers which dominated the period between 1945 and 1989, at least in public perception, were conceptualized against the blueprint of the world wars. These wars were not about the state as such but rather about who controlled the state, their ideological colour, and whether one wanted to belong to this or that state. It is true that there were protracted, smouldering civil wars that defied ideological attribution during that era, but they tended to fly under the radar of global attention.

12 Dierk Walter, *Colonial Violence: European Empires and the Use of Force* (OUP 2017).

13 Gayatri Chakravorty Spivak, 'Can the Subaltern Speak?' in: Cary Nelson and Lawrence Grossberg (eds) *Marxism and the Interpretation of Culture* (University of Illinois Press 1988) 271–313; Partha Chatterjee, *The Nation and Its Fragments: Colonial and Postcolonial Histories* (Princeton University Press 1993); Ilana Feldman and Miriam Iris Ticktin (eds), *In the Name of Humanity: The Government of Threat and Care* (Duke University Press 2010).

14 Talal Asad, *Formations of the Secular* (Stanford University Press 2003).

15 Also Makau Mutua, 'Savages, Victims, and Saviors: the Metaphor of Human Rights' (2001) 42 Harvard International Law Journal 201–45 for further critique of this agenda.

16 William Easterly, *The White Man's Burden* (Penguin Press 2006).

17 Calhoun (n 2) 41.

18 Michel Agier, 'La main gauche de l'Empire' (2003) 11(1) Multitudes 67–77.

Nowadays, types of warfare predominate in which all the regulations typical of the state wars of the past seem to have been abolished. They are not limited in time or space; they are asymmetrical and no longer distinguish between combatants and civilians. In these conflicts, the state is no longer the sole determinant of war and peace. 'New', 'hybrid', or 'fluid' wars dominate—the various terms circulating in the public sphere illustrate the difficulty of grasping the deviations from state wars. Yet, it is precisely these conflicts that are at the centre of the HDP nexus discourse.[19]

The dissolution of the order of warfare led to a dilemma for humanitarian aid. On the one hand, its necessity for alleviating suffering in war zones became increasingly clear; on the other, the humanitarian principles and boundaries to other forms of intervention that had been formed in the context of wars between states could hardly be maintained. Thus, in practice, it became increasingly clear that humanitarian aid could not live up to its own principles, such as humanity, impartiality, and neutrality. Since the 1990s we have been witnessing a profound crisis in humanitarian aid, which has manifested itself in various dimensions, to which we will turn next.

1. Permanent State of Complex Emergencies

Given the characteristics of current wars and the prevalence of fragile statehood, humanitarian aid increasingly takes the form of responding to complex emergencies. In complex emergencies, acute and chronic elements combine to create a medium- to long-term humanitarian emergency for the affected population.[20] Endemic, protracted emergencies emerge when natural disasters, famines, pandemics, or food insecurity occur in regions with violent conflict, a lack of support structures, and fragile statehood. Examples include droughts and crop failures (eg in Afghanistan, South Sudan, Somalia), floods (eg in Afghanistan, Pakistan), tsunamis (in Aceh, Sri Lanka), or earthquakes (in Haiti, Afghanistan, Pakistan).[21]

The increasing duration of such emergencies means that in many places humanitarian aid has become a permanent fixture. This is exemplified by refugee camps such as those in Dadab and Kakuma (both Kenya), Zaatari (Jordan), Katumba (Tanzania), Jalozai (Pakistan), or Nahr al-Bared (Lebanon), which have existed for decades and are managed under a humanitarian mandate. In recent years, therefore, a large proportion of humanitarian funding has been continuously devoted to protracted, unresolved crises. In such endemic, protracted emergencies, aid actors are faced with multiple and sometimes conflicting tasks. The traditional tasks of humanitarian work (mainly emergency relief) have gradually been complemented by basic services (eg education, health education), which are generally considered to be part of development cooperation. The portfolio of many humanitarian organizations has thus

[19] See Ch. 1 Section E.

[20] David Keen, *Complex Emergencies* (Polity 2008).

[21] Birgit Kemmerling, Conrad Schetter, and Lars Wirkus, 'The Logics of War and Food (In)Security' (2022) 33 Global Food Security, 100634.

expanded.[22] As a result, there are very few organizations (examples of those which do exist include MSF and the ICRC) now whose mandate is exclusively humanitarian and which maintain a clear demarcation from development cooperation.

In these contexts, humanitarian aid has been going beyond the narrow temporal limits for missions which were originally core characteristics. As a result, it has become impossible not to be drawn into tasks such as structural development, or to respond to the conflict-laden collective identities of the affected populations. Under these circumstances, it is ever more difficult to maintain the principles of impartiality and neutrality. Thus, humanitarian organizations contribute directly to normatively motivated development processes.

2. Humanitarian Aid—Part of the War Economy

Humanitarian aid often runs the risk of becoming a structuring element in protracted violent conflicts or processes of state failure.[23] As early as the 1990s, it became clear that humanitarian aid was becoming part of the political economy of violent conflicts in many places (eg DR Congo, Darfur, South Sudan), as the various parties to these conflicts came to rely on the provision of material resources and infrastructure by aid organizations or included them in their economy of violence.[24] Violent actors also often sought to gain legitimacy in the eyes of the population through access to humanitarian aid. Some regimes, often with a deficit in welfare provision, have left entire areas of emergency care to humanitarian organizations and shirked their responsibilities. The Taliban, for example, which retook power in Afghanistan in August 2021, have a vision of the state based solely on providing security, administering justice, and collecting taxes. Despite a catastrophic humanitarian emergency in the country, they have deliberately left it to international humanitarian aid to ensure the survival of the population.[25]

The criticism of such developments is that in many conflicts, humanitarian aid as a whole tends to prolong violent conflict, suffering, poverty, exclusion, and social inequality.[26] Maintaining the neutral stance of humanitarian actors while at the same time being confronted with a war economy and development tasks is an obstacle to developing perspectives for peace. Against this background, the idea of the HDP nexus initially appears as a plausible way to let any integration of humanitarian aid and development cooperation go hand in hand with a repositioning vis-à-vis the conflict parties.

[22] Mark Duffield, 'NGO Relief in War Zones: Towards an Analysis of the New Aid Paradigm' (1997) 18(3) Third World Quarterly 527–42.

[23] ibid.

[24] Gilles Carbonnier, *Humanitarian Economics. War, Disaster, and the Global Aid Market* (Hurst 2015).

[25] Since the ban on women's participation in humanitarian aid at the end of 2022, even this support is coming to an end as many international organizations have withdrawn from Afghanistan.

[26] David Chandler, 'The Road to Military Humanitarianism: How the Human Rights NGOs Shaped a New Humanitarian Agenda' (2001) 23(3) Human Rights Quarterly 678–700.

3. Politization of Humanitarian Aid

Humanitarian aid—precisely because of its proclaimed refusal to take political positions—is also repeatedly at the mercy of attempts to instrumentalize it for political interests. The majority of humanitarian organizations are now financed by (inter-)governmental donors. This creates dependencies—for instance, in the selection of countries for which resources are made available in the first place.[27] Humanitarian organizations, which have only a small amount of donations and are heavily dependent on third-party funding from donors, are particularly vulnerable to being instrumentalized by these donors. In the Western Sahel, for example, the European Union deliberately used the EU Emergency Trust Fund for Africa (EUTF) to channel humanitarian aid into regions that were pivotal for the UN's military interventions and the French-led Barkhane military mission.[28] This case is an example of how donor interests, rather than the vulnerability of the population, determine where and to whom humanitarian aid is provided. Another related concern is that governments and their agencies politically influence who has access to humanitarian aid. In the course of the Syrian war (2011–2025), a politicization of humanitarian aid has taken place since 2015. As agreed between the Syrian government and the United Nations, aid primarily benefited government-held areas, while opposition-held areas often remained cut off from humanitarian access.[29] This politicization of aid poses a dilemma for humanitarian aid organizations: if they were to protest against such politicized access restrictions with conditionalities, such as by attaching certain conditions to the provision of aid and in the worst case by stopping it altogether, they would go against the foundational humanitarian imperative. If they continued under the politicized conditions, they would undermine the principles of impartiality and neutrality of humanitarian aid.

4. Securitization of Humanitarian Aid

The increasing non-observance of the protected position of humanitarian aid workers has become an increasingly important factor for the organization of humanitarian aid. According to the Aid Worker Security Database, between 1997 and January 2026, 3,368 humanitarian workers and relief workers were killed, 2,259 kidnapped, and 3,246 injured worldwide.[30] Over the course of nearly 30 years, the number of incidents increased 18 times, from annually 35 (1997) to 611 (2024) incidents. The causes of this trend are the subject of debate: some attribute it to a deliberate military

[27] Carbonnier (n 23).

[28] Emma Fanning and Jessica Fullwood-Thomas, 'The Humanitarian-Development-Peace Nexus: What Does it Mean for Multi-Mandated Organizations?' (Oxfam, Oxfam Discussion Paper, 2019); Katja Mielke, Max Mutschler, and Esther Meininghaus, 'For a Dynamic Approach to Stabilization' (2020) 27(5) International Peacekeeping 810–35.

[29] Esther Meininghaus, 'Humanitarianism in Intra-State Conflict: Aid Inequality and Local Governance in Government- and Opposition-Controlled Areas in the Syrian War' (2016) 37(8) Third World Quarterly 1454–1482.

[30] Humanitarian Outcomes, 'The Aid Worker Security Database, 1997–present' <https://aidworkersecurity.org/> accessed 21 January 2026.

instrumentalization of humanitarian aid, others to a general increase in military operations,[31] which no longer allow for neutrality and impartiality.[32] Alternative explanations include the growing dominance of protracted civil wars or the increase in the number of humanitarian activities in conflict areas over the past three decades.[33] Regardless of which of these arguments one follows, humanitarian workers increasingly appear as 'soft targets' in violent conflicts.

In response, a securitization of humanitarian workers is emerging, with almost all humanitarian organizations tending to place the 'survival value' of their own (foreign) staff above that of the local populations and local staff. There are numerous examples of this tendency, particularly in relation to the evacuation of international staff and the abandonment of local staff.[34] The lives of foreign humanitarian workers deployed by aid organizations tend to be more securitized than those of the general population in zones of violent conflict, for example being housed in secured compounds and driven around in armoured vehicles.[35] In extreme cases, humanitarian agencies even resort to armed protection, which had been considered a taboo for decades.

Through such measures, a gradation of the value of life takes place that is diametrically opposed to the humanitarian principle of humanity which entails the equality of all human life. In other words, even humanitarian aid today is characterized by clear power asymmetries and the drawing of boundaries. These asymmetries between suffering populations and humanitarian workers and between expatriate and local staff,[36] which are reflected in varying degrees of securitization, underscore the at least partly political nature of humanitarian aid missions. The increasing insecurity of humanitarian workers leads to responses which make the self-positioning of humanitarian organizations as politically neutral, as discussed in section B, less tenable, and bolster perceptions of humanitarian aid as a party to, or object of, economies of violence.[37]

On the one hand, the challenges of humanitarian aid outlined here give an impression of the background that makes the goal of a HDP nexus plausible as a reaction to the blurring of the lines between humanitarian aid and development cooperation. On the other hand, they also illustrate the tensions inherent in the idea of the HDP nexus, especially with regard to the inclusion of the peace dimension.

Humanitarian organizations have, however, not remained unresponsive to these challenges. Humanitarian aid organizations have increasingly developed guidelines for adapting their interventions to complex conflict situations, going back, for

[31] Peter Hoffman and Thomas Weiss, *Humanitarianism, War and Politics* (Rowman & Littlefield 2017) 206.

[32] Francis Kofi Abiew, 'Humanitarian Action Under Fire. Reflections on the Role of NGOs in Conflict and Post-Conflict Situations' (2012) 19(2) International Peacekeeping 203–216.

[33] Kristian Hoelscher, Jason Miklian, and Havard Mokleiv Nygard, 'Conflict, Peacekeeping, and Humanitarian Security: Understanding Violent Attacks Against Aid Workers' (2017) 24(4) *International Peacekeeping* 538–65.

[34] Fassin (n 2).

[35] Lisa Smirl, *Spaces of Aid: How Cars, Compounds and Hotels Shape Humanitarianism* (Zed Books 2015); Mark Duffield, 'Risk-management and the Fortified Aid Compound: Everyday Life in Post-interventionary Society' (2010) 4(4) Journal of Intervention and Statebuilding 453–74.

[36] Duffield, 'NGO Relief in War Zones' (n 22).

[37] Michael Neuman and Fabrice Weissman, *Saving Lives and Staying Alive: Humanitarian Security in the Age of Risk Management* (Hurst 2016).

example, to the do-no-harm approach first developed in the early 1990s.[38] As a result, humanitarian aid workers are considering to a much greater extent the specific challenges connected to working in highly politicized environments. At the same time, such conflict sensitivity raises awareness of the fact that humanitarian action in conflict situations can have different short, medium, and long-term impacts, which again highlights the difficulty of maintaining impartiality and neutrality.

D. Attempts to Hijack Humanitarian Aid

The challenges posed to humanitarian aid mentioned in section C have led to attempts at adjustment which compromise the uniqueness and singularity of humanitarian aid. New Humanitarianism, for example, argues that the neutrality and impartiality of classical humanitarianism is subject to hypocrisy, since these principles cannot be jointly upheld at any one point in time.[39] This is because impartiality is built on the idea of equal treatment, while neutrality requires inaction. Instead of focusing on the argument of New Humanitarianism we shall identify the conceptual and practical changes that have driven the softening of the distinctiveness of humanitarian aid. We have selected concrete examples which prepared the ground for the current HDP nexus discussion.

- *Humanitarian interventions:* Since the 1990s, the labelling of interventions as 'humanitarian' has played an important role in legitimizing them.[40] In particular, the human security paradigm has become the conceptual backbone of the demand for Responsibility to Protect (r2p), which legitimizes military intervention to save lives.[41] Many critics see this labelling as an act of propaganda.[42] They warn that the label 'humanitarian intervention' conceals other interests of the intervening powers. After all, an intervention that prioritizes the protection of individual human beings is far more likely to gain political legitimacy than one that identifies tangible economic or political interests. The very dynamics of such military interventions (eg in Libya in the 2010s) also show that they quickly move from protecting life itself to structurally changing the normative political framework, resulting in regime change. Finally, the question remains as to whether military actions in the name of humanitarianism are not a contradiction in terms. Military actions may aim to protect human life at the cost of harming others. Humanitarian interventions are based on the evaluative division of victims from

[38] Mary B Anderson, *Do No Harm: How Aid Can Support Peace—or War* (Lynne-Rienner 1999).

[39] Charlotte Dany, 'Politicization of Humanitarian Aid in the European Union' (2015) 20(3) European Foreign Affairs Review 419–37.

[40] Jeff Holzgrefe and Robert Keohane (eds) *Humanitarian Intervention. Ethical, Legal, and Political Dilemmas* (CUP 2003).

[41] International Commission on Intervention and State Sovereignty (ICISS), *The Responsibility to Protect: Report of the International Commission on Intervention and State Sovereignty* (International Development Research Centre 2001).

[42] Including Mark Duffield, *Development, Security and Unending War: Governing the World of People* (Polity 2007); Mahmood Mamdani, 'Responsibility to Protect or Right to Punish?' (2010) 4(1) Journal of Intervention and Statebuilding 53–67.

perpetrators, which already goes against the humanitarian principles of neutrality and impartiality. After all, one key idea behind humanitarianism was to refuse to answer the question of which human life has a higher value.

- *LRRD:* The concept of linking relief, rehabilitation, and development (LRRD) has played a significant role in breaking down the rigid demarcation between humanitarian aid and development cooperation since the 1900s.[43] In the past, for example, it was usually argued that the transition from humanitarian to development interventions after a war was continuous (continuum approach). In the 2000s, the continuum approach prevailed, addressing the coexistence and cooperation of humanitarian and development interventions.[44] Since 2015, the United Nations has been attempting to break down the separation between humanitarian aid and development cooperation under the label The New Way of Working (NWOW). Some organizations (eg Welthungerhilfe), now combine humanitarian aid and development activities in their organizations but keep the two wings strictly separate in their internal structure. The problem with LRRD approaches is that the boundaries between humanitarian principles and politically defined development activities become blurred, and that this seems to be deliberate. In LRRD measures, an organization is often no longer able to say whether it is still adhering to humanitarian principles or not. In other words, a pragmatic view prevails, with the risk that self-reflection on the political impact of one's own actions is lost or that a creeping politicization of humanitarian aid is taking place.[45]
- *Networked approach:* Since the late 1990s, for example in the case of Germany, there have been increasing calls to overcome silo thinking and adopt a unified national policy ('whole of government' approaches) to ensure coherence and efficiency on behalf of the taxpayer. Particularly since the intervention in Afghanistan, this desire for coherence has been extended to the military level.[46] The German government developed the concept of a networked approach for the mission in Afghanistan, but its implementation failed because of the reluctance of humanitarian as well as development cooperation actors. The hurdles and gaps between the different mentalities—especially between civilian and military actors—were too great.
- *Integrated Missions:* So-called Integrated Missions, such as those pursued by the United Nations in many of its interventions, go one step further. They allow for the concentration of military, development, and humanitarian capacities (also spatially) in interventions to allow for better coordination and increased efficiency. Integrated missions are strongly influenced by normative ideas in that they aim at institution-building, even state-building. The majority of humanitarian organizations have resisted such integrated spaces and claimed their own

[43] Joanna Macrae, *Aiding Recovery? The Crisis of Aid in Chronic Political Emergencies* (Zed Books 2001).

[44] Redfield (n 5); Hoffman and Weiss (n 30).

[45] Irina Mosel and Simon Levine, *Remaking the Case for Linking Relief, Rehabilitation and Development* (Overseas Development Institute, Humanitarian Policy Group Commissioned Report, 2014).

[46] Conrad Schetter and Rainer Glassner, 'Zivil-militärische Grauzone. Integrierte Friedensmissionen und Neuer Humanitarismus schlagen neue Allianzen' (2007) 15/16 Eins Entwicklungspolitik 24–28.

humanitarian spaces.[47] However, it is increasingly a challenge in the day-to-day practice of humanitarian organizations to maintain equidistance from all political and military actors and yet receive sufficient information (eg on the security situation).

- *Privatization:* Humanitarian aid has arguably become the nucleus of a now fully developed emergency aid industry.[48] A pragmatic development in relation to this industry is the phenomenon of private (security) companies taking over tasks that used to be specific to humanitarian aid (food distribution, etc) at the request of intervening states, leading to fears of a general privatization of emergency aid and an undermining of humanitarian principles.[49] An example of this is the Israel-driven establishment of the US organization Gaza Humanitarian Foundation (GHF) in 2025, aimed at replacing UNRWA (United Nations Relief and Works Agency for Palestine Refugees in the Near East) in Gaza.

These examples of the dissolution of boundaries of humanitarian aid make the idea of a nexus between humanitarian aid, development cooperation, and peace appear as a plausible response to practice. Its emphasis on bringing in peace as a third component further seems apt to counter fears of politicization or the appropriation of humanitarian aid by the military. The question is whether the design of the HDP nexus is robust enough to avert these concerns from the humanitarian camp or whether it is merely a new approach to instrumentalizing humanitarian aid. In the following paragraph, we will examine the HDP nexus in more detail.

E. Between the HDP Nexus and the HDW Nexus

The term 'HDP nexus' emerged in the wake of the 2016 Global Humanitarian Summit in Istanbul and was given prominence by UN Secretary-General Antonio Guterres in 2017.[50] It is a term coined by the donor community and the United Nations, rather than by academia or aid agencies themselves. While humanitarian aid organizations have been seeking to evade appropriation by other logics of intervention (eg development, security) in the previous three decades with diminishing success,[51] the HDP approach opens a new chapter, which is much more complex than, for example, the continuum/contiguum approaches, as it also includes a peace component.

Initial ideas on how to bring this approach to life took a technocratic or pragmatic approach, focusing solely on synchronizing specific programme lines and their practical implementation to achieve the Sustainable Development Goals (SDGs).[52] In their

[47] Joanna Macrae (ed), 'New Humanitarianisms: A Review of Trends in Global Humanitarian Action' (*HPG Report* No 11, 2002) <http://cdn-odi-production.s3-website-eu-west-1.amazonaws.com/media/documents/293.pdf> accessed 11 July 2023.

[48] Fassin (n 2).

[49] Christopher Spearin, 'Private, Armed and Humanitarian? States, NGOs, and International Private Security Companies and Shifting Humanitarianism' (2008) 39(4) Security Dialogue 363–82.

[50] Sultan Barakat and Sansom Milton, 'Localisation across the Humanitarian-Development-Peace Nexus' (2020) 15(2) Journal of Peacebuilding & Development 147–63.

[51] Redfield (n 5).

[52] Howe (n 1).

arguments for the HDP nexus, donors and practitioners stress that the HDP nexus, as a holistic approach, can achieve synergies and efficiencies between budget lines and practical implementation which have previously been separate and conflicting. However, such ventures carry the inherent risk of simplification and of ignoring precisely the requirements that flow from the distinctive principles of humanitarian aid. Various political actors have attempted to breathe life into the HDP nexus in their own way. In the following, we will first critically outline where we see the starting points for war rather than peace becoming the frame of reference for the HDP nexus. We will then show how the HDP nexus should be conceived to reconcile humanitarian aid and peace.

1. Peace vs War/Security

In terms of its historical roots as well as its definition, humanitarian aid is more closely linked to war than peace. This fact leads to a reversal of the burden of proof. First, before we can talk about establishing a link to peace, it has to be shown that the link between humanitarian aid and development cooperation does not tend to support the logic of war.

Second, the changes in humanitarian aid and development cooperation in recent decades[53] have brought the two closer together. However, this is not a generic synergy but the result of a response to crises such as the erosion of the time and space boundaries of wars (see sections B and C). In this sense, the precondition for the HDP nexus is a crisis of the 'H' and 'D' components, each of which has moved closer to the logic of war rather than away from it. These changes make the success of an HDP nexus more difficult to achieve and suggest a tendency towards an HDW nexus.

Third, a concept such as the HDP nexus runs the risk of elevating a pragmatic, often crisis-laden chain of responses to a normative goal. This could help legitimize the status quo and possibly support trends in humanitarian aid and development cooperation in which donor logic equates security with peace, such as integrated missions or networked approaches. Due to the multifaceted erosion of the boundaries of war in recent decades, the term 'security' has increasingly been used to describe the tasks of military actors. An illustrative example of this is the case of Afghanistan, where the military mission has been linked to developmental reconstruction under the rubric of 'no development without security'. Military actions ranging from the establishment of checkpoints to patrols and even combat operations were framed as providing security. Thus, in asymmetric wars, counterinsurgency approaches, which are more akin to policing, replace conventional forms of warfare.[54] The question of whose security is at stake and what exactly is meant by security is often only vaguely answered to maximize the scope for military action. Nevertheless, at its core, we can assume an understanding of security that revolves around the establishment and enforcement of

[53] Janosch Prinz and Conrad Schetter, 'Spatial-Moral Ordering in the War on Terror: Ungoverned Spaces as a Challenge to Humanitarianism' (2021) 15(1) Journal of Intervention and Statebuilding 96–113.

[54] Connrad Schetter, 'Counterinsurgency, Anthropology, Retreat–The US Military's COIN "Strategy" in Afghanistan' (2012) 53(2) Orient 24–34.

state sovereignty (including the establishment of a monopoly on the use of force). The implementation of such an understanding of security by military means could be defined as the establishment of peace. Humanitarian organizations would be concerned about a peace component defined in such a way. Humanitarian organizations thus criticize the HDP nexus because they fear the instrumentalization of humanitarian aidfor the interests and security policies of Western donors by undermining the concept of peace.[55] The overarching problem they are facing is that nowadays, while military interventions are becoming increasingly legitimized by the concept of security, the demarcation between war and peace is being blurred.

In its current form, the HDP nexus is thus neither a normative ideal model nor a conducive practice from a perspective of peace promotion. One can arguably speak of a humanitarian-development-war nexus instead, or HDW nexus for short. An alternative conceptualization of HDP would have to focus on dissociating it from the logic of war and reorienting it towards the role of peace as binding together development and humanitarian aid. It is therefore somewhat incomprehensible that despite the criticism of the term of human security, it is still used with a positive connotation in the HDP debate.[56]

2. A Peace-Centred HDP Nexus: Building Resilience Capacities

For a peace-centred HDP nexus, it is necessary to frame the concept of peace in such a way that humanitarian aid (and also development cooperation) is not exploited by security actors or interests. Consequently, the concept of peace appropriate for the HDP nexus needs to exclude the use of physical force—in war or in order to establish security. Thus—precisely because of the erosion of the boundaries of war—the concept of peace must be narrowed to keep ambiguities and vagueness to a minimum.

One option would be to define peace less in terms of violence (negative peace = absence of war) and more in terms of positive peace (overcoming inequalities and injustices), especially since the idea of positive peace overlaps strongly with the ideas driving development cooperation. From a humanitarian perspective, the normative charge of positive peace would undoubtedly conflict with the idea of neutrality and impartiality which reproduces many of the problems discussed in sections B and C. For some humanitarian organizations, such as the ICRC, a commitment to peace remains difficult to reconcile with their core principles of neutrality and impartiality. At the same time, this would allow humanitarian aid to emancipate itself from its relationship with war and redefine itself in relation to peace.

Another option to enable the connection to peace would be to connect humanitarian aid to the concept of resilience—arguably one of the most important social sciences buzzwords of the last two decades, as Figure 3.1 is showing. At its core, resilience is

[55] Eg Emmanuel Tronc, Rob Grace and Anaïde Nahikian, 'Realities and Myths of the "Triple Nexus": Local Perspectives on Peacebuilding, Development, and Humanitarian Action in Mali' (Harvard Humanitarian Initiative, Humanitarian Action at the Frontlines: Field Analysis Series, 2019) <https://hhi.harvard.edu/publications/realities-and-myths-"triple-nexus"-local-perspectives> accessed 21 January 2026; Barakat and Milton (n 50).

[56] For example Fanning and Fullwood-Thomas (n 28).

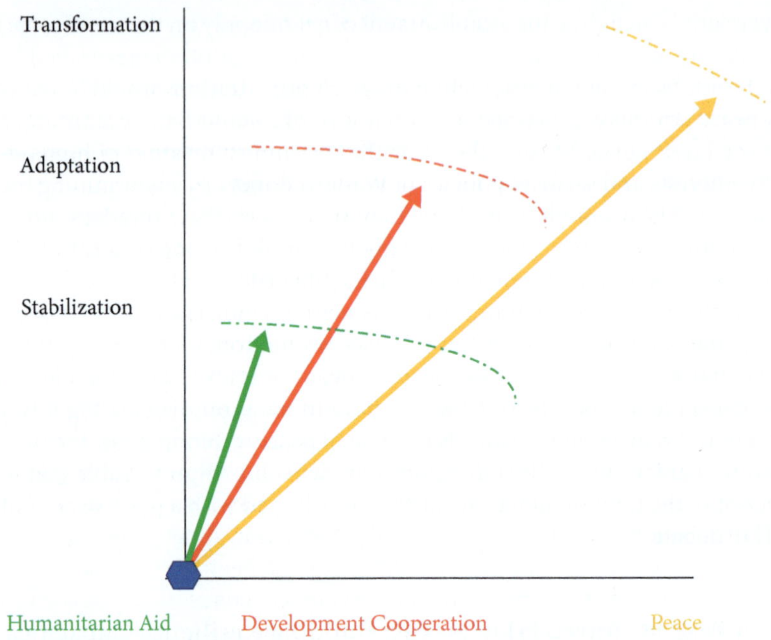

Figure 3.1 HDP nexus and resilience

about strengthening a society's ability to respond to crises. In the context of violent conflict, resilience is difficult to build because it is contextually shaped by cultural perceptions and political power relations.[57] Thus, in the context of war, resilience needs to emphasize a society's capacity not to use physical violence to resolve its conflicts (negative peace) and to find peaceful ways for marginalized groups to express their identities and access community resources (positive peace). Humanitarian aid can help to ensure basic survival with dignity, thereby strengthening existing resilience capacities. The next step on the resilience scale would be to strengthen capacities to adapt resilience forces, which would be the domain of development cooperation. The third and highest level would be the transformation of resilience capacities, which can then be understood as peace. By strengthening resilience, humanitarian aid can counter the criticism that its unreflective actions are themselves contributing to the prolongation of war and suffering. Moreover, the concept of resilience implies a radical shift in the governance of aid. The focus is no longer on the aid organization and its principles but on the communities themselves, who determine what capacities they lack to become more resilient in violent conflicts. Since it is up to the affected people themselves to identify and build the necessary resilience capacities, external normative influence is limited. This would undoubtedly be a radical break with current aid industry practices, as aid would no longer be based on the logic of international donors, IOs, and (I)NGOs, but solely on the capacity needs of the affected population.

[57] David Chandler, *Resilience: The Governance of Complexity* (Routledge 2014).

F. Conclusion

Humanitarian aid is a key component in the success or failure of the HDP nexus idea. Various organizations and scholars remain undecided about its future course. In this chapter, we have looked beyond the debates between proponents and opponents of politicized humanitarian aid and focused on the real-historical and conceptual roots of humanitarianism, noting a connection to logics of war and logics of distinction. This raised initial doubts about the plausibility of an HDP nexus. We then outlined the crises and challenges of humanitarian aid, especially through the erosion of the boundaries of war in space and time, which showed that the HDP nexus follows long-term tendencies towards the softening of the distinctiveness of humanitarian aid. This was followed by a presentation of some humanitarian responses to these crises and challenges. These responses confirmed that linking humanitarian aid to development cooperation often stabilizes security and war logics and made plausible how the current HPD nexus discussion was partly shaped by these practices. Finally, we synthesized these doubts into a critique suggesting that the HDW nexus between humanitarian aid, development, and war is in the first instance more plausible than HDP, an idea that was polemically introduced at the beginning of this chapter. By way of contrast, we then presented the options and challenges of a peace-centred re-alignment of the HDP nexus with resilience capacity building. The conclusion is that the HDP nexus remains an unstable construct that opens up many possibilities for appropriation and the continuation of the status quo, but also offers the potential for a reflexive turn of humanitarianism that could provide an impetus for a peace-centred fusion with development cooperation.

4

Gender, Protracted Conflicts, and the Triple Nexus

A Feminist Critique

Olga Jurasz, Moa Peldán, and Leena Vastapuu

A. Introduction

Public international law thrives on crises,[1] be it armed conflicts, states of emergency, environmental catastrophes, mass influx of migrants, or gross violations of human rights. Although the maintenance of international peace and security—alongside commitment to equal rights and non-discrimination—is one of the key purposes of the UN, international law continuously encounters situations that pose a threat to this objective. What is more, the allegedly shifting character of warfare, especially towards 'new wars'[2]—conflicts which are intractable, endless, directed at civilian populations, characterized by widespread human rights violations, and waged by a number of non-state actors—challenges the current normative structures of international law. This is particularly so with regard to the law on the use of force, conduct of hostilities, and protections to civilians and combatants afforded in such situations. The increasingly protracted nature of 'new wars' further disrupts neat dualities of conflict/peace, conflict/post-conflict, civilian/combatant which are well honed and preserved by international law.

The concept of 'new war' and its numerous variations has come under severe criticism. It has for instance been criticized as ahistorical,[3] Western-centric,[4] and culturalist,[5] with the consequence of leading to misguided western-led military operations in contexts such as Iraq and Afghanistan. However, much of this criticism fails to address gender essentialisms and binaries embedded in such conceptualizations,[6] which in turn has direct implications not only during the conflicts but also in their

[1] Hilary Charlesworth, 'International Law: A Discipline of Crisis' (2002) 65 Modern Law Review 377.
[2] Mary Kaldor, *New and Old Wars* (Polity Press 2012).
[3] Edward Newman, 'The "New Wars" Debate: A Historical Perspective is Needed' (2004) 35 Security Dialogue 173.
[4] Mike Smith, 'Guerrillas in the Mist: Reassessing Strategy and Low Intensity Warfare' (2003) 29 Review of International Studies 19–37; Tarak Barkawi, 'Decolonizing War' (2016) 1 European Journal of International Security 199–214.
[5] Patrick Porter, *Military Orientalism: Eastern War through Western Eyes* (Hurst & Co 2009).
[6] Leena Vastapuu, 'Beans, Bullets and Bandages? Gendered and Racialised Othering in the Depiction of Military Support Work' [2023] Civil Wars 1.

Olga Jurasz, Moa Peldán, and Leena Vastapuu, *Gender, Protracted Conflicts, and the Triple Nexus* In: *From Protracted Conflict to Sustainable Peace?* Edited by: Heike Krieger, Giedre Jokubauskaite, Asli Ozcelik, and Andreas Buser, Oxford University Press.
DOI: 10.1093/9780198967385.003.0005

aftermath, in the period of 'transition' from conflict to sustainable peace.[7] This includes the so-called triple-nexus approach that has the aim to capture interlinkages between the humanitarian, development, and peace sectors in conflict and post-conflict programming.

In this chapter, we take a critical look at the triple nexus through a feminist international law and feminist International Relations (IR) lens. Our approach allows us to examine the potential value added of the triple nexus to advance (feminist) peace and address gendered aspects of modern, protracted conflicts. We argue that despite some progress, including the adoption of the Women, Peace and Security Agenda (WPS Agenda) at the United Nations in 2000, international law is still lacking when it comes to capturing and meaningfully responding to the gendered effects of protracted conflicts. We argue that the concept of the triple nexus is not a novelty to feminists working on gender and conflict across international law and IR, who have long called for greater synchronization of efforts and complementarity in peacebuilding and addressing gender-specific impacts of conflicts on women. We further conclude that, due to the 'status' of the triple nexus (i.e. it is not a legal instrument nor legally binding), it is unlikely to exert influence on substantive developments in international law which would advance (feminist) peace. However, we do recognize that international law is reflected in, and has application to, each of the strands of the triple nexus. In that respect, viewing international law through the triple-nexus lens may spur an approach which would facilitate calls for overcoming fragmentation in international law applicable to conflict and post-conflict situations.

B. Gender and Protracted Armed Conflicts: International Law and International Relations (IR) Perspectives

To construct our argument, we approach protracted armed conflicts from three complementary perspectives in this section. First, we present the normative framework guiding international programming. Second, we provide an overview on how feminist theorizing on International Relations (IR) came about, and then do the same with feminist approaches to international law. It is noteworthy that feminist approaches in these two disciplines developed by and large as a criticism towards the mainstream approaches that seemed inadequate to grasp the lived experiences of women in and around conflict and war.

1. Protracted Armed Conflicts: A Gender Perspective

The detrimental and gender-specific position of women and girls in armed conflict was recognized at the international level during the Fourth World Conference on

[7] Leena Vastapuu, 'Not Enough Soldier, Not Enough Civilian: The Continuing Under-Representation of Female Soldiers in Disarmament, Demobilisation and Reintegration (DDR) Programmes' in Tarja Väyrynen, Élise Feron, and Catia Confortini (eds), *Routledge Handbook of Feminist Peace Research* (Routledge 2021) 231.

Women in 1995, where it was noted that 'while entire communities suffer the consequences of armed conflict and terrorism, women and girls are particularly affected because of their status in society and sex'.[8]

The WPS Agenda, inaugurated on 31 October 2000 with the adoption of United Nations Security Council Resolution 1325,[9] now includes altogether ten Resolutions (1325, 1820, 1888, 1889, 1960, 2106, 2122, 2422, 2467, and 2493). The main emphasis of Resolution 1325 was to increase the inclusion of women in all aspects of peacemaking and peacekeeping, as well as to consider women's and girls' special needs in conflict and their aftermath, including means to combat sexual violence. With the ensuing nine resolutions the Agenda has expanded significantly and incorporated a wider understanding of gender, yet the core has been and remains the goal of increasing the inclusion of women in peacebuilding efforts and security institutions in post-conflict settings.

Indeed, women's experiences of armed conflict are underscored by their gender roles within a particular social context, but they are by far not uniform. While there exist some common aspects, women's actual experiences depend on a range of factors, such as age, race, class, nationality, employment, socio-economic status and, finally, combatant or civilian status.[10] Protracted conflicts are characterized by high levels of insecurity for women, often involving high and recurring cycles of violence, not only physical but also economic. The continuum of conflict unveils a range of challenges to securing women's rights and durable peace, not least related to gender inequality, structural discrimination, and cycles of gender-based violence. Furthermore, the multi-layered consequences and complex gendered experiences of conflict are exacerbated by the existence of gender inequalities and structural discrimination in the 'new/emerging/transitional' political and legal systems, leading to further violations of women's civil and political but also socio-economic rights. This, for instance, is illustrated by the experiences of women during the Arab Spring, which saw many women becoming important socio-political players by publicly protesting against the governing regimes as well as taking on activist roles, particularly using social media. Arguably, the battles that they faced were two-fold: first, a battle against the regime and second, a fight against the existing patriarchal systems rooted in discrimination of women and reinforced by gender stereotypes which traditionally restricted participation of women in the public sphere and at such a scale. Yet, their involvement did not generally translate into greater domestic protection of women's rights or into substantive equality in the aftermath of these revolutions.[11] These realizations did not come about in a vacuum, however, but were the result of long-term advocacy of feminist activists and scholars, as exemplified in the following sections.

[8] United Nations, 'Report of the Fourth World Conference on Women' (17 October 1995) UN Doc A/CONF. 177/20, para 135.

[9] UNSCR 1325 (31 October 2000) UN Doc S/RES/1325.

[10] International Committee of the Red Cross, Women Facing War: ICRC Study on the Impact of Armed Conflict on Women (Geneva 2001); Christine Chinkin, 'Gender and Armed Conflict' in Andrew Clapham and Paola Gaeta (eds) *The Oxford Handbook of International Law in Armed Conflict* (OUP 2014) 677.

[11] Olga Jurasz, 'Women of the Revolution: The Future of Women's Rights in Post-Gaddafi Libya' in Carlo Panara and Gary Wilson (eds), *The Arab Spring. New Patterns for Democracy and International Law* (Martinus Nijhoff 2013) 123; Elisabeth Johansson-Nogués, 'Gendering of the Arab Spring? Rights and (in) security of Tunisian, Egyptian and Libyan Women' (2013) 44 Security Dialogue 393.

2. Feminist International Relations' Approaches to Protracted Armed Conflicts

Feminist International Relations (IR) theorizing emerged from the late 1980s, when several IR scholars began to critically observe the institutions and practices of world politics of the time. The question 'where are the women' was central in these efforts—simply observing war,[12] militarism and diplomatic practices,[13] the state and political economy,[14] or political theory itself[15] revealed the gendered nature of these phenomena and the workings of masculinities and femininities within them.

During the past thirty years, a significant amount of empirical work on women's involvement in protracted armed conflicts/contexts of 'irregularity' has emerged under the umbrella of Feminist IR. Leena Vastapuu[16] divides this literature into two sub-categories: projects observing women's and girls' (whose agency is further complicated by their age) roles in 'rebel governance' structures, on the one hand;[17] and projects investigating women's direct participation in armed forces in contexts of irregularity, on the other.[18] Furthermore, several scholars have investigated the 'post-war' period as a site of value contestation over accepted forms of masculinities and femininities, analysing for instance Security Sector Reform processes and

[12] Jean Elshtain, *Women and War* (1st edn, Basic Books 1987).

[13] Cynthia Enloe, *Bananas, Beaches and Bases: Making Feminist Sense of International Politics* (University of California Press 1989).

[14] V Spike Peterson (ed), *Gendered States: Feminist (Re)Visions of International Relations Theory* (Lynne Rienner Publishers 1992).

[15] J Ann Tickner, 'Hans Morgenthau's Principles of Political Realism: A Feminist Reformulation' (1988) 17 Millennium 429–40.

[16] Vastapuu (n 6) 7 f.

[17] For example, Cynthia Enloe, *Maneuvers: The International Politics of Militarizing Women's Lives* (University of California Press 2000); Nira Yuval-Davis, 'Gender, the Nationalist Imagination, War, and Peace' in Wenona Giles and Jennifer Hyndman (eds) *Sites of Violence: Gender and Conflict Zones* (University of California Press 2004) 170; V Spike Peterson, 'Gendering Informal Economies in Iraq' in Nicola Pratt and Nadje Al-Ali (eds), *Women and War in the Middle East: Transnational Perspectives* (Zed Books 2009) 35; Swati Parashar, 'Armed Resistance, Economic (In)Security and the Household: a Casestudy of the Maoist Insurgency in India' in Juanita Elias and Samanthi Gunawardana (eds), *The Global Political Economy of the Household in Asia* (Palgrave Macmillan UK 2013); Jeny Hedström, 'The Political Economy of the Kachin Revolutionary Household' (2017) 30 The Pacific Review 581; Victoria Basham and Sergio Catignani, 'War Is Where the Hearth Is: Gendered Labor and the Everyday Reproduction of the Geopolitical in the Army Reserves' (2018) 20 International Feminist Journal of Politics 153; Victoria Gilbert, 'Sister Citizens: Women in Syrian Rebel Governance' (2021) 17 Politics & Gender 552.

[18] For example, Lois Lorentzen and Jennifer Turpin (eds), *The Women and War Reader* (New York University Press 1998); Carolyn Nordstrom, 'Girls Behind the (Front)Lines' in Lois Lorentzen and Jennifer Turpin (eds), *The Women and War Reader* (New York University Press 1998) 80; Laura Sjoberg and Caron Gentry, *Mothers, Monsters, Whores: Women's Violence in Global Politics* (Zed Books 2007); Maria Eriksson Baaz and Maria Stern, 'The Gendered Subject of Violence in African Conflicts' in James Hentz (ed), *Routledge Handbook of African Security* (Routledge 2013) 157; Alexis Henshaw, 'Where Women Rebel' (2015) 18 International Feminist Journal of Politics 39; Meredith Loken and Hilary Matfess, 'Women's Participation in Violent Non-State Organizations and Terrorism' in Nukhet Sandal (ed), *Oxford Research Encyclopedia of International Studies* (OUP nd); Leena Vastapuu, 'Auto-Photographing (In) Securities: Former Young Female Soldiers' Post-War Struggles in Monrovia' in Rune Saugman and Juha Vuori (eds), *Visual Security Studies: Sights and Spectacles of Insecurity and War* (Routledge 2018); Leena Vastapuu, 'How to Find the "Hidden" Girl Soldier? Two Sets of Suggestions arising from Liberia' in Mark Drumbl and Jastine Barret (eds), *Research Handbook on Child Soldiers* (Edward Elgar 2019) 493.

Disarmament, Demobilisation, and Reintegration (DDR) programmes as interventions that more often than not fail to adequately cater for the needs of women and girls.

Feminist IR scholars have also investigated the WPS Agenda since its inception. Beyond providing general overviews and case studies,[19] critical researchers have delved into topics such as the marginalization of the Global South's agency,[20] elitisms and exclusions embedded in the Agenda,[21] and the use of essentializing language that victimizes women.[22] While not rejecting the transformative potential the Agenda still holds, many of these scholars argue that the 'add women and stir' approach is not enough, and that a truly transformative change can only take place if critical analysis is extended to the structures and norms underpinning the UN and other institutions operating in the international arena.

3. Feminist Perspectives on International Law, Gender, and Conflict

Feminist perspectives on the relationship between gender, conflict, and international law are a relatively recent development in the international law literature. The emergence of feminist critiques of international law in late 1980s and early 1990s, especially the works of Christine Chinkin, Hilary Charlesworth, Judith Gardam, and Shelley Wright, have paved the way to a feminist and gender critique of the rules governing armed conflicts (International Humanitarian Law, hereafter IHL).[23] Feminist engagements with international law—especially international humanitarian law and the use of force[24]—have uncovered many gaps and silences about women's lived experiences of armed conflicts, emphasizing that women experience armed conflict differently than men due to different male and female gender roles within the particular society as well as gender relations and power structures arising from them.[25] They unveiled the dissonance between the normative framework of international law applicable to

[19] E.g. Sara Davies and Jacqui True (eds), *The Oxford Handbook of Women, Peace, and Security* (OUP 2018); Paul Kirby and Laura Shepherd, 'Reintroducing Women, Peace & Security' (2016) 92 International Affairs 249.

[20] Soumita Basu, 'The Global South Writes 1325 (Too)' (2016) 37 International Political Science Review 362.

[21] Sheri Gibbings, 'No Angry Women at the United Nations: Political Dreams and the Cultural Politics of United Nations Security Council Resolution 1325' (2011) 13 International Feminist Journal of Politics 522.

[22] Nadine Puechguirbal, 'Discourses on Gender, Patriarchy and Resolution 1325: A Textual Analysis of UN Documents' (2010) 17 International Peacekeeping 172.

[23] Judith Gardam, 'A Feminist Analysis of Certain Aspects of International Humanitarian Law' (1988–89) 12 Australian Yearbook of International Law 265; Christine Chinkin, 'Feminist Interventions into International Law' (1997) 19 Adelaide Law Review 13; Christine Chinkin and Hilary Charlesworth, *The Boundaries of International Law: A Feminist Analysis* (Manchester University Press 2000).

[24] Christine Chinkin, 'A Gendered Perspective to the International Use of Force' (1988-1989) 12 Australian Yearbook of International Law 279; Gina Heathcote, *The Law on the Use of Force: A Feminist Analysis* (Routledge 2011); Gina Heathcote, 'Feminist Perspectives on the Law of the Use of Force' in Marc Weller (ed), *The Oxford Handbook of the Use of Force in International Law* (OUP 2015) 114.

[25] Judith Gardam, 'Women and the Law of Armed Conflict: Why the Silence?' (1997) 46 International & Comparative Law Quarterly 58; Hilary Charlesworth and Judith Gardam, 'Protection of Women in Armed Conflict' (2000) 22 Human Rights Quarterly 148, 150; ICRC, *International Humanitarian Law and Gender. Report Summary, International Expert Meeting. 'Gender Perspectives on International Humanitarian Law'* (4–5 October 2007 Stockholm, Sweden) <https://www.icrc.org/sites/default/files/external/doc/en/assets/files/other/ihl_and_gender.pdf> accessed 10 January 2025.

situations of armed conflict and the modern realities of 'new wars', especially their gendered aspects, to which these laws—in principle—apply.[26] As noted by feminist international lawyers, many modern armed conflicts—especially those protracted in nature—showed alarming patterns of gender-specific violations and the gendered effects of contemporary warfare on women, demonstrating that the provisions of the Geneva Conventions 1949 and their Additional Protocols which afford special protection to women in conflict have had little actual impact on the protection of women from atrocities and gender-based violations.

Yet, the engagement of international law with the topic of gender, conflict, and 'post-conflict' situations continues to be largely centred on war/peace, International Humanitarian Law (IHL)/International Human Rights Law (IHRL), pre-conflict/post-conflict dichotomies. While the distinction between IHL as *lex specialis* and IHRL as a general body of law applying both in peacetime and in conflict is legally correct, such an approach oversimplifies the contextual reality of protracted conflicts which see varying degrees of intensity but are underpinned by long-lasting and continuous humanitarian and human rights crises. These characteristics, combined with gender-differential experiences of conflict and insecurity, pose significant challenges to the prospect of building sustainable peace and to ensuring women's rights and their active participation in peacebuilding and transitional governance processes are prioritized. Furthermore, the dichotomous approach of international law towards viewing conflicts (and, in turn, their implications) in a linear manner does not, in general, reflect women's experiences of conflict and conflict-related insecurity, many of which are also intersectional in nature. As noted by the CEDAW Committee, 'the transition from conflict to post-conflict is often not linear and can involve cessations of conflict and then slippages back into conflict—a cycle that can continue for long periods of time'.[27]

The problematic relationship between temporality, application of international law, and women's experiences of modern conflicts has been raised as a concern among feminist international lawyers.[28] An illustrative example of this is the apparent struggle within international criminal law to adequately capture the experiences of girl soldiers—both combatants and civilians—when prosecuting international crimes committed against them, especially conflict-related sexual violence.[29]

The upwards trajectory of the feminist engagements with and interventions in international law has continued against the background of normative and policy developments, and, not least, rapidly unfolding geopolitical events, of the first quarter of the twenty-first century. In the space of approximately twenty-five years, there has been major growth in the international legal framework (including case-law) that regulates

[26] Olga Jurasz, *Gender and the Aftermath of War: the Response of International Law to the Impact of Armed Conflict on Women* (PhD thesis, Aberystwyth University 2016).

[27] CEDAW, General Recommendation No. 30 on women in conflict prevention, conflict and post-conflict situations (18 October 2013) UN Doc. CEDAW/C/GC/30, para 4.

[28] Priya Gopalan and Olga Jurasz, 'Situation in the Democratic Republic of the Congo in the case of The Prosecutor v. Bosco Ntaganda' in Kcasey McLoughlin, Rosemary Grey, Louise Chappell, and Suzanne Varrall (eds), *Feminist Judgments: Reimagining the International Criminal Court* (CUP 2025).

[29] ibid; Milla Vaha and Leena Vastapuu, '"My Heart was Already Cooked": Girl Soldiers and Situated Moral Agencies' (2018) 31 Cambridge Review of International 223.

the treatment of women in conflicts and attempts to address women's rights in conflict and transitional contexts. Importantly, in addition to major advances in ending impunity for conflict-related gender-based crimes in international criminal law,[30] IHRL also developed the law applicable to the situation of women in conflicts and in their aftermath. The application of the Convention on All Forms of Discrimination Against Women 1979 (CEDAW) to conflict prevention, conflict, and post-conflict situations was confirmed by the CEDAW Committee.[31] The Committee emphasized states' obligations to apply the Convention in diverse situations where they exercise jurisdiction (territorial and extraterritorial), including occupation, lawful and unlawful military actions in another state, peacekeeping missions, and during involvement in post-conflict reconstruction.[32] States' due diligence obligations in situations of armed conflict and in its aftermath have been stressed by the CEDAW Committee and further applied by the regional human rights courts and the Inter-American Commission on Human Rights, especially in the context of sexual violence against detainees.[33] Furthermore, regional human rights instruments, such as the Protocol to the African Charter on Human and Peoples' Rights on the Rights of Women in Africa 2003, the Belém do Pará Convention 1994, and the Istanbul Convention 2011, include substantive provisions regarding the protection of women in armed conflict.[34] Importantly, the issues of women's rights in conflict and in times of transition from conflict to peace, as well as women's participation in conflict prevention and peacebuilding, have become part of the UN Security Council's work through the adoption of the UNSC Resolution 1325 on Women, Peace and Security in 2000,[35] discussed in detail in section B.1 of this chapter.

However, these legal developments governing women's rights in conflict and in transitional contexts—while long-awaited—have been critiqued for being ostensible and contributing little towards the goal of building a feminist peace—a concept which we explore in greater detail in section D. Olga Jurasz notes that despite notable expansion of the framework on women and armed conflict, international law

[30] Maike Isaac and Olga Jurasz, 'Towards an Intersectional Understanding of Conflict-Related Sexual Violence: Gender, Sexuality, and Ethnicity at the ICTY' (2018) 18 International Criminal Law Review 858; Indira Rosenthal, Valterie Oosterveld, and Susana SáCouto (eds), *Gender and International Criminal Law* (OUP 2022).

[31] CEDAW, General Recommendation No. 30 on Women in Conflict Prevention, Conflict and Post-Conflict Situations (18 October 2013) UN Doc. CEDAW/C/GC/30.

[32] ibid, para 9.

[33] ibid, para 15; CEDAW, General Recommendation No. 19 on Violence Against Women (1992) UN Doc. A/47/38; CEDAW, General Recommendation No. 28 on the Core Obligations of States Parties under Article 2 of the Convention on the Elimination of All Forms of Discrimination Against Women (16 December 2010) UN Doc. CEDAW/C/GR/28; *Aydin v Turkey*, Application No.23178/94, 27 September 1997; *Raquel Martí de Mejía v Peru*, Inter-American Commission on Human Rights, Case 10.970, Report No. 5/96, 1 March 1996.

[34] Article 11 Protocol to the African Charter on Human and Peoples' Rights on the Rights of Women in Africa, (adopted 11 July 2003, entered into force 25 November 2005) (Maputo Protocol); Article 9 Inter-American Convention on the Prevention, Punishment, and Eradication of Violence Against Women (adopted 9 June 1994, entered into force 5 March 1995) (Belém do Pará Convention); Article 2(3) Council of Europe Convention on Preventing and Combating Violence Against Women and Domestic Violence (adopted 7 April 2011, entered into force 1 August 2014) (Istanbul Convention). The soft law developments at a regional level include Goma Declaration on Eradicating Sexual Violence and Ending Impunity in the Great Lakes Region (18 June 2008).

[35] UNSCR 1325 (31 October 2000) UN Doc.S/RES/1325.

and international institutions largely continue to view the gendered impact of armed conflict on women predominantly through the lens of sexual violence, much to the exclusion of other types of harms and rights violations experienced by women.[36] This, in turn, is reflected in 'substantial gaps in the international law regulation of these issues' and, further, contributes towards fragmentation in international law, whereby growth of highly specialized regimes (e.g. international criminal law and prosecution of conflict-related gender-based crimes) is not met with harmonization.[37] The challenges of fragmentation are also noted by Catherina O'Rourke, who notes that fragmentation 'presents practical and conceptual problems for those responsible for maintaining, understanding and complying with international law, as well as for advocates who engage international law to advance women's rights in conflict'.[38]

C. Critical Perspectives on the Triple Nexus

The triple nexus was presented as a concept in 2016, sixteen years after the introduction of WPS, when UN Secretary-General António Guterres took office. Guterres stressed that '[h]umanitarian response, sustainable development and sustaining peace are three sides of the same triangle',[39] and this was the final push within a growing international consensus on the need for linking peace with the already existing humanitarian development nexus. As conflicts today are more complex and protracted, humanitarian and development efforts need to be understood as inherently interlinked with achieving sustainable peace. The triple nexus has largely been a concept driven by the UN and aims to link bureaucratic, economic, and organizational traits of the humanitarian, development, and peace realms to work more cohesively and efficiently towards collective outcomes.[40] However, the triple nexus has been criticized mainly because it is 'yet another concept' at the UN, not sufficient to bring about substantial change. Critics have pointed to the lack of clarity around what the nexus means, both in theory and in practice, as the aim of creating a more cohesive way of working across the three domains has compromised the principles of the three individual pillars and undermined their ability to achieve their purpose.[41] Most

[36] Olga Jurasz, *Gender and the Aftermath of War: The Response of International Law to the Impact of Armed Conflict on Women* (2016) PhD thesis, Aberystwyth University, 327.

[37] ibid, 327.

[38] Catherina O'Rourke, *Women's Rights in Armed Conflict under International Law* (CUP 2020) 16.

[39] António Guterres, 'Secretary-General-designate António Guterres' remarks to the General Assembly on taking the oath of office' (New York City, 12 December 2016) <https://www.un.org/sg/en/content/sg/speeches/2016-12-12/secretary-general-designate-ant%C3%B3nio-guterres-oath-office-speech> accessed 15 January 2025.

[40] Humanitarian Learning, 'Learning Stream: Navigating the Nexus' <https://www.icvanetwork.org/uploads/2021/08/Topic-One-Briefing-Paper-The-nexus-explained.pdf> accessed 15 January 2025.

[41] Sonja Hövelmann, 'Humanitarian Topics Explained: Triple Nexus to Go' (Centre for Humanitarian Action, March 2020) <https://www.chaberlin.org/wp-content/uploads/2020/03/2020-03-triple-nexus-to-go-hoevelmann-en.pdf> accessed 15 January 2025; International Review of the Red Cross, 'Q&A: The ICRC and the "humanitarian development–peace nexus" Discussion: In Conversation with Filipa Schmitz Guinote, ICRC Policy Adviser' (2019) 101, 1051–66; Emanuel Tronc, Rob Grace, and Anaïde Nahikian, *Realities and Myths of the "Triple Nexus" Local Perspectives on Peacebuilding, Development, and Humanitarian Action in Mali* [2019] Harvard Humanitarian Initiative.

concerned is the humanitarian pillar, where many actors have highlighted the risk of politicizing humanitarianism when combining it with peace, and by doing so losing its impartiality and neutrality.[42] Peace is political in the sense that the addition of the peace pillar into the nexus may mean that state actors receive a much more central role in the work, which can affect access to people and groups in need of humanitarian support within fragmented and politicized conflicts. The ICRC maintains that this results in a 'protection gap', meaning there is a risk that protection will be prioritized to those who are politically acceptable by the government of a country—which in protracted conflicts often is a conflicting party. Blurring the lines between peace, development, and humanitarianism results in humanitarian aid not staying out of political, ethnic, religious, and military issues, as is one of the promises of humanitarian work.[43] This is worrying as this often disregards large parts of a population, often with emphasis on those on the margins. Importantly, feminist scholars of various disciplines have been pivotal in mapping out individuals and groups within these margins—who more often than not are women and girls.

As discussed earlier in this chapter, critics of the WPS Agenda have time and again emphasized that more attention needs to be placed on addressing the inherently gendered structures and customs in protracted conflicts as well as the responses of the international community to them, instead of focusing only on sexual violence or numerical increase of women. As many feminists before us have argued, the efforts towards the inclusion of women and gender aspects seem more like 'tick-box' exercises than serious efforts to address gender inequalities for achieving peace and security. The addition of the peace pillar in the triple nexus appears as a similar endeavour. It may seem like a good idea—who would be against including peace as a goal for development and humanitarian efforts?—but the inclusion of peace in the nexus risks politicizing and undermining the efforts already achieved by humanitarian and development actors. Just like the feminist claim that we should not just 'add women and stir', nor may we 'add peace and stir'. The inclusion of women, and of peace, into international efforts for a better world calls for serious consideration of who benefits substantially from the said efforts.

The introduction of the Women Peace and Security Humanitarian Action (WPS-HA) Compact in 2020 can be considered as one effort to emphasize the consideration of gendered aspects in/through/within the nexus. The Compact was announced as an initiative to address gender in humanitarian action and to ensure women's participation in humanitarian work. It 'calls for the redesign of peace and security and humanitarian processes to systematically and meaningfully include women and girls . . . in the decisions that impact their lives'.[44] Yet, it seems as though the main focus of the Compact is the inclusion of women into leadership roles and peace processes, the protection of women in conflict areas, and economic security for women. While

[42] Hövelmann (n 41); International Review of the Red Cross (n 41).

[43] International Review of the Red Cross (n 41) 1053.

[44] Generation Equality Forum, 'Compact on Women, Peace and Security and Humanitarian Action (WPS-HA)' <https://forum.generationequality.org/sites/default/files/2021-06/WPS-HA%20Compact%20Pitch%20Deck.pdf> accessed 15 January 2025.

these efforts are significant and much needed, the Compact's gender perspectives signal adding women to an already flawed system, a system that inadequately strives for gender equality and female emancipation for all women everywhere. One example of such omission is that the rhetoric on gender perspectives within the triple nexus is not met with substantial action. The addition of 'women' and of 'peace' into communal efforts within the UN and other bodies of the international humanitarian and development community approaches gender equality and peace from a liberal perspective. It is also worth noticing that the situation for women and girls across the globe is deteriorating. As an example, in a report from the UN Secretary-General from September 2023,[45] it is highlighted that the number of women and girls in conflict settings is 50 per cent higher than in 2017, that misogyny is on the rise, and that the rights of women and girls are being increasingly oppressed, especially in conflict zones. To further illustrate these challenges, the ensuing section of this chapter explores some of the feminist critiques of the triple nexus, with emphasis on the 'peace' pillar.

D. Feminist Peace and the Triple Nexus

Feminist critiques have since the 1970s highlighted the need to rethink notions of power, and, later on[46], the importance of taking an intersectional stance became an additional important element of feminist research on international relations, war and peace. This entails a serious engagement with issues such as race, class, ethnicity, gender, religion, sexuality, and indigeneity, and how they contribute to shaping uneven opportunities and dynamics of power.

That said, it is worth remembering that neither feminist IL nor feminist IR developed in a vacuum but were part of a longer feminist struggle. In the US in particular, the histories of feminism, peace activism, and anti-militarism are intricately intertwined. For example, the Women's International League for Peace and Freedom (WILPF), founded in 1915, brought together women from variegated political and religious backgrounds and actively participated in both disarmament campaigns and peace activism efforts.[47] This history has also contributed to the emergence and renaissance of Feminist Peace Research as a distinct discipline,[48] which in turn is built

[45] UNSC Report of the Secretary-General, 'Women and Peace and Security' (28 September 2023) UN Doc S/2023/725 <https://documents-dds-ny.un.org/doc/UNDOC/GEN/N23/279/08/PDF/N2327908.pdf?OpenElement> accessed 15 January 2025.

[46] The term 'intersectionality' emerged only in 1989 after being coined by Kimberlé Crenshaw, although earlier critiques called for what is now referred to as intersectional analysis.

[47] Catia Confortini, *Intelligent Compassion: Feminist Critical Methodology in the Women's International League for Peace and Freedom* (OUP 2012).

[48] Minna Lyytikäinen, Punam Yadav, Annick Wibben, Marjaana Jauhola, and Catia Confortini, 'Unruly Wives in the Household: Toward Feminist Genealogies for Peace Research' (2021) 56 Cooperation and Conflict 3; Annick Wibben, Ctia Confortini, Sanem Roohi, Sarai Aharoni, Leena Vastapuu, and Tiina Vaittinen, 'Collective Discussion: Piecing-Up Feminist Peace Research' (2019) 13 International Political Sociology 86; Tarja Väyrynen, Swati Parasha, Élise Feron, and Catia Confortini (eds), *Routledge Handbook of Feminist Peace Research* (Routledge 2021).

upon the shoulders of scholars such as Elise Boulding, Berenice Carroll, and Betty Reardon.

What should be noted here is that a variety of women—scholars as well as activists—from diverse backgrounds have actively raised concerns about women's roles in peace, development and security for more than a hundred years already. And while the emphasis and the focus of these contributions may vary depending on, for example, disciplinary orientations or the global political situation of the time, they are still united by the same basic message: that rather than assuming and generalizing, we need to take all women and their diverse experiences seriously[49] in all aspects of peace, security, and development.

Drawing from this rich historical background, we may then ask: but what makes peace a *feminist* peace? First, it necessitates that we break away from binary thinking in relation to peace, conflict, and war. Examples of binary categories include peace/war, victim/perpetrator, soldier/civilian, regular/irregular. Many feminist researchers have directed their attention precisely to the grey areas of such binaries as this is where the risks of falling through institutional cracks are the highest. Second, it is necessary to complicate the causes of insecurity when theorizing and defining peace, instead of only concentrating on the absence of war.[50] Or, as Catia Confortini[51] argues: 'there is no peace where there is oppression.' Third, many would argue that feminist research on peace, security, and war is made feminist by the questions researchers ask.[52] In addition to the obvious question of 'Where are the women', feminist researchers thus highlight the need to pose questions that are contextualized, even to the extent that in some contexts the applicability of the concept of gender might need to be questioned.[53] Fourth, for 'listening to silences' (where most persistent forms of oppression are typically hiding), feminist researchers turn often to methodological innovation and interdisciplinary collaboration.[54] With these approaches, and more, it is possible to address systematic and hidden inequalities in protracted conflicts and their aftermath, and, eventually, make the achievement of a lasting peace more likely. While *feminist peace*—a societal situation where everybody has the possibility to strive and co-exist peacefully despite their societal background, gender, or other identity categories—in itself might seem utopian, feminist researchers and activists often find it essential to locate and unravel inequalities that prevent achieving it. Such understanding of peace differs drastically from that of the UN, to which we turn next.

[49] Cynthia Enloe, *Seriously! Investigating Crashes and Crises as if Women Mattered* (University of California Press 2013).

[50] Jacqui True, 'Continuums of Violence and Peace: A Feminist Perspective' (2020) 34 Ethics & International Affairs 85.

[51] Catia Confortini, 'Feminist Contributions and Challenges to Peace Studies' *Oxford Research Encyclopedia of International Studies* (2017) <https://oxfordre.com/internationalstudies/view/10.1093/acrefore/9780190846626.001.0001/acrefore-9780190846626-e-47> accessed 15 January 2025.

[52] Annick Wibben, 'Feminist Politics in Feminist Security Studies' (2011) 7 Politics & Gender 590.

[53] Leena Vastapuu and Annick Wibben, 'Disrupting Gender in Feminist Security Narratives' in Jutta Joachim, Annica Kronsell, and Natalia Dalmer (eds), *Gender & Security: Persistent and New Security Issues* (Edward Elgar forthcoming).

[54] Annick Wibben, *Researching War: Feminist Methods, Ethics and Politics* (Routledge 2016).

E. The UN Perspective on/Engagement with 'Peace'

As many have argued before us, there exists no universal understanding of peace and therefore also its ontology varies from one context and actor to another. For the UN, peace and peacebuilding have largely been constructed in accordance with the tenets of a liberal peace.[55] As a consequence of a heavily globalized world of liberal internationalism in the post-Cold War era, with a widened concept of security, often linked to counter-terrorism and stabilization, achieving peace and reconstructing 'failed states' through humanitarian intervention has become more common.

The understanding of peace as liberal draws on the democratic peace theory, which maintains that democratic states do not go to war against each other and thus that to achieve conditions of peace, states should be democratized. As Roland Paris has argued, this perspective maintains that 'the surest foundation for peace . . . is market democracy, that is, a liberal domestic polity and a market-oriented economy'.[56] The liberal peace tendencies within the UN have been widely criticized for imposing a Western political agenda in the Global South countries, as well as for their background in Eurocentric discourses of peace. For example, scholars have argued that the liberal peace agenda within the UN entails 'martial elements' with the aim to create a liberal world order through coercive measures, or so-called liberal wars.[57] The liberal peace thus becomes interrelated with what Nicole Wegner calls a 'martial peace',[58] through the 'discursive mobilization of peace to justify martial violence'.[59] Such elements of Eurocentrism and martial peace make the addition of peace into the triple nexus problematic, since this understanding of peace risks further politicizing the humanitarian aspects of the nexus. From a feminist perspective, the addition of the peace pillar to the nexus is worrying because of these very varied and significantly militarized definitions of peace within the international community in recent decades. Such peace discourses seem to highlight the increasing responsibilities of states and military actors in global peace efforts.

Linda Åhäll argues that 'feminist scholarship has done much to highlight how the ways in which wars are fought, justified and made sense of, has everything to do with gender, which means that ideas about "security" [and peace][60] are also inherently gendered'.[61] Yet, the engagement with feminist perspectives on peace is still substantially

[55] For example David Chandler, *Empire in Denial: The Politics of State-Building* (Pluto Press 2006); Mark Duffield, *Global Governance and the New Wars: The Merging of Development and Security* (Zed Books 2001); Roland Paris, 'Peacebuilding and the Limits of Liberal Internationalism' (1997) 22 International Security 54.

[56] ibid 56.

[57] Nicole Wegner, *Martialling Peace: How the Peacekeeping Myth Legitimises Warfare* (Edinburgh University Press 2023); Caroline Holmqvist, *Policing Wars: On Military Intervention in the Twenty-First Century* (Palgrave Macmillan 2014); Bryan Mabee, 'From "Liberal War" to "Liberal Militarism": United States Security Policy as the Promotion of Military Modernity' (2016) 2 *Critical Military Studies* 242.

[58] Wegner (n 57).

[59] Wegner (n 57) 13.

[60] '[and peace]' was added by Annick Wibben in her chapter 'Genealogies of Feminist Peace Research: Themes, Thinkers and Turns' in Tarja Väyrynen, Élise Feron and Catia Confortini (eds), *Routledge Handbook of Feminist Peace Research* (Routledge 2021).

[61] Linda Åhäll, *Sexing War/Policing Gender. Motherhood, Myth and Woman's Political Violence* (Routledge 2015).

lacking in the UN's perspectives on, and engagements with, peace. The UN has aimed to 'gender mainstream' efforts for peace through the WPS Agenda, but mainly through an emphasis on introducing women to leadership roles, participation, and protection as well as prevention of sexual and gender-based violence in conflicts. The outlook on the inherently gendered structures of conflict and war, as well as on understandings of peace and peacebuilding, are largely absent in the UN. This dynamic is reinforced by the lasting and traditional view of peace within international law as an absence of hostilities. However, from a feminist perspective, the absence of hostilities/armed violence does not signify the notion of security, as we have presented in section D. To the contrary, feminists have long highlighted the 'continuum of violence'[62] which predates specific armed conflicts, is reinforced by those conflicts, and continues long after the peace agreements are reached. As noted by the CEDAW Committee, '[f]or most women in post-conflict environments, the violence does not stop with the official ceasefire or the signing of the peace agreement and often increases in the post-conflict setting . . . while the forms and sites of violence change, which means that there may no longer be State-sponsored violence, all forms of gender-based violence, in particular sexual violence escalate in the post-conflict setting'.[63] This challenges the traditional, chronological 'timeline' through which international law views conflicts and attachment to temporality that is a crucial element of defining applicability of different international legal regimes concerning conflict. This can be observed, at the very least, in the terminology adopted by the UN (and within international law instruments) referring to 'post-conflict' or 'transitional' situations which assume an 'implicit teleological temporality'[64] of moving from violence to peace and democracy which, as Ruti Teitel argues, typically implies a 'change in a liberalizing direction'.[65] Feminists in international law and IR, as well as in other disciplines, have often subverted these categories and their reliance on conventional timelines, pointing to their odd fit with women's and marginalized individuals' actual experiences of conflicts. As Cynthia Enloe eloquently explains:

> A lot of non- feminists are most comfortable with little choppy timelines: there is a wartime and pre-wartime and post-wartime. Whereas feminists, because we are interested in women's actual experiences, do not chop up time like that. In fact, some of the best researchers on women in wartime and women in armed conflict areas have advised that, if we want to fully explain what happens to women in wartime, we need to look at what women's status in the law and women's conditions economically and women's understanding of themselves and other people's understanding of them

[62] Liz Kelly, 'The Continuum of Sexual Violence' in Jalna Hanmer and Mary Maynard (eds), *Women, Violence and Social Control: Explorations in Sociology* (Palgrave Macmillan 1987) 46; Cynthia Cockburn, 'The Continuum of Violence: A Gender Perspective on War and Peace' in Werona Giles and Jennifer Hyndman (eds), *Sites of Violence: Gender and Conflict Zones* (University of California Press 2004) 24.

[63] CEDAW (n 27) para. 35.

[64] Natascha Muller-Hirth and Sandtra Rios Oyola (eds), *Time and Temporality in Transitional and Post-Conflict Societies* (Routledge 2018).

[65] Ruti Teitel, *Transitional Justice* (OUP 2000) 13.

are before the war. Don't start to take women's lives seriously just when the first gun is fired.[66]

F. Discussion

The emergence of the triple nexus, while welcomed by some, remains a contested concept when assessed from a feminist perspective. In principle, working in a more interconnected way across humanitarian, development, and peace sectors should pave the way to a more effective and inclusive peace. However, as shown in section D, an early assessment of the triple nexus from a feminist perspective shows that it is likely to have a limited impact on advancing a feminist peace. This is, not least, due to the high level of politicization of the notion of 'peace' at the UN and international levels and predominant militarized narratives of peace which, as history shows, deepens gender inequalities and violence experienced by women rather than subverts them.

Another concern relates to the dangers of (over)institutionalizing norms and principles within the UN structures, which, while well intended, may lead to creating exclusions—especially so in the sphere of women's rights. For example, a chapter in one of the major early works of Feminist IR, entitled 'Gender and International Relations',[67] provides an illuminative review of the positive and negative impacts of large-scale institutionalization upon women's causes. In the chapter, Kathleen Newland discusses the origins and evolution of the Women in International Development (WID) movement which emerged in the 1970s and 1980s as a transnational effort transcending national boundaries. The movement was sparked by women's active involvement in national liberation wars, prompting a re-examination of their roles also in post-war periods and their spread from national to international contexts in the 1970s. The movement gained momentum in an international environment receptive to new solutions, as previous development initiatives had failed in numerous ways.

The WID movement embraced intersectional ideas, considering racism, neocolonialism, class, and sexism simultaneously as obstacles to women's development. Major international institutions, including USAID, the World Bank, and the UN, recognized the women's cause. The UN's response included the creation of institutions such as INSTRAW, later becoming UNIFEM and then UN Women. Funded with often small-scale resources, diverse transnational networks of women emerged within the WID movement. Despite their diversity, women were united by their shared struggle and the need for their voices to be heard in the predominantly male-dominated development arena.

The movement engaged in profound discussions on capitalism's role in inequality and the divisions between the 'First' and 'Third World' women. Often, the latter

[66] Giti Chandra, Cynthia Enloe, and Irma Erlingsdóttir, 'No Peace without Security: Shoring the Gains of the #MeToo Movement' in Sarah Smith and Keina Yoshida (eds), *Feminist Conversations About Peace* (Bristol University Press 2022) 78.

[67] Kathleen Newland, 'From Transnational Relationships to International Relations: Women in Development and the International Decade for Women' in Rebecca Grant and Kathleen Newland, *Gender and International Relations* (Indiana University Press 1991) 122.

viewed the initiatives of the former as patronizing and disrespectful of local habits and cultural norms. As early as the 1970s and 1980s, discussions were held on whether 'development' was actually beneficial for women at all, as it seemed to introduce new pressures without addressing existing inequalities.

The UN designated the year 1975 as International Women's Year, followed by the announcement of the International Decade for Women (1976–1985). However, the institutionalization of the WID movement through UN structures had unintended consequences. Women's causes were sidelined amid more urgent global issues, and the institutionalization of diverse voices shifted focus from various geographical environments and social locations to mostly state-based approaches. The Decade was seen as a failure by many, with such criticism as 'fissures in the women's movement were exploited and widened'.[68]

Although the Decade led to international legislation and norms, the quality of life for most women did not significantly improve. Furthermore, the institutionalization of WID through UN structures redirected attention from structural constraints for equality to more programmatic and short-term responses.[69] It is highly concerning that the triple nexus may meet a similar fate as a 'toothless tiger' that, at this stage, appears to be a branding tool for how the UN wants to be seen as 'doing peace' in the twenty-first century rather than advancing the actual agenda to make change to girls' and women's lives in and emerging from modern protracted conflicts.

Finally, from the international law perspective, questions arise about the potential influence of the triple nexus on the development of international law concerning conflict and peace. As noted in sections C and D, international law rules addressing women's rights in conflicts, as well as gendered aspects of conflicts, are highly fragmented and remain inefficient despite the substantial growth of laws and policies on these issues in the past couple of decades. This results in, as argued by Ní Aoláin, a 'scattered landscape of international legal regulation for women, in which there is no evident hierarchy, a lack of substantive enforcement capacity, disjointed expertise, and ongoing norm splintering'.[70] It is highly unlikely that the emergence of a new UN institutional policy such as the triple nexus will have the power to shift that dynamic. As such, it appears a concept that may have some, albeit limited, application from the UN institutional perspective but is unlikely to contribute normatively to the advancement of peace.

G. Conclusion

As proposed in this chapter, in order to deliver sustainable, transformative, and gender-equal peace, significant shifts in approaches and attitudes towards women, peace, and security are required. With certain gaps to be filled and shortcomings to

[68] ibid 129.

[69] ibid.

[70] Fionnuala Ní Aoláin, 'International Law, Gender Regimes and Fragmentation: 1325 and Beyond' in Cecilia Bailliet (ed), *Non-State Actors, Soft Law and Protective Regimes: From the Margins* (CUP 2012) 53, 68.

be addressed, the current framework could benefit from further developments and improvements, especially in relation to enforcement measures. A greater synchronization of efforts and legal developments across various branches of international law could also contribute towards the development of a more coherent, adequate, and gender-sensitive legal framework addressing the situation of women in the aftermath of conflicts. Therefore, a trend of compartmentalizing conflict-related gendered harms and women's rights in post-conflict transitions as 'a women's only' issue in international law needs to be challenged. The development, implementation, and enforcement of a meaningful and coherent international legal framework addressing gendered impact of conflicts on women needs to be seen as an important matter for contemporary international law and addressed as an essential element in maintaining international peace and security.

The triple-nexus idea of enhancing cooperation across different spheres is not a new concept when considered from a feminist perspective. Yet, in order for the triple nexus to become feminist, it needs to seriously consider how cooperation across these areas benefits women rather than creating disadvantages, which we have noted via the introduction of the peace pillar and its politicization of humanitarian efforts, risking exacerbating the lack of protection of women and girls in conflict contexts. A feminist peace would necessitate a departure from binary ideas of war/peace, pre-conflict/post-conflict situations, and civilian/combatant. This dichotomous and linear perspective on protracted conflict does not capture women's experience of conflict and conflict-related insecurities and fails to meet the various needs of women across different times and spaces. This is further reflected in the way that women's voices and concerns are often sidelined in 'official' initiatives such as the WPS agenda and the triple nexus. The way in which women experience conflict as messy and complex does not fit with the elite UN language and mainstream vision of peace. For instance, the WPS agenda has been privileging the experiences and rights of certain women at the expense and exclusion of others—something that has become clear in DDR initiatives when perpetrator women enter the sphere. The introduction of the peace pillar into the triple nexus and its politicizing effects, where certain parts of the population are neglected because of this, may serve the same fate. Both the WPS agenda and the triple nexus give the illusion of women's rights in conflict being treated seriously, but fail to listen to women's experiences in conflict contexts and what they actually need, which can really only be comprehensively understood by asking them.

5

A Triple Nexus for Northern Central America?

Protection, Development, and Peace under Protracted Criminal Violence

Pablo Kalmanovitz[*]

A. Introduction

Countries in northern Central America—Guatemala, Honduras, and El Salvador—have gone through years of regionalized civil war that ended with UN-sponsored peace accords in the late 1980s and early 1990s, to be followed by non-ideological but intense forms of collective violence from the late 1990s to the present. A significant source of this violence has been the rivalry and feuds between two large transnational gangs traditionally called *maras*—'Barrio 18' and 'Mara Salvatrucha MS-13'—which are composed of hundreds of small *clikas* or *pandillas* of mostly male youth across northern Central America.[1]

Recent police figures estimate the total membership of *maras* to be around 65,000, but past estimates have ranged from 10,000 to 300,000.[2] They are certainly large and spread across the region—'powerful local actors that compete for control of territory and contribute to the high levels of criminal violence inflicting this region'.[3] Their

* For helpful conversations, comments, and reactions to earlier versions of this chapter, I am indebted to Adriana Alfaro, Miriam Bradley, Nuty Cárdenas, Rodrigo Chacón, Carlos Heredia, Andrew Hurrell, Heike Krieger, Samuel Moyn, Ansgar Münichsdorfer, and Margarita Petrova. Special thanks to José Ramón Tinoco for excellent research assistance. Financial support is gratefully acknowledged from the KFG International Rule of Law, Rise or Decline? and the Ministerio de Ciencia e Innovación of Spain through its Generation of Knowledge initiative (Grant Number PID2020-115145GA-I00).

[1] With Rodgers, Muggah, and Stevenson, gangs may be defined as a form of social organization that has 'institutional continuity independent of their membership at any given time' as well as 'fixed conventions and rules which can include initiation rituals, a ranking system, rites of passage, and rules of conduct, that make the gang a primary source of identity for members': Dennis Rodgers, Robert Muggah, and Chris Stevenson, *Gangs of Central America: Causes, Costs, and Interventions* (Occasional Papers of the Small Arms Survey, Graduate Institute of International and Development Studies 2009) 25.

[2] International Crisis Group (ICG), 'Life under Gang Rule in El Salvador' (ICG 2018); World Bank, 'Crime and Violence in Central America' (vol II, World Bank 2010) vii. All estimates for El Salvador and discussion refer to years prior to 2022, when President Bukele began the massive crackdown and arbitrary imprisonment of alleged gang members: El Faro, 'Documentary: How Bukele Broke the Gangs' (El Faro Website, 24 January 2024) <https://elfaro.net/en/202401/el_salvador/27221/documentary-how-bukele-broke-the-gangs> accessed 6 June 2024.

[3] Jonathan Rosen and José Miguel Cruz, 'Dancing with the Devil: Intervention Programs under Criminal Governance in Northern Central America' (2022) Criminology & Criminal Justice, <https://doi.org/10.1177/17488958221140548> accessed 12 June 2024, 2.

Pablo Kalmanovitz, *A Triple Nexus for Northern Central America?* In: *From Protracted Conflict to Sustainable Peace?*
Edited by: Heike Krieger, Giedre Jokubauskaite, Asli Ozcelik, and Andreas Buser, Oxford University Press.
 DOI: 10.1093/9780198967385.003.0006

highest concentration has been in El Salvador, where they have been reportedly active in 94 per cent of municipalities, but they are also present in Tegucigalpa, San Pedro Sula, and rural areas of Honduras, as well as Guatemala City.[4] They are keen on establishing territorial control, usually in relatively small urban areas. Their capacity to threaten and use collective force allows them to set up racketeering systems to extort local businesses, public transport, and ordinary citizens, in addition to dealing in small-scale drug trafficking and other forms of crime.

As in cases of protracted armed conflict, gang violence simultaneously results from and breeds long-term poverty, marginalization, institutional fragility, and renewed cycles of violence. Gang violence and criminal governance have overflown state capacities, thus contributing to the exacerbation and entrenchment of demands for foreign development aid and humanitarian assistance in the region. In keeping with Azar's concept of protracted social conflicts,[5] gang conflicts are highly hostile, identity-based, socially endemic, self-sustaining and prolonged in time and fluctuating in intensity. Gang conflicts also can be attributed to deep inequalities and entrenched marginalization from political and economic power, in particular lack of opportunities in education and employment for youth. So even if not technically an armed conflict in the sense of international humanitarian law (IHL),[6] gang violence has produced levels of violence, obstacles to development, and humanitarian needs comparable to those of armed conflict. In this sense, gang violence is an important case in the broader universe of protracted collective violence, which creates distinctive challenges in international law and foreign assistance, as the following shows.

Since the early 1990s, international aid in northern Central America has focused mainly on development, violence prevention programmes, improvements to the justice system, and employment creation.[7] But humanitarian demands have increased relentlessly since the early 2000s. As Jan Egeland, head of the Norwegian Refugee Council (NRC), noted in 2017, 'widespread violence has led to a crisis of protection on a scale unprecedented for areas not at war'.[8] Similarly, for the regional heads of the United Nations Office for the Coordination of Humanitarian Affairs (OCHA) and the European Civil Protection and Humanitarian Aid Operations (ECHO), 'given that large areas of these countries are effectively outside of government control, it is clear that the provision of humanitarian assistance, delivered by neutral and impartial actors, proportionate in scale and appropriate to the needs of the affected population, is urgent, relevant and should be delivered'.[9]

If the bulk of international aid has been directed to development cooperation, the most prominent domestic response has been *securitization*, particularly in the form of US-sponsored and promoted counter-narcotics and counter-crime policies centred

[4] ICG (n 2).
[5] See Ch. 1.
[6] Although organized violence in El Salvador has been qualified as a non-international armed conflict, see Ximena Galvez Lima, 'Inked or Not: Maras and Their Participation in El Salvador's Recent Armed Conflict' (2019) 10(2) Journal of International Humanitarian Legal Studies 265.
[7] Wendy Cue and Vicente Raimundo Núñez-Flores, 'According to Need? Humanitarian Responses to Violence in Central America' (2017) 69 Humanitarian Exchange 6, 9.
[8] Jan Egeland, 'The Humanitarian Consequences of Violence in Central America' (2017) 69 Humanitarian Exchange 5.
[9] Cue and Núñez-Flores (n 7) 8.

on tough criminal law enforcement.[10] Arguably the goal of such security policies is peace, even if the forms of pacification required for organized criminal violence differ fundamentally from peace negotiations to end civil wars.[11] Nonetheless, common to both enterprises is the state's two-fold objective of earning the monopoly of legitimate force and dismantling large coercive structures that capture rents largely through their capacity to threaten and extort on a vast scale.

Given the protracted character of organized criminal violence, and the manifest need for international humanitarian protection, development assistance, and peace-making for communities affected by it, it may seem straightforward that a triple-nexus approach would be fitting for northern Central America. As the introduction to this volume notes, triple-nexus approaches to international aid can be characterized by the objective of coordinating humanitarian, development, and peace goals when addressing the consequences of protracted violence.[12] They are 'holistic' in the sense of seeking institutional and on-the-ground practical cooperation and integration among separate international organizations in order to use resources more efficiently, combine capacities and expertise, 'cross-fertilize' and 'avoid siloed thinking', share data and technical expertise, and more.

This chapter reflects on the applicability of the triple nexus to northern Central America, focusing on the development-humanitarian nexus as instantiated by the World Bank and the International Committee of the Red Cross (ICRC), two of the most prominent international agencies in the development and humanitarian sectors, respectively. More broadly, the chapter provides a case study of the distinctive challenges that the expanding phenomenon of organized criminal violence can create for international aid.[13] Given the important contrasts between formal armed conflicts and organized criminal violence, it is not even clear what a triple-nexus approach would look like, much less whether it would be desirable all things considered in Northern Central America.

The chapter adopts the perspective of international agencies (specifically of the ICRC and the World Bank), not of state actors, be they national or subnational. It does not discuss the national and subnational politics of reception of international assistance. It does investigate the articulation between international agencies and national and local political actors, but only illustratively, not systematically. Nonetheless, the chapter does give a sense of what triple-nexus aid policies would look like, from the

[10] Clare Ribando Seelke, 'Gangs in Central America' (Congressional Research Service 2016).

[11] The UN-brokered and internationalized Central American peace accords are a very long way from covert government negotiations with youth gangs and *maras* in El Salvador, on which see José Miguel Cruz and Angélica Durán-Martínez, 'Hiding Violence to Deal with the State: Criminal Pacts in El Salvador and Medellin' (2016) 53(2) Journal of Peace Research 197.

[12] See Ch 1.

[13] Valuable empirical studies on the regional expansion of organized criminal violence in Latin America include Nicholas Barnes, 'Criminal Politics: An Integrated Approach to the Study of Organized Crime, Politics, and Violence' (2017) 15(4) Perspectives on Politics 967; Gustavo Duncan, *Más que Plata o Plomo: El Poder Político del Narcotráfico en Colombia y México* (Debate 2014); Enrique Desmond Arias, *Criminal Enterprises and Governance in Latin America and the Caribbean* (CUP 2017); Benjamin Lessing, *Making Peace in Drug Wars* (CUP 2018); Angélica Durán-Martínez, *The Politics of Drug Violence* (OUP 2018); Guillermo Trejo and Sandra Ley, *Votes, Drugs, and Violence* (CUP 2020).

perspective of two leading international agencies in humanitarian protection and development, in situations of protracted criminal violence.

While a normative thesis is presented and briefly defended in the last section—that triple-nexus policies are desirable in northern Central America to the extent that they can successfully counterweight national 'iron-fist' securitization policies—the chapter's main goal is to discuss the contrasts between situations of criminal violence and formally recognized armed conflicts, and to identify distinctive trade-offs and challenges that international actors may face when devising coordinated responses. Given the expansive and converging recent trajectories of humanitarian and development agencies into 'other situations of violence'—forms of collective violence that produce high social costs but do not constitute armed conflict in the IHL sense—such examination is timely and necessary.

After this introduction, the second section surveys the converging institutional paths whereby the World Bank and the ICRC came to support triple-nexus approaches in situations of protracted conflict. The third section discusses distinctive features of organized criminal violence in northern Central America and examines the World Bank's criteria for listing countries as 'situations of fragility, conflict, and violence' (FCV). It is argued that, while the Bank's instruments may be well suited for situations of armed conflict under IHL, they problematically discount distinctive features of gang violence. The fourth section turns to the humanitarian impact of criminal violence in the region and reconstructs responses by humanitarian actors and the World Bank over the past two decades.

While the Bank and the ICRC began to address the impact of criminal violence in the region some fifteen years ago, they have not (yet) conducted joint projects. The fifth and last section discusses what a triple-nexus approach would look like in situations of gang violence and considers whether it is desirable.[14] It is argued that a nexus approach could provide the institutional basis for giving more prominence to immediate humanitarian relief needs and to the social and economic dimensions of gang violence, to which widespread and popular securitization approaches have been largely blind. Preventive policies and social programmes could be leveraged through a triple-nexus articulation of international aid.

B. Institutional Convergence on the Triple Nexus: The International Committee of the Red Cross and the World Bank

Humanitarian and development agencies have traditionally followed contrasting operational logics.[15] Characteristically, humanitarian action has short time horizons and prioritizes providing effective relief impartially to the most urgent needs.

[14] The hypothetical may soon be realized. The United Nations High Commissioner for Refugees and OCHA have already adopted triple-nexus guidelines and language in recent policy documents for Mexico and Central America.

[15] Marc DuBois, 'The Triple Nexus: Threat or Opportunity for the Humanitarian Principles?' (Centre for Humanitarian Action 2022); Miriam Bradley, *The Politics & Everyday Practice of International Humanitarianism* (OUP 2023) chapter 16; François Audet, 'From Disaster Relief to Development Assistance: Why Simple Solutions Don't Work' (2015) 70(1) International Journal 110.

Humanitarian actors typically position themselves as neutrals vis-à-vis powerful actors on the ground in order to gain access to populations in need. Development cooperation, by contrast, typically aims to build state capacity, involves long-term planning and multi-year budgeting, and requires state governments as counterparts. It is, in this sense, not neutral but partisan for the state.

Reflecting this division of labour, humanitarian relief and development cooperation have traditionally been perceived as two poles in a continuum of international aid, which require some sort of 'linkage', sequencing, or transition.[16] This functional division has been found problematic in situations of protracted conflict. Fundamentally, the only way to overcome humanitarian needs in protracted conflicts is by building long-term resilience, for which development cooperation may be essential. On the other hand, without basic levels of human security and social stability, any development gains from international aid will vanish.[17] Furthermore, the longer humanitarian programmes last, the stronger the pressure to foster community participation and consider local demands, which are forms of legitimization traditionally associated with development cooperation.[18]

Reflecting this understanding, over the past two decades the ICRC and the World Bank have followed converging paths of institutional expansion into 'other situations of conflict'. This has enabled coordination efforts and formalized partnerships in the joint pursuit of humanitarian and development goals in protracted armed conflicts. The process has involved important shifts in the institutional views and operational principles of both organizations.

In the case of the ICRC, the process may be described as a 'humanitarian mandate expansion' starting in the early 2000s.[19] The ICRC began incorporating development strategies into humanitarian action in the late 1990s and early 2000s, for the discursive articulation of which the concept of '*sustainable* humanitarian impact' played an important role.[20] When the ICRC published its 2016 document on protracted conflicts, the distinction between short and long-term humanitarian needs was standard. While the former requires limited and fast action and the latter more prolonged 'structural engagements', both are deemed part of the ICRC's mandate.[21] A recent ICRC strategy document includes as one of its priorities incorporating 'longer-term and evolving needs in the design and implementation of humanitarian programmes'.[22]

16 Audet (n 15), DuBois (n 15).

17 International Committee of the Red Cross (ICRC), 'Protracted Conflict and Humanitarian Action: Some Recent ICRC Experiences' (ICRC 2016) <https://www.icrc.org/en/document/protracted-conflict-and-humanitarian-action> accessed 12 June 2024.

18 DuBois (n 15); Bradley (n 15).

19 Miriam Bradley, 'From Armed Conflict to Urban Violence: Transformations in the International Committee of the Red Cross, International Humanitarianism, and the Laws of War' (2020) 26(4) European Journal of International Relations 1061.

20 Marion Harroff-Tavel, 'Do Wars Ever End? The Work of the International Committee of the Red Cross When the Guns Fall Silent' (2003) 85(851) International Review of the Red Cross 465, 468–470; ICRC 2016 (n 17) 24.

21 ICRC 2016 (n 17) 12.

22 ICRC, 'ICRC Strategy 2019–2024' (ICRC 2022) <https://www.icrc.org/en/publication/4354-icrc-strategy-2019-2022#:~:text=The%20ICRC%20Strategy%202019–2024,relevant%20and%20sustainable%20humanitarian%20impact> accessed 12 June 2024, 14–17.

The imperative to make humanitarian action sustainable in protracted conflicts brought humanitarian action into proximity with development assistance. Both respond to social 'fragility' and seek to build 'resilience' for the longer run. Even though the ICRC has been keen to note that it has 'no ideological vision of development, nor does it favour one political vision of society over another' and 'does not intend to become a development agency with a social-change agenda',[23] it has engaged extensively in programmes traditionally associated with development assistance. For instance, in conflict areas of Iraq and Gaza, it has not only trucked water to deprived communities, but also built water pump stations and water supply systems from scratch.[24]

The World Bank's institutional trajectory has been somewhat more convoluted but originates in an expansive understanding of the role of development cooperation in what the Bank has called 'situations of fragility, conflict and violence' (FCV).[25] From the early 2000s, the Bank increasingly engaged in situations of violent conflict and state weakness, in a process that shifted from forbidding all engagement in countries undergoing civil war, to supporting post-conflict projects, to undertaking relief operations jointly with humanitarian actors during armed conflict. The Bank's 2020 'Strategy for Fragility, Conflict, and Violence' expands further its involvement to include forms of collective violence that do not constitute armed conflict but have 'major destabilizing impacts' in society, including 'interpersonal, gang-related, drug-related, and gender-based violence'.[26]

This expansion has required significant adjustments to Bank protocols and operations.[27] In response to the upsurge of civil wars in the 1990s, the Bank became involved in 'post-conflict reconstruction'. Involvement in humanitarian relief operations and peacemaking activities was allowed in 2007. The Bank's current policy on 'crises and emergencies' authorizes funding for humanitarian aid but only in partnership with other international donors and within 'integrated emergency recovery programs'.[28]

[23] ICRC 2016 (n 17) 34; ICRC 2022 (n 22) 15.

[24] ICRC 2016 (n 17) 28–31.

[25] World Bank, 'World Bank Group Strategy for Fragility, Conflict and Violence 2020 - 2025' (World Bank 2020).

[26] World Bank 2020 (n 25) 6-7; World Bank, 'Fragility, Conflict, and Violence in Middle-income Countries' (World Bank Group 2022).

[27] As Philipp Dann has noted, the Bank has long used a 'strategic mix of flexibility and rigidity' in its uses of international and institutional law, which has allowed it to chart and pursue its own chosen paths of institutional expansion, see Philipp Dann, 'The World Bank in the Battles of the "Decolonization Era"' in Jochen von Bernstoff and Philipp Dann (eds), *The Battle for International Law: South-North Perspectives on the Decolonization Era* (OUP 2019) 290–92. To see how this dynamic has played out in the triple-nexus context, see Ch. 15.

[28] World Bank, 'Updated Bank Policy: Development Cooperation and Fragility, Conflict, and Violence' (World Bank 2021) 9; Annamaria Viterbo, 'The Role of the International Financial Institutions in Fragile and Conflict-Affected Countries' in Giovanni Cellamare and Ivan Ingravallo (eds), *Peace Maintenance in Africa* (Springer 2018) 116–18. At the time, the Bank mandated the suspension of programmes if civil war resumed, see Pieter van Houten, 'The World Bank's (Post-)Conflict Agenda: The Challenge of Integrating Development and Security' (2007) 20(4) Cambridge Review of International Affairs 639, 644; World Bank 2021b (n 28) 6–7.

In parallel with this expansion into humanitarian relief territory, the Bank adopted and put into practice the concept of 'state fragility'.[29] It began compiling lists of 'low-income countries under stress' in 2006 and subsequently has published yearly lists of 'fragile states' and 'fragile and conflict-affected situations'. The purpose of these lists is to identify countries that require flexibility and adjustments to standard Bank procedures, in particular by allowing partnerships with humanitarian and peacebuilding agencies, deferring fiduciary requirements, following alternative procurement arrangements, and more.[30]

The concepts of fragility and conflict have been central to the Bank's articulation of the triple-nexus agenda. The 2020 FCV strategy includes the goal of creating partnerships with humanitarian and peacebuilding organizations, in particular the ICRC and United Nations (UN) agencies.[31] The 2018 joint World Bank and UN report 'Pathways to Peace' calls for 'integrated planning' in fragile and conflict situations, including 'pooled and combined data, analysis, and information; better coordination of planning and programming processes; and financing modalities to support closer collaboration across humanitarian, development, and peace-building operations'.[32] The Bank and the UN have formalized nexus partnerships in fragile and conflict-affected Mali, Chad, and Libya.[33]

A recent Bank review of its own actions in fragile and conflict-affected countries gives a sense of what the triple nexus can do in practice.[34] By partnering with UN agencies and the ICRC in conflict areas, the Bank has been able to reach populations otherwise unreachable due to the Bank's state bias and risk-aversion. UN agencies and the ICRC usually have field offices dispersed throughout conflict territory, while the Bank has a presence only in the capital of the country, if at all. By engaging powerful non-state actors on the ground, neutral UN agencies and the ICRC have made it possible to channel Bank funds for the provision of social services and reconstruction of infrastructure in areas outside of state control, including rebuilding water supply systems, roads, medical and school services, and more. Partnerships have also allowed for the continuous disbursement of funds in the absence of central governments.[35]

[29] Nehal Bhuta, 'Governmentalizing Sovereignty: Indexes of State Fragility and the Calculability of Political Order' in Kevin Davis and others (eds), *Governance by Indicators* (CUP 2012); Marie von Engelhardt, *International Development Organizations and Fragile States* (Palgrave Macmillan 2018) 45–59.

[30] World Bank 2022a (n 26) 83. Even though formal listing as fragile is not required for activating the Bank's emergency funds and flexible protocols, nearly all the Bank's engagements in conflict situations have been in listed countries. The recently updated OP 2.30 appears to want to change this, as it provides explicitly that 'the Updated Policy is not limited to countries listed on the Bank's classification of Fragile and Conflict-Affected Situations' but applies 'to Bank engagement in countries or situations affected by FCV [Fragility, Conflict and Violence] challenges, including those experiencing sub-national conflict, forced displacement, or high levels of interpersonal violence': World Bank 2021b (n 28) para 14.

[31] World Bank 2020 (n 25) 52.

[32] World Bank and United Nations, *Pathways for Peace: Inclusive Approaches to Preventing Violent Conflict* (World Bank 2018) 279.

[33] World Bank 2020 (n 25).

[34] Independent Evaluation Group, World Bank, 'World Bank Engagement in Situations of Conflict: An Evaluation of FY10-20 Experience' (World Bank 2021) 41–49.

[35] The Bank has signed memoranda of understanding and cooperation agreements with the ICRC and UN agencies for health provision in South Sudan (2019), food resilience in Yemen (2021), and support for water supply and health provision in the MENA region.

While the World Bank and the ICRC have converged towards the triple nexus, tensions remain in their approaches to aid. Insurmountably, there is the Bank's pro-state orientation in contrast to the neutrality of humanitarian action. There are also contrasting levels of risk tolerance; while the World Bank has been traditionally risk-averse, humanitarian organizations must tolerate risk and loss.[36] Nonetheless, the potential complementarity of their approaches, and added value of partnerships, have led to increasing joint programmes and cooperation over the past few years.

C. Fragility and Conflict in Northern Central America

Gang violence, and organized criminal violence more broadly, stands in a grey area of international law. Standard legal categories associated with the triple nexus fail to capture some of its distinctive aspects. It fits neither the 'hostilities paradigm' governed by IHL during armed conflict, nor the 'law enforcement paradigm' governed by human rights in peacetime. It can reach intensity levels and have humanitarian consequences comparable to those of armed conflicts, but its agents are usually structured loosely and lack centralized command structures or military training.[37]

In the case of *maras*, even though they have been able to coordinate strategies and repertoires of violence on a national scale, they are 'loose networks of localized gangs [which] do not necessarily communicate or coordinate with each other, either within or between countries'. It is unclear if they can be characterized as a 'federal structure, and much less a transnational one'.[38] While of course not impossible, it is rare for organized criminal violence to meet the collective organization criteria in the IHL threshold for non-international armed conflicts.[39] This does not mean that humanitarian relief is any less pressing; on the contrary, sovereignty barriers are higher and international protection mandates weaker when collective violence is not qualified as armed conflict.[40]

The international law of development cooperation, on the other hand, has over the past two decades formalized a differentiated approach to cooperation that distinguishes between 'fragile' and functional states.[41] This two-fold approach is underpinned by recognition that states that undergo protracted armed conflict are both sorely in need of development aid and incapable of assuming the obligations of functional states.[42] While none of the countries in the region has yet appeared in a World

36 Independent Evaluation Group, World Bank (n 34) 43–44.

37 Pablo Kalmanovitz, 'Can Criminal Organizations Be Non-State Parties to Armed Conflict?' (2023) 105(923) International Review of the Red Cross 618.

38 Rodgers, Muggah, and Stevenson (n 1) 8; José Miguel Cruz, 'Maras and the Politics of Violence in El Salvador' in Jennifer M Hazen and Dennis Rodgers (eds), *Global Gangs: Street Violence across the World* (University of Minnesota Press 2014); Dennis Rodgers and Adam Baird, 'Understanding Gangs in Contemporary Latin America' in Scott Decker and David Pyrooz (eds), *Handbook of Gangs and Gang Responses* (Wiley 2015).

39 Kalmanovitz (n 37).

40 Pablo Kalmanovitz and Miriam Bradley, 'Individualization and Collectivization in Contexts of Organized Criminal Violence: The Case of Mexico's War on Organized Crime' in Jennifer Welsh, Dapo Akande, and David Rodin (eds), *The Individualization of War* (OUP 2023).

41 Von Engelhardt (n 29); Viterbo (n 28).

42 Von Engelhardt (n 29) 6–8.

Bank fragility list, they all arguably meet in substance the Bank's fragility and conflict criteria. This section argues that the non-inclusion of Guatemala, El Salvador, and Honduras in the World Bank fragility lists is contestable on the basis of the Bank's own criteria. The point of this exercise is two-fold: to deconstruct and interrogate the most recent quantitative benchmarks used by the Bank to compile FCV lists, and to show that these benchmarks are biased towards political violence and blind to characteristic features of organized criminal violence.

Since 2020, the World Bank has posited two categories of states that merit inclusion in its FCV lists: those 'affected by violent conflict' and those with 'high levels of institutional and social fragility'.[43] Each category is based on several quantitative benchmarks.

- *Countries affected by conflict* have an 'absolute number of conflict deaths' above 250 per year according to the Armed Conflict Location & Event Data Project (ACLED) and 150 according to the Uppsala Conflict Data Project (UCDP), and a rate of fatalities above 2 per 100,000 people according to ACLED and above 1 per 100,000 according to UCDP.[44]
- *Fragile countries* are defined as either having a Country Policy and Institutional Assessment (CPIA) score below 3.0; or the presence of UN peacekeeping operations; or more than 2 per cent of the national population 'internationally regarded as refugees in need of international protection'.

For present purposes, CPIA scores can be left aside, as they are usually not public for middle-income countries and tend to be sensitive to internal World Bank politics.[45] And since northern Central America has had no UN peacekeeping operations since the turn of the century, the relevant criterion for fragility is having flight across borders of more than 2 per cent of the population.

Consider first the conflict indicators. Table 5.1 shows homicide data from UCDP and UNODC since 2000 and ACLED since 2018, when it began reporting. For all years reported, ACLED data is several-fold higher than UCDP data, and far above the 250 absolute and 2 per 100,000 thresholds in all countries and years reported. UNODC data on intentional homicides are not part of the fragility criteria, but they are standard measures of violence intensity and used by the Bank in other contexts. Even for Latin American standards, homicide rates in the region are very high for all years since 2000, with Honduras being the highest *in the world* for several years.

The striking discrepancy among data sources results from very different conceptualizations of violence and corresponding coding procedures. UCDP is conservative by design, meant to produce low estimates of lethality during civil wars. Its paradigmatic case is a 'battle', that is, a situation of organized violence in which belligerents seek to overcome each other's resistance through force.[46] The highest UCDP numbers

[43] World Bank, 'Classification of Fragility and Conflict Situations for World Bank Group Engagement' (World Bank 2023).

[44] There is an additional category of conflict-affected countries that have 'a rapid deterioration of the security situation', but it is not discussed here.

[45] Bhuta (n 29) 142.

[46] As UCDP notes, 'typically, battle-related deaths occur in what can be described as "normal" warfare involving the armed forces of the warring parties. This includes traditional battlefield fighting, guerrilla

Table 5.1 Measurements of homicides UCDP, ACLED, UNODC[i]

	El Salvador				Honduras				Guatemala			
	UCDP	ACLED	UNODC	Rate	UCDP	ACLED	UNODC	Rate	UCDP	ACLED	UNODC	Rate
2000	0		3551	59.60	6		3176	47.71	0		2904	24.74
2001	0		3590	59.95	0		3488	51.01	5		3230	26.9
2002	0		2835	47.16	1		3623	51.61	2		3631	29.54
2003	0		3356	55.68	47		4073	56.55	0		4237	33.71
2004	34		3897	64.57	30		3639	49.29	1		4507	62.84
2005	0		3882	64.29	0		3212	42.46	58		5338	40.65
2006	0		3927	65.08	0		3118	40.26	0		5885	43.88
2007	0		3497	57.86	0		3588	45.28	5		5781	42.21
2008	0		3179	52.39	27		4455	54.99	41		6292	45.01
2009	0		4382	71.94	3		5280	63.79	1		6498	45.57
2010	0		3987	65.21	49		6236	73.79	0		5960	40.98
2011	0		4371	71.22	18		7104	82.39	27		5681	38.3
2012	0		2594	42.1	18		7172	81.57	0		5155	34.08
2013	0		2513	40.63	17		6431	71.77	0		5155	33.42
2014	0		3921	63.14	21		5891	54.64	0		5253	33.43

Continued

Table 5.1 Continued

	El Salvador				Honduras				Guatemala			
	UCDP	ACLED	UNODC	Rate	UCDP	ACLED	UNODC	Rate	UCDP	ACLED	UNODC	Rate
2015	0		6656	106.82	0		5148	55.39	20		NA	NA
2016	0		5276	84.41	10		5150	54.44	0		NA	NA
2017	0		3962	63.22	0		3864	40.14	0		5435	32.78
2018	0	1898	3346	53.31	0	1562	3709	37.87	0	1532	4869	28.9
2019	1	1754	2398	38.18	40	2006	4078	40.95	0	2192	4387	25.65
2020	0	744	1341	21.31	1	1448	3613	35.7	0	1124	3292	18.96
2021	1	838	1147	18.17	6	1410	3931	38.25	0	1302	3520	19.99
2022	88	536	NA	NA	4	1378	NA	NA	12	1460	NA	NA

[i]All data as reported by the sources as of October 2023.

'Rate' stands for the rate of homicides per 100.000 inhabitants, with population data as provided by the World Bank.

in northern Central America belong to Honduras and result from battle-like clashes among imprisoned gangs.[47] But El Salvador, one of the most violent countries in Latin America, and (until 2022) the one with the highest concentration of *maras*, is reported as having nearly zero events since 1992, when the civil war ended.[48] UCDP understands that gang violence is not 'normal warfare' and consequently is not well suited for its coding procedure. To include an event in the database, it needs to 'clearly identify the perpetrators of different acts of violence . . . something which is difficult in . . . much of gang-related fighting'.[49]

In contrast to UCDP, ACLED began updating its coding protocols in 2018 to 'assess the prevalence of gang violence' in the region.[50] It has built indicators for classifying gang violence as political and as such fitting for reporting, including the capacity of criminal organizations to establish territorial control and build ties with politicians and state authorities.[51] But while more comprehensive than UCDP—and far above the Bank benchmarks—ACLED reports only part of the total number of intentional homicides, as Table 5.1 shows. This has to do both with the widespread availability of firearms and with variegated sources of intentional homicide.

Turning now to fragility, the relevant criterion is flight across borders of more than 2 per cent of the population 'who are internationally regarded as refugees in need of international protection'. As with the conflict criteria, there are various ways of measuring populations on the move, some more comprehensive than others.

The Bank's measure corresponds to what the United Nations High Commissioner for Refugees (UNHCR) calls 'refugees under UNHCR mandate', that is, those whose status as refugees has been formally determined either by a state or the UNHCR itself.[52] But in addition to refugees formally under its mandate, the UNHCR also counts

activities (e.g. hit-and-run attacks / ambushes) and all kinds of bombardments of military units, cities and villages etc. The targets are usually the military itself and its installations, or state institutions and state representatives, but there is often substantial collateral damage in the form of civilians killed in crossfire, indiscriminate bombings etc.' <https://www.uu.se/en/department/peace-and-conflict-research/research/ucdp/ucdp-definitions> accessed on 23 January 2025.

[47] 'Honduras' (UCDP Website) <https://ucdp.uu.se/country/91> accessed 12 June 2024.

[48] 'El Salvador' (UCDP Website) <https://ucdp.uu.se/country/92> accessed 12 June 2024. For Guatemala, the events reported refer to high-profile attacks by Mexico's Gulf Cartel against 'unarmed civilians' and public clashes between maras, see 'Guatemala' (UCDP Website) <https://ucdp.uu.se/country/90> accessed 12 June 2024.

[49] Uppsala Universitet, Frequently Asked Questions <https://www.uu.se/en/department/peace-and-conflict-research/research/ucdp/frequently-asked-questions> accessed 23 January 2025.

[50] ACLED, 'Gang Violence: Concepts, Benchmarks, and Coding Rules' (ACLED Website, 10 February 2023) <https://acleddata.com/knowledge-base/gang-violence-concepts-benchmarks-and-coding-rules/> accessed 12 June 2024. In addition to Guatemala, El Salvador, and Honduras, ACLED has reported data on 'political gang violence' in Belize, Brazil, Haiti, Jamaica, Mexico, Puerto Rico, Trinidad and Tobago, and Venezuela.

[51] ACLED does include events perpetrated by unidentified gangs or militias. Inferences are made on the basis of co-perpetration or collective modus operandi, including violence perpetrated by 'a group of two or more using sophisticated weapons' and using tactics such as 'drive-by shootings, the mutilation of bodies, public hanging of corpses, mass shootings, etc.'. Also reported are events that target 'politicians, government employees, former political actors, public prosecutors, lawyers, judges, other overtly political groups (e.g. human rights defenders), journalists, etc': ACLED (n 51).

[52] UNHCR, 'UNHCR's mandate for refugees and stateless persons, and its role in IDP situations' (UNHCR Website, 2 February 2024) <https://emergency.unhcr.org/protection/legal-framework/unhcrs-mandate-refugees-stateless-persons-and-idps#:~:text=Refugees%20are%20part%20of%20UNHCR's,mandate%2C%20or%20in%20national%20legislation> accessed 12 June 2024.

as refugees asylum *seekers*, including *prospective* seekers, which outnumber by far those formally under mandate, as well as the residual category of 'others of concern'.[53] As Table 5.2 shows, if we add refugees under mandate, asylum seekers (including prospective), and others of concern, then the 2 per cent population benchmark has been surpassed by El Salvador since 2017 and Honduras since 2019.

If the rationale for using refugee data as a benchmark is that migration 'signals a major political or security crisis' in countries of expulsion,[54] then clearly the massive outflows of migrants from El Salvador and Honduras need to be counted comprehensively rather than conservatively, as this conveys a more accurate sense of the magnitude of the crisis. Furthermore, the Bank should count comprehensively because, as the UNHCR has declared,

> the refugee definition is declaratory, i.e. a person is a refugee as soon as s/he fulfils the criteria contained in the definition. This would necessarily occur prior to a formal determination of her/his refugee status. Until such determination is made it must be assumed that those who have crossed an international border to escape a risk of serious harm in their country of origin are refugees and should be treated as such.[55]

In sum, UCDP cannot produce adequate measurements of gang violence. By looking at organized criminal violence through the lens of armed conflict, it misses some of its distinctive features, including anonymity of perpetration and ways of operation that rarely fit the battlespace image. In contrast, the ACLED instrument has been repurposed precisely to capture specific features of organized criminal violence. If an accurate representation of collective violence in the region is sought, then ACLED data should be used instead of UCDP. Furthermore, by virtue of normative principle and for the sake of technical accuracy, migration measurements should not be limited to formally recognized refugees but should be inclusive of *all* 'those who have crossed an international border to escape a risk of serious harm'.

The point of this section was not to fault the World Bank for inconsistent application of its own criteria. The benchmarks discussed in this section were implemented after 2021, and countries in northern Central America do not satisfy them as formulated. Rather, the point is to show how the Bank's seemingly objective quantitative criteria in fact presuppose contestable policy judgments on the nature of collective violence. Given the rationales presented by the Bank for its choice of benchmarks, alternative benchmarks are more adequate and fitting. Under these, El Salvador, Honduras, and Guatemala do appear as fragile and conflict-affected.

[53] The UNHCR has defined 'other people in need of international protection' as 'people who are outside their country or territory of origin, typically because they have been forcibly displaced across international borders, who have not been reported under other categories (asylum-seekers, refugees, people in refugee-like situations) but who likely need international protection'. UNHCR, 'Refugee Data Finder' (UNHCR Website) <https://www.unhcr.org/refugee-statistics/methodology> accessed 12 June 2024.

[54] World Bank 2023 (n 43).

[55] UNHCR, 'Refugee definition' (UNHCR Website, 1 March 2019) <https://emergency.unhcr.org/protection/legal-framework/refugee-definition> accessed 12 June 2024.

Table 5.2 Refugee categories as percentage of population

	El Salvador						Honduras					
	M	AS	OC	% M	% M+AS	% MN+AS+OC	M	AS	OC	% M	% M+AS	% M+AS +OC
2015	14,778	31,450	10,100	0.24%	0.74%	0.90%	6,847	19,456	5,100	0.07%	0.28%	0.34%
2016	19,617	62,163	9,800	0.31%	0.99%	1.47%	10,509	35,198	4,800	0.11%	0.48%	0.53%
2017	25,876	104,901	4,200	0.41%	1.67%	**2.15%**	14,424	59,782	3,200	0.15%	0.77%	0.80%
2018	32,562	119,271	27,285	0.52%	1.90%	**2.85%**	18,857	76,526	46,419	0.19%	0.97%	1.45%
2019	41,816	136,277	33,192	0.67%	**2.17%**	**3.36%**	26,351	122,480	72,837	0.26%	1.49%	**2.23%**
2020	45,640	149,542	20,226	0.73%	**2.38%**	**3.42%**	34,456	148,935	115,567	0.34%	1.81%	**2.95%**
2021	52,041	153,246	55,583	0.82%	**2.43%**	**4.13%**	51,687	169,994	48,926	0.50%	**2.16%**	**2.63%**
2022	58,637	148,758	53,504	0.93%	**2.35%**	**4.12%**	64,976	195,584	55,349	0.62%	**2.50%**	**3.03%**

M = refugees formally under UNHCR mandate

AS = asylum seekers, including prospective seekers

OC = others of concern

% M = percentage of national population under mandate

%M+AS = percentage of national population of refugees under mandate and refugee seekers

Data on refugees from UNHCR; population numbers as reported by the World Bank

D. Humanitarian Action and Development Aid in Northern Central America

Awareness among international agencies of the humanitarian and development impact of organized criminal violence in northern Central America began to crystallize in the late 2000s. Even though international humanitarian and development aid actors have now worked on violence-related issues in the region for more than fifteen years, the World Bank and the ICRC have yet to work jointly in Central America in projects along the development-humanitarian nexus.

A pioneering report on humanitarian action in the region by the Internal Displacement Monitoring Centre (IDMC) deemed incontrovertible the existence of a humanitarian crisis while noting that the status of humanitarian operations had been contested nationally.[56] By securitizing anti-gang policies, states put gangs in the reserved ambit of sovereignty and limited the operation and access of international agencies. Even though humanitarian responses to criminal violence in the region were still 'relatively modest and generally under-funded',[57] an important number of humanitarian organizations began operating in the mid 2010s. The ICRC and the Catholic Church in particular have played important roles 'liaising with violent groups and vulnerable communities'.[58]

Jointly with IDMC, UNHCR began collecting and reporting data on violence and displacement in 2015. Agreements to open permanent UNHCR offices in Honduras and Guatemala were made in 2016 and 2014. In 2016, NRC began reporting on the humanitarian impact of gangs on youth; it has since continued monitoring and addressing the impact of criminal violence.[59] OCHA began working in the three countries in 2008, setting up 'Humanitarian Country Teams' in Guatemala and Honduras and 'Humanitarian Assessment Teams' in El Salvador. While initially created to respond to natural disasters, since the late 2010s OCHA has increasingly turned to the humanitarian impact of criminal violence. It has followed triple-nexus guidelines and coordinated projects with the ICRC, UNHCR, ECHO, International Organization for Migration (IOM), United Nations Development Programme (UNDP), and the United Nations Children's Fund (UNICEF)—but not the World Bank.[60]

ICRC resumed its activities in El Salvador and Honduras in 2012 (its Guatemala office did not shut down after the 1996 peace accords), with the protection of victims

[56] International Displacement Monitoring Centre (IDMC), 'New Humanitarian Frontiers: Addressing Criminal Violence in Mexico and Central America' (IDMC 2015).

[57] IDMC (n 57) 18.

[58] IDMC (n 57) 18.

[59] Norwegian Refugee Council, 'Extreme Violence, Treacherous Journeys and Invisible Borders: Children on the Move in and from the Northern Triangle of Central America' (briefing note, Norwegian Refugee Council 2016).

[60] OCHA's region planning and discourse abundantly incorporate triple nexus language. For instance, its goals in El Salvador include 'supporting and strengthening sustainable solutions through humanitarian-development collaboration for restoring essential services and systems and strengthening community and institutional resilience', OCHA, 'Humanitarian Response Plan El Salvador' Humanitarian Programme Cycle August 2021 to December 2022 (OCHA 2021). In Guatemala, 'implementation will be carried out through partners in coordination with the municipalities at the district level, strengthening a triple nexus approach' OCHA, 'Humanitarian Response Plan Guatemala' Humanitarian Programme Cycle August 2021 to December 2022 (OCHA 2021) 61.

of criminal violence as one of its main goals. Among the tasks it has undertaken are providing basic relief, shelter, and health support to migrants and internally displaced persons as well as securing health services and water supplies to communities affected by gang violence.[61] The UNHCR has also undertaken humanitarian tasks, in keeping with its mandate, providing services such as 'shelter, cash and voucher assistance, community protection, case management and risk mitigation' to populations on the move.[62]

The World Bank, on the other hand, began treating criminal violence in Latin America as a development issue already in the late 2000s. A 2008 report concluded that crime and violence 'have become a development issue, and as such, cannot be ignored by the Bank'.[63] A 2010 comprehensive study of Central America concluded that crime and violence should be understood as development issues because they have 'direct effects on human welfare in the short-run and long-run effects on economic growth and social development'.[64]

The first Bank intervention addressed specifically to criminal violence in northern Central America began in 2006 with the 'Barrio Ciudad' project in Honduras (2006–13). The project was implemented in intermediate cities of Honduras and centred on the provision of small-scale 'urban upgrading' in poor neighbourhoods. The Bank contributed funds and expertise for infrastructure investments designed to 'reduce opportunities for particular crime and violence problems through spatial interventions'.[65] The project appears in the Bank's 'Fragility, Conflict, and Violence Strategy' as a model and reference for future interventions aimed at 'interpersonal, gang-related, drug-related, and gender-based violence'.[66]

The Bank subsequently undertook similar interventions in Honduras, Guatemala, and El Salvador. In Honduras, the 'Safer Municipalities Project' (2012–2018) was structured around the identification of 'hotspots' for intervention in urban areas with high concentrations of homicides, including those subject to 'organized crime (territorial control of drug and extortion markets)'.[67] Like *Barrio Ciudad* but on a larger scale, the project sought to build urban infrastructure and reduce crime through 'environmental design methods' in addition to collecting data and providing social services for at-risk youth.[68] Likewise, Guatemala's 'Urban Infrastructure and Violence

[61] As reported by the ICRC in its country humanitarian balances for 2021 and 2022.

[62] UNHCR, 'Honduras: Operational Update' (UNHCR 2023). Similar measures have been taken in El Salvador and Guatemala, as reported by the UNHCR in its country reports.

[63] World Bank, 'Urban Crime and Violence in LAC: Status Report on Activities' (World Bank 2008).

[64] World Bank 2010 (n 2), i. Remarkably, the study recommends focusing investments on preventive, not enforcement, strategies, which the Bank has subsequently largely done. As the report notes, 'governments of the region responded by implementing a variety of *mano dura* (heavy handed) policies that emphasized repression and law enforcement while minimizing prevention, rehabilitation, and social reintegration of gang members. With the passage of "Illicit Association" legislation, known and suspected gang members were rounded up in police sweeps, incarcerated, and in some instances tortured and killed through extrajudicial executions': World Bank 2010 (n 2) 60.

[65] World Bank, 'Honduras—Barrio Ciudad Project (English)' (Project Appraisal Document, report no 31238-HN, World Bank Group, 27 May 2005) 8.

[66] World Bank 2020 (n 25) 6–7, 23.

[67] Rodrigo Serrano-Berthet, 'Project Information Document (Concept Stage)—HN Safer Municipalities' (Report no PIDC497, World Bank, 13 September 2012) 2.

[68] Among the measures recommended by the Bank's Environmental Design approach are 'minimizing the number of exit and entry points to a neighbourhood; installing adequate lighting in public spaces;

Prevention Project' (2017–2023) dedicated funds to 'small-scale urban infrastructure and violence prevention interventions' in the large metropolitan area of Guatemala City.[69] In parallel to these national projects, the Bank unrolled a programme for the whole region (2014–2016) that included the 'socio-economic insertion' of at-risk youth or gang members in El Salvador.[70]

While urban areas under gang control could in principle be fitting targets for these projects, they were all executed following standard agreements with state counterparts. No humanitarian organization was involved as partner.[71] World Bank public documents do not discuss negotiation strategies for securing access to risky urban sites, nor how or whether risk assessments have been made at all. Presumably Bank operators have largely deferred to state partners for accessing sites and assessing risk.[72] The projects, it can be inferred, have followed standard procedures instead of FCV guidelines, which could also explain the absence of partnerships, joint planning, or information sharing with humanitarian actors.[73]

E. Triple Nexus as De-Securitization

We have seen that humanitarian action in response to criminal violence in northern Central America has grown steadily for the past fifteen years, providing shelter, water, health, and other basic services to displaced persons and communities at risk. A decade earlier, the World Bank began treating criminal violence as a development issue, engaging in urban crime prevention projects and systematically registering criminal violence in country diagnostics. Recently, the Bank declared that formal listing is not required for applying FCV protocols, as they can befit other situations of violence. The time is surely ripe for reflecting on what a nexus approach would look like in northern Central America and whether it would be desirable.

At an operational level, there are significant challenges associated with the fragmented structure of criminal violence. As discussed in section C, gangs are composed of large numbers of loosely federated groups, each vying for control over small, mostly urban areas. Violence in such contexts 'can flare and decline sharply in a given locality'.

facilitating natural surveillance by minimizing obstructive landscaping and structures; and avoiding hidden areas and other recesses where offenders may hide', World Bank 2005 (n 65) 10).

[69] World Bank, 'Guatemala – Urban Infrastructure and Violence Prevention Project' (report no PAD974, World Bank, 12 December 2016) 6.

[70] Sandra Lisette Flores De Mixco, 'Guatemala Proyecto Regional para la Seguridad Ciudadana—Estados Financieros al 28 de febrero 2017' (World Bank, 24 June 2017).

[71] State counterparts included the Ministry of Justice and Public Security of El Salvador, the Interior Minister and Ministry of Housing in Guatemala, and the Honduran Social Investment Fund. The Bank has also partnered with the UNDP. The only arguable exception is Catholic Relief Service (CRS) which has a mixed mandate.

[72] Fieldwork research would be required to establish this, but like other middle-income countries, governments in El Salvador, Honduras, and Guatemala may be reluctant to let the World Bank venture far into their security concerns: World Bank 2022a (n 25) 8.

[73] The final evaluation of the Safer Municipalities Project in Honduras notes the non-application of FCV guidelines, World Bank, 'Honduras—Safer Municipalities Project (P130819)' (Implementation completion and results report, report no ICR00004740, The World Bank, 11 July 2019) 18.

Communities may be subject to 'invisible coercion' but also be 'to a degree complicit' with criminal organizations.[74] In line with this assessment, recent surveys of internally displaced persons in El Salvador and Honduras have found that persons displaced by violence tend to keep their jobs and relocate to areas close to their previous residence.[75] Nonetheless, residents routinely observe curfews and walk long distances to avoid forbidden areas. Such fragmentation of territorial control and unpredictability of violence makes humanitarian access and programming difficult and hazardous.

A second significant operational hurdle is that, as noted already, governments facing criminal violence often centre their response on security and law enforcement policies and are unwilling to address—even recognize—the humanitarian impact of organized crime and iron-fist state responses. The Bank has found that middle-income countries tend to be unwilling to engage on FCV issues.[76] Third, there is significant disagreement among humanitarian actors on the wisdom of giving up neutrality and independence when partnering with development and state actors. For some, the only viable path in the region is to support and enhance weak state systems, which can eventually provide protection and basic human rights. For others, humanitarian agencies should remain fully independent and neutral until they are better established and have enough knowledge and experience with criminal violence dynamics in the region.[77]

While very important, these obstacles are not insurmountable in principle. National and international humanitarian agencies have been working in the region for more than a decade now. The ICRC and the Catholic Church have been able to broker contact with criminal organizations and mediate with local communities and other humanitarian agencies. National non-governmental organizations have found ways to work around gangs or under their permissive gaze.[78] Furthermore, the willingness of governments to work with international humanitarian agencies has varied. El Salvador and Honduras have been eager to receive international aid and cooperative with international aid agencies, Guatemala far less so.[79] For humanitarian agencies working in the region, underfunding and limited organizational capacity may be a more significant obstacle than state obstruction. A nexus approach could contribute to alleviate this, to the extent that it can facilitate co-programming and the channelling of more abundant development funds into humanitarian-development projects. Some humanitarian actors may find this form of partnership troubling, but certainly not all.

If operational obstacles could be overcome, the triple-nexus approach could operate in different ways in contexts of organized criminal violence. For instance, the World Bank's 2022 Honduras 'Systematic Country Diagnostic' proposes creating a

[74] IDMC (n 57) 10.

[75] Ministerio de Justicia y Seguridad Pública, El Salvador (MJSP), 'Caracterización de la Movilidad Interna a Causa de la Violencia en El Salvador' (Ministerio de Justicia y Seguridad Pública 2018); Comisión Interinstitucional para la Protección de las Personas Desplazadas Internamente por la Violencia (CIPPDV), 'Estudio de Caracterización del Desplazamiento Interno por Violencia en Honduras 2004–2018' (CIPPDV, Secretaría de Derechos Humanos de Honduras 2019).

[76] World Bank 2022a (n 25).

[77] IDMC (n 57) 14, 18.

[78] IDMC (n 57) 15; Rosen and Cruz (n 3).

[79] IDMC (n 57).

'mapping of services, such as education and health, against the border of gangs' which would fill an important knowledge gap in the micro-dynamics of gang control.[80] If shared with the ICRC and other humanitarian agencies, this mapping could enhance their ability to broker access and provide basic services to communities at risk; conversely, humanitarian agencies could collect and contribute real-time data to the Bank. The Bank could also provide funds for relief projects operated by humanitarian agencies, which can in turn offer risk assessments and expand the reach of the Bank to communities that governments prefer to avoid.

More concretely, under its recent policy framework for integrating violence-induced internal displacement into Bank programming,[81] the Bank could partner with humanitarian organizations already working with violence-induced displacement in the region. Furthermore, the Bank's experience with disarmament, demobilization, and reintegration programmes in situations of armed conflict could be adjusted and applied to the disarmament and social reintegration of gang members. The UNDP could be a fitting partner in such programmes, given its experience supporting small arms issues in the region.[82] More broadly, a triple-nexus approach could help leverage the provision of still undersupplied humanitarian relief by coordinating with more established development aid channels. If substantive World Bank funds were on the table, governments could be more willing to give humanitarian actors more leeway in gang contexts.

Finally, and arguably most importantly, the peace and humanitarian pillars of the triple nexus could provide a much-needed counterbalance to governmental securitization and tough law enforcement policies, which have repeatedly proven ineffective. If a well-funded development institution such as the World Bank decided to fund triple-nexus programmes directed at, for example, building protection systems for displaced persons and communities, preventive policies for at-risk youth, and disarmament and reintegration programmes for gang members, these could yield better results than traditional state iron-fist responses. Moreover, in keeping with FCV guidelines, the Bank could be more prepared to undertake riskier investments when partnering with humanitarian agencies, and even dedicate special funds on concessional terms, instead of being financially conservative and market-driven, as is usual with middle-income countries.

International agencies may be better positioned than governments to lead and fund preventive and social policies towards gangs and at-risk youth. Governments facing high levels of criminal violence are constrained by the political toxicity of any perceived leniency toward gangs, notably in truce negotiations. *Mano Dura* policies are usually in high popular demand, as the massive arbitrary imprisonments under President Bukele in El Salvador illustrate so terrifyingly. International aid organizations are not as sensitive to national public opinion as governments must be, and can in principle approach gangs differently.

[80] World Bank, 'Honduras: Paths Toward Building a Resilient Society: Systematic Country Diagnostic Update' (World Bank 2022) 24.
[81] World Bank, 'A Development Approach to Conflict-Induced Internal Displacement' (World Bank 2021).
[82] UNDP, 'Securing Development: UNDP's Support for Addressing Small Arms Issues' (UNDP 2005).

At least two important objections may be raised. First, one might react critically to this proposal and note that the underlying structural conditions for the gang phenomenon would remain untouched, while the managerial and technocratic approach of the World Bank is allowed to spread unbridled under the guise of peacemaking and neutral humanitarianism. This is hardly a promising route for the social inclusion of marginalized youth, which constitutes the bulk of potential and actual gang members. Second, even if the triple-nexus approach could contribute to a policy shift towards less iron-fist and repression, whatever social effects this may have depends on the willingness of gangs to follow suit. Why expect that triple-nexus policies would be well-received by gangs?

Starting with the second objection, the proposal admittedly points to nearly uncharted territory. We do know, however, that the least violent periods in El Salvador's recent history (before Bukele's 2022 crackdowns) were during covert truces agreed by gang leaders and governmental representatives. We also know that gang spokespersons have often called for negotiations with governments and demanded social programmes for gang members—although such pronouncements need of course to be taken with caution. It is well known that at-risk youth often prefer to avoid gangs, which can be encouraged through preventive and social policies .

The first objection is fair and fundamental. Though by no means easy to implement, the proposal of a triple nexus for northern Central America is modest. It is likely that a triple-nexus approach to international aid in the region can operate while the social and economic structures underlying gang violence remain in place. No doubt Guatemalans, El Salvadoreans, and Hondurans need to aim higher and seek deeper social chance. But meanwhile, given the current socio-political situation in the region, a triple-nexus approach to international aid may contribute to improve the social and economic conditions of people living in very dire situations. Without such basic improvements, it may be impossible to successfully plan for the longer run and aim higher via national and democratic routes.

6

Tensions Between Local and International Narratives of Conflict

USAID Discourses on Liberal Peace in Colombia*

Johanna del Pilar Cortés-Nieto, Andrés Gómez-Rey, Rafael Tamayo-Álvarez, and Andrés Rodríguez-Morales

A. Introduction

The international community has supported the Colombian Peace Accord politically[1] and financially.[2] USAID has historically been the leading international donor to Colombia.[3] Its cooperation activities in the country intensified in the late 1990s, when the ambitious military-antisubversive Plan Colombia was implemented during the Clinton administration.[4] During the peace negotiations, USAID provided financial and political aid to the Colombian government, and it has expressed its commitment to support the implementation of the Accord.[5] USAID has been the leading funder of Territorially Focused Development Programmes (PDETs), one of the tools conceived to promote rural development.[6]

In this context, the chapter presents a discourse analysis of the visions of development and peacebuilding that underpin USAID's Country Development Cooperation

* This chapter was written prior to the Trump administration's 2025 decision to permanently dismantle USAID. The authors maintain that the arguments presented remain relevant for understanding the historical impact of USAID in Colombia.

[1] Jorge Battaglino and Germán Lodola, 'Negotiations and Possible Spoilers in the Colombian Peace Process' (The Norwegian Peacebuilding Resource Centre 2013) <https://www.files.ethz.ch/isn/173189/e85f61d02af1702a4c619eb68850444e.pdf> accessed 12 August 2025.

[2] Jairo Estrada Álvarez, 'La (Des) Financiación Del Acuerdo de Paz Como Expresión de La Tendencia a La Consumación de La Perfidia' in Jairo Estrada Álvarez (ed), *El Acuerdo de paz en Colombia: Entre la perfidia y la potencia transformadora* (CLACSO 2019).

[3] Diana Marcela Rojas, 'Las Relaciones Colombia-Estados Unidos en el Gobierno Santos: ¿Llego la Hora del Post Conflicto?' (2013) 26 Análisis Político 121.

[4] Diana Marcela Rojas, 'Estados Unidos en la Construcción de la Paz en Colombia' (2017) 30 Análisis Político 37.

[5] ibid.

[6] Johanna Del Pilar Cortés-Nieto and others, 'Procesamiento Respuesta Derecho de Petición - Agencia de Renovación Del Territorio—Proyectos PDET Financiados Por Cooperación Internacional' (Universidad del Rosario 2021) <http://research-data.urosario.edu.co/citation?persistentId=doi:10.34848/FK2/EYOTAM> accessed 18 May 2023.

Johanna del Pilar Cortés-Nieto, Andrés Gómez-Rey, Rafael Tamayo-Álvarez, and Andrés Rodríguez-Morales, *Tensions Between Local and International Narratives of Conflict* In: *From Protracted Conflict to Sustainable Peace?* Edited by: Heike Krieger, Giedre Jokubauskaite, Asli Ozcelik, and Andreas Buser, Oxford University Press.

DOI: 10.1093/9780198967385.003.0007

Strategies (CDCS) for Colombia for the periods 2014–2020 and 2020–2025. We pay attention to how the roles of the state, civil society, and the private sector are portrayed in these documents, as well as how notions of the environment and natural resources are constructed. We claim that through its policies and programmes, USAID contributes to creating a 'common sense' about Colombia's post-conflict situation, positioning narratives of peacebuilding akin to liberal peace. Given USAID's powerful influence over the country, its approach to peacebuilding undermines alternative visions and closes the political space for territorial peace.

The chapter also discusses how implementing the Peace Accord redistributes power in Colombia in a way that enables donors such as USAID to influence the design of public policies on peacebuilding. It opens a political space lacking during the negotiations. This is not surprising as, historically—as the chapter shows—the law that has governed international cooperation has since its inception in the twentieth century granted donors the power to decide how development and peacebuilding should look in the context of imperial projects.

After this introduction, the chapter is divided into four sections. The first examines the imperial legacies of international law, particularly of the rules that govern international cooperation for development. In this section, we argue that the law on international development cooperation is a continuation of the imperial and colonial character of international law, and we position the development agenda as a discourse and practice aimed at governing Third World countries. The second provides some context to the 2016 Colombian Peace Accord. It discusses the tensions between the two notions of peacebuilding: liberal peace and territorial peace. This section will also examine the connections between international law and liberal peace and Colombia's emancipatory potential of territorial peace. The third section analyses USAID's most recent development strategies for Colombia and introduces our discourse analysis. The chapter ends with some conclusions.

B. The Imperialist Operation of International Law

The triple nexus is becoming the dominant paradigm in international cooperation, as evidenced by its active promotion by influential international organizations such as the OECD and leading aid donors.[7] It is based on the claim that humanitarian, development, and peacebuilding areas are interconnected processes that must be addressed simultaneously.[8] The OECD's Development Assistance Committee has recommended that such coordination entails, among other principles, prioritizing a preventive approach to conflict by investing in development and ensuring that

[7] OECD, *The Humanitarian-Development-Peace Nexus Interim Progress Review* (OECD Publishing 2022); Elizabeth Ferris, 'The Humanitarian Peace Nexus' (UN Secretary-General's High-Level Panel in Internal Displacement 2020) <https://www.un.org/internal-displacement-panel/sites/www.un.org.internal-displacement-panel/files/ferris_humanitarian_peace_nexus_0.pdf> accessed 19 May 2023.

[8] Oxfam, 'El Nexo Entre la Acción Humanitaria, el Desarrollo y la Consolidación de la Paz ¿Qué Implica Para Organizaciones Con Múltiples Mandatos?' (Oxfam 2019) <https://oxfamilibrary.openrepository.com/bitstream/handle/10546/620820/dp-humanitarian-development-peace-nexus-260619-es.pdf?isAllowed=y&sequence=10> accessed 19 May 2023.

critical humanitarian needs are met.[9] This is deemed to be possible only when local and national authority is strengthened, communities are empowered and involved in decision-making processes, and enabling conditions, especially financing, are secured.

Oxfam considers that the triple nexus 'is a continuation of long-running efforts in the humanitarian and development fields', and that the concept 'challenges the status quo of the aid system'.[10] Although we agree with the former premise, we see the triple nexus as a recent iteration of what, borrowing Pahuja's words, can be described as the 'operative mode of power in international law'.[11] Here, we refer to how international law has been shown to constantly produce political projects through narratives of progress, modernization, development, and security.[12] These narratives advance a particular understanding of the problems and needs of the Global South and propose normative solutions premised on implementing ideal institutions of the Global North, which are presented as embodying universal values. Political projects underpinning such narratives are compatible with the expansion of the capitalist mode of production, especially patterns of accumulation and integration of political communities into global circuits of production and circulation of capital. To better explain this point, we will begin by explaining what can be referred to as the imperialist logic of the functioning of international law.

A fundamental quality of modern international law is to provide discourses and practices that have justified the economic and political domination (ie exploitation and value extraction) of societies situated at the margins of the global capitalist system.[13] Specifically, through the racialization and cultural domination of peripheral societies, international law has laid down the intellectual basis for the continuous process of dispossession and concentration of natural resources operating globally. Arbitrary categorizations of specific political communities, commonly represented as 'uncivilized', 'backward', or 'underdeveloped', are used to create subjugated subjectivities, occupying a subordinated position in the global capitalist system.[14] These categorizations are relational in scope and are constructed upon comparisons with a Eurocentric paradigm of democratic values and legality.[15] Furthermore, they have given rise to a series of normative projects with a universalist scope, prescribing ways of modernizing and developing disadvantaged political communities, including the civilizing mission, the developmental state, and, more recently, the good governance agenda.[16]

[9] OECD (n 7).

[10] ibid.

[11] Sundhya Pahuja, *Decolonising International Law: Development, Economic Growth and the Politics of Universality* (CUP 2011).

[12] ibid.

[13] Bhupinder Singh Chimni, *International Law and World Order: A Critique of Contemporary Approaches* (2nd edn, CUP 2017).

[14] Pahuja (n 11).

[15] Piyel Haldar, *Law, Orientalism and Postcolonialism: The Jurisdiction of the Lotus-Eaters* (Routledge-Cavendish 2007).

[16] Luis Eslava, 'El Estado Desarrollista: Independencia, Dependencia y la Historia del Sur' (2019) 43 Revista Derecho del Estado 25.

Whereas a discursive instantiation of subaltern identities has been a pattern in the operation of the modernity project,[17] it is the specific manifestation of this process in international law that we use as the entry point for our assessment. Specifically, we draw on Ntina Tzouvala's understanding of 'civilization' as a mode of international legal argumentation that qualifies the enjoyment of international legal sovereignty by peripheral political communities to satisfy specific standards of internal governance compatible with capitalist modernity.[18] The civilizing narrative has provided the rationale justifying continuous interference in the political space of the third or developing world, which has been presented as the dissemination of allegedly universal internal governance standards beneficial to non-western territories and peoples. Furthermore, to the extent that these normative projects allow overcoming endemic dysfunctionalities such as 'backwardness' or 'underdevelopment', exploitation and extraction can be presented as part of a humanitarian enterprise regardless of their redistributive implications.[19]

This approach has similarities with Pahuja's analysis of how international law has legitimized interventions in the Third World through its promise of universality.[20] Indeed, international law's promised universality presents a view of the international legal order wherein certain institutions are projected as devices for transformation and emancipation. Pahuja argues that these political projects with aspirations of fulfilling 'universal' values can engender new rationalities in power relations, such as the concession of formal sovereignty to the Third World during decolonization.[21] Yet, the transformative potential is limited, because the promise of universality ultimately produces and justifies spheres of intervention in the Global South. Put another way, political projects promising transformation end up fostering determinate visions of the international order that facilitate capitalist expansion.

One of the mechanisms through which international law attempts to govern the Third World is the rules of international (development) cooperation.[22] This term refers here to forms of assistance and aid that move across national borders. International cooperation is increasingly structured by law. Different legal rules produced at national, supranational, and international scales govern the processes, instruments, and institutions through which aid and other forms of cooperation move across borders. Cooperation actors make decisions that shape governments' and people's behaviours while distributing goods and services essential for people's and communities' well-being.[23] International development cooperation is regulated by an area of international law that sets the mandates, competencies, institutional structures, and decision-making powers of international cooperation actors, as well as the

[17] Aníbal Quijano, 'Coloniality and Modernity/Rationality' (2007) 21 Cultural Studies 168.

[18] Ntina Tzouvala, *Capitalism as Civilisation: A History of International Law* (CUP 2020).

[19] Anthony Anghie, *Imperialism, Sovereignty and the Making of International Law* (CUP 2005).

[20] Pahuja (n 11).

[21] ibid.

[22] Philipp Dann, *The Law of Development Cooperation: A Comparative Analysis of the World Bank, the EU and Germany* (CUP 2013).

[23] ibid.

processes, instruments, and criteria on which they rely to distribute different forms of aid.[24] For us, international development cooperation law is also composed of recommendations and cooperation strategies to the extent that they shape both donors' and recipient countries' behaviours, while circulating and legitimizing specific discourses of what development and peacebuilding entail.

International development cooperation intensified at the outset of the Cold War in connection with mid-twentieth-century decolonization processes. The major powers of the time, the United States (US) and the Soviet Union, relied upon cooperation to forge political alliances. The US found international development cooperation a means to expand its imperial and economic project. Soon after the World Bank began to disburse funding to developing countries in the 1950s, the European Economic Community, created in 1958, opened a development fund; a pattern followed in 1960 by the US and Germany, which created their own cooperation funds.[25]

The agenda of international cooperation goes beyond development, from humanitarian aid to military assistance. During the twentieth century, international humanitarian cooperation focused, on the one hand, on refugees and stateless individuals as conflicts escalated across Europe and other regions, and on the other, on colonial populations in connection to imperial projects. As Gorman argues, in the colonial context, humanitarian assistance and the language of internationalism provided 'rhetorical cover for national imperial expansion'.[26] Development, in turn, has been traditionally associated with assistance aimed at improving countries and people's wealth and well-being in connection to economic goals such as growth and employment. As in the case of humanitarian aid, Escobar and others have shown how development has been central to Anglo-European projects that seek to maintain social, economic, and political control over previous colonial territories.[27]

We contend that for the triple nexus and other similar initiatives to produce structural change, it must be decoupled from the ideological roots and material interests that rely on international law for constant intervention in the political and economic affairs of the Global South, under the guise of promoting modernization and development. However, when examined more closely, the triple nexus is premised on the same narratives asserting chaos and institutional failure that have dominated the characterization of political societies in the Global South. For instance, Oxfam explains that the triple nexus must secure workable or operative humanitarian, development, and peace initiatives in zones where the most vulnerable face institutional fragility, crises, and violent conflict risk.[28] Likewise, the OECD identifies fragile and crisis-affected contexts where building resilience through holistic solutions such as those offered by the triple nexus is required.[29]

[24] ibid.
[25] ibid.
[26] Daniel Gorman, *International Cooperation in the Early Twentieth Century* (Bloomsbury Academic 2017) 117.
[27] Arturo Escobar, *Encountering Development: The Making and Unmaking of the Third World* (Princeton University Press 2011).
[28] Oxfam (n 8).
[29] OECD (n 7).

Our point is that the triple nexus is underpinned by the same narratives of failure and 'backwardness' that allow international law to serve imperialist interests by justifying perennial interventions in the Global South. It is the newest interaction of a managerial solution to deal with the problems considered endemic to societies in the Global South, just as in the nineteenth century the 'backwards' and 'uncivilized' were subjected to modernization projects. The question, however, is whether there are alternative narratives decoupled from the political projects that enable capital expansion;[30] different ways of understanding peacebuilding processes.

C. From Liberal Peace to Territorial Peace

Academic literature understands liberal peace as an attempt to build liberal democratic and effective state institutions with the help of external actors to prevent and contain conflict.[31] Democratic institutions are claimed to help resolve grievances peacefully, while imposing on governments constraints on the use of force. Furthermore, they enable governments to make public commitments that might prevent the escalation of violence. Therefore, this approach involves programmes that seek to strengthen state institutions such as the judiciary, security forces, and administrative offices, while improving the 'rule of law' and human rights protections.[32] On the economic side, liberal peacebuilding draws on the assumption that capitalism is the most efficient way of bringing prosperity to conflict-ridden societies. Hence, it promotes market-oriented development programmes that, for instance, endeavour to connect conflict-affected and poor communities to markets and global value chains.[33]

This approach has become the hegemonic understanding of what a post-conflict scenario should entail to stabilize society and empower communities in contemporary politics. This conception of peacebuilding has arguably evolved into a type of 'common sense' shared by states, international organizations, donors, and international NGOs. Indeed, according to Richmond, liberal peace is a discourse, a framework, and a structure with a specific ontology and methodology.[34] It hinges on the

[30] On the connection between capital and international cooperation, see among others Vasilios Ioakimidis and Nicos Trimikliniotis, 'Imperialism, Colonialism and a Marxist Epistemology of "Critical Peace"' in Stephen A. Webb (ed), *The Routledge Handbook of Critical Social Work* (1st edn, Routledge 2019); Antonio Donini, 'Decoding the Software of Humanitarian Action: Universal or Pluriversal?' in Volker Heins, Kai Koddenbrock, and Christine Unrau (eds), *Humanitarianism and Challenges of Cooperation* (Routledge 2016).

[31] Louis-Alexandre Berg, 'Liberal Peacebuilding' in *Peacebuilding Paradigms* (Cambridge University Press 2020); Oliver P Richmond, 'The Problem of Peace: Understanding the "Liberal Peace"' (2006) 6 Conflict, Security & Development 291; Jan Selby, 'The Myth of Liberal Peace-Building' (2013) 13 Conflict, Security & Development 57; Edward Newman, '"Liberal" Peacebuilding Debates' in Edward Newman, Roland Paris, and Oliver P Richmond (eds), *New Perspectives on Liberal Peacebuilding* (United Nations University 2009).

[32] Louis-Alexandre Berg, 'Liberal Peacebuilding: Bringing Domestic Politics Back In' in Henry F Carey (ed), *Peacebuilding Paradigms* (CUP 2020); Beate Jahn, 'Liberal Internationalism' in Oliver P Richmond and Gëzim Visoka (eds), *The Oxford Handbook of Peacebuilding, Statebuilding, and Peace Formation* (OUP 2021).

[33] Jahn (n 32).

[34] Oliver P Richmond, 'The Problem of Peace: Understanding the "Liberal Peace"' (2006) 6 Conflict, Security & Development 291.

basic tenets of liberal market democracy, including values and institutions such as the rule of law, human rights, and development. It is rooted in two main assumptions. First is that democracies and market economies are stable and peaceful, whereas undemocratic societies without competitive markets are prone to conflict. Second is that peacebuilding should help create the social and institutional conditions for the proper functioning of competitive markets.

However, the concept of liberal peace also presents internal contradictions, such as the absence of consensus on how liberal peace is meant to be implemented. At the same time, some of its implementation techniques are considered illiberal or coercive, such as conditionality derived from structural adjustment programmes, which inflicted suffering on local populations through austerity requirements.[35] Considering these internal contradictions, Jan Selby warns against understanding peacebuilding as a discrete sphere of action, made possible by a discernible collection of (liberal) mechanisms.[36]

We consider liberal peace, to put it in Foucauldian terms, as a *dispositif* aimed at governing conflict-affected societies. According to Paris, the liberal peace paradigm allows the transmission or transplanting of a particular model of domestic governance from the core to the periphery of the international system. Therefore, it resembles the operation of the colonial-era civilizing mission embedded in international law, as discussed in the previous section.[37] Conversely, we believe that liberal peace and globalization are both constitutive expressions of power relations and imperialist interests furthered by capitalist modernity. They do so by transferring authority from the local to the international. This is done primarily through the prescription of technical solutions articulated by international actors and infused with market-oriented rationalities.[38] Accordingly, the conceptualization and operation of liberal peace rely upon a vision of how local communities should organize their social and economic relations and the state's role in society in line with modernist and Western understandings. Mounting criticism of liberal peace has resulted in the quest for a paradigm shift in peacebuilding.[39] A recurring feature among alternative approaches is turning to 'the local' as a source of legitimacy,[40] which entails shifting the focus from top-down recipes for peacebuilding to embracing local participation and initiatives of communitarian origin.

Although this work claims to pay attention to local and contextual elements, like liberal peace visions, it continues to rely upon external knowledge and direction for

[35] Selby (n 31).

[36] ibid.

[37] Roland Paris, 'International Peacebuilding and the "Mission Civilisatrice"' (2002) 28 Review of International Studies 637. Yet, for Paris, this is not necessarily an undesirable outcome, as he considers the practice of peacebuilding more 'charitable' and 'consensual' than colonial domination.

[38] Michael Pugh, 'The Political Economy of Peacebuilding: A Critical Theory Perspective' (2005) 10 International Journal of Peace Studies 23.

[39] Newman (n 31).

[40] Hanna Leonardsson and Gustav Rudd, 'The "Local Turn" in Peacebuilding: A Literature Review of Effective and Emancipatory Local Peacebuilding' (2015) 36 Third World Quarterly 825; Roger Mac Ginty and Oliver P Richmond, 'The Local Turn in Peace Building: A Critical Agenda for Peace' (2013) 34 Third World Quarterly 763.

peacebuilding. Furthermore, it perceives conflict as a self-generated product of societies and local communities, meaning that peacebuilding interventions can merely play a facilitating role, support capacity building, and manage vulnerabilities at the local level.[41] Therefore, this literature is not as transformative as it claims, to the extent that it continues to identify problems from an external and Western perspective, thus engaging with local complexity mainly to strengthen supposedly technical and 'objective' knowledge on peacebuilding. As Chandler puts it, some approaches that claim to be 'bottom-up' seek to 'drill down', paying attention to the context only to pluralize the variables and localize the factors that hinder peacebuilding and statebuilding interventions.[42]

In contrast, approaches rooted in territorial relations move the debate towards hybridity,[43] the everyday scale,[44] and issues of resistance,[45] identity,[46] and relationality.[47] As Richmond points out, these works assume 'that peaceful political communities are formed through internal but networked and relational processes of legitimation rather than state-level or international processes'.[48] Richmond refers to this approach as a turn towards peace formation.

In Colombia, demands for an alternative vision of peacebuilding were a recurring topic during the peace negotiation. The emergence of the concept of territorial peace illustrates these debates. As Cairo and colleagues claim, territorial peace is a polysemic term, as it is not defined in the Accord.[49] Yet, the literature agrees that it refers to a vision of peacebuilding from the victims' and local rural populations' point of view. It pays close attention to local dynamics, that is, to the relationships between different groups that inhabit the territory, the kind of ties that exist between humans and non-humans, and grassroots political processes, among other aspects. Moreover, this approach to peacebuilding seeks to overcome the political, economic, and social conditions that have facilitated enduring violence, such as poverty, inequality, marginalization, and exclusion.[50] On the communal side, it aims to enable conflict-affected communities to design and implement peacebuilding strategies grounded on local and communal knowledge and practices.

[41] David Chandler, 'Statebuilding' in Oliver P Richmond and Gëzim Visoka (eds), *The Oxford Handbook of Peacebuilding, Statebuilding, and Peace Formation* (OUP 2021).

[42] ibid.

[43] Suthaharan Nadarajah and David Rampton, 'The Limits of Hybridity and the Crisis of Liberal Peace' (2015) 41 Review of International Studies 49.

[44] Vivienne Jabri, *War and the Transformation of Global Politics* (Palgrave Macmillan UK 2007).

[45] Vivienne Jabri, 'Shock and Awe: Power and the Resistance of Art' (2006) 34 Millennium: Journal of International Studies 819.

[46] Dorte Andersen, 'The Paradox of "the People": Cultural Identity and European Integration' (2003) 119 Radical Philosophy 17.

[47] John Paterson, 'Production Sharing Agreements in Africa: Sovereignty and Relationality' (2018) Ethiopian Yearbook of International Law 119.

[48] Richmond, 'The Problem of Peace' (n 36) 582.

[49] Heriberto Cairo and others, '"Territorial Peace": The Emergence of a Concept in Colombia's Peace Negotiations' (2018) 23 Geopolitics 464.

[50] ibid; María Carolina Olarte-Olarte, 'From Territorial Peace to Territorial Pacification: Anti-Riot Police Powers and Socio-Environmental Dissent in the Implementation of Colombia's Peace Agreement' (2019) 67 Revista de Estudios Sociales 26; Arlene B Tickner, 'Choque Ontológico y Paz Decolonial' *El Espectador* (Bogotá, 24 February 2016) <https://www.elespectador.com/opinion/columnistas/arlene-b-tickner/choque-ontologico-y-paz-decolonial-column-618449/> accessed 19 May 2023.

As Carolina Olarte-Olarte points out, territorial peace draws on two premises: on the one hand, the importance of acknowledging the intrinsic dynamics of local territories and taking them into account when implementing peacebuilding strategies; on the other hand, the need to bring state presence to the areas most marginalized or severely affected by the internal conflict and improve people's welfare.[51] The expression is also connected with popular democracy, the construction of peace from below, effective decentralization, and the strengthening of local institutions, and, for the FARC, alternative notions of development such as *Buen Vivir*.[52] Accordingly, the qualifier 'territorial' is used to recognize that some territories were more affected by the armed conflict than others and to acknowledge that the communities' participation and the incorporation of their knowledge and practices are key for lasting peace strategies.[53] Territorial peace departs from the 'localization approaches' to the extent that it does not just seek to pay attention to local dynamics, but instead takes communal/local knowledge, practices, and experiences as the basis for peacebuilding while empowering local actors to lead these processes.[54]

This seems to suggest, as Tickner indicates, that territorial peace was an 'ontological' departure from liberal values and capitalist social relations, since it acknowledges and embraces indigenous and Afro-Colombian people's visions of peace and prosperity.[55] In this sense, empowering and giving a voice should entail admitting that communities affected by the conflict have ways of thinking about social relations, living well, and the environment that might differ from the liberal development paradigm and the institutions of capitalist modernity. Nevertheless, there is a mounting perception that the transformative potential associated with the territorial peace approach in Colombian peace negotiations has not been fulfilled. Specifically, several authors raise the criticism that the government has appropriated the concept of territorial peace to promote, under the guise of participatory democracy, discourses such as the need for military state presence following a securitized logic, the importance of capacity building for modernizing the exercise of public authority, and the implementation of development and modernization projects.[56]

[51] Olarte-Olarte (n 51).

[52] Cairo and others (n 50).

[53] Kent Eaton, 'Territorial Peace Without Territorial Governments: The Centralising Logic of the 2016 Colombian Peace Accord' (2021) 16 Journal of Peacebuilding & Development 194. In any case, the literature has criticized that the logic of the Peace Accord is not really territorial. For example, it defends a logic of centralization in its implementation process (see Eaton n 53) and the processes of participation in the territory for project planning have been criticized for their methodological deficits (see Diana María Ramírez Sarmiento, 'Hacia Una Participación Ciudadana Transformadora En Colombia. Análisis de Los Programas de Desarrollo Con Enfoque Territorial (PDET)' (2021) 61 Estudios Políticos (Medellín) 73).

[54] Territorial peace in this text is therefore used to refer to a local and community-based approach to peacebuilding. Our approach is different from that of 'territorial peace theory' which studies how the stability of a country's borders influences internal conflict, Marc L Hutchison and Daniel G Starr, 'The Territorial Peace: Theory, Evidence, and Implications' *Oxford Research Encyclopedia of Politics* (Online Version, OUP 2017) <http://oxfordre.com/politics/view/10.1093/acrefore/9780190228637.001.0001/acrefore-9780190228637-e-285> accessed 19 May 2023.

[55] Tickner (n 51).

[56] Julieta Lemaitre Ripoll and Esteban Restrepo Saldarriaga, 'Law and Violence in the Colombian Post-Conflict: State-Making in the Wake of the Peace Agreement' (2019) 67 Revista de Estudios Sociales 2.

However, territorial peace remains a concept with emancipatory potential. Its 'polysemic' character means its exact content varies depending on the political actor.[57] Accordingly, it offers the possibility to re-signify peacebuilding to align its content with the effective empowerment of local communities, a different relationship between humanity and the environment, and alternative economies apart from the logic of capitalist production. Nevertheless, it should not be overlooked that 'peace agreements are essential mechanisms for restructuring power relations'.[58] In this regard, whereas the negotiation of a Peace Accord in Colombia offered an opportunity to seek an alternative approach to liberal peace, our goal is to show that international development cooperation enables a redistribution of power to allow donors to bring back hegemonic visions of peacebuilding through the back door.

D. Discourses on Peace and Development in USAID/Colombia's Country Development Cooperation Strategies

Although USAID's documents are not legally binding instruments, they have normative effects when determining peacebuilding in Colombia. As constructivist approaches have taught us, diverse discourses circulate through different forms of international law, including treaties, recommendations, strategies, indicators, policy reports, and different forms of soft law.[59] These instruments create grammar and frames of reference for understanding social problems and designing solutions accordingly. Discourses shape what is possible to think and do at a particular time, what phenomena can be counted as a problem, what type of interventions and policy options are admissible and legitimate to solve problems, and how actors (such as governments, NGOs, and international institutions) are expected to behave. In the process, hegemonic discourses distribute power across different actors and constitute subjectivities aligned with the rationalities and interests underpinning them. In short, discourses produce a common sense that governs law and policymaking.[60]

This is how we approach USAID's documents in this chapter: as discursive devices that position a particular way of understanding the Colombian conflict, its root causes, and preferable solutions. This chapter looks specifically at USAID/Colombia's Country Development Cooperation Strategies (CDCS) 2014–2018 and 2020–2025. These documents contain a diagnosis of the main causes and consequences of the

[57] Cairo and others (n 50).

[58] Selby (n 31) 76.

[59] Emanuel Adler, *Communitarian International Relations* (1st edn, Routledge 2004); Jutta Brunnée and Stephen J Toope, *Legitimacy and Legality in International Law: An Interactional Account* (1st edn, CUP 2010) <https://www.cambridge.org/core/product/identifier/9780511781261/type/book> accessed 13 February 2023; Armin Von Bogdandy and René Urueña, 'International Transformative Constitutionalism in Latin America' (2020) 114 American Journal of International Law 403; Marieke De Goede, 'Beyond Economism in International Political Economy' (2003) 29 Review of International Studies.

[60] Carol Bacchi, 'The Turn to Problematization: Political Implications of Contrasting Interpretive and Poststructural Adaptations' (2015) 5 Open Journal of Political Science 1; Michael Arribas-Ayllon and Valerie Walkerdine, 'Foucauldian Discourse Analysis' in Carla Willig and Wendy Stainton-Rogers (eds), *The SAGE Handbook of Qualitative Research in Psychology* (2nd edn, Sage 2017) 91.

Colombian armed conflict, together with prescribed solutions that USAID is willing to support. Given USAID's political and economic influence in the country, both at the level of government and local communities, its diagnosis and solutions shape and govern what peacebuilding means and entails.

USAID has been Colombia's most important international donor since at least the late 1990s. At the outset of the peace negotiations with the guerrilla group FARC-EP, the Colombian government sought support from the US government. Although the US rhetorically aligned with the peace talks, for some critics, the emphasis on territorial control and military solutions to drug trafficking continued to dominate US cooperation strategies during the early 2010s.[61]

CDCS 2014–2018 was adopted in this context. Its main objective is to 'strengthen Colombia's capacity to implement a sustainable and inclusive peace'.[62] For these purposes, the strategy focuses on four development objectives (DOs): '(1) Effective presence of democratic institutions and processes in targeted areas; (2) Reconciliation advanced among victims, ex-combatants and other citizens; (3) Improved conditions for inclusive, rural economic growth; and (4) Environmental resilience and low-emissions development strengthened.'[63]

CDCS 2020–2025, issued four years after the end of the negotiations, talks about USAID's commitment to implementing the 2016 Accord. Its main goal is defined as 'A more Stable, Peaceful, and Prosperous Colombia through Inclusive Governance and Equitable Growth', and it claims to set strategies to support Colombia in its journey to self-reliance. The document contains three DOs: (1) 'A more cohesive and inclusive society resilient to conflict', (2) 'strengthened governance to meet citizen needs and increase citizen confidence in the state', and (3) 'promote equitable and environmentally sustainable economic growth'.[64] Additionally, the strategy includes a special objective defined as 'Stability in areas impacted by migration from Venezuela'.[65]

Although the documents were drafted in different periods and under different governments, both rely upon some common assumptions akin to liberal peace. To substantiate this claim, in the following paragraphs we focus on four specific topics that cut across USAID cooperation strategies and that reveal how USAID approaches peacebuilding: development, the state, civil society, and nature.

1. Development

Both strategies portray peace as a precondition for economic development, signalling an instrumental view of peacebuilding vis-à-vis growth. Economic development, in turn, is envisioned as income generation through peasants' participation in global value chains and efficient and sustainable exploitation of the country's natural wealth.

[61] Rojas (n 4).
[62] USAID Colombia, 'Country Development Cooperation Strategy 2014–2018: A Path to Peace' (USAID Colombia 2014) 3 (accessed 19 May 2023).
[63] ibid.
[64] USAID, 'Peace, Stability and Prosperity. Country Development Cooperation Strategy 2020–2025' (USAID 2020) v.
[65] ibid.

Traditional formulas such as land formalization, infrastructure development, access to finance, and training are seen as means to further economic development. The private sector is represented as playing a crucial role in development, especially in rural areas, by providing funds and capacities to make rural production competitive at both national and global scales.

In this vein, CDCS 2014–2018 emphasizes property formalization in conflict zones to incentivize private investment and production.[66] To this end, USAID claims that it would 'support GOC [Government of Colombia] land tenure security initiatives, including land restitution and rapid extension of titles to rural citizens (including collective titles to indigenous and Afro-Colombian communities). This will include assistance to develop a modern cadaster so that the GOC can maintain accurate land ownership and titling information, a key prerequisite to guaranteeing property rights.'[67] Moreover, for USAID, 'The pervasiveness of informal land ownership and the lack of full legal protection of land rights are formidable obstacles to private investment in these regions . . . Such informality distorts the land market and discourages long-term investment.'[68] The strategy also stresses the importance of investments in infrastructure going hand in hand with the private sector, coupled with initiatives aimed at paring rural producers with the private sector, to give them access to 'higher-paying markets for competitive agricultural products'.[69]

The strategy also includes the intermediate result of '[i]ncreased private sector investment in target rural communities'.[70] It refers to financial mechanisms supported by USAID to attract investments to rural areas. The following paragraph is illustrative of how the role of the private sector is conceived:

> USAID will continue to leverage private sector investment in targeted communities through various means to reduce their costs and risks for doing business. USAID will support co-share in insurance premiums, use Development Credit Authority mechanisms, provide local workforce training in skills required for planned investment, and other tools to attract private sector investment by mitigating risk. In addition, access to financial services for rural producers will be critical for sustainable and equitable economic growth in these regions. In 2009, although 66% of Colombian farmers were smallholders, 49 large and medium-sized farmers received 78% of farm credit. USAID will support banking, microfinance, micro-insurance, and mobile money activities to expand to finance in rural areas. E-money and mobile money instruments will reduce delivery costs and inequality of access while making financial services more accessible. As a result, target populations, including ethnic communities and women heads of households, will be better integrated into the formal sector.[71]

[66] USAID Colombia (n 62).
[67] ibid 3.
[68] ibid 19.
[69] ibid 3.
[70] ibid 21.
[71] ibid.

In turn, CDCS 2020–2025 claims that 'both durable peace and stability are prerequisites for the country's social and economic prosperity'.[72] According to it, the lack of land titling is implicated in producing violence to an extent that 'weakens land governance and limits the government's ability to regulate land use and land administration, making land susceptible to illicit activities by unauthorized groups'.[73] Therefore, the strategy emphasizes land formalization to prevent conflict and bring economic prosperity to conflict-affected regions. This CDCS also stresses the importance of finance to make licit economic activities competitive and attractive to peasants. It claims that 'enabling conditions—such as job skills training, access to finance, business development services, land formalization, and cadaster updates, and investments in new or expanding local markets'[74] will allow peasants to diversify and improve livelihoods over the long-term. Private investments are expected to be incentivized through 'specialized funding instruments, such as financial guarantees, and Global Development Alliances (GDA)',[75] property rights, and public investments in strategic assets such as infrastructure, connectivity, and basic services.[76] Public–private partnerships feature prominently as means to improve public investments in these areas.[77]

Hence, growth is expected to emerge from better connections between local producers and global value chains and from the development of local capabilities to enable competition in the global economy, for instance through providing financial services to peasants.[78] The strategies qualify growth using terms such as equitable and inclusive. These qualifiers are used to talk about non-discrimination[79] and improvements in minorities and peasants' access to strategic assets such as 'land, infrastructure, energy supplies, tertiary roads, and natural resources'[80] to prompt rural development.[81] The strategies say little about indigenous, Afro-Colombian, or peasant populations' economic self-determination or control over natural resources. They do not delve into their participation in economic decision-making beyond the participatory spaces granted by accountability and transparency mechanisms.

2. The State

The documents emphasize the state's absence and fragility as a cause of the Colombian conflict, while portraying security and stability as preconditions for prosperity and growth. Against this backdrop, both strategies highlight the importance of strengthening state institutions, especially those associated with the rule of law.

[72] USAID (n 64) i.
[73] ibid 2.
[74] ibid 20.
[75] ibid 7.
[76] ibid 19.
[77] ibid 20.
[78] ibid 21.
[79] ibid 3.
[80] ibid 19.
[81] USAID Colombia (n 62).

CDCS 2014–2018 emphasizes state capacity. The rationale behind this is that the absence of effective state presence is one of the causes of the armed conflict. It claims, for instance, that state absence has enabled undemocratic rule 'imposed by force of illegal arms, and often financed by illicit sources'.[82] Therefore, its DO 1 promotes the 'effective presence of democratic institutions and processes in targeted areas'.[83] The text regards such an outcome as 'essential for a successful transition out of conflict and implementation of an eventual peace agreement'.[84] It entails USAID support to human rights, access to justice, and the rule of law.[85]

Similarly, CDCS 2020–2025 argues that the 'lack of an institutional presence is the deeper malady that ails Colombia, producing symptoms such as inequality, coca cultivation, and illegal armed actors'.[86] Furthermore, state absence is a persistent problem not solved by the Peace Accord, which has enabled illicit actors to take territorial control over rural areas and create new sources of instability. Hence, the strategy talks about strengthening state presence in the post-conflict scenario, specifically in conflict-affected regions. The strategy changes slightly as it incorporates concerns about citizens' lack of trust in public authorities due to corruption, and accountability deficits. Accordingly, the second DO advocates for 'engaging citizens and making government systems more accessible and responsive to citizen needs in historically forgotten conflict zones'.[87] The strategy also connects state presence and economic growth: 'A Colombia with a consolidated peace and expanded state presence offers new opportunities for prosperity and equitable growth.'[88]

Both strategies rely upon the assumption that state absence is at the heart of the internal armed conflict, which means that more state presence and a stronger state are part of the solution. The issue with this way of framing the problem is that it obscures how the Colombian state has been deeply implicated in producing the conflict. The problem is not only that the documents ignore that there is evidence of military complicity with massacres, selective killings, and other crimes committed by paramilitary forces.[89] It is also that USAID strategies do not take into consideration how selective state presence oriented towards creating the conditions for development projects is also connected with the root causes of the conflict.

3. Civil Society

In line with ideas of liberal peace, civil society is depicted as needing empowerment and cohesion, on the one hand, to channel its demands through democratic institutions instead of resorting to violence, and on the other hand, to exert control over state authorities, hand in hand with ideas of transparency and accountability. Although

[82] ibid 10.
[83] ibid 2.
[84] ibid 10.
[85] ibid 42.
[86] USAID (n 64) iii.
[87] ibid.
[88] ibid.
[89] Grupo de Memoria Histórica, *¡Basta Ya!: Colombia: Memorias de Guerra y Dignidad* (2013).

USAID stresses the role of civil society in democracy, in our view, democracy here is reduced to notions of participation and control through institutionalized channels to tackle corruption. Little is said about participation in allocating resources or pursuing political and economic projects different from the ones promoted by national and regional governments.

CDCS 2014–2018 refers to civil society's capacity to represent citizens' interests and participate in democratic processes as an essential component of lasting peace. Two specific functions are assigned to civil society. First, it is expected to demand accountability and transparency from public resources authorities. For instance, it argues that 'USAID will build the capacity of national and sub-national governments, as well as civil society (including ethnic minorities), to access, transparently invest and oversee public funds available via inter-governmental fiscal transfers and supplementary budget resources'.[90] Second, the strategy also seeks to encourage the participation of civil society in peace negotiations. Notably, the document argues that 'effective implementation of the Victims Law is essential to short-term and sustainable peace'[91] and highlights the importance of strengthening the institutions that implement it.

Likewise, CDCS 2020–2025 seeks to promote 'a more cohesive and inclusive society'[92] to mitigate the conditions that contribute to violence and help to provide 'mechanisms to give citizens voice' to 'increase the effective participation of citizens in state systems and channel their interests to democratic institutions rather than to illegal armed groups'.[93] Furthermore, it includes an intermediate result (IR) called 'greater citizen engagement in governance processes',[94] which aims to provide civil society with the technical and institutional capacity to engage in demanding accountability on issues such as public service delivery and resource management. CDCS 2020–2025 also has another IR entitled 'improved governance for citizen security',[95] which considers improving governance to make society safer and more resilient. This objective focuses on preventing violence and criminality through conflict mitigation and management activities, reducing impunity by enhancing the justice system, and addressing regional crime patterns. The strategy argues that they are aligned with the Colombian government's priorities regarding the end of the conflict and its victims. This claim also reveals the tensions between liberal and territorial peace within the country. In this way, civil society's role in peacebuilding is reduced to exercises of accountability and transparency along with a narrative of corruption as a problem of individuals mismanaging public funds. Discussions about the extent to which participation should entail decision-making power over resource allocation, or development strategies, are absent from the documents.

[90] USAID Colombia (n 62) 2.
[91] ibid 15.
[92] USAID (n 64) ii.
[93] ibid 4.
[94] ibid 15.
[95] ibid v.

4. Nature

An instrumental view of nature underpins the strategies, a vision whereby its importance and legal protection are mediated by the possibility of the government and rural communities exploiting it. This approach can be detected in several aspects, such as the documents' emphasis on managing conflicts about natural resources to prevent conflict and create prosperity and their insistence on securing the legal conditions required for expanding the frontier of land available for agriculture and other economic activities. That is why the concrete actions of the cooperation strategies concentrate either on formalizing property rights or securing control over ecosystems, to replace illicit economies with licit exploitative activities.

Rural economic growth is a pillar of the CDCS 2014–2018. The document stresses the importance of land security initiatives, including land restitution, formalization, and granting collective titles to minority ethnic groups. That is why the document refers to assisting in modernizing rural cadasters in Colombia to guarantee property rights.[96] The document also constantly refers to building roads and other infrastructure to foment rural economic growth.[97] Furthermore, the CDCS 2014–2018 mentions that the Colombian government has failed to secure control over areas like the Amazon Forest, inter-Andean valleys, and pacific lowlands, thus calling to improve environmental management.[98] In doing so, the document refers to these areas as biodiversity-rich and asserts that Colombia's natural resources should not be used illegally.[99]

Similarly, CDCS 2020–2025 refers to 'promote equitable and environmentally sustainable economic growth'[100] as one of its DO and associates it with expanding licit economies and livelihood opportunities. The document argues for using 'environmental interventions as a crosscutting strategic approach to achieve peace, stability, and prosperity',[101] and to consider environmental protection 'more than a means to an end, but an end in itself, as Colombia's rich environment provides countless environmental services that benefit human wellbeing end in itself'.[102] Yet, the concern is premised on the environment's utility for economic prosperity and natural wealth exploitation's role in the producing conflict. For instance, the strategy indicates: 'The CDCS has elevated the importance of environmental protection by integrating it in each of the DOs, demonstrating the transformational role a healthy natural environment plays in generating economic growth and reducing violence'.[103] The document also refers to the importance of harnessing Colombia's 'environmental resources for a stable, peaceful, and prosperous future'[104] and refers to 'promoting environmental markets and eco-friendly businesses'[105] as a means to bring sustainable economic development.

96 USAID Colombia (n 62) 3.
97 ibid 19.
98 ibid 23.
99 ibid 24.
100 USAID (n 64) v.
101 ibid 3.
102 ibid 5.
103 ibid iii.
104 ibid.
105 ibid 19.

What lies behind this conceptualization of nature is its commodification or alienation from social relations, such as the relational connections that peasants and ethnic communities have with their territories. The documents only conceive a specific relationship between society and nature: the latter is incorporated into production and accumulation patterns. This explains the insistence on better resource management and the role of infrastructure in securing the incorporation of rural areas into global value chains.

E. Conclusions

We have argued that international law on development cooperation, which includes forms of soft law such as USAID country cooperation strategies, is constitutive of peacebuilding in conflict-affected countries. International law is implicated in creating a 'common sense' of what sort of programmes and solutions peacebuilding should involve. It shapes and governs how actors, such as states and NGOs, think and act regarding post-conflict situations.

We examined the discursive process that constitutes the meaning (and ultimately, practices) of peacebuilding in Colombia through a critical perspective that explains how modern international law involves a mode of argumentation that has justified the economic and political domination of societies situated at the margins of the global capitalist system, also referred to as the Global South. Against this backdrop, we identified the idea of liberal peace as a hegemonic notion in peacebuilding, advanced by many international donors, which is instrumental in creating avenues for market expansion and natural wealth exploitation in conflict-affected regions in the Global South.

The Colombian peace negotiations replicated this model to the extent that they invited participation from government, FARC-EP representatives, and victims and conflict-affected peasant communities, providing an opportunity to imagine development and peacebuilding in other ways. The peace negotiations gave birth to what in Colombia is called 'territorial peace', an understanding of peacebuilding that considers the local dynamics of violence and enables peacebuilding initiatives grounded on rural and conflict-affected communities' peace practices and conceptions of prosperity. Although the Accord does not define territorial peace, it opened the political space to think about peacebuilding differently and counter-hegemonically.

The implementation stage entailed a redistribution of power regarding the definition of peacebuilding. Because the Accord implementation demands enormous amounts of money, international donors willing to support it have carved a new political space to influence how peacebuilding should be pursued. In this context, our chapter shows that USAID's (Colombia's main international donor) cooperation strategies since 2014 are still anchored in ideas akin to liberal peace. We argue that by advancing liberal peace, USAID disregards the alternative notion of territorial peace discussed during the negotiations and, in this sense, is only supporting the 2016 Accord rhetorically.

PART II

DRIVERS, CONSEQUENCES, AND INTERDEPENDENCIES OF PROTRACTED CONFLICTS

7
International Law on Armed Conflict and Sustainable Food Security

Antonio Coco

A. Hunger Fuelling Conflict, Conflict Fuelling Hunger

Of the 193 million people suffering from acute food insecurity around the world, according to the 2022 Global Report on Food Crises, more than 139 million live in countries plagued by an armed conflict—making this by far the 'primary driver' of hunger around the world.[1] The intrinsic connection between conflict and food insecurity is often taken as a given, and with good reason. In fact, it can be affirmed that hunger and conflict feed on each other, with one fuelling the other in a vicious cycle. On one side, food crises and—more generally—food insecurity strain societal relationships, creating opportunities and pretexts for resort to armed violence.[2] In fact, states have started using the expression 'food security' to highlight the connection between food and peace at the highest political level.[3] On the other side, armed conflict often results in the destruction of food crops and jeopardizes or disrupts processes critical to grow, store, and distribute food, including by breaking supply chains or rendering agricultural land unusable. Protracted conflict threatens or negatively impacts the four pillars of food security:[4] (i) the *availability* of a sufficient quantity of food of appropriate quality; (ii) people's *access* to resources adequate to acquire sufficient food; (iii) proper *utilization* of the available food resources to achieve a state of nutritional wellbeing; (iv) *stability* of the availability of and access to sufficient food of appropriate quality.[5] This is due to damage inflicted not just directly by military attacks but also indirectly by displacement of people onto areas which would otherwise be

[1] Global Action Network against Food Crises and Food Security Information Network, '2022 Global Report on Food Crises' (World Food Programme 2022) 6–7; Food and Agriculture Organization of the United Nations (FAO) and World Food Programme (WFP), 'Hunger Hotspots: FAO-WFP early warnings on acute food insecurity—October 2022 to January 2023 Outlook' (FAO and WFP 2022) viii and 1.

[2] Brian Lander and Rebecca Vetharaniam Richards, 'Addressing Hunger and Starvation in Situations of Armed Conflict—Laying the Foundations for Peace' (2019) 17 Journal of International Criminal Justice 675, 691.

[3] Michael Fakhri, 'Framing the Problem of Hunger and Conflict at the UN Security Council' (*Just Security*, 22 September 2022) <https://www.justsecurity.org/83173/framing-the-problem-of-hunger-and-conflict-at-the-un-security-council/> accessed 26 April 2023.

[4] Committee on World Food Security, 'Framework for Action for Food Security and Nutrition in Protracted Crises' (WFP, International Fund for Agricultural Development (IFAD) and FAO 2015) 2, para 4.

[5] FAO, 'Food Security' (Policy Brief, issue no 2, 2006) <https://www.fao.org/fileadmin/templates/faoitaly/documents/pdf/pdf_Food_Security_Cocept_Note.pdf> accessed 25 April 2023.

Antonio Coco, *International Law on Armed Conflict and Sustainable Food Security* In: *From Protracted Conflict to Sustainable Peace?* Edited by: Heike Krieger, Giedre Jokubauskaite, Asli Ozcelik, and Andreas Buser, Oxford University Press.
 DOI: 10.1093/9780198967385.003.0009

used for food production.[6] As a matter of fact, food security considerations related to armed conflicts concern not only people living in areas of active hostilities but also those who are forced to relocate and those living in areas hosting internally displaced persons, asylum seekers, and refugees.[7] At times, conflict is tied with food crises so severe that they lead to starvation, that is, suffering or death caused by lack of food or other objects indispensable for human survival.[8] The recent conflict in Yemen constitutes but one example of such deathly escalation.[9]

The war in Ukraine, ongoing at the time of writing, shows also how armed conflict could threaten to escalate to a global food crisis when the countries involved in the hostilities (in this case Russia and Ukraine) are major food producers on whose exports other countries rely.[10] Food shortages may be caused not only directly, by stopping or reducing food exports (as in the case of grains produced in Russia and Ukraine), but also indirectly, by withholding exports on goods necessary to grow food crops, such as fertilizers.[11] The food shortages caused by the Russian invasion reminded us that, in a globalized world, 'all food systems are inherently interconnected' and that 'an invasion or occupation of any place is an attack on the global food system'.[12] Of course, one should not overestimate its effects: global food insecurity was already rising prior to 2020 and was heightened further during the Covid-19 pandemic.[13] Still, if food security can be negatively impacted by armed conflict even in a relatively short time span, as shown by the speed with which the 2022 Russian invasion affected the global food markets, one may only imagine how even worse consequences may unfold in the case of protracted conflict.

Protracted armed conflict does not always involve full-scale military confrontations but can often linger in the form of low-level violence. The more a conflict lingers, the more it may jeopardize the provision of basic services—including access to food and means of livelihood—in the affected areas and society at large.[14] The economic effects of protracted armed conflict may significantly lower not only the availability

[6] Alexander Hay, Bryan Karney, and Nick Martyn, 'Reconstructing Infrastructure for Resilient Essential Services During and Following Protracted Conflict: A Conceptual Framework' (2019) 101 International Review of the Red Cross 1001, 1017.

[7] ibid.

[8] See, eg Bridget Conley and Alex de Waal, 'The Purposes of Starvation: Historical and Contemporary Uses' (2019) 17 Journal of International Criminal Justice 699, 700–02.

[9] HRC, 'Situation of Human Rights in Yemen, Including Violations and Abuses since September 2014—Report of the Detailed Findings of the Group of Eminent International and Regional Experts on Yemen' (3 September 2019) UN Doc A/HRC/42/CRP.1, paras 732ff.

[10] Diane Desierto, 'The Human Right to Food, Freedom from Hunger, and SDG 2: Global Food Crisis and Starvation Tactics from the Russian Invasion of Ukraine' (*EJIL: Talk!*, 9 June 2022) <https://www.ejiltalk.org/the-human-right-to-food-freedom-from-hunger-and-sdg-2-global-food-crisis-and-starvation-tactics-from-the-russian-invasion-of-ukraine/> accessed 18 June 2022.

[11] ibid; Moritz von Rochow, 'The Prohibition of Abusing a Dominant Position as a General Principle of International Law: Russia's Biggest Honeypot in Ukraine' (*Opinio Juris*, 13 May 2022) <https://opiniojuris.org/2022/05/13/the-prohibition-of-abusing-a-dominant-position-as-a-general-principle-of-international-law-russias-biggest-honeypot-in-ukraine/> accessed 18 June 2022. However, the positive effects of fertilizers should not be overestimated: Fakhri (n 3).

[12] ibid (n 3).

[13] HRC, 'Conflict and the Right to Food—Report of the Special Rapporteur on the Right to Food, Michael Fakhri' (29 December 2022) UN Doc A/HRC/52/40, para 13; also Fakhri (n 3).

[14] On the related notion of 'cumulative impact': ICRC, 'Protracted Conflict and Humanitarian Action: Some Recent ICRC Experiences' (International Committee of the Red Cross 2016) 10.

of sustenance but also people's purchasing power, increasing the cost of living and thereby creating so-called war-poor populations and 'lost generations' of children.[15]

Over time, continuous engagement in protracted armed conflict may contribute to or determine losses of governmental effectiveness and authority and of the government's ability to cater to basic needs of the population, either in specific areas or across the whole territory of the state. The government may grow dependent on external funding deriving from international borrowing and aid, which often becomes an indispensable source of public income.[16] If food prices increase, governments may be presented with a daunting dilemma: either incurring more debt to feed the population or prioritizing debt repayment instead of securing sufficient food, leading to more hunger.[17] Situations of this kind may also open the door to the aggressive exploitation of natural resources, leading to further depletion of the environment and poor working conditions for locals due to ineffective labour protection[18]—which in turn may prejudice the quality and quantity of available food provision and the purchasing power of the population. Furthermore, at times governments, as parties to a protracted conflict, can lose authority over certain parts of their territory, either in remote rural areas or in urban centres. Non-state actors—such as armed groups or private companies—may step in to provide governance functions, but they may not be equipped with the resources necessary to ensure food security and defeat hunger.[19]

It is imperative, thus, that efforts are made to increase global food security by combining short-term emergency relief with medium and long-term plans to build capacity and reduce the risk of both food crises and armed conflict. Such combination of efforts seems to neatly mirror the goals of the so-called humanitarian-development-peace nexus, which many governmental and non-governmental actors endeavour to adopt as a guide to their actions. Moreover, as protracted conflicts unfold and continue to exist over the years, it is crucial to take up measures and initiatives aimed at minimizing negative impacts for food security and maintain sustainability of food provision even as hostilities unfold. While conflict does commonly result in food insecurity, there may be solutions available to ensure that food systems and markets continue to function properly.[20] A government's provision of food security in emergency times, potentially with the involvement or help of external humanitarian actors, has been hailed as an effective safety net (especially for the most vulnerable), with the potential to reduce societal tensions and help affected societies to transition towards peace.[21]

[15] Tanja A Börzel and Thomas Risse, *Effective Governance Under Anarchy: Institutions, Legitimacy, and Social Trust in Areas of Limited Statehood* (CUP 2021) 34–42, 176–80.

[16] Börzel and Risse (n 15), 216–28.

[17] Fakhri (n 3).

[18] See Ch. 1 Section B.2, citing Tata Precillia Ijang and Cleto Ndikumagenge, 'Dependency on Natural Resources: Post-Conflict Challenges for Livelihoods Security and Environmental Sustainability in Goma, The Democratic Republic of Congo' (2013) 23 Development in Practice 372, 372–88; Irene Costantini, 'Statebuilding and Foreign Direct Investment: The Case of Post-2003 Iraq' (2013) 20 International Peacekeeping 263, 263–79; Leo Zulu and Sigismond Wilson, 'Whose Minerals, Whose Development? Rhetoric and Reality in Post-Conflict Sierra Leone' (2012) 43 Development and Change 1103, 1103–31.

[19] Börzel and Risse (n 15) 34–42, 176–80.

[20] Eg the measure urged by UNSC Res 2573 (27 April 2021) UN Doc S/RES/2573, para 6; HRC (n 13), para 12.

[21] Lander and Richards (n 2) 692.

For the relevant duty-bearers, these efforts are also a way of complying with applicable positive duties to which they are subject under international law. Such positive duties, deriving for instance from international humanitarian law and international human rights law, must be combined with negative ones, such as to refrain from conduct which could directly or indirectly lead to food insecurity, hunger, and starvation. An analysis grounded in international law necessarily starts from the primary actor in the international legal system, that is, states. The fact that numerous humanitarian and development organizations shoulder heavy weight in addressing food crises should not distract from the fact that states continue to bear precise legal duties—though, of course, leaving space for those organizations to operate and to fulfil their mandate or mission. Furthermore, one should not forget the duties of non-state armed groups, especially when and where they control territory: since most ongoing protracted armed conflicts in the world may be classified as non-international armed conflicts, that is, conflicts where at least one party is a non-state actor, their role is often crucial and consideration of their responsibility should not be omitted.[22]

B. The International Legal Framework on Food Crises and Starvation

Clearly, international law does not offer a magical formula to solve the problem of conflict-related food insecurity. Yet, it does offer some tools to deal with it, informing and guiding the policy and practice of the relevant duty-bearers, most notably states. The relevant legal framework is wide, and it includes various branches of international law. In this chapter, for reasons of space and expertise, I will draw the reader's attention to rules and principles deriving from two branches in particular: international humanitarian law (IHL, also known as *jus in bello*, or the law of armed conflict), and international human rights law (IHRL). These two should not, however, be mistaken as being exhaustive of all international law that has to do with conflict-related food insecurity: just to mention one more branch, the international law of the sea also provides for relevant rules, for instance those pertaining to the passage of ships carrying food crops through areas under a state's jurisdiction.[23] And above all, one must remember that international law prohibits states from using or threatening the use of force against the territorial integrity or political independence of other states, as epitomized in article 2(4) of the United Nations Charter.[24] It is plainly obvious that, if states abided by this fundamental rule, conflicts would be less numerous—with positive effects on global food security levels. Granted, respect for the ban on the use of force would not prevent internal (*rectius*, 'non-international') armed

[22] Among others and with specific respect to the right to food, Simone Hutter, 'Starvation in Armed Conflicts: An Analysis Based on the Right to Food' (2019) 17 Journal of International Criminal Justice 723, 747ff.

[23] United Nations Convention on the Law of the Sea (adopted 10 December 1982, entered into force 16 November 1994) 1833 UNTS 3, arts 17ff on the right of innocent passage.

[24] Charter of the United Nations (adopted 26 June 1945, entered into force 24 October 1945) 1 UNTS XVI (UN Charter).

conflicts—representing the vast majority of protracted conflicts on the planet—but it would be a positive contributor to the reduction of world hunger, nonetheless.

Notably, even limiting the analysis to the mentioned fields of IHL and IHRL, there are still challenges in applying international law to conflict-related food insecurity, especially regarding how well the law addresses the complexity of the issue and the practicability of legal responses. First, it is hard to clearly discern all the multiple facets of the phenomenon by using exclusively legal lenses, since *inter alia* aspects of economics, history, political science, and sociology are involved to explain the reasons for food security or insecurity in a given society at a given historical moment. Second, the context of an armed conflict may alter the relevant actors' perception: parties to an armed conflict in particular may be swayed by the military mindset to focus on the aim to gain a military advantage against the opponent, thus overlooking how their conduct affects short, medium, and long-term availability of food resources. Third, states—especially those observing a conflict from the outside—may be tempted to prioritize their own sovereign interests instead of the wellbeing of other communities. As a result, they may refrain from or delay taking action to address or alleviate food crises. Fourth, in any case, even the most altruistic and well-intentioned actors may face difficulties in adequately predicting, preventing, and responding to conflict-related food insecurity.[25]

1. International Humanitarian Law and Food Security

As is well known, IHL implicitly accepts that there will be at least *some* death and destruction in an armed conflict, including events that will inevitably affect the availability of food and the civilian population's ability to obtain an adequate amount of it. In this sense, considering how food insecurity and crises can heighten tensions and at times prolong conflicts, IHL is not necessarily and not always conducive to faster and decisive progress towards peace. Yet, the 'damage control' mentality behind IHL can be beneficial from a food-security perspective: if the rules of distinction, proportionality, and precautions are respected—by state and non-state parties to a conflict—civilian infrastructure is more often preserved, with positive effects for the civilian population both during and after the conflict.[26]

Conventional and customary IHL encompass, in fact, several provisions to counter the negative effects of conflicts on the availability of sustenance for the civilian population. First and foremost, article 54(1) of the First Additional Protocol to the Geneva Conventions (Protocol I)[27] and article 14 of the Second Additional Protocol to the

[25] These challenges are discussed more in detail in Antonio Coco, Jérôme de Hemptinne, and Brian Lander, 'International Law Against Starvation in Armed Conflict: Epilogue to a Multi-Faceted Study' (2019) 17 Journal of International Criminal Justice 913, 914–19.

[26] 'The ICRC and the "Humanitarian-Development-Peace Nexus" Discussion: In Conversation with Filipa Schmitz Guinote, ICRC Policy Adviser' (2019) 101 International Review of the Red Cross 1051, 1064–66.

[27] Protocol Additional to the Geneva Conventions of 12 August 1949 relating to the Protection of Victims of International Armed Conflicts (adopted 8 June 1977, entered into force 7 December 1978) 1125 UNTS 3 (Protocol I).

Geneva Conventions (Protocol II)[28]—which are deemed to reflect a rule of customary international law on the issue[29]—prohibit the starvation of civilians as a method of warfare. Article 54(2) of Protocol I and the second part of article 14 of Protocol II—also reflecting customary international law[30]—follow suit by prohibiting attacking, destroying, removing, or rendering useless objects indispensable to the survival of the civilian population. It is understood that objects indispensable to the survival of the civilian population comprise—among other things—'foodstuffs, agricultural areas for the production of foodstuffs, crops, livestock, drinking water installations and supplies and irrigation works'.[31] Article 54(2) of Protocol I specifies that the conduct in question is prohibited when carried out for the specific purpose of denying the objects for their sustenance value to the civilian population 'whatever the motive, whether in order to starve out civilians, to cause them to move away, or for any other motive'. Furthermore, article 54(3) of Protocol I establishes that attacks and related actions against objects indispensable to the survival of the civilian population (even when these are being used in direct support of military action) cannot be taken if they may be expected to leave the civilian population with such inadequate food or water as to cause its starvation or force its movement—and this regardless of the relevant belligerent's purpose.[32]

However, article 54(5) of Protocol I contains an exception, allowing parties to the conflict to attack, destroy, remove, or render useless even objects indispensable to the survival of civilians located on its national territory when acting with the purpose to defend such territory against an invasion, provided that the conduct in question is required by imperative military necessity.[33] This type of conduct—often referred to as a 'scorched earth' tactic or practice and intended to avoid enemy appropriation of useful goods—normally leads to devastating effects for food security in already hard times like those of armed conflict. No similar exception appears to exist in the law applicable to non-international armed conflicts.[34]

Importantly, conduct in violation of the aforementioned rules may constitute a war crime if it amounts to 'intentionally using starvation of civilians as a method of warfare by depriving them of objects indispensable to their survival, including wilfully impeding relief supplies as provided for under the Geneva Conventions'.[35] Conduct

[28] Protocol Additional to the Geneva Conventions of 12 August 1949, and relating to the Protection of Victims of Non-International Armed Conflicts (adopted 8 June 1977, entered into force 7 December 1978) 1125 UNTS 609 (Protocol II).

[29] Jean-Marie Henckaerts and Louise Doswald-Beck (eds), *Customary International Humanitarian Law*, vol 1 (CUP 2005) Rule 53, 428ff (hereafter ICRC Customary IHL Study).

[30] ibid rule 54.

[31] Protocol I, art 54(2); Protocol II, art 14.

[32] Dapo Akande and Emanuela-Chiara Gillard, 'Conflict-Induced Food Insecurity and the War Crime of Starvation of Civilians as a Method of Warfare: The Underlying Rules of International Humanitarian Law' (2019) 17 Journal of International Criminal Justice 753, 764.

[33] Protocol I, art 54(5); Yves Sandoz, Christophe Swinarski, and Bruno Zimmermann (eds), *Commentary on the Additional Protocols of 8 June 1977 to the Geneva Conventions of 12 August 1949* (Nijhoff 1987) 658–59, paras 2116–2123.

[34] ibid 1459, paras 4808–4811. ICRC Customary IHL Study (n 29) 192–193.

[35] Both in international and non-international armed conflicts, by effect of an amendment to the Rome Statute adopted on 6 December 2019: Rome Statute of the International Criminal Court (adopted 17 July 1998, entered into force 1 July 2002) 2187 UNTS 90 (Rome Statute), art 8(2)(b)(xxv) and art 8(2)(e)

which does not satisfy this definition may still be captured by other core international crimes, including crimes against humanity.[36]

In addition, as already hinted at in this section, the fundamental conduct-of-hostilities rules of distinction, proportionality, and precautions continue to apply, protecting civilian objects (including food and food-related objects) against (the effects of) attacks.[37] Notably, parties to a conflict have an obligation to take all feasible precautions against the effects of attacks with a view to protecting civilian infrastructure,[38] including infrastructure critical to the provision of food for the civilian population.

Another layer of protection, finally, is offered by the provisions on humanitarian access and relief. Parties to an armed conflict have primary responsibility for ensuring that adequate supplies of food, water, and other necessary objects are available to and accessible by the civilian population. The principle applies also to special situations such as belligerent occupation: in that respect, article 55 of Geneva Convention IV[39] places on the occupying power the duty of ensuring that the civilian population has adequate food and medical supplies. Failing that, parties to a conflict must allow and facilitate rapid and unimpeded passage of humanitarian relief for civilians in need, which is impartial in character and conducted without any adverse distinction, subject to their right of control.[40] Generally, the provision of humanitarian relief and assistance is conditional on the consent of the relevant party to the conflict.[41] However, conventional and customary IHL provide for the belligerents' duty not to arbitrarily withhold their consent to offers to conduct humanitarian relief operations.[42] After the relevant belligerent has given such consent, they have an obligation to 'allow and facilitate rapid and unimpeded passage of supplies, equipment, and personnel involved in such operations'.[43]

Yet, while these rules have the potential to contribute to food security in protracted conflict, their practical importance should not be over-estimated. For instance, the

(xix). On strategies for prosecution, Wayne Jordash, Catriona Murdoch, and Joe Holmes, 'Strategies for Prosecuting Mass Starvation' (2019) 17 Journal of International Criminal Justice 849.

36 Manuel J Ventura, 'Prosecuting Starvation under International Criminal Law: Exploring the Legal Possibilities' (2019) 17 Journal of International Criminal Justice 781.

37 Even though they do not always cover 'non-attack' situations: Christian Durisch Acosta, 'It Takes Two: The Protection of Civilians during Sieges under the IHL Prohibition against Starvation and the Right to Food' (*Opinio Juris*, 20 December 2021) <https://opiniojuris.org/2021/12/20/it-takes-two-the-ihl-protection-of-civilians-during-sieges-under-the-prohibition-against-starvation-and-the-right-to-food/> accessed 18 June 2022.

38 Protocol I, art 58; ICRC Customary IHL Study (n 29) Rule 22.

39 Geneva Conventions (adopted 12 August 1949, entered into force 21 October 1959) 75 UNTS 31, 85, 135, 287 (Geneva Conventions I-IV).

40 Geneva Convention IV, arts 10, 23, 30, 59, 108–09; Protocol I, arts 70–71; Protocol II, art 18(2); ICRC Customary IHL Study (n 29) Rule 55.

41 Geneva Convention I, art 9; Geneva Convention II, art 9; Geneva Convention III, art 9; Geneva Convention IV, art 10; Protocol II, art 18(2).

42 Consent which must be given by effect of Geneva Convention IV, art 23; Protocol I, art 70(2); Protocol II art 18(2) pursuant to rules which are deemed to be customary as witnessed in Rule 55 of the ICRC Customary IHL Study (n 29); Akande and Gillard (n 32) 770ff; Dapo Akande and Emanuela-Chiara Gillard, 'Oxford Guidance on the Law Relating to Humanitarian Relief Operations in Situations of Armed Conflict' (Oxford Institute for Ethics, Law and Armed Conflict, commissioned by the OCHA, 2017).

43 Geneva Convention IV, art 23; Protocol I, art 70(2); ICRC Customary IHL Study (n 29) Rules 55 and 56; Akande and Gillard (n 32) 770.

language of article 54(1) of Protocol I seems to support the idea that only conduct carried out with the purpose of starving civilians is prohibited—and that, therefore, incidental starvation of civilians would remain lawful[44]—even if the rest of the article makes clear that in certain situations also the incidental starvation of civilians is prohibited.[45] This has led to debates on the kind of intent (as a mental element) required for the corresponding war crime.[46] Additionally, it could be noted that the prohibition of starvation only concerns the starvation of civilians, leaving out the starvation of combatants and enemy fighters—an undoubtedly outrageous practice which clashes with the protection of non-derogable human rights such as the right to be free from cruel, inhumane, and degrading treatment.[47] Limiting the prohibition of starvation to civilians only is also out of tune with the reality that supply chains for civilians and combatants are often inextricably linked: sieges and blockades aimed at starving combatants or enemy fighters will often harm civilians as well.[48] Moreover, attacks against objects indispensable for the survival of civilians are not the only military operations which can negatively impact food security: let us think, for instance, of the longstanding effects of armed conflict on the environment, which have the potential to frustrate a population's ability to grow crops for a long time after the conflict. Rules of IHL on this point do not appear to protect food security effectively.[49]

2. Duties to Respect, Protect, and Fulfil Human Rights in Protracted Conflicts, with a View towards Food Security

There is growing consensus by now that IHRL continues to bind states during armed conflict—with debates focusing mostly on how this body of rules interacts and coordinates with IHL. The same is true with respect to those rules which concern food security.[50] From a food-security perspective, the objectives of the two regimes are often aligned, especially when considering 'negative' duties not to attack and/or render useless objects indispensable for the survival of civilians. Such duties may be easily read into the rules establishing obligations to respect the rights to life[51] and an adequate standard of living, including adequate food, clothing, housing,[52] and health.[53] In line with the chapter's overall focus, the rest of this section will consider the right to food

[44] ibid 761–62.
[45] ibid 762–65.
[46] Jordash, Murdoch, and Holmes (n 35) 854–63.
[47] HRC (n 13), para 66.
[48] ibid para 67.
[49] ibid para 64 (footnotes omitted).
[50] Similarly Simone Hutter, 'The Right to Food in Armed Conflict' in Bridget Conley and others (eds), *Accountability for Mass Starvation: Testing the Limits of the Law* (OUP 2022) 140.
[51] International Covenant on Civil and Political Rights (adopted 16 December 1966, entered into force 23 March 1967) 99 UNTS 171 (ICCPR), art 6. Cf Mona Rishmawi, 'Protecting the Right to Life in Protracted Conflicts: The Existence and Dignity Dimensions of General Comment 36' (2019) 101 International Review of the Red Cross 1149.
[52] ICCPR, Art 11; Hutter, 'Starvation in Armed Conflicts: An Analysis Based on the Right to Food' (n 22); Desierto (n 10).
[53] ICCPR, Art 12.

in particular, even though some considerations may be applicable to the other mentioned rights *mutatis mutandis*.

Guaranteeing everyone's right to adequate food has been considered an indispensable component of human dignity.[54] In particular, article 11 of the International Covenant on Economic, Social and Cultural Rights (ICESCR)[55] obliges state parties to 'take appropriate steps to ensure the realization' of the right to an adequate standard of living including adequate food (para 1) and recognizes the 'fundamental right of everyone to be free from hunger' (para 2).[56] As is common in IHRL, the legal framework on the right to food comprises a triple obligation to respect, to protect, and to fulfil the right. Full compliance with IHRL, thus, goes far beyond a mere duty to refrain from destroying food crops and from preventing access to food resources (*obligation to respect*). According to the already cited article 11(2) ICESCR,

> States Parties . . . shall take, individually and through international co-operation, the measures, including specific programmes, which are needed:
> (a) To improve methods of production, conservation and distribution of food by making full use of technical and scientific knowledge, by disseminating knowledge of the principles of nutrition and by developing or reforming agrarian systems in such a way as to achieve the most efficient development and utilization of natural resources;
> (b) Taking into account the problems of both food-importing and food-exporting countries, to ensure an equitable distribution of world food supplies in relation to need.

States must also protect the enjoyment of the right to food against harm or risk of harm posed by the conduct of third or private parties, such as companies or non-state armed groups. For instance, in the words of the Committee on Economic, Social and Cultural Rights (CESCR), states must 'ensure that enterprises or individuals do not deprive individuals of their access to adequate food' (*obligation to protect*).[57] Failure to prevent such harmful conduct or to investigate, punish, and ensure redress—where preventive measures have proven ineffective—constitutes a violation of the international legal framework on the right to food.[58] Hutter has noted that an example of such violation could be represented by the failure of Sudan's government to prevent food insecurity caused in 2003 by the Janjaweed militia's actions in the Darfur region.[59] Notably, obligations to protect the civilian population against harm to their human rights caused by third parties continue to apply even in areas where the government's authority is

[54] CESCR 'General Comment No. 12: The Right to Food' (12 May 1999) UN Doc E/C.12/1999/5, para 4. On the concept: Andrea Gattini, Rosana Garciandia, and Philippa Webb (eds), *Human Dignity and International Law* (Brill Nijhoff 2020); Ginevra Le Moli, *Human Dignity in International Law* (CUP 2021).

[55] International Covenant on Economic, Social and Cultural Rights (adopted 16 December 1966, entered into force 3 January 1967) 933 UNTS 3 (ICESCR).

[56] There is also increasing recognition that non-state actors may incur similar responsibilities, especially when they are in control of a given territory: see, among others and with specific respect to the right to food, Hutter, 'Starvation in Armed Conflicts: An Analysis Based on the Right to Food' (n 22) 747ff.

[57] CESCR (n 54) para 15.

[58] CESCR (n 54) para 19; Hutter, 'The Right to Food in Armed Conflict' (n 50) 134.

[59] Hutter, 'The Right to Food in Armed Conflict' (n 50) 134–135.

being challenged, such as in areas under the control of non-state actors—provided that the government maintains at least some degree of control.[60]

In addition to obligations to respect and protect the right to food, states must 'pro-actively engage in activities intended to strengthen people's access to and utilization of resources and means to ensure their livelihood, including food security', if need be by providing adequate food directly to those in need (*obligation to fulfil*).[61] Since the adoption of these measures may become more and more difficult in times of (protracted) conflict, it is even more crucial that some measures aimed at fulfilling the right to food are put in place in peacetime, prior to the emergence of (new) conflict.[62] Arrangements for the provision of humanitarian relief and assistance in times of (protracted) conflict may be seen as measures of compliance with the obligation to fulfil the right to food.

Compliance with positive obligations relating to the right to food, as with other rights, is measured by a standard of due diligence.[63] In other words, duty-bearers are expected to put in place measures which are 'reasonable'[64] or 'appropriate'[65] according to the extant circumstances and in light of the duty-bearer's capacity to act, with a view to protecting or fulfilling the right to food against a foreseeable risk.[66] Granted, the right to an adequate standard of living and its component, the right to food, are subject to progressive realization, which in the context of a protracted conflict may happen to be halted or slowed down. Nonetheless, even in situations of protracted conflict, states must at a minimum ensure individuals' freedom from hunger,[67] also as a means of safeguarding the right to life. Such a minimum core component of the right to food has been interpreted as a duty to ensure the 'minimum nutritional intake necessary for survival', which may appear to be a very low threshold.[68] Yet, the CESCR has clarified that duty-bearers must ensure provision of this minimum level of food

[60] *Assanidze v Georgia*, Judgment (Grand Chamber) App no 71503/01 (ECtHR, 8 April 2004) paras 139–143; *Ilaşcu and others v Moldova and Russia*, Judgment (Grand Chamber) App no 48787/99 (ECtHR, 8 July 2004) para 333; *Catan and others v Moldova and Russia*, Judgment (Grand Chamber) App nos 43370/04, 8252/05, and 18454/06 (ECtHR 19 October 2012) paras 109–110.

[61] CESCR (n 54) para 15.

[62] Hutter, 'The Right to Food in Armed Conflict' (n 50) 135.

[63] Björnstjern Baade, 'Due Diligence and the Duty to Protect Human Rights' in Heike Krieger, Anne Peters, and Leonhard Kreuzer (eds), *Due Diligence in the International Legal Order* (OUP 2020) 92 citing International Law Association (ILA), 'Study Group on Due Diligence in International Law, First Report' (ILA 2014) 14; Timo Koivurova and Krittika Singh, 'Due Diligence' in Anne Peters (ed), *Max Planck Encyclopedia of Public International Law* (Oxford Public International Law Online, last updated August 2022) <https://opil.ouplaw.com/view/10.1093/law:epil/9780199231690/law-9780199231690-e1034?prd=EPIL> accessed 31 July 2023.

[64] Among others, Baade (n 63) 97; more in general on the standard of due diligence eg, *Alabama Claims (United States v UK)* (1872) 29 RIAA 125, 127, 129, 131–132; *Application of the Convention on the Prevention and Punishment of the Crime of Genocide (Bosnia and Herzegovina v Serbia and Montenegro)*, Judgment, (2007) ICJ Rep 43, paras 430–431; International Law Association (ILA), 'Study Group on Due Diligence, Second Report' (2016) 2.

[65] *The Environment and Human Rights*, Advisory Opinion OC-23/17 (2017) Inter-American Court of Human Rights Series A No 23 paras 123 and 174.

[66] Koivurova and Singh (n 63) paras 17, 19.

[67] CESCR (n 54) para 14; Hutter, 'Starvation in Armed Conflicts: An Analysis Based on the Right to Food' (n 22) 726.

[68] Hutter, 'The Right to Food in Armed Conflict' (n 50) 133, citing UNGA, 'Interim Report of the Special Rapporteur on the Right to Food' (21 July 2017) UN Doc A/72/188, para 52.

regardless of the (un)availability of resources.[69] Even such a basic level of protection of the right to food may engender positive effects for the building or preservation of peace.[70]

C. Complying with International Law towards Sustainable Food Security and Peace

The existence of the highlighted legal framework alone is obviously not sufficient to tackle food crises and insecurity in protracted conflict. Especially given the flexibility of many of the rules presented in section B, the key to building sustainable food security lies in the policy initiatives and concrete measures taken to implement the legal framework.

Ending hunger, including conflict-related hunger, has been identified as a sustainable development goal in the 2015 UN Agenda for Sustainable Development.[71] In fact, the realization of the right to food and the achievement of global food security are long-term goals, to be achieved for present and future generations.[72] Against this backdrop, the United Nations Security Council recognized the link between armed conflict and food insecurity in its Resolution 2417 (2018), which has been viewed as a call for more decisive action to break the vicious cycle between the two phenomena, mentioned in the first section. The Resolution highlights the centrality of IHL and IHRL in this context, recalling the obligations of

> respecting and protecting civilians and taking constant care to spare civilian objects, including objects necessary for food production and distribution such as farms, markets, water systems, mills, food processing and storage sites, and hubs and means for food transportation, and refraining from attacking, destroying, removing or rendering useless objects that are indispensable to the survival of the civilian population, such as foodstuffs, crops, livestock, agricultural assets, drinking water installations and supplies, and irrigation works, and respecting and protecting humanitarian personnel and consignments used for humanitarian relief operations,[73]

and stressing that violations of IHL and IHRL can be drivers of forced displacement[74] and condemning the denial of access to humanitarian relief operations.[75] Three years after Resolution 2417, the UN Security Council followed up with Resolution 2573

[69] CESCR, 'An evaluation of the obligation to take steps to the "maximum of available resources" under an optional Protocol to the Covenant—Statement' (21 September 2007) UN Doc E/C.12/2007/1, para 4, cited by Hutter, 'The Right to Food in Armed Conflict' (n 50) 137.

[70] Lander and Richards (n 2) 690–94.

[71] UNGA, 'Transforming Our World: the 2030 Agenda for Sustainable Development' (21 October 2015) UN Doc A/RES/70/1, Goal 2.

[72] Hutter, 'The Right to Food in Armed Conflict' (n 50) 145.

[73] UNSC Res 2417 (2018) UN Doc S/RES/2417(2018), para 1.

[74] ibid para 2.

[75] ibid para 6.

(2021), which reiterated some of the same principles[76] and added further directives for parties to conflict. In particular, the Resolution urged parties to armed conflict to

> protect civilian infrastructure which is critical to the delivery of humanitarian aid including for the provision of essential services concerning vaccinations and related medical care and other essential services to the civilian population in armed conflict and to ensuring the proper functioning of food systems and markets in situations of armed conflict[77]

and encouraged 'all efforts to protect objects indispensable to the survival of the civilian population and civilian infrastructure that is critical to enable the delivery of essential services in armed conflict'.[78]

Yet, these resolutions do little to address the root causes of conflict and food insecurity. Resolution 2417, in particular, fell short of establishing proactive measures to counter food insecurity, other than recalling to duty-bearers what they must *not* do. Granted, states are urged to protect infrastructure critical to food security and to conduct prompt, impartial, and effective investigations into potential violations of relevant international law provisions,[79] but these calls do not seem to go far enough. A reporting mechanism—by which parties to an armed conflict had to explain how they took action in line with the directives of the resolution—would have undoubtedly been more incisive. Instead of that, however, Resolution 2417 simply mandates the Secretary General to include the matter of conflict-related food insecurity in its own regular reporting on country-specific situations, promptly bringing the matter to the Council's attention in the most extreme cases,[80] while Resolution 2573 requests the Secretary General to include a sub-section on the protection of objects indispensable to the survival of the civilian population in the reports on the protection of civilians.[81] The UN Special Rapporteur on the right to food has already raised the issue of how to make this reporting more frequent and robust, so that it may lead to actual action.[82]

Is this all that can be done to combat conflict-related food insecurity? Hardly so. As explained in section B, while some food-related obligations established in IHL and IHRL are obligations of result (eg the prohibition of starvation as a method of warfare, or the duty to ensure freedom from hunger), many other obligations are obligations of conduct—for instance, the obligation of parties to a conflict to protect infrastructure critical to food security as a precaution against the effects of attacks, as well as states' obligation to protect and fulfil the rights to food and to an adequate standard of living, both require duty-bearers 'only' to exercise due diligence, that is, to act to the best of their ability in order to achieve the relevant rules' aims.[83] Considering that many of

[76] UNSC Res 2573 (2021) UN Doc S/RES/2573(2021), eg at paras 1, 4, 5
[77] ibid para 6.
[78] ibid para 9.
[79] UNSC Res 2417 (2018) UN Doc S/RES/2417(2018), respectively, paras 7 and 10.
[80] ibid paras 11f.
[81] UNSC Res 2573 (2021) UN Doc S/RES/2573(2021), para 12.
[82] Fakhri (n 3).
[83] About which see, inter alia, the chapters by Björnstjern Baade and Marco Longobardo in Heike Krieger, Anne Peters, and Leonhard Kreuzer (eds), *Due Diligence in the International Legal Order* (OUP 2021).

these obligations of conduct set a flexible standard of due diligence for the duty-bearer, to be understood in light of the extant circumstances and of the duty-bearer's capacity, the protractedness of the conflict surely plays a role in defining the content of what is due. The flexible nature of these obligations also means that there will not always be a violation to investigate or about which to report. At the same time, there will almost always be room to improve the way in which a state performs its duty and to assist with compliance. Indeed, flexibility is not necessarily a detrimental feature of these obligations, allowing duty-bearers to tailor their implementation conduct to specific needs and circumstances and to seek short, medium, and long-term goals in pursuance of a strategy which seeks to tackle not only food security but also economic growth, the fight against poverty, and the improvement of nutrition practices and realities.[84]

So, what can and should states and other relevant international actors do in this sense, especially in times of protracted conflict? Possible lines of action could be divided broadly into two categories: (a) pre-conflict measures, which include institutional and legal arrangements and, more generally, capacity-building and preventive measures; (b) measures for response to crises once they manifest themselves. In both cases, measures of international cooperation play a key role. It is to these measures that I now turn.

1. Pre-Conflict Measures

Ideally, measures ensuring food security and reducing the risk of food crises should be in place already before a conflict erupts.[85] In fact, as said in section A, food security per se is likely to reduce the risk of conflict. These could include capacity-building efforts by the relevant state, sensibilization and onboarding campaigns with non-state actors,[86] initiatives (eg the building of new infrastructure) to guarantee that food production, supply, and distribution chains can operate even in emergency situations, and the effective and regular monitoring of the state of soil and its potential for agriculture.[87] Supporting 'agri-food value chains'—that is, strategic partnerships/networks of interdependent actors engaged in activities from farming to selling food products, adding value at each stage[88]—may have beneficial effects in ensuring resilience and supporting livelihoods during crises and conflict,[89] even if there is a risk that

[84] Hutter, 'The Right to Food in Armed Conflict' (n 50) 152.

[85] ibid 151.

[86] These measures have been suggested in Oxford Institute for Ethics, Law and Armed Conflict and World Food Programme, 'The Role of Law and Policy in Confronting Conflict-Induced Hunger' (Event Report, 10 and 11 November 2021) <https://www.elac.ox.ac.uk/research/the-role-of-law-and-policy-in-confronting-conflict-induced-hunger/> accessed 18 June 2022.

[87] Mentioned, as examples of necessary reconstruction efforts after the conflict, by Hay, Karney, and Martyn (n 6).

[88] Eg, Ontario Government Ministry of Agriculture, Food, and Rural Affairs, Agri-Food Network and Supply Chain as Part of the Agricultural System' <https://www.ontario.ca/page/agri-food-network-and-supply-chain-part-agricultural-system> accessed 12 August 2025.

[89] International Food Policy Research Institute (IFPRI), *Global Food Policy Report 2023: Rethinking Food Crisis Responses* (IFPRI 2023) 44ff.

the longer the crisis or conflict lasts, the more they will suffer and become unable to operate properly.

Overall, anticipatory action is key: especially in fragile and conflict-affected settings, this should be built on effective data collection and analysis, including impact assessments and developing anticipatory action frameworks that pre-identify vulnerabilities, funding triggers, and available financial resources.[90] Additionally, it is important to assess the targeting of humanitarian assistance to ensure that all groups are included and to support interventions that reflect the humanitarian-development-peace nexus, such as nutrition-sensitive programming, local procurement, and aid for permanent safety nets.[91] Mechanisms should be put in place to ensure that appropriate and sufficient funding is readily and effectively available in case there is a crisis to respond to and that investment (including private investment) in long-term resilience plans should be encouraged.[92] The UN Special Rapporteur on the right to food has also highlighted, among desirable lines of action, agrarian reforms and measures with a view to increase biodiversity, protect land rights, and curtail corporate power.[93] In addition, in pre-conflict settings as well as during conflict, school feeding programmes have been suggested as a possible helpful measure for their potential to reduce societal tension and disincentivize recruitment into armed groups,[94] and to build social cohesion after a conflict.[95] In general, the strengthening of national food systems is seen as reinforcing the legitimacy of the state and easing the relationship between the government and the people,[96] with potentially beneficial effects on the resolution or avoidance of conflict.

Such positive measures should be accompanied and supported by the establishment of institutionalized mechanisms of regular monitoring and reporting by duty-bearers, perhaps with the involvement of regional organizations, to stimulate more effective action and compliance with international law, and to provide feedback on the best ways to achieve them.[97] When it comes to monitoring specifically, there are initiatives led by some states—such as the US-led 'Famine Early Warning Systems Network'[98]—but it has been suggested that these should be complemented by 'a more independent, flexible and efficient mechanism'[99] using indicators such as 'incidents of forced displacement, market analysis in affected areas, attacks on markets and agricultural production'.[100] Steps to improve early warning systems for food crises could also include: expanding country coverage and the frequency of acute food insecurity analysis; revising procedures for declaring the existence of famines and food crises

[90] ibid 36.
[91] ibid.
[92] ibid 6 and 17f.
[93] Fakhri (n 3).
[94] Donald Bundy and others, *Rethinking School Feeding Social Safety Nets, Child Development, and the Education Sector* (World Bank 2009).
[95] Lander and Richards (n 2) 691.
[96] ibid.
[97] Oxford Institute for Ethics, Law and Armed Conflict and World Food Programme (n 86).
[98] 'About FEWS NET' (FEWS NET Website) <https://fews.net/about> accessed 26 April 2023.
[99] Lander and Richards (n 2) 696–697.
[100] Joanna Macrae and Anthony Zwi, 'Food as an Instrument of War in Contemporary African Famines: A Review of the Evidence' (1992) 16 Disasters 299.

and making them operational in conflict-affected areas; integrating various early warning systems through collaborative efforts by international and local actors; and strengthening the analysis of factors driving crises in specific locations to inform long-term responses that build resilience and reduce the risk of food crises.[101]

2. Response Measures

It may happen that preventive measures have not been taken or have proven ineffective in preventing food insecurity. Helpful guidelines for response in such a case have been formulated in the 2015 FAO 'Framework for Action for Food Security and Nutrition in Protracted Crises', which articulates eleven principles to be implemented by relevant actors.[102] The principles are organized in three groups: first, principles aimed at addressing 'critical manifestations' of food insecurity and purporting to meet the immediate humanitarian needs of those affected;[103] second, principles aimed at adapting to specific challenges, such as reaching affected populations, promoting gender equality, and promoting effective financing;[104] and third, principles—which are at the same time preventive and responsive—aimed at contributing to the resolution of underlying causes of food insecurity and undernutrition in protracted crises, which include contributions to peacebuilding through food security, managing natural resources sustainably, and promoting effective national and local governance.[105] The operationalization of these principles recalls several of the international duties described in the previous section. For instance, principle 3 ('reach affected populations') stresses the need for relevant actors to enable that food and livelihood support are effectively provided to the people affected by protracted crises, *inter alia* by 'promoting and facilitating unimpeded, safe and rapid access to affected communities in order to provide humanitarian food and livelihoods assistance' and 'refraining from unilateral measures not in accordance with international law, including the Charter of the United Nations, and which endanger food security and nutrition'.[106] Relevant stakeholders are also encouraged to take steps to 'respect the existing rights under international law of members of affected and at risk populations, and their ability to access and use their natural resources'.[107]

Effective response to food crises also necessitates strong cooperation and coordination at the international level, between the relevant states, regional organizations, and international organizations. At the very minimum, where belligerents have engaged in practices of starvation of civilians, there is a good argument—grounded in the possible characterization of the prohibition of starvation as a peremptory norm of international law—to say that other states have an obligation not to render assistance

[101] IFPRI, *Global Food Policy Report 2023* (n 89) 20.
[102] Committee on World Food Security (n 4).
[103] ibid principles 1 and 2.
[104] ibid, respectively, principles 3, 6, and 8.
[105] ibid principles 9, 10, and 11.
[106] ibid 10, para 25, respectively at (i) and (v).
[107] ibid 16 (principle 9, 'Contribute to Peacebuilding through Food Security and Nutrition'), para 32(v); 17 (principle 10, 'Manage Natural Resources Sustainably and Reduce Disaster Risks'), para 33(viii).

in maintaining the situation and to cooperate to bring it to an end.[108] But measures of international cooperation should go well beyond that: for instance, with respect to possible violations of IHL related to food and other objects indispensable to the survival of the civilian population, states other than those directly involved in the conflict have a general obligation to cooperate as required by their duty to ensure respect for IHL enshrined in article 1 common to the Geneva Conventions I–IV. International cooperation can also be seen as a way of complying with the duty to protect and fulfil the right to an adequate standard of living, for instance by the provision of technical assistance, capacity-building, and humanitarian relief to populations in need.[109]

D. Conclusion

This chapter has sought to explore the link between food crises and protracted conflict, highlighting how the two concepts feed on each other in a vicious cycle which states and other international and local actors must strive to break. While international law—especially IHL and IHRL—provides for a basic legal framework for addressing food crises in times of conflict, I have sought to show that many of the relevant obligations leave a considerable margin of appreciation and flexibility to the respective duty-bearers, be they states or non-state actors. While some may read this flexibility as a negative feature, hindering efforts to promote accountability, the chapter has sought to show that the implementation of the relevant obligations to protect civilians from hunger and to protect or ensure all individuals' right to food could comprise a vast array of measures, either preventive or responsive in nature. In fact, building sustainable food security in protracted conflict is a matter of political will more than of applicable rules. While there is always room to strengthen the relevant international legal framework and make it more detailed, the extant rules already provide valuable guiding principles and allow for tailored and inventive solutions, which could be explored in practice.

[108] cf the rules reflected in arts 40 and 41 International Law Commission, 'Articles on Responsibility of States for Internationally Wrongful Acts' (2001) UN Doc A/56/83.

[109] Actions encouraged by UNSC Res 2573 (2021) UN Doc S/RES/2573(2021), para 10.

8

The Human Right to Health in Protracted Conflicts

Duties and Responsibilities to Cooperate towards Building a Democratically Controlled Health System

Amrei Müller

A. Introduction

Protracted armed conflicts are characterized by their political intractability; that is, that finding a political path towards solving them and moving towards peace has failed over many years and even decades. As a result, armed violence might flare up and recede at irregular intervals over a long period of time.[1] Protracted conflicts can be 'episodic, cyclical [or] "frozen" [armed conflicts], long-lived insurgencies, long-standing situations of occupation, or wars between States where violence simmers at a relatively lower level than one might traditionally associate with armed conflict'.[2] Numerous international governmental and non-governmental organizations with a focus on either humanitarian, peacebuilding, or development work are regularly present in protracted conflict situations.[3]

This chapter sketches[4] various states' (and potentially also strong non-state armed groups' (NSAGs)) duties flowing from the human right to health (HRH)[5] as well as what this contribution refers to as 'responsibilities for the HRH'[6] of international organizations (IOs)[7] in protracted conflict situations. A specific focus is placed on obligations and responsibilities that could potentially assist in addressing some of

[1] ICRC, 'Protracted Conflict and Humanitarian Action: Some Recent ICRC Experiences' (ICRC 2016) 9.

[2] Ellen Policinski, 'Protracted Conflicts: The Enduring Legacy of Endless War' (2019) 101(912) International Review of the Red Cross 955, 967.

[3] ICRC (n 1) 7, 9.

[4] Space constraints preclude an analysis that goes into great depth. For example, this chapter cannot discuss the question of remedial responsibilities for violations of the HRH—be it by state human rights duty-bearers and/or by state or non-state bearers of responsibilities for the HRH.

[5] International Covenant on Economic, Social, and Cultural Rights (adopted 16 December 1966, entered into force 3 January 1967) 933 UNTS 3 (ICESCR), art 12.

[6] The subtle but important distinction between human rights duties on the one hand and responsibilities for human rights and their different bearers on the other is made convincingly by Samantha Besson, 'The Bearers of Human Rights' Duties and Responsibilities for Human Rights. A Quiet (R)Evolution' (2015) 32(1) Social Philosophy & Policy 244, and relied on throughout this chapter.

[7] It should be noted that IOs are not the only actors involved in protracted conflict countries that are addressed by 'responsibilities for the HRH'. However, due to space constraints and their prominent presence in protracted conflicts, this chapter limits itself to analysing IOs' responsibilities for the HRH.

Amrei Müller, *The Human Right to Health in Protracted Conflicts* In: *From Protracted Conflict to Sustainable Peace?*
Edited by: Heike Krieger, Giedre Jokubauskaite, Asli Ozcelik, and Andreas Buser, Oxford University Press.
 DOI: 10.1093/9780198967385.003.0010

the elements of political intractability and thus longevity of such conflicts. Among them are various actors' duties under and responsibilities for the HRH to secure the building of an (at least successively) democratically controlled health system that is responsive to the actual health needs of local populations affected by these conflicts. This arguably includes concrete duties to cooperate and coordinate the specification, allocation, and implementation of joint and complementary HRH duties and responsibilities of various actors, including duties and responsibilities to build such a health system. Focusing on such duties and responsibilities, and their coordinated implementation, could potentially also assist in clarifying one of the specifically *legal* bases in international human rights law (IHRL) obliging different actors to negotiate and work towards finding peaceful solutions despite an inevitable mistrust between them, and more broadly towards building democratic (or at least democratizing) institutions in protracted conflict countries, animated by the respect for and protection of all human rights and equality of rights-holders. This potential of the HRH and IHRL in general is grounded in the mutuality of human rights and (political) equality and, thus, democracy that permeates this body of law,[8] as well as the related right to self-determination.[9]

The analysis proceeds in three steps. Section B discusses HRH duty-bearers by briefly recalling that human rights duties depend on jurisdiction as well as the content and scope of HRH duties of various duty-bearers in protracted conflict situations. This includes duties to build democratically controlled health systems and duties of cooperation and coordination among duty-bearers to achieve this. Section C examines responsibilities for the HRH and their bearers, and their scope and content, as well as their relationship to HRH duties in protracted conflict countries. Section D concludes.[10]

B. HRH Duties in Protracted Conflict Situations and (One or Multiple) Duty-Bearers

Article 12(1) of the International Covenant on Economic, Social and Cultural Rights (ICESCR) establishes 'the right of everyone to the highest attainable standard of physical and mental health' (in short, the HRH).[11] This part examines who the HRH

[8] Henry Steiner, 'Two Sides of the Same Coin: Democracy and International Human Rights' (2008) 41 Israel Law Review 445; Samantha Besson, 'Human Rights and Democracy in a Global Context: Decoupling and Recoupling' (2011) 4 Ethics & Global Politics 19.

[9] Art 1 common to the ICESCR and International Covenant on Civil and Political Rights (adopted 16 December 1966, entered into force 23 March 1967) 99 UNTS 171 (ICCPR); also text accompanying *infra* nn 23–25.

[10] The focus here is on the HRH. Health-related IHL cannot be examined further here. However, on the interplay between health-related IHL and the HRH see: Amrei Müller, 'States' Obligations to Mitigate the Direct and Indirect Health Consequences of Non-international Armed Conflicts' (2013) 59 International Review of the Red Cross 129; and Amrei Müller, 'Social Rights in Armed Conflict Situations' in Christina Binder and others (eds), *Research Handbook on International Law and Social Rights* (Edward Elgar, 2020) 393–412. This contribution builds on this and other earlier work of the author.

[11] Note that this contribution focuses on the HRH as a right to 'equal and timely access to basic preventive, curative and rehabilitative health services' (CESCR, 'General Comment No. 14: The Right to Health' (11 August 2000) UN Doc E/C.12/2000/4, paras 17 and 43(a)) that treat both physical and mental sickness. While 'underlying determinants of health' also form part of the scope of the HRH according to the

duty-bearers are in protracted conflict situations and summarizes the scope and content of these duties.

As a preliminary remark, it can be observed that in protracted conflict situations where the situation is often volatile and formal state institutions can be weak, the character and scope of various HRH duties of one or more than one state of jurisdiction, and potentially of strong de facto regimes/NSAGs exercising de facto human rights jurisdiction, can vary based on context. These variations will be greater than in 'normal' situations where one state exercises (territorial) human rights jurisdiction over the population within its international land, sea, and aerial borders and makes a good-faith effort to comply with its HRH duties.

1. HRH Duty-Bearers in Protracted Conflicts and their Duties in the Abstract

As with all human rights duties, duties under the HRH towards concrete individuals in protracted conflicts only arise for states that exercise human rights jurisdiction.[12] This is clear from numerous jurisdiction clauses in regional and international human rights treaties.[13] 'Jurisprudence' concerning human rights treaties that do not contain explicit jurisdiction clauses, for example the ICESCR, confirms that also under these treaties, states' duties depend on jurisdiction.[14]

As a threshold criterion,[15] jurisdiction amounts to a state's 'effective, overall and normative power or control'[16] over persons. Effective control implies that state power is 'exercised, and not merely claimed'.[17] Overall control means that power is 'exercised

CESCR's General Comment 14 and their protection is of great importance in protracted conflict situations, due to space constraints and the fact that these determinants are also protected by the human rights to food, water, and housing respectively, they are not explored here further.

[12] This section summarizes the results of the author's earlier work, in Amrei Müller, 'Can Armed Non-State Actors Exercise Jurisdiction and thus Become Human Rights Duty-Bearers?' (2020) 20 Human Rights Law Review 269.

[13] Eg European Convention on Human Rights (adopted 4 November 1950, entered into force 3 September 1953) 213 UNTS 221 (ECHR) art 1; ICCPR art 2(1); Convention on the Rights of the Child (adopted 20 November 1989, enterd into force 2 September 1990) 1577 UNTS 3 (CRC) art 2(1).

[14] Eg CESCR, 'General Comment No. 4: The Right to Adequate Housing' (1 January 1992) UN Doc E/1992/23, para 13; CESCR, 'General Comment No. 15: The Right to Water' (20 January 2003) UN Doc E/C.12/2002/11, para 53; CESCR, 'General Comment No. 19: The Right to Social Security' (4 Febraury 2008) UN Doc E/C.12/GC/19, para 75; *Legal Consequences of the Construction of a Wall in the Occupied Palestinian Territory* (Advisory Opinion) 2004 ICJ Rep 136, para 112. A jurisdiction clause was included in art 2 of the Optional Protocol to the International Covenant on Economic, Social and Cultural Rights (adopted 10 December 2008, entered into force 5 May 2013) UN Doc A/RES/63/117 (OP-ICESCR).

[15] Eg *Güzelyurtlu and Others v Cyprus and Turkey*, Judgment (Grand Chamber) App no 36925/07 (ECtHR 29 January 2019) para 178.

[16] Samantha Besson, 'The Extraterritoriality of the European Convention on Human Rights: Why Human Rights Depend on Jurisdiction and What Jurisdiction Amounts To' (2012) 25 Leiden Journal of International Law 857, 865.

[17] Besson (n 16) 872; CCPR, 'General Comment No. 31: Nature of the General Legal Obligations Imposed on States Parties to the Covenant' (26 May 2004) UN Doc CCPR/C/21/Rev.1/Add.13, para 10; Francoise Hampson, 'The Scope of Extra-territorial Applicability of International Human Rights Law' in Geoff Gilbert and others (eds), *The Delivery of Human Rights—Essays in Honour of Sir Nigel Rodley* (Routledge 2010) 168.

over a large number of stakes, and not one time only and over a single matter only'.[18] Normative control—the normative element of jurisdiction—can be detected for example in the ECtHR's frequent references to (political and legal) 'authority'[19] or '*public* powers normally exercised by [a sovereign] government'.[20] It implies that control is exercised 'in a normative fashion so as to give reasons for action, and not as mere coercion';[21] or, in other words, in a non-arbitrary, (domestic) law-based and democratically controlled fashion.[22] The latter hints at the requirement under IHRL that human rights shall be protected through democratic or democratizing institutions. It is further supported by the right to self-determination, which, understood outside the colonial context,[23] obliges states to set up an institutional structure 'representing the whole people belonging to the[ir] territory without distinction of any kind'[24] that enables (internal[25]) political, social, economic, and cultural self-determination in an inclusive fashion; that is, by respecting the political equality of all individuals in this territory and, in addition, without discriminating against any sub-group.[26]

Normally, a state's human rights jurisdiction is exercised over persons on its own territory,[27] and there is a (rebuttable) presumption that states indeed exercise such jurisdiction.[28] States of jurisdiction have the full range of duties to respect, protect,

[18] Besson (n 16) 872.

[19] Eg *Al-Skeini v United Kingdom*, Judgment (Grand Chamber) App no 55721/07 (ECtHR 7 July 2011), para 137; *Öcalan v Turkey*, Judgment (Grand Chamber) App no 46221/99 (ECtHR 12 May 2005), para 91; *Al-Saadoon and Mufdhi v United Kingdom*, Judgment (Chamber) App no 61498/08 (ECtHR 2 March 2010), para 87.

[20] *Al-Skeini v United Kingdom* (n 19) para 135; *Banković v Belgium*, Decision (Grand Chamber) App no 52207/99, (ECtHR 12 December 2001), para 71; *Chiragov v Azerbaijan*, Judgment (Grand Chamber), App no 13216/05, (ECtHR 16 June 2015), para 168 (emphasis added). The CCPR also refers to 'within the power . . . of . . . [a] State Party', CCPR, 'General Comment No. 31' (n 17) para 10.

[21] Besson (n 16) 872–73 and 864–65.

[22] Also Michael Duttwiler, 'Authority, Control and Jurisdiction in the Extraterritorial Application of the European Convention on Human Rights' (2012) 30 Netherlands Quarterly of Human Rights 137, 156–59; Hampson (n 17) 166–68.

[23] The exercise of the right to self-determination by colonized peoples was limited to the three ways as set out in Princple VI in UNGA Res 1541 (XV) (15 December 1960) UN Doc A/RES/1541(XV); Antonio Cassese, *Self-Determination of Peoples: A Legal Reappraisal* (CUP 1995) 67–89; David Raič, *Statehood and the Law of Self-Determination* (Nijhoff 2002), 199–220.

[24] Vienna Declaration and Programme of Action (adopted by the World Conference on Human Rights in Vienna 25 June 1993) UN Doc A/CONF.157/23 para 2; also UNGA Res 26/25(XXV) 'Declaration on Principles of International Law concerning Friendly Relations and Cooperation with the Charter of the United Nations' (24 October 1970) UN Doc A/RES/2625(XXV); CCPR, 'General Comment No. 12: Right to Self-determination' (12 April 1984) UN Doc CCPR/C/21/Rev.1/Add.5, para 6.

[25] Outside the colonial context, arguably only in exceptional circumstances can the gross denial of 'internal' self-determination mean that a group of people can demand the exercise of 'external' self-determination, ie secession and the setting up of a new state or unification with another state; discussion on 'remedial' secession as a 'last resort mode' of the exercise of self-determination by eg Allan Buchanan, *Justice, Legitimacy, and Self-Determination: Moral Foundations for International Law* (OUP 2004) chapter 8; Frederic Mégret, 'The Right to Self-Determination: Earned, Not Inherent' in Fernando Tesón (ed), *The Theory of Self-Determination* (CUP 2018) 52–53.

[26] Reinforced by independent non-discrimination rights in human rights treaties, eg ICCPR arts 3 and 26.

[27] The ECtHR has frequently noted that jurisdiction is 'primarily' or 'essentially' territorial, ie exercised on the official territory of a state, eg *Assanidze v Georgia*, Judgment (Grand Chamber) App no 71503/01 (ECtHR 8 April 2004), para 137; *Banković v Belgium* (n 20) paras 59–61; reiterated by the ICJ in *Wall Advisory Opinion* (n 14) para 112.

[28] Eg *Assanidze v Georgia* (n 27) para 139; *Al-Skeini v United Kingdom* (n 19) para 131; *Wall Advisory Opinion* (n 14) para 109; CCPR, 'General Comment No. 31' (n 17) para 10; CRC, 'General Comment

and fulfil the HRH. However, states that have lost jurisdiction over all or parts of their own territories, for example due to a protracted conflict in which another state or states occupy or otherwise control this territory and/or a NSAG or de facto regime controls this territory, retain limited human rights obligations toward individuals on this territory over which they have also lost control.[29] These are obligations to regain control and to adopt measures to secure the HRH and other human rights of the people in such territories.[30]

Extraterritorially, states can exercise human rights jurisdiction in a general form over all people on the foreign territory over which a state has overall, effective, and normative control—often referred to as 'spatial' extraterritorial jurisdiction[31]—or in a more direct, personal form, that is, as effective, overall, and normative control over a person outside the state's official territory, often referred to as 'personal' extraterritorial jurisdiction.[32] The scope of states' duties to respect, protect, and fulfil human rights, including under the HRH, that arise from their exercise of 'spatial' or 'personal' extraterritorial jurisdiction varies in accordance with the level of control—beyond the level of control required to establish extraterritorial jurisdiction in the first place—that the respective state has over the (foreign) territory, a particular situation, and the individual(s) involved. Depending on the situation, these duties can also be 'complemented' by (limited) duties of the state that has lost its territorial jurisdiction,[33] or they can arise 'jointly' with the duties of other states when several states exercise extraterritorial jurisdiction together[34] or when extraterritorial jurisdiction by one state is exercised hand in hand with the territorial jurisdiction of the state of territorial jurisdiction.[35]

6: Treatment of Unaccompanied and Separated Children Outside Their Country of Origin' (1 September 2005) UN Doc CRC/GC/2005/6, para 78; Besson (n 16) 876. On the related idea of 'presumptive legitimacy' of statehood, also Frederic Mégret, 'Detention by Non-State Armed Groups in Non-International Armed Conflict: International Humanitarian Law, International Human Rights Law and the Question of Right Authority' in Ezequiel Heffes and others (eds), *International Humanitarian Law and Non-State Actors: Debates, Law and Practice* (Springer 2020) 180.

[29] Eg *Ilaşcu and Others v Moldova and Russia*, Judgment (Grand Chamber) App no 48787/99 (ECtHR 8 July 2004), paras 312 and 333; *Catan and Others v Moldova and Russia*, Judgment (Grand Chamber), App no 43370/04 (ECtHR 19 October 2012), para 109; *Sargsyan v Azerbaijan*, Judgment (Grand Chamber), App no 40167/06 (ECtHR 16 June 2016), para 131.

[30] Most recently confirmed by the ECtHR in *Mamasakhlisi and Others v Georgia and Russia*, Judgment (Chamber) App no 29999/04 (ECtHR 7 March 2023), para 319.

[31] *Al-Skeini v United Kingdom* (n 19) paras 138–139; reiterated most recently in *Mamasakhlisi and Others v Georgia and Russia* (n 30) para 311; and concerning socio-economic rights, Group of Experts in International Law and Human Rights, 'Maastricht Principles on Extraterritorial Obligations in the Area of Economic, Social and Cultural Rights' (Group of Experts convened by Maastricht University and the International Commission of Jurists, 28 September 2011) <https://www.fidh.org/IMG/pdf/maastricht-eto-principles-uk_web.pdf> accessed 26 March 2024 (hereafter Maastricht Principles) paras 18; Besson (n 16) 874–75; *Wall Advisory Opinion* (n 14) paras 112–113.

[32] *Al-Skeini v United Kingdom* (n 19) paras 133–137; *Mamasakhlisi and Others v Georgia and Russia* (n 30) para 312; and in relation to socio-economic rights, Maastricht Principles (n 31) principle 18; Besson (n 16) 875–76.

[33] Eg *Ilaşcu and Others v Moldova and Russia* (n 29) para 331; *Catan and Others v Moldova and Russia* (n 29) para 145–147.

[34] As in *Hassan v UK*, Judgment (Grand Chamber) App no 29750/09 (ECtHR 16 September 2014); and *Jaloud v Netherlands*, Judgment (Grand Chamber) App no 47708/08 (ECtHR 20 November 2014).

[35] On the categorization of various scenarios in which states can exercise overlapping jurisdiction and in which thus 'joint' or 'concurrent' human rights duties arise, Samantha Besson, 'Concurrent Responsibilities

Regularly, only states exercising territorial or extraterritorial ('spatial' or 'personal') jurisdiction become HRH duty-bearers. However, it is conceivable that also other entities that de facto exercise human rights jurisdiction might be recognized as de facto human rights duty-bearers, for example under customary IHRL. As analysed by the author elsewhere, there are indications that (very) strong NSAGs or de facto entities indeed exercise de facto jurisdiction and can thus be considered de facto human rights duty-bearers.[36] Such strong NSAGs or de facto entities have considerable military strength; devise and implement policies; adopt 'legislation' concerning many inter-related subject-matters and areas relating to the implementation of human rights; set up new or co-opt existing administrative structures and institutions; and engage in and encourage equal participatory, even democratic, processes that enforce their claim to act as genuine representatives of the people under their influence and control.

2. HRH Duties of Various Duty-Bearers in Protracted Conflicts

More light shall now be shed on the more concrete HRH duties in protracted conflicts, including duties of various duty-bearers to cooperate and coordinate the processes through which they specify, allocate, and implement their duties.

a) Overarching Duties to Build a Functioning (Primary) Health System

First to mention is an important overarching duty flowing from the HRH: the duty to (progressively) build a health system that provides long-term primary, secondary, and tertiary health care of good quality accessible to everyone under the respective state's jurisdiction.[37]

In a protracted conflict situation, the health system should provide as a minimum access to primary health care of good quality, as reflected in particular in the minimum core content of the HRH;[38] it should respect and safeguard people's physical and mental integrity by upholding the principle of informed consent and medical ethics;[39] it should be run by qualified health personnel;[40] non-discriminatory access to the

under the European Convention on Human Rights. The Concurrence of Human Rights Jurisdictions, Duties, and Responsibilities' in Anne van Aaken and Iulia Motoc (eds), *The European Convention on Human Rights and General International Law* (OUP 2018) 154, 166–67.

36 For more details, Müller, 'Can Armed Non-State Actors Exercise Jurisdiction?' (n 12) and Müller, 'De Facto Independent Regimes and Overarching Human Rights Duties' (2021) 32 The Hague Yearbook of International Law 31; also Mégret (n 28) 183 for a similar finding, referring to the 'public character' of NSAGs/de facto regimes and to them exercising 'right authority'.

37 Eg CESCR, 'General Comment No. 14' (n 11) para 9; HRC, 'Report of the Special Rapporteur on the Right of Everyone to the Enjoyment of the Highest Attainable Standard of Physical and Mental Health, Paul Hunt' (31 January 2008) UN Doc A/HRC/7/11 (hereafter HRC, 'Special Rapporteur on the HRH Report on Health Systems'), para 15.

38 CESCR, 'General Comment No. 14' (n 11) paras 43–44.

39 ibid paras 8 and 12(c); and section B.2.c).

40 ibid paras 12(a), 12(d), 36, and 44(e); HRC, 'Special Rapporteur on the HRH Report on Health Systems' (n 37) paras 75–86.

health system must be ensured;[41] and a comprehensive national plan for maintaining and developing the health system should exist.[42] The health system must be established and must operate on a legal basis[43] with the relevant laws conforming to the IHRL legality standard.[44] Together, these elements—also in combination with political participation rights and the right to self-determination under IHRL—indicate that the health system should function and develop under democratic control of the people who rely on it.[45]

b) Duties to Ensure Access to Primary Health Care Addressing Health Needs of Local Populations Affected by Protracted Conflicts

As a minimum, human rights duty-bearers have HRH duties in protracted conflicts to ensure access to primary health care,[46] that is, to essential health goods and services provided through a health system. According to the CESCR[47] and the Alma Ata Declaration, these include:

> At least: education concerning prevailing health problems and the methods of preventing and controlling them; . . . maternal and child health care, including family planning; immunization against the major infectious diseases; prevention and control of locally endemic diseases; appropriate treatment of common diseases and injuries; and provision of essential drugs.[48]

What the 'prevailing health problems' are, eg what the prevailing infectious and locally endemic diseases are, and what the most suitable 'methods of preventing and controlling' them would be, which essential drugs are needed as a matter of priority, and so on, must indeed be determined by taking the local context into account. This would imply procedural duties to conduct consultation processes with persons living in the respective protracted conflict country,[49] ideally democratic processes which respect the (political) equality of rights-holders, and analysis of how existing structures can be relied upon and/or adapted to provide the required essential health goods and services and how this can be done by utilizing local resources as much as possible.

41 ICESCR arts 2(2) and (3); CESCR, 'General Comment No. 14' (n 11) paras 12(b)(i), 18, 19, and 43(f); HRC, 'Special Rapporteur on the HRH Report on Health Systems' (n 37) para 42.

42 CESCR, 'General Comment No. 14' (n 11), para 43(f); HRC, 'Special Rapporteur on the HRH Report on Health Systems' (n 37) paras 88–98.

43 ibid paras 48 and 53–56.

44 As is clear from ECHR arts 2, 5(1), (2), (4), 6(1), 8(2)–11(2); ICCPR arts 6(1), 8(c)(i), (ii), 9(1), 12(1), (3), 13, 14(1), 15 (criminal law), 17(1), (2), 18(3), 19(3), 20, 21, and 22(2); ICESCR arts 4 and 8(1)(a), (c); analysed by Laurens Lavrysen, 'Protection by the Law: The Positive Obligation to Develop a Legal Framework to Adequately Protect ECHR Rights' in Eva Brems and Yves Haeck (eds), *Human Rights and Civil Liberties in the 21st Century* (Springer 2014) 69.

45 Section B.2.f).

46 CESCR, 'General Comment No. 3: The Nature of State Parties' Obligations' (14 December 1990) UN Doc E/1991/23, para 10; CESCR, 'General Comment No. 14' (n 11) para 43.

47 CESCR, 'General Comment No. 14' (n 11) paras 43–44.

48 UN International Conference on Primary Health Care (Alma-Ata 6–12 September 1978), 'Declaration of Alma-Ata' published in WHO, *Primary Health Care: Report of the International Conference on Primary Health Care Alma-Ata, USSR, 6–12 September 1978* (WHO 1978) para VII(3).

49 HRC, 'Special Rapporteur on the HRH Report on Health Systems' (n 37) paras 22, 25, 41, and 66; see section B.2.f).

There is a recognition that resourcing locally will greatly enhance the prospects for long-term access to essential health goods and services as well as local ownership of the basic health system to deliver them.[50] Of course, it might be impossible to source some essential medical equipment, medicines, and other medical products locally in protracted conflict countries. But it is not excluded that steps can be taken towards upholding existing and building new local capacities to produce (generic) drugs and/or develop and produce (new) local medicines, including those based on local traditional medical knowledge if this is identified as a possibility and priority of the local population.[51]

In protracted conflict countries it might also be the case that local populations prioritize a focus on the provision of emergency medical care,[52] especially if it is expected that violence may flare up regularly, leading to an influx of (military or civilian) wounded persons who have been injured in hostilities.

c) Duties to Respect and Safeguard Bodily and Mental Integrity

Among the HRH duties relevant in protracted conflicts are, furthermore, duties to respect and safeguard the right to physical and mental integrity, which includes respect for medical self-determination of patients—including the right not to be subjected to medical or scientific experiments[53] or to medical treatment without free and informed consent[54]—as well as duties to ensure that medical products are indeed safe and effective.[55] This would imply a medical workforce and scientists that are trained in medical ethics,[56] the adoption of domestic law to ensure quality and safety of locally or internationally resourced medicines and other medical products as well as mechanisms for controlling this quality, and safety and compliance with medical ethics.[57]

[50] Eg Alexander Hay and others, 'Reconstructing Infrastructure for Resilient Essential Services and Following Protracted Conflict: A Conceptual Framework' (2019) 101 International Review of the Red Cross 1001, 1013–14 and 1026–27.

[51] HRC, 'Report of the Special Rapporteur on the Right of Everyone to the Enjoyment of the Highest Attainable Standard of Physical and Mental Health, Anand Grover, on Access to Medicines' (1 May 2013) UN Doc A/HRC/23/42 (hereafter HRC, 'Special Rapporteur on the HRH Report on Access to Medicines') paras 11–19 on local production of medicines.

[52] This can indeed be a context-specific core HRH duty in protracted conflict situations; eg CESCR, 'General Comment No. 14' (n 11) para 16, indicating that states should create a system of 'urgent medical care' in case of accidents.

[53] ICCPR art 7; also the Convention for the Protection of Human Rights and Dignity of the Human Being with regard to the Application of Biology and Medicine (adopted 4 April 1997, entered into force 1 December 1999) ETS No 164 (Oviedo Convention); and UNESCO General Conference, 33rd Session (Paris, 3–21 October 2005) 'Universal Declaration on Bioethics and Human Rights', published in UN Educational, Scientific and Cultural Organization, 'Records of the General Conference, 33rd session' vol 1: Resolutions, Res 36.

[54] This right forms part of both the HRH, the right to privacy (ICCPR art 17); and the right not to be subjected to torture or inhuman or degrading treatment (ICCPR art 7); CESCR, 'General Comment No. 14' (n 11) para 8; and the detailed analysis offered by the UN Special Rapporteur on the HRH on informed consent, UNGA, 'Report of the Special Rapporteur on the Right of Everyone to the Enjoyment of the Highest Attainable Standard of Physical and Mental Health, Anand Grover' (10 August 2009) UN Doc A/64/272.

[55] CESCR, 'General Comment No. 14' (n 11) para 12; HRC, 'Special Rapporteur on the HRH Report on Access to Medicines' (n 51) paras 4 and 61–66.

[56] CESCR, 'General Comment No. 14' (n 11) paras 12(c) and 35; HRC, 'Special Rapporteur on the HRH Report on Access to Medicines' (n 51) paras 61–63.

[57] CESCR, 'General Comment No. 14' (n 11) para 12; HRC, 'Special Rapporteur on the HRH Report on Access to Medicines' (n 51) paras 61–66; and HRC, 'Special Rapporteur on the HRH Report on Health Systems' (n 37) para 54.

d) Duties to Secure the Availability of (Local) Qualified Medical Personnel

States' duties under the HRH include a duty to ensure the availability of 'trained medical and professional personnel', among them doctors and nurses.[58]

To ensure the long-term functioning of an essential primary health care system in a country affected by protracted conflict(s), it appears vital to recruit and train health personnel locally.[59] If primarily foreign doctors and nurses are contracted and employed through IOs, this reliance on external skills is unlikely to ensure the sustainable routine operation of the essential primary health system, including during periods of violence. Training local medical personnel will increase local employment opportunities and may contribute to building a sense of ownership and community control over the health system.[60]

e) Duties to Secure Equal Access

The HRH poses obligations on states to ensure 'access to health facilities, goods and services on a non-discriminatory basis'.[61] Working towards such equal access can contribute to building (democratically) legitimate health institutions as they will respect the (political) equality of individuals and their equal health rights. Especially in divided protracted conflict societies, this could help bridge social, ethnic, economic, and other divides and tensions, including along conflict lines.

From an economic and (public) budgeting perspective, it can be observed that an investment in a health system is only viable if this health system is indeed accessible to the local population, as only continued use ensures continued function.[62] The notion of 'accessibility' to health systems (and other infrastructure providing essential services) is further defined in IHRL as encompassing physical accessibility, (domestic) legal accessibility, and economic accessibility.[63] In protracted conflict countries, accessibility analyses can for example lead to taking into account individual conflict-related vulnerabilities of people, among them physical or mental impairment,[64] social and economic isolation of individuals arising from their role in the conflict, and the possibility that some areas cannot be accessed due to destruction or the presence of

[58] CESCR, 'General Comment No. 14' (n 11) paras 12(a), 12(d), and 36; HRC, 'Special Rapporteur on the HRH Report on Health Systems' (n 37) paras 68(b) and 75–86; and UNGA, 'Interim Report of the Special Rapporteur on the Right of Everyone to the Enjoyment of the Highest Attainable Standard of Physical and Mental Health, Dainius Pūras' (16 July 2019) UN Doc A/74/174.

[59] Hay and others (n 50) 1012–13; HRC, 'Special Rapporteur on the HRH Report on Health Systems' (n 37) para 80.

[60] Hay and others (n 50) 1026–27.

[61] CESCR, 'General Comment No. 14' (n 11) para 43(a); HRC, 'Special Rapporteur on the HRH Report on Health Systems' (n 37) paras 42–43.

[62] Hay and others (n 50) 1027.

[63] Eg CESCR, 'General Comment No. 14' (n 11) para 12(b); HRC, 'Special Rapporteur on the HRH Report on Health Systems' (n 37) paras 15, 42, 43, and 98.

[64] Eg UNGA, 'Report of the Special Rapporteur on the Rights of Persons with Disabilities, Gerard Quinn' (20 July 2022) UN Doc A/77/203, paras 64–74; Alexander Breitegger, 'Increasing Visibility of Persons with Disabilities in Armed Conflict: Implications for Interpretating and Applying IHL' (2023) 105 International Review of the Red Cross 99; Gauthier de Beco, 'Taking Economic and Social Rights Earnestly: What Does International Human Rights Law Offer Persons with Disabilities in Situations of Armed Conflict?' (2023) 105 International Review of the Red Cross 306.

unexploded ordnance (UXO) or landmines.[65] This can help to adapt plans to progressively build an essential health system controlled and run by the local community to protracted conflict situations.

f) Duties to Secure Democratic Control over Health Systems and Health Care Planning

The CESCR has emphasized that the 'participation of the population in all health-related decision-making at the community, national and international levels'[66] is an important procedural obligation under the HRH. In other words: individuals shall be able to participate 'in political decisions relating to the right to health taken at both the community and national levels'.[67] This relates to the general obligation under the HRH and IHRL of states to implement their human rights duties through legislative, executive/administrative, and judicial institutions that form a democratic state which exercises its (human rights) jurisdiction over a 'democratic society'[68] of equal individual human rights-holders.[69] This implies that the concretization of which health facilities, goods, and services an essential primary health system should provide in order to implement the HRH within the specific local protracted conflict context (mentioned in section B.2.b) should indeed be achieved through a participatory process, including, but not limited to, legislative measures of an elected parliament.[70] This legislation should comply with the IHRL legality standard and ensure the equal participation of individuals, realizing also these individuals' political participation rights set out in the ICCPR.[71] This implies that health budget allocation should be made and monitored in a democratically controlled fashion.

Conducting democratic deliberative and consultative processes on health care priorities in protracted conflict countries may be difficult, especially in periods of resurging violence and/or when control over public institutions shifts from one (state or non-state) party to the conflict to another. This should not, however, lead to a conclusion that all attempts in this direction should be abolished and/or that initiatives taken by local communities to maintain, develop, or build local health care facilities

[65] Isabel Robinson and Ellen Nohle, 'Proportionality and Precautions in Attack: The Reverberating Effects of Using Explosive Weapons in Populated Areas' (2016) 98 International Review of the Red Cross 107, 122–24.

[66] CESCR, 'General Comment No. 14' (n 11) para 11.

[67] ibid para 17; also HRC, 'Special Rapporteur on the HRH Report on Health Systems' (n 37) para 41.

[68] Eg the references to 'democratic societies' in ECHR arts 8(2)–11(2); ICCPR arts 14(1), 21, and 22(2); ICESCR arts 4 and 8(1)(a), (c); and as interpreted in CESCR, 'General Comment No. 19' (n 14) para 63; CESCR, 'General Comment No. 3' (n 46) para 8; CCPR, 'General Comment No. 25: The Right to Participate in Public Affairs' (12 July 1996) UN Doc CCPR/C/21/Rev.1/Add.7, para 1; *Ždanoka v Latvia*, Judgment (Grand Chamber), App no 58278/00 (ECtHR 16 March 2006) para 98; *Navalnyy v Russia*, Judgment (Grand Chamber), App no 29580/12 (ECtHR 15 November 2018) para 175; and World Conference on Human Rights, Vienna Declaration and Programme of Action (n 24) part I para 8.

[69] As is clear from non-discrimination and equality provisions, eg ECHR art 14 and Protocol 12 to the Convention for the Protection of Human Rights and Fundamental Freedoms (adopted 4 November 2000, entered into force 1 April 2005) ETS 177 (hereafter Protocol 12 to the ECHR) art 1; ICCPR arts 2(1), 14(1) and 26; ICESCR arts 2(2) and 3; also CCPR, 'General Comment No. 18: Non-discrimination' (10 November 1989) UN Doc HRI/GEN/1/Rev.1; CESCR, 'General Comment No. 20: Non-discrimination in Economic, Social and Cultural Rights' (2 July 2009) UN Doc E/C.12/GC/20.

[70] ICCPR art 25; Protocol I to the ECHR art 3.

[71] In particular ICCPR art 25; also Protocol I to the ECHR art 3.

should be stifled, even if they are controlled by NSGAs or de facto entities.[72] On the contrary, awarding greater weight to efforts to implement these duties might encourage various human rights duty-bearers involved in protracted conflict scenarios to cooperate in maintaining or developing existing health systems and other 'public' institutions and involve the local population in these processes and/or link to local processes in areas where it is unclear which state (or non-state actor) is the primary duty-bearer in a particular area.[73]

g) Duties to Cooperate and Coordinate HRH Duties of Various Duty-Bearers

This brings the discussion neatly to the question about duties of various duty-bearers who exercise territorial or extraterritorial jurisdiction over persons affected by a protracted armed conflict to cooperate and coordinate the specification, internal allocation, and implementation of their respective HRH duties, and to thus enable the enjoyment of the HRH and the maintenance and development of a (primary) health system.

As indicated, in protracted conflict situations, complementary HRH duties may arise under IHRL if one state exercises 'spatial' or 'personal' extraterritorial jurisdiction while the state that lost jurisdiction over its own territory still has limited positive HRH duties towards the people living on this territory,[74] and joint HRH duties may arise when two or more than two states exercise jurisdiction together.[75] In addition, strong NSAGs/de facto entities may exercise de facto human rights jurisdiction and thus de facto assume the role of human rights duty-bearers.[76] Though rarely

[72] Eg Stuart Gordon, Sarah Jane Cooper-Knock, and Louis Lilywhite, 'Dynamics of Provision of Health Services by Non-state Armed Groups—An Analysis of the Literature' (CAERUS Report 2015) <https://www.researchgate.net/publication/303374487_Dynamics_of_provision_of_health_services_by_non-_state_armed_groups_-_an_analysis_of_the_literature> accessed 24 July 2023; Chatham House, 'Non-State Armed Groups, Health and Healthcare' (Centre on Global Health Security Roundtable Summary, Foraus—the Swiss Forum on Foreign Policy, Geneva, Switzerland, 24–25 March 2015) <https://ia801701.us.archive.org/33/items/nsags-meeting-summary-in-template-final-edit-from-jo-er-pka-27.10.15/NSAGs%20Meeting%20Summary%20in%20template%20-%20final%20edit%20from%20Jo%20-%20ER-%20PKA%2027.10.15.pdf> accessed 24 July 2023.

[73] That such developments are not excluded is shown in detailed studies of protracted conflict countries conducted by political scientists, eg Ana Arjona and others (eds), *Rebel Governance in Civil War* (CUP 2015); Zachariah Mampilly, *Rebel Rulers: Insurgent Governance and Civilian Life during War* (Cornell University Press 2011); Ana Arjona, *Rebelocracy: Social Order in the Colombian Civil War* (CUP 2016) chapter 7.

[74] Eg *Ilaşcu and Others v Moldova and Russia* (n 29) para 331; *Catan and Others v Moldova and Russia* (n 29) paras 145–147.

[75] Eg *Hassan v UK* (n 34) paras 78–79, where duties arise for both the UK and the US (under the ICCPR); and *Jaloud v Netherlands* (n 34), where duties arise jointly for eg the UK and the Netherlands (paras 149–171).

[76] Eg examples given in Müller, 'Can Armed Non-State Actors Exercise Jurisdiction?' (n 12) 287–96; and Müller, 'De Facto Independent Regimes' (n 36). Though not accepting that de facto entities exercise human rights jurisdiction and thus obtain duties under the ECHR, the ECtHR reluctantly recognizes legal remedies or other measures adopted by de facto entities as legitimate for the purposes of the ECHR, eg in cases involving Turkish occupied Northern Cyprus and the de facto entity 'TRNC' (eg *Cyprus v Turkey*, Judgment (Grand Chamber), App no 25781/94 (ECtHR, 10 May 2001), paras 61 and 236–237; *Demopoulos and Others v Turkey*, Decision (Grand Chamber), App no 46113/99 (ECtHR, 1 March 2010), paras 95–96; *Foka v Turkey*, Judgment (Chamber), App no 28940/95 (ECtHR 24 June 2008), paras 83–84; and *Protopapa v Turkey*, Judgment (Chamber), App no 16084/90, (ECtHR, 24 February 2009), paras 60 and 83–89). It does so when these 'courts' are 'independent and impartial and are operating on the basis of the rule of law' (*Mozer v Moldova and Russia*, Judgment (Grand Chamber), App no 11138/10 (ECtHR, 23 February 2016) para 144; *Ilaşcu and Others v Moldova and Russia* (n 29) para 460). The ECtHR, however,

establishing a direct '*two-way* obligation [on two or more states] to *cooperate* with each other, implying [for example] at the same time an obligation to seek assistance and an obligation to afford assistance',[77] the respective duties that ECtHR jurisprudence establishes on different states involved in such situations *ex post* indirectly indicate that states should cooperate and coordinate the specification, internal allocation, and implementation of their respective duties once they exercise concurrent or joint jurisdiction. Cooperation and coordination can take various forms, as has been elaborated to some extent in jurisprudence of the ECtHR.[78] While not directly applying the HRH, the general principles developed by the ECtHR may be useful for the context of implementing the HRH in protracted conflict countries as well.

The ECtHR has, for example, regularly observed that states having lost jurisdiction over their own territories retain positive duties to re-establish control 'as an expression of jurisdiction'[79] and to take reasonable measures to ensure the enjoyment of human rights of the people over which they have lost jurisdiction.[80] Thus, among these positive duties are duties to take 'all political, judicial and other measures at their disposal'[81] towards this end, which also implies cooperation with states that exercise extraterritorial jurisdiction. More concretely, the ECtHR has in this context recognized measures taken by states which have lost control over their own territory to continue financing the education system in territories over which they have lost control;[82] the setting up of special 'judicial, investigative and civil service authorities'[83] that can be approached by individuals on territories over which the respective state has lost control and whose ECHR rights have allegedly been violated—authorities which will enter into dialogue with authorities of de facto entities and/or state(s) exercising extraterritorial jurisdiction to find ways towards securing ECHR rights of specific individuals;[84] the adoption of a new constitution granting a certain amount of autonomy to regions controlled by non-state entities supported by a third state to further a peaceful solution of an ongoing conflict and the building of democratically controlled

is always quick to observe that this does not amount to a formal recognition of the 'TRNC' as a state or a recognition of Turkish sovereignty over Northern Cyprus, eg *Cyprus v Turkey* (n 76) paras 90–101 and 238; and reiterated in *Mozer v Moldova and Russia* (n 76) para 143 and *Ilaşcu and Others v Moldova and Russia* (n 29) paras 177 and 345.

77 *Güzelyurtlu v Cyprus and Turkey* (n 15) para 233 (emphasis added).

78 Unlike the UN treaty bodies, the ECtHR has produced some jurisprudence directly concerning situations of concurrent and joint jurisdiction and is therefore relied on here.

79 *Ilaşcu and Others v Moldova and Russia* (n 29) para 339; *Mozer v Moldova and Russia* (n 76) para 151.

80 Eg *Ilaşcu and Others v Moldova and Russia* (n 29) paras 331, 333, and 339; *Catan and Others v Moldova and Russia* (n 29) paras 109–10; *Sargsyan v Azerbaijan* (n 29) paras 130–31 and 139–49; *Mozer v Moldova and Russia* (n 76) para 99; *Mamasakhlisi and Others v Georgia and Russia* (n 30) paras 318–319.

81 *Ilaşcu and Others v Moldova and Russia* (n 29) paras 340 and 313; *Catan and Others v Moldova and Russia* (n 29) para 145; *Sargsyan v Azerbaijan* (n 29) para 131; *Mozer v Moldova and Russia* (n 76) paras 100 and 151.

82 *Catan and Others v Moldova and Russia* (n 29) para 147. For the context of the HRH, this could suggest that territorial states continue to finance the functioning of a health system in territories over which they have lost control.

83 *Mozer v Moldova and Russia* (n 76) paras 205 and 215; *Sandu and Others v Moldova and Russia*, Judgment (Chamber), App no 21034/05 (ECtHR, 17 July 2018) para 99.

84 Transferred to the HRH context, this could include raising awareness about alleged violations of the HRH through such mechanisms.

state institutions;[85] the signing of agreements concerning the withdrawal of foreign troops[86] and on cooperation in various areas, such as economic and commercial matters, police and security, criminal matters, air traffic control, telephone links, sports, cultural heritage, humanitarian matters, health and environment, and even political cooperation among parliamentarians—involving both states exercising complementary jurisdiction and de facto entities.[87] For the implementation of the HRH in protracted conflicts, agreements on humanitarian and health matters might be utilized to concretize and allocate, and then implement, complementary HRH duties, including duties around maintaining and developing a (successively democratically controlled) primary health system. Often, international organizations—such as the OSCE or the UN—are involved in facilitating, negotiating, and implementing such agreements.[88] These duties of states that have lost jurisdiction over parts of their territories are 'complemented'[89] by duties of states exercising (personal or spatial) extraterritorial jurisdiction, either directly or through controlling a de facto non-state entity.[90] In cases where states exercise joint jurisdiction, and there is not usually a hostile relationship between these states, the states involved may coordinate the specification, (internal) allocation, and implementation of their respective HRH duties themselves.[91]

Concerning the duties owed towards concrete individuals, the ECtHR has established that states that have lost control over their own territories shall take all reasonable measures—in particular through negotiations with states and/or de facto entities exercising extraterritorial (personal or spatial) jurisdiction over these territories—to secure the implementation of these duties, for example by pushing for the release of unlawfully detained persons[92] and the humane treatment of detainees (including access to required medical care, family visits, and religious support);[93] by ensuring access to education for individual children;[94] by making attempts to secure access to private property;[95] and most concretely, by cooperating in criminal proceedings to comply with the procedural obligation under article 2 ECHR to effectively investigate and remedy losses of life.[96] The ECtHR specifies that such cooperation shall

[85] *Ilaşcu and Others v Moldova and Russia* (n 29) para 343.

[86] ibid para 343.

[87] ibid paras 344–45; *Güzelyurtlu and Others v Cyprus and Turkey*, Judgment (Chamber) App no 36925/07, (ECtHR 4 April 2017), para 293.

[88] *Ilaşcu and Others v Moldova and Russia* (n 29) para 344; *Güzelyurtlu v Cyprus and Turkey* (n 15) paras 106 ff and 134–36.

[89] *Sargsyan v Azerbaijan* (n 29) para 148, where the ECtHR observes that '[t]he acceptance that the territorial state had only limited responsibility under the Convention was *compensated* by the finding that another Convention state exercised jurisdiction outside its territory and thus had full responsibility under the Convention' (emphasis added).

[90] The scope of these 'complementing' duties varies depending on context, eg *Mozer v Moldova and Russia* (n 76) paras 175, 178–182, 184, 201, 217–218, concerning duties of the Russian Federation complementing Moldova's duties; and *Mamasakhlisi and Others v Georgia and Russia* (n 30) paras 412, 429, and 441.

[91] Eg *Hassan v UK* (n 34) paras 78–79; and *Jaloud v Netherlands* (n 34) paras 149–151.

[92] *Ilaşcu and Others v Moldova and Russia* (n 29) paras 348–352; *Mozer v Moldova and Russia* (n 76) paras 153–155.

[93] *Mozer v Moldova and Russia* (n 76) paras 183 and 200; *Mamasakhlisi and Others v Georgia and Russia* (n 30) paras 402–408.

[94] *Catan and Others v Moldova and Russia* (n 29) para 147.

[95] *Sandu and Others v Moldova and Russia* (n 83) para 87.

[96] *Güzelyurtlu v Cyprus and Turkey* (n 15).

happen through diplomatic channels, but if states—due to being on opposing sides of an ongoing protracted conflict—have no formal diplomatic relations, states 'may be required to use other more informal or indirect channels of cooperation, for instance through third States or international organizations'.[97]

Formulating direct duties on states exercising complementary or joint jurisdiction to concretely cooperate on the specification, (internal) allocation and implementation of human rights duties—including the HRH duties set out in sections B.2.a)–f)—could be conducive to setting in motion processes that may not only help to concretely secure the HRH in protracted conflict situations where multiple duty-bearers are involved but also start a dialogue among all states (and potentially NSAGs exercising de facto jurisdiction) affected that are based on and appeal to concurrently arising *legal* HRH obligations of all parties. The institutionalization of such processes may be encouraged, underpinned by states' general duty under IHRL to organize themselves institutionally in a way that enables them to comply with all their human rights duties, including HRH duties.[98] Given the already mentioned grounding of IHRL in the mutuality of human rights, equality, and democracy, as well as the related presumptive (democratic) legitimacy of the territorial state underlying the ECtHR's understanding of jurisdiction, in the case of conflicting claims as to how the HRH should be realized through the coordination and implementation of complementary duties of various states (and potentially of NSAGs exercising de facto jurisdiction) in a particular protracted conflict situation, the interpretations of the territorial state should arguably be given priority.[99] This does not exclude, but indeed encourages, taking on board in an institutionalized cooperation process the results of quasi-legal bottom-up developments concerning the implementation of the HRH in protracted conflict countries (including the building of an accessible health system) that may have taken place due to the absence of reliable health authorities run by the state of territorial jurisdiction, especially when the protracted conflict has been ongoing over many years. Some of these informal processes may be driven by NSAGs or states exercising extraterritorial jurisdiction but may have originally built on existing local health law and institutions which have been developed and adapted through participatory processes involving local populations respecting their (political) equality and equal rights to address an evolving situation and concrete emerging health needs of the local population. In its jurisprudence, the ECtHR tentatively recognizes such possibilities by accepting that 'laws' and 'tribunals/courts' operated by de facto entities may be regarded as '(domestic) law' and 'tribunals/courts' for the purposes of the ECHR when they conform to the ECHR's legality requirements and when the 'tribunals/courts' form 'part of a judicial system operating on a "constitutional and legal basis" reflecting a judicial tradition compatible with the Convention'.[100]

Overall, taking seriously duties to cooperate towards the specification, allocation, and implementation of complementary and joint HRH duties in protracted conflict

[97] ibid para 237.
[98] Besson (n 35) 169.
[99] ibid.
[100] *Cyprus v Turkey* (n 76) paras 231 and 236–237; reiterated in *Ilaşcu and Others v Moldova and Russia* (n 29) para 460 and most recently in *Mamasakhlisi and Others v Georgia and Russia* (n 30) paras 419–424.

countries could potentially open the door to full-fledged peace negotiations. Through such negotiations various components of a de facto essential primary health system under the control of various states of territorial and extraterritorial jurisdiction and/or strong non-state entities may be integrated and then run as a unitary health system via deliberative, democratic, or democratizing processes involving the local population. This may be helped by supranational courts such as the ECtHR or UN treaty bodies if they place more emphasis on such duties which are to arise even if the level of trust among the various parties involved is low.

C. Responsibilities for the HRH and Their Bearers

In addition to HRH duties that arise for states (and potentially strong non-state actors) that exercise jurisdiction under article 12 ICESCR, so-called responsibilities for the HRH arise as well. They address all states (that do not exercise jurisdiction) and IOs, but also other private entities and even individuals. The CESCR has referred to 'responsibilities for the HRH' in its General Comment No. 14 as follows:

> While only States are parties to the Covenant and thus ultimately accountable for compliance with it, all members of society—individuals, including health professionals, families, local communities, intergovernmental and non-governmental organizations, civil society organizations, as well as the private business sector—have *responsibilities* regarding the realization of the right to health. States parties should therefore provide an environment which facilitates the discharge of these responsibilities.[101]

Responsibilities for the HRH are thus to be distinguished from states' human rights duties that, as explained, arise from relationships of jurisdiction. Responsibilities for the HRH are, however, closely related to HRH obligations: their overarching aim, which, in turn, determines their scope and character, is to enable and assist states of jurisdiction to discharge the HRH obligations that they owe to the people under their jurisdiction and also not to undermine the efforts of states of jurisdiction in this regard.[102] Responsibilities for the HRH are thus collective or multilateral responsibilities of all states, IOs, and other non-state entities to cooperate[103] with states of jurisdiction towards this end and even to establish a multi-level (institutional) international order in which the HRH and all other human rights can be fully realized.[104] The notion of 'responsibilities for human rights' in general is omnipresent in the CESCR's and, to a lesser extent, in other UN treaty bodies' 'jurisprudence', even though the terminology

[101] CESCR, 'General Comment No. 14' (n 11) para 42 (emphasis added).

[102] Besson (n 6) 262. This is confirmed by various statements of the CESCR: see discussion in section C.

[103] Eg ICESCR art 2(1); Charter of the United Nations (adopted 26 June 1945, entered into force 24 October 1945) 1 UNTS XVI (UN Charter) arts 55–56.

[104] Universal Declaration of Human Rights, adopted 10 December 1948 by UNGA Res 217 A(III) (UDHR) art 28.

used to describe them has not been consistent.[105] This inconsistency can also be observed in statements of other UN treaty bodies[106] and legal literature.[107]

1. International Organizations as Bearers of Responsibilities for the HRH

Given their extensive involvement in protracted conflict countries, and due to space constraints, the following paragraph focuses on IOs as holders of responsibilities for the HRH. The CESCR and the Committee on the Rights of the Child (CRC) highlight IOs' responsibilities for the HRH[108]—including those of the World Health Organization (WHO), strengthened via the WHO's Constitution[109]—but also other UN organizations and specialized agencies such as UNDP, UNICEF, UNESCO, ILO, and FAO, as well as the World Bank and the IMF,[110] are addressed by responsibilities for human rights. Moreover, given its special role in securing compliance with IHL in armed conflicts, including health-related provisions, the ICRC may also be considered as a bearer of responsibilities for the HRH, complementing, where reasonable, its rights and duties under IHL.[111]

In general, the legal basis for UN organizations' responsibilities for human rights (including the HRH) is articles 1 and 2 as well as articles 55 and 56 UN Charter and customary IHRL.[112] Moreover, they can be bound by implied terms relating to the protection of human rights under their constituent instruments[113] as well as by obligations arising under institutional acts of the organization itself, such as resolutions of the UN Security Council[114] or resolutions of other UN organs expressing customary

[105] In its General Comments, the CESCR inconsistently refers to 'international obligations' or 'responsibilities', often using these terms interchangeably; to 'obligations/responsibilities of actors other than states'; and/or to 'obligations/responsibilities of international assistance and cooperation' and occasionally to 'extraterritorial obligations/responsibilities'. It does not offer definitions of the different terms it uses.

[106] Eg CRC, 'General Comment No. 15, The Right to Health' (17 April 2013) UN Doc CRC/C/GC/15, section D, using the terms 'obligations' and 'responsibilities' interchangeably.

[107] For an overview of the myriad terminology found in academic literature, Mark Gibney, 'On Terminology: Extraterritorial Obligations' in Malcolm Langford and others (eds), *Global Justice, State Duties* (CUP 2013), 32–50.

[108] CESCR, 'General Comment No. 14' (n 11) para 42; CRC, 'General Comment No. 15' (n 106) para 77.

[109] Eg preamble of the Constitution of the World Health Organization (adopted 22 July 1946, entered into force 7 April 1948) 14 UNTS 185, referring directly to the human right to health. There is no question that international organizations are bound by their constituent instruments, even if they are not a party to these instruments. On this see *Reparations for Injuries Suffered in the Service of the United Nations* (Advisory Opinion) (1949) ICJ Rep 174, para 180.

[110] Eg CESCR, 'General Comment No. 2: International Technical Assistance Measures' (2 February 1990) UN Doc E/1990/23, para 2; CESCR, 'General Comment No. 11: Plans of Action for Primary Education' (11 May 1999) UN Doc E/C.12/1999/4, para 11; and CESCR, 'General Comment No. 12: The Right to Food' (12 May 1999) UN Doc E/C.12/1999/5, para 30.

[111] Eg Geneva Convention I arts 9 and 23; Geneva Convention II art 9; Geneva Convention III arts 9, 73, and 125–26; Geneva Convention IV arts 10, 14, 59, 61, and 142–43; also CESCR, 'General Comment No. 14' (n 11) para 65; and CESCR, 'General Comment No. 15' (n 14) para 60.

[112] *Interpretation of the Agreement of March 1951 between the WHO and Egypt* (Advisory Opinion) (1980) ICJ Rep 73, para 37.

[113] For the detailed argument, Guglielmo Verdirame, *The UN and Human Rights: Who Guards the Guardians?* (CUP 2011) 75–82.

[114] This is clear from UN Charter arts 1 and 2 read in conjunction with the provisions of Chapter VII of the UN Charter.

human rights law.[115] Various international human rights treaties also refer to the role of the UN, its subsidiary organs, and its specialized agencies to assist in the implementation of human rights[116] and/or recall articles 55 and 56 UN Charter in their preambles.[117] Responsibilities for human rights are fully binding on IOs, in particular when their scope and content is (relatively) clearly defined under treaty (eg their constituting instrument) or customary IHRL.

2. Holders of Responsibilities for the HRH

Responsibilities for the HRH are not owed to concrete individuals but to all states and their institutions, and only indirectly to the individuals whose equal HRH should be secured through these domestic (democratic) institutions, including an accessible health system. In other words, the holders of responsibilities for the HRH are states of jurisdiction, and, if one were to accept that de facto entities or strong NSAGs can also exercise de facto (human rights) jurisdiction and thus become human rights duty-bearers, these entities too would become responsibility-holders. This is often expressed implicitly in the statements of the CESCR. The Committee has highlighted, for example, that IOs should cooperate effectively 'in relation to the implementation of [human] right[s] at the domestic level',[118] that is, in supporting states in their efforts to discharge their HRH obligations, indicating that IOs owe these responsibilities to states. Similarly, the CRC has held that any measures undertaken by IOs should be 'targeted as supporting States to fulfil their obligations under the Convention [on the Rights of the Child]'.[119]

Overall, this is justified by the grounding of IHRL in the mutuality of human rights, equality, and thus democracy (political community), as well as the right to self-determination as mentioned in section A. Only entities—usually (democratic) states—that exercise (territorial and, in exceptional cases, extraterritorial) jurisdiction have the institutional, normative, and coercive capacities to secure the equal human rights and the right to self-determination of equal rights-holders that form a 'democratic society' as foreseen under IHRL. IOs and other non-state actors do not have jurisdiction-based human rights duties but indeed (only) responsibilities for human rights owed to (democratic) states, which can also be described as supportive but subordinate[120] to states' (primary[121]) human rights duties.

[115] Verdirame (n 113) 82. The UDHR can be of particular importance in this context, as it provides an authoritative guide to the interpretation of the generic human rights provisions of the UN Charter. On its customary status, William Schabas, *The Customary International Law of Human Rights* (OUP 2021).

[116] Eg ICESCR art 22; CRC art 45; Convention on the Rights of Persons with Disabilities (adopted 13 December 2006, entered into force 3 May 2008) 2515 UNTS 3 (CRPD), art 38.

[117] Eg preambles of the ICCPR and CRPD.

[118] CESCR, 'General Comment No. 15' (n 14) para 60; CESCR, 'General Comment No. 14' (n 11) para 46.

[119] CRC, 'General Comment No. 5: General Implementation Measures' (27 November 2003) UN Doc CRC/GC/2003/5, para 64.

[120] Eg Margot Salomon, 'Deprivation, Causation and the Law of International Cooperation' in Malcolm Langford and others (eds), *Global Justice, State Duties* (CUP 2011) 278–79, referring to them as 'secondary', 'subsidiary' or 'complementary' 'duties'.

[121] Eg Wouter Vandenhole and Wolfgang Benedek, 'Extraterritorial Human Rights Obligations and the North–South Divide' in Malcolm Langford and others (eds), *Global Justice, State Duties* (CUP 2011) 335;

3. The Scope and Content of Responsibilities for the HRH in Protracted Conflicts

The foregoing already indicates that the scope and content of IOs' responsibilities for the HRH in protracted conflict situations will be shaped in relation to (democratic) state(s)-of-jurisdictions' duties to secure the HRH of the persons under their jurisdiction. This makes them highly context-dependent and may be one reason why UN treaty bodies rarely make specific indications about the scope and content of responsibilities for human rights in general, and for the HRH in particular. However, mirroring some of the HRH duties set out in section C.2, responsibilities for the HRH will inter alia have (a) a minimum core; and (b) a 'negative' and 'positive' dimension.

a) Minimum Core Responsibilities for the HRH

One focus of the content of IOs' responsibilities for the HRH is to enable states of jurisdiction to implement their minimum core HRH duties. This is clear from the CESCR's general statement that 'it is particularly incumbent on States parties, and other actors in a position to assist [including IOs], to provide international assistance and cooperation, especially economic and technical, to enable developing countries to fulfil their core obligations',[122] adding that, for the context of 'national and international developmental policies', core rights 'when grouped together establish an international minimum threshold that all developmental policies should be designed to respect [, protect, and fulfil]'.[123] This focus on the minimum core is grounded in the fact that core rights build on fundamental human interests, first and foremost interests to survive (and thus also: basic equality),[124] and states should therefore implement core rights as a matter of priority.[125] Where they are unable to do so—for example, due to lack of resources or capacities, an ongoing protracted conflict, or the like—it is in this area that there is a particularly urgent need for support by responsibility-bearing IOs.

More concretely, this would imply that responsibility-bearers support state(s) of jurisdiction involved in protracted conflicts to build up a functioning health system, providing primary health care of good quality and equal access to everyone living in the protracted conflict country, respecting and safeguarding people's physical and mental integrity by upholding the principle of informed consent and medical ethics and run by qualified medical staff.[126] Given the great importance of the HRH core

and UNGA Res 41/128, 'Declaration on the Right to Development' (4 December 1986) UN Doc A/RES/41/128, art 3(1).

[122] Eg CESCR, 'General Comment No. 19' (n 14) para 61; similarly, CESCR, 'General Comment No. 14' (n 11) para 45; and CESCR, 'General Comment No. 15' (n 14) para 38.

[123] CESCR, 'Substantive Issues Arising in the Implementation of the International Covenant on Economic, Social and Cultural Rights: Poverty and the International Covenant on Economic, Social and Cultural Rights—Statement adopted by the Committee on Economic, Social and Cultural Rights' (10 May 2001), UN Doc E/C.12/2001/10, para 17.

[124] As argued by David Bilchitz, *Poverty and Fundamental Rights. The Justification and Enforcement of Socio-economic Rights* (OUP 2007) 187–222.

[125] CESCR, 'General Comment No. 3' (n 46) para 10; and CESCR, 'General Comment No. 14' (n 11) para 47.

[126] Section B.2.

duty to ensure that the basic health system indeed addresses *locally* prevailing health problems,[127] even under their core responsibilities for the HRH, international organizations should ensure that they respond indeed to the results of local consultative (or even democratic) processes through which state(s) of jurisdiction may have established which essential health goods and services local populations would need access to as a matter of priority, which existing elements of a health system and local health staff they may wish to rely on and develop/train, and what local resources they wish to utilize. If such processes have not been conducted, international organizations might encourage state(s) of jurisdiction to do so, instead of imposing their technocratic blueprint understanding of minimum health care facilities, goods, and services that protracted conflict societies allegedly 'need' from the top down, delivered by foreign health personnel hired by IOs.

b) Negative and Positive Dimensions of Responsibilities for the HRH

The overarching aim of responsibilities for the HRH implies that responsibility-bearers have responsibilities (a) to preserve (or not to undermine)[128] the ability of state(s) of jurisdiction to implement their HRH duties through a functioning (democratically controlled) health system and broader institutional framework; and (b) to (pro-actively) support[129] states of jurisdiction to do so. In other words, responsibilities for human rights encompass all types of responsibilities—'negative' responsibilities to respect, as well as 'positive' responsibilities to protect and to fulfil.

Concerning 'negative' responsibilities of IOs for all human rights in general, the CESCR has observed that IOs should refrain from adopting and promoting programmes, policies, laws, and so on that undermine the capacity of states to respect, protect, and fulfil their human duties owed to the people under their jurisdiction.[130] State capacity can be undermined for example through IO-driven adoption of far-reaching sanctions and embargos;[131] the promotion of structural adjustment programmes;[132] debt-related policies;[133] the adoption and entrenchment of undue trade, investment, or intellectual property rules, or rules protecting commercial interests;[134] or more generally any development, humanitarian, and peacebuilding policies that

[127] Section B.2.b).

[128] Eg CESCR, 'General Comment No. 15' (n 14) para 31, albeit concerning the right to water.

[129] Generally on this responsibility: CESCR, 'General Comment No. 15' (n 14) para 60 ('promotion of the right to water' through activities of IOs); CESCR, 'General Comment No. 17: Protection of Moral and Material Interests resulting from Scientific, Literary or Artistic Production' (12 January 2006) UN Doc E/C.12/GC/17, para 57 (UN agencies to take measures 'likely to contribute to the effective implementation of ICESCR art 15(1)(c)); CESCR, 'General Comment No. 19' (n 14) para 83 (addressing in particular the IMF).

[130] Generally: Maastricht Principle (n 31) principle 16.

[131] CESCR, 'General Comment No. 8: Economic Sanctions and Respect for Economic, Social and Cultural Rights' (12 December 1997) UN Doc E/C.12/1997/8, paras 11–14.

[132] CESCR, 'General Comment No. 2' (n 110) para 9; CESCR, 'General Comment No. 4' (n 14) para 19 (addressing international financial institutions); CESCR, 'General Comment No. 15' (n 14) para 60; CESCR, 'General Comment No. 19' (n 14) para 83.

[133] CESCR, 'General Comment No. 2' (n 110) para 9; CESCR, 'General Comment No. 12' (n 110) para 41.

[134] Eg CESCR, 'General Comment No. 15' (n 14) para 60; CESCR, 'General Comment No. 17' (n 130) para 57; Maastricht Principles (n 31) principle 16.

undermine human rights.[135] These general responsibilities of IOs can be concretized for the HRH in protracted conflict countries: for example, sanctions and embargos adopted by IOs have undermined the ability of state(s) of jurisdiction to secure their HRH duties;[136] UN peacekeeping forces have brought cholera into their host country;[137] and WHO-driven health policies—such as the focus on expensive vertical biomedical single-disease interventions and thus neglect of long-term health system building[138]—have undermined state(s)' of jurisdictions' abilities to comply with their duties under the HRH set out in section B.3

Though rarely specifying IOs' responsibilities for the HRH further, the CESCR has indicated that among the procedural responsibilities of IOs are responsibilities to conduct impact assessments of their health-related policies, programmes, legal measures, and so on[139] and carry out broader monitoring activities of the impact of policies and programmes once they were adopted.[140] More importantly, the CESCR has observed that IOs have responsibilities to adopt HRH-based policies and programmes.[141] This would imply a more interactive, context-dependent determination of the scope of specific IOs' responsibilities for the HRH in relation to state(s) of jurisdictions' HRH duties and these states' capacity gaps to implement them, rather than responsibilities to carry out mere technical 'impact assessment' of top-down health programmes unilaterally developed and implemented by IOs in protracted conflict countries. Indeed, proactive responsibilities of IOs to cooperate with states of jurisdiction towards the implementation of these states' HRH duties would arise.[142]

This brings the analysis to IOs' more 'positive' responsibilities for the HRH, to enhance the capacity of states of jurisdiction to secure the HRH for individuals under their jurisdiction in protracted conflict situations. Among the more concrete examples of responsibilities, albeit not limited to responsibilities for the HRH, the CESCR has called on IOs to provide development assistance or to adopt rights-based

[135] Eg CESCR, 'General Comment No. 22: Right to Sexual and Reproductive Health' (4 March 2016) UN Doc E/C.12/GC/22, para 52; CESCR, 'General Comment No. 14' (n 11) para 64; CESCR, 'General Comment No. 4' (n 14) para 19.

[136] Concerning the effects of sanctions imposed on Iraq in the 1990s, eg Hans von Sponeck, *A Different Kind of War: The UN Sanctions Regime in Iraq* (Berghahn Books 2006); and on the devastating effects of the current (2023–24) sanctions regime against Syria, HRC, 'Report of the Special Rapporteur on the Negative Impact of Unilateral Coercive Measures on the Enjoyment of Human Rights on his Mission to the Syrian Arab Republic, Idriss Jazairy' (8 October 2018) UN Doc A/HRC/39/54/Add.2, paras 24–52; OHCHR, 'UN Expert Calls for Lifting of Long-Lasting Unilateral Sanctions "Suffocating" Syrian People' (Press Release, 22 November 2022) <https://www.ohchr.org/en/node/104160> accessed 24 July 2023.

[137] UNGA, 'Report of the Special Rapporteur on Extreme Poverty and Human Rights, Philip Alston' (26 August 2016) UN Doc A/73/367.

[138] Eg critical analysis by Regien Biesma and others, 'The Effects of Global Health Initiatives on Country Health Systems: A Review of the Evidence from HIV/AIDS Control' (2009) 24 Health Policy and Planning 239; Krishna Rao and others, 'When Do Vertical Programmes Strengthen Health Systems? A Comparative Assessment of Disease-specific Interventions in India' (2014) 29 Health Policy and Planning 495; Gorik Ooms and others, 'The "Diagonal" Approach to Global Fund Financing: A Cure for the Broader Malaise of Health Systems?' (2008) 4(6) Globalization and Health 1.

[139] Eg CESCR, 'General Comment No. 8' (n 131) para 12.

[140] ibid paras 13–14; CESCR, 'General Comment No. 15' (n 14) para 60.

[141] CESCR, 'General Comment No. 14' (n 11) para 64; also, CESCR, 'General Comment No. 15' (n 14) para 60; CESCR, 'General Comment No. 19' (n 14) paras 84.

[142] CESCR, 'General Comment No. 14' (n 11) para 64 referring to 'coordinated efforts' of states and IOs to realize the HRH.

policies and programmes,[143] including via providing financial assistance,[144] technical assistance/guidance,[145] humanitarian assistance (disaster relief),[146] or relevant information.[147] Positive responsibilities to support the development of national plans for the implementation of the HRH,[148] including drafting and implementing framework legislation[149]—or, in protracted conflict situations, promoting ad hoc agreements between various states and non-state actors involved—could be read as a responsibility of IOs in the specific context of protracted conflicts to ensure that various states (and potentially NSAGs/de facto entities) exercising complementary or joint jurisdiction indeed coordinate the specification and implementation of their respective HRH duties through IOs. This would complement and support states' HRH duties to cooperate and coordinate the specification, (internal) allocation, and implementation of their HRH duties discussed in section C.2.g), including by acting through IOs. Once more, this would ideally link back all duty-bearers' and responsibility-bearers' efforts to secure the HRH in protracted conflict situations to the health priorities and preferences of local populations, expressed by state (and non-state) duty-bearers ideally representing these populations via democratic institutions and processes, including a democratically controlled local health system.

D. Concluding Remarks

This chapter outlined states' (and potentially de facto entities') HRH duties and IOs' responsibilities for the HRH in the specific context of protracted conflicts. The analysis shows that there are comprehensive duties and responsibilities under IHRL addressing various state actors, IOs, and even non-state/non-IO entities to secure the HRH of everyone affected by a protracted conflict. The chapter emphasized duties under and responsibilities for the HRH to maintain and develop an accessible (primary) health care system which provides essential health goods, facilities, and services addressing the prevailing local health problems of people affected by protracted conflicts and to promote broad participation in, and even local democratic control over, this health system. This also encompasses emerging duties and responsibilities addressing all actors involved to *cooperate* towards this end, including by recognizing and potentially integrating 'informal' participatory bottom-up processes and

[143] ibid and CESCR, 'General Comment No. 2' (n 110) para 8(a); CESCR, 'General Comment No. 15' (n 14) para 60; CESCR, 'General Comment No. 12' (n 110) para 40; and CESCR, 'General Comment No. 19' (n 14) para 84.

[144] CESCR, 'General Comment No. 2' (n 110) para 13; CESCR, 'General Comment No. 12' (n 110) para 64.

[145] CESCR, 'General Comment No. 14' (n 11) para 63; CESCR, 'General Comment No. 15' (n 14) para 38; CESCR, 'General Comment No. 22' (n 135) para 53.

[146] CESCR, 'General Comment No. 14' (n 11) para 40; CESCR, 'General Comment No. 12' (n 110) para 38; CESCR, 'General Comment No. 15' (n 14) para 60.

[147] CESCR, 'General Comment No. 22' (n 135) para 53.

[148] CESCR, 'General Comment No. 14' (n 11) para 63; CESCR, 'General Comment No. 11' (n 110) para 9.

[149] CESCR, 'General Comment No. 14' (n 11) para 56; CESCR, 'General Comment No. 12' (n 110) para 30; CESCR, 'General Comment No. 11' (n 110) para 11.

activities relating to health system maintenance and development even if controlled and promoted by de facto entities or NSAGs.

A renewed focus on these obligations and responsibilities could arguably assist in overcoming some of the political intractability and thus longevity of protracted conflicts. At the same time, it could promote processes that address the true local health priorities of the specific local population affected by such conflicts. Of course, by their very nature protracted conflict situations involve parties that mistrust each other, and IHRL has clear limits to accommodate de facto entities and NSAGs even if they comply with the HRH and their health-related duties under IHL. But reiterating and further specifying all parties' legally binding duties and responsibilities to cooperate in relation to the HRH might assist in building trust and thus move towards a political solution for protracted conflicts. UN treaty bodies and regional human rights courts like the ECtHR could assist such processes by further clarifying the scope and content of relevant duties under and responsibilities for the HRH and other human rights.

9

A (Limited) Role of International Law in Tackling Environmental Degradation During Protracted Conflicts

Britta Sjöstedt

A. Introduction

This chapter explores issues in protracted armed conflicts related to climate change and environmental degradation, and the available tools offered by international law to protect the environment and climate in this context. The degradation of the environment has become increasingly apparent with changes in weather patterns, rising sea-level, pollution, and loss of biodiversity and ecosystem services. In 2023, six of the nine planetary boundaries were exceeded, which potentially can endanger the conditions for human life on earth.[1] Given the threats to ecological integrity and climate change, the environment in states experiencing protracted armed conflicts is particularly vulnerable and often without sufficient protection, with the risk of long-term and irreversible damage to the ecosystem. Environmental issues are present in protracted conflicts in various ways, including: contributing to conflict outbreaks, when several groups are competing for access to arable land and resources; sustaining hostilities, as natural resources play a role in financing the warring parties; acting as direct as well as indirect targets during hostilities to gain military advantage; and/or obstructing peacebuilding efforts.[2] Protracted armed conflicts often lead to governance collapse, resulting in a lack of functioning judiciary, crumbling infrastructure, growing corruption and an informal economy with a less attractive setting for investments and with halted conservation work. War-torn societies are therefore in a worse condition to respond to the challenges posed by climate change and environmental degradation, becoming captured in a vicious cycle of violence and further environmental degradation that is difficult to break.[3]

[1] Katherine Richardson and others, 'Earth Beyond Six of Nine Planetary Boundaries' (2023) 9 Science Advances.

[2] United Nations, 'A More Secure World: Our Shared Responsibility Report of the High-level Panel on Threats, Challenges and Change' (2004); Onita Das, *Environmental Protection, Security and Armed Conflict* (Edward Elgar Publishing 2013) 66f; UNEP, 'From Conflict to Peacebuilding: The Role of Natural Resources and the Environment' (2009) 8, 10.

[3] For instance ICRC, 'When Rain Turns to Dust: Understanding and Responding to the Combined Impact of Armed Conflicts and the Climate and Environment Crisis on People's Lives' (2020).

Britta Sjöstedt, *A (Limited) Role of International Law in Tackling Environmental Degradation During Protracted Conflicts*
In: *From Protracted Conflict to Sustainable Peace?* Edited by: Heike Krieger, Giedre Jokubauskaite, Asli Ozcelik, and Andreas Buser, Oxford University Press. © Britta Sjöstedt 2026. DOI: 10.1093/9780198967385.003.0011

In past years, climate change and environmental degradation have been elevated on the international security agenda. The United Nations (UN) Security Council has discussed environmental security on several occasions, including the protection of the environment during armed conflict, climate change, and natural resources as root causes of armed conflict. As a result, the Security Council has adopted several resolutions highlighting the connection between security and environmental degradation.[4] Also, in 2024 the UN Environment Assembly adopted a resolution addressing environmental protection in conflict situations,[5] building on previous resolutions adopted in 2016 and 2017 respectively.[6] Furthermore, in 2020, the International Committee of the Red Cross (ICRC) published revised Guidelines on the Protection of the Environment during Armed Conflict (ICRC Guidelines).[7] At the same time, the ICRC also published a report highlighting the essential steps that the ICRC and the broader humanitarian community should take to mitigate these risks, emphasizing the pressing need to bolster climate action and financial support in regions affected by conflict.[8] Finally, the UN International Law Commission (ILC) has developed a set of Draft Principles to Enhance the Environmental Protection in Relation to Armed Conflicts (PERAC Principles),[9] which the UN General Assembly adopted in December 2022.[10]

Despite the plethora of international legal or quasi-legal instruments, the overall international legal framework addressing environmental protection and climate change in relation to armed conflicts is seldom enforced in situations of protracted armed conflict and often disregarded by parties of armed conflicts. Against this backdrop, the chapter argues that during protracted armed conflicts, multilateral environmental agreements (MEAs) may guide environmental interventions carried out in protracted armed conflict as they offer mechanisms that can carry out implementation work in fragile states. MEAs rely heavily on other actors than the state party in their implementation, including international organizations, non-governmental organizations (NGOs), other state parties, local communities, local authorities, and even organized armed groups (OAGs). While MEAs are often regarded as toothless instruments in armed conflicts,[11] they may become prominent depending on the actors

[4] In April 2007, the Security Council held its first meeting studying the linkages between climate change and security. In 2011, the Security Council issued a statement that highlighted possible security implications of consequences of climate change acknowledging that the climate change and security are connected.

[5] UN Environmental Assembly (6th session), Draft Resolution on Environmental Assistance and Recovery in Areas Affected by Armed Conflict (29 February 2024) UN Doc UNEP/EA.6/L.15

[6] UN Environment Assembly (2nd session), Resolution 2/15 on Protection of the Environment in Areas Affected by Armed Conflict (4 August 2016) UN Doc UNEP/EA.2/Res.15; UN Environment Assembly, Resolution 3/1 on Pollution Mitigation and Control in Areas Affected by Armed Conflict or Terrorism (30 January 2018) UN Doc UNEP/EA.3/Res.1.

[7] These guidelines revised the 1994 guidelines and will replace them for military manuals and instructions on the protection of the environment in times of armed conflict, UN Doc A/49/323, 49.

[8] ICRC, 'When Rain Turns to Dust' (n 3).

[9] ILC, Draft Principles on Protection of the Environment in Relation to Armed Conflicts: Texts and Titles of the Draft Preamble and the Draft Principles adopted by the Drafting Committee on Second Reading (20 May 2022) UN Doc A/CN.4/L.968.

[10] UNGA Res 77/104 (7 December 2022) UN Doc A/RES/77/104.

[11] For instance Michael Bothe and others, 'International Law Protecting the Environment During Armed Conflict: Gaps and Opportunities' (2010) 92 International Review of the Red Cross 569.

implementing them and their mode of operation.[12] Yet, MEAs, like most legal frameworks, are unable to address the underlying structural issues in conflict situations. The issues of illegal informal economies, along with frequently corrupt political authorities engaging in layers of governance structures and unofficial decision-making, contribute to the violence that exacerbates environmental degradation, poverty, and further unrest. Thus, the dynamics of protracted armed conflicts are difficult to address by solely legal means.

Section B of the chapter explores the environmental issues that occur in the context of protracted armed conflicts and how these affect the conflicts. Section C studies how the applicable international law may contribute to hamper the adverse effects of climate change and prevent further environmental degradation in the context of protracted armed conflicts. To this end, the chapter studies the application of the PERAC Principles to international humanitarian law (IHL) mainly by looking at the ICRC Guidelines, and to international environmental law primarily in the form of MEAs. Section D of the chapter studies environmental interventions in protracted armed conflicts to address environmental degradation and climate change. Finally, the chapter provides a conclusion.

B. Linking Protracted Armed Conflict, Climate Change, and Environmental Degradation

The term 'protracted armed conflict' lacks a clear legal as well as conceptual definition.[13] In this chapter the term is used to describe a particular condition of 'endless wars'.[14] A common characteristic of protracted armed conflict is that the state has limited control or ability to govern certain parts of its territory. In regard to environmental protection, it may result in illegal exploitation of natural resources, halted conservation work, increased number of displacement camps, often informal, lacking basic services for displaced persons which causes pressure on the local environment, and so on. In these situations, the population and the state are often dependent on international interventions.[15] Similarly, environmental protection relies frequently on external actors to protect national parks and endangered animal species and conduct conservation as well as environmental recovery projects, as for instance in the Virunga National Park in the Democratic Republic of Congo (the DRC).[16]

[12] The role of MEAs in gaining in recognition in the area of armed conflict. Britta Sjöstedt, *The Role of Multilateral Environmental Agreements: A Reconciliatory Approach to Environmental Protection in Armed Conflict* (Hart Publishing 2021); Helen Obregón Gieseken and Vanessa Murphy, 'The Protection of the Natural Environment under International Humanitarian Law: The ICRC's 2020 Guidelines' (2023) 105 International Review of the Red Cross 1180.

[13] See Ch. 1.

[14] In this regard the term 'protracted armed conflict' is similar to the term 'post-conflict', a situation of prolonged hostilities with periods of calmness.

[15] See Ch. 1 Section B.1.

[16] Britta Sjöstedt, 'The Role of Multilateral Environmental Agreements in Armed Conflict: "Green-keeping" in Virunga Park. Applying the UNESCO World Heritage Convention in the Armed Conflict of the Democratic Republic of the Congo' (2013) 82 Nordic Journal of International Law 129.

The relation between protracted armed conflict, climate change, and environmental degradation is complex and will be dealt with in three categories in this section. First, climate change and environmental degradation are partly *drivers* of protracted armed conflict; second, the *consequences* of the warfare and knock-on effects, that is, the collapsed institutional infrastructure, worsen impacts of climate change and environmental degradation; third, the conflicts affect the *ability* to mitigate and adapt to climate change and prevent further environmental degradation. These three categories influence each other negatively, which accelerates the problems, making it difficult to break the destructive patterns of environmental degradation and protracted conflict. Nevertheless, there are some examples when protracted armed conflicts may have certain positive outcomes for the *environment* by blocking large infrastructure or exploitation projects such as building roads or building mines and preventing people from visiting forests and hunting animals, and so on.[17] However, this chapter focuses on the negative environmental impacts of armed conflict.

1. Drivers

According to the ICRC, states experiencing conflicts are excessively affected by climate change.[18] Nevertheless, it is crucial to emphasize that conflicts and instability are not directly caused by climate change and environmental degradation alone.[19] Instead, it is the interplay between the impacts of climate change and socio-economic challenges in regions marked by inadequate governance, social unrest, and political instability that gives rise to these issues. The resource scarcity can create competition and tensions between different groups. It can result in human displacement, as people are forced to move due to drought, flooding, or other climate-related disasters, which can further strain resources and exacerbate existing tensions between the displaced persons and the local population fighting over the same resources.[20] For this reason, the Security Council has described climate change and environmental degradation as a 'threat-multiplier'.[21] In a resolution adopted in 2017 addressing the Lake Chad basin, the Security Council recognized 'the adverse effects of climate change and ecological changes among other factors on the stability of the Region, including through water scarcity, drought, desertification, land degradation, and food insecurity'.[22]

[17] The conflict may block certain commercial activities and discourage people from staying in certain areas. Hence, for security reasons, protracted armed conflicts can prevent these areas to be exploited, which means that the nature can flourish in peace.

[18] ICRC, 'When Rain Turns to Dust' (n 3).

[19] Nils Petter Gleditsch, 'Armed Conflict and the Environment: A Critique of the Literature' (1998) 35 Journal of Peace Research 381.

[20] ICRC, 'When Rain Turns to Dust' (n 3).

[21] UN News, 'Climate Change Recognized as 'Threat Multiplier', UN Security Council debates its impact on peace' <https://www.un.org/peacebuilding/news/climate-change-recognized-'threat-multiplier'-un-security-council-debates-its-impact-peace> accessed 10 January 2025.

[22] UNSC Res 2349 (31 March 2017) UN Doc S/RES/2349 para 26.

2. Consequences

Protracted armed conflicts cause environmental degradation mainly in two ways. First, the warfare leads to environmental damage, either by parties directly targeting the environment or as collateral damage when attacking other (military) targets. Attacks targeting the environment directly may involve damaging farmlands to disrupt the food supply, destroying forests to eliminate potential hiding places for the enemy, or targeting dikes and dams to cause flooding and hinder the enemy's movement. They could also be attacks deliberately harming the specific environment crucial for a group's livelihood or natural resources it relies upon, impacting the group's ability to survive. When these acts are carried out with the intent to destroy a national, ethnic, racial, or religious group (in whole or in part), it can be classified as ethnic cleansing or even genocide.[23] In armed conflicts, the environment is typically impacted indirectly as collateral damage from hostilities, for instance by attacking military targets such as energy facilities or industry complexes, leading to toxic leaks polluting the land, air, and water. A single attack can lead to devastating and long-lasting environmental impacts, as noted in the attack on the Kakhovka Dam in Ukraine, leading to devastating flooding that kills not only people but also animals, and damages farmland, infrastructure, and nature.[24]

Second, particularly prevalent in protracted armed conflicts, environmental damage ensues from the disruption of established governmental structures and functions, leading to adverse impacts on the environment in various ways. The collapsed infrastructure can result in failure to handle basic services such as sewage, sanitation, and waste as well as inability to carry out restoration or conservation work.[25] These issues are problematic both from a public health and an environmental perspective. Because of the institutional collapse and lack of infrastructure, war-torn societies are ill-equipped to handle the flow of the large number of displaced persons, who often flee due to the hostilities but also leave for environmental reasons, as mentioned above. They often settle in temporary, informal camps, which become permanent over the years due to the protracted conflicts. The displaced population often relies on humanitarian agencies to provide for their basic needs, which they are often unable to fully meet.[26] The lack of assistance in combination with the fact that the camps

[23] Article II(c) in the Convention on the Prevention and Punishment of the Crime of Genocide (adopted 9 December 1948, entered into force 12 January 1951) 78 UNTS 277 (Genocide Convention). Also ethnic cleansing as part of crimes against humanity in Article 7(1)(h) in the Rome Statute of the International Criminal Court (adopted 17 July 1998, entered into force 1 July 2002), 2187 UNTS 90 (1998 Rome Statute). These types of acts have taken place in protracted armed conflicts such as those in Iraq and Sudan, during which certain habitats were attacked, making these areas unlivable in order to drive groups away, for instance in Darfur or in the Mesopotamian marshlands.

[24] Britta Sjöstedt and Karen Hulme, 'Re-evaluating International Humanitarian Law in a Triple Planetary Crisis: New Challenges, New Tools' (2023) 924 International Review of the Red Cross 1238.

[25] Hassan Partow, 'Environmental Impact of Wars and Conflicts' (Future Arab Environmental Challenges" Arab Forum for Development Report, Lebanon, 2008) 167; UNEP, 'From Conflict to Peacebuilding' (n 2) 17.

[26] This was evident in the DRC, when the UN High Commissioner for Refugees (UNCHR) allowed the displaced persons fleeing the Rwandan genocide to cut firewood inside the Virunga National Park, also listed as a world heritage site. At its peak, the site of Virunga National Park lost around 90 hectares of forest per day. The cutting of the firewood imperilled the unique ecosystem and threatened the endangered mountain gorillas in the park. These problems remain in the eastern DRC, even after more than two

become permanent results in very negative impacts on the surrounding environment, which is often polluted and deforested by the displaced population, and may cause tensions with the local communities.[27]

The lack of state control and of functioning state organs creates a milieu of corruption of public officials that weakens the legal system and more importantly the trust in it, feeding informal economies. In some cases, the result is that exploitation of natural resources is widespread and tolerated, supported, or even directly carried out by state officials.[28] The exploitation of natural resources contributes to financing the hostilities; thus the uncontrolled exploitation will in turn add fuel to sustain the conflict. This has been noted in several protracted armed conflicts taking place in Angola, Sierra Leone, Sudan, Liberia, the DRC, the Central African Republic, and elsewhere. The uncontrolled exploitation of natural resources has considerable environmental impacts, including deforestation and pollution, often taking place in sensitive ecological areas.[29] Overall, the governance collapse becomes a fertile ground for new layers of informal governance that develop along with the duration of the conflict in certain regions, including the emergence of 'rebel governance'.[30] These informal parallel systems become a 'new normal' and disrupt normal societal functions.[31]

3. Ability

The lack of a healthy governance structure in protracted conflicts hinders the ability to mitigate and adapt to climate change and prevent further environmental degradation. This is because political, economic, and social stability are crucial factors to carry out necessary measures.[32] Aside from the lack of ability of the war-torn states, they are perceived as fragile and unsafe, which affects their chances of being considered as stable or credible partners for loans, investments, cooperation, or trade. These states tend to be seen as overly risky by international investors/institutions and have a poor credit rating, making it difficult, if not impossible, for them to access funding from external sources. Thus, investment in mitigation and adaptation measures, including building irrigation systems, dams, energy plants, and walls to prevent flooding; investing in early warning systems; improving access to clean water; promoting sustainable land use; and supporting disaster risk reduction efforts will be put on hold. This means that crucial resilience-building investments that would have been able to mitigate the

decades. Informal camps have been established around, as well as inside, the world heritage sites, and the huge number of displaced persons, the presence of armed groups, the low production in agriculture, and the interrupted activities of conservationists have all led to an increase in wildlife poaching.

[27] For instance, IOM, Deforestation in Sudan (2021) <https://environmentalmigration.iom.int/sites/g/files/tmzbdl1411/files/documents/deforestation-report-in-s.-sudan-2021.pdf> accessed 2 October 2024.

[28] UNEP, 'From Conflict to Peacebuilding' (n 2).

[29] Daniëlla Dam-de Jong., 'International Law and Resource Plunder: The Protection of Natural Resources During Armed Conflict' (2008) 19 Yearbook of International Environmental Law 27.

[30] Ana Arjona, Nelson Kasfir, and Zachariah Mampilly (eds), *Rebel Governance in Civil War* (CUP 2015).

[31] ibid.

[32] Malin Mobjörk and others, Climate-Related Security Risks: Towards an Integrated Approach' [2016] Stockholm International Peace Institute.

impacts of climate change from a long-term perspective to ensure stability are not taking place,[33] which may deepen and intensify the existing problems related to climate change and environmental degradation. As a result of protracted conflict and its repercussions on governance, affected states are less prepared to deal with the adverse side effects of climate change and environmental degradation and unable to invest in techniques to mitigate and adapt to climate change. Hence, the difficulties within the war-torn states in seeking to adapt and improve the environmental situation also bring in a notable 'external' dynamic lying outside the war-torn states' control that adds to the problems.[34]

C. The International Legal Framework

Protracted armed conflict triggers the application of several international legal frameworks, as pointed out in Chapter 1.[35] The PERAC Principles bring together rules and recommendations from different international legal fields trying to remedy the patchy and often inadequate international law protecting the environment in relation to armed conflict. This is noted for instance in PERAC Principles 19–21, applicable in situations of occupation, which include obligations of international environmental law in addition to the IHL.[36] While IHL, mainly directed at the warring parties, has the ability to limit the adverse effects of warfare on the environment and infrastructure, it is limited in its support to states to deal with environmental degradation and climate change impacts. On the contrary, international environmental law has little ability to affect the warfare but may instead be able to provide support to states, mainly aiming at preventing environmental damage. However, both these international legal fields have a poor record in terms of compliance by states.

1. IHL

IHL applies in the case of armed conflict and distinguishes between international and non-international conflict. The majority of protracted armed conflicts are of non-international character.[37] IHL has been criticized for not fully embracing the development of environmental protection law, reflecting the existing awareness and concerns for environmental issues.[38] Nevertheless, two recent initiatives have attempted to enhance the environmental protection in armed conflict, namely the ICRC Guidelines from 2020 and the PERAC Principles from 2022. The two instruments have

[33] ICRC, 'When Rain Turns to Dust' (n 3).

[34] Jeroen de Zeeuw, 'Building Peace in War-Torn Societies: From Concept to Strategy' [2001] The Clingendael Institute.

[35] See Ch. 1.

[36] For example, Principle 20 states that the occupation power shall comply with the obligation of sustainable use in the occupied territories, being an update of the usufruct rules in the Haag Regulations in the light of international environmental obligations.

[37] ICRC, 'Increasing Respect for International Humanitarian Law in Non-International Armed Conflicts' 2008.

[38] Sjöstedt and Hulme, 'Re-evaluating International Humanitarian Law' (n 23).

overlapping scope, but the twenty-eight PERAC Principles go beyond IHL and elaborate on an international legal framework that safeguards more broadly the environment in the context of armed conflicts before, during, and after armed conflict.[39] Thus, the PERAC Principles apply throughout the conflict cycle, taking into account the indeterminable protracted conflicts without separating those of international and non-international character. Several of the PERAC Principles refer to 'parties to an armed conflict', which refers to state armies as well as OAGs.[40] While the ICRC Guidelines provide detailed guidance on how the IHL rules protect the environment in warfare, the PERAC Principles seek to address *all types* of environmental damage occurring in relation to armed conflict, including the type of damage that is not a result of the hostilities but involves adverse knock-on environmental effects. Several rules set out in the ICRC Guidelines are to some degree mirrored in the work of the ILC.[41] The replication of certain rules and principles in the two instruments is a strong indication that they represent customary international law, although the wording of them implies whether they are intended to be binding or merely recommendations. In particular, being a product of the authoritative ILC, the PERAC Principles, apart from adding weight to IHL rules to reflect international customary law, underscore the importance of other applicable legal fields to protect the environment in relation to armed conflict. Consequently, the two instruments complement and re-enforce each other in protecting the environment in times of armed conflict.[42]

The ICRC Guidelines build on and develop the previous ICRC Environmental Guidelines adopted in 1994. The updated Guidelines consist of thirty-two rules and recommendations intended to clarify the existing IHL rules with a view to protect the environment. Apart from being incorporated into military manuals and national legal frameworks, the ICRC Guidelines seek to be of use for non-state actors such as OAGs and other actors that are in a position to influence parties to a conflict.[43] The Guidelines contain *inter alia* rules providing direct environmental protection set out in articles 35(3) and 55 in the Additional Protocol I. The direct protection is absolute and applies if an attack is intended or might be expected to cause widespread, long-term, *and* severe environmental damage. The application of direct environmental protection requires an extremely high threshold. As both the ICRC Guidelines and the PERAC Principles have incorporated these provisions, it indicates that they reflect customary international law, at least in international armed conflicts. Additional Protocol I only applies in international armed conflict and Additional Protocol II, applicable to non-international conflict, does not contain any corresponding rules on environmental protection. Yet, the 2005 Customary Law Study undertaken by the ICRC takes the position that articles 35(3) and 55 in Additional Protocol I may

[39] ILC, 'Report of the International Law Commission on the Work of Its Seventy-Third Session' (15 September 2022) UN Doc A/77/10 Chap. V.

[40] ibid.

[41] PERAC Principles 12–18 apply during armed conflict and consist largely of IHL rules also included in the 2020 Guidelines.

[42] Obregón Gieseken and Murphy (n 12) 1186.

[43] ICRC, 'Guidelines on the Protection of the Natural Environment in Armed Conflict: Rules and Recommendations Relating to the Protection of the Natural Environment under International Humanitarian Law, with Commentary' (2020) para 11.

arguably apply in non-international armed conflict.[44] However, little state practice is provided to support this position and several states have opposed it.[45] In addition, and more importantly, most of the environmental consequences of protracted armed conflicts are not the result of an attack intended or expected to cause damage that reaches the threshold of widespread, long-term, and severe, and thus they fall outside of its scope.

The ICRC Guidelines contain a prohibition on using destruction of the environment as a weapon, which was incorporated into the ICRC Customary Law Study as well.[46] This prohibition may be of relevance in protracted armed conflicts when attacking the environment for the purpose of making places inhabitable and thereby attacking the population and forcing them to move. Furthermore, the ICRC Guidelines include specific prohibitions or restrictions on the use of methods and means of warfare having adverse impacts on the environment, such as use of poison, herbicides, weapons of mass destruction, landmines, starvation of civilians, and unexploded remnants.[47] While the use of poison, herbicides, incendiary weapons, and weapons of mass destruction is limited in protracted armed conflicts, the presence of landmines and unexploded remnants is a widespread problem. Apart from personal injuries and deaths, they cause damage to wildlife and contaminate agricultural land, soil, and water systems. The existence of mines and unexploded remnants can force the local population to abandon areas, which causes displacement and puts pressure on other parts of the environment that may prove unsustainable.[48]

In the context of protracted armed conflict, the general IHL rules of protection are perhaps of most relevance to limit environmental damage from warfare. The ICRC Guidelines affirm that the general rules are applicable as long as the environment or parts of it does not contribute to the war efforts, and thus constitutes a civilian object.[49] The PERAC Principles also state that the general IHL rules of protection apply to protect the environment when not considered a military objective.[50] The ICRC Guidelines contain detailed support on how to apply the general rules of protection under IHL with regard to the environment. For instance, Rule 9 in the ICRC Guidelines on passive precautions prescribes that parties to a conflict must take all feasible precautions to protect civilian objects under their control against effects of attacks.[51] The commentary states that this rule requires that OAGs controlling parts of a territory take precautions to protect areas of major ecological importance or of particular fragility. Such areas include ground water aquifers, national parks, and habitats of endangered species. The warring parties should take precautions such as informing opposing parties of the existence and location of ongoing conservation efforts. Furthermore, such precaution could involve refraining from having troops or

44 Rules 43–45; Jean-Marie Henckaerts and Louise Doswald-Beck (eds), *Customary International Humanitarian Law Study* (CUP 2005) Volume I, 143 f.

45 For instance Elisabeth Wilmshurst and Susan Breau (eds), *Perspectives on the ICRC Study on Customary International Humanitarian Law* (CUP 2007).

46 Rules 1–4 in the ICRC Guidelines.

47 Rules 19–22 in the ICRC Guidelines.

48 ICRC Guidelines, paras 265–266.

49 Rules 5–18 in the ICRC Guidelines.

50 PERAC Principle 4, 13(3), and 14.

51 Rule 9 in the ICRC Guidelines is a restatement of articles 57–58 in the API.

military material in these areas. This would then prohibit use of inaccessible nature reserves, which are frequently used in many protracted armed conflicts as hiding places for OAGs and for exploitation of natural resources and wildlife poaching.[52] The PERAC Principles make reference to the principle on precautions.[53] Principles 4 and 18 specifically endorse parties to armed conflict to designate areas of major ecological or cultural importance as protected zones. The principles highlight the possibility to protect areas of major ecological importance or of particular fragility, and enable a special regime for safeguarding protected zones.[54]

Rule 10 of the ICRC Guidelines prohibits attacks or other methods of denying objects indispensable to the survival of the civilian population.[55] As mentioned above, protracted conflicts in environmentally vulnerable areas have a considerably higher risk of damaging access to clean water, food stocks, arable agricultural land, and livestock. Rule 10 covers acts such as poisoning water wells, flooding, or burning agricultural land. Rule 10 provides indirect environmental protection as it protects certain man-made elements, such as irrigation installations, attacks on which may have negative impacts on the surrounding environment. Attacks on these objects can also result in large-scale population displacement, which may have negative impacts as described above. Rule 10 is silent on whether the acts have to be committed with a specific intent to deny the civilians the objects. This is, however, a requirement in Article 54 in the Additional Protocol I, which Rule 10 is re-stating, which also represents customary international law. Most military manuals do not require intent, which is also pointed out in the Commentary to Rule 10.[56] Removing the special intent expands the scope of the rule and provides more substantial protection. However, such interpretation is unlikely to represent the common understanding of this prohibition.

Related to exploitation of natural resources and poaching—which is a frequent issue in protracted armed conflict, as explained in section B.2—both the ICRC Guidelines[57] and the PERAC Principles[58] specifically state that pillage of property constituting part of the natural environment is prohibited.[59] Both instruments reaffirm the 2005 ruling of the International Court of Justice (ICJ) on Armed Activities on the Territory of the Congo, in which the Court held that the prohibition on pillage extends to looting, plundering, and illegal exploitation of natural resources by members of the Ugandan armed forces on the territory of the DRC.[60] The prohibition of pillage covers both organized pillage that is authorized or ordered by a party to a conflict and individual acts of pillage, whether they are committed by civilians or military personnel.[61] Accordingly, the prohibition provides direct and indirect protection of

[52] ICRC Guidelines, paras 144–145.

[53] PERAC Principle 14.

[54] ILC commentary (n 39).

[55] Rule 10 ICRC Guidelines restates articles 54 AP I and 14 AP II.

[56] Paras 153, 66–67. For further details on the protection of objects indispensable to the survival of the civilian population, see Ch. 7.

[57] Rule 14 ICRC Guidelines.

[58] PERAC Principle 16.

[59] Restated articles 28 and 47 in the Haag Regulations, Article 33(2) Fourth Geneva Convention and Article 4(2)(g) AP II.

[60] *Armed Activities on the Territory of the Congo (Democratic Republic of the Congo v Uganda)* (2005) ICJ (Judgment) ICJ Rep 116.

[61] Commentary to ICRC Guidelines, para. 183, 76.

the environment, since the exploitation causes damage to the surrounding nature.[62] Furthermore, the ICRC Guidelines provide rules on implementation and dissemination. In the context of protracted armed conflicts, 'better respect for IHL can limit the impact of armed conflict on the natural environment and the deeply interlinked consequences for conflict-affected populations who depend on it', as stated by the ICRC.[63] However, while this statement is correct, IHL is seldom respected in protracted armed conflicts. In fragile states, the lack of enforcement undermines the deterrent effect of punishment for IHL violations.

2. International Environmental Law

International environmental law addresses various issues to hamper the adverse effects on the environment and the climate. Sustainable development is often central in environmental interventions, as discussed in section D, and represents a cornerstone in most modern international environmental law. The MEAs are the main vehicles to implement international environmental law. Most commentators would argue that MEAs remain applicable in times of armed conflict, unless the treaty states otherwise.[64] This is supported by the previous work of the ILC in regard to the topic Effects of Armed Conflict on Treaties in which the continued application of environmental treaties was presumed.[65] Still, a lot of uncertainty remains in regard to *how* the MEAs apply. In a few cases, the treaty bodies of the MEAs have adopted resolutions, plans, and strategies that acknowledge that armed conflicts have implications in relation to the treaties' implementation. Still, the treaty bodies provide scarce guidance on how to apply the instruments in relation to armed conflict.[66]

In the case of a conflict of rules, IHL would have priority as the *lex specialis* over the MEAs.[67] However, MEAs seldom cause conflicts as they often have open-ended

[62] ibid para. 186, 77.

[63] ICRC website, <https://www.icrc.org/en/publication/4382-guidelines-protection-natural-environment-armed-conflict> accessed 13 January 2025.

[64] For instance, Silja Vöneky, 'Armed Conflict, Effect on Treaties' (1 January 2012). Available at SSRN: <https://ssrn.com/abstract=3369609> or <http://dx.doi.org/10.2139/ssrn.3369609>; Britta Sjöstedt, *The Role of Multilateral Environmental Agreements* (n 12); Bothe and others (n 11).

[65] Criticism with respect to the lack of guidance provided by the ILC on the applicability of international environmental treaty obligations in situations of armed conflict is reflected in the statements of various state delegations in the Sixth Committee and by UN Environment. Eg, Italy, UN GAOR, 74th Sess., 28th meeting, 24, UN Doc A/C.6/74/SR.28 (29 Nov 2019).

[66] The most prominent example is perhaps the pilot project under the World Heritage Convention protecting the five World Heritage Sites in the DRC conflict. For a detailed elaboration, Britta Sjöstedt, 'The Role of Multilateral Environmental Agreements' (n 16). Also Decision 42 COM 7 by the World Heritage Committee, <https://whc.unesco.org/en/decisions/7112/>. Furthermore, the COP of Biological Diversity Convention has launched the Peace and Biodiversity Dialogue Initiative promoting transboundary conservation to prevent conflicts <https://www.cbd.int/peace/about/objectives> The CBD has also adopted a few decisions related to conflict over natural resources in conservation: Decision XI/2, para 27; Decision V/23, Activity 8 (c). The COP of the Ramsar Convention has also acknowledged armed conflict in a few of its decisions: Draft Resolution 18.19, para 13 adopted by 13th Meeting of the Conference of the Contracting Parties to the Ramsar Convention on Wetlands (2018); Resolution XII/6, para. 10 adopted by 12th Meeting of the Conference of the Parties to the Convention on Wetlands (2015); Resolution VIII/31, para 5 adopted by 8th Meeting of the Conference of the Contracting Parties to the Convention on Wetlands (2002).

[67] *Legality of the Threat or Use of Nuclear Weapons* (Advisory Opinion) 1996 ICJ Rep 96, 226.

drafted provisions enabling context-based solutions. They set out general objectives and provide guidance on how to achieve them. They are, in general, preventative and/or precautionary-orientated and, at least in MEAs adopted after the 1992 Rio Declaration, built around the concept of sustainable development. This concept goes beyond nature conservation and deals with broader questions of socio-economic issues and the uneven relation between developed and developing states. For example, the so-called Rio Conventions—the Convention on Biological Diversity (CBD),[68] the UN Framework Convention on Climate Change (UNFCCC),[69] and the Convention to Combat Desertification (UNCCD)[70]—contain cross-sectorial priorities for sustainable development. The conventions emphasize sustainable use of natural resources, poverty reduction, and strengthening equality and social justice as a part of protecting the environment. The priorities are materialized in the Conventions by including provisions opting for integration of the environment and development, civil society participation, and that developed states shall provide assistance to developing states. For instance, in Article 2 the UNFCCC sets out that reaching a level of concentration of greenhouse gas emissions in the atmosphere 'should be achieved within a time-frame sufficient to allow ecosystems to adapt naturally to climate change, to ensure that food production is not threatened, and to enable economic development to proceed in a sustainable manner'. The broad notion of how to protect the environment is of significance when applied in armed conflicts as it attempts to address also the root causes of the environmental degradation (and possibly also the conflict).

Although they have a limited number of prescriptive rules, MEAs are still able to influence changes in the behaviour of states because of their structure and *modus* of operation. MEAs have a complex legal structure that relies on treaty bodies and other structures for their application. In protracted armed conflicts, the institutional structures that are necessary for implementing international environmental obligations may be non-existent or inadequate. As a result, environmental protection work may be obstructed. However, MEAs have the potential to reinforce weak state institutions and engage other actors in conservation work through their treaty bodies and financial mechanisms. The treaty bodies can adopt binding decisions; provide recommendations and guidance; and initiate projects, programmes, and capacity-building initiatives to enhance compliance with treaty obligations by relying on other state parties and collaborative partners.[71] This structure facilitates cooperation between various actors, such as international organizations, NGOs, and the private sector, in various projects or programmes to respond to environment-related demands set out (at least partly) in the MEAs.[72] The reliance of other actors than states is significant in

[68] Convention on Biological Diversity (adopted 5 June 1992, entered into force 29 December 1993) 1760 UNTS 79.

[69] UN Framework Convention on Climate Change (adopted 9 May 1992, entered into force 21 March 1994) 1771 UNTS 107.

[70] UN Convention to Combat Desertification in Those Countries Experiencing Serious Drought and/or Desertification, Particularly in Africa (adopted 14 October 1994, entered into force 26 December 1996) 1954 UNTS 3.

[71] Geir Ulfstein, 'Treaty Bodies' in Daniel Bodansky, Jutta Brunnée, and Ellen Hey (eds), *Oxford Handbook of International Environmental Law* (OUP 2007).

[72] Louis Kotzé, *Global Environmental Governance: Law and Regulation for the 21st Century* (Edward Elgar 2012) 7.

the context of protracted armed conflict. Although the cooperating actors cannot substitute domestic institutions, they can minimize environmental destruction by providing funding, capacity-building, equipment, data analysis, consultation on national regulation, and coordination of international and local actors outside the state organs involved in protection work. Certain MEAs have established funding systems in order to channel support and capacity-building, even though the financial support under each MEA is limited. For instance, the Global Environment Facility (GEF) is the financial mechanism for several MEAs.[73] The GEF has carried out projects in various conflicts, either in the form of a project carried out by NGOs or by other entities to further the aims of an MEA. Thus, the MEAs are influential to ensure that conservation work is carried out to some extent to respond to climate change and environmental degradation in vulnerable states, due to concerns for not only the environment but also socio-economic issues. However, funding from MEAs may also be affected by the instability in war-torn states.

3. PERAC Principles Relevant for Protracted Armed Conflict

Several of the PERAC Principles address other environmental issues not occurring as a direct result of the hostilities. These include the principles on designation of protected zones, presence of military forces, peace operations, human displacement, due diligence and liability of business enterprises, peace processes, sharing and granting access to information, post-conflict environmental assessment, and remedial measures. In the following, a few of the key principles are analysed.

In protracted conflicts with a large presence of military and humanitarian actors, some of the PERAC principles seek to mitigate environmental impacts of states and international organizations when involved in peace operations. Principle 6 aims at mitigating the impact of military forces, while Principle 7 targets peace operations of any types, also including other actors than military forces. The environmental impacts of these can be substantial. The two principles take into account the practice that is already in place and in that sense, they do not add much in terms of normativity. For instance, the UN Department of Field Support (DFS) has adopted a strategy on environmental protection and management for UN peacekeeping operations. Both principles are formulated in a manner providing a lot of discretion to states and international organizations by adding the wording 'as appropriate' with regard to the measures to mitigate harm to the environment. Thus, the Principles mostly serve as a reminder to consider environmental effects of peace operations or other engagements when military forces are present.

Principle 8 deals with the environmental impacts of displacement of persons, which are often of a significant scale, as explained above. The principle targets states, international organizations, and other actors, including OAGs, to take measures to prevent and mitigate the environmentally adverse effects of displacement.[74] It seeks

[73] For instance the CBD, Ramsar Convention, etc.

[74] The principle builds from art 9 of the African Union Convention for the Protection of Internally Displaced Persons in Africa (adopted 23 October 2009, entered into force 6 December 2012) (Kampala Convention).

to incorporate efforts already being made by aid organizations such as the UN High Commissioner for Refugees (UNHCR) and its Environmental Guidelines to minimize the environmental impacts of displacement camps. The UNHCR Guidelines highlight the need to incorporate environmental elements as early as the planning stage and note the importance of avoiding certain environmentally sensitive areas as locations for the camps, such as internationally recognized protected areas or other sensitive areas.[75] The UNHCR Guidelines include measures to provide the camps with firewood or alternative material, water supply, and food supply and to ensure the design and installation of appropriate sanitation facilities, including waste management, to avoid impacts on the surrounding environment.[76] The UNHCR Guidelines also contain directions for the rehabilitation of the camp sites once the displaced persons are repatriated.[77] However, in protracted armed conflicts, camps are in reality long-term settlements. Such long-term settlements of the camps tend to affect relations with the local population due to the need to compete for resources. The UNHCR Guidelines state that activities related to the camps should ensure consultation with the local population and comply with local laws and regulations concerning the environment. If local laws are not in place, the activities should comply with internationally recognized standards. Activities should, as far as possible, respect the customary rights of local people over the use of or access to land and natural resources,[78] which may assist in easing the tensions between the displaced and the local communities.

In most protracted armed conflicts, as previously mentioned, the exploitation of natural resources contributes to the development of an informal war economy, from which certain business enterprises profit. To hinder such practices, PERAC Principles 10 and 11 address the responsibilities of states to regulate business enterprises and to hold them liable for environmental harm occurring in armed conflict. Principle 10 addresses states' responsibility to adopt appropriate legislation and to take other measures to ensure that business enterprises operating in territories of conflict contexts comply with due diligence requirements with regard to environmental protection. Principle 11 addresses the liability of business enterprises, requiring that 'States should provide adequate and effective procedures and remedies, in particular for the victims of such harm'. Both principles aim to regulate states to control business enterprises in order to block the financial means generating the environmentally destructive practices. There are a number of documented cases where business enterprises have been directly involved with OAGs through negotiations, payments, or providing them with facilities or logistical support in order to exploit natural resources.[79] Although the business enterprises are seldom in direct control of the exploitation, they are part of the system sustaining this practice by providing a monetary flow. The

[75] UNHCR 'Environmental Guidelines' (Geneva 1996), 16

[76] ibid 22.

[77] ibid 18–20.

[78] ibid 10 f.

[79] For instance, the report by Crisis Group on the illicit relations noted between armed groups, local traders, and foreign companies: Thierry Vircoulon, 'Behind the Problem of Conflict Minerals in DR Congo: Governance' (*International Crisis Group*, 19 April 2011) <https://www.crisisgroup.org/africa/central-africa/democratic-republic-congo/behind-problem-conflict-minerals-dr-congo-governance> accessed 28 October 2024.

PERAC principles may not add much to target business enterprises' direct responsibility under international law.[80] But they are part of a greater trend aiming to close the impunity gap for these business enterprises. Together with other initiatives such as the UN Guiding Principles (UNGPs) on Business and Human Rights,[81] they highlight the issue of the need to include environmental protection in human rights law when advocating for greater responsibility of private entities and states' responsibility to prevent such harmful practice, also extra-territorially.[82]

Several PERAC Principles are aimed at restoration efforts. Principle 22 calls on parties to armed conflict as well as international organizations to specially address environmental protection and restoration during a peace process. This principle may be important for protracted armed conflicts as many of these have environmental elements considered crucial for maintaining peace in line with the notion of 'environmental peacebuilding'.[83] Furthermore, Principles 24, 25, and 26 are highly relevant in protracted armed conflicts addressing assessment and restoration of the environment. Principle 24 focuses on the need for relevant actors to cooperate in order to carry out post-armed conflict environmental assessments and remedial measures. Post-conflict environmental assessments are important for rebuilding the environment in war-torn countries and as a vehicle to stop the vicious cycle of environmental destruction and hostilities. The UN Environment Programme has carried out several such assessments, which map out the environmental damages occurring as a consequence to armed conflicts and suggest measures to address them directed mainly at national authorities.[84] The ILC commentary explains that the post-conflict assessments are a way to discover security risks related to the environment that can contribute to destabilizing the society and trigger a conflict outbreak.[85] Principle 24 also aims to foster cooperation in these efforts, but without explaining how to address the environmental risks to ensure peace. As discussed in section B., climate change and environmental degradation in protracted armed conflict spur conflicts and even lead to new ones; therefore environmental assessments may be essential tools to initiate restoration efforts through cooperation when and where it is most needed.

D. Environmental Interventions in Protracted Armed Conflict

Despite the challenges, there are several examples of environmental interventions being carried out in protracted armed conflicts to protect the environment and the

[80] Daniëlla Dam-de Jong and Britta Sjöstedt, 'Enhancing Environmental Protection in Relation to Armed Conflict: An Assessment of the ILC Draft Principles' (2021) 44 Loyola of Los Angeles International and Comparative Law Review 129.

[81] UNCHR 'Human Rights and Transnational Corporations and other Business Enterprises' (16 June 2011) UN Doc A/Res/17/4.

[82] For a more detailed analysis, see for instance Amanda Kron, 'At the Frontlines of Implementing the Right to a Healthy Environment: Understanding Human Rights and Environmental Due Diligence in Relation to Armed Conflicts' (2023) 105 International Review of the Red Cross 1623.

[83] Daniëlla Dam de Jong and Britta Sjöstedt (eds), *Research Handbook on International Law and Environmental Peacebuilding* (Edward Elgar 2023).

[84] UNEP's Website <https://www.unep.org/topics/disasters-and-conflicts> accessed 28 October 2024.

[85] ILC, 'Report on the Work of Its Seventy-Third Session' (n 39) 289.

climate. For instance, the GEF, the financial mechanism of several MEAs, is operating in numerous areas affected by conflicts, often in collaboration with several external and internal actors. In fact, the majority of the GEF's projects are conducted in fragile or conflict-affected areas.[86] The GEF is one of the main contributors of the Great Green Wall (GGW) project initiated and led by the African Union in the Sahel region. The GGW project aims to respond to climate change and environmental degradation, including in the many states in the Sahel region that are experiencing protracted armed conflicts. Apart from combating land degradation, desertification, and drought, the project incorporates strategies to eradicate poverty, fight hunger, build local resilience to climate change, improve public health, create jobs, boost economic opportunities, and stabilize the region and social peace, which are also promoting sustainable development.[87] To this end, the GGW applies the Rio Conventions. In particular, the project is consistent with the objective of the UNCCD[88] and implements Article 4(2)(c) in the UNCCD which requires the parties to integrate strategies for poverty eradication into efforts to combat desertification and mitigate efforts of drought.[89]

A recent assessment of the GEF's work in fragile and conflict-affected states underscored that many of the projects lack strategies to manage conflict-related risks.[90] At the same time, the environmental interventions are both impacting the armed conflicts and being influenced by them. This interaction is demonstrated in three distinct ways.[91] First, environmental interventions can aggravate the conflict by adding to the tensions. For instance, an intervention may be carried out without significant knowledge of the conflict and may appear to take one party's side or restrict access to certain areas. This was the case in a project in Guatemala that planned a hydroelectric dam funded by the UNFCCC's Clean Development Mechanism that threatened the indigenous Mayan communities' access to food, waters, and sacred sites. The disputes over the dam project escalated to violence. The project was later cancelled as it lacked the free prior consent of the indigenous peoples. Conservation work that restricts access for local communities is often a problem that may recall to historic injustices done to the local communities, in particular to indigenous peoples in the name of conservation.[92] Second, conflicts may affect the ability to perform the environmental intervention. Conservation activities can be hindered by not getting access to certain regions and/or communities. For safety reasons, some areas may be too dangerous for the

86 Global Environment Facility Independent Evaluation Office (GEF IEO), GEF Support in Fragile and Conflict-Affected Situations, Evaluation Report No. 151, (2024) <https://www.gefieo.org/sites/default/files/documents/evaluations/fragility-2020.pdf> ix accessed 28 October 2024.

87 Great Green Wall, 'Ambition' <https://www.greatgreenwall.org/2030ambition/> accessed 28 October 2024; also One step, GEF document, Annex A1 <OnestepMSPApprovaldocument_GGWI One Step MSP Document Resubmission_28092020.docx> accessed 12 January 2025 (hereafter GEF Approval Document).

88 GEF Approval Document (n 87).

89 For instance, a session was held to highlight the multiple benefits of investment in soil health beyond acting as carbon sinks, of sustainable landscapes, their simultaneous contribution to the objectives of three UN conventions: UNFCCC, UNCBD and UNCCD, and explore possibilities for effective public-private collaboration, a key for transformative action: Great Green Wall, 'Ambition' (n 87).

90 GEF (n 86) x.

91 ibid 9.

92 ibid.

conservation staff to enter. Conservation staff may be threatened or even murdered; there may be mines or other unexploded remnants in the areas. Third, environmental interventions may help contribute to building peace.[93] This is in line with the notion of environmental peacebuilding. Environmental peacebuilding refers to a multidisciplinary approach that considers 'the integration of natural resource management and environmental protection in conflict resolution and recovery strategies to prevent conflict relapse and to lay the foundations for sustainable peace and development'.[94] By fostering dialogue, resource-sharing, and joint management of natural resources, conservation can contribute to building trust, enhancing stability, and mitigating conflicts in the region.

Frequently in environmental interventions, the reliance on external actors for environmental protection work in a war-torn country may risk creating a 'parallel system' that bypasses or undermines the authority of the state, as well as local leaders. The involvement of external actors in environmental protection work can lead the state to become dependent on foreign aid and financial means to protect the environment and create a perception that the state is not capable of fulfilling its responsibilities. This may further erode public trust in state institutions and exacerbate political instability, and thus exacerbate the dynamic that perpetuates protracted conflict. It can be particularly problematic if the state is weak or non-functional, as external actors may unintentionally undermine the state's legitimacy or sovereignty, but also on a local level the communities may feel excluded from the decision-making regarding their surrounding environment. In addition, external actors may have different priorities or agendas than the state and/or local communities, which can lead to conflicts or misunderstandings. Instead, in protracted armed conflict in which conservation work continues, it should occur with the help of local authorities and/or surrounding communities. Empowering communities to actively participate in the project may foster a sense of ownership, encourage local stewardship, and promote social cohesion.

International law could be key here—in particular the MEAs, to ensure local decision-making, not only to make the decisions legitimate but also to incorporate local and traditional knowledge for understanding of the local environment. By prioritizing inclusive decision-making, local ownership, and transparent mechanisms, these projects can mitigate risks and contribute to sustainable development and peace. To enable this prioritization, MEAs can be of use in providing obligations for the state to include the local communities in the decision-making and provide for context-based environmental protection. In protracted armed conflicts, over time, communities affected by armed conflict may develop resilience and adaptive strategies to cope with environmental challenges without assistance form the government. This can involve innovative approaches to resource management, the emergence of local governance systems, or the adoption of sustainable practices. Understanding these dynamics requires context-specific analysis and tailored approaches.[95] Therefore, how the environment is protected will depend on the conflict itself. The forms of governance must be adapted to the particular socio-ecological context. Each conflict situation

[93] ibid. 21 f.
[94] Dam de Jong and Sjöstedt (n 83).
[95] UNEP, 'From Conflict to Peacebuilding' (n 2) 19.

is unique and influenced by various factors, including the specific geographic location, the nature of the conflict, and the capacity for environmental management and governance.

E. Conclusion

While the rules of IHL are able to limit some of the environmental *consequences* of protracted armed conflicts related to warfare, MEAs may play a more prominent role in terms of preventing climate change and environmental degradation by boosting war-torn states' ability to respond to the adverse impacts. This can help address *drivers* of conflicts related to resource scarcity and competition. By restoring ecosystems and promoting sustainable resource management, the environmental interventions guided by MEAs can increase the *ability* to respond to environmental degradations and climate change in protracted armed conflicts. Yet, these interventions are unable to solve the underlying structural issues in the protracted armed conflicts. These demand political solutions rather than those that can be solved by international law.

10

Terrorism, Counter-Terrorism, and the Humanitarian-Development-Peace Nexus

Ben Saul

A. Introduction

Terrorism and international and national counter-terrorism laws, policies, and practices pose numerous challenges to the humanitarian-development-peace nexus, although the inter-relationships vary widely between countries. First, terrorism can generate humanitarian crises and endanger humanitarians in armed conflict, but excessive counter-terrorism responses can also impede medical and humanitarian activities protected under international humanitarian law (IHL), from Somalia to Gaza. Second, terrorist goals and ideologies can be resistant to peace negotiations, but many insurgencies nonetheless end through negotiated settlements, reintegration, and reconciliation. Excessive counter-terrorism laws and policies can present additional barriers to peacemaking, evident in the conflicts from Sri Lanka to Afghanistan. Counter-terrorism can also pose related challenges for peacekeeping and peacebuilding. In turn, the failure to resolve protracted conflict can itself stimulate terrorist threats.

Third, terrorism can inflict serious economic harm, undermine development, and thus exacerbate conditions conducive to further terrorism. Despite the difficult operating environment, development activities remain necessary in the face of terrorist threats not only to ensure human rights, but to address the conditions conducive to terrorism. This is formally recognized in national and UN policies. However, in practice, repressive law enforcement and military responses to terrorism continue to take priority at the expense of more structural remedies, and terrorist financing and sanctions regimes can disrupt essential development financing. Where development activities do occur, there are often risks of their militarization or securitization, which can undermine principles of good development practice, the local legitimacy and sustainability of development programmes, and the safety of development actors. A recent example is the failure of development and peacebuilding activities in Afghanistan.[1]

[1] UNDP, 'Prevention of Violent Extremism: 2021 Annual Report' (UNDP 2022) 3.

Ben Saul, *Terrorism, Counter-Terrorism, and the Humanitarian-Development-Peace Nexus* In: *From Protracted Conflict to Sustainable Peace?* Edited by: Heike Krieger, Giedre Jokubauskaite, Asli Ozcelik, and Andreas Buser, Oxford University Press. © Ben Saul 2026. DOI: 10.1093/9780198967385.003.0012

B. Interface with Humanitarian Action

1. Impacts of Terrorism on Humanitarian Action

Terrorism, including by organized armed groups that are legally designated as terrorist organizations, can generate humanitarian crises in armed conflicts. Terrorist groups may deliberately target civilian populations for political, sectarian, or instrumental reasons, resulting in personal injury and disabilities, disruption of livelihoods, denial of basic needs and services, forced displacement, and separation of families. In addition to war crimes, such groups may commit crimes against humanity and even genocide (as in the case of ISIL attacks on the Yezidi minority in Iraq).[2]

Further, having generated humanitarian crises, terrorist groups may seriously impede impartial humanitarian action to assist civilians in need. They may deliberately attack humanitarian, medical, or peacekeeping personnel or objects (such as relief convoys or hospitals). They may refuse or impose arbitrary restrictions on access to vulnerable populations or 'tax' or divert aid. They may be suspicious of the motives or allegiance of NGOs or UN entities.

While some terrorist ideologies enable violence against civilians and humanitarian crises, it is important to maintain perspective. In the absence of an international definition of terrorism, abusive national designations of armed groups as 'terrorist' may be designed to delegitimize them but may not accurately reflect their true nature. Many national laws deem any non-state violence against the state as terrorism, thus proscribing and criminalizing all insurgent groups, even if they generally respect IHL and spare civilians. Some 'terrorist' groups in control of territory may indeed facilitate unimpeded humanitarian relief and, as de facto governmental authorities, provide security and other public goods to gain support of civilians, especially where populations have been victims of state repression.

Further, state violence, including that to counter terrorism, may stimulate greater humanitarian crises than terrorist violence. States have greater capacities and resources to wage war than terrorist groups and may systematically commit violations of IHL—including terror tactics—and/or international human rights law. They may also punish populations suspected of sympathizing with terrorist groups, including by denying, restricting, or diverting humanitarian relief on a partisan basis.

2. Counter-terrorism Law Impacts on Humanitarian Action

National counter-terrorism laws proliferated globally after the terrorist attacks of 11 September 2001. Security Council Resolution 1373 (2001) requires all states to criminalize the financing, planning, preparation, or perpetration of, or support for, 'terrorist acts'. Due to legal and political disagreements, the Council did not define 'terrorist acts' or the scope of the various preparatory acts states must criminalize, but left these matters to national implementation. Many states have enacted expansive

[2] United Nations Investigative Team to Promote Accountability for Crimes Committed by Da'esh/Islamic State in Iraq and the Levant (UNITAD), 'Sixth Report' (3 May 2021) UN Doc S/2021/419.

offences relating to terrorist acts or terrorist organizations, including preparatory offences such as financing, training, support, or association.

The resolution also did not specify the relationship of terrorist crimes to IHL governing armed conflict. In contrast, six international counter-terrorism conventions, starting with the Terrorist Bombings Convention 1997, exclude the activities of armed forces in armed conflict, governed by IHL, from their scope. 'Armed forces' under IHL include non-state organized armed groups in non-international armed conflicts.[3] As such, these treaties distinguish insurgency from terrorism, leaving the regulation of armed conflict exclusively to IHL and other applicable legal regimes (including international criminal law and international human rights law).

The Council largely side-stepped these issues, leaving them to national discretion. Yet, the Council has listed certain entities, such as Al Qaeda, the Taliban, and ISIL, for arms, travel, and financial sanctions purposes. While such listings are not 'terrorist' designations as such, Council resolutions descriptively refer to these groups in a counter-terrorism context. The Council has thus signalled that such groups are not excluded from being 'terrorist' simply because they are armed groups in NIACs.

Various national counter-terrorism laws have adversely affected protected humanitarian and medical activities under IHL in numerous ways. Humanitarian action, including aid, assistance, relief, and protection, is essential to protect life, basic needs, and human rights, from food and medical care to humane treatment in detention. Under IHL, all parties to a conflict must allow and facilitate the rapid and unimpeded passage of impartial humanitarian relief for civilians in need,[4] subject to reasonable measures of control. The wounded and sick must also receive the necessary medical care,[5] and medical personnel, units, and activities are protected.[6] IHL does not prohibit humanitarian negotiations with armed groups, whether to enable medical or food relief or to facilitate the release of prisoners.[7] States may not override these obligations in countering terrorism.

Many humanitarian actors have expressed concern at the impact of counter-terrorism laws on their protected activities under IHL, including preparatory and group-based terrorism offences, financial sanctions, and the intrusive regulation of non-profit organizations. First, overbroad laws conflict with IHL where they prohibit

[3] Ben Saul, 'From Conflict to Complementarity: Reconciling International Counter-Terrorism Law and International Humanitarian Law' (2021) 103 International Review of the Red Cross (IRRC) 157.

[4] Jean-Marie Henckaerts and Louise Doswald-Beck (eds), *Customary International Humanitarian Law*, vol 1 (CUP 2005), Rule 55 (hereafter ICRC Customary IHL Study); Geneva Convention IV relative to the Protection of Civilian Persons in Time of War (adopted 12 August 1949, entered into force 21 October 1959) 75 UNTS 287 (Geneva Convention IV) art 23; Protocol Additional to the Geneva Conventions of 12 August 1949 relating to the Protection of Victims of International Armed Conflicts (adopted 8 June 1977, entered into force 7 December 1978) 1125 UNTS 3 (Protocol I) art 70(2); Protocol Additional to the Geneva Conventions of 12 August 1949, and relating to the Protection of Victims of Non-International Armed Conflicts (adopted 8 June 1977, entered into force December 1978) 1125 UNTS 609 (Protocol II) art 18; Rome Statute of the International Criminal Court (adopted 17 July 1998, entered into force 1 July 2002) 2187 UNTS 90 (Rome Statute) art 8(2)(b)(xxv).

[5] ICRC Customary IHL Study, Rule 110.

[6] ICRC Customary IHL Study, Rules 25–30.

[7] UNGA, 'Report of the Special Rapporteur on the Promotion and Protection of Human Rights and Fundamental Freedoms while Countering Terrorism, Fionnuala Ní Aoláin, Impact of Counter-terrorism on Peacemaking, Peacebuilding, Sustaining Peace, Conflict Prevention and Resolution' (16 September 2022) UN Doc A/77/345 para 29.

or criminalize the provision of medical or humanitarian assistance to any person entitled to it, whether terrorist fighters *hors de combat* (including those wounded or detained), civilian members or sympathizers of terrorist organizations, or 'suspect' populations living in areas under the control of a terrorist group.[8]

Second, some national laws and policies have restricted or prohibited certain forms of engagement with 'terrorist' groups.[9] Humanitarian actors need to cooperate with all parties to a conflict, including 'terrorist' groups, to effectively undertake their impartial activities. Counter-terrorism laws normally do not prohibit mere contact with non-state actors.[10] Some purely humanitarian dealings with terrorist groups have nonetheless been prohibited or criminalized. For example, some national terrorist financing laws and UN and national sanctions regimes prohibit giving any funds to persons or entities involved in terrorist acts,[11] which could include incidental payments to armed groups to facilitate the passage of humanitarian relief. National laws countering the travel of 'foreign terrorist fighters' also pose a risk of criminalizing the mere entry or presence of any person in a 'declared area' unless humanitarian exceptions exist and are properly applied.[12]

Further, it is an offence under United States law to provide 'material support or resources to a foreign terrorist organization',[13] which is defined to include any training, advice, finance, or other assistance to a group. The US Supreme Court strictly interpreted this law to prohibit the training of armed groups on IHL, peaceful dispute settlement under international law, and petitioning the UN.[14] Any support was thought to indirectly facilitate a group's terrorist activity, for instance by lending it legitimacy, straining the US's relationship with its allies, enabling the group to use the international legal system to buy time, 'threaten[ing], manipulat[ing], and disrupt[ing]',[15] or seeking humanitarian financial aid that could be diverted to terrorism.

Third, some donors have adopted 'no contact' policies as a condition of funding, which prohibit humanitarian actors receiving these donors' funding (such as aid agencies or NGOs) from dealing with certain groups (such as Hamas in Gaza), whether to secure access or safety for humanitarian personnel or the passage of relief supplies. Fourth, many donors, such as the European Union and the US, have imposed other restrictive conditions on funding to prevent diversion of funds to terrorist activities, which require humanitarian actors as well as their partners and contractors to exercise due diligence in their operations and impose vetting, screening, or monitoring

[8] Saul, 'From Conflict to Complementarity' (n 3); Françoise Bouchet-Saulnier, 'How Counter-terrorism Throws Back Wartime Medical Assistance and Care to Pre-Solferino Times' (2021) 103 IRRC 479; Alejandro Pozo Martin and Rabia Ben Ali, 'Guilt by Association: Restricting Humanitarian Assistance in the Name of Counter-terrorism' (2021) 103 IRRC 539.

[9] Kate Mackintosh and Ingrid Macdonald, 'Counter-terrorism and Humanitarian Action' (2013) 58 Humanitarian Exchange Magazine, 23, 24.

[10] Kate Mackintosh and Patrick Duplat, 'Study of the Impact of Donor Counter-Terrorism Measures on Principled Humanitarian Action' (Commissioned by UN Office of the Coordination of Humanitarian Affairs and the Norwegian Refugee Council, July 2013).

[11] Eg UNSC Res 1373 (2001) UN Doc S/RES/1373 para 1(d).

[12] Eg Australian Criminal Code s 119.2.

[13] 18 US Code § 2339B.

[14] *Holder v Humanitarian Law Project*, 561 US (2010) Nos 08-1498 and 09-89 (US Supreme Court) (21 June 2010).

[15] ibid at 37.

requirements.[16] Some donors even adopt a 'zero tolerance' approach to risk.[17] Banks have also 'de-risked' their operations, limiting legitimate access to financial services, including essential international transactions, by humanitarian actors.[18]

In addition to increasing the administrative burdens on humanitarian actors, restrictive laws and policies have led to humanitarian actors becoming 'risk-averse' and self-limiting their activities, even if they were strictly lawful, because of uncertainty about legal liabilities and reputational damage. Such chilling effects can result in actors refusing funding from some donors, ceasing operations in some places or to some populations, including Syria, Iraq, Somalia, and Palestine, or passing on risks to partners and contractors.

Restrictive laws and policies have adversely impacted on humanitarian operations, for instance by limiting funding to particular places, populations, partners, or programs. For example, after Al Shabaab was labelled as a terrorist group, US aid to southern Somalia was reduced by almost 90 per cent between 2008 and 2010[19]—in the midst of a famine that had killed 260,000 people by 2012.[20] Islamic charities have been particularly hard-hit by restrictions.[21] The UK terminated cash aid to 50,000 civilians in north-eastern Syria after the displacement of people from areas previously controlled by ISIL, to avoid perceptions of financing terrorist sympathizers.[22] USAID imposes higher thresholds for assisting former kidnapped victims of Boko Haram in Nigeria.[23]

Some humanitarian actors, such as the ICRC and UN, enjoy international immunities from national legal liabilities,[24] but NGOs, civil society actors, and contractors do not. Informal engagement is often tolerated in practice, although this can still leave organizations facing legal uncertainty or self-restriction.[25] In some cases, specific UN mandates enable limited engagement, as with Hamas in Gaza or Al Shabaab in Somalia,[26] but this does not necessarily immunize NGOs from the laws of their home states or third states. Restrictive measures have also affected NGOs and civil society actors working in conflict areas, such as human rights and development actors engaged in advocacy, monitoring, or fact-finding.

[16] Emanuela-Chiara Gillard, Sangeeta Goswami, and Fulco van Deventer, 'Screening of Final Beneficiaries: A Red Line in Humanitarian Operations—An Emerging Concern in Development Work' (2021) 103 IRRC 517.

[17] Emma O'Leary, 'Politics and Principles: The Impact of Counterterrorism Measures and Sanctions on Principled Humanitarian Action' (2021) 103 IRRC 459, 464.

[18] Sue Eckert, 'Counterterrorism, Sanctions and Financial Access Challenges: Course Corrections to Safeguard Humanitarian Action' (2021) 103 IRRC 415, 431–436.

[19] Mackintosh and Duplat (n 10).

[20] BBC News, 'Somalia famine "killed 260,000 people"' (2 May 2013) <www.bbc.com/news/world-africa-22380352> accessed 17 May 2023.

[21] Mackintosh and Duplat (n 10).

[22] O'Leary (n 17) 465.

[23] ibid.

[24] Mackintosh and Macdonald (n 9) 25.

[25] Naz Modirzadeh, Dustin Lewis and Claude Bruderlein, 'Humanitarian Engagement under Counterterrorism: A Conflict of Norms and the Emerging Policy Landscape' (2011) 93 IRRC 1, 19–20.

[26] UNGA Res 46/182 (19 December 1991) UN Doc A/RES/46/182 para 35(d) mandated UN humanitarian actors to negotiate with relevant parties. On Somalia, UNSC Res 1916 (2010) UN Doc S/RES/1916 para 5 (creating a temporary humanitarian exception to counter-terrorism financing sanctions).

Fifth, at a policy level, the designation of some armed groups as 'terrorist' also challenges the principles of humanitarianism.[27] The four principles of humanitarian action are: humanity (addressing suffering wherever it is found); neutrality (not taking sides in hostilities or preferring some political, racial, religious, or ideological causes over others); impartiality (acting on the basis of need and without discrimination); and independence (remaining autonomous from the political, economic, military, or other agendas of other actors).[28] Counter-terrorism laws 'take sides' by criminalizing and/or ostracizing some groups. Neutrality and independence can be compromised by humanitarian actors being pressured to participate in counter-insurgency/terrorism or stabilization efforts,[29] in which humanitarian assistance is co-opted and militarized as part of strategies to win civilian 'hearts and minds'. Humanity and impartiality are further undermined by restrictive policies which discourage aid to certain populations or places even if they are in most need.

The legal polarization of relations with 'terrorist' groups may also make such groups suspicious of engaging with humanitarian actors. Humanitarian actors may be seen as closely affiliated with state counter-terrorism efforts, including by collaborating in humanitarian assistance, political stabilization, and development-oriented civilian 'hearts and minds' campaigns; by fulfilling their contractual or other legal requirements to report suspicious behaviour to governments, thus 'surveilling' populations; or because UN agencies, including humanitarian and development actors, are part of the 'whole of UN' approach to counter-terrorism under the UN Global Counter-terrorism Coordination Compact 2018 and the UN Global Counter-terrorism Strategy 2006. Armed groups may consequently be reluctant to allow humanitarian access or assistance, or may even target humanitarian actors as perceived counter-terrorism actors.

Counter-terrorism law may additionally criminalize non-state participants in armed conflict as 'terrorists' irrespective of whether they comply with IHL. The ICRC warns against criminalizing 'any act of violence' by armed groups as unlawful terrorism when it is not unlawful under IHL, since doing so 'is likely to diminish any incentive to comply with IHL'[30]—including its rules on respect for medical and humanitarian activities.

[27] Ashley Jackson and Eleanor Davey, *Humanitarian Policy Group Working Paper: From the Spanish Civil War to Afghanistan: Historical and Contemporary Reflections on Humanitarian Engagement with Non-state Armed Groups* (Overseas Development Institute 2014) 1, 2.

[28] UNGA Res 46/182 (1991) UN Doc A/RES/46/182 and 58/114 (2003) UN Doc A/RES/58/114.

[29] Jackson and Davey (n 27) 17; Ashley Jackson, 'Talking to the Other Side: Humanitarian Engagement with Armed Non-state Actors' (Humanitarian Policy Group Brief 47, Overseas Development Institute 2012) 3.

[30] ICRC, 'International Humanitarian Law and the Challenges of Contemporary Armed Conflicts' (ICRC 2019) 58; ICRC, 'Terrorism and International Law: Challenges and Responses: The Complementary Nature of Human Rights Law, International Humanitarian Law and Refugee Law' (ICRC 2002); Lindsey Cameron and others, 'Article 3: Conflicts not of an international character' in Dörmann and others (eds), *International Committee of the Red Cross Commentary to the Second Geneva Convention* (CUP 2017) para 895; also ICRC, 'The Applicability of IHL to Terrorism and Counterterrorism' (ICRC 2015); Jelena Pejic, 'Armed Conflict and Terrorism' in Ana Maria Salinas de Frias, Katja Samuel and Nigel White (eds), *Counter-Terrorism: International Law and Practice* (OUP 2012) 171, 177; Tristan Ferraro, 'Interaction and Overlap between Counter-Terrorism Legislation and International Humanitarian Law' in 'Proceedings of the 17th

3. Incremental Improvements

Over time, the Security Council has become more sensitive to the adverse impacts of counter-terrorism measures on humanitarian action. From 2005 onwards, the Security Council encouraged, but did not require, states to comply with international law, including IHL, when implementing their counter-terrorism obligations.[31] Since 2019, Resolution 2462 makes IHL compliance binding ('decides'),[32] following a trend pioneered in respect of human rights in 2017,[33] but it does not specifically mention protected humanitarian and medical activities.

Resolution 2482 (2019) urges—but does not require—states to 'take into account' the effect of counter-terrorism measures on 'exclusively humanitarian activities, including medical activities, that are carried out by impartial humanitarian actors in a manner consistent with' IHL.[34] The clause is, however, non-binding and merely suggests that states procedurally 'take into account' humanitarian impacts—rather than substantively respect the IHL rules.

However, such guidance has been adopted long after most states had already adopted new counter-terrorism laws infringing on humanitarian action. In many states, counter-terrorism imperatives are viewed as weightier objectives than strict IHL or human rights law compliance. A general exhortation to respect IHL is not sufficiently specific or detailed enough to ensure that the many different elements of counter-terrorism laws are compliant with the particular human rights that are affected by them. Supervision of the consistency of national laws with IHL has also, arguably, not been sufficiently robust. It is desirable that the Council should unambiguously affirm, in a binding paragraph, that states must specifically comply with IHL concerning medical and humanitarian assistance,[35] and such a requirement should be closely monitored by the UN counter-terrorism bodies.

An example of good practice in relation to counter-terrorism is in EU law, which excludes '[t]he provision of humanitarian activities by impartial humanitarian organizations recognized by international law, including international humanitarian law'.[36]

Bruges Colloquium: Terrorism, Counter-Terrorism and International Humanitarian Law' (College of Europe and ICRC 20–21 October 2016).

[31] Eg UNSC Res 1624 (2005) UN Doc S/RES/1624 para 4; 2178 (2014) UN Doc S/RES/2178 para 5; 2253 (2015) UN Doc S/RES/2253 preamble; 2368 (2017) UN Doc S/RES/2368 preamble; 2396 (2017) UN Doc S/RES/2396 preamble and paras 4, 18, 34 and 40; and 2462 (2019) UN Doc S/RES/2462 para 5.

[32] UNSC Res 2462 (2019) UN Doc S/RES/2462 para 6.

[33] UNSC Res 2396 (2017) UN Doc S/RES/2396 paras 11–13; David McKeever, 'International Humanitarian Law and Counter-terrorism: Fundamental Values, Conflicting Obligations' (2020) 69 ICLQ 43, 63.

[34] UNSC Res 2482 (2019) UN Doc S/RES/2482 para 16, also UNSC Res 2462 (2019) UN Doc S/RES/2462 para 24 (financing measures only).

[35] UNGA, 'Report of the Special Rapporteur on the Promotion and Protection of Human Rights and Fundamental Freedoms while Countering Terrorism, Fionnuala Ní Aoláin' (3 September 2020) UN Doc A/75/337 para 34; McKeever (n 33) 74–75.

[36] EU Directive 2017/541 of 15 March 2017 on combating terrorism and replacing Council Framework Decision 2002/475/JHA and amending Council Decision 2005/671/JHA (2017) OJ L88/6, recital 37.

An increasing number of states are adopting humanitarian exceptions in national laws or taking humanitarian issues into account in policies on prosecutorial discretion.[37]

In relation to counter-terrorism sanctions, after the Security Council first imposed sanctions in relation to Al Qaeda under Resolution 1267 in 1999, there was no humanitarian exception until December 2021.[38] After the Taliban returned to power in August 2021, sanctions on persons who were now in government contributed to an economic crisis and chronic food insecurity in Afghanistan. The Council belatedly recognized the problem in Resolution 2615 (2021) in deciding 'that humanitarian assistance and other activities that support basic human needs in Afghanistan are not a violation of [sanctions] and that the processing and payment of funds, other financial assets or economic resources, and the provision of goods and services necessary to ensure the timely delivery of such assistance or to support such activities are permitted'.[39] Under Resolution 2664 (2022), a similar humanitarian exception is applied to all Security Council sanctions regimes, including those addressing Al Qaeda and ISIL.[40] Again, effective implementation of these exceptions will be the test of its success.

Other improvements have also been made to ameliorate the adverse effects of counter-terrorism laws on humanitarian action, although these are typically jurisdiction-specific, and there remains considerable inconsistency between states. For example, conditions in some grant agreements have become less excessively restrictive; there has been better guidance and dialogue about sanctions and de-risking; more humanitarian exceptions or exemptions have emerged;[41] and the Financial Action Task Force moderated its excessively punitive anti-terrorist financing regulations on non-profit organizations.[42]

C. Interface with Peacemaking

The involvement of terrorist groups in armed conflict can adversely affect prospects for peacemaking and peacebuilding. Much depends on the characteristics of the group.[43] The more radical or extreme its goals, the less the likelihood of a negotiated peace,[44] since such goals are especially difficult to accommodate in a political settlement, and the group may be ideologically unwilling to compromise. Contemporary examples of groups resistant to dialogue include ISIL, Al Qaeda, Al Shabaab, Boko Haram, Abu Sayyaf, and Jemaah Islamiyah. This is not necessarily distinctive to

[37] Eg UK Crown Prosecution Service, 'New Legal Guidance for Humanitarian, Development and Peacebuilding Work Overseas' (4 October 2022).

[38] There was only a 'basic expenses' exception granted on a case-by-case basis.

[39] UNSC Res 2615 (2021) UN Doc S/RES/2615 para 1.

[40] UNSC Res 2664 (2002) UN Doc S/RES/2664 paras 1–2.

[41] O'Leary (n 17) 470–73.

[42] Financial Action Task Force, 'The FATF Recommendations 2012: International Standards on Combating Money Laundering and the Financing of Terrorism and Proliferation' (Paris, FATF 2012, amended March 2022) Recommendation 8: Non-profit Organisations.

[43] Audrey Cronin, *How Terrorism Ends: Understanding the Decline and Demise of Terrorist Campaigns* (Princeton University Press 2009) 40–42.

[44] Seth Jones and Martin Libicki, *How Terrorist Groups End: Lessons for Countering al Qa'ida* (Rand Corporation 2008) 21–22.

terrorism; other extreme groups, such as the Lord's Resistance Army or the Khmer Rouge, were also long resistant to peacemaking. Religious terrorist groups particularly tend to fight longer[45] than secular, political, or territorial movements. Extremist ideologies may also make post-conflict reconciliation more difficult.

Nonetheless, one study suggests about half of terrorist insurgencies end through a negotiated settlement with the government.[46] Again, armed groups classified as 'terrorist' are not necessarily all extreme movements but encompass a range of political adversaries, from conventional rebels in civil war to national liberation movements. Popular support for a group may make it amenable to a political resolution, although sectarianism and state intransigence can also entrench division and inhibit dialogue.

Settlements have been reached, for example, with 'terrorist' groups such as the Irish Republican Army, Palestine Liberation Organization, Revolutionary Armed Forces of Colombia (FARC), Free Aceh Movement, and Moro liberation groups in the Philippines, among others. Even extreme groups, such as the genocidal Khmer Rouge or the fundamentalist Taliban, have eventually entered into dialogue and peace settlements, although the Taliban seemingly did so for tactical reasons rather than due to a genuine commitment to a participatory and inclusive political settlement.

Pillar I of the UN Global Counter-Terrorism Strategy identifies 'prolonged unresolved conflicts' as one of the conditions conducive to terrorism[47] and recommends efforts to resolve conflict, including through conflict prevention, negotiation, mediation, conciliation, judicial settlement, rule of law, peacekeeping, and peacebuilding. However, in practice, repressive law enforcement and military responses have tended to predominate in response to terrorism, and sometimes excessive measures have counter-productively exacerbated terrorism.

1. Counter-terrorism Laws as Impediments to Peacemaking

The ultimate aim of counter-terrorism laws is to suppress and, in the context of armed conflict, defeat terrorist groups. Paradoxically, however, in some situations excessive state counter-terrorism responses, including violations of IHL and human rights, can diminish prospects for peacemaking by fuelling the grievances that stimulate recourse to violence and mobilizing public support for the terrorists' cause.[48] Specifically, the legal proscription of terrorist groups and the related criminalization of activities related to them can impede efforts to both make peace during conflict and consolidate the peace after conflict.[49]

[45] ibid xiv.

[46] ibid xv (whereas the government 'wins' the conflict in about one fifth of cases, and the terrorist group 'wins' in a quarter of cases).

[47] ibid.

[48] ibid 31; Cronin (n 43) 204.

[49] Also Sophie Haspeslagh, *Proscribing Peace: How Listing Armed Groups as Terrorists Hurts Negotiations* (Manchester University Press 2021); Saul, 'From Conflict to Complementarity' (n 3); Harmonie Toros, '"We Don't Negotiate with Terrorists!": Legitimacy and Complexity in Terrorist Conflicts' (2008) 39 Security Dialogue 407; Daragh Murray, 'Non-State Armed Groups and Peace Agreements' in Marc Weller, Mark Retter and Andrea Varga (eds), *International Law and Peace Settlements* (CUP 2021) 187; UNGA, 'Special Rapporteur Report' (2022) (n 7) paras 34–40.

First, classifying armed groups as terrorist symbolically vilifies and politically delegitimizes them, thus hardening public attitudes against them, legitimizing and empowering repressive state responses and mobilizing international support for the state's cause.[50] This can seriously hinder the political space and willingness and the legal ability of governments to enter into peace negotiations. Adverse labelling also deters the involvement of third party mediators (such as foreign states or NGOs),[51] which can be essential in maintaining confidence between the parties. They can also affect the scope of any eventual negotiations that may arise and limit the range of political concessions that are considered acceptable in any settlement.

The hardening of attitudes towards terrorism after 9/11 resulted, for example, in Colombia resiling from negotiations with FARC;[52] Spain feeling constrained by popular opinion from dialogue with ETA in the Basque region; international interlocutors refraining from engaging with the increasingly isolated LTTE in Sri Lanka[53] or, later, Hamas in Gaza; and international solidarity diminishing from long-standing national liberation struggles as in Palestine.

Proscription and criminalization may likewise undermine the willingness of terrorist groups themselves to negotiate, since such measures may make them feel ostracized from any partnership for peace, deepen their sense of grievance, and harden their resolve against the victimising state. For example, the LTTE refused an EU-supported ceasefire monitoring mission after the EU listed the LTTE;[54] and the EU's credibility as a neutral mediator in relation to the PKK was undermined by its listing of the PKK.[55]

In contrast, when Colombia later reframed FARC not as a terrorist group but as insurgents or guerrillas, more space opened for an ultimately successful dialogue for peace.[56] The loosening of sanctions on the Taliban, such as travel restrictions, and their increasing political differentiation from Al Qaeda and ISIL also enabled Taliban leaders to participate in US negotiations abroad,[57] ultimately resulting in a peace agreement (albeit lacking essential Afghan government participation).

Second, proscription and criminalization also pose practical impediments to peacemaking. As in relation to humanitarian action, such measures may directly or indirectly prohibit or restrict engagement with terrorist groups. Travel bans and border restrictions may prevent attendance at negotiations; financial sanctions or terrorist

[50] Haspeslagh (n 49); UNGA, 'Special Rapporteur Report' (2022) (n 7) paras 34–40.

[51] Flavia Eichmann, 'Naming Terror: Impact of Proscription on Negotiations with Non-State Armed Groups' (2019) Journal of Public and International Affairs <https://jpia.princeton.edu/news/naming-terror-impact-proscription-negotiations-non-state-armed-groups> accessed 17 May 2023.

[52] Haspeslagh (n 49).

[53] Øystein Birkeland, 'The Impact of Terrorist Proscriptions on Peace Processes—Sri Lanka's 5th Peace Process' (Master thesis, University of Oslo 2014); Vidar Helgesen, 'How Peace Diplomacy Lost Post 9/11: What Implications Are There for Norway?' (2007) 3 Oslo Files on Defence and Security 1, 12–13.

[54] William Zartman and Guy Olivier Faure, *Engaging Extremists: Trade-Offs, Timing, and Diplomacy* (US Institute of Peace 2011); Véronique Dudouet, 'Mediating Peace with Proscribed Armed Groups' (Special Report 239, US Institute of Peace 2010); Helgesen (n 53).

[55] Eichmann (n 51).

[56] Haspeslagh (n 49); Sophie Haspeslagh, 'The "Linguistic Ceasefire": Negotiating in An Age of Proscription' (2021) 52(4) Security Dialogue 361.

[57] UNSC 'As Taliban Offensive Escalates, Afghanistan at Dangerous Turning Point' (6 August 2021) Press Release SC/14596.

financing offences may prevent reimbursement of travel, accommodation, and food; and offences of providing 'material support' for, 'associating' with, or training terrorist groups may incriminate third party mediators or NGOs.[58]

2. Impediments to Reintegration and Reconciliation

Third, the criminalization of IHL-compliant fighters and their civilian supporters as terrorists undermines IHL's encouragement to states to confer the widest possible amnesty for (IHL-compliant) acts during conflict.[59] Such recommendation aims to encourage post-conflict reconciliation and heal social divisions between warring sides. If an armed group has been labelled or its members criminalized as terrorist, such stigmatization may render it legally and politically difficult for governments and the population to accept the release of 'terrorists'. The same is true of 'terrorist' eligibility for participation in transitional justice frameworks, which may intertwine elements such as prosecution, amnesty, leniency, truth commissions, reparations, reconciliation, and healing.[60]

Relatedly, counter-terrorism laws can complicate or even preclude eligibility of persons for disarmament, demobilization, and reintegration (DDR),[61] which may be necessary for a lasting peace. An estimated 10,000 ISIL fighters have been detained by the rebel Syrian Democratic Forces in north-eastern Syria since ISIL's territorial 'Caliphate' was suppressed in 2017, without a clear roadmap for their reintegration. In total there are 30,000 former ISIL members and their associates—including family members—from 80 countries in camps in Syria and Iraq 'without a clear policy and operational framework to support their effective repatriation, rehabilitation and re-socialization'.[62] DDR is, however, eventually necessary in most terrorist campaigns, whether with the LTTE in Sri Lanka, FARC in Colombia, Boko Haram in Nigeria, Al Shabaab in Somalia, the Taliban (when captured under the previous Afghan government), or others.[63]

UN DDR standards emphasize that neither those suspected of terrorist acts nor individuals or groups listed by the Security Council can be eligible for DDR, as is the case for those suspected of international crimes.[64] However, the standards operate

58 Eichmann (n 51).

59 Protocol II art 6(5); ICRC Customary IHL Study, Rule 159; ICRC, 'The Applicability of IHL' (n 30); Pejic (n 30); ICRC, 'Terrorism and International Law' (n 30).

60 Institute for Integrated Transitions (IFIT) and United Nations University Centre for Policy Research (UNU-CPR), *The Limits of Punishment: Transitional Justice and Violent Extremism* (United Nations University 2018).

61 ICRC, 'The Applicability of IHL' (n 30); Pejic (n 30); ICRC, 'Terrorism and International Law' (n 30); UNGA, 'Special Rapporteur Report' (2020) (n 35) para 42.

62 UNDP, 'Prevention of Violent Extremism' (n 1) 3.

63 IFIT and UNU-CPR (n 60); Saïbou Issa and Nadine Machikou, 'Reintegrating Former Boko Haram Associates: Perspectives from Far North Region in Cameroon' (Policy Brief, Global Center on Cooperative Security 2019); Omar Ashour, 'Islamist Deradicalization in Algeria: The Case of the Islamic Salvation Army and Affiliated Militias' in Rohan Gunaratna, Jolene Jerard, and Lawrence Rubin (eds), *Terrorist Rehabilitation and Counter-Radicalization* (Routledge 2011) 11.

64 UN Inter-Agency Working Group on DDR (IAWG), 'Integrated Disarmament, Demobilization and Reintegration Standards' (UN DDR Centre 2020) <https://www.unddr.org/the-iddrs/> accessed 17 May 2023, module 2.11, section 4.2.6.

by *renvoi* to the definition of terrorism not only in international counter-terrorism treaties—some of which exclude all activities of armed forces (that is, including insurgents) in armed conflict—but also in Security Council resolutions—which do not define terrorism and allow states to decide the issue—including whether to criminalize mere membership in or support of an armed group or participation in hostilities, even when not prohibited by IHL. Exclusion from DDR can thus be overbroad: terrorist offences in national law are not necessarily of equivalent gravity to international crimes warranting exclusion from DDR. The same is true of excluding anyone associated with a Security Council listed group, which of itself does not reveal anything about whether the individual's conduct was harmful.

The UN standards note, however, that DDR knowledge may be relevant to implementing the 'prosecution, rehabilitation, and reintegration' (PRR) measures which the Security Council has indicated should be used in relation to foreign terrorist fighters.[65] PRR is thus posited as an alternative framework to DDR, despite the lack of conceptual clarity about the 'terrorism' trigger for PRR and exclusion from DDR. In 2017, Security Council Resolution 2396 recommended (but did not require) that states 'develop and implement comprehensive and tailored prosecution, rehabilitation, and reintegration strategies' in relation to foreign terrorist fighters (including returnees) and their spouses and children.[66] Such strategies should include comprehensive risk assessments for individuals and appropriate prosecution, rehabilitation, and reintegration measures, taking into account that some individuals may be victims of terrorism.

By way of example, an African sub-regional response to Boko Haram/ISIL, adopted in 2018, has indicated that 'screening, prosecution, rehabilitation, and reintegration' (SPRR) is preferred to DDR, since regular disarmament and demobilization efforts do not formally apply to a terrorist group listed by the Security Council and where that group has not signed an agreement with a state to surrender arms.[67] Members of terrorist groups who lay down their arms voluntarily may be entitled to more lenient treatment.

Security Council and related guidance do not provide specificity regarding who precisely is or is not eligible for PRR (or more conventional DDR) in the context of terrorism, for instance in relation to the kind of terrorist activity of a certain person. There is a spectrum and balance between ensuring accountability for serious acts of terrorism—that is, those involving attacks on civilians or acts proximately connected with such attacks—and pursuing amnesties or other non-prosecutorial methods in relation to, for example, IHL-compliant fighters, members of armed groups who

[65] ibid; eg UNSC Res 2178 (2014) UN Doc S/RES/2178 para 4 and UNSC Res 2396 (2017) UN Doc S/RES/2396 para 18, 29–30 ('prosecution, rehabilitation, and reintegration' measures for 'foreign terrorist fighters').

[66] UNSC Res 2396 (2017) UN Doc S/RES/2396 para 30; paras 29–41; UNSC 'Security Council Guiding Principles on Foreign Terrorist Fighters: The 2015 Madrid Guiding Principles and its 2018 Addendum' (23 December 2015 and 13 February 2018) UN Docs S/2015/939 and S/2018/117; UNSC 'Technical Guide to the Implementation of Resolution 1373 (2001) and Other Relevant Resolutions' (18 August 2017) UN Doc S/2017/716.

[67] African Union Lake Chad Basin Commission, 'Regional Strategy for the Stabilization, Recovery and Resilience of the Boko Haram-affected Areas of the Lake Chad Basin Region' (African Union 2018) annex 3; Issa and Machikou (n 63).

performed non-combat functions, lesser conduct such as minor terrorist financing, or wider circles of supporters or family members.

Somalia's national programme for the rehabilitation and reintegration of former Al Shabaab combatants was limited to those who voluntarily disengaged (some due to government promises of amnesties) and who were assessed as low security risk after renouncing extremist ideology, although prior to 2015 higher-risk individuals had also taken part.[68] While low-risk security assessment may be based partly on an evaluation of the nature of prior activities with Al Shabaab, screening does not explicitly exclude those low-risk persons who may have committed terrorist crimes in the past—and whose victims demand justice. The appropriate balance between terrorist prosecution and PRR alternatives, including transitional justice, requires further clarification at the policy level and in concrete conflict settings.

3. Peacekeeping, Peacebuilding and Counter-Terrorism

Counter-terrorism efforts may also adversely affect UN peacekeeping. In 2015 a UN policy review noted that UN peacekeeping missions 'are not suited to engage in military counter-terrorism operations', due to their composition and character.[69] Empowering a peacekeeping operation with counter-terrorism and/or stabilization mandates in support of a state can compromise its impartiality and neutrality and thus undermine its legitimacy, credibility, trustworthiness, and reputation as perceived by the armed group and parts of the host state's population.[70] UN forces may become directly implicated in human rights violations or be complicit in violations by the state forces they support.[71] This in turn may stimulate more terrorism, retaliation against UN forces and local partners, and greater risks to the other components of a hybrid UN operation, including humanitarian, human rights, development, and peacemaking personnel.[72] Support for counter-terrorism operations by the UN Multidimensional Integrated Stabilization Mission in Mali (MINUSMA), for example, may have contributed to the targeting of MINUSMA personnel.[73] Concerns have also been expressed about the UN operations in Somalia and the Democratic Republic of Congo.[74] There is also a risk that empowering UN operations with

68 James Khalil and others, 'Deradicalisation and Disengagement in Somalia: Evidence from a Rehabilitation Programme for Former Members of Al-Shabaab' (Whitehall Report 4-18, Royal United Services Institute for Defence and Security Studies 2019).

69 UNGA and UNSC, 'Report of the High-level Independent Panel on Peace Operations on uniting our strengths for peace: politics, partnership and people' (17 June 2015) UN Doc A/70/95-S/2015/446 para 119.

70 UNGA, 'Special Rapporteur Report' (2022) (n 7); Naureen Chowdhury Fink and Arthur Boutellis, 'Between a Rock and a Hard Place: Counterterrorism and Peacekeeping in the Sahel' (IPI Global Observatory, 20 July 2021) <https://theglobalobservatory.org/2021/07/between-a-rock-and-a-hard-place-counterterrorism-and-peacekeeping-in-the-sahel/> accessed 17 May 2023.

71 UNGA, 'Special Rapporteur Report' (2022) (n 7) paras 26–27, 31.

72 ibid paras 26–27.

73 ibid para 33.

74 Charles Hunt and Shannon Zimmerman, 'Counter-Terrorism & Peace Operations: The Impacts of UN Security Council Approaches to Tackling Terror on the Pursuit of Peace' (SFI Research Brief, Resolve Network 2022).

counter-terrorism functions may strengthen state repression, thus reducing incentives to negotiate, prolonging conflict,[75] and failing to address the underlying conditions conducive to terrorism—including state violations.

Post-conflict, there are risks in counter-terrorism efforts co-opting, securitizing, and distorting peacebuilding activities, reflecting donor priorities rather than local needs.[76] Peacebuilding funding has been increasingly allocated for programmes to prevent and counter violent extremism, as in Burkina Faso, Chad, Kyrgyzstan, Mali, Mauritania, the Niger, Nigeria, Tajikistan, and Togo.[77] Such projects, particularly in collaboration with state security forces, may undermine human rights and the principles of consent, 'do no harm', legality, necessity, and proportionality.[78] At the institutional level, UN counter-terrorism budgeting and staffing are increasing exponentially, in contrast to the struggle to support the UN Peacebuilding Fund.[79]

D. Interface with Development

Development can address conditions conducive to terrorism and armed conflict, including socio-economic marginalization, and thus weaken support for terrorist groups and terrorist recruitment.[80] However, development activities are typically disrupted by armed conflict, particularly where the violence is on a substantial scale and is geographically extensive. Terrorist violence imposes substantial economic and development costs,[81] including due to personal injury and disability, property damage, and disruption of formal and informal economic activity. Conflict may destroy or impede the infrastructure (including transport, industry, agriculture, and essential utilities), services, labour, markets, and trade on which development projects depend. It may displace populations and thus disrupt agricultural and industrial production and the availability of labour. It may be unsafe for development actors to operate, and a narrower humanitarian response may predominate, although the boundaries are increasingly blurred in practice.[82] The parties may not agree to the continuation of projects, including to prevent the other side from gaining political legitimacy and popular support through successful development projects. Government resources may also be directed away from development towards security, and the indirect costs of conflict may further squeeze funds available for development. Even where the violence is not especially intense or is geographically limited, the unpredictable risk of terrorism may

[75] Kaisa Hinkkainen Elliott, Sara Polo, and Liana Eustacia Reyes, 'Making Peace or Preventing It? UN Peacekeeping, Terrorism, and Civil War Negotiations' (2021) 65 International Studies Quarterly 29, 40.

[76] UNGA, 'Special Rapporteur Report' (2022) (n 7) para 22.

[77] ibid.

[78] ibid para 22.

[79] Jordan Street, 'UN Budget vs. Rhetoric: Touting "Agenda for Peace" But Investing in Counterterrorism Instead?' (Just Security, 1 December 2022) <https://www.justsecurity.org/84334/un-budget-vs-rhetoric-touting-agenda-for-peace-but-investing-in-counterterrorism-instead/> accessed 17 May 2023.

[80] Kim Cragin and Peter Chalk, *Terrorism and Development: Using Social and Economic Development to Inhibit a Resurgence of Terrorism* (RAND 2003).

[81] UNDP, 'Measuring the Economic Impact of Violent Extremism Leading to Terrorism in Africa' (UNDP 2019) 1.

[82] Gillard and others (n 16) 532.

mean foreign public and private sector partners may be too risk-averse to invest. Since weakly governed and less developed states are more prone to terrorism, the economic burden of terrorism often falls on states least equipped to effectively respond to it.

1. National Responses

Armed conflicts involving terrorist groups and consequent counter-terrorism strategies bring distinctive legal and policy dynamics to the interface with development. In the immediate aftermath of the 11 September 2001 attacks, counter-terrorism efforts focused principally on military and criminal suppression of terrorism. The emphasis on repression was, however, increasingly seen as too one-dimensional and even counter-productive in the absence of more preventive strategies, including those addressing the root 'causes' of terrorism.

At the national level, there was a creeping militarization of development activities in some settings, such as the US-led civilian 'hearts and minds' efforts as part of state rebuilding in Afghanistan and Iraq. Such efforts are not new but part of a historical continuum, from British efforts to subdue the Malayan Emergency in the 1950s to US counter-insurgency doctrine in the Vietnam War in the 1960s. Providing social and economic programmes and livelihood opportunities to improve living standards is seen as a way of undermining support for insurgencies and legitimating newly installed governments supported by foreign powers.

From the perspective of international development actors and NGO partners, however, such efforts involve acute risks. In some cases, official development assistance and state budgets have been skewed towards security sector activities, which may reduce spending on education, health, social services, and public infrastructure, in turn aggravating grievances conducive to terrorism.[83] Military-led activities may instrumentalize the design and delivery of development activities in a manner inconsistent with 'good' or 'best' development practices and principles, such as consultation and participation, local ownership and empowerment, aid effectiveness and sustainability, 'do no harm', 'human'-centred rather than purely economic development, human rights consistency, and sensitivity to gender and other vulnerabilities.[84] For example, counter-terrorism screening of beneficiaries has disrupted and delegitimized some development projects in Burkina Faso and Mozambique.[85]

Further, where development actors partner with military forces or governments in conflict, they may be perceived as political collaborators with the regime, thus endangering the safety of their personnel and compromising their ability to operate. Unlike humanitarian actors, development actors also do not benefit from the same protections in armed conflict under IHL,[86] although they do enjoy general protection as civilians, and some may have further protection, in or outside conflict, under the

[83] UNDP, 'Measuring the Economic Impact' (n 81) 28, 30–31, 33, 35.
[84] Eg Gillard and others (n 16) 533–36; Amartya Sen, *Development as Freedom* (Alfred A Knopf 1999).
[85] Gillard and others (n 16) 535–36.
[86] ibid 531.

UN Convention on the Safety of United Nations and Associated Personnel.[87] State forces may be unwilling to allow development actors to operate independently, or it may not be safe to do so in the absence of security provided by state forces.

Terrorist financing laws and sanctions may particularly chill development financing, presenting similar concerns as in the context of humanitarian activities discussed earlier. Inadequately funded and poorly delivered development projects may result in social disenchantment and push populations towards armed groups for assistance.[88]

2. United Nations Responses

At the multilateral level, in 2006, the UN General Assembly adopted the Global Counter-Terrorism Strategy, which seeks to rebalance counter-terrorism policy in a more holistic manner. While its Pillars II (prevent and combat terrorism) and III (build states' capacity to prevent and combat terrorism) reinforce traditional repressive approaches, Pillars I and IV sought to promote neglected policy areas by addressing the conditions conducive to terrorism (Pillar I) and respect for human rights and the rule of law (Pillar IV).

Pillar I declares that 'conditions conducive to terrorism'—a more acceptable euphemism for what was described, too deterministically, as root 'causes' at the UN in the 1970s—cannot 'excuse or justify' terrorism but must be addressed.[89] It identifies such conditions as non-exhaustively including 'prolonged unresolved conflicts, dehumanization of victims of terrorism . . . lack of rule of law and violations of human rights, ethnic, national and religious discrimination, political exclusion, socio-economic marginalization, and lack of good governance'.[90]

The bulk of the recommended measures in response concern development and inclusion,[91] assisting victims,[92] promoting civilizational and religious understanding,[93] and efforts to resolve conflict[94] and improve the rule of law, human rights, and good governance.[95] Such recommendations conceive of a wider and more participatory approach than militarized or securitized 'stabilization'-type development activities mentioned in the previous section.

[87] Also Andrej Zwitter, 'Humanitarian Action, Development and Terrorism' in Ben Saul (ed), *Research Handbook on Terrorism and International Law* (2nd edn, Edward Elgar 2019) 300.

[88] Cragin and Chalk (n 80).

[89] UNGA Res 60/288 (20 September 2006) 'The United Nations Global Counter-terrorism Strategy' UN Doc A/RES/60/288.

[90] ibid.

[91] Specifically, pursuing development, economic growth and social inclusion and eradicating poverty and reducing marginalization: ibid paras 5–6.

[92] ibid para 8.

[93] ibid paras 2–3.

[94] Specifically, conflict prevention, negotiation, mediation, conciliation, judicial settlement, rule of law, peacekeeping, and peacebuilding: ibid para 1.

[95] ibid para 7.

Pillars I and IV have been further advanced by the more controversial UN Secretary-General's Plan of Action to Prevent Violent Extremism of 2015.[96] The Plan recognizes the need for more 'systematic preventive measures which directly address the drivers of violent extremism that have given rise to the emergence of these new and more virulent groups'.[97] It is based on the premise that violent extremism undermines peace and security, sustainable development, human rights, the rule of law, and humanitarian action.[98] The 'push factors' driving violent extremism which it identifies include lack of socio-economic opportunities; marginalization and discrimination; poor governance; violations of human rights and the rule of law; prolonged and unresolved conflicts; and radicalization in prisons.[99]

The Plan contains more than seventy recommendations to states and the UN system, including the development of national and regional Plans of Action to prevent violent extremism (PVE), in which priority areas include development-relevant matters such as dialogue and conflict prevention; strengthening good governance, human rights, and the rule of law; engaging communities; empowering youth; gender equality and empowering women; education, skill development, and employment facilitation; and strategic communications.[100] Plans should also align national development policies with the Sustainable Development Goals.[101]

In practice, the Security Council has occasionally been attentive to the conditions conducive to terrorism in specific situations. For example, in Resolution 2349 (2017) addressing Boko Haram and ISIL in West Africa, it called for UN entities to assist states and African regional organizations to address the conditions conducive to the spread of terrorism and violent extremism that can be conducive to terrorism.[102] It devoted five paragraphs of the resolution to 'root causes and development'.[103] On causes, it referred to inequalities, environmental challenges, violent extremist narratives, conditions conducive to violent extremism and terrorism, and the adverse effects of climate change and ecological changes (such as water scarcity, drought, desertification, land degradation, and food insecurity). In response, it recommended measures such as investment in vital services (such as health care and education), agriculture, infrastructure, social cohesion, good governance, and the rule of law; addressing inequalities, as well as long-term development needs; managing climate and ecological risks; and empowering civil society, including in conflict prevention, conflict resolution, and peacebuilding and humanitarian efforts. These are nonetheless non-binding

[96] UNGA, 'Plan of Action to Prevent Violent Extremism, Report of the Secretary-General' (24 December 2015) UN Doc A/70/674. UNGA recommended that states implement relevant recommendations of the Plan of Action in UNGA Res 70/291 (1 July 2016) UN Doc A/RES/70/291.

[97] ibid para 6.

[98] ibid paras 12–22.

[99] ibid paras 24–31.

[100] ibid paras 48–55.

[101] ibid para 44(e) (specifically by: ending poverty (Goal 1); ensuring inclusive and equitable quality education (Goal 4); achieving gender equality (Goal 5); promoting sustained, inclusive and sustainable economic growth, full and productive employment, and decent work for all (Goal 8); reducing inequality within and among countries (Goal 10); making cities and human settlements inclusive, safe, resilient, and sustainable (Goal 11); and promoting peaceful and inclusive societies for sustainable development, providing access to justice for all, and building effective, accountable, and inclusive institutions (Goal 16)).

[102] UNSC Res 2349 (2017) UN Doc S/RES/2349 para 8.

[103] ibid paras 22–27.

recommendations, which contrasts starkly with the willingness of the Council to require states to implement repressive law enforcement measures against terrorism.

While the more holistic and balanced approach in the Global Strategy and Plan of Action has undoubted advantages, it also has potential costs. It risks relabelling as counter-terrorism a range of policy areas addressing disparate phenomena, when states remain deeply divided over the conditions conducive to terrorism.[104] It requires the UN 'to address numerous policy objectives at once—promotion of development, good governance, human rights and the rule of law, conflict prevention and resolution'.[105] Indeed, many activities claimed by the Secretary-General as progress towards implementing the Strategy count (or 'double hat') existing UN programmes in those broad fields but which are not specifically designed as counter-terrorism projects.[106] The UN is nonetheless integrating PVE into its activities in the field. The UN Development Programme, for example, undertakes PVE activities in forty-two states, focusing on promoting inclusive governance, equitable access to services and economic opportunity, gender equality, and human rights.[107]

Further, the blurring of counter-terrorism with these other UN goals has brought tensions between and resistance from many UN actors concerning their roles and participation in counter-terrorism. For example, labelling their activities as counter-terrorism can jeopardize humanitarian principles of impartiality and neutrality, or otherwise bring reputational and security risks for actors engaged in a variety of activities based on their own dedicated mandates—humanitarian, development, peacebuilding, conflict prevention, human rights and rule of law, good governance, educational reform, and inter-faith dialogue. Even if terrorism may undermine all of those activities, integrating counter-terrorism objectives into them may be tactically 'a marriage best kept quiet',[108] since labelling them as counter-terrorism may politicize them and make them more difficult to implement in the field. It can also divert resources or shift priorities based on counter-terrorism or PVE considerations rather than being driven by the legal or policy frameworks of human rights or development.

The PVE agenda in particular has been controversial because of the lack of definition of terms such as 'violent extremism' and 'radicalization',[109] which are understood differently by different states and other actors. As with terrorism, the UN has side-stepped the issue by declaring that definition is a state prerogative,[110] despite expecting common global action on PVE. Some (poorly designed or executed) PVE programmes have adversely affected human rights.

[104] Alistair Millar and Naureen Chowdhury Fink, 'Blue Sky III: Taking UN Counterterrorism Efforts in the Next Decade from Plans to Action' (Global Center on Cooperative Security 2016) 23.

[105] James Cockayne, Alistair Millar, and Jason Ipe, 'An Opportunity for Renewal: Revitalizing the United Nations Counterterrorism Program' (Global Center on Cooperative Security 2010) 23.

[106] To give just one example, in 2008 the Secretary-General mentioned that '90 countries received support from UNDP for the rule of law, access to justice and human rights': UNGA, 'UN Global Counter-Terrorism Strategy: Activities of the United Nations System in Implementing the Strategy' (7 July 2008) UN Doc A/62/898, 4.

[107] UNDP, 'Prevention of Violent Extremism' (n 1) 6.

[108] Cockayne and others (n 105) 25.

[109] Alistair Millar, 'Blue Sky IV: Clouds Dispersing? An Independent Analysis of UN Counterterrorism Efforts in Advance of the Sixth Review of the UN Global Counter-Terrorism Strategy' (Global Center on Cooperative Security 2018) 8.

[110] UNGA 'PVE Plan of Action' (n 96) para 5.

In practice (reflected in the number of UN projects), there was still initially more attention to Pillars II and III on repression than the more preventive Pillars I and IV.[111] Over time greater attention has been paid to Pillars I and IV, although human rights and the rule of law are still marginalized and have not been 'mainstreamed' across all areas of counter-terrorism, including peace and security and development.[112] The imbalance is also reflected in the resources allocated between the Pillars and dedicated UN counter-terrorism staffing.[113]

3. Development in Non-State Territories

Most of the counter-terrorism measures assume governmental control over the territories in which preventive developmental activities should occur. Governments and development partners may be precluded or restricted from accessing territories controlled by armed groups, since they must respect state sovereignty and domestic jurisdiction, and 'political prohibition' clauses may limit the competence of international financial institutions to work without government (or de facto government) consent.[114] Here a normative gap arises under IHL. Rebel administrations are simply illegal under national law. A state has the right to repress the threat to national sovereignty and law and order that violent political rebellions represent. Unlike in international armed conflicts, there is no recognition of any capacity of insurgent rulers to be quasi-'occupying powers' under IHL, so as to accord them any legal rights to provide public administration, regulate economic activity (including development), and ensure law and order for civilians. This is despite rebel governments often providing these things in practice. The extent to which human rights law binds armed groups remains unsettled, albeit with support growing for its partial application.

All of this makes it legally and politically challenging for lawful development activity to occur in rebel-held areas, even where it is for the benefit of civilians living in poverty and has the incidental benefit of addressing conditions conducive to terrorism and violent extremism. Extraction of natural resources by armed groups, even for the benefit of populations or provision of services, is treated as theft or looting. International development actors and foreign companies are understandably averse to the legal and investment risks, including the barriers posed by any applicable terrorist financing laws and sanctions regimes. The lack of legitimate economic pathways inevitably entrenches the reliance of armed groups on organized criminal activities, including narcotics trafficking or 'taxation', illicit resource extraction (whether mining, logging, or wildlife), or illicit trade in antiquities. Affected states are generally opposed

[111] ibid para 7.

[112] Hanny Megally, 'UN Global Counter-Terrorism Strategy Review' (NYU Center on International Cooperation 2018) 4.

[113] Millar (n 109) 8; Eric Rosand and others, 'A Roadmap to Progress: The State of the Global P/CVE Agenda' (The Prevention Project and Royal United Services Institute 2018) 32.

[114] Eg Articles of Agreement of the International Bank for Reconstruction and Development (adopted 27 December 1945, entered into force 25 April 1947) 2 UNTS 134 art 10; Agreement establishing the African Development Bank (adopted 4 August 1963, entered into force 10 September 1964) 510 UNTS 3 and 569 UNTS 353 art 38; World Bank, 'Operational Policies' <https://policies.worldbank.org/en/policies#1> accessed 17 May 2023, 2.30 (conflict), 7.30 (de facto governments), and 8.00 (emergency response).

to regularizing development activities for the benefit of populations living under rebel control, since doing so could cement rebel control and popular legitimacy.

Ultimately, civilians under rebel control are deprived of opportunities for economic and human development and thus of dignity and the necessary opportunities for human flourishing; they are hostage to a criminal war economy and squeezed by indiscriminate counter-terrorism laws.

E. Conclusion: Harmonizing Counter-terrorism with the 'Triple Nexus'

The configuration of any nexus between terrorism/counter-terrorism and humanitarian, peace, and development activities varies greatly by context, not least because counter-terrorism laws are often jurisdiction-specific and highly variable. Security conditions on the ground may also dictate that, at particular moments and in certain areas, a mainly humanitarian response, rather than concurrent development and peacemaking, -keeping, or -building activities, is feasible.

Across the board, counter-terrorism efforts in conflict settings have tended to emphasize repressive law enforcement and military responses to the detriment of humanitarian, peace, and development activities—with potential to aggravate, not lessen, terrorism. Sometimes these adverse impacts are inadvertent, but they can also reflect deliberate policy choices to prioritize a repressive—and potentially ineffective—counter-terrorism model over more preventive, structural approaches involving development and peace activities. Even where a wider approach is taken, counter-terrorism initiatives may seek to co-opt humanitarian, peace, and development actors, which not only compromises them but undermines the effectiveness of counter-terrorism.

Given the shared risks of adverse impacts, humanitarian, peace, and development actors should coordinate[115] to identify and articulate shared concerns and mobilize within the relevant UN and other fora to effectively mitigate counter-terrorism excesses. A cross-cutting concern among all actors should be greater attention to mainstreaming human rights, which not only counter-terrorism but also the 'triple nexus' too often overlook.

[115] Inter-Agency Standing Committee and UN Working Group on Transitions 'Background paper on Humanitarian-Development-Peace Nexus' (Joint Workshop, New York, 20–21 October 2016) 3.

11

Refugees in Protracted Conflicts

The Lasting Legal Status of Multigenerational Palestinian Refugees

Mutaz M. Qafisheh and Jinan Bastaki

A. Introduction

The passage of time seems to pose a problem for the application of law in protracted conflicts. On the one hand, legal claims may weaken over time. Domestically, for example, there may be statutes of limitation. On the other hand, one looks to the law to ensure justice, preservation of rights, and reparations for violations of those rights regardless of the passage of time. South Africa, for instance, had to deal with the issue of land restitution after the fall of a centuries-old Apartheid regime.[1] What happens, then, to the rights of people forcibly displaced from their homes and denied return for decades or more?

In this respect, the European Court of Human Rights (ECtHR) in *Demopoulos* ruled:

> the passage of time and the continuing evolution of the broader political dispute must inform the Court's interpretation and application of the Convention which cannot, if it is to be coherent and meaningful, be either static or blind to concrete factual circumstances.[2]

The ECtHR then indicated that 'it must be recognised that with the passage of time the holding of a title may be emptied of any practical consequences'.[3] The case concerned a number of applicants—Cypriot nationals of Greek Cypriot origin—who owned property in the Northern part of Cyprus, which came under the control of the Turkish Republic of Northern Cyprus (TRNC). Since the August 1974 Turkish military intervention, the claimants had fled to the South, and maintained that they had been deprived of their property rights due to the Turkish occupation. However, this judgment departed from previous ECtHR jurisprudence (the *Loizidou* case, for example[4]) and was widely criticized as it contradicted fundamental legal

[1] Wouter Veraart, 'Redressing the Past with An Eye to the Future. The Impact of the Passage of Time on Property Rights Restitution in Post-Apartheid South Africa' (2009) 27 Netherlands Quarterly of Human Rights 45.

[2] *Demopoulos and Others v Turkey* (Demopoulos), Grand Chamber, European Court of Human Rights, 1 March 2010, para 85.

[3] ibid, para 111.

[4] *Loizidou v Turkey*, Grand Chamber, European Court of Human Rights, 18 December 1996.

Mutaz M. Qafisheh and Jinan Bastaki, *Refugees in Protracted Conflicts* In: *From Protracted Conflict to Sustainable Peace?*
Edited by: Heike Krieger, Giedre Jokubauskaite, Asli Ozcelik, and Andreas Buser, Oxford University Press.
 DOI: 10.1093/9780198967385.003.0013

principles.[5] The question is still relevant for displaced persons in protracted conflicts, particularly the Palestinians, who have been denied return since their displacement in the late 1940s.

Indeed, Palestinians have been the victims and survivors of more than a century of colonization, ethnic cleansing, and conflict,[6] which has given rise to the largest and oldest protracted refugee group in the world.[7] As of 2025, there were close to six million Palestinians registered with the United Nations Relief and Works Agency for Palestine Refugees in the Near East (UNRWA), which operates in five areas: the West Bank, Gaza, Jordan, Syria and Lebanon.[8] This number does not account for those who were displaced to areas where UNRWA does not operate, such as Egypt and Iraq;[9] nor those who were displaced after UNRWA ceased registering new refugees; nor those who emigrated to third states where they may have subsequently obtained citizenship. Indeed, one of the most salient features of the Palestinian–Israeli conflict is the continuous displacement of Palestine's natives that endures to this day.[10]

As a settler colonial project, and with its desire to maintain a Jewish-majority state in historic Palestine, Israel's displacement of Palestinians and prevention of their return have accompanied the conflict since its inception.[11] Palestinians have concurrently retained their demand for the right to return—a right enshrined in international law—despite the prolonged nature of their displacement. Major political actors have meanwhile insisted on resettlement as the preferred solution.[12] The exercise of the right to self-determination through the establishment of an independent Palestinian state has been thwarted by successive Israeli governments, coupled with expanding settlements, construction of the Wall, and effective annexation via an indefinite occupation.[13]

[5] Elena Proukaki, 'The Right of Displaced Persons to Property and to Return Home after Demopoulos' (2014) Human Rights Law Review 701.

[6] Rashid Khalidi, *The Hundred Years' War on Palestine: A History of Settler Colonialism and Resistance, 1917–2017* (Metropolitan 2020); Ilan Pappe, *The Ethnic Cleansing of Palestine* (Simon and Schuster 2007); Nur Masalha, *A Land without a People: Israel, Transfer and the Palestinians 1949–96* (Faber and Faber 1997).

[7] Francesca Albanese and Lex Takkenberg, *Palestinian Refugees in International Law* (OUP 2020).

[8] Riccardo Bocco, 'UNRWA and the Palestinian Refugees: A History within History' (2009) 28 Refugee Survey Quarterly 229.

[9] Oroub El-Abed, *Unprotected: Palestinians in Egypt since 1948* (Institute for Palestine Studies; International Development Research Centre, 2009); Palestine Liberation Organization—Refugee Affairs Department, 'Palestinian Refugees in Iraq' (1999).

[10] Penny Green and Amelia Smith, 'Evicting Palestine' (2016) 5 State Crime Journal (1 April 2016); BADIL Resource Center for Palestinian Residency and Refugee Rights, 'Ongoing Forced Displacement of the Palestinian Population on Both Sides of the "Green Line"', Al-Majdal Magazine, No 39–40 (Autumn 2008).

[11] The UN General Assembly defined certain actions as constituting 'ethnic cleansing' which include acts 'aimed at forcing individuals to leave their homes'—UN General Assembly Resolution 49/196, 23 December 1994. L Veracini, 'What Can Settler Colonial Studies Offer to an Interpretation of the Conflict in Israel–Palestine?' (2015) 5 Settler Colonial Studies 268; Sari Hanafi, 'Spacio-Cide: Colonial Politics, Invisibility and Rezoning in Palestinian Territory' (2009) 2 Contemporary Arab Affairs 106; Patrick Wolfe, 'Settler Colonialism and the Elimination of the Native' (2006) 8 Journal of Genocide Research 387.

[12] Jinan Bastaki, 'The Meanings of Citizenship between Resettlement and Return: The Case of Displaced Palestinians' (2020) 24 Citizenship Studies 154.

[13] International Court of Justice, *Advisory Opinion on the Legal Consequences arising from the Policies and Practices of Israel in the Occupied Palestinian Territory, including East Jerusalem*, 19 July 2024 ('Policies and Practices AO'), paras 230–264.

This chapter argues that, while prolonged conflicts may seem to impact the rights of refugees, this is, in fact, not the case. This is particularly so when it comes to Palestinians, who have additionally developed a distinctive status that survives the passage of time. After this introduction, the chapter consists of three sections. Section B introduces the debates around the passage of time and rights. Section C highlights the four waves of Palestinian exodus through a century-plus conflict, starting from the first generation of refugees in 1925 (1), through the 1948 *Nakba* (2) and the 1967 flights (3), up to the 2023–2025 displacement during the Gaza war (4). Section D explores the effects of the protracted conflict on the legal status of these refugees that derives from the ongoing *Nakba* (1), uninterrupted refuge (2), and failure of the political attempts to end the plight of Palestinians by resettlement (3), which led to the creation of a special law pertinent to Palestinian refugees under international law (4).

B. Protracted Conflicts, Reparations, and the Passage of Time

The right of return, particularly after conflict, is today considered paramount. This was reaffirmed in, for example, the insistence on the right to return of Bosnians to Bosnia and Herzegovina to reverse the effects of ethnic cleansing,[14] as well as that of Kuwaitis back to Kuwait after Saddam's invasion.[15] Yet, more protracted conflicts may impact the rights of displaced persons. As William Schabas notes, 'That legal rights and entitlements are subject to temporal limitation is not a controversial proposition.'[16] In the above-mentioned *Demopoulos* case, when it came to notions of home, the Court held that

> it is not enough for an applicant to claim that a particular place or property is a 'home'; he or she must show that they enjoy concrete and persisting links with the property concerned . . . The nature of the ongoing or recent occupation of a particular property is usually the most significant element in the determination of the existence of a 'home' . . . However, where 'home' is claimed in respect of property in which there has never been any, or hardly any, occupation by the applicant or where there has been no occupation for some considerable time, it may be that the links to that property are so attenuated as to cease to raise any, or any separate, issue . . . Nor can the term 'home' be interpreted as synonymous with the notion of 'family roots'.[17]

As mentioned, this case departed from the ECtHR's prior findings, particularly as the reason for the lack of 'persisting links' is a foreign occupation. Yet the issue of

[14] Catherine Phuong, '"Freely to Return": Reversing Ethnic Cleansing in Bosnia-Herzegovina' (2000) 13 Journal of Refugee Studies 165, 181.

[15] The Security Council 'Invites the International Committee of the Red Cross to keep the Secretary-General apprised as appropriate of all activities undertaken in connection with *facilitating the repatriation or return of all Kuwaiti and third country nationals* or their remains present in Iraq on or after 2 August 1990' (emphasis added): UN Security Council 2981st Meeting, 'Resolution 687', 8 April 1991, S/RES/687, para 31.

[16] William A Schabas, 'Time, Justice, and Human Rights: Statutory Limitation on the Right to Truth?' in Nanci Adler (ed) *Understanding the Age of Transitional Justice* (Rutgers University Press 2019) 37.

[17] *Demopoulos* (n 2), para 136.

the passage of time persists. In a 2001 piece on reparations, Human Rights Watch stated that

> there are practical limits to how long, or through how many generations, such claims [of descendants of victims] should survive. Because human history is filled with wrongs, many of which amount to severe human rights abuse, significant practical problems arise once a certain time has elapsed in building a theory of reparations on claims of descendancy alone. If one goes back far enough, most everyone could make a case of some sort for reparations, trivializing the concept.[18]

This echoes resistance to reparations and restitution from States. Germany, for example, has had to contend with its genocide in Namibia against the Ovaherero and Nama peoples in 1904–1908. Germany's arguments against reparations rest mainly on the contention that it was a 'historical genocide'—as opposed to a 'legal' one—and that the international law principle of inter-temporality would preclude reparations.[19]

Arguments about the colonial nature of the principle of inter-temporality notwithstanding (as well as when it is conveniently deployed),[20] these would not apply currently to protracted conflicts, particularly not after the Second World War, as the right to return of refugees after armed conflict can be considered to have become part of customary international law.[21]

Furthermore, the right itself is found in human rights law, the laws of nationality, state succession, international humanitarian law, and self-determination. A general principle of international law is that where there is a legal right, there is also a legal remedy when that right is breached.[22] In fact, when Spain and Portugal enacted their

[18] Human Rights Watch, "An Approach to Reparations," July 19, 2001, <https://www.hrw.org/news/2001/07/19/approach-reparations> accessed 31 August 2025.

[19] Sinja Graf, 'Law, Time, and (in) Justice after Empire: Germany's Objection to Colonial Reparations and the Chronopolitics of Deflection,' (2025) 17 International Theory 1 The governments of Germany and Namibia signed a Joint Declaration in 2021, where Germany admitted moral responsibility and pledged development aid. See: United in Remembrance of our Colonial Past, United in our Will to Reconcile, United in our Vision of the Future, Ger.— Namib., 2021, <https://dialogue-on-namibias-past.org/germany-namibia-2021-joint-declaration/#:~:text=Resources%20%2F%20Primary%20Sources-,German%20Government%20and%20Namibian%20Government%20(15,05-2021)%3A%20Joint%20Declaration&text="UNITED%20IN%20REMEMBRANCE%20OF%20OUR,OUR%20VISION%20OF%20THE%20FUTURE"> accessed 31 August 2025.

[20] 'German legal doctrine itself has successfully relied on arguments of natural justice to deal with the difficulty that many crimes committed during the Nazi period were legalized by discriminatory and inhumane laws or were at the time when they were committed not explicitly prohibited in Germany's positive law.' See Office of the United Nations High Commissioner for Human Rights, 'Joint Communication by the Mandates of the Special Rapporteur on the Promotion of Truth, Justice, Reparation and Guarantees of Non-Recurrence; the Special Rapporteur in the Field of Cultural Rights; the Special Rapporteur on Extrajudicial, Summary or Arbitrary Executions; the Special Rapporteur on Adequate Housing as a Component of the Right to an Adequate Standard of Living, and on the Right to Non-Discrimination in This Context; the Special Rapporteur on the Rights of Indigenous Peoples; the Special Rapporteur on Contemporary Forms of Racism, Racial Discrimination, Xenophobia and Related Intolerance and the Special Rapporteur on Violence against Women and Girls, Its Causes and Consequences', 23 February 2023, 9, <https://spcommreports.ohchr.org/TMResultsBase/DownLoadPublicCommunicationFile?gId=27875> accessed 31 August 2025.

[21] Vic Ullom, 'Voluntary Repatriation of Refugees and Customary International Law' (2001) 29 Denver Journal of International Law & Policy 115, 144.

[22] Ian Brownlie, *State Responsibility* (Clarendon 1983) 1.

respective Laws of Return in 2015 enabling Sephardic Jews to apply for citizenship, the language used was one of historic reparations in the form of restitution—going back to the status quo ante—for the wrongful act of expulsion.[23]

These principles apply more broadly to refugees and even in protracted conflict situations, and Palestinians have had their right of return specifically reaffirmed in consecutive General Assembly resolutions.

C. Palestinian Refugees and Multiple Displacements

The expulsion of Palestine's native population and their replacement with Israeli settlers has been at the heart of the Zionist policy since the end of the nineteenth and early twentieth centuries and is still in place today.[24] This policy has been executed gradually through at least four systematic waves, each coinciding with a major conflict. Each wave of refugees was somewhat overshadowed by a subsequent one, often larger in number at the time in which the flight took place. The first wave emerged with the British occupation of Palestine during the First World War through the wording of the 1925 British-enacted Palestine Citizenship Order. The second wave, which occurred during the Israeli–Arab war in 1947–1949, formally led to what are today known as Palestinian refugees; this category still incorporates the largest number of Palestinian refugees. The 1967 war generated a third refugee wave fleeing the West Bank and Gaza. In the aftermath of the 7 October 2023 attack, nearly all Gaza inhabitants were forcibly displaced.

We will recount four generations of Palestinian dispossession to show that, although the century-long conflict aggravated the issue of refugees, the refugee status has never been factually and legally altered.

1. The First Generation: The 1925 Denationalized Palestinians

With more than a century of conflict, the status of this group of Palestinian refugees, which includes those who were born in Palestine but residing abroad when the 1925 Palestinian Citizenship Order was enacted, has not been widely recognized. Unlike natives residing in the territory of Palestine in 1925, who became Palestinian citizens automatically, the citizenship of the former group raised legal and humanitarian concerns. The debate in relation to this group continued until the end of the British Mandate for Palestine (when the British controlled Palestine for almost three decades, from shortly after the end of the First World War, under the League of Nations Mandate system).[25] The Mandate system was ostensibly meant to provide assistance to

[23] Jinan Bastaki, 'Reading History into Law: Who Is Worthy of Reparations? Observations on Spain and Portugal's Return Laws and the Implications for Reparations' (2017) 4 Islamophobia Studies Journal 115–28.

[24] Ilan Pappé, *The Ethnic Cleansing of Palestine* (Oneworld 2006), Nur Masalha, *Expulsion of the Palestinians: The Concept of 'Transfer' in Zionist Political Thought, 1882–1948* (Institute of Palestinian Studies 1992).

[25] See Article 22, Covenant of the League of Nations, 28 June 1919.

former Ottoman territories until they were able to stand alone.[26] The formidable subsequent developments, particularly the problem of the 1948 refugees, overshadowed the significance of the case of this group despite its legal relevance.[27]

The problem arose from the wording of Article 2 of the Palestinian Citizenship Order, which gave those Palestine natives residing abroad on 1 August 1925, the day on which the Order came into force, the right to opt for Palestinian citizenship.[28] This option had to be exercised within two years after the coming into force of the Order. However, on 12 November 1925, the British High Commissioner for Palestine proclaimed that the right of option should commence retroactively as of 6 August 1924, terminating the right to exercise that right on 5 August 1926. The British-run Government of Palestine denied, as a result, thousands of persons the right to become Palestinian citizens solely because they happened to be abroad at a given date.[29]

For most of Palestine's natives abroad, the nine-month period to apply for citizenship under Article 2 was inadequate. For example, representatives of these natives residing in Mexico complained, through a letter sent to the British Secretary of Foreign Affairs dated 9 September 1929, that the 1925 Citizenship Order 'did not become known to Palestinians resident abroad because the [British-run] Palestinian Government would not authorize advertisements in foreign countries to bring the instructions to their notice'.[30]

Palestine's natives were also excluded by Britain from obtaining visas even to visit their relatives or look after their property in Palestine. Those who applied for visas received advice of rejection of their application, thus making it physically impossible for them to travel home. In justifying its refusal to grant Palestinian citizenship, the British government asserted that the intention of such natives was solely to receive diplomatic protection from the British authorities, not to return home. In 1927 the League of Nations Mandates Commission expressed hope, based on the principle of equity, that the British government would show a 'liberal spirit' in dealing with these persons.[31]

A recommendation on resolving the status of this group was presented to the British government by the Palestine Royal Commission, which had visited Palestine to investigate the causes of the disturbances of 1936. The Commission suggested that at least those who were able to establish an unbroken personal connection with Palestine could return.[32] In practice, however, only a limited number of persons were able to

[26] For more on the mandate system as well as its legality, see Victor Kattan, *From Coexistence to Conquest: International Law and the Origins of the Arab-Israeli Conflict, 1891–1949* (Pluto 2009) 38–77.

[27] Mutaz Qafisheh, 'An Ongoing Anomaly: Pre- and Post World War II Palestinian Refugees' (2015) 27 International Journal of Refugee Law 52.

[28] Robert Drayton (ed), *The Laws of Palestine in Force on the 31st Day of December 1933* (Waterlow and Sons 1934) 3404.

[29] Mutaz Qafisheh, 'Genesis of Nationality and Migration in Palestine and Israel 1917–1925' (2009) 11 Journal of the History of International Law 1.

[30] Centro Social Palestino in Mexico, *Letter to the British Minister of Foreign Affairs* (with a cover letter to the League of Nations), 9 September 1929, 2, available in the League of Nations archives in Geneva.

[31] Permanent Mandates Commission, *Minutes of the Twelfth Session* (League of Nations 1927) 128–29.

[32] Palestine Royal Commission, *Report presented by the Secretary of State for the Colonies by Command of His Britannic Majesty* (His Majesty's Stationery Office, July 1937), *Summary of Report*, 21.

return home. In a time span of 20 years, only 465 natives residing abroad managed to acquire citizenship and return after 1925.[33]

It is hard to determine the concrete number of persons belonging to this category today. As has been the case across the globe, people travelled as traders, as students, and for pleasure. A French consular report published in 1907, for instance, indicated that emigrants from Palestine to the United States alone totalled 4,000 people in 10 years.[34] Half of these emigrants brought their families over. Yet most of Palestine's immigrants targeted Latin America, notably Argentina, Brazil, Chile, Honduras, Mexico, and El Salvador.[35] In 1927, it was estimated that the number of native Palestinians in Europe and the Americas constituted 25,000.[36] By 1936, it was reported by the aforementioned Palestine Royal Commission that this figure had risen to 40,000.[37]

In conclusion, the status of this class of Palestinians and their descendants remains unresolved. This group constitutes today the most protracted class of Palestinian refugees. As the majority of these persons had supposedly acquired other citizenships by the passage of time, their main right would be the right of return, as is the case for other refugees. Members of this category originate from various areas of pre-1948 Palestine. If individuals had been habitual residents of the parts of Palestine in which the state of Israel was established, they should be, legally speaking, allowed to return to Israel and acquire Israeli citizenship. Those who were habitual residents in today's West Bank or Gaza should be granted citizenship of the state of Palestine.[38]

2. The Nakba: 1948 Palestinian Exude

The largest numbers of Palestine citizens were driven out during the Israeli–Arab war in the 1948–1949 period. The majority ended up in Jordan (including the then Jordanian-annexed West Bank), Syria, Lebanon, and Gaza, with a smaller number settling in Egypt and Iraq, while others dispersed all over the world.[39] This wave of refugees created what is named in Arabic *the Nakba*, or the Catastrophe. Somewhere between 750,000 and 1,000,000 citizens departed the territory of Palestine that constitutes today's Israel.[40] As of 2024, nearly six million individuals from this group

[33] Government of Palestine, *A Survey of Palestine* (Government Printer 1946), vol I, 206.

[34] Kemal Karpat, 'The Ottoman Emigration to America, 1860–1914' (1985) 17 International Journal of Middle East Studies 185.

[35] Cecilia Baeza, *Palestinians in Latin America: Between Assimilation and Long-distance Nationalism* (Jerusalem Fund, 21 November 2013) 1.

[36] Committee of the Defenders of the Rights of Palestine Arab Emigrants in Palestinian Naturalization, *Memorandum submitted to the High Commissioner for Palestine* (League of Nations Doc 60395, 29 July 1927) para 5.

[37] Palestine Royal Commission (n 32) 21.

[38] Mutaz Qafisheh, 'What Is Palestine? The *de jure* Demarcation of Boundaries for the ICC's *ratione loci* Jurisdiction and Beyond' (2020) 20 International Criminal Law Review 908.

[39] UNRWA, Memo Ref. 1.191, 1 April 1950, cited by Albanese and Takkenberg (n 7) 90–91. cf B Morris, *The Birth of the Palestine Refugee Problem, 1947–1949* (CUP 1987), S Flapan, *The Birth of Israel: Myths and Realities* (Pantheon 1987).

[40] Mutaz Qafisheh, 'Citizens of the State of Palestine and the Future of Palestinian Refugees', in Mutaz Qafisheh (ed), *Palestine Membership in the United Nations: Legal and Practical Implications* (Cambridge Scholars 2013), 45–133, 76–81.

are registered with UNRWA.[41] Hundreds of thousands of others were not registered with the Agency, as we will see. The vast majority of this category were recognized Palestinian citizens,[42] and were entitled to Israeli citizenship through the law of State succession. Count Folke Bernadotte, the UN Mediator for Palestine who was assassinated in West Jerusalem on 17 September 1948 by the Stern Gang, a designated terrorist organization,[43] stated:

> The Arab inhabitants [of Palestine] are not citizens or subjects of Egypt, Iraq, Lebanon, Syria and Transjordan, the States which are at present providing them with a refuge and the basic necessities of life. As residents of Palestine, a former mandated territory for which the international community has a continuing responsibility until a final settlement is achieved, these Arab refugees understandably look to the United Nations for effective assistance.[44]

Yet the final settlement and repatriation have never materialized. Palestinian refugees were denationalized and denied return.[45] The selectivity of Israel's denationalization is apparent as the Israeli government permitted the 17,000 Palestinian Jews who were displaced by the war in 1948 to return to their homes, whereas the overwhelming majority of Palestinian Muslims and Christians were prevented from doing so.[46]

Israel's adamant refusal to allow the return of refugees made other durable solutions politically unfeasible. In the absence of an agreed-upon solution, the role of UNRWA became crucial. The Agency had an explicit legal protection mandate tailored to the circumstances of the refugees it had to assist and protect, who needed their presence in the host countries to be regularized.[47] Conversely, Palestinian refugees needed international legal support to voluntarily repatriate, to regain control of their possessions left behind in Israel, and, at the same time, to be provided with assistance to survive the harsh conditions in the refugee camps across which they were scattered.[48]

It is for this category of refugees that the concept of the 'right of return' emerged (though later it became an established legal norm that collectively applies to all types of Palestinian refugees). Israel constantly opposes the right of return to its territory. As an individual title, the right of return cannot be compromised, even if Palestine, as a state, gives up this right. The right has a firm basis in international law and can only be

[41] UNRWA, *Palestine Refugees* (2024), <www.unrwa.org/palestine-refugees> accessed 31 December 2024.

[42] Mutaz Qafisheh, *The International Law Foundations of Palestinian Nationality: A Legal Examination of Palestinian Nationality under Britain's Rule* (Nijhoff 2008).

[43] Thomas Suarez, *State of Terror: How Terrorism Created Modern Israel* (Olive Branch Press 2017).

[44] General Assemble Official Records: Third Session Supplement No 11 (A/648): 'Progress Report of the United Nations Mediator on Palestine' (16 September 1948) (emphasis added).

[45] Victor Kattan, 'The Nationality of Denationalized Palestinians' (2005) 74 Nordic Journal of International Law 90.

[46] Victor Kattan, *From Coexistence to Conquest: International Law and the Origins of the Arab–Israeli Conflict, 1891–1949* (Pluto 2009) 211.

[47] Michael Fischbach, *Records of Dispossession: Palestinian Refugee Property and the Arab–Israeli Conflict* (Institute for Palestine Studies 2003).

[48] Benjamin N Schiff, *Refugees unto the Third Generation: UN Aid to Palestinians* (Syracuse University Press 1995).

ended by a refugee himself or herself, as mentioned above. The particulars of this issue have been more systemically addressed elsewhere in the literature.[49]

3. The 1967 Naksa

The 1967 Palestinian refugee wave began with the Israeli occupation of the West Bank and Gaza during the so-called Six-Day War.[50] The Arab defeat by Israel is named in Arabic *the Naksa*, meaning 'backward' or, simply, the Second Catastrophe. More than 400,000 individuals in this category were forced to depart the occupied Palestinian Territory.[51] It is difficult to reach an exact number of those displaced in 1967 at present as there is no formal agency tasked with collecting data pertinent to the individuals in this category. Yet considering that the population in the West Bank and Gaza increased more than fourfold after the *Naksa*, it can be estimated that number of the displaced exceeds one million.[52]

Under international law, and according to the practice of UNRWA and UNHCR, these peoples are, to this day, considered ordinary refugees.[53] The difference is that, if they are originally from areas in the West Bank, they do not have the right of return to Israel. Once they settle in the state of Palestine, they lose their refugee status. However, as long as Israel refuses their admission to the new state of Palestine (ie the 1967-occupied territory), members of such a group would continue to be refugees. The ICJ in its 2024 OPT AO reaffirmed the right of return for the individuals of this group.[54] By obtaining Palestinian passports, such people can be protected abroad by Palestinian embassies, participate in referendums, vote in elections, and be elected.[55]

4. The 2023–2025 Gaza War

After 16 years of Israeli blockade and a series of wars in which more than 5,000 Palestinian civilians were killed and thousands others injured and detained,[56] armed groups launched an attack on Israel on 7 October 2023 with the aim of a prisoner

[49] Mutaz Qafisheh, 'Bases for the Palestinian Refugees' Right of Return under International Law: Beyond General Assembly Resolution 194' (2012) Cambridge International Law Journal. See also W Thomas Mallison and Sally V Mallison, 'The Right of Return' (1980) 9 Journal of Palestine Studies 125; John Quigley, 'Displaced Palestinians and a Right of Return' (1998) 39 Harvard International Law Journal 171; G Boling, 'The 1948 Palestinian Refugees and the Individual Right of Return: An International Law Analysis' (BADIL 2007).

[50] Nayef Al-Rodhan, Graeme Herd, and Lisa Watanabe, 'The Six-Day War and its Consequences', in *Critical Turning Points in the Middle East* (Palgrave Macmillan 2011) 99–115.

[51] Qafisheh, 'Citizens of the State of Palestine and the Future of Palestinian Refugees' (n 40) 65–67.

[52] Albanese and Takkenberg (n 7) 49–52.

[53] Tom Segev, 'The June 1967 War and the Palestinian Refugee Problem' (2007) 36 Journal of Palestine Studies 6.

[54] *Policies and Practices AO* (n 13) para 270.

[55] Mutaz Qafisheh, 'Palestinian Citizenship Law: A Proposal' (2021) 20 Yearbook of Islamic and Middle Eastern Law 60, 72–73.

[56] OCHA, *Data on Casualties*, <www.ochaopt.org/data/casualties> accessed 31 December 2024.

exchange.[57] It is estimated that around 1,200 Israelis were killed as a result, while around 200 were taken hostage. This precipitated a large-scale assault by Israel. One year into the war, out of the 2.1 million people in Gaza, 1.9 million were internally displaced and an estimated 100,000 fled to Egypt.[58] More than 3,000 Palestinians were forcibly displaced in the West Bank.[59] At least 45,000 Palestinians (2 per cent of the population) have been killed so far,[60] and more than 107,000 have been injured.[61] More than 66 per cent of buildings in Gaza have been destroyed.[62] South Africa brought a case against Israel at the ICJ for genocide claims in December 2023,[63] on which the Court issued three provisional measures between January and May 2024.[64]

On 24 October 2023, a document leaked from Israeli Intelligence Minister Gila Gamliel detailed that a durable post-war solution for Gaza had to include the transfer of Palestinians to the Egyptian Sinai.[65] Israeli officials were openly calling for a 'second *Nakba*',[66] making explicit the intent to forcibly and permanently displace the Palestinian population from Gaza. It was also reported that Israeli Prime Minister Benjamin Netanyahu had attempted to convince EU leaders to pressure Egypt into accepting Palestinian refugees from Gaza.[67]

During this war, Israel displaced civilians within Gaza under artillery fire and warplane bombardment. Starting on 13 October 2023, the military gave the one million people in northern Gaza and Gaza city 24 hours to 'evacuate' to the south of the Strip.[68] Thus, nearly 90 per cent of the population was confined in an area smaller than 11 per cent of the total size of Gaza.[69] The UN Special Rapporteur on the human rights of internally displaced persons (IDPs) indicated in March 2024 that 'Israel's evacuation

[57] Einav Halabi, Itamar Eichner, and Meir Turgeman, 'Hamas Chief: All Israeli Hostages for All Palestinian Prisoners', *Ynetnews*, 28 October 2023, 7, <https://www.ynetnews.com/article/hjv5rrqz6> accessed 31 August 2025; United Nations Human Rights, '7 October: UN Experts Call for End of Violence and Accountability after Year of Human Loss and Suffering and Blatant Disregard for International Law', OHCHR, 7 October 2024, <https://www.ohchr.org/en/press-releases/2024/10/7-october-un-experts-call-end-violence-and-accountability-after-year-human> accessed 31 August 2025, 'Why Are So Many Palestinian Prisoners in Israeli Jails?', Al Jazeera (8 October 2023).

[58] David Lemmi and Arianna Pagani, 'In Egypt, Displaced Gazans Organize in Grassroots Movements', *Al-Monitor* (8 June 2024).

[59] OCHA, *Humanitarian Situation Update #213: West Bank* (4 September 2024).

[60] Rasha Khatib, Martin McKee, and Salim Yusuf, 'Counting the Dead in Gaza: Difficult but Essential' (2024)404 The Lancet 237–38.

[61] OCHA, *Humanitarian Situation Update #249: Gaza Strip* (24 December 2024).

[62] UN Satellite Center, *UNOSAT Gaza Strip Comprehensive Damage Assessment* (29 September 2024).

[63] Riccardo Mazzeschi and Eugenio Carli, 'Proof of Specific Intent in the Crime of Genocide: The Case of *South Africa v. Israel* before the International Court of Justice' (2024) 22 Journal of International Criminal Justice 429.

[64] Andrew Sanger, 'Genocide Cases before the International Court: Community Action to Enforce Fundamental Norms' (2024) 83 The Cambridge Law Journal 199.

[65] Yuval Abraham, 'Expel All Palestinians from Gaza, Recommends Israeli Gov't Ministry', *+972 Magazine* (30 October 2023).

[66] Chantal Da Silva, 'Israel Right-Wing Ministers' Comments Add Fuel to Palestinian Fears', *NBC News* (13 November 2023).

[67] Henry Foy and others, 'Israel's Netanyahu Lobbied EU to Pressure Egypt into Accepting Gaza Refugees', *Financial Times* (30 October 2023).

[68] Al-Haq, *Israel's Evacuation Order to 1.1 Million Palestinians in Gaza Is Direct Forcible Transfer, Urgent Intervention Is Needed* (13 October 2023).

[69] OCHA, *Humanitarian Situation Update No. 209: Gaza Strip* (26 August 2024).

orders have not made the people of Gaza safer; on the contrary, they have been used to forcibly transfer and confine the civilian population in unlivable conditions'.[70]

In May 2024, the ICJ's third provisional measures order stated that the Court was 'not convinced that the evacuation efforts and related measures that Israel affirms to have undertaken to enhance the security of civilians in the Gaza Strip . . . are sufficient to alleviate the immense risk to which the Palestinian population is exposed'.[71]

On the contrary, the UN Special Rapporteur on the Situation of Human Rights in Occupied Palestinian Territory concluded that '[t]he total siege and near-constant carpet-bombing, along with draconian evacuation orders and ever-shifting "safe zones", have created an unparalleled humanitarian catastrophe' in Gaza.[72] She added that 'the sheer scale of evacuations, amidst an intense bombing campaign . . . increased levels of panic, forced displacement and mass killing'.[73]

Forced displacement and genocide are not mutually exclusive. In the *Krstić* case, the International Criminal Tribunal for the former Yugoslavia (ICTY) found that forcible transfer of civilian population could be used as evidence of genocidal intent.[74] The Court, therefore, held that 'forcible transfer could be an additional means by which to ensure the physical destruction of [the group]'.[75] Hence, the ICTY Trial Chamber in *Prosecutor v Blagojevic and Jokic* ruled:

> The forcible transfer of the women, children and elderly *is a manifestation of the specific intent to rid the Srebrenica enclave of its Bosnian Muslim population. The manner in which the transfer was carried out* . . . clearly indicates that it was a means to eradicate the Bosnian Muslim population from the territory where they had lived.[76]

In parallel, Israel intensified its attacks on UNRWA.[77] This is significant because UNRWA is meant to fulfil its mandate of providing services to Palestine refugees until a just and durable solution is found, including the right of return. Israel bombarded UNRWA's headquarters and flattened most of its offices, schools, and facilities in Gaza. Israeli authorities evicted the Agency from its historical building in East Jerusalem and turned its property into a settlement.[78] On 28 October 2024, the Israeli parliament (Knesset) passed a law banning UNRWA from operating in Gaza, the West Bank, and East Jerusalem.[79] In response, the UN General Assembly, in December

[70] Paula Gaviria Betancur, 'Gaza: Israel's Dehumanisation of Displaced Persons Must End, Says UN Expert' (OHCHR, 6 March 2024); P Betancur, 'Israel Working to Expel Civilian Population of Gaza, UN Expert Warns' (OHCHR, 22 December 2023).

[71] OPT case, Provisional Measures, ICJ Doc No 2024/47, 24 May 2024.

[72] Francesca Albanese, *Anatomy of a Genocide*, UN Doc A/HRC/55/73, 1 July 2024, para 37.

[73] ibid, para 77.

[74] *Prosecutor v Radislav Krstic*, Appeals, 19 April 2004, Case No: IT-98-33-A, para 33.

[75] ibid, para 31.

[76] *Prosecutor v Blagojevic and Jokic* (Trial Judgment), 17 January 2005, IT-02-60-T, para 675 (emphasis added).

[77] Ekin Deniz Uzun, 'Palestinian Refugees in Gaza: The UNRWA and Beyond' (2024) 28 Law and Justice Review 19; UN News, 'Israel's new laws banning UNRWA already taking effect', <https://news.un.org/en/story/2025/01/1159586> accessed 29 January 2025.

[78] UNRWA, 'Situation Report #147 on the Humanitarian Crisis in the Gaza Strip and the West Bank, including East Jerusalem' (12 November 2024).

[79] 'Israel's Parliament Passes Laws Banning UNRWA from Operating Inside Israel, Occupied Palestine', *Middle East Eye* (28 October 2024).

2024, requested the ICJ to deliver an advisory opinion on 'the obligations of Israel, as an occupying Power and as a member of the United Nations, in relation to the presence and activities of the United Nations, including its agencies and bodies . . . in and in relation to the Occupied Palestinian Territory'.[80]

Further to this is US President Trump's pressure on neighbouring states to transfer Palestinians from Gaza, and for the United States to effectively annex the territory.[81] In combination with the attacks on UNRWA, this constitutes a fresh attempt to disregard the right of return for Palestinian refugees by eliminating the Agency charged with their assistance and then 'resettling' Palestinians to neighbouring states.[82]

D. Effects of the Protracted Conflict on Refugee Status

1. An Ongoing Nakba

The previous section has shown the systematic violence that triggered the displacement of Palestinians since the British occupation and then Mandate, as well as how Palestinians continue to be uprooted to this day by various means. Many also move abroad for economic opportunities and are then prevented from return to Gaza or the West Bank, including East Jerusalem.[83] While the above waves of displacement are often discussed separately, all emanate, in essence, from the same continuous event. The same group of people, Palestinians, are being uprooted from the same historical land— Mandate Palestine.[84] This policy is carried out by Zionists and Israel as a settler colony with an 'uninterrupted continuity of intent',[85] that is, to remove the native population from the land through ongoing displacement, domination, extermination and the denial of return.[86]

Rabea Eghbarieh has demonstrated that the *Nakba* has undergone a metamorphosis.[87] The mass expulsion of civilians by Zionist paramilitary forces, and then by the army of Israel, transformed the *Nakba* into a tenacious system of domination:

[80] UN Doc A/79/L.28/Rev.1, 12 December 2024, para 10.

[81] Moses Dirk, "Trump's Gaza Plan May Mark the End of the Postwar Order," Jacobin, 16 February 2025, <https://jacobin.com/2025/02/gaza-trump-postwar-order-genocide/> accessed 31 August 2025; Matt Viser and Michael Birnbaum, 'Trump Proposes U.S. "Take over" Gaza, Permanent Displacement of Residents', *Washington Post*, 4 February 2025, <https://www.washingtonpost.com/politics/2025/02/04/trump-netanyahu-meeting/> accessed 31 August 2025.

[82] Anne Irfan, *Refuge and Resistance: Palestinians and the International Refugee System* (Columbia University Press 2023); Shihadeh Mtanes, 'UNRWA Closure as Prelude to the Elimination of Palestinians' Right of Return', Arab Center Washington DC, 2 December 2024, <https://arabcenterdc.org/resource/unrwa-closure-as-prelude-to-the-elimination-of-palestinians-right-of-return/> accessed 31 August 2025.

[83] J Mohammad, 'Identity Card Losers' (Palestinian Independent Commission for Citizen's Rights 1998); Jinan Bastaki, 'The Meanings of Citizenship between Resettlement and Return: The Case of Displaced Palestinians' (2020) 24 Citizenship Studies 154–75.

[84] Hanafi (n 11) 110.

[85] Lorenzo Veracini, 'The Other Shift: Settler Colonialism, Israel, and the Occupation' (2013) 42 Journal of Palestine Studies 28.

[86] Morad Elsana, *Indigenous Land Rights in Israel: A Comparative Study of the Bedouin* (Routledge 2020).

[87] Rabea Eghbariah, 'Toward Nakba as a Legal Concept' (2024) 124 Columbia Law Review 889.

> [a] *Nakba* regime that is grounded in the destruction of Palestinian society and the denial of self-determination. The patterns of violence, conquest and dispossession evolved into a brutally sophisticated regime of colonial oppression. Across Israel, the West Bank, Gaza, East Jerusalem, refugee camps in the Levant and displaced people in the diaspora, Palestinians occupy distinctive and discounted coordinates in a convoluted matrix of law, whereas Jewish Israelis maintain a singular and claimed superior status.[88]

If one looks deeper at the 1967 war, the methods of displacement were no different to those used in 1948. An interview with a displaced 23-year-old Palestinian woman reveals that after she and her family returned to their village of Beit Nuba two days after leaving for safety, 'they saw their homes being demolished. Red soil was put over the place where houses had been.'[89] French missionaries saw the three villages of Beit Nuba, Imwas, and Yalu 'systematically destroyed by dynamite and bull-dozers'.[90] While it might be assumed that the West Bank was simply occupied and escaped the complete destruction that befell the 1948 villages, an additional four villages in the West Bank (Bayt Marsam, Awa, Habla, and Jifliq) were razed to the ground.[91] There was a total depopulation of the three refugee camps near Jericho.[92] Buses were arranged to take people out on the condition that they signed a statement that they were leaving voluntarily.[93] In July 1967, Israel announced that it would allow the West Bank refugees to return to their homes.[94] About 175,000 applications were filed by the end of July alone, but the Israeli government stopped the re-admittance of the refugees at the end of August, after allowing only 14,000 people to return.[95]

As with the refugees of 1948, then, the majority of those displaced in 1967 were not allowed to return after the cessation of hostilities. Historians have shown that those who tried to return without the permission of Israel were either sent back or shot dead.[96] In Gaza, the Israelis forcibly deported young men and sent them to Jordan or Egypt.[97] While the right of return is viewed as the main concern of those who were made refugees in 1948, those displaced in 1967 were also prevented from return in a similar way. Displacement has never been specific to any one war and continues today. Since October 2023, northern Gaza, in particular, has witnessed systematic demolition of entire cities, towns, villages, refugee camps, neighbourhoods, schools, hospitals, and other infrastructure, combined with civilian massacres *en masse*,

88 ibid.

89 Peter Dodd and Halim Barakat, *River without Bridges: A Study of the Exodus of the 1967 Palestinian Arab Refugees* (Institute for Palestine Studies 1968) 39.

90 ibid.

91 Nur Masalha, *A Land Without a People: Israel, Transfer and the Palestinians 1949-96* (Faber and Faber 1997) 83.

92 Nur Masalha, *The Politics of Denial: Israel and the Palestinian Refugee Problem* (Pluto 2003) 200–04.

93 Ann M Lesch, 'Israeli Deportation of Palestinians from the West Bank and the Gaza Strip, 1967–1978' (1979) 8 Journal of Palestine Studies 104.

94 Dodd and Barakat (n 89) 57.

95 ibid.

96 Tom Segev, *1967: Israel, the War and the Year That Transformed the Middle East* (Little, Brown 2007) 540.

97 Masalha, *A Land without a People* (n 91) 83–84.

starvation, and evictions, in order to force them south and clear the north for Israeli occupation and possibly new Jewish settlements.[98]

While some tend to think about the Palestinian dispossession in terms of 'events' or dates, displacement has been an ongoing feature of the settler colonialist regime. Legally, the modes of displacement, such as house demolition, deportation, land confiscation, and building settlements, are often viewed as human rights violations or breaches of humanitarian law. While methods vary, the result is one: domination over land and immediate or eventual displacement of the population. Thus, in essence, these acts constitute not simply norm breaches but rather diverse tactics to achieve a strategic goal: expelling a native people from their land; an ongoing *Nakba* that binds together those who are conventionally thought of as 'refugees' and those who are not.

2. Uninterrupted Refugee Status

The UNRWA developed a needs-based definition of refugees in order to fulfil its mandate, but it does not encompass all displaced Palestinians. The Agency has one particular group to look after: 'people whose normal place of residence was Palestine between June 1946 and May 1948, who lost both their homes and means of livelihood as a result of the 1948 Arab-Israeli conflict'.[99] Currently, when one thinks about refugees displaced from Palestine, this is the category that is referred to; namely, 'Palestine refugees' as defined by UNRWA. These registered refugees have a legally recognized status. Indeed, under Article 1D of the 1951 Refugee Convention, if UNRWA's protection or assistance ceases for any reason, Agency refugees are *ipso facto* entitled to the benefits of the Convention like other refugees.[100]

The expansion of UNRWA's definition of Palestine refugees in 1992, which removed the criteria of need, offered the opportunity for non-registered refugees to register.[101] However, the definition is still limited to those who were displaced as a result of the 1948 war. As a result, while many have registered with UNRWA, others have not. For example, the majority of nomadic Bedouin could not register as they did not lose their 'homes', but rather their grazing land.[102] Some expelled residents of West Jerusalem did not lose their livelihood and thus were not counted as refugees.[103] One-fourth still live in refugee camps, while the rest settled in cities.[104] Those who were not registered with the UNRWA also include refugees with an independent income

[98] B'tselem, *The World Must Stop the Ethnic Cleansing of Northern Gaza* (22 October 2024).

[99] UNRWA, *Palestine Refugees*, <www.unrwa.org/etemplate.php?id=86> (accessed 31 December 2024).

[100] Mutaz Qafisheh and Francesca Albanese, 'Article 1D: Definition of the Term "Refugee"' in Andreas Zimmermann and Terje Einarsen (eds), *The 1951 Convention Relating to the Status of Refugees and Its 1967 Protocol: A Commentary* (2nd edn, OUP 2024) 629–68; Hasan Bülbül, 'Recognising Palestinian Refugees: Applicability of Article 1D of the 1951 Refugee Convention in Turkey' (2024) 45 Refugee Survey Quarterly 280.

[101] BADIL, *What Role for UNRWA?* (February 2000).

[102] Alice Panepinto, 'Jurisdiction as Sovereignty over Occupied Palestine: The Case of Khan-al-Ahmar' (2017) 26 Social & Legal Studies 311.

[103] Helena Schulz, *The Palestinian Diaspora: Formation of Identities and Politics of Homeland* (Routledge 2003) 36.

[104] UNRWA, 'Palestine Refugees', <www.unrwa.org/palestine-refugees> accessed 31 December 2024.

or property and those residing out of UNRWA operation areas, such as Egypt[105] and Iraq.[106] The UNRWA refuses to register children of refugee mothers and non-refugee fathers.[107] In Lebanon, thousands of post-1948 Palestinian refugees, known as non-IDs, were denied registration with the UNRWA due to the refusal of the Lebanese government.[108] Hundreds of thousands of displaced Palestinians lost home and property but remained inside Israel.[109] In addition, more than a million refugees were displaced for the first time in 1967 but were not included in UNRWA's registration criteria.[110] It is also estimated that more than two million eligible refugees are currently not registered with the Agency.[111]

The UN Conciliation Commission for Palestine (UNCCP), the entity created and tasked with promoting a durable solution for the Palestinian refugees, had its own definition for the purpose of determining 'eligibility for both repatriation and compensation'.[112] It provided:

> Are to be considered as refugees under paragraph 11 of the General Assembly resolution of 11 December 1948 persons of Arab origin who, after 29 November 1947, left territory at present under the control of the Israel authorities and who were Palestinian citizens at that date. Are also to be considered as refugees under the said paragraph stateless persons of Arab origin who after 29 November 1947 left the aforementioned territory, where they had been settled up to that date.[113]

International law characterizes as a refugee any person who crosses a state frontier for reasons of conflict, human rights violations, breaches of humanitarian law or other serious harm; these would fall within the UNHCR's mandate.[114] Combining the UNCCP and international law definitions, all Palestinians who were displaced from the territory of historic Palestine can be considered refugees. They possess the rights of repatriation and compensation.[115] Some might argue that under the 1951 Refugee Convention, refugee status ceases once a person obtains a durable solution

[105] Oroub El-Abed, *Unprotected: Palestinians in Egypt since 1948* (Institute for Palestine Studies 2009).

[106] Gabriela Wengert and Michelle Alfaro, 'Can Palestinian Refugees in Iraq Find Protection?' *Forced Migration Review* (Palestinian Displacement: A Case Apart?), No 26 (August 2006).

[107] Christine Cervenak, 'Promoting Inequality: Gender-Based Discrimination in UNRWA's Approach to Palestine Refugee Status' (1994) 16 Human Rights Quarterly 300.

[108] Rosemary Sayigh and Katharina El Masri, *Non-Identified Palestinians in Lebanon—A Life without a Legal Existence* (American University of Beirut 2012).

[109] Qafisheh, 'Citizens of the State of Palestine and the Future of Palestinian Refugees' (n 40) 96.

[110] UNRWA is of the position that Palestine refugees are 'the descendants of Palestine refugee males, including adopted children, are also eligible for registration': in UNRWA, 'Palestine Refugees', <www.unrwa.org/etemplate.php?id=86> accessed 31 December 2024.

[111] BADIL estimates this number based on UNRWA's approximation that it represents three-quarters of Palestine refugees worldwide. Nidal Al-Azza and Amaya Al-Orzza, 'Survey of Palestinian Refugees and Internally Displaced Persons 2013–2015' (BADIL 2015) 51.

[112] UNCCP, 'Definition of a "Refugee" under Paragraph 11 of the General Assembly Resolution of 11 December 1948', UN Doc A/AC.25/W/61, 9 April 1951.

[113] ibid, art 1.

[114] Guy Goodwin-Gill and Jane McAdam, *The Refugee in International Law* (OUP 2007) 49.

[115] Basheer Alzoughbi, 'International Law on State Responsibility and the Exodus of Palestinian Refugees', *Conference on Palestinian Refugees in the Arab World: Reality and Prospects* (Al Jazeera Center for Studies and Palestinian Return Centre 2012).

(repatriation, host country integration, third-state resettlement); notably the acquisition of citizenship. Yet, the Refugee Convention is *not* one of the sources of the right of return. On the contrary, the main provision of the Convention is the right *not* to be returned, or *non-refoulement*.[116] The purpose of the Convention is rather to provide 'the most comprehensive codification of the rights of refugees at the international level',[117] and to lay down 'basic minimum standards for the treatment of refugees'.[118] Acquiring citizenship simply means that protection shifts from the global to the national level. Examining whether or not the Convention applies to Palestinian refugees' right of return is misguided, as the purpose of the Convention is to provide international support for those who lack state protection.[119]

Additionally, the right of self-determination has been repeatedly affirmed for Palestinians. As self-determination is a right of 'peoples',[120] '[t]o secure the collective self-determination the *people* must be able to stay on the *territory*, or if they leave, they must have a right to return'.[121] The ICJ has reaffirmed the right to self-determination in a number of cases, notably *Namibia* (1971),[122] *Western Sahara* (1975),[123] *East Timor* (1995),[124] and *Wall* (2004).[125] In these four instances, significant numbers of people were displaced. In the *Namibia* case, in particular, refugees had been fleeing to the neighbouring States from the 1960s to the 1980s.[126] Some of the Namibian exiles did not fit the definition of a refugee, but were nevertheless viewed to be in the same category when it came to repatriation. In 1978, the representatives of Canada, France, Germany, the UK, and the United States drew up a settlement plan, endorsed in Security Council Resolution 435.[127] The plan stipulated that 'the key to an internationally acceptable transition to independence is free elections for the whole of Namibia as one political entity'. Regarding refugees, the plan outlined:

> (c) All Namibian refugees or Namibians detained or otherwise outside the territory of Namibia will be permitted to return peacefully and participate fully and freely in the electoral process without risk of arrest, detention, intimidation or imprisonment.
>
> (d) The Special Representative with the assistance of the United Nations High Commissioner for Refugees and other appropriate international bodies will ensure

[116] *Convention Relating to the Status of Refugees*, 28 July 1951, 189 UNTS 137, art 33(1).

[117] UNHCR, *Introductory Note by the Office of the United Nations High Commissioner for Refugees* (December 2010).

[118] ibid.

[119] Mazen Masri, 'The Implications of the Acquisition of a New Nationality for the Right of Return of Palestinian Refugees' (2015) 5 Asian Journal of International Law 356.

[120] *Charter of the United Nations*, 24 October 1945, 1 UNTS XVI, art 1A(2).

[121] M Cherif Bassiouni, *The Palestinians' Right of Self-Determination and National Independence* (Association of Arab-American University Graduates 1978) 19 (emphasis in original).

[122] *Legal Consequences for States of the Continued Presence of South Africa in Namibia (South West Africa) notwithstanding Security Council Resolution 276 (1970)*, Advisory Opinion of 21 June 1971, ICJ Reports (1971) 16.

[123] *Western Sahara*, Advisory Opinion of 16 October 1975, ICJ Reports (1975) 12.

[124] *Case Concerning East Timor (Portugal v Australia)*, Judgement of 30 June 1995, ICJ Reports (1995) 90.

[125] *Legal Consequences of the Construction of a Wall in the Occupied Palestinian Territory*, Advisory Opinion of 9 July 2004, ICJ Reports (2004) 136.

[126] Ngila RL Mwase, 'The Repatriation, Rehabilitation and Resettlement of Namibian Refugees at Independence' (1990) 25 Community Development Journal 114.

[127] UN Security Council Resolution 435, 29 September 1978.

that Namibians remaining outside of Namibia are given a free and voluntary choice whether to return. Provision will be made to attest to the voluntary nature of decisions made by Namibians who elect not to return to Namibia.[128]

In order for the return to materialize, it required, among other things, the repeal of the discriminatory colonial laws that caused people to flee. This began in 1989 with Proclamation No. 14, First Law Amendment.[129] Approximately 40,000 refugees were repatriated before the elections that took place that year.[130] Repatriation was viewed as part of self-determination, since the people had been dislocated as a result of the denial of the right to self-determination. Thus, when people are denied their right to self-determination through, inter alia, displacement and dispossession, they must be able to return in order to exercise the right, as was the case in Namibia, and as is directly applicable to Palestinians.

3. Claims of Refugee Resettlement

Israel has long argued that resettlement, not repatriation, is the 'solution' to the refugee issue. As early as 1948, Israeli Foreign Minister Moshe Sharrett pointed to the 'vast potentialities of absorption [of refugees] in Syria and Iraq'.[131] In 2004, US President George W. Bush exchanged letters with the Prime Minister of Israel at the time, Ariel Sharon, aimed at achieving a settlement between Israel and the Palestine. In his letter, Bush wrote that 'a solution to the Palestinian refugee issue as part of any final status agreement will need to be found through the establishment of a Palestinian state, and the settling of Palestinian refugees there, rather than in Israel'.[132]

Politically, it has always been asserted that resettlement or citizenship is a 'solution' for refugees, since citizenship comes with basic rights, including the right to enter/return to the country of one's citizenship and, thus, this would cancel the right of return to one's original 'home'.[133] Again, as early as June 1948, Sharett told an Israeli cabinet meeting that '[w]e will pay for assets and land [of Palestinian refuges] and this will serve for their settlement in other countries. But they are not returning. And this is our policy.'[134] This was met with broad support in the cabinet.[135] In August that year, a committee was appointed by Prime Minister David Ben-Gurion to submit a proposal for refugee resettlement.[136] The committee concluded that the 'solution' to the refugee

[128] UN Doc S/12636, 10 April 1978.

[129] Charles Gasarasi, 'UN Resolution 435 and the Repatriation of Namibian Exiles' (1990) 3 Journal of Refugee Studies 342.

[130] Susan Akram, 'Self-Determination, Statehood, and the Refugee Question under International Law in Namibia, Palestine, Western Sahara, and Tibet' in Susan Akram and Tom Syring (eds), *Still Waiting for Tomorrow: The Law and Politics of Unresolved Refugee Crises* (Cambridge Scholars 2014) 84.

[131] Jacob Tovy, *Israel and the Palestinian Refugee Issue: The Formulation of a Policy, 1948–1956* (Routledge 2014) 18.

[132] 'Letter from US President George W. Bush to Prime Minister Ariel Sharon', available at: Israel Ministry of Foreign Affairs, 'Exchange of Letters between PM Sharon and President Bush' (14 April 2004).

[133] Donna Arzt, *Refugees into Citizens* (Council on Foreign Relations 1997).

[134] Tovy (n 131) 14.

[135] ibid 15.

[136] ibid 17.

problem was resettlement.[137] This remains the Israeli position at present, supported by some states.[138]

Nonetheless, international law perceives the issue differently. With regard to the *Namibia* case, for instance, refugees returned almost twenty years after the ICJ ruling. Thus, Mwase emphasized:

> The majority of the Namibian refugees are a coherent group of people whose extremely strong organization, SWAPO, was a more or less de facto Government of independent Namibia . . . Since Namibian refugees are due to go home . . . integration in the normal sense is not desirable. Since countries do not easily confer citizenship status to outsiders, the fact that Namibian refugees did not want permanent residential status, made things easier for host countries.[139]

The negotiations between the PLO and Israel that started in the late 1980s have been viewed as confining the right of return to the West Bank and Gaza. Initially, the PLO saw self-determination and return as essentially the same matter, applicable to all of historic Palestine, and that includes the return of refugees.[140] Over time, however, the PLO shifted its focus to self-determination within the Occupied Territories and the establishment of a State. The refugee issue has been deferred during the process, particularly regarding the 1948 refugees.[141] The 1993 Israel–PLO Declaration of Principles on Interim Self-Government Arrangements deferred the issue of refugees until the final stage of negotiations.[142] It was unclear what a 'just settlement' on the refugee issue would look like.[143] A Refugee Working Group was set up, but it did not address the right of return or compensation. Rather, it focused on the conditions of refugees and raising funds to improve life in the refugee camps.[144] It secured, too, the return of about 80,000 Palestinians to the West Bank.[145]

Under international law, Palestinians still retain the individual right to return to their homes. Gros Espiell, the UN Special Rapporteur of the Sub Commission on Prevention of Discrimination and Protection of Minorities, pointed out that '[t]o assert that self-determination constitutes a collective right of peoples does not mean that an individual right, to which all human beings are entitled, cannot exist at the same time'.[146] Quigley reaffirms this argument, by concluding:

[137] ISA, MFA 2445/3, Memorandum on an Arrangement for Arab Refugees, undated, in Tovy (n 131) 19–20.

[138] Bill Clinton, 'Proposals for a Final Settlement' (2001) 30 Journal of Palestine Studies 150.

[139] Mwase (n 126) 117.

[140] Palestinian National Council, 'The Palestinian National Charter' (10 July 1968) art 2.

[141] Saeb Erakat, 'Palestine Liberation Organization Legal Brief in Support of Recognition of the State of Palestine', in Qafisheh, *Palestine Membership in the United Nations* (n 40) 15–29.

[142] *Declaration of Principles on Interim Self-Government Arrangements* (Washington, DC, 13 September 1993), 32 ILM 1525 (1993), art V.

[143] Richard Falk, 'Some International Law Implications of the Oslo/Cairo Framework for the PLO/Israeli Peace Talks', in Stephen Bowen (ed), *Human Rights, Self-Determination and Political Change in the Occupied Palestinian Territories* (Brill 1997) 1–23, 6, 17.

[144] Salim Tamari, 'Palestinian Refugees and the Palestinian-Israeli Negotiations' (1999) 29 Journal of Palestine Studies 81.

[145] Schulz (n 103) 212–13.

[146] Hector Espiell, 'The Right to Self-Determination: Implementation of United Nations Resolutions' (United Nations 1980), UN Doc E/CN.4/Sub.2/405 (1980), para 57.

> The right of self-determination relates to a people and its right to exercise sovereignty in particular territory. Repatriation [of Palestinian refugees] relates to individuals and their right, as individuals, to return to a locality and a piece of property from which they were displaced.[147]

While the UNHCR lists the durable solutions for refugees as repatriation, integration, and resettlement, availing oneself of one solution does not negate the other. In November 1990, the tripartite Chile–IOM–UNHCR repatriation agreement provided for the return of refugees including 'those persons who lost their Chilean nationality because they have acquired the nationality of their country of asylum or refuge' (Article II).[148] The UNHCR was first set up in Chile 1973 under Pinochet's regime to help refugees from other states who had previously fled to Chile as well as Chilean refugees who escaped to other states.[149] As the UNHCR supervises the implementation of the 1951 Convention, technically those refugees who naturalized in their host States were no longer refugees, and thus not the responsibility of UNHCR. However, they were included in the repatriation agreement and allowed to return. This was due to the Chilean government's law No. 18 994, which created the National Bureau of Return, 'to assist and support all Chileans willing to return'.[150] The Chilean authorities and the UNHCR enabled the return of those who were considered as already having a 'home'. The return was based on the root causes that created the refugee status.

A similar context-adapted process may apply to Palestinians. In other words, Palestinians who fled historic Palestine at any point in time since the detachment of that territory from the Ottoman Empire in 1917–1918 are eligible to return either to the present Israel or to the State of Palestine (the West Bank and Gaza), depending on the individual's former area of residence before his or her flight.[151]

4. The Special Regime for Palestinian Refugees

As we have seen, international law provides several bases for the right of return that apply to all refugees. For Palestinians, the passage of time has produced a distinct customary regime for Palestinian diaspora,[152] particularly as two specialized UN agencies were created to tend to their plight and facilitate the implementation of their rights. This regime can only cease to exist once the factors that created it disappear. Hence, Palestinian refugee status would not terminate pursuant to the acquisition of other citizenships or by social integration.[153]

[147] John Quigley, 'Self-Determination in the Palestine Context', Ohio State Public Law Working Paper No. 101 (24 September 2007).

[148] Amnesty International, *Bhutan: Nationality, Expulsion, Statelessness and the Right to Return* (2000), 17.

[149] UNHCR, 'Chile: When We're No Longer Needed', *Refugees Magazine* (1 June 1996).

[150] Jaime Llambias-Wolff, 'The Voluntary Repatriation Process of Chilean Exiles' (1993) 31 International Migration 590.

[151] Qafisheh, *The International Law Foundations of Palestinian Nationality* (n 42) 209–217.

[152] cf Michael Kagan, 'The (Relative) Decline of Palestinian Exceptionalism and Its Consequences for Refugee Studies in the Middle East' (2009) 22 Journal of Refugee Studies 417.

[153] Masri (n 119) 356.

With regard to the right of return to one's homeland in pre-1948 Palestine, that is either the state of Israel or the state of Palestine within the 1967-occupied territory, depending on the original place of habitual residence of each individual or his/her descendant.[154] Such individuals may legally continue to invoke the right to compensation for, and restitution of, their property and damages sustained over the years.[155] As the practice proves, such persons would continue to be regarded as UNRWA-registered refugees, including benefiting from the Agency's services, whenever they reside in any of the five UNRWA areas of operation.[156] In short, it can be safely concluded that international law has developed a *lex specialis* regime for Palestinian refugees, which is either equal or 'heightened',[157] and in no means inferior, to other refugees in the world.

This status encompasses far-reaching consequences. An agreed-upon political solution relating to Palestinian refugees between Israel and Palestine would not affect the international legal status of these refugees until their status (ie return and/or reparation) is restored.[158] Similarly, the State of Palestine can confer its citizenship to Palestinian refugees worldwide without the fear that these refugees will lose their status vis-à-vis the State of Israel.[159] In this case, Palestine will be considered as any other state that confers citizenship to refugees without affecting their rights. Palestinian refugees, despite being attributed to pre-1948 Palestine, possess the right of return to Israel. Under the law of state succession,[160] refugees who were expelled from the territory of Palestine that became Israel are presumed to become Israeli citizens. If such refugees are empowered to return, they may become dual Palestinian–Israeli citizens.[161]

The special regime pertinent to Palestinians also affects the UNRWA–UNHCR relationship. Whereas the UNHCR possesses the general mandate to protect refugees worldwide, the UNRWA applies the special mandate to protect Palestinians. The consequence of such relationship is two-fold. First, whenever the UNRWA ceases to function, the UNHCR should take over the UNRWA's role. The UNRWA may stop providing aid due to the presence of a refugee outside UNRWA areas, the inability of the UNRWA to register certain refugees due to the policies of host States, and the abolishment of the UNRWA operation in some of its areas, such as the Israeli decision to terminate the Agency's presence in the Palestinian territory as early as 2025.[162] Second, the special regime imposes an obligation on the UNRWA, as a General Assembly subsidiary organ, to provide refugees with similar assistance and protection

[154] Qafisheh, 'Palestinian Citizenship Law: A Proposal' (n 55) 60.

[155] Albanese and Takkenberg (n 7), 452–90.

[156] Lance Bartholomeusz, 'The Mandate of UNRWA at Sixty' (2010) 28 Refugee Survey Quarterly 452.

[157] Susan Akram and Terry Rempel, *Temporary Protection for Palestinian Refugees: A Proposal* (BADIL 2014) 31.

[158] Justus R Weiner, 'The Palestinian Refugees' "Right to Return" and the Peace Process' (1997) 20 Boston College International and Comparative Law Review 1.

[159] Mutaz Qafisheh, 'Who Has the Right to Become a Palestinian Citizen? An International Law Analysis' (2017) 18 Yearbook of Islamic and Middle Eastern Law 112.

[160] Jeffrey Blackman, 'State Succession and Statelessness: The Emerging Right to an Effective Nationality under International Law' (1998) 19 Michigan Journal of International Law 1160.

[161] Mutaz Qafisheh, Rama Sahtout, Francesca Albanese, and Lex Takkenberg, 'The *Lex Specialis* Regime Pertinent to Palestinian Refugees' (2023) Global Jurist 43.

[162] UNRWA, *Statement of the Secretary-General on Israeli Legislation on UNRWA* (29 October 2024).

as those provided by the UNHCR. This is because the absence of the UNCCP does not relinquish the UN responsibility towards the refugees, and the functions that were rendered by the UNCCP could be well served by a body which was created somewhat in an ancillary position to it.[163] While the exclusion of Palestinians from the 1951 Convention intended to eliminate the overlapping mandate between UN bodies, it should by no means render the protection or assistance given to Palestinians inferior to that assigned to other refugees.[164] This, in turn, places an obligation on the UN to protect Palestinian refugees on the same footing as the UNHCR does. Although the Convention itself might not be invoked with regard to Palestinians, as the majority of them reside in non-member states to the Convention (Jordan, Lebanon, Syria and Palestine), the UN should guarantee that the rights of these refugees are the same as those enshrined in the Convention.[165]

E. Conclusion

The protracted conflict that created four generations of dispossessed Palestinians does not preclude the constant relevance of the refugee status of these peoples. Creeping legal evidence, coupled with numerous factual indicators, implies that the passage of time would not affect the ongoing rights of Palestinian refugees as a group and as individuals under international law.

The 1925 citizenship legislation that converted Palestinian natives upon the Palestine's territory detachment from the Ottoman Empire in 1917–1918 functions as the baseline for determining the status of those who were gradually displaced in subsequent periods. Since then, Palestinian citizens who were dispossessed from their homeland have retained their claims across generations. Palestine's natives insisted that they were entitled to recover their citizenship during the Mandate period (1918–1948). They brought their plight to the highest international body at the time, namely the League of Nations. With new waves of Palestinian flights during the 1948–1949 and 1967 wars and throughout sporadic conflicts up until the 2023–2025 Gaza war, the status of Palestinian refugees remained legally intact and, rather, reinforced.

Palestinian refugees form the only class of refugees in the world for whom an ongoing specialized UN agency has been commissioned to protect. The inception of the UNRWA shortly before the UNHCR by the General Assembly infers that this agency is a complementary and equal UN body to the UNHCR and Palestinian refugees hold a status akin to the status of other refugees. Following the legislation adopted by the Israeli Knesset on 28 October 2024 to eradicate the UNRWA, the General Assembly held an emergency special session on 12 December 2024. The Assembly, by a 159-vote resolution, warned 'against any attempts to dismantle or diminish the operations and mandate of the Agency'.[166]

[163] Qafisheh and Albanese (n 100) 633–36.
[164] ibid 654.
[165] Ardi Imseis, 'Negotiating the Illegal: On the United Nations and the Illegal Occupation of Palestine, 1967–2020' (2020) 31 European Journal of International Law 1055.
[166] UN Doc A/ES-10/L.32, 5 December 2024, para 9.

The international community has likewise created other bodies to preserve the case of Palestine, especially the issue of refugees. These bodies include the UNCCP as early as December 1948,[167] the UNRWA a year later, and the UN Committee on the Exercise of the Inalienable Rights of the Palestinian People in November 1975.[168] The issue of Palestinian refugees was placed at—and it is still at—the heart of the UN's mandate. Subsequently, the General Assembly passed dozens of resolutions that aimed to assist and protect Palestinian refugees and to preserve their status.

The mandate of the UN Palestine refugee agency and relevant UN General Assembly resolutions were converted into hard law by Article 1D of the 1951 Convention on the Status of Refugees. This paragraph sets up a distinctive regime for Palestinian refugees by providing a permanent basis for their protection until the settlement of their plight. Thus, Article 1D provides protection by the UN, either through the UNRWA or UNHCR, whenever and wherever they find themselves. In other words, the situation of Palestinian refugees has been placed under the permanent responsibility of the international community represented by the United Nations, however the conflict is prolonged.[169]

The case of Palestinian refugees is supported by comparative civil law logic: the right to private property, reparation for damages sustained by wrongful acts or omissions, and the statute of limitation. Rights to possess real estate and other assets as well as compensation for damages under tort law would remain intact and can be passed on to one's heirs as long as reparation is unsettled, particularly when the right holders reaffirm their uninterrupted claims. Thus, the refugee status and its combined rights would not cease to exist by the passage of time as long as the claims persist.

It is but natural, therefore, for the ICJ to resolve in its advisory opinion of 19 July 2024 the ongoing existence of the right of displaced Palestinians that comprises repatriation and reparation, at least for those refugees removed from the 1967 occupied territory, as the scope of the advisory opinion was limited to the Israeli occupation of the West Bank, including East Jerusalem, and Gaza. There is no reason to believe that the Court would rule otherwise regarding the status of Palestinian refugees from previous or later epochs, as all belong to the same category of people.

The foregoing shows that the conflict, despite spanning more than a century, has not altered the status of Palestinian refugees and its associated rights under international law, particularly repatriation and reparation. On the contrary, a customary law for refugees has emerged, which keeps the case legally active as long as the incumbent rights are unrecovered for however long the cycle of conflict may last.[170]

[167] UN Doc A/RES/194(III), 11 December 1948, para 11.

[168] UN Doc A/RES/3376(XXX), 10 November 1975, para 2.

[169] Ardi Imseis, *The United Nations and the Question of Palestine: Rule by Law and the Structure of International Legal Subalternity* (CUP 2023).

[170] Ghassan Elkahlout, 'Sisyphus but the Boulder Gets a Little Heavier Every Time' in Ghassan Elkahlout (ed), *Gaza Cycle of Destruction and Rebuilding: Understanding the Actors, Dynamics, and Responses* (Palgrave 2024) 1–16.

12

Potential and Limitations of International Law in Addressing Protracted Displacement in the Sahel

Sâ Benjamin Traoré

A. Introduction

The Sahel region is one of the areas most affected by displacement globally.[1] What is called the 'Sahel' is a strip of land that crosses Africa from west to east, stretching from Mauritania to Sudan.[2] Due to its climatic characteristics, the Sahel region has been naturally prone to displacements since time immemorial.[3] In recent times, however, such displacements have dramatically increased to become a major regional and international concern. While climate-induced displacement accounts for a considerable amount of the region's total displacement figures, armed conflicts have been the primary driver of such displacements over the past decade. Once predominantly concentrated in the easternmost part of the Sahelian strip, conflict-induced human displacement has spread across West Africa, particularly in the Central Sahel, which encompasses Mali, Niger, and Burkina Faso. Its close vicinity includes the northern part of Nigeria[4] and large parts of Chad that are also experiencing staggering levels of conflict-related human displacement.[5]

In its most recent report on the 'Activities of the United Nations Office for West Africa and the Sahel', the United Nations Secretary-General (UNSG) indicated that internal and cross-border displacement in the Central Sahel region is dramatically increasing.[6] According to the UNSG, as of November 2024 there were more than 6.5 million internally displaced persons (IDPs) in Burkina Faso, Mali, the Niger, and Nigeria, compared with 6.2 million in the first half of 2024.[7] Many people from the same countries have also fled to neighbouring countries such as Mauritania, Ghana, Côte d'Ivoire, Benin, and Togo.[8] The intricate and interwoven socio-historical,

[1] Internal Displacement Monitoring Centre, *Internal Displacement in Africa: An Overview of Trends and Developments (2009–2023)* (IDMC 2024) 31.

[2] OJ Walther and D Retaillé, 'Mapping the Sahelian Space', in LA Villalón (ed) *The Oxford Handbook of the African Sahel* (OUP 2021) 29.

[3] ibid, 30.

[4] IDMC (n 1) 31.

[5] IDMC (n 1) 23.

[6] United Nations Security Council, *Report of the Secretary-General on the Activities of the United Nations Office for West Africa and the Sahel* (2 December 2024) UN Doc S/2024/871, para 32.

[7] ibid.

[8] ibid.

Sâ Benjamin Traoré, *Potential and Limitations of International Law in Addressing Protracted Displacement in the Sahel*
In: *From Protracted Conflict to Sustainable Peace?* Edited by: Heike Krieger, Giedre Jokubauskaite, Asli Ozcelik, and Andreas Buser, Oxford University Press. © Sâ Benjamin Traoré 2026. DOI: 10.1093/9780198967385.003.0014

cultural and geographical realities of the Sahel region make the distinction between IDPs and refugees often artificial. Communities exist across borders in the region, and many have a very low consciousness of crossing an international border when seeking greater safety outside their habitual residences. The international borders existing between these states are strikingly fluid, if not porous, and more often than not the same (ethnic) communities exist across borders. Nonetheless, this contribution focuses on IDPs, although the protection challenges faced by IDPs and refugees in the region are undoubtedly similar.[9]

Under international law, IDPs are distinct from refugees in that the latter have crossed an internationally recognized border while the former have, despite their displacement, remained within their country of residence.[10] The UN Guiding Principles on Internal Displacement define IDPs as 'persons or groups of persons who have been forced or obliged to flee or to leave their homes or places of habitual residence, in particular as a result of or in order to avoid the effects of armed conflict, situations of generalized violence, violations of human rights or natural or human-made disasters, and who have not crossed an internationally recognized border'.[11] The African Union's Convention for the Protection and Assistance of Internally Displaced Persons in Africa (the Kampala Convention) defines internal displacement in similar terms.[12]

Internal displacement dynamics in the (Central) Sahel region are complex but undoubtedly fuelled by the outbreak of an avalanche of armed conflicts in the region over the last decade. The region is currently characterized by political and social instability, with the presence of countless insurgent groups. It is hard to trace the origins of this security crisis. However, there is little doubt that the collapse of Gadhafi's regime following NATO's 2011 military intervention in Libya created a volatile situation that exacerbated the mushrooming of armed groups in the region.[13] These armed groups, with more or less articulated political objectives, have operated across the region, engaging in regular hostilities with both state and international/multinational forces. Most of these armed groups operate across borders, adding a significant transnational or cross-border dimension to the conflict and the displacements it engenders.

However, the security situation in the Central Sahel region has become more intricate due to—at least—three combining factors. First, it has served as the primary justification for dramatic political transformations, with the overthrow of civilian governments by military juntas.[14] The '*just-war-style*' counter-terrorism narrative and

[9] UNHCR, *Project 21 Supporting IDPs and Refugees in the Central Sahel and Lake Chad Basin regions | Advocacy and Briefing Note for the Organization of Islamic Cooperation Donor Conference* (October 2024) <https://data.unhcr.org/es/documents/details/86713> accessed 12 June 2025.

[10] United Nations Commission on Human Rights, 'Report of the Representative of the Secretary-General on Internally Displaced Persons, submitted pursuant to Commission resolution 1992/73' UN Doc E/CN.4/1993/35 (1993); R Adeola, *The Internally Displaced Person in International Law* (OUP 2020) 3.

[11] United Nations, 'Guiding Principles on Internal Displacement' (1998) UN Doc E/CN.4/1998/53/Add.2, para 2.

[12] African Union, Convention for the Protection and Assistance of Internally Displaced Persons in Africa (adopted 23 October 2009, entered into force 6 December 2012) (Kampala Convention) art 1(l).

[13] International Crisis Group, *The Central Sahel: A Perfect Sandstorm*, Africa Report No 227 (25 June 2015); R Marchal, 'The Reshaping of West Africa after Muammar Qadhafi's Fall' (Norwegian Peacebuilding Resource Centre, October 2012).

[14] Ibrahim Yahaya Ibrahim, 'Insurrections djihadistes en Afrique de l'Ouest: idéologie mondiale, contexte local, motivations individuelles' (2019) 72 *Hérodote* 123–42; A Loada, 'Le souverainisme de l'État sahélien à l'épreuve du défi sécuritaire: le cas du Burkina Faso' (2024) 2 *Afrique Contemporaine* 209–26;

practices adopted by the military juntas have entailed considerable consequences both for internal displacement dynamics and for the effective protection of IDPs. Second, this new political context has also manifested in a tense relationship between states and the traditional international partners, including the United Nations and many humanitarian organizations.[15] This situation affects the way responses to internal displacement are shaped in the region. Last, the multifaceted nature of the Sahelian context is only made more complex by the fact that the region is on the front lines of the climate crisis, which has deepened conflicts over scarce resources and displacement patterns.[16] Illegal trafficking and other criminal activities taking place in the region further reinforce this volatility, further complicating the life of those already forced to flee.[17] The Sahel situation is therefore rightly described as 'a complex web of interconnected crises, marked by persistent political and social instability, a deteriorating security situation, and the inexorable creep of climate change'.[18]

It appears that the issues of IDPs in the Sahel region are embedded in structural social, political, and environmental realities. One might therefore wonder whether traditional responses of international law to the IDPs question are well designed to address such a multifaceted issue. The aim of this chapter is to discuss the nature, relevance, and limits of this legal framework in responding to this 'severe humanitarian and protection crisis' in the Sahel.[19] The chapter proceeds from the understanding that while any type of internal displacement presents considerable challenges, the protractedness of the conflicts in the Sahel region (essentially due to a continuous climate and development crisis) compels a radically different approach to the issue of displacement. The chapter will therefore discuss the extent to which this protracted character of the Sahelian conflicts requires renewed ways of thinking about the legal framework as well as practical responses. The chapter argues that in addition to its limited nature, the current legal framework governing internal displacement is set to fail and therefore needs to be rethought. The multiplicity of factors at play requires an approach that extends beyond traditional legal frameworks relating to the protection of victims of armed conflicts, which tend to isolate or be oblivious to structural dynamics shaping the Sahelian conflicts and context. The chapter will investigate the content and co-existence of these regimes, discuss the protection opportunities they offer, and highlight the challenges and structural limitations they face.

This contribution contains five sections. After this introduction, section B focuses on the classification of the conflict in the Sahel. Section C examines the legal

N Wilén and K Aning, *Countering Extremism in West Africa: What Options Are Left?* (Konrad Adenauer Stiftung, March 2025).

[15] International Crisis Group, *Minusma: négocier un départ sans accroc* (2 June 2023) <https://www.crisisgroup.org/fr/africa/sahel/mali/minusma-negocier-un-depart-sans-accroc> accessed 15 May 2025; Wilén and Aning (n 14).

[16] Cristiano d'Orsi and Gino J Naldi, 'Climate-Induced Displacement in the Sahel: A Question of Classification' (2021) 103 (918) *IRRC* 1029–65.

[17] UNHCR, 'Sahel Emergency' <https://www.unhcr.org/emergencies/sahel-emergency> accessed 13 May 2025.

[18] OCHA, 'Regional Focus: Central Sahel' (Humanitarian Action 2024) <https://humanitarianaction.info/article/regional-focus-central-sahel> accessed 13 May 2025.

[19] UNHCR (n 17).

framework that can be mobilized in the search for ways to address protection issues and section D discusses some practical challenges that undermine the effective protection of IDPs in the Sahel region. Section E examines the limits of the current international legal framework in addressing development challenges in the Sahel. It also explores the relevance, and the limitations, of the climate change regime within an integrated approach to understanding the complex interplay between climate change, conflict, and displacement in the region.

B. Legal Classification and Protractedness of the Armed Violence in the Sahel

1. Context and Legal Classification of the Armed Violence in the Sahel

Under international law, conflict classification is the first step to determine the relevant legal framework applicable in situations characterized by armed violence. Precisely, the exercise of classification aims to determine whether international humanitarian law (IHL)—the body of international law applicable during armed conflict—is relevant in the first place and, if so, the exact applicable rules depending on the nature of such conflict. Simply put, there are two categories of armed conflict under international law, with two corresponding bodies of rules: international armed conflicts (IACs) and non-international armed conflicts (NIACs).[20] Although the underlying principles are admittedly identical in the two categories of conflict, significant differences may exist between rules. While the corpus related to IACs provides significantly more protective rules, NIAC rules are rather minimalistic and 'chaotic'.[21] Notwithstanding recent tendencies both by scholars and international courts to conflate the two frameworks, the distinction between the two types of conflicts remains relevant due to the critical conceptual and political assumptions it bears.[22]

Before delving into the intricacies of the legal classification of the armed violence in Central Sahel countries, it is worth briefly depicting the main actors involved. First, opposition between state military forces and insurgent groups is not new in the region, especially in Mali and Niger.[23] However, after decades of relative lull and cyclical reemergence, the violence has sparked at an unprecedented level in Mali since

[20] Nils Melzer and Etienne Kuster, *International Humanitarian Law: A Comprehensive Introduction* (ICRC 2019) 49–73; Marko Milanovic and Vidan Hadzi-Vidanovic, 'A Taxonomy of Armed Conflict' in Nigel White and Christian Henderson (eds), *Research Handbook on International Conflict and Security Law* (Edward Elgar 2012).

[21] Robert Kolb, *Advanced Introduction to International Humanitarian Law* (Elgar 2014) 32.

[22] ibid; see also Jerome de Hemptinne, *Les conflits armés en mutations* (Pedone 2019) 91–129.

[23] Since independence, Mali has witnessed the rise of Touareg rebellions. Most significant are the ones that happened in 1963, 1990, 2006, and 2012 and in which arms were taken up against the Malian government and were met with an armed response. In a similar vein, Niger faced Touareg insurgencies, although less frequently—there are two major instances of such a phenomenon, one between 1990 and 1995 and another between 2007 and 2009. See Angel Rabasa and others, 'The Tuareg Insurgency in Mali, 2006–2009' in Angel Rabasa and others (eds), *From Insurgency to Stability: Volume II: Insights from Selected Case Studies* (RAND Corporation 2011); Kassimm Kone, 'A Southern View on the Tuareg Rebellions in Mali' (2017) 60(1) *African Studies Review* 53; Dorina A Bekoe, 'Niger's Tuareg Rebellions' in *Niger: Will There Be a Third Tuareg Rebellion?* (Institute for Defense Analyses 2012).

2012, when the Movement for the Liberation of Azawad (MNLA)—a Tuareg separatist movement—took control of several Malian cities before having to face a coalition of two jihadist groups[24] that not only reclaimed the said territories but were making their way to Bamako, the Malian capital city. This led to French military intervention in Mali after an invitation from the Malian authorities, followed by a United Nations Security Council (UNSC) resolution.[25] Since then, countless jihadist organizations have emerged on the Malian territory, leading to various international responses, notably marked by the presence of French military forces from 2012 to 2022. Meanwhile, from 2015 onwards, many of the Islamist insurgent groups spread across the borders and started operating in Niger and Burkina Faso. This also led to the creation of the G5 Sahel, a multinational force which engaged in intense hostilities with armed groups especially between 2015 and 2022.[26] Moreover, the United Nations Mission in Mali, MINUSMA, received a robust mandate from the UNSC to combat non-state armed groups in Mali[27]. The Mission was later dismissed by the Malian military junta, and the UNSC terminated it in June 2023.[28] To date, no international force is operating in any of the Central Sahel countries.[29] The number of insurgent groups in the region is not known accurately. In addition to Tuareg insurgency groups such as MNLA and its allies,[30] various jihadist groups are present in the Central Sahel. They are all emanations of one of two main jihadist terrorist organizations active in the Sahel region: Jama'at Nasr al-Islam wal Muslimin (JNIM) and the Sahel province of the Islamic State (ISIS).[31] It is not uncommon for these groups to fight each other.[32]

In addition to official governmental forces and multinational/international forces, two other critical actors deserve mention. First, the rise of jihadi insurgency and the constellation of armed groups has led to the emergence and/or reinforcement of

[24] In June 2012, Ansar Dine and MUJAO took control of Kidal, Gao, and Timbuktu after driving out the MNLA. OECD, *Conflict over Resources and Terrorism: Two Facets of Insecurity* (OECD Publishing 2013).

[25] Karine Bannelier and Theodore Christakis, 'Under the UN Security Council's Watchful Eyes: Military Intervention by Invitation in the Malian Conflict' (2013) 26(4) LJIL 855.

[26] International Crisis Group, *Finding the Right Role for the G5 Sahel Joint Force* (12 December 2017) <https://www.crisisgroup.org/africa/west-africa/burkina-faso/258-force-du-g5-sahel-trouver-sa-place-dans-lembouteillage-securitaire> accessed 12 May 2025; International Crisis Group, 'The Social Roots of Jihadist Violence in Burkina Faso's North' (International Crisis Group 2017) Report n 254; International Crisis Group, *Mali: Avoiding the Trap of Isolation* (9 February 2023) <https://www.crisisgroup.org/africa/sahel/mali/b185-mali-eviter-le-piege-de-lisolement> accessed 12 May 2025.

[27] See for instance UN Security Council Resolution 2391 (8 December 2017) UN Doc S/RES/2391.

[28] UN Security Council Resolution 2690 (30 June 2023) UN Doc S/RES/2690.

[29] The G5 Sahel came to a conclusion in December 2023 after the withdrawal announced by Burkina Faso and Niger in the same month and the previous exit of Mali in 2022. French forces were also forced to leave after the coups, as a result of deteriorating relations. However, the Multinational Joint Task Force (MNJTF) is still in operation. It is a combined multinational formation, comprising units, mostly military, from Benin, Cameroon, Chad, Niger, and Nigeria.

[30] MLNA and its allies had at some point created the Coordination of Azawad Movements (CMA) with two other groups: the Haut Conseil pour l'Unité de l'Azawad (HCUA) and the Mouvement Arabe de l'Azawad 1 (MAA1).

[31] UNSC (n 6).

[32] Abdelhak Bassou and Ihssane Guennoun, *Al Qaeda vs. Daech in the Sahel: What to Expect?* (Policy Center for the New South 2017); M Guidère, 'Les rivalités islamistes au Sahel' in *La guerre des islamismes* (Gallimard 2017) 180–88; R Ferraro, 'Challenges to Implementation of Humanitarian Access Norms in the Sahel' (2021) 103(918) IRRC 859–82.

vigilantism in the region. In the absence of state-provided security, many 'self-defence' groups have proliferated, especially in Burkina Faso and Mali. These groups are frequently involved in armed activities and other forms of violence.[33] For this reason, they have become central actors in the deepening of inter- and intra-community violence, causing more displacement in the Sahel region.[34] Second, facing staffing challenges in confronting the surge of violence by armed groups, governments in the region have chosen to rely on paramilitary groups and militias. In Burkina Faso, for instance, the government created the *Volontaires pour la Défense de la Patrie* (VDP/ Volunteers for the Defense of the Homeland) in 2020.[35] One may argue that they are 'members of militias or volunteer corps forming part of such armed forces' under the Third Geneva Convention.[36]

This mapping of actors highlights the complexity of the legal classification of armed violence in the Sahel. Yet, things could have been much easier, since it is beyond serious doubt that there is no IAC in (any of) the Central Sahelian countries currently. Following Common Article 2 of the Geneva Conventions,[37] there is no 'declared war' or 'any other armed conflict' arising between two or more states in the Sahel region. While tensions between certain states have marked the overall context, such tensions have never escalated to reach the threshold of an IAC.[38] Similarly, even considering the extension of IACs to national liberation wars,[39] it appears that none of the current armed confrontations in the Sahel can reasonably fall under that category. Some of the armed groups involved in the conflict in Mali have long claimed that they were fighting for 'self-determination' and independence, but such claims have never succeeded. None of them have been internationally recognized as a national liberation

[33] Viljar Haavik, 'Self-Defence Militias and State Sponsorship in Burkina Faso' (ACCORD Conflict Trends, March 2022) <https://www.accord.org.za/conflict-trends/self-defence-militias-and-state-sponsorship-in-burkina-faso/> accessed 11 June 2025; UN High Commissioner for Refugees (UNHCR), *UNHCR Position on Returns to Burkina Faso—Update I* (July 2023) <https://www.refworld.org/policy/countrypos/unhcr/2023/en/124330> accessed 4 June 2025; R Le Cour Grandmaison and others, *Self-defence Groups as a Response to Crime and Conflict in West Africa: Learning from International Experiences* (OCWAR-T Research Report 10, November 2023).

[34] See Human Rights Watch, '"We Used to Be Brothers": Self-Defense Group Abuses in Central Mali' (7 December 2018); M Pellerin, 'Les groupes d'autodéfense, pompiers pyromanes du Sahel' (Notes de l'Ifri, Ifri, December 2022).

[35] Loi no 028-2022/ALT instituant les Volontaires pour la Défense de la Patrie (Burkina Faso, 2022); ACLED, 'Actor Profile: Volunteers for the Defense of the Homeland (VDP)' (26 March 2024) <https://acleddata.com/2024/03/26/actor-profile-volunteers-for-the-defense-of-the-homeland-vdp/> accessed 12 May 2025; A Tisseron, *Pandora's Box: Burkina Faso, Self-Defense Militias and VDP Law in Fighting Jihadis* (Clingendael 2023).

[36] Geneva Convention (III) relative to the Treatment of Prisoners of War (adopted 12 August 1949, entered into force 21 October 1950) 75 UNTS 135, art 4.

[37] See Geneva Conventions of 12 August 1949 (hereinafter GCs) Common art 2.

[38] See Julia Grignon, 'Le début de l'application du droit international humanitaire. Discussion autour de quelques défis' (2014) 96 *IRRC, Sélection française* 1. (Over the past six years, tensions have escalated between France and each of the three countries (Mali, Burkina Faso, and Niger). Similar tensions have also arisen between these countries and their neighbours—namely, between Burkina Faso and Côte d'Ivoire, between Mali and Côte d'Ivoire, and between Niger and Benin. In addition, ECOWAS has threatened to use force against Niger.

[39] See Additional Protocol I to the Geneva Conventions of 12 August 1949, and relating to the Protection of Victims of International Armed Conflicts (adopted 8 June 1977, entered into force 7 December 1978) 1125 UNTS 3, art 1, para 4 (hereinafter AP I).

movement making it impossible to apply IAC rules by virtue of Article 1(3) of the first Additional Protocol to the Geneva Conventions.[40]

It is therefore apparent that the ongoing armed violence in the Sahel region does not pertain to an IAC. Consequently, it may only fall within the category of a NIAC. Although there is no definition of the concept of NIAC in IHL treaties, the International Criminal Tribunal for the former Yugoslavia (ICTY) famously ruled that a NIAC exists whenever there is protracted armed violence 'between governmental authorities and organized armed groups or between such groups within a state'.[41] What makes the difference between an IAC and NIAC is essentially the nature of the actors involved. An IAC exists when there is a state on both sides of a conflict.[42] Common Article 3 of the Geneva Convention sets lower criteria for the existence of NIACs, compared to Additional Protocol II, which adds criteria relating to the duration of hostilities and territorial control by the non-state armed groups involved in a NIAC.[43] However, under customary international law, for a NIAC to exist it is sufficinet for two criteria to be met: (i) the hostilities must reach a certain intensity; (ii) the armed group involved must reach a minimum level of organization.[44] These criteria must be considered *in concreto*. In the context of the Sahel, this requires that each specific opposition/confrontation be scrutinized in order to verify the existence of a NIAC.

Be that as it may, there is little doubt that most of the armed violence in the Sahel pertains to NIACs.[45] However, the specificities of the context require at least three observations. First, it is doubtful that some instances of armed violence occurring in the Sahel countries meet the minimum intensity and organization criteria. Over the years, the region has experienced many sporadic attacks for which no armed group has claimed responsibility. Moreover, the volatile security situation in the region has permitted banditry and various forms of organized crime that would not meet the traditional criteria of a NIAC. Some of these groups clearly lack an organizational

[40] Quite to the contrary, the AU and the UNSC have expressly condemned the proclamation of AZAWAD independence by the MLNA. See, for instance, 'African Union, The African Union totally rejects the so-called declaration of "Independence" by a rebel group in northern Mali' (<https://www.peaceau.org/en/article/the-african-union-totally-rejects-the-so-called-declaration-of-independence-by-a-rebel-group-in-northern-mali>).

[41] *Prosecutor v Tadic* (Decision on the Defence Motion for Interlocutory Appeal on Jurisdiction) IT-94-1-A (International Criminal Tribunal for the former Yugoslavia, 2 October 1995) para 70.

[42] ibid.

[43] Marco Sassòli, *International Humanitarian Law: Rules, Controversies, and Solutions to Problems Arising in Warfare* (2nd edn, Edward Elgar 2023) 180, para 6.31.

[44] *Tadic* (n 41); see also *Prosecutor v Callixte Mbarushimana* (Decision on the Confirmation of Charges) [2011] ICC-01/04-01/10, para 103; *Prosecutor v Ramush Haradinaj et al* (Trial Chamber I) Case No IT-04-84-T, Judgment, 3 April 2008, para 60.

[45] See RULAC, 'Non-international Armed Conflicts in Burkina Faso' (Geneva Academy 2023) <https://www.rulac.org/browse/conflicts/non-international-armed-conflicts-in-burkina-faso> accessed 3 June 2025; RULAC, 'Non-international Armed Conflicts in Mali' (Geneva Academy 2023) <https://www.rulac.org/browse/conflicts/non-international-armed-conflits-in-mali> accessed 3 June 2025; RULAC, 'Non-International Armed Conflicts in Niger' (Geneva Academy 2024) <https://www.rulac.org/browse/conflicts/non-international-armed-conflicts-in-niger> accessed 3 June 2025; C Redaelli, 'A Common Enemy: Aggregating Intensity in Non-International Armed Conflicts' (Humanitarian Law & Policy Blog, 22 April 2021) <https://blogs.icrc.org/law-and-policy/2021/04/22/common-enemy/> accessed 3 June 2025.

structure, making them unidentifiable.[46] Some chose tactically to undertake sporadic 'terrorist attacks' with no clear intention to control a territory or reveal their structure. In that regard, it should be recalled that according to the ICTY, 'banditry, unorganized and shortlived insurrections, or terrorist activities' may not reach the threshold of armed conflict.[47] However, the phenomenon of armed groups having a decentralized structure, operating often as alliances of smaller armed groups in geographic proximity, is not exclusive to the Sahel region. Some even claim it is an inherent feature of contemporary armed conflicts.[48]

In the specific context of Mali, the International Criminal Court (ICC) was faced with this issue in the recent *Al Hassan* case.[49] Al Hassan's defence called into question the existence of a NIAC, disputing whether both the organization and the intensity requirements were met. However, in its judgment, the Trial Chamber concluded that instead of strictly examining bilateral relationships that may not meet the traditional criteria of organization and intensity, it is possible to rely on the *aggregation of intensity* in configurations where many groups operate in the same geographical space with some form of coordination of their actions.[50] The International Committee of the Red Cross (ICRC) had previously adopted a similar approach.[51] This has opened the way for a more flexible interpretation of the intensity and organization criteria.

Second, the lack of territorial control by many armed groups in the Sahel may suggest that Additional Protocol II is not applicable to these situations. This is an important issue due to the more protective framework offered by this Protocol compared to Common Article 3. Although the situation can only be properly assessed on a case-by-case basis, the rather broad interpretation of the Additional Protocol II criteria applied in practice suggests that a large proportion of the armed operations concerned fall under the definition set out in this instrument.[52] Although each country has its own particularities, the situations are similar in Mali and Burkina Faso, and to a great extent in Niger.[53] Finally, the examination of the presence of international forces in the Sahel region—before their dismissal by the new military regimes—does not entail

[46] See Sa Benjamin Traoré and Tiérowé G Dabiré, 'The Right to Water for Internally Displaced Persons in the Sahel Region' (2021) 103(918) IRRC 959–80.

[47] *Prosecutor v Duško Tadić* (Trial Chamber) Case No IT-94-1-T, Opinion and Judgment, 7 May 1997, para 562; *Prosecutor v Boškoski and Tarčulovski* (Trial Chamber) Case No IT-04-82-T, 10 July 2008, para 190.

[48] International Committee of the Red Cross, 'The Roots of Restraint in War' (12 June 2018).

[49] *Prosecutor v Al Hassan Ag Abdoul Aziz Ag Mohamed Ag Mahmoud* [2024] ICC-01/12-01/18, paras 427–43.

[50] ibid, para 1266, footnote 4064: 'Given the holistic nature of the assessment of the facts that is required, the Chamber also finds unpersuasive the Defence's arguments relating to individual confrontations taken in isolation, to show that they were not 'intense' enough by themselves.'

[51] See International Committee of the Red Cross, *International Humanitarian Law and the Challenges of Contemporary Armed Conflicts* (ICRC, Geneva 2019) 51 explaining that 'When several organized armed groups display a form of coordination and cooperation, it might be more realistic to examine the intensity criterion collectively by considering the sum of the military actions carried out by all of them fighting together'.

[52] Such broad interpretation is confirmed in the *Al Hassan* case (n 49) paras 1267–1269.

[53] The number of armed groups operating in Niger was relatively fewer than those in Mali and Burkina Faso. See Council on Foreign Relations, 'Violent Extremism in the Sahel' (Global Conflict Tracker 2024) <https://www.cfr.org/global-conflict-tracker/conflict/violent-extremism-sahel> accessed 4 June 2025.

any meaningful conclusion regarding a possible 'internationalization' of some of the hostilities. While the intervention of foreign forces in a NIAC may influence its classification, this has not been the case in the Sahel.[54] Similarly, the involvement of foreign-controlled military firms such as Wagner in Mali may entail some IHL consequences but does not change the overall nature of these conflicts as NIACS; neither does the cross-border dimension of the activities of most insurgent groups in the Central Sahel.[55]

2. Protractedness of the Conflicts and Displacements in the Sahel

Although long-running conflicts are not a new phenomenon, the concept of 'protracted armed conflicts' has given rise to considerable doctrinal controversies.[56] In its ordinary meaning, the term 'protracted' refers to something that is lengthened, extended, or prolonged in time. This definition may be helpful in certain cases where the conflict is manifestly lengthy. However, the qualification remains very subjective as no minimum passage of time can be objectively provided. Nonetheless, there is a consensus around its essential characteristics. Some international instruments refer to the notion of 'protractedness', especially to define their scope of applicability or the context in which some war crimes can be committed.[57] International tribunals have also refer to the concept when assessing the existence of an armed conflict.[58] However, the concept of *protracted conflict* is not a legal category under international law. Protractedness is a factual reality with considerable implications for the applicability and effectiveness of international norms.

The ICRC defines protracted conflicts using two main criteria: *intractability* and *longevity*, the latter being precisely a consequence of the former. There are several dimensions to these two elements. First, protracted conflicts can be of different forms. They can take the form of either a linear protraction of a single conflict or a series of several conflicts. Based on the ICRC's assessment, one can consider that (i) protracted conflicts are habitually *fragmented and mutating*; they are (ii) *episodic* in that they involve 'periods of differing conflict intensity over time and space'; (iii) they are *internationalized* in the sense that they either implicate other states and international organizations or they have themselves a cross-border dimension; they (iv) *reflect a social reality* and result in *a profound de-structuring of the social fabric.* This includes extreme fragility, poor service delivery, and significant human suffering requiring immediate humanitarian assistance.[59] In a nutshell, protracted conflicts stand out regarding the particularity of the armed violence, time, scope, and intensity; they

[54] See Traoré and Dabiré (n 46); Diakonia, *Qualification juridique de la situation au Mali et droit international applicable* (October 2019).
[55] Diakonia (n 54) 24.
[56] International Committee of the Red Cross, *Protracted Conflict and Humanitarian Action: Some Recent ICRC Experiences* (ICRC 2016).
[57] See Rome Statute of the International Criminal Court (adopted 17 July 1998, entered into force 1 July 2002) 2187 UNTS 90, art 8(2)(f).
[58] Mona Rishmawi, 'Protecting the Right to Life in Protracted Conflicts: The Existence and Dignity Dimensions of General Comment 36' (2019) 101(912) IRRC 1149.
[59] ICRC (n 56).

possess an internationalized dimension and result in overlapping social issues and widespread human suffering. All these traits exist in the Sahelian conflicts.

First, although the eruption of extreme violence might seem relatively recent in the Sahel region—from 2012 onwards—the situation has rapidly evolved into multiple coexisting and mutating conflicts. As with other protracted conflicts, its root causes are more intricate than what is too often portrayed as random violent Islamist extremism. It is now well established that there are deeper, structural factors driving and perpetuating the present situation, such as group grievances and social injustices entrenched in the local history, cultural practices, and lack of opportunities.[60]

Furthermore, Mali and Niger had experienced cyclical conflicts for decades. It is no surprise that the more recent conflict spread after the reemergence of an old Tuareg rebellion in Mali.[61] The political aims of Tuareg nationalism were quickly overshadowed, giving way to other motives, ranging from the spread of jihadist ideologies to more overtly self-serving interests such as organized crime.[62] Other structural grievances build on historical antagonisms between certain communities—such as the Fulani, composed of mostly herders and other agricultural communities—or the fight over resources due to the dramatic effects of climate change in the region.[63] The conflict in the Sahel is also embedded in failed political choices imposed both internationally, with the waves of neoliberalism since the 1980s, and domestically, by successive corrupt regimes.[64] Another characteristic of protracted conflict present in the Sahel is its episodic nature. Relative peace in large parts of the affected countries coexists with constant outbreaks of violence in specific and frequently changing hotspots.[65]

Second, the Central Sahel conflict has an 'internationalized' dimension in multiple respects. The conflagration of the security crisis in the Sahel commenced after the regime change in Libya, when some fighters moved south into Niger and Mali and reactivated the Tuareg rebellion. This situation paved the way for international insurgent extremist groups, such as Al Qaeda and later the Islamic State, to turn the Sahel region into the new frontier of the jihad. The early presence of Boko Haram in Nigeria, the poor presence of robust state institutions in large parts of the Sahel, and the existing traffic routes—especially with southern Algeria—made it easier for these groups to create regional connections and become key actors in the violent extremism in the Sahel.[66] Another aspect of the internationalized character of the conflict in the Sahel relates to the intervention of external actors. Protracted conflicts usually attract

[60] ICG (n 26); IDMC (n 1).

[61] Andre Bourgeot, 'Sahel, terres de conflits' (Présentation) (2020) 117 *Recherches Internationales* 45, 55; Amy Niang, 'Le "boom" des saisons dans l'espace sahélo-saharien: Proto-révolution, désintégrations et reconfigurations sociopolitiques' (2013) 245 *Afrique contemporaine* 53; Bruce Whitehouse, 'Mali: Collapse and Instability' in LA Villalón (ed), *The Oxford Handbook of the African Sahel* (OUP 2022) 127.

[62] United Nations and World Bank, *Pathways for Peace: Inclusive Approaches to Preventing Violent Conflict* (World Bank 2018) 23.

[63] Alexandre Marc, Neelam Verjee, and Stephen Mogaka, *Relever les défis de la stabilité et de la sécurité en Afrique de l'Ouest* (Agence Française de Développement 2015) 14.

[64] Jean-Pierre Olivier de Sardan, 'The Construction of States and Societies in the Sahel' in LA Villalón (ed) *The Oxford Handbook of the African Sahel* (OUP 2024) 51–58; Bourgeot (n 61).

[65] ICRC (n 56) 10.

[66] Marc-Antoine Pérouse de Montclos, *L'Afrique, nouvelle frontière du djihad?* (La Découverte 2018).

many international actors operating directly or through proxies.[67] Indeed, the Sahel has become a centre of geopolitical confrontations between traditionally present external actors, such as France, and newcomers. While a lot of emphasis has been put on Russia's presence, especially through the Wagner group, other actors such as China, Turkey, and Iran are also present in the region. The list of international actors involved in the region extends to the United Nations, the European Union, the African Union, ECOWAS, and many non-governmental organizations.

Finally, the Sahelian situation also qualifies as a protracted conflict because it has rendered the socio-political structures in the region extremely fragile. The concerned states have been unable to maintain core state functions in the different regions affected by the conflict. The prime example of this is the widespread inability of states to provide a minimum level of security to their populations. Occurrences of violence are repetitive and the state security apparatus is overwhelmed. A significant number of schools and medical infrastructures have closed down due to the security situation.[68] Moreover, in all three Central Sahelian states, the conflict has entailed critical structural changes in governance. Not only has it been used to justify the re-emergence of military rule, but it has also served as the main reason for exponentially increasing military budgets in these countries to the detriment of the delivery of basic services. The conflict has, therefore, turned into a widespread humanitarian crisis, with close to 20 million people in need of humanitarian assistance and protection services in Central Sahel. Large parts of the population in these countries face food insecurity due to violence, climate shocks, and increasing inflation. These vulnerabilities were further exacerbated by the Covid-19 pandemic.[69] Besides the outbreak of recent conflicts, the current humanitarian crisis in the Sahel has its roots in the structural fragilities of the Sahelian states, which have made the region a humanitarian chasm for decades.[70]

As is apparent, the conflict in the Sahel exhibits all of the defining features of a protracted conflict. For IDPs, such protractedness can only result in the protractedness of their displacement. Conflict-related displacement is the primary form of suffering in today's protracted conflicts.[71] Like *protracted conflict*, no clear definition exists for the concept of *protracted displacement*. Part of the explanation for this lies in the fact that it is difficult to determine exactly when a particular instance of displacement is resolved.[72]

The duration-based approach to protractedness was first embraced by the UNHCR vis-à-vis refugees. The UNHCR defines protracted refugee situations as those where at least 25,000 have been in asylum for five years or more without any immediate

[67] ICRC (n 56).
[68] UNSC (n 6).
[69] Steve Tiwa Fomekong, 'Plaidoyer pour une protection juridique effective et renforcée des communautés d'accueil des personnes déplacées internes au Sahel' (2022) 103(3) *IRRC, Sélection française*.
[70] Isaline Bergamaschi, 'The Political Economy of Aid in the Sahel' in LA Villalón (ed), *The Oxford Handbook of the African Sahel* (OUP 2022); G Mann, *From Empires to NGOs in the West African Sahel: The Road to Nongovernmentality* (CUP 2014).
[71] ICRC (n 56) 11.
[72] Walter Kälin, *Internal Displacement and the Law* (Oxford University Press 2023) 237.

prospect for a durable solution.[73] Protracted displacements have therefore often been defined on such a temporal basis. The exact number of years suggested in these definitions has varied between one and five years.[74] However, as pointed out by Kälin and Chapuisat, the use of duration as the only criterion for defining protracted displacement can prove inconclusive.[75] Other definitions insist on criteria such as the inability to return for a prolonged time, or the continued reliance on humanitarian action. All these definitions of protracted displacement have strengths and weaknesses. Based on the shortcomings of these previous conceptions, the United Nations Office for the Coordination of Humanitarian Affairs (OCHA) defines protracted displacements as

> situations in which tangible progress towards durable solutions is slow or stalled for significant periods of time because IDPs are prevented from taking or are unable to take steps that allow them to progressively reduce the vulnerability, impoverishment and marginalization they face as displaced people, in order to regain a self-sufficient and dignified life and ultimately find a durable solution.[76]

Protracted displacements are therefore characterized by profound vulnerability for a long period of time marked especially by absolute poverty, inadequate housing, limited or no access to basic services, food insecurity, and reliance on humanitarian assistance.[77] Due to the 'complex web of interconnected crises' in the Sahel, these characteristics have been the dominant reality of the majority of IDPs in the region.[78] Most Sahelian IDPs cannot return safely to their places of origin. They lack the means to meet their basic needs and must endure the dire consequences of recurring violence as well as climate change.

C. The Legal Framework of Protection: The Need for an Integrated Approach

1. The Relevance of Traditional IHL Rules in the Sahelian Context

a) IHL Preventive and Protective Regime

Before proceeding, it is worth recalling that conflicts are the main drivers of recent internal displacements in the Sahel. As previously shown, most of the ongoing violence in the region falls within the category of armed conflict under IHL. IHL is the first

[73] UNHCR, *Executive Committee of the High Commissioner's Programme, Standing Committee, 'Protracted Refugee Situations'* (EC/54/SC/CRP.14, 2004) 5.

[74] See Walter Kälin and Hannah Entwisle Chapuisat, *Breaking the Impasse: Reducing Protracted Internal Displacement as a Collective Outcome* (OCHA 2017) note 23.

[75] ibid 17. They explain that 'some IDPs may have succeeded in resuming a more or less normal life without being able to return. Their situation is not comparable to those who remain in a long-lasting vulnerability situation.'

[76] ibid, 20.

[77] ibid.

[78] OCHA, *2024 Sahel Humanitarian Needs and Requirements Overview* (6 June 2024) <https://reliefweb.int/report/burkina-faso/2024-sahel-humanitarian-needs-and-requirements-overview> accessed 25 May 2025.

entry point when it comes to assessing the framework of protection of IDPs in a conflict situation. In that sense, contrary to what has sometimes been suggested, it cannot be said that traditional international law instruments had ignored IDPs' protection until the adoption of the 1998 UN Guiding principles.[79] However, only IHL rules relative to NIACs are relevant in the context of the Sahel, given the nature of the Sahelian conflicts. Although IHL does not provide detailed rules exclusively dedicated to internal displacement, many of its principles and rules are useful in this context. Here, the logic of IHL rules is twofold. First, IHL provides sufficient guidance to prevent internal displacement during armed conflict. Its application can therefore prevent internal displacements from happening in the first place. Second, it also contains important provisions dealing with the consequences of displacement through effective protection and assistance in instances of conflict-related displacements.[80] While IHL rules applicable to internal displacement are even more limited in number when concerning NIACs, most IHL displacement-related rules have arguably reached the status of customary international law.[81]

IHL expressly imposes on parties to an armed conflict the obligation not to forcibly displace civilians. This rule derives logically from one of the underlying principles of all IHL rules, which is the distinction between civilians and combatants and the correlative principle that the civilian population must be protected against the effects of the conflict. However, this prohibition is subject to narrowly defined exceptions, namely when the security of the civilians is at stake or for imperative military reasons.[82] IHL rules dealing with the effects of displacement revolve around the same principle of protection of civilians against the effects of armed conflicts. Provided they do not directly participate in hostilities, IDPs must be protected as part of the civilian population. Just like all civilians, IDPs cannot be the target of attacks by the parties to the conflict.[83] The IHL principles of humane treatment and respect for human dignity also applies to IDPs. They must not be subjected to violence or any form of inhumane treatment. Their life must be protected. Parties to the conflict cannot take them hostage or subject them to collective punishment.[84] The use of IDPs as human shields is also prohibited.[85]

[79] See for instance Phil Orchard, 'Protection of Internally Displaced Persons: Soft Law as a Norm-generating Mechanism' (2010) 36 Review of International Studies, 281, 282; Eilidh Beaton, 'Internal Displacement and International Protection' in Jamie Draper and David Owen (eds), *The Political Philosophy of Internal Displacement* (OUP 2024) 119.

[80] See eg Jean-Marie Henckaerts and Louise Doswald-Beck, *Customary International Humanitarian Law, Vol. I: Rules* (3rd edn, ICRC/CUP 2009) Rules 131–133 (hereinafter CIHL).

[81] CIHL, Rules 129–133.

[82] See for instance Geneva Convention (IV) relative to the Protection of Civilian Persons in Time of War (adopted 12 August 1949, entered into force 21 October 1950) 75 UNTS 287 (hereinafter GC IV) arts 49 and 147; Protocol Additional to the Geneva Conventions of 12 August 1949, and relating to the Protection of Victims of International Armed Conflicts (Protocol I) (adopted 8 June 1977, entered into force 7 December 1978) 1125 UNTS 3 (hereinafter AP I) art 85(4)(a); Protocol Additional to the Geneva Conventions of 12 August 1949, and Relating to the Protection of Victims of Non-International Armed Conflicts (Protocol II) (adopted 8 June 1977, entered into force 7 December 1978) 1125 UNTS 609 (hereinafter AP II) art 17.

[83] AP I art 51 and 75; AP II art 4,5; CIHL Rules 1 and 7.

[84] CIHL rule 97; CIHL rule 103, AP II art 13(1).

[85] AP II art 13(1); CIHL Rule 97.

Civilian property, including temporal shelters and places of residence, must be protected against attacks. This protection stands as long as such objects are not used for military purposes. In case of military use, they may lose the protection accorded by IHL.[86] IHL also provides that IDPs must not be subject to any form of discrimination. This means specifically that they should not be given treatment which is less than that afforded to the general population. Moreover, IDPs must not be treated with specific adversity because of their status.[87] They must be protected against all forms of physical or mental violence, including rape and other forms of sexual violence.[88] They must also be given the right to move freely, and they must not be subject to arbitrary arrest or detention.[89] Many IHL rules also guarantee civilians the right to an adequate standard of living. IDPs must therefore enjoy access to basic necessities such as shelter, hygiene, health, safety, and nutrition.[90] It should be added that violations of some of these protection rules may amount to war crimes under international law.[91]

Finally, some IHL rules protect IDPs' right to return. Such a right to voluntarily and safely return to their homes or places of habitual residence emerges as soon as the reasons for their displacement cease.[92] Parties to an armed conflict bear the primary obligation to meet the basic needs of the civilian population, including IDPs. While impartial organizations are entitled to undertake humanitarian activities in IACs, the situation in a NIAC is quite different. Humanitarian activities undertaken in these situations are subject to the consent of the parties to the conflict.[93] However, it is generally agreed that this consent cannot be denied arbitrarily. According to the ICRC, 'effective and repeated access to internally displaced persons by impartial humanitarian organizations is a key factor in meeting the basic needs of the displaced and the host communities', especially in instances where large influxes of IDPs overwhelm the state's capacity to fulfil their primary role and duty of addressing internal displacement, or are unwilling to do so.[94]

b) Relevance and (In)effectiveness in the Sahel

The broad IHL framework for preventing internal displacement and protecting IDPs bears significant relevance in the Sahel context. Indeed, it is well established that many of these rules are frequently—if not systematically—violated by the duty bearers, namely the parties to the conflicts. For instance, there have been various reports of continued attacks against IDP camps in each of the Central Sahelian states.

[86] AP I art 51; AP II article 13; CIHL rules 1, 7, 14, 15, and 22.
[87] GC IV art 3, 13 and 27; AP I; art 75 (1); AP II art 2(1) and 4(1); CIHL rules 87 and 88.
[88] GC IV art 27.
[89] CIHL Rule 99.
[90] AP II art 17(1); CIHL Rule 131.
[91] The Rome Statute of the International Criminal Court (adopted 17 July 1998, entered into force 1 July 2002) 2187 UNTS 3, art 8(2)(b)(xxv).
[92] GC IV art 49; CIHL Rule 132.
[93] GCs common art 3; AP II art 18.
[94] International Committee of the Red Cross, *Internally Displaced Persons and International Humanitarian Law* (ICRC 2022) 5.

These attacks are conducted not only by non-state armed groups[95] but also by government forces.[96] Moreover, it is not a secret that IDPs have been confronted with stigma and discrimination. Many IDPs in the region have been targeted on account of their belonging to specific ethnic groups—such as the Fulani—accused of conspiring with terrorist organizations.[97]

More specifically, the implementation of IHL rules relating to the obligation to meet the basic needs of IDPs is clearly challenged as evidenced by the dire humanitarian situation. Similarly, there are good reasons to believe that IHL rules regarding the right to return have been violated vis-à-vis many IDPs. Indeed, under IHL return is a right and not an obligation. However, the return of IDPs has become politicized both by governments and by armed groups in the region. For instance, in many instances, government forces have forced IDPs to return to their regions and villages. The objective of such policies is to instrumentalize the return of IDPs as evidence of high performance of military regimes in Central Sahel countries in their 'fight against terrorist organization'.[98] In such conditions, with the reoccurrence of violence, many IDPs have been (re)exposed to attacks. Returning IDPs are particularly exposed to attacks by armed groups because they are suspected of being loyal to government

[95] Sam Mednick, 'Thousands of Malian Refugees Flee Burkina Faso Camps after Attacks' (The New Humanitarian, 29 May 2020) <https://www.thenewhumanitarian.org/feature/2020/05/29/Burkina-Faso-Mali-refugees-extremists> accessed 3 June 2025; OCHA, *OCHA Niger—Flash Update #1: Attaque contre des civils dans la commune de Tondikiwindi (département de Ouallam) dans la région de Tillabéri, situation au 12 janvier 2021* (OCHA 2021) <https://www.unocha.org/publications/report/niger/ocha-niger-flash-update-1-attaque-contre-des-civils-dans-la-commune-de-tondikiwindi-d> accessed 3 June 2025; Le Monde, 'Au Mali, une attaque djihadiste sur un convoi civil fait une trentaine de morts' (*Le Monde*, 9 February 2025) <https://www.lemonde.fr/afrique/article/2025/02/09/au-mali-une-attaque-djihadiste-sur-un-convoi-civil-fait-une-trentaine-de-morts_6538108_3212.html> accessed 3 June 2025.

[96] MINUSMA, *Quarterly Note on Human Rights Trends: April–June 2020* (MINUSMA 2020); United Nations Security Council, *Report of the Secretary-General on the Situation in Mali* (1 June 2023) UN Doc S/2023/402; Human Rights Watch, 'Mali: L'armée et le groupe Wagner ont commis des atrocités' (Human Rights Watch, 12 December 2024) <https://www.hrw.org/fr/news/2024/12/12/mali-larmee-et-le-groupe-wagner-ont-commis-des-atrocites> accessed 3 June 2025; Bassillioh Rukanga, 'Burkina Faso military accused of killing over 100 civilians by Human Rights Watch' (*BBC News*, 12 May 2025) <https://www.bbc.com/news/articles/cgj871wej3lo> accessed 3 June 2025.

[97] Dougoukolo Alpha Oumar Ba-Konaré, 'Au Mali, le monstre du terrorisme ethnique a ôté plus de vies que le djihadisme' (14 April 2019) *Le Monde* <https://www.lemonde.fr/afrique/article/2019/04/14/au-mali-le-monstre-du-terrorisme-ethnique-a-ote-plus-de-vies-que-le-djihadisme_5450086_3212.html> accessed 4 June 2025; TV5MONDE, 'Burkina Faso: la communauté peule stigmatisée, amalgame et risque de "guerre civile"' (23 August 2022) *TV5MONDE—Informations* <https://information.tv5monde.com/afrique/burkina-faso-la-communaute-peule-stigmatisee-amalgame-et-risque-de-guerre-civile-1157591> accessed 4 June 2025; R Hammond, '"I Pray to You Not to Shoot Us": Mali's Fulani Herders Languish in Camps after Violence—in Pictures' *The Guardian* (23 May 2024) <https://www.theguardian.com/global-development/gallery/2024/may/23/mopti-mali-violence-fulani-herders-internally-displaced-people-idp-camps-dogon-farmers-islamist-rebels> accessed 4 June 2025; Human Rights Watch, 'Burkina Faso: Government-Allied Militias Linked to Massacre' (14 March 2025) <https://www.hrw.org/news/2025/03/14/burkina-faso-government-allied-militias-linked-massacre> accessed 4 June 2025.

[98] See for instance the Russia-influenced media Sputnik praising the Burkina Faso government for having allowed the return of more than 1 million IDPs; Sputnik, 'Plus d'un million de déplacés au Burkina ont pu retourner chez eux' (9 December 2024) *Sputnik Afrique* <https://fr.sputniknews.africa/20241209/plus-dun-million-de-deplaces-au-burkina-ont-pu-retourner-chez-eux-1069621038.html> accessed 4 June 2025. This contrasts with what the UNHCR considers as forced return of IDPs (considering that the return to areas still embroiled in fighting would endanger IDPs' lives): UNHCR (n 33).

forces.[99] Finally, as discussed below, the application of IHL rules on humanitarian assistance has been rather limited.

2. The Kampala Convention and Its Broader (Human Rights-Centred) Approach

a) Overview of the Kampala Convention Protective Regime

The Kampala Convention, the only international treaty on internal displacement, is a binding instrument applicable to all situations of internal displacement in Africa. Interestingly, Burkina Faso, Mali, and Niger are all parties to the Convention.[100] Because it deals with all forms of displacement (not just conflict-related), the Convention has a comprehensive scope. It therefore extends beyond the scope of IHL concerns as strictly defined. Significantly, the Convention draws from international instruments such as the 1998 UN Guiding Principles on Internal Displacement. According to its preamble, the Convention is the expression of a common African vision in 'providing durable solutions to situations of internally displaced persons by establishing an appropriate legal framework for their protection and assistance'.[101] The comprehensive approach to the causes of internal displacement adopted by the Kampala Convention is particularly relevant in the Sahel context, where displacement dynamics involve several combining factors. The Convention's preventive and protective framework extends to displacements causes by natural disasters, development projects, generalized violence, and human rights violations.[102]

The large scope of application of the Kampala Convention offers a broader protective framework to IDPs in the Sahel for at least two reasons. First, while armed conflicts constitute their primary driver, ongoing displacement in the region has been fuelled by other factors, such as climate change, which could fall under the notion of natural disaster as provided under the Kampala Convention. Extreme weather events have increasingly contributed to displacement in recent years.[103] Second, as pointed out above, the legal classification of the violent situation in the Sahel is not always clear-cut. Instances of violence that lead to large-scale displacement may not always fall within the category of armed conflicts. Some situations fall short of the threshold

[99] For instance, see ICG (n 26); U.S. Department of State, 2022 Report on International Religious Freedom: Burkina Faso (May 2023) <https://www.state.gov/reports/2022-report-on-international-religious-freedom/burkina-faso/> accessed 4 June 2025; UNCHR Position—July 2023 (n 33).

[100] See African Union, *Status List: African Union Convention for the Protection and Assistance of Internally Displaced Persons in Africa (Kampala Convention)* <https://au.int/en/treaties/african-union-convention-protection-and-assistance-internally-displaced-persons-africa> accessed 12 May 2025.

[101] UN, *Guiding Principles* (n 11) preamble para 5.

[102] African Union, *African Union Convention for the Protection and Assistance of Internally Displaced Persons in Africa (Kampala Convention)* (adopted 23 October 2009, entered into force 6 December 2012) preamble, art I(k) and art X (hereafter Kampala Convention).

[103] United Nations Office of the Special Coordinator for Development in the Sahel and United Nations High Commissioner for Refugees, *Moving from Reaction to Action: Anticipating Vulnerability Hotspots in the Sahel* (eds Sophie Charlotte von Loeben, Jana Birner, Kira Vinke and Christoph Gornott) (UNOSCDS and UNHCR 2023) <https://reliefweb.int/report/world/moving-reaction-action-anticipating-vulnerability-hotspots-sahel> accessed 7 June 2025; Bendangwapang Ao and Namrata Saha, 'Internally Displaced Persons and the Right-Based Approach: An Inquiry into the Legal Platforms of the African Union' in

for NIAC. For example, recurrent inter-community violence, particularly in central Mali and many parts of Burkina Faso, has resulted in considerable displacements. Such situations fall under the Kampala Convention's reference to 'situations of generalized violence and human rights violations'.[104] Although the Convention does not define 'generalized' violence, article 3(1)b identifies underlying factors such as political, social, cultural, and economic exclusion as well as targeting of persons based on identity, religion, or political opinion. Indeed, as pointed out already, many IDPs in the Sahel have been forced to leave their villages because of their ethnic identity.[105]

While drawing on IHL rules on the protection of civilians during armed conflict,[106] the Kampala Convention is primarily rooted in human rights law. It is also true that these two branches of international law share more than is often assumed. There is arguably a 'human rights thinking' behind most IHL rules.[107] The reason for the human rights-centred approach seems self-evident. Although international human rights law (IHRL) does not explicitly recognize a general right not to be displaced,[108] internal displacement poses basic human rights issues as it ultimately affects the enjoyment of IDPs' human rights.[109] It is apparent that the Kampala Convention not only refers to several human rights instruments, but it is crafted in a human rights language.

The list of international instruments recalled in the preamble includes all major international and African human rights texts, starting with the 1948 Universal Declaration of Human Rights.[110] State Parties are obligated to respect, protect and fulfil the human rights of IDPs. The Convention refers to 'inherent rights of internally displaced persons' while affirming that 'all persons have a right to be protected against arbitrary displacement'.[111] It therefore imposes an obligation on states to ensure respect for and the protection of the human rights of internally displaced persons, including humane treatment, non-discrimination, equality, and equal protection of

Pardeep Singh, Bendangwapang Ao, and Anamika Yadav (eds), *Global Climate Change and Environmental Refugees* (Springer 2023).

[104] Kampala Convention art IV(4)(d).
[105] Patricia Huon, 'Mali Conflict: "It's Not about Jihad or Islam, but Justice"' *The Guardian* (15 March 2021) <https://www.theguardian.com/global-development/2021/mar/15/mali-conflict-its-not-about-jihad-or-islam-but-justice> accessed 5 June 2025; Hammond (n 97); Human Rights Watch, 'Burkina Faso: Army Directs Ethnic Massacres' (12 May 2025) <https://www.hrw.org/news/2025/05/12/burkina-faso-army-directs-ethnic-massacres> accessed 5 June 2025.
[106] Fomekong (n 69).
[107] Boyd van Dijk, *Preparing for War: The Making of the Geneva Conventions* (OUP 2022), 67; Yves Sandoz, 'Droit international humanitaire et droits de l'homme: mariage d'amour ou de raison?' in Andréas Auer, Alexandre Fluckigerm and Michel Hottelier (eds), *Les droits de l'homme et la constitution, Études en l'honneur du Professeur Giorgio Malinverni* (Schulthess 2007) 339.
[108] UNHCR, 'Manuel pour la protection des déplacés internes' (2008) 189.
[109] The First UN Expert on the issue captured the nature of such rights. According to Deng: 'Among these are the right to food, the right to shelter and adequate living conditions, the right to health care, the right to life and personal integrity, the right to work and to an adequate wage, freedom of residence and movement, family unity, the right to education, legal personality, and freedom of thought, association, expression and assembly.' See Francis M Deng, *Comprehensive Study on the Human Rights Issues Related to Internally Displaced Persons: Report of the Representative of the Secretary-General, Pursuant to Commission on Human Rights Resolution 1992/73* (21 January 1993) UN Doc E/CN.4/1993/35, 10, para 30.
[110] Kampala Convention preamble.
[111] Kampala Convention art IV (4).

law, which are central foundational human rights principles.[112] Furthermore, IDPs' rights to freedom of movement, to property, and to asylum must also be protected. It further provides specific protection for and assistance to internally displaced persons with special needs, including separated and unaccompanied children, female heads of households, expectant mothers, mothers with young children, the elderly, and persons with disabilities or with communicable diseases.[113]

Despite its innovations, the Kampala Convention retains the traditional state-centric approach common to human rights instruments. While some of the rules are rather innovatively addressed to non-state actors such as armed groups and multinational corporations, the Convention focuses on State Parties' duty to regulate the conduct of these non-state actors and ensure they do not violate IDPs' rights.[114] The Convention imposes on states the duty to incorporate its provisions in their domestic laws.[115] Some obligations require states to refrain from violating IDPs' human rights, while many others impose duties on states to take positive measures to prevent internal displacements, protect IDPs, and find durable solutions to their situation. This includes criminal accountability for non-respect of the preventive and protective obligations set forth in the Convention.[116] The right to information and consultation is also provided for IDPs, especially regarding all decisions that may affect their situation. Similarly, article 11 recalls the right of IDPs to voluntary return, prohibiting forced return to their place of habitual residence.

It is worth noting that the Kampala Convention establishes an individual right of IDPs 'to peacefully request or seek protection and assistance, in accordance with relevant national and international laws, a right for which they shall not be persecuted, prosecuted or punished'.[117] This right to assistance echoes the state's primary duty and responsibility for providing protection and humanitarian assistance to internally displaced persons within their territory or jurisdiction without discrimination.[118] This raises the somewhat controversial issue of the right to humanitarian assistance. According to article 5(3) of the Convention, States Parties have an obligation to respect the mandates of the African Union, the United Nations, and the roles of international humanitarian organizations in providing protection and assistance to internally displaced persons, in accordance with international law.[119] This provision builds on and reinforces article 30 of the UN Guiding Principles.[120]

b) Domestication of the Kampala Convention in Sahel Countries

The Central Sahelian countries have not approached the implementation of the Kampala Convention in the same way. There is no domestic legislation in Mali

112 Kampala Convention art III, IV (4), V, IX, inter alia.
113 Kampala Convention art IX (2) (c).
114 Allehone M Abebe, *The Emerging Law of Forced Displacement in Africa: Development and Implementation of the Kampala Convention on Internal Displacement* (1st edn, Routledge 2016) 151–90.
115 Kampala Convention art III(2)(a).
116 Kampala Convention art III (1) (H) (G) and (I).
117 Kampala Convention art V(9).
118 Kampala Convention art V(1).
119 Kampala Convention art V(3).
120 See UN (n 11) principle 30.

incorporating the Kampala Convention into domestic law. However, in 2015, the Malian government adopted a National Strategy for the Management of Internally Displaced Persons and Returnees. This policy framework contains limited references to the Kampala Convention.[121] Among other things, it aims at contributing to post-conflict stabilization by providing people in emergency situations with coordinated and integrated assistance necessary for their survival, and ensuring the socioeconomic reintegration of IDPs and returnees by strengthening social cohesion.[122] It is unclear what has become of this strategy following the two successive military coups in Mali.

Niger, on the other hand, adopted national legislation in 2018 implementing the Kampala Convention into domestic law.[123] The Nigerien legislation reflects the obligations enshrined in the Kampala Convention in a concise yet comprehensive manner. The legislation also established some institutional responsibilities including obligations assigned to various state administrative bodies. The National Human Right Commission of Niger is vested with the power to denounce violations of IDPs' rights and refer cases for investigation to the competent authorities.[124] Under this legislation, the Nigerien state holds the primary responsibility for humanitarian assistance to IDPs. Only in cases of resource insufficiency may the state seek assistance from national and international humanitarian organizations.[125]

Burkina Faso does not have specific legislation on IDPs. However, several scattered domestic laws in Burkina Faso address aspects of IDP protection and could be considered as implementing large parts of the Kampala Convention.[126] The primary legislation in this regard is the 2014 Framework legislation for the prevention and management of risks, humanitarian crises, and disasters.[127] The institutional framework in Burkina Faso is centred on the National Council for Emergency Relief and Rehabilitation (*Conseil national de secours d'urgence et de rehabilitation*, CONASUR), which is the governing and decision-making body for disaster prevention, emergency relief management, and rehabilitation. There is also the General Directorate for Solidarity and Humanitarian Action. However, the absence of a clear legislative framework comprehensively implementing the

[121] République du Mali, *Stratégie Nationale de Gestion des Personnes Déplacées Internes et des Rapatriés* (2015) (accessible here <https://www.refworld.org/policy/strategy/natlegbod/2015/fr/121353>); Moreover, although the Malian government withdrew from it, Article 15 of the 2015 Agreement for Peace and Reconciliation in Mali Resulting from the Algiers Process deals with humanitarian issues including the issue of IDPs referring to the Kampala convention. (<https://www.un.org/en/pdfs/EN-ML_150620_Accord-pour-la-paix-et-la-reconciliation-au-MaliIssu-du-Processus-d'Alger.pdf>).

[122] Mali (n 121).

[123] Law No 2018-74 of 10 December 2018 on the Protection and Assistance of Internally Displaced Persons [Niger].

[124] Law No 2018-74 (n 123) art 15.

[125] Law No 2018-74 (n 123) art 17.

[126] Kienou Medard, Étude de la compatibilité de la législation Burkinabè à la convention de Kampala (2019), Unpublished Report (On file with the author).

[127] See Law No 012-2014/NA on the Prevention and Management of Risks, Humanitarian Crises and Disasters (Burkina Faso).

Kampala Convention remains a considerable loophole in the protection of IDPs in Burkina.[128]

D. Practical Protection Challenges in the Current Sahelian Context

1. The Uncertainty of Domestic Protection amidst the (Neo-)Sovereign Political Turn

'Neo-sovereignism' refers to over-reliance on the concept of state sovereignty, a political posture displayed by Central Sahelian military regimes since their arrival in power.[129] Since 2019, a new political context has emerged in the Central Sahelian countries. The degraded security situation and the accusations of incompetence levelled against civilian regimes were used as justification for military coups in these countries. The military leaders, therefore, gained considerable support from the population based on their pledge to eradicate terrorism in record times. It is unclear whether substantial progress has been made in that direction. However, this new political context has been marked by a strong reaffirmation of state sovereignty and demands for non-interference in domestic affairs. In addition to the strict security agenda that has shaped their domestic and international legitimacy agenda, these military regimes have also proclaimed an 'anti-imperialist' agenda. Anti-imperialist and non-interference narratives led to, among other things, the withdrawal from the regional organization ECOWAS, the ending of military cooperation with France, and the denunciation of many other security initiatives in the region.[130] Even more striking was the demand for the end of the UN mission in Mali (MINUSMA) by the Malian authorities. Their counter-terrorism operations have had significant implications on the protective and operational frameworks relating to internal displacements.

The first consequence of the current political context is the approach adopted by the military regime: that the perceived 'legitimacy' of their fight against armed groups trumps human rights obligations. Massive human rights violations have been reported in this context both by domestic and international organizations.[131] Moreover, the current context is characterized by a shrinking civic space, in which both domestic and international human rights organizations as well as critical civil society organizations are constantly attacked or silenced by state authorities. This systematic rollback

[128] Ministère de la Justice et des Droits Humains en charge des Relations avec le Parlement, *Rapport analytique sur la situation des personnes déplacées internes écoutées en 2024* (October 2024) (On file with the author).

[129] Achille Mbembe, 'Afrique-France: neuf thèses sur la fin d'un cycle' (2023) *Le Grand Continent* <https://legrandcontinent.eu/fr/2023/09/04/afrique-france-la-fin-dun-cycle-fr/> accessed 6 June 2025; International Crisis Group, *Le tournant souverainiste au Mali* (Rapport Afrique No 315, 3 December 2024).

[130] Wilén and Aning (n 14).

[131] Amnesty International, *Human Rights Violations by Security Forces in the Sahel* (9 June 2020); Human Rights Watch, 'Sahel: End Abuses in Counterterrorism Operations' (Human Rights Watch, 2021) <https://www.hrw.org/news/2021/02/13/sahel-end-abuses-counterterrorism-operations> accessed 4 June 2025; Adama Dieng, 'The Sahel: Challenges and Opportunities' (2022) 104(918) IRRC; Human Rights Watch (n 105).

of human rights is not conducive to IDPs' protection. Additionally, the issue of IDPs has been highly politicized due to this context. Such politicization manifests in different ways. For instance, there has been strong resistance from political authorities in the Central Sahelian countries to granting access to critical information on the situation of IDPs.[132]

Indeed, having justified their legitimacy through the populations' aspirations for safety and security, the military regimes have become very sensitive to revealing accurate information about the state of displacements in their countries. Figures on internal displacements may serve as indicators of the security situation of these countries. The military authorities in the region are not willing to display accurate information on terrorist attacks and IDPs, which may contradict the narrative of military success that they have promoted so far. It should be noted that, in an era of fake news and social media propaganda, non-state armed groups in the region have also used images and figures to display their alleged successes and supremacy over governmental armed forces.

Second, the politicization of displacement raises another issue which relates to accusations leveled against IDPs themselves. IDPs are often suspected of belonging to terrorist armed groups. This has repeatedly led to attacks against IDP camps, arrests of IDPs, or discrimination against or lack of support of IDPs by host communities.[133] Non-state armed groups are equally suspicious of IDPs, particularly when they return from regions under the control of government forces. While IDPs are prohibited under the Kampala Convention from engaging 'in subversive activities', the problem with such accusations is their lack of substantiated evidence and how often they are rooted in discriminatory considerations. Indeed, these individuals pay the double price of being massively displaced but also suspected of complicity with terrorist groups.[134]

2. The Challenges of International Assistance

The context described above has also considerably affected the provision of international assistance to IDPs in the Sahel. The legal framework relating to the protection of IDPs acknowledges the primary responsibility of states in dealing with displacement issues within their territories. According to the UN Guiding Principles, 'national authorities have the primary duty and responsibility to provide protection and humanitarian assistance to internally displaced persons within their jurisdiction'.[135] The term 'national authorities' refers here to state bodies. This is clarified by the Kampala Convention's statement that 'States Parties bear the primary duty and

[132] Henry Wilkins, 'Journalists in Burkina Faso Blocked from Accessing IDP Sites' (Al Jazeera, 25 May 2021) <https://www.aljazeera.com/news/2021/5/25/journalists-in-burkina-faso-blocked-from-accessing-idp-sites> accessed 6 June 2025. https://www.aljazeera.com/news/2021/5/25/journalists-in-burkina-faso-blocked-from-accessing-idp-sites

[133] Human Rights Watch (n 105).

[134] ibid.

[135] UN (n 11) principle 3.

responsibility for providing protection of and humanitarian assistance to internally displaced persons within their territory or jurisdiction without discrimination of any kind'.[136] It is, therefore, apparent that international assistance and the role of international actors in dealing with displacement issues is subject to the principle of state sovereignty. There is no right of IDPs to request international assistance. Hence, there is no correlative obligation on states to accept such international assistance.[137] Even under the strict IHL rules, such an obligation is absent in a context such as the Sahel due to the non-international character of the conflicts in the region.[138] The preeminence of state sovereignty in NIAC contexts such as the Sahel has entailed a series of consequences for the protection and assistance of IDPs. First, the strong reaffirmation of state sovereignty, along with demands for non-interference, has fostered increasing hostility towards humanitarian and development assistance in the Sahel countries.[139] While many organizations have halted their operations in the Sahel, the rejection of MINUSMA is the clearest example of this dynamic. This followed a series of criticisms raised against the mission by the Malian transitional authorities. MINUSMA was accused not only of failing to carry out its mandate, but also of interfering in Malian internal affairs.[140] As a multidimensional peace operation, MINUSMA's mandate included humanitarian assistance and stabilization activities. Another example is the French Development Agency (AFD), which had to shut down following the considerable deterioration of the relations between French and Malian authorities.[141]

Second, even for international actors that have been able to maintain their presence in Sahelian countries, the security crisis and political dynamics have rendered their work highly difficult. Operational obstacles have multiplied due to the difficulty of accessing certain parts of these countries where humanitarian needs are urgent. In addition to such operational obstacles, humanitarian personnel have had to face accusations of supporting terrorism in many Sahelian countries. The first aspect of this issue relates to the highly dangerous nature of humanitarian work in a context marked by widespread terrorist activity. As different 'terrorist organizations' have increased their control over large parts of Sahelian countries, humanitarian actors have been obliged to considerably limit their activities to main urban centres.[142] Yet, humanitarian action in NIAC is subject to the consent of the parties controlling the territory to which it is destined, although, in principle, such consent must not be arbitrarily denied. In a context of suspicion by state actors and reprisal by armed groups, many IDPs in remote regions have been deprived of their right to receive humanitarian assistance.

[136] Kampala Convention art V (1).

[137] The terms of Article V of the Kampala Convention are more mandatory than the UN Guiding Principles. However, they can hardly be interpreted as acknowledging a right to international assistance.

[138] IHL's rules related to IAC are more precise on the right to humanitarian assistance, especially in situations of occupation. See GC IV, 23, 30, 59; AP I, 54(1), 70; Sassòli (n 43).

[139] Hanafi Dicko, 'De la difficulté d'intervenir au Sahel' (MSF CRASH, 24 June 2024) <https://msf-crash.org/fr/guerre-et-humanitaire/de-la-difficulte-dintervenir-au-sahel> accessed 12 May 2025.

[140] UNSC (n 96).

[141] Taïs Brouck, 'Afrique–France: Poussée Hors du Sahel, l'AFD Forcée à se Réinventer' (*Jeune Afrique*, 2024).

[142] Bourgeot (n 61); Ferraro (n 32).

Accusations of supporting terrorist organizations have been levelled against humanitarian organizations as well as individual humanitarian workers. The spread of fake news on social media has contributed to amplifying such accusations and has fuelled a hostile climate for humanitarian operations in some countries such as Niger, where the military junta has recently banned the ICRC despite worldwide recognition of its credibility and its special status under IHL. Alongside other humanitarian organizations, the ICRC has been accused without substantiated evidence of 'supporting terrorists' in Niger.[143]

This stance regarding international actors might be fully justified under the principle of sovereignty. It also falls within the ongoing backlash against various international rules and institutions fuelled by populist narratives across the globe.[144] However, from a legal perspective, it raises the question of the extent to which state sovereignty may hinder international assistance in the context of IDP protection. In other words, would an overly rigid understanding of non-interference place IDPs in what some have termed as a 'sovereignty trap', especially when state authorities are not willing or able to address displacement issues themselves? Yet, this question is not new in international law discourse. The entire IDPs issue has always been framed keeping in mind the necessary balance between state sovereignty and international assistance. Special Rapporteur Deng had already indicated that sovereignty in this context should also equate to responsibility.[145] According to Deng, it must be understood as a responsibility to ensure that basic human rights are respected. When governments fail to discharge this responsibility in assisting the IDPs, the international community should be entitled to step in to fill protection gaps.[146]

In the context of humanitarian assistance in NIAC, the principle of sovereignty is understood as requiring that states do not arbitrarily refuse humanitarian access.[147] However, while such an approach to sovereignty was once generally shared in the post-Cold War context, the current geopolitical context has shown that many agreed-upon international standards are subject to significant erosion. In the Sahel context, deep scepticism about the benefits of international rules and institutions amid decades of Western interference, disillusionment with liberal democracy and its associated values, and the growing resistance to Western narratives generally, including within the humanitarian domain, all contribute to the current security situation. It is indeed a fact that humanitarian actions cannot be dissociated from geopolitical dynamics; manipulation of humanitarian assistance for (geo)political interests is also a reality.[148] In this context, the attitude of the military juntas towards Western-led humanitarian initiatives in Sahelian countries may not be entirely unwarranted.

143 Le Monde, 'Le Niger demande au Comité international de la Croix-Rouge de quitter le pays' (6 February 2025) <https://www.lemonde.fr/afrique/article/2025/02/06/le-niger-demande-au-comite-international-de-la-croix-rouge-de-quitter-le-pays_6534235_3212.html> accessed 6 June 2025.

144 See on this issue, Heike Krieger, "Populist Governments and International Law" (2019) 30 EJIL 971.

145 Deng (n 109) 45, para 183.

146 Roberta Cohen and Francis M Deng, *Masses in Flight: The Global Crisis of Internal Displacement* (Brookings Institution Press 1998).

147 Lindsey Cameron, Eve La Haye, Heike Niebergall-Lackner, Bruno Demeyere, and Jean-Marie Henckaerts, 'The Updated Commentary on the First Geneva Convention—A New Tool for Generating Respect for International Humanitarian Law' (2016) 97(900) IRRC 1219.

148 Antonio De Lauri (ed), *The Politics of Humanitarianism: Power, Ideology and Aid* (I.B. Tauris 2016).

While these considerations may have explained the willingness of military juntas in the Sahel to closely monitor humanitarian assistance, the legal framework applicable to humanitarian assistance, particularly regarding IDPs, to which these states are party, provides some indication of the limits to their margin of appreciation. Although IHL does not establish a general right to humanitarian assistance in NIACs, it recognizes a right to humanitarian initiative to certain organizations, such as the ICRC.[149] Moreover, humanitarian activities strictly related to the provision of medical services cannot be prevented even in NIACs. According to Additional Protocol II, 'Under no circumstances shall any person be punished for having carried out medical activities compatible with medical ethics'. While this strict protection of the medical personnel in NIAC should benefit humanitarian organizations carrying out medical activities in the Sahel, it could arguably extend to all impartial humanitarian activities as well.[150]

This approach is also provided under the Kampala Convention. According to Article V (3), 'States Parties shall respect the mandates of the African Union and the United Nations, as well as the roles of international humanitarian organizations in providing protection and assistance to internally displaced persons, in accordance with international law'. Given recent developments in the Sahel, one may wonder to what extent this obligation has been complied with by central Sahelian governments. It remains unclear whether this provision of the Kampala Convention can be interpreted as trumping the states' sovereignty when it comes to international assistance to IDPs on their territories. Although there is often a fine line between humanitarian and development activities, IHL and the Kampala Convention frameworks are humanitarian-focused and would not cover development actors. As pointed out above, some international actors intervening in development activities, which used to also provide assistance to IDPs, have been banned in the Sahel.[151] Despite these hindrances, international actors have remained critical in the delivery of humanitarian assistance to IDPs. In Burkina Faso, for instance, the UNHCR has a robust operational presence through its seven offices. The UNHCR is deploying its 2022–2025 Multi-Year Multi-Partner Strategy and localization agenda despite an unprecedented budgetary deficit.[152]

E. Beyond Emergency-Centred Approaches: International Law's Limits in Addressing Root Causes of Internal Displacement in the Sahel

1. Intrinsic and Extrinsic Limits of Traditional Legal Frameworks

Despite their usefulness in addressing the issue of internal displacement in the Sahel, IHL and even more specific instruments such as the Kampala Convention are

[149] Yves Sandoz, Christoph Swinarski and Bruno Zimmermann (eds), *Commentary on the Additional Protocols of 8 June 1977 to the Geneva Conventions of 12 August 1949* (ICRC/Martinus Nijhoff 1987) 1417–23.

[150] ICRC commentaries of GC I (2016) 782 para 832.

[151] Wilén and Aning (n 14); On this issue see J Antouly, 'Les conflits de régimes entre la lutte contre le financement du terrorisme et la protection de l'assistance humanitaire' (DPhil thesis, Université Paris Nanterre 2024).

[152] UNHCR, 'Burkina Faso, Multi-Year Multi-Partner Strategy and Localization Agenda 2022–2025' (2022).

insufficient to decisively transform the realities of IDPs. First, these bodies of law are not only limited in their provisions but they suffer from a lack of implementation, reducing them to mere 'rhetorical' instruments.[153] There are inherent reasons for that. For instance, as pointed out above, IHL rules do not provide for a specific category of IDPs. IHL rules and principles extend to IDPs by virtue of the latter's civilian status. While still being relevant, including for preventive and protective purposes, these rules have not been designed to address the specificities of IDPs' experiences.[154] Moreover, the nature of the violence and the intricacies of displacement causes in the Sahel may imply, in some cases, the non-pertinence of IHL rules. This happens when the specific occurrence of violence at hand does not reach the threshold of a NIAC. Even assuming that IHL rules applicable to internal displacement remain relevant, they face the same profound ineffectiveness that has long characterized IHL in many armed conflicts. Despite their noble objectives, the open texture of most critical IHL rules leaves them at the mercy of potentially contradicting and bad faith interpretations.[155]

In the context of the Sahel, although there is no doubt that many rules concerning the conduct of hostilities are *manifestly* violated by armed actors, IHL rules are open enough to allow some attempts to justify such violations under the same law. For instance, IHL rules, under certain conditions, allow parties to the conflict to decide that a population can be displaced for military purposes. Moreover, under a certain interpretation of rules concerning the conduct of hostilities, a party to the conflict may consider that an IDP camp is being used for hostile activities. In that case, except for the rules of precaution and proportionality, such a camp may be targeted by the threatened party. As discussed above, in the context of the Sahel, IDP camps have been recurrently suspected of hosting terrorists, and IDP groups have been accused of supporting one side of the conflict.

Furthermore, international instruments, such as the UN Guiding Principles or the Kampala Convention, have intrinsic limitations. Despite their unquestionable qualities, these instruments approach the issue from an individual rights perspective. They strive to ensure that IDPs' human rights are respected. It is not a coincidence that such human rights-oriented approaches to the issue of internal displacement emerged precisely after the end of the Cold War, when human rights promotion became an essential pillar of the (neo)liberal consensus. This rights-based approach is often presented as the panacea to the issue of internal displacement and was embraced in various regional approaches to the issue.[156] Its contours have been defined as a requirement for emphasizing the centrality of human dignity, non-discrimination and prioritization of vulnerable persons, and involvement and empowerment of IDPs as rights holders, and through participation in decision-making processes.[157]

[153] Phil Orchard, *Protecting the Internally Displaced: Rhetoric and Reality* (Routledge 2018) 168.
[154] Deng (n 109).
[155] See Helen M Kinsella and Giovanni Mantilla, 'Contestation before Compliance: History, Politics, and Power in International Humanitarian Law', *International Studies Quarterly* (2020) 0, 1–8.
[156] Dug Cubie, 'Complementarity between Human Security and Legal Frameworks for Humanitarian Action' in G Oberleitner (ed), *Research Handbook on International Law and Human Security* (Edward Elgar 2022) 258, 264.
[157] Adeola (n 10).

However, such a human rights-based approach raises important difficulties. First, intrinsically, this approach is set to encounter the same technical and political hindrances as the implementation of human rights in general. Most human rights are not absolute and states can legitimately take measures to derogate from their obligations or to limit certain rights under specific circumstances and conditions.[158] Most displacement causes, such as armed conflict and natural catastrophes, would justify the adoption of measures limiting human rights. In the context of Sahelian states, due to the ongoing security crisis, states have adopted a number of measures limiting human rights in general. While there is no doubt that many of these measures fall outside the permissible scope of derogations and limitations, it is a fact that the human rights framework does allow such legitimate infringements.[159] This opens up the possibility of depriving IDPs of their human rights on a 'valid basis'. In contexts where the general population suffers human rights limitations and violations, it becomes unreasonable to expect that IDPs are miraculously protected. Extrinsically, the current ineffectiveness of the human rights-based approach speaks to the ontological limitations of human rights as a transformative tool. The current human rights project has failed to deliver, especially on the front of economic, social, and cultural rights for the majority of humans.[160] It is therefore naïve, if not cynical, to believe that IDPs' human rights could be an exception to that reality.

Finally, both IHL and human rights frameworks applicable to IDPs are emergency management-oriented. Despite the insistence of international instruments, such as the Kampala Convention, on the concept of lasting solutions, durable solutions must efficiently address the root causes of internal displacement and massive human rights violations.[161] So far, such effective solutions are absent or not complied with, which reflects the structural limitations of international legal frameworks in addressing internal displacement.

2. International Law's Limitations to Address Development Issues in the Sahel

In the first comprehensive international study on the issue of internal displacement, Francis Deng rightly indicated that the regulatory framework vis-à-vis internal displacement has suffered a 'chronic lack of implementation'.[162] He further observes that this ineffectiveness 'itself may be an indication that existing human rights and humanitarian standards may not be adequately tailored to meet the challenge of the crisis'.[163] Deng concluded that the inadequacy of the responses to internal displacement issues was a symptom of a deeper normative deficiency. Despite the important normative

[158] International Covenant on Civil and Political Rights (adopted 16 December 1966, entered into force 23 March 1976) 999 UNTS 171 (ICCPR) art 4.

[159] Samson MS Mé Dabire, *La dérogation aux droits de l'homme en Afrique: Le droit africain des droits de l'homme et des peuples à l'épreuve des circonstances exceptionnelles* (Schulthess Verlag 2021).

[160] Samuel Moyn, *Not Enough: Human Rights in an Unequal World* (Harvard University Press 2018).

[161] On durable solutions to the issue of IDPs see Kälin (n 72).

[162] Deng (n 109) 20, para 74.

[163] ibid.

developments on internal displacement, both at the international level with the adoption of the UN Guidelines and more specifically at the African level with the adoption of the Kampala Convention, the situation of IDPs has arguably not improved. This state of affairs is due to the inability of the current legal framework to address the root causes of internal displacement. In fact, international law has not been able to address structural development issues, which explains the misfortune of the majority of IDPs in the world. This issue was captured by Deng in his 1993 Report:

> A crucial factor in understanding the problem of displacement is that most displaced persons are in and from developing countries with acute problems of nation-building: crises of national identity and unity, ineffective authority and control, limited capacity for economic productivity and resource distribution and, above all, tension between central political and economic forces and the demand for autonomy and equitable participation on the part of component constituencies. While international legal standards and enforcement mechanisms are critically important to remedying the gross violations of human rights that emanate from internal conflicts, appreciating the underlying causes of these conflicts is crucial, both to designing appropriate measures aimed at addressing the problems at their domestic roots and to initiating ameliorative actions before problems reach the crisis level.[164]

This assessment is particularly accurate in the Sahel context. The current conflicts in the Sahel are primarily rooted in development issues. Heavy colonial legacies, internal political failures, and structural conditioning by neo-liberal economic institutions contributed not only to the proliferation of multiple conflicts but also to the continuous instability of the states, rendering them unable to effectively address displacement issues. All Central Sahelian countries are struggling with development issues and usually ranked among the less developed countries in the world. Over the past twenty years, Burkina Faso, Mali, and Niger have always been among the lowest ten—and often the lowest five—countries in the UNDP's Human Development Index.[165] For a country such as Burkina Faso, nearly half of the population is considered as 'poor'.[166] In central Sahelian countries, the state has long been unable to provide meaningful social and economic development to the majority of the population. Some regions in the periphery have been particularly neglected, which has fuelled resentment towards the state and created fertile ground for recruitment by jihadist groups. In that sense, the situation in the Sahel should better be characterized as a social insurrection rooted in significant underdevelopment.[167] Such social and political issues ensure the protractedness of the conflicts in the region.

[164] ibid 34, para 132.

[165] See United Nations Development Programme (UNDP), *Human Development Report 2023/2024: Breaking the Gridlock—Reimagining Cooperation in a Polarized World* (UNDP 2024).

[166] 'Of the 20,505,155 inhabitants in Burkina Faso in 2019, 8,065,679 are classed as poor, equating to 39.3 per cent. The depth of poverty, that is the average gap in percentage terms between the consumption of poor households and the poverty threshold, is 11.6 per cent.' See Institut National de la Statistique et de la Démographie (INSD), *Cinquième recensement général de la population et de l'habitation du Burkina Faso*, vol 3: *Mesure et cartographie de la pauvreté* (2022) 27.

[167] Niang (n 61); de Sardan (n 64).

The idea that effectively addressing the IDPs crisis requires us to tackle the root causes of displacement is not novel. There is arguably no recent international framework on this issue that does not underscore such necessity.[168] Concepts such as 'durable solutions', 'integrated approach', 'holistic approach', or 'humanitarian-development nexus' are often used to highlight the need for effective and lasting responses. However, international law, in its current form, is structurally incapable of addressing development issues both in general and in the countries of the Sahel, grappling with conflicts, climate change, and development issues.[169] While they are not the only cause of development issues, structural dynamics within the international system have amplified and perpetuated such development gaps and unequal North–South relationships. Developing countries undertook significant efforts to reform the international economic system. However, their struggles for a New International Economic Order, the right to development, and a fairer international economic system have (lamentably) all failed.[170] The United Nations was unable to dismantle the deeply rooted legacies of colonial exploitation. The system has instead been used to maintain patterns of structural domination and was not able to deliver on its human rights and economic development mandate for many.[171] Moreover, although one of the most critical purposes of the current international system, based on the UN Charter, was to address root causes of conflicts, in recent years international law has arguably been reduced to a managerial tool of the neo-liberal project. The right to development for which African countries advocated evaporated into various forms of economic cooperation led by donor countries, international financial institutions, and various agencies, with little to no impact.[172] Having failed to address the root causes of underdevelopment and conflict, international law can only make a limited contribution to addressing their symptoms, such as internal displacement.[173] When massive displacement of populations occurs, such as in the Sahel, international law's regulatory framework strives to contain the emergency but fails to provide long-term effective strategies.[174] Lasting solutions to the issue of IDPs cannot be effective without sufficient economic resources and strong institutional structures—or, put simply, without development. Such a development approach to internal displacement is critical.[175]

[168] See for instance, United Nations, 'Shining a Light on Internal Displacement A Vision for the Future, Report of the United Nations Secretary-General's High-Level Panel on Internal Displacement' (2021).

[169] See for instance Joel Ngugi, 'Making New Wine in Old Wineskins: Can the Reform of International Law Emancipate the Third World in the Age of Globalization' (2002) 8 UC Davis Journal of International Law and Policy 73.

[170] James Thuo Gathii, 'Africa and the Radical Origins of the Right to Development' (2020) 1 TWAIL Review 28–50; Umozurike Oji Umozurike, International Law and Colonialism in Africa (Nwamife 1979); Mohammed Bedjaoui, *Pour un nouvel ordre économique international* (UNESCO 1979).

[171] Antony Anghie, *Imperialism, Sovereignty and the Making of International Law* (CUP 2005).

[172] Peter Uvin, 'From the Right to Development to the Rights-Based Approach: How "Human Rights" Entered Development' (2007) 17 Development in Practice 597; Gathii (n 170).

[173] Ntina Tzouvala, 'Aggression, Capitalism, and International Law: Missed Opportunities or Structural Constraints?' (2024) 77(1) *Current Legal Problems* 201–32.

[174] Kälin (n 72).

[175] United Nations (n 168), 13; Kälin (n 72).

3. The Relevance and Constraints of a Progressive Climate Change Regime

An important dimension of international law's failure to deal with root causes of the complex conflicts in the Sahel concerns the lack of proper response from international law to the ongoing climate crisis, which has severe implications for the Sahel. The correlation between climate change, conflicts, and displacement in the Sahel region is widely recognized. According to the UN Secretary General:

> Risks from conflict, disasters and climate change are often interconnected and mutually reinforcing: Natural resource constraints caused by climate change may create tensions and lead to violence within communities, or communities displaced by conflict might not be able to return because of the impact of climate change in their areas of origin. Individuals and communities with pre-existing vulnerabilities are often most at risk of repeated harm.[176]

The UN Security Council has also finally recognized the adverse impact of climate and ecological changes on the security situation in the Sahel.[177] In the Central Sahel, climate change has led to extreme weather events, desertification, and land degradation. This has caused socio-economic challenges and exacerbated conflicts over the control of natural resources.[178] The vulnerability of Sahel countries to climate change effects is also linked to the structure of their economies, whereby most of the population makes a living from subsistence agriculture. In its Written Statement before the ICJ in the *Advisory proceedings on Obligations of States in respect of Climate Change*, Burkina Faso observed:

> climate change has had certain socio-political consequences in Burkina Faso, as it has in other countries on the Sahelian strip. The growing scarcity of resources caused by climate change reduces the margins of manoeuvre of those in power to create social goods through ambitious public policies, while low rainfall and desertification lead to impoverishment and increased competition between communities for the few resources that are available, in particular water points and grazing and agricultural land. The decline in natural resources resulting from climate change is thus one of the causes of political instability and security issues within the Sahelian strip, including in Burkina Faso.[179]

[176] The United Nations Secretary-General's Action Agenda on Internal Displacement. Follow-Up to the Report of the UN Secretary-General's High-Level Panel on Internal Displacement (2022), 20.

[177] UN Security Council, *Presidential Statement S/PRST/2024/3* (24 May 2024) <https://docs.un.org/en/S/PRST/2024/3> accessed 4 June 2025.

[178] ibid.

[179] Burkina Faso, *Written Statement in the Advisory Proceedings on the Obligations of States in respect of Climate Change* (2 April 2024) <https://www.icj-cij.org/case/187/written-proceedings> accessed 12 May 2025.

While the countries in the Central Sahel have contributed insignificantly to global greenhouse gas emissions, they are among the most vulnerable to the effects of climate change.[180] Climate change now has broader implications for the development of Sahelian countries. In this context, *durable solutions* to displacement issues in the Sahel cannot ignore the need to address the climate crisis in the region. However, so far, international law seems ill-equipped to provide serious responses to the climate crisis, especially in developing countries. Adaptation initiatives in developing countries have not been supported by industrialized countries despite the responsibilities that they bear regarding climate change. Developing countries have stressed that—as a matter of law and morality—industrialized countries must substantially contribute to their adaptation efforts.[181]

Moreover, in the specific Sahelian context, the UN Security Council has (somewhat reluctantly) acknowledged the United Nations Framework Convention on Climate Change and the Paris Agreement as the primary international, intergovernmental forums for negotiating the global response to climate change.[182] Yet, there is no international consensus on the meaning and scope of states' obligations deriving from the climate change regime under international law. Industrialized countries strive to limit as much as possible their obligations vis-à-vis Global South countries. One need only examine the written submissions by states in the above-mentioned advisory proceedings before the ICJ to appreciate such a divide between states. Irrespective of what the ICJ will *advise* in this case, substantial shifts in state practice remain unlikely, especially in the current international context where climate scepticism and denial are promoted at the highest political level of the most industrialized countries.[183]

F. Conclusion

The unprecedented number of IDPs in the Sahel countries has led to a humanitarian crisis in the region. One of the primary causes of internal displacement in the region is the ongoing NIACs in the Sahelian countries. However, such conflicts themselves are interlinked with other complex social, political, climate, and ecological dynamics which explain their protractedness. This contribution showed that the current international legal frameworks on IDP issues are articulated around IHL and IHRL. These frameworks may provide important preventive and protective principles and rules. IHL rules related to IDPs apply to a large extent to the situation in the Sahel, given that most of the ongoing violence in the region meets NIAC criteria. More specific

[180] For instance, a country like Burkina Faso has contributed not more than 0.12 percent of global emissions. UNDP, 'Climate Promise: Burkina Faso' (UNDP Climate Promise, 2025) <https://climatepromise.undp.org/what-we-do/where-we-work/burkina-faso#:~:text=Ahead%20of%20COP26%2C%20Burkina%20Faso,to%20a%20reduction%20of%2030.76%25> accessed 6 June 2025.

[181] Burkina Faso (n 179).

[182] UNSC (n 177).

[183] David Gelles, 'The US under Trump: Alone in Its Climate Denial', New York Times, 19 May 2025, <https://www.nytimes.com/2025/05/19/climate/trump-climate-denial.html> accessed 21 June 2025; See also Timo Busch and Lena Judick, 'Climate Change—That Is Not Real! A Comparative Analysis of Climate-Sceptic Think-Tanks in the USA and Germany' (2021) 164 *Climatic Change* 1–23.

frameworks such as the UN Guiding Principles and the Kampala Convention represent significant progress in developing a normative framework for the prevention and protection of internal displacements in the Sahel.

While such rules may offer useful tools to deal with IDPs matters, they are essentially concerned with dealing with the immediate consequences of internal displacement. In so doing, they prove intrinsically and extrinsically limited. They suffer implementation challenges in addition to their structural inability to address the root causes of internal displacements. This chapter argued that protracted displacement issues are related to more structural, political, and economic realities that the most pertinent (international) legal regimes are not designed to address. With very limited resources and profound development issues, Sahelian countries cannot respond effectively to the ongoing displacement crisis. In addition, the actual political context in the Sahel makes international assistance highly politicized and uncertain. Dealing decisively with IDPs' issues requires radical ways of rethinking global power balances, inequality between and within states, and development, for no durable solutions can be reached without acting on root causes.

Acknowledgements

I wish to thank Ms Mariam Mestari for her assistance in editing the references in the chapter. A special thanks also to Dr Habiba Abubaker for carefully reading this chapter and making pertinent remarks.

PART III
CREATING THE DIVIDE?
(In)compatible Institutional Frameworks

13

Aligning Humanitarian Principles with Peace and Development Objectives

Marc DuBois

A. Introduction

A nexus resides in the staggering tangle of human needs. In the fragmented, sectoral international systems responding to those needs, the remarkable disregard for this nexus has given rise to demands and policies to operationalize the humanitarian-development-peace nexus (hereinafter 'HDP nexus' or 'triple nexus'). At best, the triple nexus largely remains a work in progress, impeded by sticky strategic and programmatic factors such as poor interoperability, disjointed architecture, disconnected funding streams, major cuts to the humanitarian budget, or the formidable self-interest and entrenched habits of the status quo. At worst, it is vilified as the latest attempt to 're-cast humanitarian action entirely', subsuming it to development assistance and 'giving priority to domestic and foreign policy objectives above the humanitarian needs'.[1]

B. The HDP Nexus: A Challenging Approach in the Response to Protracted Crisis

1. Briefly, the Triple Nexus

Faced with protracted conflict, dramatic increases in migration and the duration of this displacement, climate change, rising inequality, state fragility, and budgetary pressure on United Nations (UN) agencies, the HDP nexus was galvanized in various policy agendas in the build-up and production of the 2016 World Humanitarian Summit (WHS).[2] At the WHS, UN Secretary-General Ban Ki-moon declared the

[1] Christos Christou, 'MSF International President Moral Report 2019–2020' (unpublished MSF report, copy on file with author) 7.

[2] United Nations General Assembly (UNGA), 'Review of the United Nations Peacebuilding Architecture' (27 April 2016) UN Doc A/RES/70/262; United Nations Security Council Res 2282 (27 April 2016) UN Doc S/RES/2282 (2016); 'Agenda for Humanity' (United Nations Office for the Coordination of Humanitarian Affairs, Agenda for Humanity, 2016) <https://agendaforhumanity.org/agendaforhumanity.html> accessed 7 July 2024; World Bank and others, 'The Grand Bargain' (Inter-Agency Standing Committee 2017) <https://interagencystandingcommittee.org/grand-bargain/grand-bargain-sha

Marc DuBois, *Aligning Humanitarian Principles with Peace and Development Objectives* In: *From Protracted Conflict to Sustainable Peace?* Edited by: Heike Krieger, Giedre Jokubauskaite, Asli Ozcelik, and Andreas Buser, Oxford University Press. © Marc DuBois 2026. DOI: 10.1093/9780198967385.003.0016

necessity for 'genuine change in the way we deliver assistance . . . in the way we resolve to reduce the fragmentation of international assistance . . . [and] in the greater investments we make to prevent and resolve conflicts and human suffering'.[3] In its attention to the causes of conflict and poverty, in its conviction that conflict fuels vulnerability, the HDP nexus presages a greater institutional and operational recognition that protracted crisis is ill-addressed by the protracted delivery of 'short-term assistentialist' responses.[4]

> Nexus approach refers to the aim of strengthening collaboration, coherence and complementarity. The approach seeks to capitalise on the comparative advantages of each pillar—to the extent of their relevance in the specific context—in order to reduce overall vulnerability and the number of unmet needs, strengthen risk management capacities and address root causes of conflict.[5]

In more concrete terms, complementarity provides a seemingly straightforward division of labour: 'humanitarian response to save lives and protect people, development assistance to address multi-dimensional structural challenges, and peace action to ensure that countries can sustain peace, ie prevent the outbreak, escalation, continuation and recurrence of conflict.'[6] Yet describing the HDP nexus has proven easier than realizing the HDP nexus: the operational linking of H, D, and P has prompted considerable conceptual struggle (section D.1). Pragmatic impediments similarly abound, arising from the differences in, *inter alia*, goals, methodologies, time frames, and funding mechanisms.

2. A New Formula for Wine in a New Age of Cocktails

Critics and proponents alike rightly suggest that improved intersectoral coordination is far from new, and over the past decades has been proposed under a number of different policy banners—Linking Relief, Reconstruction, and Development (LRRD), Disaster Risk Reduction, Resilience, and so on—lending credence to accusations that

red-commitment-better-serve-people-need-2016> accessed 7 July 2024; Council of the European Union, 'Operationalising the Humanitarian-Development Nexus—Council Conclusions' (19 May 2017) Doc No 9417/17.

[3] UNGA, 'One Humanity; Shared Responsibility. Report of the Secretary-General for the World Humanitarian Summit' (2 February 2016) UN Doc A/70/709, 48.

[4] Marc DuBois, 'The New Humanitarian Basics' (HPG working paper, Overseas Development Institute, May 2018) 5–6.

[5] Development Assistance Committee (DAC) of the OECD, 'Recommendation on the Humanitarian-Development-Peace Nexus' (2019) Doc No OECD/LEGAL/5019, 6. More glibly, DAC sees this as prioritizing 'an approach that prioritises "prevention always, development wherever possible, humanitarian action when necessary"': ibid 3.

[6] Inter-Agency Standing Committee (IASC) Results Group 4 on Humanitarian-Development Collaboration, 'Exploring Peace within the Humanitarian-Development-Peace Nexus (HDP NEXUS)' (issue paper, endorsed by IASC Operational Policy and Advocacy Group, October 2020) 1 (hereafter IASC Results Group 4).

the triple nexus is merely 'old wine in a new bottle'.[7] In the late 1980s, when LRRD first sought to strengthen humanitarian development linkages, the policy posited little nexus or programmatic commingling, as the prevailing ideology viewed societies as developing linearly, progressing along a 'continuum' from crisis to early recovery (rehabilitation) to development and so forth.[8] As the 1990s progressed, 'continuum' thinking was replaced by recognition of a 'contiguum' in which various aid instruments might be simultaneously applied.[9] 'Whole-of-government' responses to protracted crisis then gained momentum in the period leading up to the articulation of the HDP Nexus,[10] and experts now regularly tout the need for holistic rather than sectoral modes of engagement.

C. The HDP Nexus: The Challenge Posed to Humanitarians on the Basis of Their Principles

1. Briefly, the Core Principles of Humanitarian Action

The Fundamental Principles of the International Red Cross and Red Crescent Movement were approved by the International Conference of the Red Cross in 1965 (and revised in 1986).[11] From the Movement's seven principles, the international humanitarian sector has considered humanity, impartiality, independence, and neutrality as the four core principles of humanitarian action (see Box 13.1)[12]

> Persons taking no active part in the hostilities ... shall in all circumstances be treated humanely, without any adverse distinction founded on race, colour, religion or faith,

[7] Eg, Sonja Hövelmann, 'Triple Nexus to Go' (2020) Centre for Humanitarian Action <https://www.chaberlin.org/wp-content/uploads/2020/03/2020-03-triple-nexus-to-go-hoevelmann-en-online.pdf> 3 accessed 07 July 2024.

[8] Irina Mosel and Simon Levine, 'Remaking the Case for Linking Relief, Rehabilitation and Development' (report commissioned by Humanitarian Policy Group, Overseas Development Institute, March 2014).

[9] Joanna Macrae and Adele Harmer, 'Beyond the Continuum: An Overview of the Changing Role of Aid Policy in Protracted Crises' (Humanitarian Policy Group research report, Overseas Development Institute, July 2004) (hereafter Macrae and Harmer, Humanitarian Policy Group research report). There have been consistent attempts, particularly in the UN, to join the international intervention together within a single chain of command and/or plan. Throughout the post-'Global War on Terror' 2000s, the humanitarian sector chafed at the proximity to these political objectives, criticising the UN's 'integrated' approach and the 'blurring of the lines' between aid being used to accomplish military or political objectives and the humanity-driven aid delivered by neutral and independent organizations. Eg, Nicolas De Torrente, 'Humanitarian Action under Attack: Reflections on the Iraq War' (2004) 17 Harvard Human Rights Journal 1.

[10] Mosel and Levine (n 8) 3.

[11] ICRC, 'The Fundamental Principles of the International Red Cross and Red Crescent Movement' (proclaimed in by the 20th International Conference of the Red Cross and Red Crescent, Vienna, 1965) <https://www.ifrc.org/who-we-are/international-red-cross-and-red-crescent-movement/fundamental-principles> accessed 3 October 2024.

[12] The definitions and their explanation presented in the textbox below can be found in HAP International, People In Aid, and the Sphere Project, *The Core Humanitarian Standard on Quality and Accountability* (Groupe URD) 8 (hereafter *The Core Humanitarian Standard*). The Core Humanitarian Standard explains that these definitions were derived from the sources listed below in nn 22–24).

Box 13.1 The Core Humanitarian Principles

The Core Humanitarian Principles

- **Humanity**: Human suffering must be addressed wherever it is found. The purpose of humanitarian action is to protect life and health and ensure respect for human beings.
- **Impartiality**: Humanitarian action must be carried out on the basis of need alone, giving priority to the most urgent cases of distress and making no adverse distinction on the basis of nationality, race, gender, religious belief, class, or political opinion.
- **Independence**: Humanitarian action must be autonomous from the political, economic, military, or other objectives that any actor may hold with regard to areas where humanitarian action is being implemented.
- **Neutrality**: Humanitarian actors must not take sides in hostilities or engage in controversies of a political, racial, religious, or ideological nature.

> sex, . . . An impartial humanitarian body, such as the International Committee of the Red Cross, may offer its services to the Parties to the conflict.[13]

All four principles contribute to access to people in need and territories in conflict, principally by fostering trust in the intentions and actions of the organization on the part of armed groups and people affected by crisis.[14] Of importance for the discussion in section C.2, neutrality and independence are strictly operational and 'have no intrinsic moral value', whereas humanity and impartiality are substantive principles which hold an ethical purpose.[15]

Although the core humanitarian principles have not been formally adopted by or extended to cover development and peace agencies, these actors nonetheless also share the commitment to humanity and follow complementary principles,[16] and for many objectives of either peace or development work, there are no barriers to their implementation.[17]

> Mentions of humanitarian principles are omnipresent in policy documents relating to [the HDP Nexus], but these references are usually end-of-sentence caveats and are

[13] On impartial humanitarian actors, Geneva Convention IV arts 10, 23, 59, 63; Protocol Additional to the Geneva Conventions of 12 August 1949 relating to the Protection of Victims of International Armed Conflicts (adopted 8 June 1977, entered into force 7 December 1978) 1125 UNTS 3 (Protocol I) art 70; Protocol Additional to the Geneva Conventions of 12 August 1949, and relating to the Protection of Victims of Non-International Armed Conflicts (adopted 8 June 1977, entered into force 7 December 1978) 1125 UNTS 609 (Protocol II) art 17. The Geneva Conventions provide the specific legal privilege to impartial humanitarian actors to offer relief (so-called right of initiative), and this should be facilitated rather than obstructed. In contrast, the principle of neutrality is not mentioned in the Geneva Conventions or their Additional Protocols.

[14] Jérémie Labbé and Pascal Daudin, 'Applying the Humanitarian Principles: Reflecting on the Experience of the International Committee of the Red Cross' (2015) 97 International Review of the Red Cross 183.

[15] ibid 187.

[16] IASC Results Group 4 (n 9).

[17] Macrae and Harmer, Humanitarian Policy Group research report (n 12) 4.

> rarely developed further ('while fully respecting humanitarian principles'). This perpetuates the idea that humanitarian principles are a constraint to the nexus. Yet, what humanitarian principles aim to enable – access, trust, impartial response, management of security risks – is equally valuable for development or peace actors.—Filipa Schmitz Guinote, ICRC Policy Advisor[18]

Moreover, there is considerable support for the notion that humanitarian principles offer a common ideological ground to bridge the cultural barriers between the three sectors.[19] The perspective of the Interagency Standing Committee (IASC—a standards-setting body for the humanitarian sector) on the role played by the principle of humanity is unequivocal: 'Giving priority to protecting and saving lives and ensuring respect for the rights, wellbeing and dignity of human beings *is a core commitment for actors within all three fields*—humanitarian, development and peace—and thus offers a potential common ground for engagement.'[20] This common ground is also shaped by deployment of the guardrail function of the principles (see section D).

Common ground is a familiar role for the principles. As the historian Andrew Thompson explains, the principles 'provided a way of talking across different cultures and societies about the best means of protecting people during times of war'.[21] This is in part because the principle of humanity serves as an overarching norm or goal and in part because the principles provide a point of departure for a common vocabulary and an understanding of each other's language.[22] Tellingly, Nexus Academy programming, an initiative delivered by the UN-DAC Dialogue Group, includes a module on 'Building Trilingualism' in its course to foster HDP nexus solutions.[23]

2. Using the Principles as an Argument Against the HDP Nexus

Humanitarians have often overstated the challenge of the HDP nexus to the core humanitarian principles.[24] Their sharpest argumentation regarding the HDP nexus centres on the objectives and actions of 'Big P' (eg a perceived political coherence with

[18] ICRC, 'Q&A: The ICRC and the "Humanitarian-Development-Peace Nexus" Discussion—In Conversation with Filipa Schmitz Guinote, ICRC Policy Adviser' (2019) 101 International Review of the Red Cross 1051, 1060.

[19] A note of caution is warranted. Establishing common ground or agreeing to a common interpretation of the humanitarian principles can be difficult to achieve even among humanitarian actors. The Royal Institute of International Affairs (Chatham House), 'The Normative Framework of Humanitarian Action in Armed Conflict' (summary report on workshop 1, London, 22 and 29 November 2021, Chatham House 2022) <https://chathamhouse.soutron.net/Portal/Public/en-GB/RecordView/Index/191239> accessed 8 July 2024 (hereafter Chatham House, Summary report on workshop 1).

[20] IASC Results Group 4 (n 9) 11 (emphasis added). Indeed, the principle of humanity gives rise to the restraints on war and hence is the fundamental idea behind IHL. It thus offers common ground with armed actors and government authorities as well.

[21] Andrew Thompson, 'Humanitarian Principles Put to the Test: Challenges to Humanitarian Action during Decolonization' (2015) 97 International Review of the Red Cross 45, 75.

[22] Eg, IASC Results Group 4 (n 9) 17.

[23] 'Nexus Academy—Learning, Community, and Capacity for HDP Solutions' (*IASC*, January 2022) <https://interagencystandingcommittee.org/system/files/2022-01/Nexus%20Academy%20Explainer%20Jan%202022.pdf> accessed 8 July 2024.

[24] Marc DuBois, 'The Triple Nexus–Threat or Opportunity for the Humanitarian Principles' (2020) Centre for Humanitarian Action <https://www.chaberlin.org/wp-content/uploads/2020/05/2020-05-triple-nexus-threat-or-opportunity-dubois-en.pdf> accessed 27 February 2026.

military intervention, peacekeeping efforts, or diplomatic peace negotiations). This has sparked calls for distinctions to be maintained; for the principles to function as a firewall safeguarding the neutral, 'apolitical' essence of humanitarian endeavour that is integral to access.[25] Further, the positioning of development and of peace efforts has been viewed as an embedded political component of politics and global security. For example, supporting D and P might suggest differential worthiness among groups needing assistance, or impair the establishment of neutrality (trust) if an organization becomes linked to a particular, political analysis of the causes of conflict.[26] Hence, the argument concludes, tackling the structural causes and solutions to conflict, injustice, and vulnerability is incompatible with principled humanitarian action.

D. The Principles of Humanitarian Action Offer a Framework that Supports Thinking and Acting in Nexus Terms

In its engagement with the HDP Nexus, principled action challenges humanitarians to redefine some operational interventions *and* to retain sufficiently independent decision-making and political neutrality.[27] It is with the principles that humanitarian deliberation should begin, not where it must end. This discussion then unfolds in three subsections. First, the principles function as a common ground upon which all three sectors can engage with one another (not to mention, potentially, military actors, political authorities, climate agencies, etc).[28] Further, the principles are well designed to act as guardrails for these interactions with the D and P sectors, just as they do vis-à-vis armed actors or the state.[29] Second, the principle of humanity should drive interventions on the basis of a nuanced, iterative, and comprehensive understanding of context and people's needs. Third, it is with a revaluing of the principles—normative development that updates the sector's conceptualization and/or implementation of them—that the humanitarian system can reform its approach to people, contexts, and protracted crisis.

[25] Eg Emmanuel Tronc, Rob Grace, and Anaide Nahikian, 'Realities and Myths of the Triple Nexus: Local Perspectives on Peacebuilding, Development, and Humanitarian Action in Mali' (*Harvard Humanitarian Initiative*, June 2019) <https://hhi.harvard.edu/publications/realities-and-myths-"triple-nexus"-local-perspectives> accessed 8 July 2024.

[26] Dorothea Hilhorst and Eline Pereboom, 'Multi-Mandate Organisations in Humanitarian Aid' in Sezgin and Dijkzeul (eds) *The New Humanitarians in International Practice: Emerging Actors and Contested Principles* (Routledge 2016) 94.

[27] Former President of the ICRC Peter Maurer sets out the contours of just such a balancing of imperatives: 'In theory we all share the same aspirations for global peace, development and security, as well as the understanding about the limits of humanitarian action in addressing or preventing the causes of crisis. In practice however, our experience shows that emergency access to vulnerable populations . . . depends on the ability to isolate humanitarian goals from other transformative goals, be they economic, political, social or human rights related.' Peter Maurer, 'Humanitarian Diplomacy and Principled Humanitarian Action, speech given by Mr Peter Maurer' (conference organized by the Graduate Institute of International and Development Studies, Geneva, 2 October 2014) 97 International Review of the Red Cross 445, 451.

[28] Eg, IASC Results Group 4 (n 9).

[29] In many conflict contexts, this guardrail function is critical to avoiding that new (nexus) ways of working lead to 'triple hatting', where key individuals and agencies may be perceived as champions of H, D, and P at once, Chatham House, Summary report on workshop 1 (n 19).

In sum, and contrary to their function as a barrier, this chapter sees the principles, and in particular the principle of humanity, as *requiring* that the humanitarian sector engage differently with development and peace, and at a minimum to understand and mitigate the impact of humanitarian programming upon development and peace.

1. The Humanitarian Principles: A Common Ground on Which Nexus Actors Can Engage Both Conceptually and Programmatically

The vision behind the HDP nexus is not one that ignores the challenges to developing and strengthening a nexus, but one that recognizes the costs of not doing so. In attempting to strengthen the HDP nexus, much effort and ink pertains to overcoming a multitude of pragmatic challenges to operationality. Yet the primary obstacle to the commingling of perspectives and people lies at the conceptual level: some level of shared institutional objectives, vocabulary, principles, and ideology is required to confront the 'inherent trade-offs' and differences between the agendas of the three sectors, as well as the cultural differences between approaches and staff.[30] The crux of the problem is blockage: even between two sectors that know each other well, the 'humanitarian and development communities continue to largely talk past each other on humanitarian principles'.[31]

The difference between the sectors, and the recalcitrance of some humanitarians, both highlight the criticality of establishing a common ground. In a protracted crisis such as Yemen or Somalia or in responding to a more specific crisis such as an Ebola outbreak or an earthquake, humanity serves well as all three sectors' overarching goal. Humanity is, and should be, inescapable; triple nexus policies are hence riven with principle. For example, a core recommendation of OECD's Development Assistance Committee (DAC) on the HDP nexus calls for all actors to 'put people at the centre'.[32]

The essential call of this chapter is for the respective interventions of the three sectors to be designed on the basis of (1) intentional (rather than general or assumed) complementarity and comparative advantage, and (2) an understanding of how their efforts might undermine, reinforce, or explicitly contribute to the efforts of the other sectors. A peace actor might thereby engage with humanitarians because the latter's health clinic is inadvertently exacerbating tensions between local communities. The peace NGO could frame this engagement with the humanitarians around the actual or perceived compromises to the neutrality and impartiality of their work due to the grievance that the other community receives more aid. Or a local development NGO might comprehend better the negative impact of malaria on certain community development projects and approach the local humanitarian actor through the principle of

[30] Christina Bennett, 'The Development Agency of the Future—Fit for Protracted Crises?' (working paper, Overseas Development Institute, April 2015) <http://cdn-odi-production.s3.amazonaws.com/media/documents/9612.pdf> accessed 8 July 2024, 10.

[31] Joanna Macrae, '"Linking Thinking": Why Is It So Hard and What Can We Do About It?' (*KUNO Humanitarian Exchange Platform*, June 2019) <https://www.kuno-platform.nl/wp-content/uploads/2019/06/Linking-Thinking-KUNO_Macrae.pdf> 6 accessed 8 July 2024; also Mosel and Levine (n 8).

[32] OECD-DAC (n 23).

impartiality, providing evidence that changes the agency's calculation of local needs, leading to the agency developing its programming devoted to malaria prevention.

2. The Principle of Humanity Instructs Aid Interventions to Recognize the Dignity of All Human Beings, and to Recognize the Individuality of Persons, Communities, and Contexts

As Pictet described it, the principle of humanity occupies hallowed ground in humanitarian discourse—'a special place because it is the expression of the profound motivation of the Red Cross, from which all the other principles are derived'.[33] Beyond its inspirational role in charters and mission statements, humanity should be fundamental to programme decision-making. For example, the Sphere Handbook's Humanitarian Charter translates international humanitarian law into a set of core legal principles that are most relevant to the well-being of people affected by disaster or conflict. Their declared starting point is the universalist conviction that 'all people affected by disaster or conflict have a right to receive protection and assistance to ensure the basic conditions for life with dignity,' the legal force of which is derived from the moral principle that 'all human beings are born free and equal in dignity and rights'.[34] Yet a more contemporary interpretation of humanity would recognize the inherent tension within the principle, placing greater weight on articulating a more 'localized' humanity that (1) operationalizes local individuality and the specificities of the particular context, (2) acknowledges and engages with the full scope of human needs, and (3) manifests substantial 'operationalized' respect for human agency.

- *Insufficient valuation of context.* Context does not lead programme design.[35] Attributing insufficient value and time/resources to understanding context results in part from situating context in the realm of programming rather than in the realm of ethics/principles (ie humanity), hence it being easily compromised or abandoned in the name of more rapid or 'effective' intervention.[36] There is an associated devaluation of context knowledge which supports the maintenance of foreign decision-making structures, leaving context analysis supplanted by necessary though lesser initiatives such as security management or continuity across a global organization.
- *Poor implementation of conflict sensitivity.* An essential component of 'little p' activities and Do No Harm, conflict sensitivity is generally embraced across the

[33] Jean Pictet, 'The Fundamental Principles of the Red Cross: Commentary' (1979) 19 International Review of the Red Cross 130, 135.

[34] Sphere Association, *The Sphere Handbook: Humanitarian Charter and Minimum Standards in Humanitarian Response* (4th edn, Sphere Association 2018) 28.

[35] Anita Ernstorfer, Anne-Sofie Stockman, and Frauke de Weijer, 'Peace Responsiveness: A Paradigm Shift to Deliver on Conflict Sensitivity and Sustaining Peace' (2023) 33 Development in Practice 584.

[36] Eg, Dominic Naish, 'Not a Priority: the Lack of Contextual Understanding in Humanitarian Missions' (opinion article, Overseas Development Institute Humanitarian Practice Network, 4 May 2021) <https://odihpn.org/publication/not-a-priority-the-lack-of-contextual-understanding-in-humanitarian-missions/> accessed 8 July 2024. Naish, a former analyst in three different humanitarian agencies, left the sector with

humanitarian sector yet unsystematically implemented. Reinforcing the linking of context to the principle of humanity, conflict insensitivity is wrongly blamed on poor capacity or skills yet is 'more often due to a lack of political will, organizational culture, and individual and organizational mindsets and practices'.[37] In the end, the call is to be 'peace sensitive' as well conflict sensitive.

- *Short-termism in a protracted crisis joined with the siloed lens of humanitarian response.* Crucially, humanitarianism's dominant short-termism[38] is justified by conceptualizing the context as a 'humanitarian crisis', in which extraordinary circumstances demarcate such a significant departure from 'normalcy' as to justify an ahistorical exceptionalism.[39] In turn, this exceptionalism—the emergency need to move swiftly and assure biological sustenance—serves as an ideological mooring for standardized responses to generic victims and an exclusivity in the engagement with power. Empowering the principle of humanity, in contrast, grounds a more unexceptional humanitarian action, bringing people into the tent to create 'a more ordinary, more accessible, place for engagement with power'.[40]

As described throughout this book,[41] protracted conflicts are anything but a classic humanitarian crisis that temporarily overwhelms societal capacity. In response, for example, the Sphere Handbook calls specific attention to protracted crisis, recommending that humanitarian work 'consider different means of meeting needs and supporting life with dignity', taking such measures as working with local service providers and communities and exploring long-term or permanent solutions.[42] As argued in section A, embedding such programmatic advice within the principles raises the priority of delivering on these objectives. Protracted crises generate prodigious *structural* human suffering, from the prolonged 'destitutionization' of civilians to the destruction and erosion of a people's state (economy, institutions, environment, services, etc), environment, communities, and lives.[43]

If viewed through the lens of humanity, the protracted crisis is arguably most distinguished by neither its temporal duration nor its political complexity, but by the nature of its impact on people. In their exploration of protracted crisis, the International Committee of the Red Cross's (ICRC) Hugo Slim and Ariana Lopes Morey foregrounded the 'cumulative impact': 'As a protracted conflict progresses, it gradually

the 'conviction that the humanitarian sector's *raison d'être* is to implement projects, and it will pursue this regardless of how much or little it understands the contexts it works in, or the ripple effects of its interventions': ibid.

[37] Ernstorfer, Stockman, and de Weijer (n 35) 584f.

[38] Ernstorfer, Stockman, and de Weijer (n 35) 589.

[39] Eleanor Davey, John Borton, and Matthew Foley, 'A History of the Humanitarian System: Western Origins and Foundations' (HPG working paper, Overseas Development Institute 2013).

[40] Alasdair Gordon-Gibson, 'Engagement and Disengagement' (*Norwegian Centre for Humanitarian Studies Blog*, 17 March 2023) <https://www.humanitarianstudies.no/engagement-and-disengagement/> accessed 8 July 2024.

[41] Eg Ch. 1.

[42] Sphere Association (n 34) 17.

[43] Hugo Slim and Ariana Lopes Morey, 'Protracted Conflict and Humanitarian Action: Some Recent ICRC Experiences' (International Committee of the Red Cross 2016).

degrades infrastructure, services, living conditions and, with them, human dignity. This cumulative impact is typically felt across all sectors—education, health care, food security, water, electricity and law and order.'[44] Appreciating protracted crises as having a cumulative impact is useful yet insufficient. A protracted crisis generates less a crisis of addition than of multiplication, less a quantitative than a qualitative intensification. Focusing on its impact on people and their communities, protracted crisis can be better described as a *compounding* crisis.

As time progresses, a multi-faceted, interlocked impoverishment of people and society occurs. The direct harm falls upon the human in the compounding of grief, fear, anxiety, and illness and the loss of confidence, community, home, social capital, and hope. In turn, compounding societal effects radiate from this compounded impact on the human. For example: 'Over time, refugees can develop into . . . highly organized and militant states-in-exile. In addition, protracted situations result in reduced expectations for the future, increasing feelings of hopelessness and desperation among refugees/displaced person. Further, host societies are likely to become less hospitable the longer a refugee/IDP crisis lasts.'[45]

As crisis intervention settles into decades of relief programming and substitution for the state, the specificity of protracted crises does not yet sufficiently oblige relief efforts to more directly confront the overlap and entanglement with development, peace, securitization, governance, justice, and other more politically driven interventions. Essentially, the situation is no longer exceptional, which raises questions related to the 'the dignity of temporary humanitarian solutions permanently implemented, the dependence on the continuation of this type of support, and the degree to which they truly continue to meet people's evolving needs'.[46] At a minimum, context, seen through the lens of humanity, demands recognition of (1) the weight of greater needs (that is—solutions to the structural problems of conflict, immiseration, entrenched displacement, economic ruin, healthcare system collapse, etc); and (2) how the interconnectedness, regularity, and duration of harm compound the effects in exponential fashion.

[44] ibid 10. Following publication of this report, Slim, then ICRC's Head of Policy and Humanitarian Diplomacy, explained further: when 'dealing with this cumulative impact of protracted conflict, IHL might expect humanitarian action to become more deeply engaged in war-torn societies, in a way that some may stereotype as "developmental" but which is humanitarian in such a context in support of basic needs'. Hugo Slim, 'Keynote Address: Nexus Thinking in Humanitarian Policy: How Does Everything Fit Together on the Ground?' (WFP Annual Partnership Consultations, Rome, 25 October 2017) <https://www.icrc.org/en/document/nexus-thinking-humanitarian-policy-how-does-everything-fit-together-ground> accessed 8 July 2024.

[45] Huma Haider, 'Refugee, IDP and Host Community Radicalisation' (GSDRC Applied Knowledge Services, 31 October 2014) <https://assets.publishing.service.gov.uk/media/57a089a640f0b652dd00033c/hdq1162.pdf> accessed 8 July 2024.

[46] Cara Kielwein, 'Can We Make Better Use of Humanitarian Data for an Impartial and Humane Response to Crisis?' (*Humanitarian Practice Network*, 24 November 2023) <https://odihpn.org/publication/can-we-make-better-use-of-humanitarian-data-for-an-impartial-and-humane-response-to-crisis/> accessed 8 July 2024.

3. The Principles Call Upon Humanitarian Actors to Improve Their Performance in Relation to Development, Peace, and Humanitarian Objectives

a) Nexus Thinking as the Way Forward

The principles thus offer a gateway to 'Nexus thinking': 'a future culture and ideology where the mindset within the three sectors is sufficiently cross-pollinated that the differences become technical, not normative and not hierarchical.'[47] Less densely, nexus thinking points to the need for H, D, and P actors to resemble the aforementioned cardiologist: competent specialists in their field and significantly more mindful of the relationship of their work to the whole body, and more willing to bring other specialists into the consultation. Fitzpatrick and colleagues summarize such nexus thinking as 'focusing on the needs of the population and being aware of the interactions of the (sectors) but not being limited by them.'[48] For example, this requires humanitarians to deliver relief, and at the same time to struggle to improve the sustainability of their efforts.

b) See More Harm in Order to Do No Harm

Derived from medical ethics, the Do No Harm (DNH) principle requires humanitarian and development actors to endeavour to minimize the inadvertent harm they may do by their presence and by their aid programming.[49] Put more bluntly, via meaningful engagement with people's need for development and peace, humanitarians will render visible how their work may exacerbate conflict and undermine development. Following on from this, humanity should be construed as requiring the concomitant accountability—humanitarians must operationalize a recognition of their responsibility for the impact of their actions and omissions. Though certainly such considerations have long existed in the standards and frameworks humanitarians should follow, the imperative of principled action adds potency. Perhaps most importantly, the principles offer civil society, including the development and peace sectors, a vocabulary with which they can more persuasively engage with humanitarians, urging them to respect and protect humanity rather than arguing about improvements to programming.

More fundamentally than joint programming or coherent planning, humanity should push humanitarians to engage with or even to strengthen their understanding of human society; of community structures related to conflict/stability, the social contract with the state, social cohesion among groups, the production of social capital, conflict sensitivity, and the role of government. Nexus thinking offers ingress to discussions that neither technical guidelines nor evaluations regularly broach. Critically, humanity makes it clear that 'local' actors and populations must drive the understanding and interpretation of key questions. For example:

[47] DuBois (n 24) 10.

[48] Merry Fitzpatrick and others, 'Making the Nexus Real: Moving from theory to practice' (Tufts University, December 2021) 25.

[49] International Federation of the Red Cross and Red Crescent Societies (IFRC), 'Applying Better Programming Initiative—Do No Harm' (IFRC 2016).

- In terms of delivering services such as healthcare or water supply in a protracted crisis, how does long-term 'substitution' for the state undermine the development of people's trust in the state?
- How does the belief in the superiority of high-expenditure ('foreign'—International Non-Governmental Organizations (INGO) UN) institutions impact upon stability or grievance and trust in government?
- How does such substitution stunt the growth of civil society?
- Or in terms of humanitarian protection, how does denunciation reinforce divisions, grievances, and conflict (note the contrast with potential approaches steeped in notions of transitional justice)?

A diverse set of questions with one common denominator—the more protracted the intervention, the greater the risk of harms accruing.

c) The Contours of the Principle of Humanity Infused with Twenty-First-Century Thinking

At a minimum, the need to protect human dignity in protracted crisis should push humanitarians to address human suffering beyond 'mere' immediate needs. Surveys conducted in the WHS consultation process revealed that when those receiving assistance in situations of protracted crisis rated their needs, 'unemployment' (identified by roughly 35%) and 'poverty/destitution' (26%) occupied first and second position.[50] These needs involve the common aspiration of development, even if development as a globalized venture is a highly contested notion. Similarly extensive research by the Collaborative Learning Projects (CDA) as part of their highly regarded Listening Project showed that people very much appreciate relief assistance, and yet when viewed in a long-term and wider society perspective, the negative aspects of this aid, such as dependency, outweighed the positive.[51] As in the WHS consultation, the CDA's research found that people wanted aid to focus on economic betterment and improved political and security conditions, and for aid to be delivered in a sense of solidarity, colleagueship, and support. As more recent research concludes, '[i]n many respects, a demand to think beyond survival is bound up in the core humanitarian principle of humanity'.[52]

E. Conclusion

For the purpose of humanitarian action to be fulfilled, 'it is necessary for each generation to pay renewed attention to the essential and inspirational principle of a shared humanity'.[53] However, enmeshed in the power dynamics of the sector, 'the broad

[50] World Humanitarian Summit secretariat, 'Restoring Humanity: Synthesis of the Consultation Process for the World Humanitarian Summit' (United Nations 2015) 55.

[51] Mary B Anderson, Dayna Brown, and Isabella Jean, *Time to Listen: Hearing People on the Receiving End of International Aid* (CDA Collaborative Learning Projects 2012).

[52] Oliver Lough and others, 'Beyond Survival: Exploring Wellbeing in Humanitarian Action' (HPG Working paper, Overseas Development Institute, June 2023) 13.

[53] Thompson (n 21) 76.

acceptance of this commitment to humanity means it is often lost as an operational or orienting principle'.[54] This sectoral *assumption* of its humanity, then, misses the principle of humanity as challenging humanitarians to operationalize humanity in an expansive fashion: 'humanity implies that no service whatsoever for the benefit of a suffering human being is to be dismissed out of hand.'[55] Effective humanitarian action—alleviating hunger, illness, rooflessness—serves humanity and also clears obstacles to other urgent bedrocks of human fulfilment, such as development and peace.

[54] Larissa Fast, 'Unpacking the principle of Humanity: Tensions and Implications' (2016) 97 International Review of the Red Cross 111, 113.

[55] ICRC, 'The Fundamental Principles of the Red Cross and Red Crescent' (ICRC publication ref no 0513, ICRC 1996).

14

Overcoming Boundaries

Protracted Conflict, Inter-Institutional Cooperation, and the World Bank's Legal Constraints

Ansgar Münichsdorfer

A. Introduction

The dire socio-economic needs caused by protracted conflicts by far exceed the financial capacity of humanitarian assistance.[1] Protracted conflicts require more extensive, more diversified, and longer-term financing.[2] The humanitarian-development-peace nexus is in part a response to this inadequacy in funding—an agenda to 'broaden the resource base' of international responses to protracted conflicts.[3] It builds on development finance to provide both different approaches to and additional means of financing. Accordingly, multilateral development banks have been an essential component of the triple nexus from the outset. In fact, a central concern of many initiatives is to harness the financial resources of multilateral development banks for crisis- and conflict-affected areas.[4] Key initiatives such as the 'New Way of Working' and the 'Grand Bargain', as well as the *Sustaining Peace* resolutions, emerge from or explicitly call for intensified collaboration between the World Bank Group and UN agencies.[5]

At the same time, multilateral development banks are the development actors most constrained in implementing the nexus. In their case, the sectoral peculiarities that have so far impeded collaboration with other sectors involved in the triple nexus are of a distinct nature: for multilateral development banks, more than for most development actors, mode of operation, project types, and relevant stakeholder relationships

[1] High-level Panel on Humanitarian Financing, 'Too Important to Fail—Addressing the Humanitarian Financing Gap' (Inter-Agency Standing Committee (IASC) 2016) 2–3, 6–7.

[2] ibid 7; United Nations Office for the Coordination of Humanitarian Affairs (OCHA), 'The New Way of Working' (OCHA 2017) 11.

[3] High-level Panel on Humanitarian Financing (n 1); United Nations Office for the Coordination of Humanitarian Affairs (n 2) 11.

[4] Emma Fanning and Jessica Fullwood-Thomas, 'The Humanitarian-Development-Peace Nexus: What Does it Mean for Multi-mandated Organizations?' (discussion paper, Oxfam 2019) 13, 17; World Bank et al, 'The Grand Bargain' (Inter-Agency Standing Committee 2017) <https://interagencystandingcommittee.org/grand-bargain/grand-bargain-shared-commitment-better-serve-people-need-2016> accessed 27 March 2024 ('Grand Bargain') commitment 10(5); Development Assistance Committee (DAC) of the Organisation for Economic Co-Operation and Development (OECD), 'Recommendation on the Humanitarian-Development-Peace Nexus' (2019) Doc No OECD/LEGAL/5019 ('OECD DAC Recommendation') s V.

[5] International Council of Voluntary Agencies (ICVA), 'The "New Way of Working" Examined' (ICVA 2017) 3–4; Grand Bargain (n 4) commitment 10(5); UNSC Res 2282 (27 April 2016) UN Doc S/Res/2282, para 20.

Ansgar Münichsdorfer, *Overcoming Boundaries* In: *From Protracted Conflict to Sustainable Peace?* Edited by: Heike Krieger, Giedre Jokubauskaite, Asli Ozcelik, and Andreas Buser, Oxford University Press.
 DOI: 10.1093/9780198967385.003.0017

are highly juridified. Their constituent treaties contain limited mandates and constrain both how they operate and with whom they interact. Over the past decades, they have also developed an extensive body of norms on project design, due diligence, and accountability, which has further anchored their distinctive approaches in law.[6]

Owing to those legal constraints, the World Bank had long remained largely absent from (post-) conflict situations since its establishment in 1944.[7] Over the past twenty-five years, however, it has gradually increased its engagement in conflict-affected areas, so much so that the Bank now professes to operate in contexts that cover the full spectrum of fragility and conflict.[8] In some respects, this has involved a far-reaching reinterpretation of its constituent treaties. In other respects, though, the Bank's legal framework and practice have remained relatively unchanged throughout.

Taking a closer look at the legal (and institutional) constraints and the changes and continuities in their interpretation is worthwhile for two reasons: first, there is a reciprocal relationship between the humanitarian-development-peace nexus and the World Bank's legal framework. Legal constraints affect whether and to what extent the World Bank can engage in the cooperation and collaboration envisaged by the triple nexus. Conversely, the triple nexus also finds its way into the Bank's legal framework and may influence the interpretation of its constituent treaties. Exploring how this unfolds can shed light on the function the nexus assumes and the purpose it serves for the institution. After all, the nexus is not an externally imposed concept, but was devised with active participation of multilateral development banks. Its origins lie in part in the core commitment to a 'New Way of Working' made by the UN Secretary-General, UN agencies, and the World Bank at the 2016 World Humanitarian Summit.

Second, the legal framework has an impact on whether the World Bank undertakes projects that contribute to the objectives of ending protracted conflicts and building sustainable peace. Legal constraints influence the types of projects the Bank finances, in which geographies, for which considerations and in which form it does so, by whom they are implemented, and what risks are assumed along the way. The way aid is provided and distributed, in turn, determines whether aid successfully mitigates or exacerbates conflict and violence:[9] research has identified several categories of aid projects that may be associated with an increase in violence. These include projects that are perceived by non-state armed groups as part of government strategies to prevent recruitment or to foster relations with communities, and projects that focus on the (re)construction of infrastructure which could potentially be used for military

[6] On their legal nature, Marie von Engelhardt, *International Development Organizations and Fragile States: Law and Disorder* (Palgrave Macmillan 2017) 83–84; Giedre Jokubauskaite, 'The Legal Nature of the World Bank Safeguards' (2018) 51 Verfassung und Recht in Übersee/Law and Politics in Africa, Asia and Latin America 78.

[7] Kristen E Boon, '"Open for Business": International Financial Institutions, Post-Conflict Economic Reform and the Rule of Law' (2007) 39 International Law and Politics 513, 521–22; Jan Wouters and Philip De Man, 'Post-Conflict Reconstruction' in Jan Wouters, Philip De Man and Nele Verlinden (eds), *Armed Conflicts and the Law* (Intersentia 2016) 535.

[8] World Bank, 'World Bank Group Strategy for Fragility, Conflict and Violence 2020–2025' (World Bank 2020) ('FCV Strategy') 8.

[9] Daniel Karell and Sebastian Schutte, 'Aid, Exclusion, and the Local Dynamics of Insurgency in Afghanistan' (2018) 55 Journal of Peace Research 711, 712; Christoph Zürcher, 'What Do We (Not) Know About Development Aid and Violence? A Systematic Review' (2017) 98 World Development 506, 508.

purposes.[10] Armed groups regularly resort to (indiscriminate) violence against civilians and development actors to sabotage these stabilization efforts.[11] In addition, an increase in violence is associated with projects that lack impartiality and exacerbate tensions within or between communities by excluding or disadvantaging certain individuals,[12] (ethnic) minorities, sub-national groups, or geographical areas.[13] Finally, the fungibility of development assistance is critical, since fungible aid facilitates the capture of additional resources by belligerents and may thus prolong conflict and/or increase violence.[14] Governments, in particular, may be able to reallocate freed-up resources to their military budgets. These few findings illustrate that the World Bank's legal framework, by shaping what and how it finances, can have an impact on the success of international responses to protracted conflicts.

This chapter argues that the World Bank avails itself of the humanitarian-development-peace nexus to support an expansion of its operations, while its legal and institutional framework otherwise prevents a paradigm shift towards conflict-sensitive interventions. As section B will detail, the notion of protractedness blurs essentials terms, concepts, and boundaries that define the mandate and have occupied a central place in the Bank's legal thinking. Likewise, thematic linkages at the triple nexus serve as, or underpin, legal arguments used by the World Bank to overcome the limitations of its mandate, thereby enabling operational expansion in conflict-affected settings. While some of the projects enabled in this way were previously considered to be thematically outside the Bank's mandate, others simply extend the Bank's traditional investment and economic reform projects to conflict environments. This reveals a certain instrumentality and selectivity in the reinterpretation of the mandate. Section C will, in turn, focus on inter-institutional cooperation as an enabling factor. It not only serves as an argument in expanding the mandate, but also provides the Bank with the basis of an alternative to its government-centric operational model that extends its spatial reach into areas of limited statehood. The Bank's institutional and legal framework, however, ensures that this alternative modus operandi retains an exceptional character, thus reaffirming its default priority for government-led economic stabilization. In summary, the concept of 'protracted conflict' and the promotion of the humanitarian-development-peace nexus primarily serve to clear constitutional and operational hurdles. In doing so, they have opened vast thematic and spatial areas for World Bank interventions. Given the Bank's prevailing priority placed upon neoliberal economic reform, traditional investment projects, and economic stabilization

[10] Christoph Zürcher, 'The Folly of "Aid for Stabilisation"' (2019) 40 Third World Quarterly 839, 842–44, 847.

[11] ibid.

[12] Karell and Schutte (n 9) 713–14, 720–22.

[13] Mary B Anderson, *Do No Harm: How Aid can Support Peace—or War* (Lynne Rienner Publishers 1999) 46–47; Gilles Carbonnier, *Humanitarian Economics: War, Disaster and the Global Aid Market* (Hurst & Co 2015) 88–89; Paul Fishstein and Andrew Wilder, 'Winning Hearts and Minds? Examining the Relationship between Aid and Security in Afghanistan' (Feinstein International Center 2012) 62–64; World Bank and United Nations, *Pathways for Peace: Inclusive Approaches to Preventing Violent Conflict* (World Bank 2018) ('Pathways for Peace') 250.

[14] Michael G Findley et al, 'The Localized Geography of Foreign Aid: A New Dataset and Application to Violent Armed Conflict' (2011) 39 World Development 1995, 1998–99; Carbonnier (n 13) 88; Anderson (n 13) 49f.

by governments involved in conflict, this expansion should be approached with caution.

B. Overcoming and Circumventing Legal Mandate Constraints

The World Bank Group consists of five institutions with slightly different yet overlapping and complementary mandates. The original institution, the International Bank for Reconstruction and Development (IBRD), was established to facilitate both post-war reconstruction and development through financial instruments.[15] The International Development Association (IDA), as the other core institution, likewise has the purpose of 'promoting economic development', albeit with a particular focus on 'rais[ing] standards of living in the less-developed areas of the world'.[16] Also of interest here is the International Finance Corporation (IFC), whose mandate is to further economic development by encouraging and facilitating private investment.[17] All three institutions have in common that their Articles of Agreement require the projects they support to be 'productive' or to 'increase productivity'.[18] They also share a prohibition of 'political activity' as a central legal constraint (on their mandates). Enshrined in various manifestations in their constituent treaties, this prohibition bars the organizations from interfering in the 'political affairs' of their members and from relying on political considerations in their decisions:[19]

> The Bank and its officers shall not interfere in the political affairs of any member; nor shall they be influenced in their decisions by the political character of the member or members concerned. Only economic considerations shall be relevant to their decisions, and these considerations shall be weighed impartially in order to achieve the purposes stated in Article I.[20]

Elsewhere, the Articles of Agreement stipulate that loans are to be used exclusively for the intended purposes 'without regard to political or other non-economic influences'.[21] In this provision, the juxtaposition of 'political' and 'economic' considerations as a false dichotomy, central to the political prohibition, is particularly visible.[22] This juxtaposition reflects an underlying rationale. Apart from the aim of achieving a broad membership base across the ideological divides of the emerging Cold War, the

[15] Articles of Agreement of the International Bank for Reconstruction and Development, (adopted 27 December 1945, entered into force 27 December 1945) 2 UNTS 134 ('IBRD AoA') art I.

[16] Articles of Agreement of the International Development Association (adopted 26 January 1960, entered into force 24 September 1960) 439 UNTS 249 ('IDA AoA') art I.

[17] Articles of Agreement of the International Finance Corporation Association, (adopted 25 May 1955, entered into force 20 July 1955) 264 UNTS 117 ('IFC AoA') art I.

[18] IBRD AoA (n 15) art I (i)–(iii); IDA AoA (n 16) art I; IFC AoA (n 17) art I (i), (iii).

[19] IBRD AoA (n 15) art IV (10); IDA AoA (n 16) art V (6); IFC AoA (n 17) art III (9).

[20] IBRD AoA (n 15) Art IV (10).

[21] IBRD AoA (n 15) art III (5)(b); IDA AoA (n 16) art V (1)(g).

[22] On the limits of this dichotomy Stefanie Killinger, *The World Bank's Non-Political Mandate* (Heymann 2003) 80ff; Sundhya Pahuja, *Decolonising International Law: Development, Economic Growth and the Politics of Universality* (CUP 2011) 18–22.

prohibition served to ensure the World Bank's credibility with capital markets and private investors guided exclusively by economic profitability and economic risks.[23]

Consequently, the political prohibition does not prohibit the World Bank from engaging with economic repercussions of political situations.[24] It does however prohibit the Bank from taking sides in political and ideological controversies and from getting involved in political dynamics, including those of an armed conflict.[25] More than that, according to the traditional interpretation, it must stay out of arenas where sovereign functions and political power are exercised, or where engagement would inevitably involve political considerations.[26] Therefore, the World Bank has traditionally avoided politically sensitive issues such as peace and reconciliation, security and defence, organized crime, and criminal justice.[27] These issues were also considered too far removed from productive economic activity for projects addressing them to qualify as 'productive'.[28] Thus, despite an explicit mandate to 'restore economies destroyed or disrupted by war' and to facilitate 'transition from a wartime to a peacetime economy',[29] the World Bank has for a long time rarely engaged with conflicts or 'post-conflict' reconstruction.[30] Owing to the political prohibition, active hostilities and political instability were merely addressed in terms of their economic impact and the risks they posed to World Bank investments. At least until the end of the Cold War, the emphasis was on whether conflict affected the realization of projects, including their development objectives; impaired the borrower's creditworthiness; or impeded on-site monitoring.[31]

However, as has been argued more generally elsewhere and as will be illustrated throughout this chapter in relation to engagement in conflict-affected areas, the World Bank has over time demonstrated a 'strategic mix of flexibility and rigidity' in interpreting its mandate and the political prohibition.[32] Specifically, the notion

[23] Ronald Janse, '(Why) Was the World Bank Supposed to Be a Nonpolitical Organization? An Interpretation of the Original Meaning and Rationale of Article 4(10) of the Articles of Agreement of the International Bank for Reconstruction and Development, 1941–1948' (2014) 16 Journal of the History of International Law 113; Ibrahim F I Shihata, *The World Bank Legal Papers* (Martinus Nijhoff Publishers 2000) 226; Hassane Cissé, 'Should the Political Prohibition in Charters of International Financial Institutions Be Revisited? The Case of the World Bank' in Hassane Cissé, Daniel Bradlow, and Benedict Kingsbury (eds), *The World Bank Legal Review: Volume 3: International Financial Institutions and Global Governance* (World Bank 2012) 60.

[24] Shihata (n 23) 229; Engelhardt (n 6) 108–109; on the evolution of the test whether a decision was based on an economic rationale, Ronald Janse, 'Entering the Forbidden Zone: The World Bank, Criminal Justice Reform and the Political Prohibition Clause' (2013) 10 International Organizations Law Review 81, 96–98.

[25] Shihata (n 23) 270–271; Janse, 'Forbidden Zone' (n 24) n 46 and accompanying text.

[26] Rigo Sureda, 'Eligibility of Police Expenditures for Bank Financing' (1997) (as cited in Dimitri van den Meerssche, *The World Bank's Lawyers: The Life of International Law As Institutional Practice* (OUP 2022) 132).

[27] Boon (n 7) 522; Jon H S Lie, 'The World Bank and Conflicts: From Narrow Rules to Broader Principles' (NUPI Series on Security in Practice 9, Norwegian Institute of International Affairs 2008) 1, 7; Janse, 'Forbidden Zone' (n 24) 101.

[28] Sureda (n 26) (as cited in van den Meerssche (n 26) 132).

[29] IBRD AoA (n 15) art I (i), (v).

[30] Lie (n 27) 6–8; Boon (n 7), 519–22; Wouters and De Man (n 7) 535.

[31] Shihata (n 23) 198–99; Cissé (n 23) 66.

[32] Philipp Dann, 'The World Bank in the Battles of the "Decolonization Era"' in Jochen von Bernstorff, Philipp Dann and Max H Mayer (eds), *The Battle for International Law: South-North Perspectives on the Decolonization Era* (OUP 2019) 291–92; Antony Anghie, 'International Financial Institutions' in Christian Reus-Smit (ed), *The Politics of International Law* (CUP 2009) 232–33, 235–37.

of 'economic considerations', as an antonym to 'political considerations', has been subject to recurrent reinterpretations: 'economic' was gradually superseded by ever broader notions of 'development', with additional aspects being incorporated through concepts such as 'good governance', 'sustainable development'[33] and the 'security-development nexus'.[34] Since the mid-1990s, the World Bank has thus increasingly ventured into areas of activities in conflict situations that were previously considered beyond its mandate.[35]

Within this process, the conceptualization of protracted conflicts and the thematic interlinkages at the humanitarian-development-peace nexus have been instrumental (section B.1). They either serve as legal arguments by the Bank's General Counsel to circumvent or overcome the different limitations of the mandate, or indirectly inform these arguments. On a more abstract level, they have been involved in dissolving the categorizations that underlie the mandate and that have structured the Bank's internal legal documents. In doing so, they have successfully facilitated a thematic expansion of activities and the World Bank's penetration into fragile and conflict-affected situations. However, the continued focus on traditional investment and economic reform projects in conflict areas testifies to a certain selectivity and instrumentality in the re-interpretation of the mandate (section B.2).

1. Protractedness as a Boundary-Blurring Concept

The notion of 'protracted conflicts' does not only denote particularly long-lasting conflicts; it also subsumes, as a single enduring condition, heterogeneous and complex situations that undergo major transformations over time. As set out in the introduction to this volume, protracted conflicts are characterized by fluctuating intensity over time, ie, episodic outbursts of violence and hostilities alternating with comparatively calm periods.[36] Conflict intensity also varies spatially, resulting in the co-existence of active fighting and relative peace, as well as varying degrees of state control and functioning in different geographical areas.[37] The notion of protractedness thus spans the categories of 'war' and 'peace',[38] and to some extent could both normalize conflicts and create a permanent state of exception. Within the World Bank, it operates to blur

[33] Anghie (n 32) 230–32; Bhupinder S Chimni, 'International Financial Institutions and International Law: A Third World Perspective' in Daniel D Bradlow and David B Hunter (eds), *International Financial Institutions and International Law* (Wolters Kluwer 2010) 39–40.

[34] Lie (n 27) 4, 7–10; John D Ciorciari, 'A Prospective Enlargement of the Roles of the Bretton Woods Financial Institutions in International Peace Operations' (1998) 22 Fordham International Law Journal 292, 294–95; World Bank, *World Development Report: Conflict, Security and Development* (World Bank 2011). The interrelationship between peace, security, and development is also emphasized in Sustainable Development Goal 16 and the *sustaining peace* resolutions, UNGA Res 70/262 (27 April 2016) UN Doc A/Res/70/262; UNSC Res 2282 (27 April 2016) UN Doc S/Res/2282.

[35] On the changes at the World Bank in the 1990s, Boon (n 7) 522–25; Wouters and De Man (n 7) 535. Ciorciari (n 34) 300–01 argues that the rigid interpretation of the political prohibition was contingent on the Cold War context.

[36] Pathways for Peace (n 13) 18–19; International Committee of the Red Cross, 'Protracted Conflict and Humanitarian Action: Some Recent ICRC Experiences' (ICRC 2016) 10; Ch. 1, Section B.2.

[37] International Committee of the Red Cross (n 36) 10; Ch. 1, Section B.2.

[38] See Ch. 1, Section B.

previously rigid boundaries and to challenge the binary logics that underpin the constraints of the mandate and have structured legal documents. Primarily concerned are the conflict/post-conflict binary (section B.1.a)) and the productive/non-productive binary (section B.1.b)). Throughout, protractedness contributes to the de-contouring of the mandate-defining notion of 'development'.[39]

a) Conflict—Post-Conflict Binary

One binary that has been overcome by means of the conceptualization of 'protracted conflicts' is the conflict/post-conflict binary. This binary is central to the IBRD's reconstruction mandate, which only commences once a conflict is ending. This emerges clearly from its formulations in the Articles of Agreement: the IBRD is supposed to 'assist in . . . the restoration of economies destroyed or disrupted by war, the reconversion of productive facilities to peacetime needs' and, 'in the immediate postwar years, to assist in bringing about a smooth transition from a wartime to a peacetime economy'.[40] So when, after a long period of abstinence, the Bank eventually began to engage in conflict-affected areas in the 1990s, considerable emphasis was placed on the 'post-conflict' dimension.[41] Initially, the World Bank Group rediscovered the IBRD's mandate for 'post-conflict reconstruction' and then transformed it into a mandate for 'post-conflict peacebuilding'.[42] In doing so, it adopted a framing that also ties in with the IDA's development mandate.[43] Correspondingly, the distinction between conflict and post-conflict phases was a key structuring device of Operational Policy 2.30 ('Development Cooperation and Conflict'). Activities during ongoing conflicts were to be significantly reduced and primarily of an observational nature.[44] A report accompanying the policy explained that 'larger-scale operations' would only commence 'when peaceful conditions have persisted for some time'.[45]

However, the classification as 'post-conflict' often did not accurately characterize the actual environments in which the Bank was operating. As early as 1998, the World Bank's Evaluation Department noted that 'among the countries with identified Bank-financed 'post-conflict reconstruction' operations, about half are experiencing

[39] In this respect, the economic development/politics binary is also affected.

[40] IBRD AoA (n 15) art I (i), (v).

[41] World Bank, 'Transcript of the Meeting of the Executive Directors: A Framework for World Bank Involvement in Situations of Conflict' (held on 18 February 1997, World Bank 1997) <https://documents.worldbank.org/en/publication/documents-reports/documentdetail/225911521016631337/transcript-of-meeting-of-the-executive-directors-of-the-ibrd-and-ida-held-on-tuesday-february-18-1997> accessed 13 October 2023, 7, 16, 48, 87.

[42] Francesco Seatzu, 'Speculating on the World Bank's Involvement in Post-Conflict Reconstruction Operations and Activities' (2019) 16 International Organizations Law Review 192, 203; Ana Palacio, 'Legal Opinion on Peace-Building, Security, and Relief Issues under the Bank's Policy Framework for Rapid Response to Crisis and Emergencies' Annex to World Bank, 'Toward a New Framework for Rapid Bank Response to Crisis and Emergencies' (Board Report, World Bank 2007) <https://documents.worldbank.org/en/publication/documents-reports/documentdetail/528631468136803309/toward-a-new-framework-for-rapid-bank-response-to-crisis-and-emergencies> accessed 27 September 2023, para 12.

[43] Ciorciari (n 34) 304–05.

[44] World Bank, 'OP 2.30: Development Cooperation and Conflict' (Operational Policy, World Bank 2001) ('OP 2.30') para 2. All World Bank Policies and Procedures can be accessed via 'Policies and Procedures' <https://policies.worldbank.org/en/policies#1> accessed 13 October 2023.

[45] World Bank, *Post-Conflict Reconstruction: The Role of the World Bank* (World Bank 1998) 47.

ongoing conflict'.[46] The characterization of a situation as 'post-conflict' rather served to create a pretence of 'normalcy', legitimizing the Bank's reengagement and the resumption of its traditional activities.[47]

Things have since changed. The Bank began to explicitly 'lean in to conflict'[48] as it became involved in the security sector, increasingly financed projects targeting conflict-affected and displaced populations, and aimed to address drivers of fragility and conflict.[49] It now acknowledges that it operates in contexts that cover the full spectrum of conflict. Recognizing that conflict prevention, engagement during active conflict, transition out of conflict, and post-conflict reconstruction can all take place simultaneously, these categories no longer structure the Bank's current policies.[50] The fact that heterogeneous and complex situations—spanning previous categorizations of conflict and post-conflict—are now grouped together as protracted conflicts has contributed to overcoming the limitation to the post-conflict phase.

In terms of the World Bank's mandate, the increased engagement with conflict was primarily justified by articulating a development-security nexus. That is, peace, security, and justice are identified as preconditions for (economic) development, which has prompted and enabled the Bank 'to position fragility, conflict, and violence at the core of its development mandate'.[51] This development-security nexus occupies a central position in the General Counsels' legal opinions.[52] Engagement in conflict-affected settings has, however, also been significantly facilitated by the blurring of the conflict/post-conflict distinction. Concepts such as 'protracted conflict', 'fragility', and 'resilience', by encompassing both the realm of conflict and the post-conflict realm, have normalized conflict as an environment in which development interventions take place.[53] Within these concepts, conflict and violence are no longer seen as exceptional phenomena that need to be resolved politically before development interventions can resume. Instead, they are seen as an enduring reality that needs to be managed and worked within, requiring depoliticized interventions.[54]

[46] Alcira Kreimer et al, *The World Bank's Experience with Post-Conflict Reconstruction* (World Bank 1998) 9.

[47] Bhupinder S Chimni, 'Refugees, Return and Reconstruction of "Post-Conflict" Societies: A Critical Perspective' (2002) 9 International Peacekeeping 163, 165–66.

[48] Independent Evaluation Group, 'World Bank Engagement in Situations of Conflict: An Evaluation of FY10-20 Experience' (World Bank 2021) 25–28.

[49] World Bank, 'Bank Policy on Development Cooperation and Fragility, Conflict, and Violence' (Bank Policy, World Bank 2021) ('FCV Policy') s III paras 6–7; World Bank, 'Updated Bank Policy: Development Cooperation and Fragility, Conflict and Violence (Board Paper)' (World Bank 2021) <https://documents.worldbank.org/en/publication/documents-reports/documentdetail/498771628797344998/updated-bank-policy-development-cooperation-and-fragility-conflict-and-violence> accessed 28 September 2023 ('Board Paper') para 7.

[50] FCV Policy (n 49) s III para 2.

[51] World Bank, 'Operationalizing the 2011 World Development Report: Conflict, Security and Development' (World Bank, 2011) iii (as cited in Anne-Marie Leroy, 'Legal Note on Bank Involvement in the Criminal Justice Sector' (World Bank 2012) para 2).

[52] Leroy, 'Criminal Justice Sector' (n 51) paras 11–15.

[53] David Chandler, 'Rethinking the Conflict-Poverty Nexus: From Securitising Intervention to Resilience' (2015) 4 Stability: International Journal of Security & Development 5; Hani Sayed, 'The Humanization of the Third World' in Luis Eslava, Michael Fakhri, and Vasuki Nesiah (eds), *Bandung, Global History, and International Law: Critical Pasts and Pending Futures* (CUP 2017) 446.

[54] Chandler (n 53) 8; Sayed (n 53) 446, 448.

In combination, the development-security nexus and the normalization of conflict as an operating environment associated with the relinquishment of the conflict/post-conflict binary have allowed for a shift in the interpretation of the political prohibition clause. Interventions in security and conflict-related sectors are no longer *categorically* precluded on the grounds that they are deemed too politically sensitive. Instead, the Bank now evaluates on a *case-by-case* basis whether projects in those sectors (justified on the basis of the development-security nexus) amount to political interference.[55] In 2012, a Legal Note by the Bank's General Counsel 'evolved' the interpretation of the Articles of Agreement in this way to allow for individual projects in the criminal justice sector.[56] This was subsequently extended to projects involving or implemented by security actors,[57] a move formalized by the recent Bank Policy on Development Cooperation and Fragility, Conflict, and Violence (FCV Policy).[58] While the World Bank still does not provide financing for armaments, military infrastructure, or peacekeeping missions,[59] several forms of involvements of security actors are now conceivable. Apart from their engagement to provide security for projects, these include support to 'civilian functions' performed by (para-)military actors, such as humanitarian assistance[60] or maintenance of essential infrastructure in highly unstable regions.[61] Implementation by military units must, however, remain a last resort and be limited to emergency situations in otherwise inaccessible and/or insecure locations.[62]

In sum, the notion of protracted conflict has dissolved the conflict/post-conflict binary on which the World Bank's mandate is partly premised, thereby not only dispensing with a temporal and contextual constraint on its interventions, but also facilitating a substantial expansion into new thematic areas.

b) Productive/Non-Productive Binary

Protracted conflict as a concept and the humanitarian-development nexus as an institutional response have also been instrumental in challenging the distinction between humanitarian assistance and development cooperation. Within the World Bank's legal framework, this is relevant in terms of the 'developmental' mandate and as a manifestation of the productive/non-productive binary. In the past, humanitarian relief was considered insufficiently 'productive' and thus outside the World Bank's mandate, given its focus on short-term consumption.[63] In the early 2000s, the now retired OP 2.30 § 3 (a)—which like all Bank Policies is legally binding, at least internally, on

[55] This change of practice is discussed extensively in van den Meerssche (n 26) ch 7.
[56] Leroy, 'Criminal Justice Sector' (n 51).
[57] Anne-Marie Leroy, 'Legal Aspects of the World Bank's Involvement in the Security Sector: An Essay' in 'Legal Vice Presidency: Annual Report FY 2014' (World Bank 2014) VII.
[58] FCV Policy (n 49) s III paras 13, 16.
[59] FCV Policy (n 49) s III para 15.
[60] On the permissibility of funding humanitarian assistance: Section B.1.b).
[61] Leroy, 'Security Sector' (n 57) VIII; FCV Strategy (n 8) para 131.
[62] FCV Policy (n 49) s III para 16.
[63] World Bank, 'Operational Policy on Emergency Recovery Assistance (OP 8.50)' (Operational Policy, World Bank 1995) ('OP 8.50') para 2; Annamaria Viterbo, 'The Role of the International Financial Institutions in Fragile and Conflict-Affected Countries' in Giovanni Cellamare and Ivan Ingravallo (eds), *Peace Maintenance in Africa: Open Legal Issues* (Springer 2018) 116; Maurizio Ragazzi, 'Role of the World Bank in Conflict-Affected Areas' (2001) 95 American Society of International Law Proceedings 240, 243.

the World Bank's staff[64]—still stipulated that the Bank 'does not provide humanitarian relief'.[65] OP 8.50 § 2 even provided a list of activities or items that were ineligible for Bank financing, including food and water supplies, temporary health care and shelter, and the restoration of essential transport links. By 2007, however, the Bank's General Counsel had invoked the relief-development continuum to justify increasing engagement in humanitarian emergencies.[66] In continuation, the current FCV Policy of 2021 is based on the recognition that 'that there is a continuum between emergency relief activities, recovery, and rebuilding'.[67]

This conceptualization as a continuum, which substitutes for the delineation between humanitarian and development assistance, is closely linked to the identification of multidimensional and protracted crises. Protracted conflicts create humanitarian emergencies, the duration of which corresponds to the typical time horizon of development assistance, that is, the medium and long-term.[68] The cumulative impacts of protracted conflicts require, and the intermittent low intensity of violence allows for, system-supporting and resilience-oriented approaches to humanitarian emergencies.[69] In protracted conflicts, humanitarian assistance and development cooperation blur into one. The identification of a continuum is thus supported by the conceptualization of certain realities as protracted conflicts.

This continuum, as a description, forms the basis of the *legal* argument that enables operational engagement in humanitarian emergencies. Of course, such engagement must still be able to be subsumed under the World Bank's developmental mandate and must therefore invariably rely on a 'robust development rationale'.[70] However, in view of the cumulative impact of protracted conflict on countries' infrastructures and institutions, 'protect[ing] human capital, institutions and [past] development gains' and 'mitigating development impacts' are deemed sufficient.[71] Accordingly, emergency cash transfers or the supply of equipment/consumables to sustain health care and shelter are eligible if these relief activities can have an impact on future reconstruction needs and works.[72] Interestingly, the Bank's choice of words closely resembles the formulation used by the International Committee of the Red Cross (ICRC) to describe its humanitarian action in protracted conflict—it refers to 'achieving development holds'.[73] The notion of protracted conflict has thus helped to frame humanitarian activities as 'productive' and 'developmental', a framing which is relied upon to legally justify the expansion of operations in humanitarian emergencies.

In addition, the continuum also acquires legal significance through a second, distinct pathway, reflecting not its descriptive, but its normative dimension. This

64 World Bank, 'Bank Policy: Policy and Procedure Framework' (Bank Policy, World Bank 2014) s III para 3.

65 OP 2.30 (n 44) para 3 (a).

66 Palacio, 'Legal Opinion' (n 42) paras 23–24, 27.

67 Board Paper (n 49) para 37.

68 FCV Strategy (n 8) ix, 52.

69 ibid 24; International Committee of the Red Cross (n 36) 20–21.

70 FCV Policy (n 49) s III para 8.

71 FCV Policy (n 49) s III paras 2 (b),(d), 8; Board Paper (n 49) n 17; FCV Strategy (n 8) 24.

72 World Bank, 'OP 8.00: Rapid Response to Crises and Emergencies' (Operational Policy, World Bank 2007) ('OP 8.00') n 3; Palacio, 'Legal Opinion' (n 42) paras 23, 26, n 41.

73 International Committee of the Red Cross (n 36).

normative dimension is embodied in external soft-law instruments, which the Bank recognises as authoritative points of reference. Thus, the 'principles associated with the humanitarian-development-peace nexus' as set out in the OECD DAC Recommendations[74] have been elevated to 'applicable principles and standards' to which the FCV Policy demands adherence.[75] They are mentioned alongside the Articles of Agreements, without any differentiation in terms of their legal force.[76]

2. A New Environment for Persisting Priorities

The expansion by the Bank of its scope of action does not, however, necessarily translate into a reorientation of its operations and priorities in conflict-affected countries. Having normalized conflict as an environment for development interventions, it frequently pursues its traditional agenda within them and sticks to established practices. This indicates a certain instrumentality behind the reinterpretation of the mandate, which can be viewed critically irrespective of how one assesses the actual expansion of the mandate, such as engagement in humanitarian emergencies.

In protracted armed conflict, the World Bank Group continues to extend loans conditional on policy reforms and to finance traditional investment projects, notably in geographic areas that are hardly affected by active hostilities and during periods of relative normality.[77] The World Bank may have overcome the notion of clearly distinguishable conflict and post-conflict phases and acknowledges that fragility, active conflict, and transition out of conflict can coexist.[78] However, it still differentiates spatially between 'areas of conflict' and 'relatively stable areas' in which it would proceed with conventional investments.[79] The World Bank has even made facilitating private sector development one of its four overarching guiding principles for conflict-affected states.[80] To this end, it introduced financial instruments through which the IDA partially underwrites the financial and political risks of private investment in conflict environments.[81] As a result, projects in the transport, energy, extractive industries, and agribusiness sectors account for a significant share of projects in protracted conflicts.[82]

Moreover, the World Bank does not hesitate to advance neoliberal policy reforms in conflict contexts and even perceives conflicts as opportunities to do so.[83] This was

[74] OECD DAC Recommendation (n 4).

[75] Board Paper (n 49) para 38.

[76] FCV Policy (n 49) s III para 8.

[77] On the World Bank's routine operations in Bogotá (Colombia), Luis Eslava, *Local Space, Global Life: The Everyday Operation of International Law and Development* (CUP 2015).

[78] FCV Policy (n 49) s III para 2; Board Paper (n 49) paras 19–20; FCV Strategy (n 8) para 60.

[79] FCV Strategy (n 8) 26.

[80] ibid 16, 20.

[81] Elliot Dolan-Evans, 'Making War Safe for Capitalism: The World Bank and its Evolving Interventions in Conflict' (2022) 53 Security Dialogue 531, 541–42; World Bank, 'Operationalizing the IDA18 IFC-MIGA Private Sector Window' (World Bank 2017).

[82] FCV Strategy (n 8) 89; Independent Evaluation Group, 'The International Finance Corporation's and Multilateral Investment Guarantee Agency's Support for Private Investment in Fragile and Conflict-Affected Situations' (World Bank Group 2022) 16–18.

[83] Kreimer et al (n 46) 46, holding that 'the immediate post-conflict period can be a window of opportunity to pursue policy reforms'.

already the case in East Timor and during the occupation of Iraq, where the World Bank pursued agricultural reforms aimed at commercialization, privatization, and export orientation of agriculture,[84] among other liberalizations.[85] It also remains the case, particularly in protracted conflicts, where institutions are often still strong enough to adopt reforms. Most notably, the World Bank—seeking to support private sector development—promotes business environment reforms in fragile and conflict-affected states, with the stated aim of improving the climate for foreign investment, reducing regulation for businesses, and increasing competition in markets.[86]

Not only does the World Bank stick to its conventional practices in spite of an expanded mandate, but it even occasionally continues to invoke former, more restrictive interpretations of the mandate to discount the conflict environment. A recent example is the continued financing of infrastructure projects in Ethiopia as armed conflicts in the Tigray region were intensifying.[87] The World Bank merely deplored what it called an 'unfortunate unrest' and noted: 'As a development focused organization, the World Bank does not have the mandate to get involved in the internal governance issues of its member states.'[88] Similarly, the Bank continues to rely on an interpretation of the political prohibition from the early 1990s, allowing it to disregard the fungibility of its financing.[89] In spite of the above-mentioned expansion into the security sector that has since taken place, the Bank still explicitly holds that loan 'conditionalit[ies] related to security or military expenditures' are impermissible.[90] Invoking the political prohibition, it deprives itself of the ability to prevent its loans from being indirectly used to increase military spending in ongoing conflicts.

In summary, the World Bank—in areas into which it has only expanded through the dissolution of the conflict/post-conflict binary—continues to a considerable extent to pursue the investment projects and economic reforms for which it has been widely criticized in the past. The expanded scope of action it has carefullyconstructed has not resulted in a comprehensive paradigm shift. Rather, the foregoing analysis suggests a certain selectivity and opportunism in reinterpreting the mandate.

C. Inter-Institutional Cooperation: An Enabler in Two Dimensions

In addition to the concept of protracted conflict and the interlinkages discussed in the previous section, another element of the humanitarian-development-peace nexus

[84] Ntina Tzouvala, 'Food for the Global Market: The Neoliberal Reconstruction of Agriculture in Occupied Iraq (2003–2004) and the Role of International Law' (2017) 17 Global Jurist 117.

[85] Boon (n 7).

[86] Tania Ghossein and Ahmed N Rana, 'Business Environment Reforms in Fragile and Conflict-Affected Situations: What Works and Why?' (World Bank 2022).

[87] World Bank, 'New World Bank Financing Supports Ethiopia's Goal of Universal Electricity Access by 2025' (2022) <https://www.worldbank.org/en/news/press-release/2021/03/29/new-world-bank-financing-supports-ethiopia-s-goal-of-universal-electricity-access-by-2025> accessed 28 September 2023.

[88] World Bank, 'World Bank Group Statement on Current Situation in Ethiopia' (World Bank 2021) <https://www.worldbank.org/en/news/statement/2021/03/05/world-bank-group-statement-on-current-situation-in-ethiopia> accessed 28 July 2022.

[89] Board Paper (n 49) para 48; for the interpretation in the 90s Shihata (n 23) 205–06.

[90] FCV Policy (n 49) s III para 14; Leroy, 'Security Sector' (n 57) VIII–IX.

serves as an argument in stretching the World Bank's mandate: inter-institutional co-operation (section C.1). At the same time, inter-institutional cooperation is also of relevance in a second dimension, as it provides the Bank with the basis of an alternative modus operandi (section C.2).

1. Inter-Institutional Cooperation as Legal Tool

Initially, one reason for the World Bank to consider peacebuilding and humanitarian relief as beyond its remit was that these functions were assigned to other international organizations (IO).[91] This reasoning arguably aligned with the ICJ's concept of a division of exclusive functional responsibilities between specialized agencies within the UN system.[92] Subsequently, however, the World Bank reversed the conclusions it drew from the principle of speciality. Legal documents permitted support for 'activities *outside* the Bank's traditional' mandate *provided* the Bank did so in partnership with other organizations—including in the form of multi-donor trust funds—and in the context of integrated programmes.[93] Since then, the World Bank has continuously emphasized partnerships, in terms of situational assessment as well as in operational engagement in humanitarian emergencies, forced displacement crises, and peacebuilding.[94] In other words, the Bank has legitimized new practices by associating them with legitimate organizations in their respective fields,[95] at least until these practices became established as World Bank practices.

As another recent example also illustrates, the World Bank seems to view the reference to partnerships with competent organizations as something it can use to cope with the constraints of its mandate. Under two funding lines for fragile and conflict-affected states, it has made continued funding conditional on the achievement of agreed milestones.[96] Some of these milestones, the Bank acknowledges, relate to issues outside its mandate, such as holding elections, increasing the number of security forces, or resuming peace talks.[97] Nevertheless, the Bank apparently deems this legal

[91] OP 2.30 (n 44) para 3(a); OP 8.50 (n 63) para 2; Cissé (n 23) 66; Viterbo (n 63) 113; Palacio, 'Legal Opinion' (n 42) para 25, specifying that the Bank's operations 'must remain consistent with the prevailing division of labor among international organizations'.

[92] *Legality of the Use by A State of Nuclear Weapons in Armed Conflict (Advisory Opinion)* [1996] ICJ Rep 66, 79–81.

[93] OP 8.00 (n 72) para 5; Palacio, 'Legal Opinion' (n 42) paras 2, 15, 19; Giovanna Adinolfi, 'The Role of International Financial Institutions' in Andrea de Guttry, Marco Gestri, and Gabriella Venturini (eds), *International Disaster Response Law* (TMC Asser Press 2012) 619.

[94] FCV Policy (n 49) s III paras 1, 3(d), 8, 11; FCV Strategy (n 8) 52.

[95] On this strategy, Rafael Biermann, 'Legitimizing Inter-Organizational Relations' in Joachim A Koops and Rafael Biermann (eds), *Palgrave Handbook of Inter-Organizational Relations in World Politics* (Palgrave Macmillan 2016) 350–52.

[96] International Development Association, 'IDA20—Building Back Better from the Crisis: Toward a Green, Resilient and Inclusive Future' (World Bank 2022) <https://documents.worldbank.org/en/publication/documents-reports/documentdetail/163861645554924417/ida20-building-back-better-from-the-crisis-toward-a-green-resilient-and-inclusive-future> accessed 28 September 2023 Annex 4, n 5, 17.

[97] International Development Association, 'IDA19: Mid-term Review of the Operationalization of the Fragility, Conflict and Violence (FCV) Envelope' (World Bank 2021) <http://documents.worldbank.org/curated/en/280011636535499521/IDA19-Mid-term-Review-of-the-Operationalization-of-the-Fragility-Conflict-and-Violence-FCV-Envelope> accessed 15 February 2022 para 11, table A1.1.

as long as the respective milestones are not monitored and supported by the Bank itself, but rather by competent partner organizations.[98] Inter-institutional cooperation is thus deployed as justification for practices that might otherwise be considered ultra vires.

To a limited extent, inter-institutional interaction might indeed increase the World Bank's discretionary powers. Article V(8)(b) IBRD AoA prompts the Bank to consider the views and recommendations of 'international organizations having specialized responsibilities in related fields' in decision concerning matters within their competence.[99] This could be interpreted to mean that even political judgments turn into 'technical expertise' if they emanate from functionally competent international organizations. In decisions on its development projects, it could therefore lawfully draw on such expertise. Yet, at the same time, Article V(8)(a) IBRD AoA clearly states that any cooperation with other international organizations needs to remain within the terms of the Articles of Agreement.

2. Bypassing Government: The World Bank's Alternative Modus Operandi

Having illustrated how inter-institutional cooperation has been instrumental in expanding the mandate, this section now highlights that it also adds an option in terms of the Bank's modus operandi: inter-institutional cooperation offers an alternative to the norm of government-led economic stabilization (section C.2.a)). While the IDA AoA are in principle conducive to this alternative (section C.2.b)), the World Bank's secondary law ensures that it retains an exceptional character, thus reflecting the Bank's continued priority for government-led stabilization (section C.2.c)). Lastly, section C.2.d) explores factors that may explain this divergence between the Bank's Articles and its Policies.

a) An Exception to the Norm of Government-Led Stabilization

The World Bank's predominant operational model is to provide (concessional) loans to governments for specific projects or policies. Projects thus financed are to be implemented by government agencies and their contractors, which are occasionally specified at the project design stage and otherwise selected through procurement procedures. It is the operational model of a financial institution that is reliant on governments, both in legal terms as borrowers or guarantors, and in practical terms for project implementation.[100] It also aligns with the state-centric conception of development cooperation, which considers governments to be the 'natural counterparts' of donor states and international organizations.[101]

[98] ibid para 11.

[99] Contrarily, within its core mandate, the Bank insulates itself from recommendations by reference to its status as 'independent organisation' under its Relationship Agreement with the UN.

[100] Viterbo (n 63) 119.

[101] Engelhardt (n 6) 49–50.

In relation to conflict-affected areas, the World Bank's orientation towards working with governments translates into a default priority for government-led economic stabilization. Typically, early recovery projects target conflict-affected communities and aim to reinforce or re-establish the presence of the state in areas directly affected by conflict as well as adjacent areas.[102] In some cases, projects also seek to prevent the recruitment of fighters by non-state armed groups.[103] To these ends, such projects tend to focus on restoring livelihoods and economic opportunities through cash-for-work programmes and the revitalization of small businesses, providing basic services and rehabilitating selected infrastructure. The World Bank frequently cooperates with security actors, including UN peacekeeping missions, to implement such projects in insecure areas or to rapidly initiate them once areas have been recaptured.[104] After all, state institutions that are perceived as neutral and trustworthy by all parties to a conflict and can therefore implement projects across frontlines are only rarely available.[105]

In a particularly striking example, the World Bank announced cash-for-work programs in Myanmar's Rakhine State 'to create the underlying conditions to foster peace and stability'.[106] Despite the 'clearance operations' and the ongoing persecution of the Rohingya in the state,[107] the World Bank would have entrusted Myanmar's government with implementing the supposedly 'inclusive' project. The Bank initiated the project fully aware that it might exacerbate inter-ethnic tensions and violence, and only dropped it after heavy criticism.[108] As this example underscores, the World Bank is, due to institutional constraints, prone to support precisely those government-led stabilization projects that research has identified as often being associated with an increase in violence.[109]

[102] World Bank, 'Project Appraisal Document: Central African Republic LONDO ('Stand-Up') Project' (report no PAD1469, World Bank 2015) <https://documents1.worldbank.org/curated/en/962531468189561818/pdf/PAD1469-PAD-P152512-IDA-R2015-0205-1-Box385353B-OUO-9.pdf> accessed 3 October 2021, paras 32, 41; World Bank, 'Project Appraisal Document: Mozambique Northern Crisis Recovery Project' (report no PAD4389, World Bank 2021) <https://documents1.worldbank.org/curated/en/305051619834459880/pdf/Mozambique-Northern-Crisis-Recovery-Project.pdf> accessed 28 September 2023.

[103] Independent Evaluation Group, 'World Bank Engagement in Situations of Conflict' (n 48) 60–61.

[104] FCV Strategy (n 8) 53.

[105] Examples are the Social Fund for Development and the Public Works Project in Yemen, which undertake cash-for-work programmes, rehabilitation of local infrastructure, and revitalization of small businesses. Both institutions were specifically selected as partners because of their 'geographic outreach' and 'reputation for political neutrality [and] credibility': World Bank, 'Project Appraisal Document: Yemen Emergency Crisis Response Project' (Report No PAD1797, World Bank 2016) <https://documents1.worldbank.org/curated/en/276821468242019652/pdf/PAD1797-PAD-P159053-IDA-R2016-0183-1-Box396273B-OUO-9.pdf> accessed 3 October 2021, paras 43, 49, 64; Lamis Al-Iryani, Alain de Janvry, and Elisabeth Sadoulet, 'The Yemen Social Fund for Development: An Effective Community-Based Approach amid Political Instability' (2015) 22 International Peacekeeping 321.

[106] World Bank, 'Rakhine Recovery and Development Support Project' (Project Information Document, World Bank 2019) <http://documents1.worldbank.org/curated/en/734311557488220009/pdf/Concept-Project-Information-Document-PID-Rakhine-Recovery-and-Development-Support-Project-P168797.pdf> accessed 8 October 2021.

[107] UNHRC, 'Report of the Independent Fact-finding Mission on Myanmar' (2019) UN Doc A/HRC/42/50 paras 76–90.

[108] Mohammad Shahabuddin, *Minorities and the Making of Postcolonial States in International Law* (CUP 2021) 260.

[109] For a few findings of this research, Section A.

Gradually, however, inter-institutional cooperation at the humanitarian-development-peace nexus is emerging as a viable alternative to government-led economic stabilization and, more generally, the Bank's state-centric operational model. This alternative lies in *directly* financing UN agencies and humanitarian (international) non-governmental organizations ((I)NGOs), without involving governments at the design and implementation stage. While the involvement of UN agencies and (I)NGOs has long been common practice, they previously merely used to be involved in the implementation of projects as contractors of the borrowing government, that is, under the prevailing operational model. One example of this emerging approach is the Essential Health Services Project in South Sudan, which provides grants to UNICEF and the ICRC. The corresponding financing agreements were concluded *directly* between those organizations and the World Bank. Under this project, direct cooperation, particularly with the ICRC due to its commitment to neutrality and independence, allows the World Bank to extend the project to 'insecure' regions controlled by non-state armed groups.[110] Similar projects have been undertaken mainly in Somalia, Yemen, South Sudan, Sudan, Afghanistan, and Myanmar, as the use of the operational model increased in recent years.

Inter-institutional cooperation thus forms the basis of a fundamentally different modus operandi that primarily expands the World Bank's spatial reach. It provides the ability to operate in areas previously considered inaccessible, that is, in conflict-affected states without effective or fully functioning governments and in areas controlled by non-state armed actors. As an institutional arrangement without direct involvement of government authorities, it also offers a way to engage without legitimizing those effectively in power,[111] for example where the incumbent authorities are sanctioned or not internationally recognized. This is equally relevant with respect to non-state armed actors. Incidentally, many of the projects implemented through this cooperation only became thematically conceivable as a result of the extension of the mandate, which—as outlined in section B.1—is likewise partly based on the humanitarian-development nexus.

b) Potentials under the Articles of Agreement

From a legal point of view, the Articles of Agreement are in principle oriented towards government-led projects, yet allow for inter-institutional cooperation on a larger scale. Pursuant to them, financing may be extended to a member state's government, a political sub-division thereof, or a private or public entity in the territory of a member state.[112] Whenever a loan is not provided directly to a state's government, the World

[110] World Bank, 'Project Appraisal Document: South Sudan Provision of Essential Health Services Project' (Report No PAD3140, World Bank 2019) <https://documents.worldbank.org/en/publication/documents-reports/documentdetail/885611551582069381/south-sudan-provision-of-essential-health-services-project> accessed 28 September 2023, paras 108, 109.

[111] Jeff Chelsky, Sengphet Lattanavong, and Mees van der Werf, 'When the Financing Stops: the World Bank, Chad, and Shades of Engagement' (Independent Evaluation Group, June 28 2022) <https://ieg.worldbankgroup.org/blog/when-financing-stops-world-bank-chad-and-shades-engagement> accessed 28 September 2023.

[112] IBRD AoA (n 15) art III (4); IDA AoA (n 16) art V (2)(c).

Bank must—in the case of IBRD loans[113]—or is entitled to require a governmental guarantee.[114] Additionally, however, the IDA may also duly provide financing 'to a public international or regional organization', according to article V (2)(c) IDA AoA.

Generally, all projects and operations are subject to the concerned state's consent.[115] The World Bank derives this requirement, among other things, from the political prohibition clause. The clause is commonly interpreted to mean that the Bank must not question the choice of a particular form of government or political ideology[116] and must not cooperate or engage with representatives of the opposition, local governments, or non-governmental actors without governmental approval.[117] As regards the IBRD, government approval in the form of consent to either the financing or guarantee agreement is required anyway. In respect of the IDA, it can additionally be deduced from a dedicated paragraph in the Articles of Agreement:

> The Association shall not provide financing for any project if the member in whose territory the project is located objects to such financing, except that it shall not be necessary for the Association to assure itself that individual members do not object in the case of financing provided to a public international or regional organization.[118]

The second half of this provision holds remarkable potential if it is understood to mean that the concerned state's consent is not required for the financing of projects carried out by other international organizations. The cautious, almost procedural formulation raises doubts in this respect. The reference to 'individual members' could be interpreted to imply that the provision only refers to members who are concerned exclusively by virtue of their membership in the receiving IO. It would not waive the consent of the state on whose territory the IO intends to undertake the project, though. Its systematic position as an explicit exception to the consent requirement, on the other hand, speaks in favour of such an understanding. While the provision has hardly been applied or even mentioned in relation to current inter-institutional cooperation, it did appear in an older legal memorandum. The Bank's then General Counsel, Ibrahim Shihata, summarized it as allowing the Bank to provide financing to IOs 'without requiring . . . approval of the member in whose territory the project is located'.[119] Hence, the Articles of Agreement arguably provide a general basis for financing projects implemented by other IOs, bypassing the concerned government and its consent.

c) Limitation to Exceptional Constellations in Bank Policies

As a matter of Bank policy, however, this alternative modus operandi remains of an exceptional character rather than becoming the new norm for engagement in

[113] IBRD AoA (n 15) art III (4)(i).
[114] IDA AoA (n 16) art V (2)(d).
[115] FCV Policy (n 49) s III para 17 in connection with para 3(b); Board Paper (n 49) para 24.
[116] Janse, 'Nonpolitical Organization' (n 23) 116.
[117] Shihata (n 23) 231, 270; Engelhardt (n 6) 108 n 47.
[118] IDA AoA (n 16) art V (1)(e).
[119] Shihata (n 23) 812.

conflict-affected areas. The World Bank continues to prioritize government-led projects, as various Bank policies severely restrict the cases in which it can directly finance IOs and/or bypass the consent of the states on whose territory the projects are ultimately undertaken.

In fact, Bank policy explicitly stipulates that IDA financing is in principle provided to governments only.[120] Accordingly, Bank policies limit *direct* legal arrangements and disbursements between the Bank and other international organizations (or NGOs) to 'exceptional circumstances'.[121] They are only permitted if (1) countries experience humanitarian crises and emergencies because of natural or man-made disasters,[122] (2) government capacities are severely constrained, especially during high-intensity conflict,[123] (3) there is 'no government in power', or (4) project sites are controlled by a de facto regime ineligible for cooperation. Section 3 paragraph 12(d) Policy on Investment Project Financing reveals the *ratio* behind this restrictive approach by further confining the arrangements—*directly* funding UN agencies and (I)NGOs is an option only *as long as* the borrower's capacity is constrained *while* capacity is (re)built.[124]

This objective is also reflected in project design, as can be observed in the example of the already mentioned South Sudan Essential Health Services Project. The neutral and independent ICRC is the partner of choice *only* for 'insecure' regions controlled by non-state armed groups.[125] Conversely, implementation in government-controlled areas is carried out by UNICEF and aims at enhancing capacity and ultimately a 'transition towards a government-led implementation modality'.[126] The project itself is thus designed to ensure that its institutional arrangement is only a transitional solution and limited to the necessity out of which it arose.

Regarding the consent requirement, too, Bank policies impose restrictions compared to the IDA Articles of Agreement. The FCV Policy, guided solely by the political prohibition, stipulates that 'the Bank does not operate in the territory of a member country without the approval of that member['s] [government]' and subjects all partnerships with international organizations to this principle.[127] Accordingly, the government of South Sudan, for example, has made a standing request to provide financing to third parties, acknowledging that its access to certain regions is limited for political reasons and that neutral implementation is required given the non-international

[120] World Bank, 'Bank Policy: Lending Operations: Choice of Borrower and Contractual Agreements' (Bank Policy, World Bank 2017) s III para 6.

[121] Adinolfi (n 93) 620–21.

[122] World Bank, 'Bank Policy on Investment Project Financing' (Bank Policy, World Bank 2018) ('IPF Policy') s III para 12.

[123] International Development Association, 'IDA20' (n 96) Annex 4, paras 11–13; IPF Policy (n 122) s III para 12.

[124] Also FCV Strategy (n 8) 53.

[125] World Bank, 'Provision of Essential Health Services Project' (n 110) paras 108–09.

[126] ibid para 103; World Bank, 'Project Paper: Additional Financing for Provision of Essential Health Services Project' (Report No PAD4018, World Bank 2021) <https://documents1.worldbank.org/curated/en/894031611630103393/pdf/South-Sudan-Provision-of-Essential-Health-Services-Project-Additional-Financing.pdf> accessed 28 September 2023, para 32.

[127] FCV Policy (n 49) s III paras 3(b), 17(a); Board Paper (n 49) para 24.

armed conflict.[128] By contrast, faced with authorities unwilling to approve such projects, the Bank has no option but to disengage.[129]

A narrow exception in this respect is provided by a 'noteworthy'[130] or 'astonishing'[131] provision in the FCV Policy. For the exceptional constellation to which it applies, this provision offers a solution that neither explicitly refers to or relies on article V (1)(e) IDA AoA nor calls into question the general consent requirement:

> If there is no government in power, Bank assistance may be initiated by requests from the international community as properly represented (e.g. by the United Nations) and subject in each case to the prior approval of the Bank's Executive Directors.[132]

Until recently, the only case of the rule's application was unambiguous and concerned Somalia.[133] The World Bank would, however, also apply the provision in absence of a '*proper* government', that is, in the presence of a de facto regime with which it is unable to engage.[134] Under the Policy on *Dealings with De Facto Governments*, the launch of projects in collaboration with a de facto government is dependent on whether it is 'in effective control of the country, enjoys a reasonable degree of stability and public acceptance' and honours the country's (financial) obligations.[135] In other words, creditworthiness is the main factor.[136] Additionally, the de facto government must be recognized by the international community, including other international organizations.[137] If these conditions are not fulfilled, as in the case of the Taliban in Afghanistan after August 2021, the Bank authorizes itself to intervene at the request of the international community.[138]

Pursuant to the FCV Policy, the Policy on *Dealings with De Facto Governments* is also to be followed as soon as more than one entity asserts power.[139] The implications of this referral, however, contradict the traditional position in international law, which

[128] World Bank, 'Project Appraisal Document: South Sudan Enhancing Community Resilience and Local Governance Project' (Report No PAD3655, World Bank 2020) <https://documents.worldbank.org/en/publication/documents-reports/documentdetail/824121596765983121/south-sudan-enhancing-community-resilience-and-local-governance-project> accessed 28 March 2024 para 59.

[129] Yet, the option to disengage confers a powerful position on the Bank: Sanbèlè Dominique Da, 'Les Organisations Internationales Économiques et la Consolidation de la Paix dans les Etats Sortant de Conflits Armés' (Thèse de doctorat, Université Grenoble Alpes 2015) 86.

[130] Engelhardt (n 6) 112.

[131] Sanbèlè Dominique Da (n 129) 99.

[132] FCV Policy (n 49) s III para 3(b).

[133] Engelhardt (n 6) 117.

[134] Palacio, 'Legal Opinion' (n 42) para 20; International Development Association, 'IDA19 Second Replenishment Meeting: Special Theme—Fragility, Conflict and Violence' (World Bank Group 2019) <http://documents.worldbank.org/curated/en/515831563779134705/IDA19-Second-Replenishment-Meeting-Special-Theme-Fragility-Conflict-and-Violence> accessed 28 September 2023, 14, n 44.

[135] World Bank, 'OP 7.30: Dealings with De Facto Governments (Operational Policy, World Bank 2013) ('OP 7.30') para 5(a)–(c).

[136] Engelhardt (n 6) 119; Michael Nesbitt, 'The World Bank and De Facto Governments: A Call for Transparency in the Bank's Operational Policy' (2007) 32 Queen's Law Journal 641, 647, 652–53.

[137] OP 7.30 (n 135) para 5(d), (e).

[138] World Bank, 'Emergency Support for the People of Afghanistan' (World Bank 2022) <https://www.worldbank.org/en/country/afghanistan/brief/afghanistan-emergency-support> accessed 28 September 2023.

[139] FCV Policy (n 49) s III para 3(b).

assumes that the de jure government remains the appropriate interlocuter during internal conflicts, even if they result in the loss of control over substantial parts of the territory.[140] Closer to that traditional position is Section III paragraph 18 FCV Policy, subjecting engagement with non-state actors in relation to territories controlled by them to the consent of the de jure government. The co-existence of these two provisions raises the question of the distinction between a non-state actor exercising control over certain territory and a non-state actor's territorial control leading to the de jure government's loss of 'effective control of the country'. The insofar decisive criterion for the application of the Policy on de facto governments seems to be whether the de jure government and the non-state actor raise competing claims to control the national government.[141] In Yemen, the World Bank believes that this is currently the case. Although it still refers to the 'internationally recognized Government of Yemen led by President . . . Hadi' and although other actors rely on his consent,[142] it assumes that there is 'no government in power'.[143] The Bank therefore financed numerous projects by UN agencies and (I)NGOs ranging from emergency nutrition to education and urban services based exclusively on the UN Resident Coordinator's request.[144]

So, instead of applying the provisions of the IDA AoA as a function of conflict sensitivity considerations, Bank policies largely limit the alternative modus operandi to engagement in areas of limited statehood. In its efforts to avoid recourse to article V(1)(e) IDA AoA, the Bank even enters legally controversial terrain.

d) Motivations for Non-Exhaustion of the Legal Options

How can we explain this divergence between the IDA AoA, which provide for a general possibility to finance projects implemented by IOs without the concerned state's consent, and Bank policies, which limit this option to the circumstances just described? One aspect that can explain the limitation of Bank policies to some extent is the funding modalities and, concomitantly, the financial resources required. Direct financing of international organizations and non-governmental organizations has so far been exclusively in the form of non-repayable grants.[145] Of course, most states experiencing protracted conflict receive grants anyway because they are classified as being at high risk of debt distress or in debt distress.[146] However, with respect to some conflict-affected states, including Myanmar, Mali, Iraq, Ukraine, and the Democratic

[140] Hersch Lauterpacht, *Recognition in International Law* (CUP 2012) 93. Tom Ruys and Luca Ferro, 'Weathering the Storm: Legality and Legal Implications of the Saudi-led Military Intervention in Yemen' (2016) 65 International & Comparative Law Quarterly 61, 82–86.

[141] OP 7.30 (n 136) para 4(a).

[142] World Bank, 'FY20-21 Country Engagement Note for Yemen' (Report No 136046-RY, World Bank 2019) <https://documents1.worldbank.org/curated/en/757121557938303017/pdf/Yemen-Country-Engagement-Note-for-the-Period-FY20-FY21.pdf> accessed 28 September 2023, para 13; Ashley Deeks, 'International Legal Justification for the Yemen Intervention: Blink and Miss It' (*Lawfare*, 30 March 2015) <https://www.lawfareblog.com/international-legal-justification-yemen-intervention-blink-and-miss-it> accessed 28 September 2023.

[143] Afrah Alawi Al-Ahmadi and Samantha de Silva, 'Delivering Social Protection in the Midst of Conflict and Crisis: The Case of Yemen' (World Bank 2018) 10, 38–39.

[144] World Bank, 'FY20-21 CEN Yemen' (n 142) para 32.

[145] The FCV Policy (n 49) s III para 3(b) n 5 explicitly prescribes this for cases with no government in power.

[146] International Development Association, 'IDA20' (n 96) 80–81.

Republic of Congo, it does make a difference financially for the World Bank, as these states are in principle only eligible for repayable concessional loans.[147] To provide these, the World Bank is not equally dependent on finite donor contributions, but can draw on the financial markets. Where the Bank relies on recurring replenishments by donors to provide grants, contributing countries can additionally set priorities and attach earmarks and conditions.[148] Hence, some of the limitations may also be attributed to donor preferences.

Another aspect is that the World Bank, in order not to expose itself too much to accusations of political interference, emphasizes country ownership in its conflict-related engagements.[149] It also insists that it will only undertake them at the request of the government in power. This applies in particular to engagement in the security sector, peacebuilding, or cooperation with non-state actors. However, it also pertains to cooperation with international organizations, provided of course that there is a government the World Bank can deal with.[150] The World Bank seeks to compensate for an expanded mandate by deference to the government.

An additional influence in this respect may be that the principle of ownership is prominently enshrined in key soft law documents of the law of development co-operation.[151] Moreover, in practical terms, the World Bank would deprive itself of its leverage with governments and its ability to push for reforms if it did not work predominantly with and through governments.[152]

Finally, Bank Policies attempt to provide a uniform regulatory framework—and thus legal basis—for both IBRD and IDA operations. While the IDA AoA provide room to directly finance IOs and/or bypass government consent, similar policies are often difficult or impossible to justify under the IBRD AoA.[153] Bank policies are therefore relatively restrictive and seek to get by without recourse to those IDA AoA provisions that have no counterpart in the IBRD AoA, although most countries experiencing protracted conflict are IDA countries to begin with.

This demonstrates that inter-institutional cooperation at the nexus serves as a fundamentally different modus operandi, deployed primarily to expand the World Bank's spatial reach—into areas controlled by non-state armed actors and into conflict-affected states without effective, internationally recognized, or fully functioning governments. By and large, however, the World Bank is not exploiting the potential of the IDA AoA in this respect, sticking with government-led stabilization projects even when they are not the most conflict-sensitive solution.

[147] Those countries are either not IDA countries or are not classified as in (high risk of) debt distress.

[148] Dann (n 32) 289.

[149] Van den Meerssche (n 26) 235–36.

[150] FCV Policy (n 49) s III para 13; IPF Policy (n 122), s III para 12(c); Board Paper (n 49) paras 24, 46; Leroy, 'Security Sector' (n 57) IX.

[151] Ownership is emphasized both in general documents, ie the Paris Declaration on Aid Effectiveness, the Accra Agenda for Action, and the Busan Partnership for Effective Development Cooperation, and in documents relating to fragile and conflict-affected states in particular, ie the Principles for Good International Engagement in Fragile States or the New Deal, Engelhardt (n 6) 51–53, 58–61.

[152] Sarah Charles et al, 'The Role of the World Bank in Fragile and Conflict-Affected Settings: Lessons for IDA19 and the FCV Strategy' (International Rescue Committee 2019) 4–6. <https://www.rescue.org/sites/default/files/document/4291/theroleoftheworldbankinfragileandconflict-affectedsituations-002.pdf> accessed 12 June 2023.

[153] See the distinction made in Shihata (n 23) 810–13.

D. Conclusion

As the World Bank faces increasing competition from new donors in its traditional field of activity, and as the interest of its major shareholders in avoiding spillover effects and ensuring the availability of global public goods increases, it has been expanding into the conflict realm. On a purely practical level, the associated reinterpretation of its mandate is enabled by the fact that the Bank's organs themselves are entrusted with authoritative interpretation.[154] With a view to the Bank's self-perception as a technocratic institution and its rational-legal authority, however, it is crucial for the Bank to also provide acceptable justifications.[155] This is where the concept of protracted conflict and the triple nexus come into play. They are instrumental in blurring the binaries on which the mandate is premised and in circumventing legal constraints, thus enabling the Bank to operate in conflict phases and contexts and to thematically expand its operations. Inter-institutional cooperation at the triple nexus provides legitimacy and justification for ultra vires considerations as well as the basis for an alternative operational model that extends the Bank's spatial reach. Throughout, however, the World Bank has remained a state-centric financial institution, prioritizing economic stabilization and privatization. It continues to also support those activities that research has identified as often being associated with an increase in violence. Together with the choice not to exhaust the legal options available, this illustrates that conflict sensitivity considerations only guide action within the framework set by the priorities chosen. This is troublesome given that the Bank's due diligence standards and accountability mechanisms are very slow to adapt to conflict contexts.

[154] IBRD AoA (n 15) art IX (a), (b); IDA AoA (n 16) art X (a), (b); Killinger (n 22) 52–54; Anghie (n 32) 234; also Guy F Sinclair, *To Reform the World: International Organizations and the Making of Modern States* (OUP 2017) 210–11.

[155] Anghie (n 32) 224; Michelle Miller-Adams, *The World Bank: New Agendas in a Changing World* (Routledge 1999) 22 as cited by Cissé (n 23) 83.

15

Inter-Institutional Cooperation, Limited Mandates, and Challenge to Functional Immunities of International Institutions

Héloïse Guichardaz

A. Introduction

The aim of this chapter is to examine the difficulties caused by the different existing standards of immunity among international organizations, and the impact these differences could have in conflict situations. In particular, the de facto absolute immunity from which the United Nations (UN) continues to benefit is distinct from a current observable phenomenon of limiting the immunity of other international organizations, for instance through court cases. As a consequence of this extensive protection, the UN is able to fulfil a wide mandate, while other organizations are more limited in their scope of actions. In conflict situations, this could potentially lead to the UN becoming the centre point of peacebuilding operations, to the detriment of smaller organizations. Since one of the main components of the triple nexus argument is to facilitate cooperation between actors—an aspect that is also put forward when it comes to conflict resolution—such a centring could have a grave impact.

While long conflicts have always existed, so-called protracted conflicts have been increasingly discussed on the international stage in recent years. The UN has identified them as one of the main challenges faced by their peacekeeping missions.[1] Protracted conflicts as addressed here have multiple characteristics that set them apart from other, more 'typical' conflicts. Social unrest (with causes such as economic and/or social exclusion), weak State institutions, and an increase in civil wars have rendered conflicts 'more intractable, harder to resolve with traditional tools of statecraft and mediation'.[2] Due to the broad range of issues in current conflict situations, cooperation between different international organizations with different types and levels of expertise is essential to conflict resolution and the maintenance of peace, including organizations with humanitarian, development, and peace mandates. This is the rationale behind the triple nexus agenda, aiming at combining

[1] United Nations, 'A4P: Our Agenda for Peacekeeping' (*United Nations*) <https://www.un.org/en/A4P/> accessed 27 July 2023.

[2] Adam Day, 'The Future of UN Peace Operations in a Changing Conflict Environment' (*United Nations Peacekeeping*, 2020) <https://peacekeeping.un.org/sites/default/files/future_of_peacekeeping_operations_in_a_changing_conflict_environment.pdf> 2.

Héloïse Guichardaz, *Inter-Institutional Cooperation, Limited Mandates, and Challenge to Functional Immunities of International Institutions* In: *From Protracted Conflict to Sustainable Peace?* Edited by: Heike Krieger, Giedre Jokubauskaite, Asli Ozcelik, and Andreas Buser, Oxford University Press. © Héloïse Guichardaz 2026.
DOI: 10.1093/9780198967385.003.0018

humanitarian, development, and peace initiatives.[3] The formation of the triple nexus requires cooperation between all three sectors of activity—humanitarian, peace, and development—which automatically means cooperation between the actors operating in these sectors. These actors include different international organizations, with different mandates and normative frameworks.

Mandates and the level of immunity (and therefore protection) that an international organization is afforded are linked. An organization's immunity would extend to the scope of its mandate, as the wider the scope of immunities is, the wider the reach of a mandate can be. In other words, the high level of protection afforded gives an organization enough space to expand its mandate. In that sense, a mandate is to be understood in a broader sense than strictly textual. If an organization is given *both* the mandate to intervene in a conflict situation *and* absolute immunity, it can perceive (correctly) that it is allowed to act in as many ways as possible to resolve the conflict.

International organizations have generally benefited from absolute immunity rather than restrictive immunity,[4] either in their constitutive instruments or in the domestic legal systems of most States. Their immunity allows them to execute their mandates without interference from lawsuits that could hinder their functioning. However, a recent trend has started to emerge, particularly in the United States: the restriction of immunity for international organizations. This would not necessarily be a major issue if this trend was not combined with another phenomenon, which has been a constant since 1946: the continuous granting of absolute immunity to the UN. These two phenomena run parallel to each other: while the UN can continue to do what it needs to fulfil its mandates unperturbed, other international organizations are starting to see their immunity restricted, and therefore their mandates are at risk of being restricted as well to avoid lawsuits. This leads to a potential imbalance of effectiveness between the UN and other international organizations.

The potential imbalance in the freedom of action of the UN and other international organizations could in turn have a negative effect on cooperation within the triple nexus, as the UN's role in handling conflicts may be given much more importance, to the detriment of other, potentially more successful approaches. Furthermore, the absolute immunity from which the UN benefits prevents any form of judicial accountability in case of death or damage inflicted upon the vulnerable populations already in a complex and volatile situation, which may lead to even more causes of

[3] United Nations General Assembly (UNGA) 'Review of the United Nations Peacebuilding Architecture' 70th sess, (27 April 2016), UN Doc A/RES/70/262; United Nations Security Council (UNSC) Res 2282 (27 April 2016) UN Doc S/Res/2282; UNGA 'One Humanity: Shared Responsibility' UN GAOR 70th sess, Agenda Item 73(a) (2 February 2016) UN Doc A/70/709 ('*Agenda for Humanity*'), World Bank Group and others, 'The Grand Bargain' <https://interagencystandingcommittee.org/grand-bargain> accessed 15 June 2023 ('*Grand Bargain*'); General Secretariat of the Council of the European Union, 'Council Conclusions: Operationalising the Humanitarian-Development Nexus' (19 May 2017) Doc No 9383/17; World Bank Group and United Nations, *Pathways for Peace: Inclusive Approaches to Preventing Violent Conflict* (Washington DC/World Bank 2018) ('*Pathways for Peace*'); Organisation for Economic Co-Operation and Development, 'Development Assistance Committee (DAC) Recommendation on the Humanitarian-Development-Peace Nexus' (2019) OECD/LEGAL/5019 ('*OECD DAC Recommendation*').

[4] 'Restrictive', in the context of immunities, means that certain actions by an international organization or a State are not considered to be covered by immunity. In the case of States, the category of action is defined as *acta jure gestionis*, or private acts, as opposed to *acta jure imperii*, or sovereign acts. Absolute immunity, on the contrary, means that any action is covered by immunity.

protractedness. In short, while the consequences of the recent trend of restricting immunity for international organizations but not the UN might seem a very minor issue, it has the potential of having a snowball effect on the continuation of protracted conflicts and the success of the triple nexus approach.

After this introduction, this chapter is divided into three sections, showing that the United Nations benefits from absolute immunity to a degree other organizations generally do not (B); that absolute immunity, or the lack thereof, has an effect on the mandate and effectiveness of international organizations (C), and that this disparity in both degrees of immunity and scopes of their mandates creates an environment that does not facilitate cooperation and the sharing of expertise between international organizations in situations such as protracted conflicts, creating a major obstacle for the application of the triple nexus and the prevention of protracted conflicts (D). It will ultimately show that an unequal application of restrictive immunity has a domino effect in sensitive situations such as endless conflicts, leading to a lack of cooperation and a lack of accountability likely to lead to further violence.

B. Immunities of International Organizations: A Patchwork of Varying Degrees of Coverage

International organizations have long benefited from immunities in order to carry out their activities effectively. While State immunity is granted on the basis of the *par in parem non habet imperium* principle (an equal has no power over an equal), the basis for international organization immunity is functional necessity: they cannot function effectively without immunities.[5] In practice, this often translates as de facto absolute immunity, granted either through treaties or through domestic legislations (B.1), though recent judicial development has shown the start of a trend towards restrictive immunity—but not for the United Nations (B.2).

1. The De Facto Absolute Immunity of International Organizations

If one were to take a look at the constitutive instruments of most international organizations, the words 'absolute immunity' would not appear. These instruments usually set out a functional immunity, based on the functions of the organizations. It is only in the treaty relative to the privileges and immunities that the de facto absolute immunity is set out. As for organizations that do not have such a provision, domestic legislation takes over as long as the international organization is recognized as such in the relevant domestic legal system.

The Charter of the United Nations, for instance, establishes the *functional* immunity—to be understood as restrictive, only applying to the functions of the organization—from which the UN benefits via its article 105, paragraph 1: 'The Organization shall enjoy in the territory of each of its members such privileges and

[5] Niels Blokker, 'International Organizations: The Untouchables?' (2013) 10 International Organizations Law Review 259, 260.

immunities as are necessary for the fulfilment of its purposes.'[6] Paragraph 3 adds that the General Assembly will detail the exact application of paragraph 1 in 'recommendations' or 'conventions' proposed to the member States.[7] The following year, the Convention on the Privileges and Immunities of the United Nations (hereafter the General Convention or CPIUN) was adopted, and with it a shift from functional immunity to absolute immunity. Article 2, Section 2 of the Convention states:

> The United Nations, its property and assets wherever located and by whomsoever held, shall enjoy immunity from every form of legal process except insofar as in any particular case it has expressively waived its immunity. It is, however, understood that no waiver of immunity shall extend to any measure of execution.[8]

This marked change from functional to absolute immunity, with very few caveats,[9] was generally adopted by domestic courts and is still consistently upheld,[10] despite the perceived incompatibility with the UN Charter.[11]

Many other organizations have followed suit. The Charter of the Association of South East Asian Nations (ASEAN) states that 'ASEAN shall enjoy in the territories of its Member States such immunities and privileges as are necessary for the fulfilment of its purposes.'[12] Following this functional setting, its 2009 Privileges and Immunities Agreement of the Association of South East Asian Nation (ASEAN Agreement) adopts the same clause as the General Convention, almost word for word:

> ASEAN and the property and assets of ASEAN shall enjoy immunity from every form of legal process except insofar as in any particular case it has expressly waived its immunity. It is, however, understood that no waiver of immunity shall extend to any measure of execution.[13]

[6] Charter of the United Nations (signed on 26 June 1945, entered into force on 24 October 1945) 1 UNTS XVI (UN Charter) art 105, paragraph 1.

[7] ibid para 3.

[8] Convention on the Privileges and Immunities of the United Nations (adopted on 13 February 1946, entered into force 17 September 1946) 1 UNTS 15 (General Convention) art II, section 2.

[9] ibid section 29 ('disputes arising out of contracts', 'other disputes of a private law character', disputes involving an official of the UN who enjoys immunity 'by reason of his official position', and if the Secretary General has waived the immunity of either the organization or of the official). However, in practice, immunity is rarely waived and disputes of a private law character are not defined (and the concept is therefore easily abused and restricted). As a result, despite these caveats, the UN benefits from de facto absolute immunity.

[10] For instance *Delama Georges v United Nations* 834 F 3d 88 (2nd Cir. 2016) and *Laventure v United Nations* 279 F. Supp. 3d 394 (E.D.N.Y. 2017), both on the Haiti cholera crisis.

[11] The change of scope of immunity between the UN charter (functional, as necessarily needed for its purposes) and the General Convention (absolute with only a couple of caveats) has been the subject of a few articles. The general consensus seems to be that there is a logical path from the former to the latter, despite the apparent incompatibility. This topic is outside of the remit of this chapter, but for more information, Eric de Brabandere, 'Immunity of International Organizations in Post-conflict International Administrations' (2010) 7 International Organizations Law Review 79, 87–88; Rosalyn Higgins and others, *Oppenheim's International Law: United Nations* (1st edn, Oxford University Press, Oxford 2017) 558.

[12] Charter of the Association of Southeast Asian Nations (adopted on 20 November 2007, entered into force on 15 December 2008), 2624 UNTS 223, art 17, para 1.

[13] Agreement on the Privileges and Immunities of the Association of Southeast Asian Nations, <https://asean.org/wp-content/uploads/2021/09/Agreement-on-Privileges-and-Immunities.pdf> accessed 7 August 2023, art 3.

Other examples include the 2012 Privileges and Immunities Agreement of the International Renewable Energy Agency (IRENA Agreement)[14] and the Convention on the Privileges and Immunities of the Specialised Agencies.[15]

However, the strict UN model is not the only way in which international organizations have benefitted from absolute immunity. Organizations such as the International Finance Corporation (IFC, part of the World Bank Group) or the Organisation for Economic Cooperation and Development (OECD) also have immunities provisions. In the case of the IFC, the section of its 1955 Articles of Agreement dedicated to privileges and immunities reads quite differently from the UN equivalent:

> Actions may be brought against the Corporation only in a court of competent jurisdiction in the territories of a member in which the Corporation has an office, has appointed an agent for the purpose of accepting service of process, or has issued or guaranteed securities. No actions shall, however, be brought by members or persons acting for or deriving claims from members. The property and assets of the Corporation shall, wheresoever located and by whomsoever held, be immune from all forms of seizure, attachment or execution before the delivery of final judgment against the Corporation.[16]

Section 10 adds that '[e]ach member shall take such action as is necessary in its own territories for the purpose of making effective in terms of its own law the principles set forth in this Article'.[17] This means that the degree of immunity accorded to the IFC in a given State relies upon its domestic legislation. The United States has for instance established that the IFC falls under the remit of the 1945 International Organizations Immunities Act (IOIA), which until very recently granted de facto absolute immunity to the organizations in its remit.

The OECD, despite its Supplementary Protocol No. 1 being almost identical to similar provisions in the General Convention,[18] opens itself to the same situation as the IFC due to its Supplementary Protocol No. 2, laying out inter alia the rules

[14] IRENA Doc. A/3/13 <https://www.irena.org/-/media/Files/IRENA/Agency/About-IRENA/Assembly/Third-Assembly/A_3_13_Privileges-and-Immunities.pdf> accessed 7 August 2023, art III, section 3: 'The Agency, its property and assets, wherever located and by whomsoever held, shall enjoy immunity from every form of legal process except in so far as in any particular case the Assembly has expressly waived the immunity of the Agency. It is, however, understood that no waiver of immunity shall extend to any measure of execution.'

[15] Convention on the Privileges and Immunities of the Specialized Agencies (opened for signature 21 November 1947, entered into force 2 December 1948) 33 UNTS 261, art III, section 4: 'The specialized agencies, their property and assets, wherever located and by whomsoever held, shall enjoy immunity from every form of legal process except in so far as in any particular case they have expressly waived their immunity. It is, however, understood that no waiver of immunity shall extend to any measure of execution.'

[16] Articles of Agreement of the International Finance Corporation (adopted on 25 May 1955, entered into force 20 July 1956) 264 UNTS 117, art VI, section 3.

[17] ibid section 10.

[18] Convention on the Organisation for Economic Cooperation and Development (with Supplementary Protocols Nos. 1 and 2) (signed on 14 December 1960, entered into force on 30 September 1961) 888 UNTS 179, Supplementary Protocol No. 1, art 2: 'The Organisation, its property and assets wherever located and by whomsoever held, shall enjoy immunity from every form of legal process except insofar as in any particular case it has expressly waived its immunity. It is, however, understood that no waiver of immunity shall extend to any measure of execution.'

that should be applied in case a State has not signed and ratified Protocol No. 1. The United States and the IOIA get a direct mention, with Protocol No. 2 setting out that the OECD shall benefits from privileges and immunities 'as follows . . . (c) in the United States, the legal capacity, privileges, exemptions, and immunities under the International Organisations Immunities Act provided for in Executive Order No. 10133 of 27th June, 1950'.[19] In other words, both the IFC and the OECD rely on the IOIA for absolute immunity in the United States.

One might conclude from this analysis that there is no apparent difference between the United Nations and other organizations, including the IFC and the OECD, when it comes to immunity. The road to absolute immunity may be different, but they all benefit from it. However, recent developments in domestic law—particularly in the United States—have created a marked contrast between the United Nations and the rest.

2. A Trend towards Restrictive Immunity—Excluding the UN

The first of these developments concern case law, whereby the UN's absolute immunity remains unchallenged in the courts, even when faced with a human rights-based argument. The second development is that the IFC, as well as other organizations also benefiting from absolute immunity via domestic legislation, have found themselves subjected to a more restrictive immunity following a controversial US Supreme Court case: *Jam v IFC* (hereafter *Jam*).[20]

The absolute immunity of the UN is not only stated in conventions; it is also buttressed by domestic legal decisions. The consolidation of the UN's absolute immunity in the United States dates back to 2010 and the case of *Brzak v United Nations*.[21] This case is significant in that while it deals with accusations of sexual harassment and victimization in the foreground, it also confirms a vitally important element for the United Nations and its privileges and immunities in the United States: that the General Convention is self-executing. Indeed, the US Court of Appeals for the Second District stated in its March 2010 decision, in opposition to the plaintiffs' argument that the General Convention was not self-executing, that 'the CPIUN is self-executing and applies in American courts without implementing legislation' (and is therefore 'binding on American courts').[22] The decision was supported by the fact that the treaty 'contains stipulations which . . . require no legislation to make them operative'[23] and by the executive branch's own assessment of the General Convention. As it is, the United Nations is therefore protected not only by the IOIA, but by its own General Convention. As the protection accorded by the IOIA would ultimately not last, the self-executing status of the General Convention has allowed the United Nations to fully retain its absolute immunity, 'without exception'.[24]

19 ibid Supplementary Protocol No. 2 OECD, para (c).
20 *Jam v International Finance Corp.*, 586 U.S. ___ (2019).
21 *Brzak v United Nations*, 597 F.3d 107 (2d Cir. 2010).
22 ibid 8.
23 ibid 5.
24 ibid 7.

This position was consolidated by the recent decision in the Haiti cholera case, heard first in the United States District Court for the Southern District of New York[25] and subsequently in the United States Court of Appeals for the Second Circuit.[26] Brought by Nepalese peacekeepers following the 2010 earthquake, the disease spread through the country, aided by the damaged infrastructures as a result of the natural disaster. The negligence in testing the peacekeepers before their arrival, and the resulting 10,000 deaths and millions more of infected cases, were deemed the judicial responsibility of no one, as the UN successfully invoked its absolute immunity.[27] The UN did recognize a moral responsibility[28] and started a trust fund for Haiti.[29] However, out of the $400 million promised,[30] '[a]s of 31 December 2022, the UN Haiti Cholera Response MPTF received an overall total amount of $21,888,101',[31] about 5 per cent of the original goal.

The United States courts are not the only ones dismissing plaintiffs' actions based on the UN's absolute immunity. While its decision was not based on self-executing status, the European Court of Human Rights (ECtHR) closed the door on any argument invoking the right to access justice as a challenge to the United Nations' absolute immunity, despite keeping it open for other international organizations. Indeed, the Court recognized that the right of access to justice (derived from Article 6 of the European Convention on Human Rights)[32] was violated if an organization could not prove that it fell within the remit of a three-pronged test developed in *Ashingdane v UK* (1985):[33] a legitimate aim to limit the right of access to justice, proportional to the means employed, and in a way that does not 'restrict or reduce the access left to the individual in such a way or to such an extent that the very essence of the right is impaired'.[34] Despite these clear rules, the ECtHR did not apply them to their full extent with regard to the United Nations in the case of *Stichting Mothers and Srebrenica and Others v Netherlands*.[35] Though it recognized that the presence of a 'reasonable alternative means to protect effectively their rights under the Convention'[36] was enough

[25] *Delama Georges v United Nations* 84 F Supp 3d 246 (SDNY 2015).
[26] *Delama Georges* v *United Nations* 834 F 3d 88 (2nd Cir. 2016).
[27] ibid 22.
[28] United Nations Secretary-General, 'Statement Attributable to the Spokesman for the Secretary-General on Haiti' (2016) <https://www.un.org/sg/en/content/former-secretary-general/statements/2016-08-19/statement-attributable-the-spokesman-for-the-secretary-general-haiti> accessed 16 October 2023.
[29] United Nations, 'United Nations Haiti Cholera Response Multi-Partner Trust Fund Launched to Help Country Overcome Epidemic, Build Sound Systems, Strengthen Resilience' (14 October 2016) <https://www.un.org/press/en/2016/dev3248.doc.htm> accessed 20 July 2023.
[30] United Nations, 'Secretary-General Apologizes for United Nations Role in Haiti Cholera Epidemic, Urges International Funding of New Response to Disease' (1 December 2016)<https://press.un.org/en/2016/sgsm18323.doc.htm> accessed on 20 July 2023.
[31] Office of the UN Resident Coordinator in Haiti and the Director of the Sustainable Development Unit of the Executive Office of the Secretary-General's and UN Multi-Partner Trust Fund Office, *UN Haiti Cholera Response Multi-Partner Trust Fund* (2022) < https://mptf.undp.org/sites/default/files/documents/2023-06/haiti_cholera_mptf_report_updated_by_rc.pdf> accessed 20 July 2023, 3.
[32] *Golder v United Kingdom* (1975) 1 EHRR 524.
[33] *Ashingdane v United Kingdom* (1985) 7 EHRR 528.
[34] ibid para 57. More recently, the three-pronged test was reiterated (and used) in *Waite and Kennedy v Germany* (1999) 30 EHRR 261, para 59 and *Beer and Reagan v Germany* (1999) 33 EHRR 19, para 49.
[35] *Stichting Mothers of Srebrenica and Others v Netherlands* (2013) 57 EHRR SE10.
[36] *Waite and Kennedy v Germany* (1999) 30 EHRR 261, para 68 and *Beer and Reagan v Germany* (1999) 33 EHRR 19, para 58.

to fulfil the proportional means condition in landmark cases *Waite and Kennedy v Germany*[37] and *Beer and Reagan v Germany*,[38] the absence of such means was not enough for the ECtHR to recognize that the *Mothers of Srebrenica* case presented clear evidence of a violation of the rights of the plaintiff to have access to justice. Likewise, the 'essence of the right' condition is simply ignored. In other words, while the ECtHR fully assessed the extent to which the right of access to justice was potentially violated by other organizations—such as the European Space Agency in the *Beer and Reagan* and *Waite and Kennedy* cases—it does not show the same commitment for the UN. The UN therefore benefits from the protection of its absolute immunity in both domestic and regional courts. However, the same cannot be said for other international organizations.

The European Space Agency in *Beer and Reagan* and *Waite and Kennedy*, while ultimately found not in violation of the right of access to justice, did not benefit from the leeway given to the UN by the court. The presence of an internal Appeals Board—'reasonable alternative means'—was key in the assessment that it had not violated Article 6 of the convention,[39] unlike in *Mothers of Srebrenica*. In France, a similar case saw the appeal by international organization Banque Africaine de Développement struck down and its *pourvoi en cassation* rejected on the basis that the Banque had not installed an internal tribunal to deal with the issue at hand—an employment dispute. One could argue that an organization would therefore not need much change to fit within the accepted standards of the court: setting up an internal tribunal, or rather any alternative means 'to protect effectively their right under the Convention',[40] should be enough to ward off most lawsuits. Moreover, all the cases looked at thus far, with the exception of *Mothers of Srebrenica*, have dealt with issues of employment, where the alleged victims were internal to the organization itself as current or former employees. However, a recent legal development has gone even further, and the decision and its ramifications have the potential to have an effect on the mandate of the organizations themselves: this is the US Supreme Court case *Jam v IFC*.[41]

Jam and others v IFC is a case before the Supreme Court of the United States (thereafter Supreme Court, or simply SCOTUS) decided on 27 February 2019, opposing the World Bank Group International Finance Corporation (the aforementioned IFC) and a group of petitioners made up of local fishing and farming communities. It followed a lengthy procedure before the United States District Court for the District of Columbia and the United States Court of Appeals for the District of Colombia Circuit, both of which agreed with the IFC's argument that it benefited from absolute immunity under the International Organizations Immunities Act.

The IFC had entered into a loan agreement with the India-based company Coastal Gujarat Power Ltd to finance the construction of a coal-fired power plant in Gujarat. However, following allegations that pollution from the plant has 'destroyed

[37] *Waite and Kennedy v Germany* (1999) 30 EHRR 261.
[38] *Beer and Reagan v Germany* (1999) 33 EHRR 19.
[39] *Waite and Kennedy v* Germany (1999) 30 EHRR 261, para 68 and *Beer and Reagan v Germany* (1999) 33 EHRR 19, para 58.
[40] ibid.
[41] *Jam* v *International Finance Corp.*, 586 U.S. ___ (2019).

or contaminated much of the surrounding air, land, and water',[42] petitioners sued the IFC. Both the District Court[43] and the Court of Appeals[44] ruled—based on precedents—that the IFC was immune from suit, as the IOIA contained a disposition stating that international organizations falling under the remit of the Act (such as the IFC, per Executive Order 10680)[45] 'shall enjoy the same immunity from suit and every form of judicial process as is enjoyed by foreign governments'.[46] Since, at the time the IOIA was enacted, 'foreign governments' (States) enjoyed de facto absolute immunity, the interpretation of this disposition remained static and fixed in time. However, State immunity evolved to become restricted—for instance in cases of 'commercial activities'.[47] This shift from absolute to restricted immunity was cemented in the Foreign Sovereign Immunities Act, or FSIA (1976).[48]

When the case went before the Supreme Court, the Court chose to go against the already established precedents and both of the lower courts, and ruled that the IFC could no longer rely on absolute immunity. It chose to interpret the IOIA dynamically with the FSIA. This meant that any international organization falling under the remit of the IOIA (including the IFC) would now see the rule on its immunity interpreted as having evolved in the same manner as State immunity did—from absolute to restrictive.[49]

While initial reactions to the decision were mixed,[50] as it would only impact organizations under the remit of the IOIA and the decision on remand from the Supreme Court still led to the lower court upholding the organization's immunity as it did not meet all the requirement for the commercial activity exception,[51] the decision now constituted a precedent. Such precedent was followed a couple of years later, in the case of *Rodriguez v Pan-American Health Organization*[52] (thereafter *Rodriguez*). It is this case, more than *Jam*, that cements the concerning trend of a blanket reduction of immunity coverage for international organizations—and its impact on mandates.

[42] ibid 6.

[43] *Jam* v *International Finance Corp.*, 172 F.Supp.3d 104 (2016).

[44] *Jam* v *International Finance Corp.*, 860 F.3d 703 (2017).

[45] Executive Order 10680 (2 October 1956).

[46] 22 USC §288a(b): 'international organizations, their property and their assets, wherever located and by whomsoever held, shall enjoy the same immunity from suit and every form of judicial process as is enjoyed by foreign governments.'

[47] 28 USC §1602: 'Under international law, states are not immune from the jurisdiction of foreign courts insofar as their commercial activities are concerned.'

[48] ibid: 'Subject to existing international agreements to which the United States is a party at the time of enactment of this Act a foreign state shall be immune from the jurisdiction of the courts of the United States and of the States except as provided in sections 1605 to 1607 of this chapter.'

[49] *Jam* v *International Finance Corp.*, 586 U.S. ___ (2019) 10.

[50] For example Sachintha Dias, 'Jam v IFC before the D.C. District Court: Forget the Floodgates, there won't even be a Trickle' (*EJIL:Talk!*, 1 April 2020) <https://www.ejiltalk.org/jam-v-ifc-before-the-d-c-district-court-forget-the-floodgates-there-wont-even-be-a-trickle/> accessed 22 October 2024, for a nuanced take on the situation following the Supreme Court decision.

[51] *Jam* v *International Finance Corporation*, Civil Action No. 2015-0612 (D.D.C. 2020).

[52] *MATOS RODRIGUEZ and others* v *PAN AMERICAN HEALTH ORGANIZATION*, 502 F. Supp. 3d 200 (D.D.C. 2020).

C. The Negative Impact of Restricted Immunity on the Mandates of International Organizations

The case of *Rodriguez* arose from allegations of forced labour and human trafficking following the development of the Mais Médico programme between Cuba and Brazil—a programme in which the Pan-American Health Organization (PAHO) served as a financial intermediary between the two States. As the plaintiffs went against PAHO instead of either of the two involved States, the organization responded with a motion to dismiss, arguing that it benefited from immunity under the IOIA, the UN Charter, and the WHO Constitution. The latter two arguments were dismissed as neither of the two instruments are considered self-executing,[53] while the argument of the IOIA was dismissed as some of the plaintiffs' claims fell under the remit of the commercial activity exception.[54] This examination of the commerciality of PAHO's actions would not have needed to happen had *Jam* not been a precedent. In this case, it was argued that PAHO acted as a financial intermediary between Brazil and Cuba, a conduct which was therefore considered to be within the remit of the commercial activity exception, as the conduct 'is "the sort of action" "typically performed by participants in the market"'.[55] The application of what is originally a rule for States only was not easy for the court, who agreed with the Supreme Court in *Jam* that 'applying this test to "international organizations . . . is fraught with difficulty"'.[56] However, this decision was upheld on appeal.[57]

Both *Jam* and the subsequent *Rodriguez* cases show two concerning developments for international organizations and their immunity. First, while the courts all recognize the difficulty of applying a made-for-States rule to an international organization, they have all so far chosen to follow the precedent set by *Jam* (with harsher consequences for PAHO so far), despite arguments that by doing so the courts had 'failed to accurately capture the nature of the Mais Médicos program and PAHO's role in it'.[58] This blurring of the lines between States and international organizations is even more grating when considering that this has not, and most certainly will not, affect the United Nations' activities as long as *Brzak* is upheld. In other words, unlike the UN, some organizations face the risk of seeing courts 'fitting the square peg of states' choice to engage in commercial activities into the round hole of international organizations performing functions mandated by their member states or authorized by their constitutions'.[59] In other words, their mandates can now be targeted by lawsuits where they had previously been protected by immunity.

[53] ibid 227 (UN Charter) and 228 (WHO Constitution). Interestingly, the UN Charter is therefore not self-executing while the General Convention, with its rules on absolute immunity, is.
[54] ibid 223.
[55] ibid 213.
[56] ibid 212.
[57] *MATOS RODRIGUEZ and others v PAN AMERICAN HEALTH ORGANIZATION* 29 F.4th 706 (D.C. Cir. 2022)
[58] Gian Luca Burci, 'Jam v IFC's Complications: The Pan-American Health Organization' (*EJIL:Talk!*, 4 January 2021) <https://www.ejiltalk.org/jam-v-ifcs-complications-the-pan-american-health-organization/> accessed 22 October 2024.
[59] ibid.

This is not a new argument, and it is widely accepted within the doctrine as a very good reason as to why international organizations should be able to benefit from immunity. Kristen Boon writes that '[w]ithout immunity, the U.N. would be subject to pesky lawsuits, retaliatory acts by member states against its representatives and organs, and suits that could drain its resources'[60] and that 'acknowledging liability for harms in peacekeeping operations'—such as could have happened in the *George v UN* case—'may set a precedent that will frighten off potential troop contributing countries (TCC) from future peacekeeping missions and hamper the U.N.'s ability to provide assistance in future emergency situations'.[61] Supreme Court Justice Breyer, in his dissenting opinion on *Jam*, affirms that the IOIA sought to 'facilitate fully the functioning of international organizations in this country',[62] implying that the majority decision would mean the opposite of facilitating and, ergo, affect its mandate negatively. He then uses the example of the United Nations Relief and Rehabilitation Administration (UNRRA), which he explains would not have been able to achieve its missions if it had not been protected by immunity on its commercial activities, as it regularly used 'contracts, often made in the US, for transportation and for numerous commercial goods'.[63] In other words, such a limitation would negatively impact the UNRRA's mandate, in the same way it will certainly impact PAHO's.

The argument that the limitation of immunity equates to a negative impact on mandates requires several caveats. One of them is the recency of these developments: the *Jam* SCOTUS case is from 2019, and the latest development in *Rodriguez v PAHO* was delivered in the first half of 2022. As such, the real impact of these cases has not been observed yet. However, there is a definite tendency in US courts to reduce the immunity of international organizations. While it is conceivable that the courts will be able to adapt the FSIA dispositions to international organizations more adequately, this seems unlikely, given that the courts refused PAHO's suggestion to consider activities based on whether or not they were 'outside of their mission'[64] —and to only consider such activities as potentially commercial. Moreover, the assessment of the General Convention as self-executing—accentuating the gap between the UN and the IOIA-covered international organizations—seems firmly entrenched in the jurisprudence, from *Brzak* to *George*.

The second caveat would be that the majority of the cases mentioned so far have originated from the US. Focusing on one country inevitably limits the remit of analysis, but there are a couple of counterpoints to this argument. First, the large number of international organizations with headquarters in the United States is behind the prevalence of cases in this particular jurisdiction. Second, and most importantly, the US cases are not the only ones attempting to limit international organizations' immunity. As shown in section B.2, there are multiple cases both at the ECtHR level and

[60] Kristen Boon, 'The United Nations as Good Samaritan: Immunity and Responsibility' (2016) 16 Chicago Journal of International Law 341, 351.

[61] ibid 346.

[62] *Jam* v *International Finance Corp.*, 586 U.S. ___ (2019), Justice Breyer's dissent, 6.

[63] ibid 10.

[64] Gian Luca Burci, 'Jam v IFC's Complications: the Pan-American Health Organization' (*EJIL:Talk!*, 4 January 2021) <https://www.ejiltalk.org/jam-v-ifcs-complications-the-pan-american-health-organization/> accessed 22 October 2024.

in domestic courts, though they have so far only addressed 'internal' issues (involving current or former employees), demonstrating a similar approach. Notably, the only case at the ECtHR dealing with the immunity of an international organization that goes against the trend of limiting said immunity is *Mothers of Srebrenica*, focusing on the United Nations. In other words, there are two different trends being consistently followed in multiple jurisdictions. On the one hand, there is an increasing amount of domestic court cases restricting immunity for international organizations. On the other hand, this tendency towards restriction is not present when it comes to the UN, as evidenced by, inter alia, the ECtHR jurisprudence.

In conclusion, the recent trend towards limiting absolute immunity for international organizations has the potential to have a severe impact on their mandates, with the notable exception of the UN, which continues to benefit from absolute immunity. This leaves the UN's mandate unimpeded.

D. The Difference in Levels of Immunity: Impact on Protracted Conflicts and the Triple Nexus

As shown in section B.2, there is a trend towards a reduction of absolute immunity for many international organizations, while the UN remains wholly protected. However, while the resulting impact on these organizations' mandates is also generally accepted, the link with the triple nexus and protracted conflicts is more tenuous. It is by looking through the lenses of cooperation between different actors with different mandates as a core component of the nexus that the impact of having different levels of immunity for these actors can be established. Different actors work on different aspects of the nexus—humanitarian, development, and peace—and cooperation between the three branches is key to the triple nexus policy. Yet, actors of the same broad category on the international stage—international organizations—now have to contend with being treated differently with regard to their immunity.[65] Though the trend towards restrictive immunity for international organizations is recent and so far limited, the precedent set by *Jam* remains, and has already influenced decisions made in other cases (D.1). From this point, the chapter will examine the recent trend of ever-expanding mandates of peacekeeping missions, coupled with the lack of accountability for the UN, as an argument for the potentially severe impact of this patchwork of immunities and limited mandates on protracted conflicts (D.2).

1. An Obstacle to Inter-Institutional Cooperation

One of the key features of the nexus policy prescriptions is increased cooperation among actors from all three branches. The nexus itself, aiming to involve actors from the humanitarian, peace, and development sectors, has to deal with a diversity of

[65] While a certain set of international organizations—financial organizations, including the IFC—are somewhat different from other organizations in that their constitutive instruments did not technically grant them absolute immunity as discussed earlier, they were treated as such in the US under the IOIA.

approaches and methods. The UN General Assembly, in its 27 April 2016 resolution,[66] recognizes 'that the scale and nature of the challenge of sustaining peace' (of which protracted conflicts are a big part) 'calls for close strategic and operational partnerships between the United Nations, national Governments and other key stakeholders, including international, regional and sub regional organizations'.[67] It also stresses 'the importance of partnership and cooperation between the United Nations and relevant regional and sub regional organizations, including the African Union, to improve cooperation and coordination in peacebuilding'.[68] In his 2018 report,[69] the Secretary-General also makes a mention of 'pilot projects at the country level suggest[ing] that an institutionalized partnership between the United Nations and the World Bank can unlock significant financial flows towards peacebuilding and sustaining peace'.[70] In short, the United Nations has always considered cooperation, and inter-institutional cooperation with other international organizations in particular, to be paramount to what would then take form as the humanitarian-development-peace triple nexus, as well as to maintain sustainable peace and prevent conflict situations from becoming protracted. This sentiment is shared by the doctrine: in her 1998 article on the Dayton Agreement,[71] Fionnuala Ní Aoláin writes that 'the international intervention in Bosnia was marked by a decentralized peace implementation, splintered into multiple supra-national mandates'.[72] Coupled with the 'profound ambivalence' regarding 'the shape of post-war Bosnia',[73] the result is that '[t]he lesson to be learned here is that international efforts need to be internally unified and organizationally coherent'.[74]

However, there is an argument to be made that the different levels of immunity granted to international organizations, even if it is so far limited to certain jurisdictions, would constitute an important obstacle to such cooperation. As shown in Section B.2, while the UN continues to enjoy globally undisputed absolute immunity, international organizations such as the IFC, PAHO, or OECD have seen their immunity go from absolute to restrictive. This difference of treatment and its impact on mandates can cause issues regarding coordination and cooperation. On the one hand, the UN has a large mandate for which it is generally protected through de facto absolute immunity (reinforced by court decisions consistently in its favour). On the other hand, an organization such as the IFC or PAHO finds itself with restricted immunity and a limited mandate, the combination of which can cause difficulties when it comes to being able to carry out its main activities. The case of *Rodriguez* constitutes a very

[66] UNGA 'Review of the United Nations Peacebuilding Architecture' (27 April 2016) UN Doc A/RES/70/262. Considered an inaugural step in the emphasis of the triple nexus at UN level.

[67] ibid 3.

[68] ibid para 19.

[69] UNGA, UNSC 'Peacebuilding and Sustaining Peace: Report of the Secretary-General' (18 January 2018) UN Doc A/72/707-S/2018/43.

[70] ibid para 58.

[71] Fionnuala Ní Aoláin, 'The Fractured Soul of the Dayton Peace Agreement: A Legal Analysis' (1998) 19 Michigan Journal of International Law 957.

[72] ibid 993.

[73] ibid 993.

[74] ibid 993–94; also Elizabeth M Cousens, 'Making Peace in Bosnia Work' (1997) 30 Cornell International Law Journal 789, 815, where she describes 'senior officials at most major implementing agencies described a chaotic blend of different mandates, incompatible timetables, and divided leadership among their respective executive bodies', the agencies in question being UN Civil Affairs, the UNHCR, OSCE, etc.

good example of the precarious position in which an organization can find itself if the activities that allows it to carry out its mandate can be considered commercial and open to court scrutiny.

The need for cooperation between different actors has also been demonstrated during the Balkan war and associated conflicts—years before the current focus on the triple nexus. The experience of both the conflict and the UN's handling of Kosovo in the 1990s—when the UN exercised territorial administration arguably amounting to acting as a de facto state—showed the need for cooperation not only in the heart of the conflicts but even in a post-conflict situation, so as to prevent the rising of tensions and the protractedness of the situation. Holohan writes that '[e]very organisation and actor fed into the source of, escalation or de-escalation of, and solution to or addressing of security issues',[75] adding that '[t]he UN as the "lead" agency in the mission was critical but needed observation, intelligence and intervention from every actor to even be aware of emerging flashpoints'.[76] Indeed, the UN that she describes 'is run by a combination of career international civil servants and short-term contract hires', relying on procedures that were 'heavily bureaucratic and centralised'.[77] The UN today is not markedly different: its approach to peacebuilding has been described as 'state-centric', as opposed to NGOs such as Oxfam viewing peacebuilding as 'a bottom-up, community process'.[78] The hierarchal, bureaucratic culture of the UN is still largely present, making it vitally important—for all elements of the triple nexus—for there to be NGOs, local actors, and specialized international organizations to take care of the bottom-up approach, to use their specific expertise, and to lead the actions on the ground.

However, with the current decrease in protection for international organizations excluding the UN, the current set-up on the ground would mean that the UN would be able to take on an ever-expanding set of functions while specialized organizations such as PAHO or the IFC see their mandates reduced and their actions targeted by lawsuits—lawsuits that can actually succeed. This shift in the dynamic between international organizations can have severe consequences for the situation on the ground, from lack of expertise to lack of accountability.

2. A Precarious Centring of the UN in Conflict Situations

This section of the chapter sets out different situations in which this differentiation between international organizations can cause issues with coordination and cooperation, one of the core elements of the triple nexus and a safeguard against the escalation of tensions and the protractedness of conflicts. The UN remains currently in a privileged position and, particularly through its peacekeeping missions, now has a very broad mandate, supported by its absolute immunity. Other international

[75] Anne Holohan, 'Peacebuilding and SSR in Kosovo: an Interactionist Perspective' (2016) 17(3–4) Global Crime 331, 335.
[76] ibid 335.
[77] ibid 338.
[78] Emma Fanning and Jessica Fullwood-Thomas, *The Humanitarian-Development-Peace Nexus: What Does It Mean for Multi-mandated Organizations?* (Oxfam 2019) 37.

organizations, increasingly lacking the protection given by absolute immunity, are not able to function as easily as the UN and will have to either limit their mandates or deal with costly and time-consuming lawsuits, hindering their functioning. The resulting loss of specific expertise could lead to a mishandling of sensitive situations. In other words, international organizations with a more specific mandate would see a decrease in their protection due to the lack of absolute immunity, while the UN would be able to continue with its mandate relatively undisturbed. This is despite the fact that these organizations may be more capable of handling a particular conflict or overall better equipped to deal with a specific issue in a conflict than the very bureaucratic UN. On the other hand, as the UN still benefits from absolute immunity, there are issues of accountability and perceived impunity, causing reputational damage for the UN. Overall, the imbalance of immunity coverage among international organizations leads to a centring of the UN and its lack of accountability, while also starting to have an effect on the core functions of other organizations.

UN peacekeeping missions used to be limited in scope and mandate during the Cold War, often including activities such as maintaining ceasefires and stabilizing situations on the ground. While the missions evolved during the course of the Cold War, including a very early armed peacekeeping mission in 1956,[79] there was a shift from the 1990s onwards (once the Cold War had ended). Peacekeeping missions became multidimensional, multifaceted enterprises, with mandates going far beyond the traditional supervision and maintenance of a ceasefire. Such mandates now include, inter alia, assistance for the organization of free and fair elections,[80] disarmament, demobilization, and reintegration (DDR),[81] and protection, promotion, and restoring of human rights and the rule of law.[82] Thus, UN peacekeepers remain in one place for a lengthy amount of time, often in close proximity with vulnerable populations. Despite the very likely risk of harm to these populations in part due to this length of proximity (as already seen in the Haiti case), the UN still benefits from absolute immunity. As such, the UN cannot be compelled to provide financial reparations to the victims of its actions, and cannot be considered judicially responsible. This situation is, for now, beneficial for the UN: it allows it to continue its activities without major interference from lawsuits that could hinder its functioning.

However, as seen in section D.1, the UN still follows a top-down, bureaucratic approach to a large extent. While there has been emphasis in the doctrine and in policy papers on working with other international organizations and NGOs in order to achieve a more bottom-up and less bureaucratic approach, the recent trend of international organizations seeing their protections lifted and their mandates being reduced means that any potential partnership would now become inherently and increasingly unequal. Furthermore, the usual approach to conflict prevention by the UN can carry a significant risk to sustainable peace and security by causing or worsening the protractedness of a conflict, as 'State-led processes [that the UN favours] risk prioritizing state security and state-led security services over human security and a sense

[79] First United Nations Emergency Force UNEF I (November 1956 – June 1967).
[80] For instance UNSC Res 1159 (27 March 1998) UN Doc S/RES/1159, para 10.
[81] For instance UNSC Res 2100 (25 April 2013) UN Doc S/RES/2100 para 16.
[82] For instance UNSC Res 1473 (4 April 2003) UN Doc S/RES/1473 para 1.

of safety for individuals, especially women, children and minority groups'.[83] This prioritization 'also risks contributing further to insecurity',[84] in turn increasing the risk of creating a protracted conflict. In other words, a diversity of approaches is preferable to be truly inclusive when it comes to conflict prevention. In turn, this inclusivity and participation from all actors in conflict prevention has a better chance to succeed than a single, top-to-bottom approach.

Additionally, while there are many contributions from the doctrine and policy papers on what the triple nexus should encompass, one stands out in particular for this chapter: flexibility, as opposed to the siloed approach of three separated and isolated pillars in humanitarian aid, peace, and development. However, the centring of the UN, and particularly of the UN's *façon de faire*, leads to a severe lack of flexibility. Indeed, 'issues arise when not all staff across departments embody adaptive, flexible and context-specific mindsets'.[85] While the UN can claim a broad mandate, its top-down and bureaucratic approach has not significantly changed. In other words, while flexibility is favoured in a triple-nexus context, the established structure and processes of the UN make this difficult. This lack of flexibility can also be seen in the mandates of other organizations, which are now facing limitations due to the lack of protection via absolute immunity.

On the other hand, the centring of the UN has other consequences, this time as a direct result of what the organization has managed to keep: absolute immunity. Over the years, and following high-profile cases such as the cholera crisis in Haiti, the UN has faced increasing criticism and accusations of lack of accountability and impunity. Demonstrations in Haiti following the revelation that UN peacekeepers had brought and spread cholera in the country[86] have shown that the UN is facing severe reputational damage. From that point, it is not difficult to imagine that further cases of death, injury, damage, or destruction caused by peacekeeping missions could lead to a general rejection of the UN and its missions altogether. In other words, the very absolute immunity that protects its mandate could have consequences that would render the UN unable to execute its general mandate of maintaining international peace and security.

This section on the lack of accountability and its link to further episodes of violence and conflicts is buttressed by the experience of the UN in Kosovo, where the United Nations Interim Administration Mission in Kosovo (UNMIK) acted as a de facto state, and where several instances of violations of human rights by peacekeepers occurred. Indeed, the example of Kosovo 'illustrates how the unaccountable governance of the UN administration of war-torn societies breaks with the very basic principles that the UN is mandated to establish'.[87] Not only does this have an impact

[83] Emma Fanning and Jessica Fullwood-Thomas, *The Humanitarian-Development-Peace Nexus: What Does it Mean for Multi-mandated Organizations?* (Oxfam 2019) 37.

[84] ibid 37.

[85] Tilly Alcayna, *Organisational Flexibility and Programming Across the Humanitarian–Development–Peace Nexus* (ALNAP Spotlight Study 2019) 32.

[86] Rory Carroll, 'Protesters in Haiti Attack UN Peacekeepers in Cholera Backlash' *The Guardian* (London, 16 Nov 2010) <https://www.theguardian.com/world/2010/nov/16/protestors-haiti-un-peacekeepers-cholera> accessed 21 December 2022.

[87] Gezim Visoka, 'The "Kafkaesque Accountability" of International Governance in Kosovo' (2012) 6(2) Journal of Intervention and Statebuilding 189, 206.

on the reputation of the UN, but 'peacekeeping operations risk undermining their local missions as negative practices concerning the use of power, a lack of compliance with the relevant human rights standards, and unprofessional conduct could lose the trust of the local population, and encourage undemocratic practices by weak and fragile local institutions'.[88] In other words, the lack of accountability following human rights abuses and/or negligence leads to general distrust in the institutions in charge (UNMIK; MINUSTAH for Haiti, though it did not have the same position domestically as UNMIK had), leading to more violence and the failure of the democratic, sustainable, and peace-centred agenda that the UN aims to apply.

In short, the lack of accountability also causes issues with regard to the prevention of the escalation of violence leading to a conflict. Compounded by the fact that international organizations that are not on an equal footing struggle to create meaningful instances of cooperation and coordination with each other, there is real danger to the effectiveness of the triple nexus and the prevention of (protracted) conflicts. While there is no ideal solution, the imbalance of protection would need to be addressed. However, as seen through the example of Haiti, absolute immunity—in other words, coming back to the state of affairs before *Jam*—is not the answer when it comes to the prevention of protracted conflicts. An alternative solution would be to bring all international organizations to the same level of protection—restrictive—while also making sure that organizations are not at a risk of being unable to function because of lawsuits. One possible way to do that would be to have more robust internal review mechanisms. In the case of the UN, this could mean focusing on the standing claims commissions present in every Status of Forces Agreements.[89] These commissions are to be as impartial as possible and equipped to handle cases regarding private law disputes for each UN peacekeeping missions.[90] At the time of writing, none has ever been implemented.

E. Conclusion

In conclusion, while the major developments mentioned in this chapter are relatively recent, a few early predictions can already be made. The restrictions on immunity for international organizations are not affecting all of them equally. The UN, in particular, finds itself in a privileged situation where it might be the only institution able to carry out its broad mandate effectively. This causes a range of issues, from the loss of expertise and bottom-up approach that other organizations provide, to the lack of accountability as a result of absolute immunity in cases of negligence or human rights violation from the UN. The triple nexus, with its emphasis on diversity of actors and

[88] ibid 207.

[89] Agreement signed by the UN and the host State of a peacekeeping mission, addressing any potential issues associated with the presence of an armed force in the State (such as tax liabilities and terms of employment for national staff). It also contains a section on death and/or injury caused by the mission.

[90] UNGA, 'Comprehensive Review of the Whole Question of Peace-Keeping Operations in All Their Aspects: Model Status-of-Forces Agreement for Peace-Keeping Operations' (9 October 1990) UN Doc A/45/594, para 51.

flexibility of approaches, would then be severely affected, as would the prevention of violence and protracted conflicts. This is a thorny issue, as the general rejection of absolute immunity for international organizations is promoted as a way to achieve accountability. However, going too far (*Rodriguez*) or not far enough (the UN) also has its downsides, particularly regarding the triple nexus.

16
The UN and Protracted Conflict

Martin Wählisch

A. Introduction

The enduring legacy of endless wars remains a pain point for the United Nations (UN), which was founded with the aspiration to bring about lasting peace. The Middle East peace process and the situations in Kashmir, Nagorno-Karabakh, Western Sahara, Syria, and other places are sore reminders of how difficult it is to end cycles of recurring violence and instability worldwide. The interconnectivity of socio-political factors, the complex multitude of concerned intrastate stakeholders, and tendencies of regionalization have made conflicts less responsive to traditional forms of UN peace efforts—this makes any conflict increasingly prone to potentially become protracted. The UN Secretary-General outlined in the Common Agenda in 2021 that the multilateral architecture needs a new agenda for peace to counter growing risks to the fragile international order.[1] The Common Agenda explicitly points out that this includes protracted conflicts involving transnational networks and new actors, frequently associated with terrorism, rapidly evolving weapons technologies, and a growing willingness of regional actors to participate directly in wars.

Protracted conflicts typically result from a complex mix of factors, spanning security, economic, social, and environmental dimensions. In the most challenging cases, political interests become intricately entangled at domestic, regional, and international levels, making solutions appear nearly unattainable until significant shifts occur. Protracted conflicts present formidable obstacles to achieving the SDGs. They exacerbate poverty, hinder access to education and healthcare, impede economic growth, and perpetuate inequality and social injustice. Furthermore, these conflicts often lead to long-term forced displacement, exacerbating refugee crises and straining the resources and infrastructure of host countries. Navigating the intricate interplay between protracted conflicts and the SDGs necessitates a multidimensional approach. This approach prioritizes not only peace and security but also investment in long-term development initiatives, while addressing immediate humanitarian needs, encapsulating the essence of the triple-nexus concept. The fundamental idea is that sustainable development, humanitarian support, and peace efforts are mutually reinforcing. Embracing this concept allows for progress in resolving protracted

[1] UNGA, 'Our Common Agenda: Report of the Secretary-General' (2 September 2021) UN Doc A/75/982 <https://www.un.org/en/content/common-agenda-report/assets/pdf/Common_Agenda_Report_English.pdf> accessed 27 March 2025.

Martin Wählisch, *The UN and Protracted Conflict* In: *From Protracted Conflict to Sustainable Peace?* Edited by: Heike Krieger, Giedre Jokubauskaite, Asli Ozcelik, and Andreas Buser, Oxford University Press.
 DOI: 10.1093/9780198967385.003.0019

conflicts by tackling their root causes, promoting inclusive institutions, and fostering social cohesion.

This chapter focuses on the UN's perspective on protracted conflicts in the context of the Sustainable Development Goals (SDGs) and the organization's overall Sustaining Peace framework. In addition, it explores the promising framework of the humanitarian-development-peace (HDP) nexus for addressing protracted conflicts and advancing the SDGs. However, it also explores the practical challenges, especially within the United Nations, that impede the effective implementation of this approach. These challenges encompass coordination among UN agencies, resource allocation, engagement with local actors, measuring impact, and navigating complex political environments. Recognizing and addressing these challenges is pivotal for the UN to harness the potential of the HDP nexus in conflict-affected regions. Overall, the chapter unpacks aspects of the policy debate in the UN regarding systemic challenges related to the intractability and longevity of conflicts, distills lessons learnt from programmatic initiatives, and reflects on the circumstances for the normalization of protracted conflicts. It concludes that the multilateral system is ill equipped to transform existing protracted conflict structures and draws attention to the urgency of continuously revitalizing debate about historic hot spots.

B. Protracted Conflicts: A Tour d'Horizon

A replica of the Kadesh Peace Treaty dating from c. 1259 BC, the earliest peace treaty whose text is known to have survived, is placed next to the entrance of the Security Council Chamber in the New York City headquarters of the UN. Originally signed by Hattusillis III, King of the Hittites, and Ramses II, King of the Egyptians, the treaty brought to an end the well-documented Battle of Kadesh that had been fought some sixteen years earlier. After the peace treaty was carved into stone, attacks on the Hittite holdings in now-central Syria followed.[2] The artefact is a reminder of the common circumstance that conflicts often drag on and take massive amounts of time to be resolved. Peace agreements do not guarantee an end of hostilities, and attacks and violence can quickly recur.

'When one looks at today's situation in the world, we see protracted conflict situations everywhere. We see new conflicts that emerge or re-emerge . . . And we badly need to find solutions', noted Antonio Guterres in September 2017 at the launch of the UN Strategy on Libya in his first year of tenure as UN Secretary-General.[3] 'Protracted', 'intractable', and 'frozen conflicts' seem to be frequent agenda items for the UN Security Council. Besides the situation in Libya, which has 'only' been on the Security Council's agenda since 2011, some topics have been pending for decades. These include the India-Pakistan question regarding Kashmir (1948) and the situations in

[2] Historically, the Hittites and Egyptians maintained peace until the fall of Hatti to Assyria, nearly a century later. For details, Antonio Santosuosso, 'Kadesh Revisited: Reconstructing the Battle between the Egyptians and the Hittites' (1996) 60(3) Journal of Military History 423.

[3] UNSG, 'Secretary-General Remarks on the Launch of the UN Strategy on Libya at the High-Level Event on Libya' (20 September 2017) <https://unsmil.unmissions.org/secretary-general-remarks-launch-un-strategy-libya-high-level-event-libya> accessed 28 March 2025.

Cyprus (1963), the Middle East (1967), Western Sahara (1975), Iraq and Kuwait (1990), Liberia (1991), Somalia (1992), Georgia (1992), Bosnia and Herzegovina (1992), Haiti (1993), Burundi (1993), Afghanistan (1994), the Great Lakes region (1996), the Democratic Republic of the Congo (1997), Central African Republic (1997), Guinea-Bissau (1998), Sudan and South Sudan (2004), Iraq (2005), Myanmar (2006), Mali (2012), and Ukraine and Russia (2014), just to name a few.[4]

Scholarly research confirms that most conflicts since 1990s are predominantly recurrent, following the credo that 'war begets war'.[5] Gates, Nygård, and Trappeniers, from the Peace Research Institute Oslo (PRIO), concluded that peace agreements usually only last seven years before conflict reoccurs.[6] Based on their studies, 135 countries experienced the recurrence of conflict, with 60 per cent of all conflicts recurring in the post-Second World War era. There is a historical logic to it, as the world experienced a surge in new conflicts following decolonialization in the 1970s and the end of the breakup of the Soviet Union in 1990s.

The problem is that the longer a conflict lasts, the more difficult it becomes to resolve.[7] One reason for this is that prolonged conflict duration tends to increase complexity as political, humanitarian, security, economic, and social dimensions accumulate and intertwine.[8] Recurring conflict is often driven by unaddressed grievances, which must be addressed for any lasting peace.[9] Yet, because of behavioural preferences, conflict parties often prefer to maintain the status quo; clashing political interests of regional and international players can also keep the conflict in a state of limbo.[10] Protracted conflict can also face a fragmentation of conflict parties, which increases the complexity of political fault lines that need to be reconciled for compromise. Because of the long conflict duration, the conflict economy also often benefits trans-national organized crime, money laundering, smuggling, human trafficking, illegal arms sales, and other illegal trade, which often brings spoilers into the conflict resolution process that have an interest in keeping fragility alive for their own benefits.[11] All this makes protracted conflict important to the UN in the search for lasting and eternal peace worldwide.

But there are also protracted conflicts that eventually found resolution. Although the list of success stories is limited, Colombia is a popular example in this regard. In September 2016, the Government of Colombia and the Revolutionary Armed Forces of Colombia-People's Army signed the Final Peace Agreement. Then UN Secretary-General Ban Ki Moon noted: 'Colombia's ability to end its protracted conflict has

[4] The date indicated when the agenda item was first taken up by the Security Council at a formal meeting. See UNSC, 'Summary Statement by the Secretary-General of Matters of Which the Security Council Is Seized and of the Stage Reached in Their Consideration' (8 March 2021) UN Doc S/2021/10/Add.10.

[5] Scott Gates, Håvard Mokleiv Nygård, and Esther Trappeniers, *Conflict Recurrence*, Conflict Trends Series (PRIO, 2016).

[6] ibid.

[7] UN and World Bank, *Pathways for Peace: Inclusive Approaches to Preventing Violent Conflict* (World Bank, 2018).

[8] Jacob Kathman and Michelle Benson, 'Cut Short? United Nations Peacekeeping and Civil War Duration to Negotiated Settlements' (2019) 63(7) Journal of Conflict Resolution 1601–1629.

[9] Gates and others (n 6), 1.

[10] Miriam Fugfugosh, *Operationalising Mediation Support: Lessons from Mediation Experiences in the OSCE*, GCSP Geneva Papers No 3 (2018) 16.

[11] ibid.

inspired the world. Hard work lies ahead in bringing peace to life across the country. The United Nations is proud and committed to accompany Colombia on this historic journey.'[12] 'We will remain vigilant to the human rights and other challenges that persist notwithstanding the end of the conflict', Ban concluded.[13] The experience gleaned from the Colombian peace process instils caution, yet also fosters optimism that even the most enduring and entrenched conflicts can be resolved.

The United Nations also played a pivotal role in resolving the long-standing 'name issue' between the Former Yugoslav Republic of Macedonia (FYROM) and Greece, culminating in the historic Prespa Agreement in 2018. Under the guidance of UN mediator Matthew Nimetz, both parties engaged in a series of negotiations, which ultimately led to FYROM agreeing to change its name to North Macedonia. This decision marked a turning point in diplomatic relations, as it addressed Greece's concerns about potential territorial claims and the appropriation of its historical heritage. The ratification of the Prespa Agreement by both countries' parliaments paved the way for North Macedonia's accession to NATO and the European Union, fostering regional stability and cooperation. The relentless diplomatic initiatives by the UN in this respect underscore its capacity to assume a pivotal role in facilitating dialogue and promoting peaceful conflict resolution for seemingly never-ending disputes.[14]

C. How Does the UN Address Protracted Conflicts?

1. From Diplomatic Efforts to Peacekeeping

There is no explicit guidance, handbook, or instruction issued by the UN regarding how to specifically address protracted disputes or conflict, apart from the usual rules in the UN Charter. Although it might sound simplistic, the main instrument to counter continuous frictions is dialogue. In this spirit, the UN Secretary-General continuously offers 'good offices' to help conflict parties and regions to resolve conflicts and tensions peacefully.[15]

For instance, with a view to addressing the situation in Kashmir, the Secretary-General has consistently urged both sides to exercise maximum restraint and take immediate steps to de-escalate the situation, while calling on them to address their outstanding issues, including regarding Kashmir, peacefully through diplomacy and dialogue, and stressing that 'his good offices are available, if accepted by both

[12] UNSG, 'Remarks to the Press Following the Signing of the Colombia Peace Agreements' (26 September 2016) <https://www.un.org/sg/en/content/sg/speeches/2016-09-26-0> accessed 28 March 2025.

[13] ibid.

[14] For the mediator's perspective, Matthew Nimetz, 'The Macedonian "Name" Dispute: The Macedonian Question—Resolved?' (2020) 48(2) Nationalities Papers 205–14.

[15] For details, Thomas M. Franck and Georg Nolte, 'The Good Offices Function of the UN Secretary-General' in A Roberts and B Kingsbury (eds), *United Nations, Divided World: The UN's Roles in International Relations* (Clarendon Press 1993) 143–82.

sides'.[16] The Security Council considered the volatile situation surrounding Kashmir in August 2019, for the first time since 1965.[17] Pakistan had requested the Security Council meeting, and it was subsequently called for by China, as Permanent Member of the Council. The consultations remained inconclusive, but the Secretary-General's commitment to be helpful as a third party remains valid.[18] It is therefore of utmost importance for the United Nations to persist in its efforts, embodying the very essence of its mission. No matter the challenges, the UN must maintain hope and continue to work tirelessly towards fostering dialogue and peace, keeping its faith in the transformative power of diplomacy and negotiation.

Cyprus is another example of continuing efforts despite a historical heritage of unsuccessful attempts to bring the conflict to an end. Negotiations to reach a comprehensive and durable settlement to the long-standing Cyprus question are ongoing. The Secretary-General has emphasized on various occasions that both he personally and the United Nations are 'at the disposal of the two Cypriot communities and of the guarantor powers to support the search for a solution that is acceptable to all'.[19] In 2019, both sides agreed that achieving a comprehensive and durable settlement to the Cyprus problem within a foreseeable horizon is of utmost importance, but a solution remained pending.[20] Subsequently to a series of other attempts, an informal 5 + 1 meeting on Cyprus was held in Geneva by the UN in April 2021, but efforts had 'not yet found enough common grounds to allow for the resumption of formal negotiations in relation to the settlement of the Cyprus problem'.[21] 'But I do not give up', stressed Secretary-General Guterres in the press conference at the end of the unsuccessful talks.[22] He concluded:

> My agenda is very simple. My agenda is strictly to fight for the security and well-being of the Cypriots, of the Greek Cypriots and the Turkish Cypriots, that deserve

[16] UNSG, 'Statement Attributable to the Spokesman for the Secretary-General on the Situation in Kashmir (30 September 2016) <https://www.un.org/sg/en/content/sg/statement/2016-09-30/statement-attributable-the-spokesman-for-the-secretary-general-the-situation-kashmir> accessed 28 March 2025. See also UNSG, 'Statement Attributable to the Spokesman for the Secretary-General on the Situation in Jammu and Kashmir' (8 August 2019) <https://www.un.org/sg/en/content/sg/statement/2019-08-08/statement-attributable-the-spokesman-for-the-secretary-general-the-situation-jammu-and-kashmir> accessed 28 March 2025.

[17] 'UN Security Council Discusses Kashmir, China Urges India and Pakistan to Ease Tensions' *UN News: Global Perspective, Human Stories* (16 August 2019) <https://news.un.org/en/story/2019/08/1044401> accessed 28 March 2025.

[18] UNSG, 'Press Conference by Secretary-General António Guterres at United Nations Headquarters' (21 January 2022) SG/SM/21115, United Nations, Meetings Coverage and Press Releases <https://www.un.org/press/en/2022/sgsm21115.doc.htm> accessed 28 March 2025.

[19] UNSG, 'Secretary-General's Remarks to the Security Council Open Debate on Conflicts in Europe' (21 February 2017) <https://www.un.org/sg/en/content/sg/statement/2017-02-21/secretary-generals-remarks-security-council-open-debate-conflicts> accessed 28 March 2025.

[20] UNSG, 'UN Secretary-General's Statement on Cyprus' (25 November 2019) <https://www.un.org/sg/en/content/sg/statement/2019-11-25/un-secretary-general%E2%80%99s-statement-cyprus> accessed 28 March 2025.

[21] UNSG, 'Opening Remarks at Press Conference Following the Informal 5+1 Meeting on Cyprus' (29 April 2021) <https://www.un.org/sg/en/content/sg/speeches/2021-04-29/opening-press-remarks-following-informal-51-meeting-cyprus> accessed 28 March 2025.

[22] ibid.

> to live in peace and prosperity together. And being so, we have been able to agree that I will convene in the near future another meeting of the 5+1, the five plus the United Nations, again with the objective to move in the direction of reaching common ground to allow for formal negotiations to start. We are determined to do everything we can to make this dialogue move on and to make this dialogue at one moment be able to reach positive results.[23]

So in other words, there is nothing the UN can do but try to address protracted conflict with patience and endurance.

In addition to its diplomatic and soft power efforts, UN peacekeeping plays a critical role in addressing protracted conflicts by authorizing military interventions and deploying peacekeeping forces. These missions are often authorized to use force when necessary and remain engaged in protracted conflict zones for extended periods, sometimes spanning decades. While UN peacekeepers are committed to upholding ceasefires and creating conditions for lasting peace, the logic of peacekeeping is that they also serve as a deterrent against potential escalations of violence. This dual approach, combining diplomatic efforts with the presence of peacekeeping forces, underscores the UN's comprehensive strategy to address protracted conflicts, emphasizing both the 'soft' aspects of peacebuilding and the necessity of robust security measures in ensuring long-term stability and peace. An example is the United Nations Interim Force in Lebanon (UNIFIL) that has tried to address the protracted conflict between Lebanon and Israel which began in 1978 and expanded after 2006. UNIFIL's primary mission is to monitor ceasefires, maintain regional stability, and facilitate humanitarian aid delivery. It plays a crucial role in preventing hostilities along the Blue Line and the wider southern Lebanon area. UNIFIL's efforts include fostering dialogue, building trust between conflicting parties, and facilitating communication between the Lebanese Armed Forces and the Israel Defense Forces. Additionally, UNIFIL supports the Lebanese government in extending its authority, developing infrastructure, and strengthening local institutions. By addressing both immediate security concerns and underlying socio-economic issues, UNIFIL aligns with the broader UN strategy for sustainable peacebuilding. Despite the complexities of the conflict and critique of the effectiveness of UN peacekeeping at large, UNIFIL's continuous presence underscores the UN's commitment to maintaining stability and working towards a just and lasting resolution in this protracted conflict zone.

2. The Humanitarian-Development-Peace Nexus for 'Sustaining Peace'

There has been increased discussion among Member States and parts of the UN system on parameters that can help break through the circle of conflict and violence. In 2016, the General Assembly recognized that 'sustaining peace', as drawn from the Secretary-General's Advisory Group of Experts report in 2015, should be

[23] ibid.

> broadly understood as a goal and a process to build a common vision of a society, ensuring that the needs of all segments of the population are taken into account, which encompasses activities aimed at preventing the outbreak, escalation, continuation and recurrence of conflict, addressing root causes, assisting parties to conflict to end hostilities, ensuring national reconciliation, and moving towards recovery, reconstruction and development, and emphasizing that sustaining peace is a shared task and responsibility that needs to be fulfilled by the Government and all other national stakeholders, and should flow through all three pillars of the United Nations engagement at all stages of conflict, and in all its dimensions, and needs sustained international attention and assistance.[24]

The Advisory Group of Experts had previously advocated that 'peacebuilding' needs to be liberated from the strict limitation to post-conflict contexts, and proposed the term 'sustaining peace instead'.[25] The recommendation was that such an approach would critically rely on 'uniting the peace and security, human rights and development "pillars" of the UN'.[26] In resolutions A/RES/70/262 and S/RES/2282 (2016), the General Assembly and Security Council also stressed the importance of the Peacebuilding Commission maintaining international attention to the sustaining peace agenda and support efforts with targeted programming.

As a practical response, the UN and World Bank signed a partnership framework in 2017 that focuses on building resilience for the most vulnerable people by reducing poverty, promoting shared prosperity, enhancing food security, and sustaining peace in crisis-affected situations.[27] The framework was a 'response to global calls for our institutions to work more closely together on prevention and reducing needs, risks, and vulnerability as the world faces a spike in violent conflict.'[28] Under this framework, the UN and World Bank agreed to work in complementary ways to 'reduce the multidimensional risks of crisis and help prevent violent conflict; develop joint analyses and tools for more effective solutions; coordinate support to address protracted crises including forced displacement; and scale up impact by leveraging financing'.[29]

The concept of strengthening relations between humanitarians, development, and peace actors is often described as a triple nexus to frame interlinkages of the UN's sustaining peace agenda. UN Deputy Secretary-General Amina Mohammed stressed in her remarks to the World Humanitarian Forum in 2020:

> We will only break the cycle of risk and vulnerability by joining forces behind coherent, coordinated and integrated approaches. The 2030 Agenda for Sustainable

[24] UNGA, Res 70/262 (12 May 2016) UN Doc A/RES/70/262.

[25] The Challenge of Sustaining Peace: Report of the Advisory Group of Experts for the 2015 Review of the United Nations Peacebuilding Architecture (29 June 2015) UN Doc A/70/621-S/2015/490 <https://reliefweb.int/attachments/b3884d6d-8cb0-331a-94e7-1796b90640e5/150630%20Report%20of%20the%20AGE%20on%20the%202015%20Peacebuilding%20Review%20FINAL.pdf>accessed 28 March 2025.

[26] ibid.

[27] UNSG, 'Joint Statement on Signing of New UN–World Bank Framework to Build Resilience and Sustain Peace in Conflict Areas', SG/SM/18473 (22 April 2017) <https://www.un.org/sg/en/content/sg/note-correspondents/2017-04-22/joint-statement-signing-of-new-un-world-bank-framework-build-resilience-and-sustain-peace-conflict-areas> accessed 28 February 2025.

[28] ibid.

[29] ibid.

> Development remains our agreed road map for addressing the humanitarian-development-peace nexus. The Sustainable Development Goals are our best tools for prevention and, with concerted action and political will, we can not only survive this crisis but thrive as we recover better.[30]

She then further elaborated that this is about aligning decision-making during the response and recovery: 'We need to bring together the development and humanitarian communities, and—in certain country contexts—the peace actors. This is not only about responding to the current emergency, but rather about dealing with its root causes and ensuring that we are better prepared to recover and address future crises.'[31] It also requires to 'work closely with Governments to mobilize and align a wide range of financing sources—public and private, domestic and international'.[32]

From a practical standpoint, the triple nexus offers a valuable platform for the UN to overcome some of its institutional limitations, especially concerning protracted intra-state conflicts vis-à-vis complex and interconnected challenges of the modern world, including climate change, forced displacement, and poverty-driven instability. For example, the UN and World Bank partnership enables the UN to leverage the expertise and resources of the World Bank, bridging the gap between peace and development efforts. This collaborative approach helps the UN extend its reach and impact in addressing protracted crises, ultimately enhancing its ability to fulfil its mandate. However, the effectiveness of such international cooperation hinges on the careful navigation of inherent complexities. While collaboration is undoubtedly a positive step, it also raises questions about potential challenges, such as coordinating joint efforts, ensuring alignment with the diverse objectives of various stakeholders, and managing expectations. Moreover, the degree to which these partnerships can overcome the institutional limits set out in the UN Charter depends on the commitment of member states, political will, and the ability to adapt to evolving global dynamics. The UN and World Bank partnership represents a promising avenue for addressing multifaceted global challenges and advancing the UN's mandate. It embodies the spirit of international cooperation and demonstrates the UN's capacity to adapt and extend its reach beyond the confines of the UN Charter. However, the success of such initiatives depends on diligent implementation, sustained commitment, and the ability to navigate the complexities of contemporary global affairs.

D. What Role Does International Law Play in All This?

As the backbone of the global rules-based order, international law is a critical element in addressing prolonged conflicts and maintaining peace within the UN framework. It governs the behaviour of states and other international entities, formulates norms

[30] UN Press Release, Deputy Secretary-General Urges Support to Fragile Countries amid COVID-19, Calls for Long-Term Transition Out of Crises, DSG/SM/1451 (22 September 2020) <https://www.un.org/press/en/2020/dsgsm1451.doc.htm>accessed 28 March 2025.

[31] ibid.

[32] ibid.

and principles for harmonious coexistence, and offers mechanisms for conflict prevention, resolution, and post-conflict reconstruction.[33]

1. Dispute Settlement under the UN Charter

The UN Charter spells out in Chapter VI on the Pacific Settlement of Disputes in Article 33 that dangers to international peace and security shall be addressed through 'negotiation, enquiry, mediation, conciliation, arbitration, judicial settlement, resort to regional agencies or arrangements, or other peaceful means of their own choice', which applies to disputes between states but also gives guidance for the resolution of intra-state conflict. The Charter does not differentiate between long-standing or brief disputes, but instead concentrates on the issue at hand, determining whether a threat to international peace and security exists or not. Implicitly, the UN Charter requires tenacity, as it is assumed that efforts towards peace should be sustained until a dispute is fully resolved. Nevertheless, a challenge is that prolonged conflicts tend to establish the current state of affairs as the new norm, making it incrementally difficult to determine the original baseline for peace as the spectrum for compromises increases while the conflict endures. This phenomenon hinders the pursuit of lasting peace. In light of this, we can conclude that the Charter's principles are invaluable but require adaptation to the complex realities of protracted conflicts. The international community must recognize that a tenacious, evolving approach to mediation is essential, one that maintains a focus on addressing the underlying grievances and objectives of the parties involved. Only then can protracted conflicts be effectively resolved, allowing peace to take root and flourish. The logical mechanics of prioritizing peaceful means of conflict resolution, as advocated in the UN Charter, are undoubtedly clear and rational. However, the practical implementation of these principles often faces significant challenges, primarily driven by the complexities of power politics. In many cases, power dynamics, vested interests, and geopolitical considerations can hinder the swift and effective application of peaceful solutions. This reality underscores the critical need for international actors to navigate these political obstacles and work diligently towards the Charter's goals of maintaining international peace and security through peaceful means, even in the face of formidable power politics.

Regarding the 'good offices' of the Secretary-General, the UN Charter provides limited instructions on temporal perspectives, as the effectiveness and persistency of diplomatic efforts basically depends on the style of the person in office.[34] In the same vein, given that the UN Charter's directives for peaceful conflict resolution do not carry a specific expiry date, the 'good offices' of the Secretary-General call for an extensive level of patience. This involves perseverance in maintaining the readiness of conflicting parties to participate, steadfastness in waiting for shifts in regional or

[33] For a useful overview on protracted conflicts and international law, Dustin Lewis, 'The Notion of "Protracted Armed Conflict" in the Rome Statute and the Termination of Armed Conflicts under International Law: An Analysis of Select Issues' (2019) 912 International Review of the Red Cross 1091–15.

[34] Adam Day, 'Politics in the Driving Seat: Good Offices, UN Peace Operations, and Modern Conflict' in Cedric de Coning and Mateja Peter (eds), *United Nations Peace Operations in a Changing Global Order* (Palgrave 2018), 67–89.

international dynamics, and resilience in staving off disillusionment among those working tirelessly to solve the conflict. The rules-based international order demands restoration, and every possible measure must be undertaken until this sacred goal is reached.

2. Temporal Rules in the Practice of the UN Security Council

Undoubtedly, conflicts can gradually lose their prominence and priority as time passes, yet this diminishing attention does not render them devoid of validity or insignificance.[35] On the contrary, these conflicts continue to exist in their tangible reality, even when international focus wanes. As more urgent issues arise and capture the world's attention, persistent conflicts may appear less pressing or essential. However, it is crucial to recognize that the passing of time does not erase the underlying causes or invalidate the suffering and turmoil endured by those affected. It serves as a reminder that in international conflict resolution, peace mediators must maintain focus on the ultimate goal, even when, or perhaps especially when, conflicts prove to be complex and difficult to solve. One crucial aspect is the notion of the 'ripeness of conflict', which often requires a significant passage of time, spanning years or even decades, before the desired fruits of peace can be achieved.[36]

Temporality is an important notion also for the UN Security Council's consideration of conflicts. Some indications on temporal rules can be found in the practice of the UN Security Council related to its agenda-setting procedures. At the beginning of each year, the Security Council reviews its summary statement in order to determine if the Council has concluded its consideration of any of the listed items—in particular, those items that were considered for the first time during the preceding year—and whether, consequently, such items should be deleted from the statement. Any item which has not been considered by the Security Council at a formal meeting during the preceding three calendar years will also be deleted.[37] Protracted conflicts, which often exhibit a lack of significant developments or noticeable changes over time, may find themselves relegated to the background. The annual review process, which assesses whether the Council has concluded its consideration of listed items, can inadvertently push protracted conflicts down the priority list. Since these conflicts may lack new developments or major shifts, they may not attract immediate attention during the agenda review. In essence, this procedural approach might mean that protracted conflicts are more likely to be 'shelved' or deferred in favour of newer, more pressing issues. The Council's effort to maintain a focused and manageable agenda can inadvertently result in the postponement of discussions related to these long-standing conflicts. This could potentially lead to frustrations among parties involved in protracted

[35] For insights, Joel Blaxland, 'Thinking Outside the (Temporal) Box to Explain Protracted Intrastate Conflict' (2021) 58(6) Journal of Peace Research 1271–1283.

[36] For the critique of the theoretical underpinnings of ripeness in conflict resolution, Eamonn O'kane, 'When Can Conflicts Be Resolved? A Critique of Ripeness' (2006) 8(3) Civil Wars 268–84.

[37] UNSC, S/2017/507 (30 August 2017) para 15.

conflicts, as they may perceive their issues as being deprioritized or overshadowed by more recent crises.

However, the deletion of an item does not imply that such an item cannot be taken up by the Security Council as and when it deems necessary in the future.[38] The Security Council retains the flexibility to revisit protracted conflicts as and when it deems necessary in the future. This flexibility acknowledges that the dynamics of conflicts can evolve, and the Council can adjust its priorities accordingly. Rather than being forgotten, matters are essentially postponed until circumstances align for a suitable resolution to be pursued. Nonetheless, the procedural rules do create a dynamic where protracted conflicts may struggle to maintain a consistent presence on the Council's agenda, as the focus shifts towards addressing emerging concerns. In conclusion, the UN Security Council's temporal rules for agenda setting reflect its complex task of balancing immediate crises with emerging issues. While these rules can result in protracted conflicts being temporarily 'shelved', they do not preclude the possibility of future consideration. The challenge lies in ensuring that the Council remains responsive to evolving conflicts while also addressing the enduring issues that contribute to protracted conflicts in the first place.

3. The UN within a Changing Conflict Landscape

An additional challenge faced by international law in addressing protracted conflicts lies in the fact that the rules established in the UN Charter were primarily designed to address inter-state disputes, as exemplified by the cases of Kashmir and Cyprus mentioned earlier. There has indeed been a gradual expansion of the notion of a 'threat to peace' in Chapter VII of the UN Charter to encompass intra-state armed conflicts. However, the specific circumstances triggering this designation remain subjects of intense debate in each case and are often shrouded in ambiguity. This ambiguity frequently results in divisions within the UN Security Council and undermines the effectiveness of multilateral efforts to address protracted intra-state conflicts. Consequently, there is a greater degree of uncertainty when it comes to resolving intra-state conflicts. Intra-state conflicts are typically left to the discretion of the involved states, as long as they do not result in significant regional or global spillover effects and do not trigger the international community's responsibility to protect the human rights of affected populations. While the Charter remains silent on explicit guidance for protracted disputes or conflicts, it reflects the era in which it was conceived, where the pressing concern was the prevention of large-scale international conflicts. This historical context helps explain why the Charter's tools for dispute resolution are primarily inter-state focused. Despite this focus, the fundamental principle of dialogue emerges as a universal and adaptable instrument for addressing a wide spectrum of conflicts, whether inter-state or intra-state. In line with this spirit, the UN Secretary-General consistently deploys 'good offices' to foster peaceful resolutions, emphasizing the enduring relevance of diplomacy in a world marked by evolving conflict

[38] ibid para 17.

dynamics. This all explains the inherent tension within international law, where the UN Charter's original design geared toward inter-state disputes has left a deliberate gap in specific guidance for addressing protracted intra-state conflicts, requiring the international community to navigate a complex landscape where diplomacy and dialogue play pivotal roles in securing peaceful resolutions. Indeed, this insufficiency in international law may be a contributing factor to the prevalence of protracted intra-state conflicts over inter-state conflicts.

4. Rethinking the UN Security Council's Role in Protracted Conflicts

The approach of the United Nations Security Council towards prolonged conflicts is complex, as its members are usually advocating for peaceful resolutions and for safeguarding civilians involved in these conflicts, yet the Council has been often divided on many conflicts. Critics contend that the extended duration of certain conflicts could potentially be attributed to the Council's inaction in those specific instances.[39] This has sparked debate and scrutiny regarding the Security Council's effectiveness in resolving and mitigating protracted conflicts.[40]

The Arria-formula Meeting on 'Transitioning from Protracted Conflict and Fragility into Peace Through Sustainable Development', in December 2022, shed some light on the ongoing deliberations in the Security Council on how to strengthen links between conflict, peace, and development to overcome protracted conflict. Kenya, then President of the Security Council, noted as a pain point in the concept note of its initiative that UN peace operations are sometimes deployed for decades in protracted conflicts, or, conversely, that often missions are withdrawn amid incomplete peace processes.[41] Kenya argued that the Security Council could benefit from a 'fresh appraisal' of the interaction between sustainable development and conflict to guide the Council's decisions and resolutions. Kenya also underscored the potential of the SDGs—with their comprehensive scope, defined objectives, and capacity to attract international backing for vulnerable nations—in supplying a significant blueprint for tackling the primary triggers of instability and conflict. It also recalled Security Council resolution 2282 of 27 April 2016 that sought to establish greater overlap among the activities of the General Assembly, ECOSOC, the Security Council, and the UN system, including the Council's intention to regularly seek the Peacebuilding Commission's advice.

However, most Security Council members remained hesitant to make new commitments beyond the usual words of support to international peace and development. The US admitted that the root causes of protracted conflicts 'remain largely

[39] See also Elena Kropatcheva, 'The Evolution of Russia's OSCE Policy: From the Promises of the Helsinki Final Act to the Ukrainian Crisis' (2015) 23(1) Journal of Contemporary European Studies, 6–24.

[40] Thomas D Grant, 'Frozen Conflicts and International Law' (2017) 50(3) *Cornell International Law Journal*, 361–414.

[41] Arria formula Meeting on 'Transitioning from Protracted Conflict and Fragility into Peace Through Sustainable Development', *What's In Blue*, 19 December 2022 <https://www.securitycouncilreport.org/whatsinblue/2022/12/arria-formula-meeting-on-transitioning-from-protracted-conflict-and-fragility-into-peace-through-sustainable-development.php> accessed 28 March 2025.

unaddressed', while advocating for a revitalization of the 2030 SDG Agenda and inclusive and collaborative international development efforts to tackle protracted conflicts.[42] China stressed that there is 'no one-size-fits-all solution', arguing that 'conflict and post-conflict countries have different national realities, different security issues, and different endowments for development' and stressed that 'the international community should not impose external solutions or attach any political strings'.[43] Instead, China noted that it has 'always been a staunch supporter, advocate, and practitioner of the concept of development for peace', as seen in its Belt and Road Initiative and the Global Development Initiative put forward to 'help developing countries overcome the difficulties in achieving common development, and realize lasting peace through sustainable development'. This Arria-formula Meeting demonstrated contrasting world views on how protracted conflicts should be addressed. In this author's view, it revealed that the multilateral system is ill equipped to transform existing protracted conflict structures. There is little international consensus regarding the strategies and methodologies employed in dealing with prolonged conflicts.

Just a month later in January 2023, the Security Council held an Open Debate on the theme 'Investment in people to enhance resilience against complex challenges' under the agenda item of peacebuilding and sustaining peace, which repeated the same mantra of good will but took no further action. The Permanent Observer for the League of Arab States found some harsher words, describing the 'Council's failure' in being unable 'to resolve protracted conflicts'.[44] Many of the participating Member States agreed that raging wars and protracted conflicts require decisive actions from the Council to fulfil its primary responsibility under the Charter of the United Nations, noting that sustaining peace can be achieved only by Member States' strong adherence to the principles of the Charter and the presence of strong accountability.[45] This means that the Security Council should play a more proactive role in addressing conflicts and promoting peace to effectively fulfil its obligations. However, the current circumstances of global realpolitik have rendered compromises arduous, impeding efforts to tackle both enduring and newly emerging conflicts.

The absence of international consensus on how to concretely address protracted conflicts, as demonstrated in the aforementioned Arria-formula Meeting and Security Council Open Debate, reveals complex challenges within the design of the international peace and security system. This lack of consensus is indicative of both political differences among key Security Council members and other stakeholders, driven by varying interests and priorities, and deeper structural issues within international

[42] Ambassador Lisa Carty, US Representative to the UN Economic and Social Council, 'Remarks at a UNSC Arria-formula Meeting on "Transitioning from Protracted Conflict and Fragility into Peace Through Sustainable Development"' (22 December 2022) <https://usun.usmission.gov/remarks-at-a-unsc-arria-formula-meeting-on-transitioning-from-protracted-conflict-and-fragility-into-peace-through-sustainable-development/> accessed 28 March 2025.

[43] Ambassador Zhang Jun, 'Remarks at the Arria Formula Meeting on "Transitioning from Protracted Conflict and Fragility into Peace Through Sustainable Development"' (22 December 2023) <http://un.china-mission.gov.cn/eng/chinaandun/202212/t20221224_10994734.htm> accessed 28 March 2025.

[44] UNSC, 'With Highest Number of Violent Conflicts Since Second World War, United Nations Must Rethink Efforts to Achieve, Sustain Peace, Speakers Tell Security Council' SC/15184 (26 January 2023) <https://press.un.org/en/2023/sc15184.doc.htm> accessed 28 March 2025.

[45] ibid.

organizations like the United Nations. These structural issues include power imbalances favouring certain countries or groups, institutional constraints ill-suited to prolonged conflicts, limited enforcement capacity, resource constraints, and the tendency to overlook local ownership and engagement. Furthermore, the complexity of protracted conflicts, deeply rooted in historical, social, economic, and political factors and involving multiple actors, underscores the need for tailored and context-specific strategies to address these enduring challenges. In summary, the absence of international consensus highlights the imperative for ongoing reform and adaptation within the global peace and security system, fostering dialogue, cooperation, and flexible solutions that can accommodate diverse perspectives and adapt to evolving conflict dynamics.

E. Lessons Learned and Ways Forward to Better Address Protracted Conflict

With the growing professionalization of international peace mediation over the past decades, the intellectual understanding of prolonged conflicts has deepened in recent years.[46] Typically, a complicated amalgamation of factors keeps protracted conflicts in limbo, encompassing security, economic, social, and environmental aspects. In the worst cases, entanglements of political interests on the domestic, regional, and international level make solutions seemingly impossible until circumstances change radically.

Protracted conflicts pose significant challenges to the achievement of the SDGs. They exacerbate poverty, hinder access to education and healthcare, impede economic growth, and perpetuate inequality and social injustice. Moreover, these conflicts often lead to long-term forced displacement, an exacerbating refugee crisis, and straining resources and infrastructure in host countries. To address the complex interplay between protracted conflicts and the SDGs, a multi-dimensional approach is required. This entails not only promoting peace and security but also investing in more long-term development projects and serving short-term humanitarian needs—this is the essence of the discussed triple nexus. The idea is that sustainable development, humanitarian support, and peace are mutually reinforcing, and efforts to achieve the SDGs can contribute to resolving protracted conflicts by addressing root causes, building inclusive institutions, and promoting social cohesion.

The concept of the HDP nexus indeed offers a promising framework for addressing protracted conflicts and advancing the Sustainable Development Goals (SDGs). However, the practical implementation of this approach faces several significant challenges, especially when viewed through the lens of the United Nations. First, coordination among different UN agencies and international organizations can be a formidable hurdle. The UN is a complex and decentralized system with numerous specialized agencies, each with its own mandate and funding mechanism. Ensuring seamless cooperation and information sharing among these entities to

[46] Among others, Michal Smetana and Jan Ludvík, 'Between War and Peace: A Dynamic Reconceptualization of "Frozen Conflicts"' (2023) 18 Asia Europe Journal 1.

deliver integrated responses in conflict-affected regions can be a logistical nightmare. Second, the allocation of resources is a persistent challenge. Balancing short-term humanitarian needs with long-term development projects and peacebuilding efforts requires substantial financial resources. However, securing consistent and sustainable funding for such initiatives remains a challenge, often subject to the fluctuating priorities of donor nations and organizations. Third, engaging with local actors and communities effectively is crucial for the success of the HDP nexus. However, navigating the complex political landscapes of conflict-affected areas, building trust, and involving local stakeholders in decision-making processes can be exceptionally challenging. Local ownership and participation are essential but require delicate diplomacy and cultural sensitivity. Furthermore, measuring the impact of HDP initiatives and ensuring accountability presents difficulties. Traditional indicators for measuring success may not adequately capture the multifaceted outcomes of such integrated approaches, making it challenging to demonstrate the effectiveness of HDP programmes to stakeholders and donors. Last, the HDP nexus relies on the assumption that peace, development, and humanitarian efforts are mutually reinforcing. While this is an appealing concept in theory, it can be hard to achieve in practice, especially in regions with deeply rooted conflicts and political instability. The interplay between these three pillars can be unpredictable and may not always lead to positive synergies.

In conclusion, while the HDP nexus offers a promising approach to addressing protracted conflicts and advancing the SDGs, the United Nations faces numerous practical challenges in its implementation. These include coordination among UN agencies, resource allocation, engaging with local actors, measuring impact, and navigating complex political environments. Recognizing and addressing these challenges will be critical for the UN to effectively realize the potential of the HDP nexus in conflict-affected regions.

Finally, persistence and patience are key to tackle protracted conflicts. As illustrated in this chapter, by adhering to international law and utilizing its mechanisms, the international community can work towards achieving peaceful and just resolutions to protracted conflicts. International law provides a structured framework that encompasses several principles crucial for conflict resolution. These include the principles of sovereignty, self-determination, non-intervention, and the prohibition of the use of force except in self-defense or with the approval of the United Nations Security Council. These principles serve as guiding principles for both states and non-state actors involved in protracted conflicts. However, it is essential to distinguish between the multilateral system and international law. While international law sets the rules and norms governing state behaviour, the multilateral system involves the mechanisms and institutions through which states cooperate to implement and enforce these laws. The enforcement and effectiveness of international law can be complex and challenging, particularly in contexts where political will and cooperation among states may be lacking. In other words, the multilateral system can sometimes be ill equipped to effectively address protracted conflicts if it hinders the enforcement and effectiveness of international law. Nonetheless, international law still provides a framework and avenue towards achieving the SDGs. To overcome the complexities of protracted conflicts, collective efforts are required. This entails fostering collaboration, dialogue, and negotiation among all parties involved, as well as the support of regional and international actors. By combining the principles of international law with the aspirations of the SDGs, it becomes possible to address the underlying causes of conflicts, promote inclusive societies, and achieve sustainable development.

PART IV
BRIDGING THE DIVIDE
A Key Role for Human Rights?

17
The Humanitarian-Peace-Development Nexus
What Role for Human Rights?

Andreas Buser

A. Introduction

The humanitarian-development-peace nexus (triple nexus) appears as the latest incarnation of calls for a reform of international responses to protracted conflicts.[1] This nexus seeks to strengthen cooperation between humanitarian, development, and peace actors to better address the needs of people affected by protracted conflict and to work towards sustainable peace.[2] Such cooperation raises many questions, in particular whether the mandates, objectives, and operating principles of central actors engaging in cooperation along the nexus are compatible.[3] From a human rights perspective, this also concerns the overall framework in place to respect, protect, fulfil, and promote the human rights of populations affected by protracted conflict.

In that regard it is notable that triple-nexus debates again spotlighted the many compounded human rights impacts of protracted conflicts. Grave and systematic human rights violations are depicted as a particular feature of protracted conflicts[4] and the promotion of human rights is seen as an inclusive measure to prevent violent conflicts.[5] Some statements and reports on the nexus also promote stronger linkage with human rights. As António Guterres has put it:

> The UN is uniquely placed to connect the dots . . . To succeed, it must further strengthen the nexus between peace and security, sustainable development and

[1] For an overview of the concept see Ch. 1 Section E. and Sonja Hövelmann, 'Triple Nexus to Go' (Centre for Humanitarian Action, March 2020) <https://www.chaberlin.org/en/publications/triple-nexus-to-go-2/> accessed 25 March 2024.

[2] On actors present in such conflicts: ICRC, 'Protracted Conflict and Humanitarian Action: Some Recent ICRC Experiences' (ICRC 2016) 9.

[3] In more depth: Ch. 13.

[4] Council of the European Union, 'Operationalising the Humanitarian-Development Nexus' (19 May 2017) Doc No 9383/17, para 1; World Bank, 'Strategy for Fragility, Conflict, and Violence 2020–2025' (World Bank 2020) <https://documents.worldbank.org/en/publication/documents-reports/documentdetail/844591582815510521/world-bank-group-strategy-for-fragility-conflict-and-violence-2020-2025> accessed 25 March 2024, 6, 18, 21, 87.

[5] World Bank and United Nations, *Pathways for Peace: Inclusive Approaches to Preventing Violent Conflict* (Conference edition, World Bank 2018) 163ff.

Andreas Buser, *The Humanitarian-Peace-Development Nexus* In: *From Protracted Conflict to Sustainable Peace?*
Edited by: Heike Krieger, Giedre Jokubauskaite, Asli Ozcelik, and Andreas Buser, Oxford University Press.
 DOI: 10.1093/9780198967385.003.0021

> human rights policies—a holistic approach to the mutually-reinforcing linkages between its three pillars.[6]

Relatedly, one central recommendation of the Organisation for Economic Cooperation and Development's (OECD) Development Assistance Committee (DAC) on the nexus is:

> To put people at the centre . . . Recognising this, joined-up programming will seek to: Ensure an inclusive, people-centred approach in all crises and violent conflicts that respects international human rights principles and standards.[7]

In a similar direction, the Norwegian Foreign Ministry argued that a 'rights-based approach also draws more attention to the transition between humanitarian and long-term assistance, especially in protracted crises'.[8] From this perspective, human rights as a common legal language could help to overcome the much deplored 'silo thinking' in each respective field.[9]

This chapter analyses the promise of human rights as a common language to facilitate cooperation along the nexus from a legal standpoint. It first sets out the legal framework human rights provides for states and international organizations (IOs) seeking to provide integrated humanitarian, peace, and development assistance in settings of protracted conflicts. In doing so, it highlights that legal debates on the relevance of human rights law for international development, humanitarian, and peace cooperation are ongoing in each sector but that key actors remain averse to accept human rights as a legal language to cover their own impacts rather than a mere policy commitment. Even where they accept requirements for human rights due diligence (eg for misconduct by United Nations (UN) troops) or some form of social or ethical standards (World Bank (WB) and International Committee of the Red Cross (ICRC)), implementation and access to judicial review remain an issue.

The final section outlines institutional responses by these key actors to increase 'conflict sensitivity' within their human rights/social policy frameworks and the role these reforms played to facilitate cooperation between these sectors. Importantly, it finds that for common projects in settings of protracted conflicts between the ICRC,

[6] António Guterres, 'Challenges and Opportunities for the United Nations' (Vision Statement, United Nations, 4 April 2016) <https://www.un.org/pga/70/wp-content/uploads/sites/10/2016/01/4-April_Secretary-General-Election-Vision-Statement_Portugal-4-April-20161.pdf> accessed 25 March 2024.

[7] Development Assistance Committee of the OECD, 'Recommendation on the Humanitarian-Development-Peace Nexus' (2024) Doc No OECD/LEGAL/5019.

[8] Ministry of Foreign Affairs of Norway, 'Opportunities for All: Human Rights in Norway's Foreign Policy and Development Cooperation' (Meld. St. 10 (2014–2015) Report to the Storting (white paper), translation from Norwegian, 12 December 2014) 50, <https://www.regjeringen.no/contentassets/261f255d028b42cab91ad099ee3f99fc/en-gb/pdfs/stm201420150010000engpdfs.pdf> accessed 25 March 2024.

[9] For the assessment that human rights can provide a common language to facilitate cooperation between the World Bank, the UN, governments, NGOs, and academics: World Bank, 'Lessons from the Human Rights, Inclusion and Empowerment HRIE Trust Fund Grants' (World Bank 2022) <https://documents.worldbank.org/en/publication/documents-reports/documentdetail/322581647864309466/lessons-from-incorporating-human-rights-in-human-rights-inclusion-and-empowerment-trust-fund-grants-human-rights-in-hrie-grants>, 9; generally on human rights as a language: David S Law, 'The Global Language of Human Rights: A Computational Linguistic Analysis' (2018) 12(1) The Law & Ethics of Human Rights 111.

UN agencies, and the World Bank, the World Bank's Environmental and Social Framework applies. Consequently, the ICRC and UN agencies, when acting as borrowers and implementation agencies in these projects, indirectly fall under the oversight of the World Bank. Whether this strengthens human rights accountability,[10] or only provides a fig leaf for economic interests of national and global elites,[11] remains a matter of perspective.

B. Humans as Rights-Holders vis-à-vis Humanitarian, Peace, and Development Actors

Providing a common language for humanitarian, peace, and development actors starts with the question of responsibility. Are key actors responsible vis-à-vis people affected by protracted conflict individually or even collectively? To this date the primary duty bearer for the protection and fulfilment of human rights remains the territorial state. However, in protracted conflicts governments are often weak and either not willing or incapable of protecting and fulfilling human rights within their territory.

In such scenarios, an expansive interpretation of human rights may imply a secondary obligation on the international community and non-governmental actors, encompassing private non-governmental organizations (NGOs) and even armed groups.[12] Consequently, individuals may hold a right towards the international community to receive assistance, and a corresponding right towards the territorial state to permit such assistance.[13] Furthermore, within the framework of the Responsibility to Protect (R2P), the potential for serious human rights violations may necessitate an intervention by the international community or, at the very least, the provision of assistance to restore security and uphold human rights.[14]

Hence, human rights could be interpreted to establish a collective duty of the territorial state (in some cases also armed groups exercising effective control over large territories), IOs, and foreign states to assist people affected by protracted crises in a holistic manner. Based on the insight that human rights violations in protracted conflicts are particularly severe due to their compounded nature and long duration, such a collective obligation would require humanitarian, peace, and development actors to coordinate their action and put an emphasis on preventing armed conflict. Such a collective obligation may not require individual organizations to overstep their mandate

[10] On the World Bank's Inspection Panel's role in strengthening human rights accountability: Lynn M Ta and Benjamin A T Graham, 'Can Quasi-Judicial Bodies at the World Bank Provide Justice in Human Rights Cases?' (2018) Georgetown Journal of International Law 113; Dilek Barlas and Tatiana Tassoni, 'Improving Service Delivery through Voice and Accountability: The Experience of the World Bank Inspection Panel' in Jan Wouters and others (eds), *The World Bank Legal Review Volume 6 Improving Delivery in Development: The Role of Voice, Social Contract, and Accountability* (The World Bank 2015).

[11] Cf Giedre Jokubauskaite and David Rossati, 'A Tragedy of Juridification in International Development Finance' (2022) 43(1) Canadian Journal of Development Studies 39, 41.

[12] Cf CESCR 'General Comment No. 3: The Nature of State Parties' Obligations' (14 December 1990) UN Doc E/1991/23, para 14; also Ch. 8.

[13] For a critical discussion of such dimensions within art 2 ICESCR: Ben Saul, David H Kinley, and Jacqueline Mowbray, *The International Covenant on Economic, Social and Cultural Rights: Commentary, Cases and Materials* (OUP 2014) 381 ff.

[14] UNGA, '2005 World Summit Outcome' (24 October 2005) UN Doc A/RES/60/1, para 138–140.

or engage in work where they have no expertise. Rather, it would highlight the need for cooperation among different actors to pursue a common objective: the realization of human rights.

As the following sections demonstrate, such a progressive reading, however, remains contested. It is telling that rights to development, to peace, and humanitarian assistance are often discussed separately and in a siloed way. Even more, within these separate discussions, the conceptualization of recipients of foreign assistance as rightholders has not taken deep root in legal practice and institutional settings.[15] Only for negative duties does some consensus appear to be emerging, providing affected populations with at least a right not to be harmed directly by international interventions purportedly in their interest.

1. Right to Development and Right to Humanitarian Assistance?

Among the three issue areas of the nexus, development is the sector where rights language is most pervasive. Debates on a right to development have been ongoing for decades and currently a Draft Convention on the Right to Development is being negotiated.[16] As a long-standing demand by states and other actors from the Global South, such a right has often been promoted as a paradigm shift in development discourses.[17] Negotiations on the Draft Convention are important, as the adoption of a binding multilateral treaty on the matter could bring clarity to many disputed substantial questions regarding the content and justiciability of such a right.

This said, the Draft Convention's provisions on development cooperation remain rather vague. They do not contain a specific obligation of states to engage in development cooperation vis-à-vis individual rights holders, let alone any specification of the amount due (eg a proportion of GDP as envisaged by developing countries). Whereas the duty to cooperate foreseen in the draft at first sight has many far-reaching implications, concrete measures proposed to implement the duty (eg official development assistance, debt cancellation, technology transfer) are only 'encouraged' rather than required.[18] Even more, obligations of IOs foreseen in the draft are limited to negative duties, such as to refrain from conduct that aids or assists a recipient state in human rights violations.[19] All in all, the external dimension of the right to development, so prominent in earlier discussions, has become downplayed.[20]

[15] For an overview of such efforts see: Petra Minnerop, Naomi Roht-Arriaza, and Sara C Aminzadeh, 'Solidarity Rights (Development, Peace, Environment, Humanitarian Assistance)' in Anne Peters and Rüdiger Wolfrum (eds), *Max Planck Encyclopedia of International Law* (OUP, last updated February 2018).

[16] Cf Roman G Teshome, 'The Draft Convention on the Right to Development: A New Dawn to the Recognition of the Right to Development as a Human Right?' (2022) 22(2) Human Rights Law Review 1; Rumu Sarkar, *International Development Law: Rule of Law, Ruman rights & Global Finance* (2nd edn, Springer 2020), 123–178.

[17] See also Ch. 22 Section D.

[18] Human Rights Council, 'Revised Draft Convention on the Right to Development, with Commentaries' (6 April 2022) UN Doc A/HRC/WG.2/23/2/Add.1, art 13 para 4.

[19] ibid art 7 and 9.

[20] Arne Vandenbogaerde, 'The Right to Development in International Human Rights Law: A Call for its Dissolution' (2013) 31(2) Netherlands Quarterly of Human Rights 187.

Rights language is less prominent in the field of humanitarian assistance. Nonetheless, there is discussion of a (human) right to humanitarian assistance.[21] Such a right could fill gaps existing under humanitarian law which are identified in the following, but currently its legal status and content remain controversial.

International humanitarian law does not explicitly foresee such a right, as rules on international armed conflicts only foresee the possibility to make an 'application to the Protecting Powers, the International Committee of the Red Cross, the National Red Cross (Red Crescent, Red Lion and Sun) Society of the country where they may be, as well as to any organization that might assist them', but not a right that such assistance is granted.[22] Even more, rules on non-international armed conflict—the predominant setting of protracted conflict—lack such a provision.[23]

Nonetheless, state parties to an armed conflict are explicitly required to meet several basic needs of civilians within their effective control[24]—particularly so in situations of (prolonged) occupations.[25] Outside such situations, common article 3 Geneva Conventions I–IV[26] and article 27 Geneva Convention IV can be read to require parties to an armed conflict—including armed groups (also article 4 Protocol II[27])—to treat humanely persons in the power of a party, which may include the obligation to ensure the basic needs of the population under their control.[28]

Given that protracted armed conflicts are often characterized by low-level but enduring armed violence, with isolated, sporadic 'outbreaks' of conflict, human rights law also remains in most instances fully applicable.[29] For people in territories under enemy control, some limited obligations may continue for territorial states, such as not cutting freshwater supplies via established water pipes or even continuing the payment of pensions and social support when basic needs of people dependent on such payments would otherwise not be fulfilled.[30] Even more, albeit controversial, armed

[21] Boško Jakovljevic, 'The Right to Humanitarian Assistance: Legal Aspects' (1987) 27 IRRC 469; International Institute for Humanitarian Law, 'Guiding Principles on the Right to Humanitarian Assistance' reprinted in (1993) 33 IRRC 519; Yoram Dinstein, 'The Right to Humanitarian Assistance' (2000) 53(4) Naval War College Review 77; Ruth A Stoffels, 'Legal Regulation of Humanitarian Assistance in Armed Conflict: Achievements and Gaps' (2004) 86 IRRC 515, 516ff.

[22] Geneva Convention IV relative to the Protection of Civilian Persons in Time of War (adopted 12 August 1949, entered into force 21 October 1959) 75 UNTS 287 (Geneva Convention IV) art 30.

[23] Stoffels (n 21) 521.

[24] Eg: Geneva Convention IV art 24 (child welfare), 39 (means of existence for non-repatriated persons).

[25] Geneva Convention IV, art 55 and Protocol Additional to the Geneva Conventions of 12 August 1949, and relating to the Protection of Victims of Non-International Armed Conflicts (adopted 8 June 1977, entered into force 7 December 1978) 1125 UNTS 609 (Protocol II), art 69; Vaios Koutroulis, 'The Application of International Humanitarian Law and International Human Rights Law in Situation of Prolonged Occupation: Only a Matter of Time?' (2012) 94(885) IRRC 165.

[26] Geneva Conventions (adopted 12 August 1949, entered into force 21 October 1959) 75 UNTS 31, 85, 135, 287 (Geneva Conventions I–IV).

[27] Protocol II (n 25).

[28] Knut Dörmann and Tristan Ferraro, 'Humanitarian Assistance' in Dieter Fleck and Michael Bothe (eds), *The Handbook of International Humanitarian Law* (4th edition, OUP 2021) para 11.01; Dapo Akande and Emanuela-Chiara Gillard, *Oxford Guidance on the Law Relating to Humanitarian Relief Operations in Situations of Armed Conflict* (commissioned by the United Nations Office for the Coordination of Humanitarian Affairs, 2016), 12.

[29] Eg: Saul, Kinley, and Mowbray (n 13) 152 f.

[30] Amrei Müller, *The Relationship Between Economic, Social and Cultural Rights and International Humanitarian Law: An Analysis of Health-related Issues in Non-International Armed Conflicts* (Martinus Nijhoff Publishers 2013) 253.

groups which factually exercise state functions may be required to protect and fulfil human rights within 'their' territory.[31]

However, neither international humanitarian law (IHL) nor human rights law contains clear obligations of states and IOs which are not parties to the conflict in this respect, even though parties themselves often are unable or unwilling to fulfil basic needs without international support, particularly in situations of protracted conflicts. An international dimension of providing humanitarian assistance is sometimes read into international cooperation requirements under the UN Charter[32] and the International Covenant on Economic, Social, and Cultural Rights (ICESCR).[33] However, such a duty to cooperate is often seen to be of a merely declaratory character.[34] Accordingly, most UN resolutions on the matter only reaffirm IHL duties, but do not create a general obligation to cooperate on humanitarian matters.[35] According to many governments, international law so far has not given rise to a standalone right to receive foreign humanitarian assistance.[36]

Aside from debates over an explicit right to development or humanitarian assistance, scholars have long sought to establish related obligations with reference to established human rights treaties, most notably the ICESCR. The absence of a limiting jurisdiction clause and the Covenant's repeated reference to 'international cooperation' have led the Covenant's Committee (CESCR) to promote a collective obligation to cooperate in order to protect and fulfil economic, cultural, and social rights.[37] However, what is required to fulfil the duty to cooperate has not been established more precisely so far. Proposals range from certain percentage points of GDP (eg 0.7%) to be spent on development cooperation to non-regression[38] and targeting requirements (eg populations most in need).[39] Whereas scholars have identified potential factors

[31] On such notions: Daragh Murray, *Human Rights Obligations of Non-State Armed Groups* (Bloomsbury Publishing 2016) 10; Gilles Giacca, *Economic, Social, and Cultural Rights in Armed Conflict* (OUP 2014) 242–70; Katharine Fortin, *The Accountability of Armed Groups under Human Rights Law* (OUP 2015) 166; rather critically: Andreas T Müller, 'Human Rights Obligations of Armed Groups' in Robin Geiß, Heike Krieger and Henning C Lahmann (eds), *The 'Legal Pluriverse' Surrounding Multinational Military Operations* (OUP 2020).

[32] Charter of the United Nations (adopted 26 June 1945, entered into force 24 October 1945) 1 UNTS XVI (UN Charter) arts 1 para 3 and 56.

[33] International Covenant on Economic, Social, and Cultural Rights (adopted 16 December 1966, entered into force 3 January 1976) 993 UNTS 3 (ICESCR).

[34] Rüdiger Wolfrum, 'Cooperation, International Law of' in Anne Peters and Rüdiger Wolfrum (eds), *Max Planck Encyclopedia of International Law* (OUP, last updated April 2010), para 17.

[35] Eg: UNSC Res 1701 (2006) UN Doc S/RES/1701 para 6; UNSC Res 2139 (2014) UN Doc S/RES/2130 para 16 (Syria); UNGA Res 43/131 (1988) UN Doc A/RES/43/131; UNGA Res 45/100 (1990) UN Doc A/RES/45/100.

[36] For an overview of state opposition to such a right within ILC procedures: Maria G Pietropaolo, 'A Human Rights-Based Approach to Humanitarian Assistance' (2016) 7(2) The Journal of International Humanitarian Legal Studies 257, 261ff.

[37] CESCR, 'General Comment No. 3' (n 12) para 14; also: Group of Experts in international law and human rights, 'Maastricht Principles on Extraterritorial Obligations in the Area of Economic, Social and Cultural Rights' (Group of Experts convened by Maastricht University and the International Commission of Jurists, 28 September 2011) <https://www.fidh.org/IMG/pdf/maastricht-eto-principles-uk_web.pdf> accessed 26 March 2024, paras 15–18.

[38] HRC, 'Report of the Special Rapporteur on the Right to Food, Olivier de Schutter: The Role of Development Cooperation and Food Aid in Realizing the Right to Adequate Food: Moving from Charity to Obligation' (11 February 2009) UN Doc A/HRC/10/5, para 9.

[39] For overviews, see: Malcolm Langford, Andy Sumner, and Alicia E Yamin, 'Introduction: Situating the Debate' in Malcolm Langford (ed), *The Millennium Development Goals and Human Rights: Past, Present*

to be taken into account to allocate individual shares to states obliged by a shared responsibility to fulfil human rights globally (such as causation, vicinity and capacity),[40] most donor states so far retain their discretion in deciding whom to support and by which means.[41] As of now, a right to receive assistance vis-à-vis foreign states or the international community as such has not received state support.[42]

The same remains true for IOs. Whereas it is relatively settled that IOs are bound by human rights law as established in international customary law, general principles, signed treaties, and—if containing human rights requirements—their mandates,[43] it is quite doubtful whether these obligations entail positive obligations towards people not within their 'jurisdiction' (effective control).[44] Although important development actors, such as the World Bank, moved considerably from the outright rejection of human rights approaches towards embracing the Universal Declaration on Human Rights in its 'vision statement', this policy goal remains merely an ethical one.[45]

2. Right to Peace and the Responsibility to Protect?

The outlook for a right to peace and a secondary obligation of the international community to prevent or restore peace is not much brighter. Despite numerous efforts to reform the traditional conception of peace as an inter-state issue, such as the development of the notions of a right to peace,[46] positive

and Future (CUP 2015) 26; Léonie J Wagner, *Menschenrechte in der Entwicklungspolitik* (Springer VS 2017) 118–20.

[40] Wouter Vandenhole and Wolfgang Benedek, 'Extraterritorial Human Rights Obligations and the North-South Divide' in Malcolm Langford and others (eds), *Global Justice, State Duties: The Extraterritorial Scope of Economic, Social and Cultural Rights in International Law* (CUP 2013) 335.

[41] Eg: Alhagi Marong, 'Development, Right to, International Protection' in Anne Peters and Rüdiger Wolfrum (eds), *Max Planck Encyclopedia of International Law* (OUP, last updated August 2010) para 1; Sarkar (n 16) para 152f.

[42] Cf Minnerop, Roht-Arriaza, and Aminzadeh (n 15) para 19–20; Emilie Kuijt, *Humanitarian Assistance and State Sovereignty in International Law: Towards a Comprehensive Framework* (Intersentia 2015) 214ff; for a critical assessment of the idea of a collective duty: Saul, Kinley, and Mowbray (n 13) 139 ff; but affirmatively for a collective *duty* see Ch. 8.

[43] Among the plethora of legal inquiries eg: Sigrun Skogly, *The Human Rights Obligations of the World Bank and the International Monetary Fund* (Cavendish 2001); Rachel Hammonds and Gorik Ooms, 'World Bank Policies and the Obligation of Its Members to Respect, Protect and Fulfill the Right to Health' (2004) 8(1) Health and Human Rights 26; Cornelia Janik, *Die Bindung Internationaler Organisationen an Internationale Menschenrechtsstandards: Eine Rechtsquellentheoretische Untersuchung am Beispiel der Vereinten Nationen, der Weltbank und des Internationalen Währungsfonds* (Mohr Siebeck 2012).

[44] Against an obligation to provide assistance eg: Philipp Dann, *The Law of Development Cooperation: A Comparative Analysis of the World Bank, the EU and Germany* (CUP 2013) 232–234; but for the opposing view eg: Wagner (n 39) 132.

[45] World Bank, 'Environmental and Social Framework' (World Bank 2017) <https://www.worldbank.org/en/projects-operations/environmental-and-social-framework> accessed 26 March 2024, 1, para 3; see: Philipp Dann and Michael Riegner, 'The World Bank's Environmental and Social Safeguards and the Evolution of Global Order' (2019) 32(3) Leiden Journal of International Law 537, 551.

[46] Eg: UNGA, 'Declaration on the Right of Peoples to Peace' (12 November 1984) UN Doc A/RES/39/11 and UNGA, 'Declaration on the Right to Peace' (19 December 2016) UN Doc A/RES/71/189; William A Schabas, 'The Human Right to Peace' in Asbjørn Eide, Jakob T Möller and Ineta Ziemele (eds), *Making Peoples Heard* (Brill Nijhoff 2011) 47–49.

peace,[47] human security,[48] and responsibility to protect,[49] peoples and individuals in (protracted) conflict are usually not seen as rights-holders vis-à-vis foreign states, the UN, or the international community as such.

This is not to say that no different interpretations exist. Early scholarly work concluded that a right to peace is 'firmly established' as an individual and collective right and actually represents the 'sine qua non for the full realization of all human rights'.[50] At least in inter-state conflicts, a violation of the prohibition of the use of force may also amount to a human rights violation of every civilian harmed by this conflict (eg right to life, private and family life).[51] As early as 1982, the Committee on Civil and Political Rights (CCPR) promoted a 'supreme duty to prevent wars . . . and other acts of mass violence causing arbitrary loss of life'.[52] According to Alston, such a right could include positive obligations 'to support measures at the local, national, regional and international levels which are designed to promote the achievement and maintenance of peace', but, the argument continues, concretizing the right would need further legal development.[53]

However, almost thirty years later, not much concretization has been achieved, even for treaties such as the Banjul Charter[54] which explicitly cover a right to peace.[55] In its reformed comment, the CCPR even neutralized its above statement by highlighting only that '[e]fforts to avert the risks of war, and any other armed conflict, and to strengthen international peace and security, are among the most important safeguards for the right to life'.[56] Several newer UN documents on the right to peace exist, but in each case the issue also met strong resistance.[57]

While it is important to acknowledge that the concept of peace has substantially changed since 1945, it did not develop as far as promoters of a right to peace argue. Under the concept of positive peace, grave human rights violations allow UN Security Council (UNSC) interference in internal conflicts but this does not seem to entail a right of affected populations.[58] Neither does the responsibility to protect give individuals a right to foreign intervention. The 2005 World Summit Outcome document

[47] Cf Johan Galtung, 'Positive and Negative Peace' in Charles Webel and Jørgen Johansen (eds), *Peace and Conflict Studies: A Reader* (Routledge 2011).

[48] Barbara von Tigerstrom, *Human Security and International Law: Prospects and Problems* (Hart Publishing 2007).

[49] UNGA, '2005 World Summit Outcome' (n 14) para 139.

[50] Philip Alston, 'Peace as a Human Right' (1980) 4(11) Journal of Peace Research 319, 328.

[51] ibid 328.

[52] CCPR, 'General Comment No. 6—Article 6: right to life' (30 April 1982) UN Doc HRI\GEN\1\Rev.1, 6, para 2.

[53] Alston (n 50) 329.

[54] African Charter on Human and Peoples' Rights (concluded 27 June 1981, entered into force 21 October 1986) 1520 UNTS 217.

[55] Rachel Murray, *The African Charter on Human and Peoples' Rights: A Commentary* (OUP 2019), art 23, 538.

[56] CCPR, 'General comment No. 36—Article 6: right to life' (3 September 2019) UN Doc CCPR/C/GC/36, para 69.

[57] UNGA, 'Declaration on the Right to Peace 2016' (n 46); and HRC, 'Promotion of the Right of Peoples to Peace' (18 June 2008) UN Doc A/HRC/RES/8/9; for an example of resistance, see: UNGA 'Explanation of Vote by Germany (on behalf of the EU)' (17 June 2009) UN Doc A/HRC/11/L.11,

[58] UNSC Res 794 (1992), UN Doc S/Res/794 (1992) (Somalia); Frédéric Mégret, 'The Security Council' in Frédéric Mégret and Philip Alston (eds), *The United Nations and Human Rights: A Critical Appraisal* (2nd edn, OUP 2020) 49, 51, 54, 57.

accepts a subsidiary responsibility of the international community to adopt peaceful measures as well as 'collective action' to protect populations from 'genocide, war crimes, ethnic cleansing and crimes against humanity'.[59] However, the subsequent UNSC practice has been far from consistent in this respect. Whereas in some cases the UNSC acted accordingly and cited the R2P in its resolutions,[60] the cases of Syria and Ukraine exemplify the ongoing political nature of whether the UNSC acts or not. Accordingly, the case of Syria has been described as the graveyard for R2P.[61]

The recent turn to the Uniting for Peace Resolution procedure in the case of Ukraine[62] and initiatives by the UN General Assembly (UNGA) to demand justification of the exercise of the veto from a permanent UNSC member[63] can be seen as small steps towards legal reform. Still, at present, the idea of a collective international 'responsibility to protect' and a right to such protection mostly remains a political notion and an ethical expectation, rather than a legal one.[64]

3. Towards a Right not to be Harmed by Humanitarian, Development, and Peace Actors

Whereas donor states and IOs intervening in situations of protracted conflicts might not be obliged by human rights law to provide assistance in the first place, it is increasingly accepted that they must avoid negative human rights impacts.[65] Although effective control over concrete projects or funded policies is often lacking, the concept of complicity can give rise to donor state accountability, and the same applies for IOs, including the World Bank and UN.[66]

Obligations for IOs to respect human rights law can be based on international customary law, general principles, treaty obligations of member states, and individual mandates (articles 55(c), 57 and 59 of the UN Charter).[67] Lacking effective control over individual projects on the ground, states and IOs nonetheless can become responsible under concepts of complicity or 'aid and assistance'.[68] Thus, IOs are at least

[59] UNGA, '2005 World Summit Outcome' (n 14) para 139.

[60] UNSC Res 1674 (28 April 2006) UN Doc S/RES/1674 (2006) para 4, 8; for an overview of all references see: 'UN Security Council Resolutions and Presidential Statements Referencing R2P' (Global Centre for the Responsibility to Protect Website, 19 December 2023) <https://www.globalr2p.org/resources/un-security-council-resolutions-and-presidential-statements-referencing-r2p/> accessed 26 March 2024.

[61] Mégret (n 58) 62.

[62] UNGA, 'Uniting for Peace' (3 November 1950) UN Doc A/Res/377(V).

[63] UNGA Res 76/262 (26 April 2022) UN Doc A/Res/76/262; also: UNGA and UNSC, 'Code of Conduct Regarding Security Council Action Against Genocide, Crimes Against Humanity or War Crimes' (14 December 2015) UN Doc A/70/621–S/2015/978 Annex I.

[64] Cf Andreas S Kolb, *The UN Security Council Members' Responsibility to Protect: A Legal Analysis* (Springer 2017) 529.

[65] Eg for development assistance: Dann (n 44) 283, 296; Thomas Stubbs and Alexander Kentikelenis, 'Conditionality and Sovereign Debt' in Ilias Bantekas and Cephas Lumina (eds), *Sovereign Debt and Human Rights* (OUP 2018).

[66] Dann (n 44) 265ff.

[67] For an overview of these arguments: Janik (n 43); Dann (n 44) 269ff.

[68] International Law Commission, 'Articles on Responsibility of States for Internationally Wrongful Acts' (2001) UN Doc A/56/83, art 16; International Law Commission, 'Draft Articles on the Responsibility of International Organisations, with Commentaries' (2011) UN Doch A/66/10 para 88ff, art 14 para 5; cf

subject to a due diligence duty to assess impacts on human rights of their operations.[69] These duties are irrespective of whether organizations or states pursue development, humanitarian, peacebuilding, or integrated assistance, but the duty of care required in protracted conflicts may require particular vigilance, given the particular vulnerability of people and the increased potential to do more harm than good.

The establishment of such a responsibility is more difficult for the ICRC, which has the status of a private NGO incorporated in Switzerland. According to the ICRC statutes, however, the ICRC 'enjoys a status equivalent to that of an international organization and has international legal personality in carrying out its work'.[70] Indeed, IHL provides the ICRC with partial subjectivity under international law. As such, the ICRC arguably is required to at least respect the corpus of human rights law under international customary law. This may not give rise to an obligation to fulfil and protect, but it nonetheless allows for the conceptualization of individuals vis-à-vis the ICRC as rights holders not to be harmed.[71]

C. Institutional Practice: Human Rights as Operational Guidance?

Legal doctrine is important but what matters in practice is whether key actors providing assistance in protracted conflicts actually embrace human rights as a common langue and legal framework to guide their operations. Thus, the following sections focus on these practices, highlighting notable developments but also severe shortcomings in particular with regard to cooperation between different actors along the triple nexus.

1. UN Peacebuilding and Human Rights

The UN has a clear mandate to promote human rights and increasingly takes this mandate more seriously in its peace pillar. Human rights obligations of the UN stem from the UN Charter (articles 1 and 2 as well as articles 55 and 56 UN Charter), customary international law, and general principles of law.[72] The UN, in principle, accepts its

August Reinisch, 'To What Extent Can and Should National Courts "Fill the Accountability Gap"?' (2014) 10(2) International Organizations Law Review 572, 573.

[69] Dann (n 44) 365; Stubbs and Kentikelenis (n 65).

[70] ICRC, 'Statutes of the ICRC' (adopted 21 December 2017, entered into force 1 January 2018) <https://www.icrc.org/en/document/statutes-international-committee-red-cross-0> accessed 31 January 2026, art 2 para 2.

[71] Note that for example that the CESCR does not acknowledge positive obligations of the ICRC: CESCR 'General Comment No. 14: The Right to Health' (11 August 2000) UN Doc E/C.12/2000/4, para 65; and CESCR 'General Comment No. 15: The Right to Water' (20 January 2003) UN Doc E/C.12/2002/11, para 60.

[72] For an overview of different doctrinal constructs: Guglielmo Verdirame, *The UN and Human Rights: Who Guards the Guardians?* (CUP 2011); Janik (n 43).

duty to respect human rights, for example with regard to conduct of peacekeepers,[73] and at times also takes up the role of protecting and fulfilling human rights.

Many activities carried out in modern complex peace missions factually contribute to protecting and fulfilling human rights in territorial states, such as the provision of basic essential services, exercise of police functions, election control, or the demobilization of armed groups and their reintegration into society.[74] Human rights work by the UN is legally permissible because of the now established broad conception of peace—so-called positive peace—that views human rights violations as root causes and drivers of conflict. Increasingly, this also includes social, economic, and cultural rights.[75] Explicit UN human rights work, depending on the mandate of the individual mission, may include human rights reporting, investigating and verifying past human rights violations, promoting and protecting human rights, conducting capacity-building initiatives, assisting in transitional justice efforts, collaborating with UN and international development and humanitarian organizations, designing and conducting human rights training programmes for local institutions, and identifying and integrating human rights perspectives into programmes of disarmament, demobilization, and reintegration of combatants.[76] Modern peacekeeping missions are regularly mandated to protect civilians against physical violence (so-called PoC mandates).[77]

However, alignment of peace work with human rights remains an ongoing process and mandates largely differ in terms of their incorporation of human rights language and measures.[78] In recent years the UN restructured its peace and security pillar to prioritize prevention and sustaining peace and to align peace and security more closely with the development and human rights pillars.[79] Notably, under the human rights pillar, the United Nations High Commissioner for Human Rights promotes national ownership, non-discrimination, accountability, transparency, and participation as principles derived from human rights to inform peacebuilding efforts.[80] In protracted conflicts, applying these principles could increase effectiveness of peace negotiations,

[73] United Nations Department of Peacekeeping Operations and Department of Field Support 'United Nations Peacekeeping Operations—Principles and Guidelines' (UN 2008).

[74] For an overview of such activities: Michael Bothe, 'Peacekeeping' in Anne Peters and Rüdiger Wolfrum (eds), *Max Planck Encyclopedia of International Law* (OUP, last updated August 2016) 15.

[75] Eg Resolution on 'Sustainable Peace': UNSC Res 2282 (27 April 2016) UN Doc S/RES/2282 (2016) and UNGA Res 70/262 (27 April 2016) UN Doc A/RES/70/262.

[76] UN Department of Peacekeeping Operations and Department of Field Support, 'United Nations Peacekeeping Operations: Principles and Guidelines' (United Nations 2008) <https://www.un.org/ruleoflaw/blog/document/united-nations-peacekeeping-operations-principles-and-guidelines-the-capstone-doctrine/> accessed 26 March 2024, chapter 1.2; also: Ben F Klappe, 'The Law of International Peace Operations' in Dieter Fleck and Michael Bothe (eds), *The Handbook of International Humanitarian Law* (4th edn, OUP 2021), para 20.04.

[77] For an overview: 'Protection of Civilians Mandate' (UN Peacekeeping Website) <https://peacekeeping.un.org/en/protection-of-civilians-mandate> 26 March 2024.

[78] For an overview: Mégret (n 58) 70.

[79] UNSC Res 2282 (n 75) and UNGA Res 70/262 (n 75); UNGA, 'Restructuring of the United Nations Peace and Security Pillar Report of the Secretary-General' (13 October 2017) UN Doc A/72/525; for an overview: Klappe (n 76) 667.

[80] OHCHR, 'Review of the Peacebuilding Architecture: The Contribution of Human Right to Peacekeeping and Sustaining Peace' (thematic paper, OHCHR 2020) <https://www.un.org/peacebuilding/sites/www.un.org.peacebuilding/files/1._ohchr_thematic_paper_on_the_contribution_of_hr_to_sp_and_recommendations.pdf> accessed 26 March 2024, 3.

for example by requiring peace negotiations to include marginalized groups and especially women.[81]

However, the UN at times has shown a lack of sensitive institutional responses to allegations of misconduct, and complexity concerning overlapping spheres of control makes it difficult to attribute responsibility.[82] Partially in response to these criticisms, the UN installed due diligence safeguards which are in line with legal requirements under the law of state responsibility.[83] Nonetheless, internal UN responses remain limited and fragmented, and accountability and access to justice remain an issue. Some status of forces agreements installed human rights advisory panels (eg UNMIK) but this has not become standard practice.[84] Whereas status of forces agreements allow for the settlement of disputes of a 'private law character' by standing claims commissions, it remains questionable whether such claims would cover human rights violations.[85] In addition, accountability before national courts is limited for functional reasons by the law of immunity.[86] In any case, the UN often appears financially ill-equipped to cover compensation for human rights infringements.[87] Overall, rhetorical commitment by UN peacebuilding activities to human rights thus often faces practical implementation problems.

2. Human Rights 'Light'? The Role of Social and Ethical Standards within the Development and Humanitarian Sectors

Unlike the UN, both the ICRC and WB so far neither explicitly promote human rights nor accept an obligation to respect human rights.[88] Nonetheless, both institutions have in place numerous policy guidelines which have been reformed in the context of

[81] ibid 3; also: CESCR, 'Concluding Observations on the Sixth Periodic Report of Colombia' (19 October 2017) UN Doc E/C.12/COL/CO/6, paras 25–26.

[82] On these complexities: Paulina Starski, 'Accountability and Multinational Military Operations' in Robin Geiß and Heike Krieger (eds), *The 'Legal Pluriverse' Surrounding Multinational Military Operations* (OUP 2020) 314; Gisela Hirschmann, 'Cooperating with Evil? Accountability in Peace Operations and the Evolution of the United Nations Human Rights Due Diligence Policy' (2020) 55(1) Cooperation and Conflict 22.

[83] Helmut P Aust, 'The UN Human Rights Due Diligence Policy: An Effective Mechanism against Complicity of Peacekeeping Forces?' (2015) 20(1) Journal of Conflict and Security Law 61.

[84] Mégret (n 58) 85.

[85] Eg Agreement between the United Nations and the Government of Haiti concerning the Status of the United Nations Operation in Haiti (adopted 9 July 2004, entered into force 9 July 2004) 2271 UNTS 235, s 55. For such an argument: UNGA, 'Report of the Special Rapporteur on Extreme Poverty and Human Rights' (26 August 2016) UN Doc A/71/40823, paras 28–30.

[86] For overviews of related court cases and reform proposals: Heike Krieger, 'Addressing the Accountability Gap in Peacekeeping: Law-Making by Domestic Courts As a Way to Avoid UN Reform?' (2015) 62(2) Netherlands International Law Review 259, 275; Reinisch (n 68) 578–87; Nico Schrijver, 'Beyond Srebrenica and Haiti' (2014) 10(2) International Organizations Law Review 588, 599.

[87] The example of cholera in Haiti is revealing, where the UN accepted 'moral responsibility' but faced difficulties in delivering the promised \$400 million, only \$8.7 million had been raised up to 2020: see Tamer Morris, 'State Responsibility and Accountability in UN Peacekeeping: The Case of The Mothers of Srebrenica v. The Netherlands' (2022) 29(2) International Peacekeeping 204, 208.

[88] For an overview of the ongoing struggle between the WB and human rights lawyers and NGOs to change this, see: Dimitri van den Meersche, 'A Legal Black Hole in the Cosmos of Virtue—The Politics of Human Rights Critique Against the World Bank' (2021) 21(1) Human Rights Law Review 80.

the nexus (a) and b)) and arguably also played a role in facilitating inter-institutional cooperation (c)). Nexus-related reforms, however, did not address more fundamental concerns with the WB's Environmental and Social Safeguard framework.

a) Human Rights-Based Approaches to Development Cooperation

At least in theory, the past three decades of development cooperation have seen a remarkable shift towards a people-centred approach in formulating development policy.[89] A variety of important donors, including UN agencies[90] and NGOs, pursue human rights-based approaches (HRBAs) to development cooperation.[91] These approaches differ in detail but generally have several common elements: linkage to rights, accountability, empowerment, participation, non-discrimination, and particular attention to vulnerable groups.[92] In practice, such approaches require the conduct of impact assessments, the participation of affected people, and some form of accountability, such as internal grievance mechanisms.[93] Although these approaches highlight a 'linkage' to human rights, they must not be mistaken for an acknowledgement of legal obligations.

The WB does not explicitly adopt such a HRBA. Efforts exist within the Bank to promote more explicit human rights language.[94] However, the evaluation of these initiatives found that impact within the Bank was slim and no homogeneous acceptance of HRBAs persisted among its staff.[95]

Nonetheless, language adopted by the WB in several policy documents comes close to what is usually understood to be the main contents of a HRBA. The WB has numerous policies in place that highlight the importance of participation, transparency, and a focus on the most vulnerable, and the Environmental and Social Framework (ESF) puts in place numerous social and environmental standards.[96] The World Bank's Inspection Panel provides potentially affected persons with a formalized grievance mechanism to address failures concerning WB staff's oversight over individual projects, a mechanism sometimes associated by scholars with human rights accountability.[97]

[89] Cf Dann (n 44) 219, 235ff.

[90] Eg UN Sustainable Development Group, 'The Human Rights Based Approach to Development Cooperation: Towards a Common Understanding Among UN Agencies' (UN Sustainable Development Group, September 2003) <https://unsdg.un.org/resources/human-rights-based-approach-development-cooperation-towards-common-understanding-among-un> accessed 31 January 2026.

[91] For an overview: Varun Gauri and Siri Gloppen, 'Human Rights-Based Approaches to Development: Concepts, Evidence, and Policy' (2012) 44(4) Polity 485.

[92] Eg: Jae-Eun Noh, 'Review of Human Rights-based Approaches to Development: Empirical Evidence from Developing Countries' (2022) 26(5) International Journal of Human Rights 883.

[93] Wagner (n 39) 140.

[94] Notably, the Nordic Trust Fund and its successor the Human Rights, Inclusion, and Empowerment Umbrella Trust Fund promoted HRBAs, see: 'Human Rights, Inclusion and Empowerment' (World Bank Website) <https://www.worldbank.org/en/programs/humanrights/strategic-priorities#3> accessed 26 March 2024.

[95] 'Nordic Trust Fund Completion Report' (World Bank 2019) <https://documents.worldbank.org/pt/publication/documents-reports/documentdetail/838261570087406932/ten-years-of-building-knowledge-on-human-rights-in-the-world-bank-group> accessed 26 March 2024, 5.

[96] World Bank (n 45).

[97] Eg Ta and Graham (n 10); Dann and Riegner (n 45).

With the turn of the WB towards funding projects and development policies in settings of protracted conflicts, it has also reformed its ESF. Many development actors and scholars stress the need for conflict-sensitive approaches in such settings to mitigate negative human rights effects, as development projects have played into conflict lines, such as in Afghanistan, Colombia, and Zimbabwe.[98] Such an approach is also pursued by the WB.[99] The WB's environmental and social standards and operational policies require its staff to take into account a number of risks related to protracted conflict, such as 'threats to human security through the escalation of personal, communal or interstate conflict, crime or violence' and 'risks related to conflict or contestation over land and natural resources' in due diligence impact assessments.[100]

Additionally, borrowers may be required to carry out 'Social and Conflict Analysis' of relevance for human rights, such as the human right to life, physical integrity, and non-discrimination, to assess the degree 'to which the project may (a) exacerbate existing tensions and inequality within society (both within the communities affected by the project and between these communities and others); (b) have a negative effect on stability and human security; and (c) be negatively affected by existing tensions, conflict and instability, particularly in circumstances of war, insurrection and civil unrest'.[101] In its 'Strategy for Fragility, Conflict and Violence' the WB also explicitly promotes a people-centric approach focused on inclusion, participation, and a focus on the most vulnerable.[102] Moreover, the WB seeks to scale up its efforts in addressing root causes of violence, including human rights violations.[103] What is missing so far is a conflict-sensitive approach for development policy financing (DPF) building on insights from peacebuilding.[104]

On a more structural level and from the perspective of critics, these reforms may however be seen as another attempt to whitewash the WB's operations and pursue business-as-usual practices.[105] More holistic reforms such as rethinking the need for market-driven reforms and economic growth in settings of protracted conflicts, which

[98] SIDA, 'A Human Rights Based Approach to Peace Building' (SIDA, January 2015) <https://cdn.sida.se/app/uploads/2021/05/06122535/human-rights-based-approach-peace-building.pdf> accessed 26 March 2024, 4; OECD, *Conflict and Fragility: Do No Harm – International Support for Statebuilding* (OECD 2010); FAO, 'Corporate Framework to Support Sustainable Peace in the Context of Agenda 2030' (FAO 2018) <https://openknowledge.fao.org/items/cb7bc1ca-b565-48d8-b21b-1882f99d27b9> accessed 26 March 2024, 9, 26; more generally also: Michael G Findley, 'Does Foreign Aid Build Peace?' (2018) 21(1) Annual Review of Political Science 359.

[99] World Bank (n 4) 18.

[100] World Bank (n 45) 4, 19.

[101] ibid 23.

[102] World Bank (n 4) 18.

[103] ibid 18, 21, 87.

[104] NYU Center on International Cooperation and Center for Global Development, 'Strengthening Approaches to Conflict Prevention and Peacebuilding at the UN and IFIs: Key Ideas and Recommendations' (research note, Center for Global Development, December 2020) <https://www.cgdev.org/publication/strengthening-approaches-conflict-prevention-and-peacebuilding-un-and-ifis-key-ideas-and> accessed 26 March 2024, 6.

[105] Among various critiques, eg: María VC Ormaza and Franz C Ebert, 'The World Bank, Human Rights, and Organizational Legitimacy Strategies: The Case of the 2016 Environmental and Social Framework' (2019) 32(3) Leiden Journal of International Law 483; Radu Mares, 'Securing Human Rights through Risk-management Methods: Breakthrough or Misalignment?' (2019) 32(3) Leiden Journal of International Law 517; Jokubauskaite and Rossati (n 11); for a less critical more technical assessment also highlighting the need for moderate reforms eg: Ta and Graham (n 10).

might interfere with peace processes and economic and social rights, seem not to have taken place.[106] As argued by Cahill-Ripley, an alternative approach to 'transitional or post-conflict development would use economic and social rights as a tool with which to ensure that basic needs and services are prioritized as a challenge to economic free market development, which may not benefit the existing marginalized or poor in the state'.[107]

In essence, the World Bank's approach can be seen as a form of human rights 'light', as it incorporates human rights terminology without explicitly acknowledging responsibility under human rights law. Moreover, it exhibits a somewhat selective and ideologically influenced stance concerning the specific content of safeguards and the appropriateness of policies in protracted conflict environments.

b) Human Rights-Based Approaches to Humanitarian Assistance

The sector most resistant to human rights-based approaches and the triple nexus more generally remains the humanitarian sector.[108] Based on its operating principles of neutrality and independence, the ICRC in particular must avoid to be associated by parties to a conflict as a (politicaly motivated) human rights actor, in order not to be denied access. This also has some legal underpinnings, as IHL only provides 'impartial' humanitarian actors with the so-called right of initiative.[109] Whereas the argument could be made that parties to the ICESCR are in any case required to accept assistance when they are unable to meet the 'minimum core' of economic and social rights,[110] factual concerns remain that the ICRC and other humanitarian actors may lose access if they more openly adopted HRBA.[111]

[106] For an overview of recent reforms: Jenimah Kolo and Megan Fahrney, 'The World Bank Inspection Panel Literature Review' (report, Helen Kellogg Institute for International Studies, 3 April 2022) <https://policycommons.net/artifacts/2367426/the-world-bank-inspection-panel-literature-review-jemimah-kolo-and-megan-fahrney/3388438/.> accessed 26 March 2024; on the need for more structural reform: International Council on Human Rights Policy, *Negotiating Justice? Human Rights and Peace Agreements* (International Council on Human Rights Policy 2006) 101; Michael O'Flaherty, 'Future Protection of Human Rights in Post-Conflict Societies: The Role of the United Nations' (2003) 3(1) Human Rights Law Review 53, 56.

[107] Amanda Cahill-Ripley, 'Reclaiming the Peacebuilding Agenda: Economic and Social Rights as a Legal Framework for Building Positive Peace—A Human Security Plus Approach to Peacebuilding' (2016) 16(2) Human Rights Law Review 223, 240.

[108] For a historical overview and the argument that practice changed towards making some limited usage of human rights: Sergey Sayapin, 'The International Committee of the Red Cross and International Human Rights Law' (2009) 9(1) Human Rights Law Review 95; Filipa Schmitz Guinote, 'The ICRC and the "Humanitarian–Development–Peace Nexus" Discussion' (2019) 101(912) IRRC 1051, 1053.

[109] ICRC, *Commentary on the Third Geneva Convention: Convention (III) Relative to the Treatment of Prisoners of War* (CUP 2020) para 828; This right of initiative is based on art 3 for non-international armed conflict and Geneva Convention I art 9, Geneva Convention II art 9, Geneva Convention III art 9 and Geneva Convention IV art 10; also: Dapo Akande and Emanuela-Chiara Gillard, 'Arbitrary Withholding of Consent to Humanitarian Relief Operations in Armed Conflict' (2016) 91 International Law Studies 484, 487; Müller (n 30) 245, 270.

[110] CESCR 'General Comment No. 12: The Right to Food' (12 May 1999) UN Doc E/C.12/1999/5, para 17; Olivier de Schutter and others, 'Commentary to the Maastricht Principles on Extraterritorial Obligations of States in the Area of Economic, Social and Cultural Rights' (2012) 34(4) Human Rights Quarterly 1084, principle 34; recently eg CESCR, 'Concluding Observations on the Sixth Periodic Report of the Democratic Republic of the Congo' (28 March 2022) UN Doc E/C.12/COD/CO/6, para 5.

[111] For an overview of examples (Colombia, Myanmar, Palestine, and Pakistan) where states denied access to humanitarian actors applying rights-based approaches: Kaja Borgrevink and Kristin B Sandvik,

This of course must not mean that the ICRC could not accept a duty to respect human rights. In fact, it already has in place numerous policies which also endorse the principle of 'do no harm', which, if interpreted broadly, could include negative impacts on human rights.[112] Complaints about ICRC staff misconduct can be filed with an internal non-judicial grievance mechanism.[113] Moreover, these policies embrace HRBA-related language, such as putting people at the centre of protective measures,[114] accountability,[115] transparency and information sharing,[116] participation,[117] and non-discrimination.[118] The Federation of the Red Cross and Red Crescent Societies (IFRC) is even a signatory of the Sphere Handbook, which explicitly adopts a human rights-based approach to humanitarian work.[119] As with the WB, the approach of the ICRC however only qualifies as human rights 'light', because legal accountability is rejected and the organization mostly refrains from adopting human rights more explicitly as operational guidance.

c) Common Projects and Oversight by the WB

An interesting side effect of WB cooperation with the ICRC and UN agencies is that it enables an oversight of these joint operations by the World Bank Inspection Panel. Within common projects, such as in South Sudan, Yemen, and Myanmar, the ICRC takes up the role of a borrower in relation to the WB. Thus, it prepared extensive documentation and risk assessments in line with the WB's ESF.[120] The same should apply to cooperation with the UN Food and Agriculture Organisation (FAO), although documents on these projects are not publicly available so far. Nonetheless, FAO essentially also takes up the position of a borrower from the WB, which is why the WB's ESF becomes indirectly applicable. Thus, environmental and social standards of the

'The Afterlife of Buzzwords: The Journey of Rights-based Approaches through the Humanitarian Sector' (2022) 26(2) International Journal of Human Rights 285, 297.

[112] ICRC, 'Professional Standards for Protection Work: Carried Out by Humanitarian and Human Rights Actors in Armed Conflict and Other Situations of Violence' (3rd edn, ICRC 2018) <https://reliefweb.int/report/world/professional-standards-protection-work-carried-out-humanitarian-and-human-rights-0> accessed 26 March 2022, 22, 27.

[113] ibid 30.

[114] ibid 22.

[115] ICRC, 'Accountability to Affected People, Institutional Framework' (ICRC, January 2019) <https://www.icrc.org/en/publication/accountability-affected-people-institutional-framework> accessed 26 March 2024, 1.

[116] ICRC (n 112), 23, 24, 62, 64.

[117] ibid 28.

[118] ibid 28.

[119] Sphere Association, *The Sphere Handbook: Humanitarian Charter and Minimum Standards in Humanitarian Response* (4th edn, Sphere Association 2018); for a critique: Helen Ouyang, Michael Vanrooyen, and Sofia Gruskin, 'The Sphere Project: Next Steps in Moving toward a Rights-based Approach to Humanitarian Assistance' (2009) 24(3) Prehospital and Disaster Medicine 147.

[120] These documents are available online at: ICRC, 'ICRC Joins the World Bank in Yemen Food Security Response and Resilience Project' (ICRC Website, 17 March 2023) <https://www.icrc.org/en/document/icrc-joins-world-bank-yemen-food-security-response-and-resilience-project> accessed 26 March 2024; ICRC, 'South Sudan: World Bank and ICRC Partner to Save and Change Lives' (ICRC Website, 15 July 2021) <https://www.icrc.org/en/document/south-sudan-world-bank-and-icrc-partner-save-and-change-lives> accessed 26 March 2024; and ICRC, 'ICRC and World Bank Partner to Support Violence-affected Communities in Myanmar' (ICRC Website, 20 October 2022) <https://www.icrc.org/en/document/icrc-and-world-bank-support-violence-affected-communities-myanmar> accessed 26 March 2024.

WB become the common framework for cooperations between the WB, ICRC, and FAO, such as in food security projects in Yemen.[121] Whereas this could in principle be seen as increasing the accountability of actors involved, it must be stressed that many concerns remain with WB oversight and the inspection panel, such as a lack of independence and transparency and limitations of remedies.[122] Thus, scholarship should follow the developments here closely and critically, as it will be interesting to analyse how practice evolves in that regard in particular when the first cases related to common projects in protracted conflicts reach the Inspection Panel.

D. Conclusion

The analysis has demonstrated that human rights have so far not been mainstreamed along the nexus, although related language can be found within policies and internally binding instruments among all key actors. Whereas the UN promoted some internal reform and more clearly accepts a duty to respect human rights along all its pillars, remaining concerns include neglect of economic and social dimensions in its peace and security pillar and, on a more fundamental level, access to justice concerns.

Given the reluctance of the ICRC and World Bank to engage with human rights and accept legal accountability, it is not surprising that a common human rights approach to protracted conflicts so far has not materialized. Whether such a human-rights based approach would however differ substantially from what is already out there in terms of policy documents is questionable. The further 'juridification' of these polices by bringing the ICRC and UN agencies within the ESF framework and by adjusting social and environmental standards to particular challenges of protracted conflicts is a notable development that could increase accountability. These reforms are unlikely to mute more fundamental critiques against these standards and their implementation in practice and thus critical scholarship should closely follow developments here, in particular when the first cases set in protracted conflict reach the WB Inspection Panel.

All in all, human rights may have become a common language among critics of policy and practice in each sector, but not so much of key institutional actors themselves.[123] Given this state of affairs, it is probably unrealistic that the promotion of human rights law and true respect for its contents will become an overarching objective of institutional cooperation of peace, development, and humanitarian actors in the near future beyond the established forms of human rights 'light' analysed in this

[121] For an overview of the project's agenda: 'Yemen: Acute Food Insecurity Projection Update October–December 2022' (Integrated Food Security Phase Classification Info Website, 16 November 2022) <https://www.ipcinfo.org/ipc-country-analysis/details-map/en/c/1156028/?iso3=YEM> accessed 26 March 2024.

[122] Kolo and Fahrney (n 106); Yvonne Wong and Benoit Mayer, 'The World Bank's Inspection Panel: A Tool for Accountability?' in Jan Wouters and others (eds), *The World Bank Legal Review Volume 6 Improving Delivery in Development: The Role of Voice, Social Contract, and Accountability* (World Bank 2015), 495–530.

[123] On the limited transformational impact of HRBA to humanitarian aid: Borgrevink and Sandvik (n 111), 302: on the inability to transform power relations in the development sector: Andrea Cornwall and Celestine Nyamu-Musembi, 'Putting the "Rights-based Approach" to Development into Perspective' (2004) 25(8) Third World Quarterly 1415, 1432.

article. However, this does not mean that referring to human rights is no viable tactic for critics of the status quo. As Cornwall and Nyamu-Musembi put it:

> Rights talk is above all talk of politics, of power and of social justice. It is talk that inspires and impassions, talk that animates and mobilises, talk that restores to people a sense of their agency and their rightful claim to dignity and voice.[124]

Learning from history and the fate of other 'buzzwords' in the field requires observers to remain vigilant that promised reforms under the triple-nexus agenda, most notably notions of 'putting people at the centre', go beyond mere rhetoric and 'window-dressing'.

[124] Cornwall and Nyamu-Musembi (n 123) 1433.

18
Protracted Conflicts and the Right to Water

Sofie-Marie Terrey

A. Introduction

Access to sufficient clean drinking water is a multidimensional problem in many of today's protracted conflicts. As the situations in Syria and Yemen show,[1] water supply can be severely impaired during protracted conflicts. This is not only because water resources and infrastructure are directly targeted and weaponized by conflict parties;[2] protracted conflicts also imply many indirect negative consequences for water access which are most severe in the long term: the progressive loss of critical infrastructure, consumables, and staff can lead to the continuous erosion of access to and sufficient quality of water and sanitation services.[3]

This is detrimental because a lack of adequate water can be significantly more deadly than the direct use of force, especially if it is prolonged. Inadequate water supply also negatively impacts a wide range of other socio-economic concerns, such as healthcare and food security. In Sub-Saharan and Middle Eastern countries experiencing protracted conflicts, the chance of young children dying due to a lack of adequate water and sanitation supply is more than twenty times higher than the chance of dying from violence in conflict.[4] In the future, conflict-related impairments of the affected population's water supply could be further compounded by climate change, for example through a growing overlap of conflict- and climate-induced displacement: conflict-induced displacement already poses challenges for water supply,[5] and

[1] ICRC, 'Bled Dry: How War in the Middle East is Bringing the Region to the Brink of a Water Catastrophe' (ICRC 2015); ICRC, 'Syria Water Crisis: Up to 40% Less Drinking Water after 10 Years of War' (ICRC, 1 October 2021) <https://www.icrc.org/en/document/syria-water-crisis-after-10-years-war> accessed 17 May 2023.

[2] Eg Peter Gleick, 'Water as a Weapon and Casualty of Armed Conflict: A Review of Recent Water-related Violence in Iraq, Syria, and Yemen' (2019) 6 (4) WIREs Water; Pacific Institute, 'Water Conflict Chronology' <http://www.worldwater.org/conflict/map/> accessed 17 May 2023.

[3] ICRC, 'Urban Services during Protracted Armed Conflict' (ICRC 2015) 21ff.; also Schillinger and others, 'Water in War: Understanding the Impacts of Armed Conflict on Water Resources and Their Management' (2020) 7(6) WIREs Water 11ff.

[4] World Bank, ICRC, and UNICEF, 'Joining Forces to Combat Protracted Crises: Humanitarian and Development Support for Water and Sanitation Providers in the Middle East and North Africa' (The World Bank 2021) 1.

[5] Generally UNGA 'Report of the Special Rapporteur on the Human Rights to Safe Drinking Water and Sanitation' (3 August 2018) UN Doc A/HRC/39/55.

Sofie-Marie Terrey, *Protracted Conflicts and the Right to Water* In: *From Protracted Conflict to Sustainable Peace?*
Edited by: Heike Krieger, Giedre Jokubauskaite, Asli Ozcelik, and Andreas Buser, Oxford University Press.
 DOI: 10.1093/9780198967385.003.0022

most cases of such conflict-induced displacement occur in already arid regions which are especially prone to climate change[6] and thus to climate-related displacement.[7]

Addressing the harms caused by inadequate water supply for people living in protracted conflict settings thus requires not only the prevention of attacks on water infrastructure and short-term emergency measures. It also requires approaches aiming at the sustainable rehabilitation and capacity building of the water and sanitation sector that makes it resilient to future impairments[8]—conflict but also climate-related ones. In international legal research, however, contributions on water and conflict have often focused instead on the legal protection of water in international humanitarian law (IHL) from *direct* interferences during the conduct of hostilities.[9] Yet, especially due to the non-international nature of many protracted conflicts, IHL as a normative basis can be insufficient to address many *indirect*, rather structural impairments on water supply. This does not justify neglecting them as unavoidable 'side effects' of conflict, though: they can constitute violations of the human right to water (HRtW) and related economic, social, and cultural rights (ESCR) for which legal accountability can be fostered.[10] So far, the interplay of armed conflict and the HRtW has received rather less attention from scholars.[11]

Accordingly, this chapter addresses some aspects related to the HRtW with regard to the idiosyncrasies of protracted conflicts. Section B demonstrates the need for and the possibilities of complementarity of the HRtW with IHL in protracted conflicts. Section C examines the guarantees arising from the HRtW in protracted conflicts in more detail, including the repercussions that a very long conflict duration can have on the realization of the HRtW. Section D then briefly points at adequate measures on the international level to foster compliance with the HRtW in protracted conflicts.

[6] Internal Displacement Monitoring Centre and Norwegian Refugee Council, 'Global Report on Internal Displacement 2021—Internal displacement in a changing climate' (Internal Displacement Monitoring Centre 2021) 96ff.

[7] Eg UN Special Rapporteur on the human rights to safe drinking water and sanitation, 'Special Thematic Report on Climate Change and the Human Rights to Water—Part 2: The Impacts of Climate Change on the Human Rights to Safe Drinking Water and Sanitation of Groups and Populations in Situations of Vulnerability' (UN OHCHR 2022) para 46.

[8] Also UNICEF, 'Water under Fire Report' (UNICEF 2019) 15ff.

[9] Eg Théo Boutruche, 'Le Statut de l'eau En Droit International Humanitaire' (2000) 82 International Review of the Red Cross 887; Lorenz, 'The Protection of Water Facilities under International Law' (UNESCO 2003); Mara Tignino, *Water During and After Armed Conflicts* (Brill Research Perspectives on International Water Law Series, Brill 2016) 1; Ameur Zemmali, 'The Protection of Water in Times of Armed Conflict' (1995) 35 International Review of the Red Cross 550; Geneva Water Hub, 'Geneva List of Principles for the Protection of Water Infrastructure' (Geneva Water Hub and The Platform for International Water Law of the University of Geneva 2019).

[10] Also Simone Hutter, 'Starvation in Armed Conflicts: An Analysis Based on the Right to Food' (2019) 17 Journal of International Criminal Justice 723, 730.

[11] Besides more general contributions on ESCR in armed conflict, especially Gilles Giacca, *Economic, Social, and Cultural Rights in Armed Conflict* (OUP 2014) and Amrei Müller, *The Relationship between Economic, Social and Cultural Rights and International Humanitarian Law* (Brill 2013), a couple of authors have focused on the HRtW in armed conflict: Elizabeth Mottershaw, 'Economic, Social and Cultural Rights in Armed Conflict: International Human Rights Law and International Humanitarian Law' (2008) 12 The International Journal of Human Rights 449; Ameur Zemmali, 'The Right to Water in Times of Armed Conflict' in Liesbeth Lijnzaad, Johanna van Sambeek and Bahia Tahzib-Lie (eds), *Making the Voice*

B. Sustainable Water Provision in Protracted Conflicts—Legal Frameworks

While IHL provides for various prohibitive rules for the conduct of hostilities related to water,[12] it also contains, to a certain extent, *positive* obligations to provide safe drinking water during conflict. They can mainly be found in rules on persons specifically protected by IHL, notably persons deprived of their liberty[13] and displaced persons,[14] which focus on adequate conditions of health and nutrition of those persons. An obligation to provide for water is implicit in many IHL rules containing minimal socio-economic guarantees, such as the rules on medical care for the wounded and sick, since sufficient clean water is often essential for their fulfilment.[15] A certain standard of water access is also secured through the prohibition on using starvation of civilians as a method of warfare[16] by denying a minimum amount of water to the population[17] and the protective rules on humanitarian assistance that aim to provide water services.[18] These rules are especially relevant here because starvation as a method of warfare is a recurrent issue in several current protracted conflicts. In Syria, Yemen, and Ethiopia, for example, conflict parties have been accused of deliberately exacerbating food and water insecurity, especially by denying humanitarian access.

However, overall, the approach of IHL to water supply appears narrow, and especially so in protracted conflicts. The existing rules are rather fragmented and mostly do not even mention water explicitly. In particular, their regulatory content is too scant when the situations they are designed to address last significantly longer than may have been contemplated when they were drafted. The case of protracted displacement is particularly illustrative here. While article 49 Geneva Convention IV and article 17 Protocol II demand that the socio-economic conditions of the displaced shall be 'satisfactory', what constitutes such 'satisfactory' water access in situations of decades-long internal displacement remains unclear. Furthermore, the obligation to

of Humanity Heard (Nijhoff 2004) 307; Tignino (n 9) 74ff; Amanda Cahill-Ripley, *The Human Right to Water in the Occupied Palestinian Territories* (Routledge 2011).

12 For an extensive analysis: Mara Tignino, *L'eau et La Guerre: Éléments Pour Un Système Juridique* (Bruylant 2011) 77–97, 127–54.

13 Geneva Convention III relative to the Treatment of Prisoners of War (adopted 12 August 1949, entered into force 21 October 1959) 75 UNTS 135 (Geneva Convention III) art 20 (2), 26 (3), 46 (3), Protocol Additional to the Geneva Conventions of 12 August 1949, and relating to the Protection of Victims of Non-International Armed Conflicts (adopted 8 June 1977, entered into force December 1978) 1125 UNTS 609 (Protocol II) art 5 (1) (b); Jean-Marie Henckaerts and Louise Doswald-Beck (eds), *Customary International Humanitarian Law*, vol 1 (CUP 2005), Rule 118, 428ff (hereafter ICRC Customary IHL Study). Also, the prohibition on inhuman treatment in Common Article 3 Geneva Conventions was defined to comprise a lack of sufficient water provision, ICRC Customary IHL Study Rule 90, 318f.

14 Geneva Convention IV relative to the Protection of Civilian Persons in Time of War (adopted 12 August 1949, entered into force 21 October 1959) 75 UNTS, 287 (Geneva Convention IV) art 49(3); Protocol II art 17 (1); ICRC Customary IHL Study (n 13) Rule 131, 465 and Rule 132, 471.

15 Zemmali, 'The Protection of Water' (n 9) 556.

16 Protocol Additional to the Geneva Conventions of 12 August 1949 relating to the Protection of Victims of International Armed Conflicts (adopted 8 June 1977, entered into force 7 December 1978) 1125 UNTS 3 (Protocol I) art 54 I; Protocol II art 14; ICRC Customary IHL Study (n 13) Rule 53, 186ff.

17 Cahill-Ripley, *The Human Right to Water* (n 11) 105, 106.

18 Protocol I art 70 (1); Protocol II art 18 (2); ICRC Customary IHL Study (n 13) Rule 55, 193ff.

facilitate voluntary and safe return of displaced persons in customary law includes the provision of basic needs, such as water.[19] Yet, no guidance exists, for example, on obligations to provide long-term sustainable water supply (eg by reconstructing water infrastructure or cleaning polluted water resources) to make the permanent resettlement of displaced persons in an area possible. In addition, arguably, the rules on starvation and humanitarian assistance are similarly characterized by an 'emergency lens'.[20] The prohibition of starvation of civilians essentially protects against extreme water deprivation that can be directly linked to specific conduct of hostilities, while more structural impairments that may not be immediately life-threatening but lead to damage in the long term are not covered. Also, with regard to water provision through humanitarian action, IHL does not regulate, for example, which (water) services the population is entitled to receive and for how long, and how relief actions should be designed.[21]

1. The Right to Water as a Holistic Approach to Water Supply in Protracted Conflicts

To address structural impairments on water access in protracted conflicts, it thus seems essential to rely on international human rights law (IHRL), and specifically the HRtW. Not originally foreseen in the ICESCR,[22] the HRtW has been contested from various sides[23] during its emergence as a codified right—the Committee on Economic, Social, and Cultural Rights (CESCR) derived it in 2003 from articles 11 and 12 of the ICESCR.[24] Nonetheless, it has not only been recognized at the UN level for more than a decade now[25] but also recognition has grown in regional human

[19] ICRC Customary IHL Study (n 13) Rule 132, 471.

[20] Also Riccardo Vecellio Segate, 'Hidden Hunger in Peacetime and Wartime: Retailoring the "Responsibility to Protect" to Food-Power Discourses in Burundi and North Korea, Between International Politics and International Law' (2021) 46 North Carolina Journal of International Law and Commercial Regulation 181, 214.

[21] Eg a definition of what constitutes 'inadequate supply' (Protocol I art 70 (1)) or 'undue hardship' (Protocol II art 18 (2)) does not exist: Yves Sandoz, Christophe Swinarski, and Bruno Zimmermann (eds), *Commentary on the Additional Protocols of 8 June 1977 to the Geneva Conventions of 12 August 1949* (Nijhoff 1987) paras 2794, 4881. It is also disputed whether IHL at all confers a right of the population to receive assistance: Heike Spieker, 'Humanitarian Assistance, Access in Armed Conflict and Occupation', *Max Planck Encyclopedia of Public International Law* (last updated 2015) <https://opil.ouplaw.com/display/10.1093/law:epil/9780199231690/law-9780199231690-e1701?rskey=Um2kwi&result=1&prd=MPIL> accessed 18 May 2023, paras 25–26.

[22] International Covenant on Economic, Social, and Cultural Rights (adopted 16 December 1966, entered into force 3 January 1976) 993 UNTS 3 (ICESCR).

[23] Nina Reiners, 'Despite or Because of Contestation? How Water Became a Human Right' (2021) 43 Human Rights Quarterly 329.

[24] CESCR, 'General Comment No. 15: The Right to Water (Arts. 11 and 12 of the Covenant)' (20 January 2003) UN Doc E/C.12/2002/11; for details: Ndjodi Ndeunyema, 'Unmuddying the Waters: Evaluating the Legal Basis of the Human Right to Water Under Treaty Law, Customary International Law, and the General Principles of Law' (2020) 41 Michigan Journal of International Law 455, 457ff.

[25] HRC Res 15/9 (30 September 2010) UN Doc A/HRC/RES/15/9; UNGA Res 64/292 (28 July 2010) UN Doc A/RES/64/292. For details: Laurence Boisson de Chazournes, *Fresh Water in International Law* (2nd edn, OUP 2021) 190ff; also Amnesty International and WASH United, 'Recognition of the Human Rights to Water and Sanitation by UN Member States at the International Level' (Amnesty International 2015).

rights systems, which is important with respect to the geographic areas most affected by both protracted conflicts and water scarcity.[26] For example, the incorporation of the HRtW in the African human rights system by the African Commission on Human and People's Rights will be relevant regarding protracted conflicts in the Sahel region, while regarding conflicts in the MENA region it is notable that the Arab Charter on Human Rights also includes a HRtW.

Like the ICESCR in general,[27] the HRtW continues to apply during armed conflict.[28] The right entitles every person to an adequate supply of water.[29] Water must be consistently and sufficiently available, accessible for everyone without discrimination, and of sufficient quality to be safe.[30] These guarantees are subject to progressive realization according to article 2(1) ICESCR; however, states have an obligation to immediately take steps towards such realization.[31] In addition, the CESCR has specified a minimum core content of the right, which must be fulfilled immediately.[32] Over the course of the past decades since its initial codification, the right has been elaborated with increasing specificity in its content and scope by human rights bodies as well as academic literature, so that it now provides an extensive catalogue of standards with which states are obliged to comply.

The HRtW thus not only provides a higher norm density than IHL; also, it compensates for protection weaknesses occurring especially in protracted conflicts that result from the application scope of IHL. In protracted internal conflicts marked by a persistent state of fluctuation in the intensity of violence and insecurity, the application of IHL can be difficult to determine.[33] Economic, social, and cultural rights (ESCR), including the HRtW, are applicable at all times since they also cannot be derogated from during conflict.[34] Additionally, problems arising due to the conflict

[26] For the African human rights system, ACHPR 'Guidelines on the Right to Water in Africa' (ACHPR 2019); the African Commission has explicitly included the right to water in its reporting procedures, eg ACHPR, 'Concluding Observations and Recommendations – Malawi, adopted at the 70th Ordinary Session (23 February–9 March 2022)' (ACHPR 2022) 8, and ACHPR, 'Concluding Observations – Niger, adopted at the 23rd Extraordinary Session (13–22 February 2018)' (ACHPR 2018) 17. For the Inter-American human rights system: *Indigenous Communities of the Lhaka Honhat Association (Our Land) v Argentina* (Judgment on Merits, Reparations and Costs) Inter-American Court of Human Rights Series C No 400 (6 February 2020) para 222; for Arab countries: Arab Charter on Human Rights (adopted 22 May 2004, entered into force 15 March 2008) reprinted in (2005) 12 Int'l Hum Rts Rep 893 art 39 (2) (e).

[27] *Legal Consequences of the Construction of a Wall in the Occupied Palestinian Territory* (Advisory Opinion) (2004) ICJ Rep 178 para 106; Manisuli Ssenyonjo, *Economic, Social and Cultural Rights in International Law* (Hart 2016) 54ff.

[28] CESCR, 'General Comment No. 15' (n 24) para 22; ACHPR, 'Guidelines on the Right to Water' (ACHPR 2019) Guideline 34.1.

[29] For a detailed elaboration: eg Inga Winkler, *The Human Right to Water: Significance, Legal Status and Implications for Water Allocation* (Hart 2012) 125ff.

[30] CESCR, 'General Comment No. 15' (n 24) paras 11, 12.

[31] ibid para 17.

[32] ibid para 37.

[33] Robin Geiß, 'Armed Violence in Fragile States: Low-intensity Conflicts, Spillover Conflicts, and Sporadic Law Enforcement Operations by Third Parties' (2009) 91 International Review of the Red Cross 127, 134ff.

[34] The CESCR routinely emphasizes that at least core obligations are non-derogable, eg CESCR, 'General Comment No. 15' (n 24) para 40; CESCR, 'General Comment No. 14: The Right to the Highest Attainable Standard of Health (Art. 12)' (11 August 2000) UN Doc E/C.12/2000/4 para 47. However, authors have argued that except for labour rights, ESCR should generally be considered as non-derogable during

nexus requirement of IHL can be overcome through a focus on the HRtW. This could, for example, address the complexities of an overlap of conflict- and climate-induced displacement: the HRtW provides protection of displaced people regardless of the reasons for their displacement.[35] It could also potentially fill protection gaps regarding treaty law as Protocol II has not been ratified by all countries affected by or at risk of protracted conflicts.[36]

More broadly, the HRtW contributes an important vantage point by being essentially forward-looking. The HRtW, but also interconnected rights such as the right to food, health, housing, or a healthy environment, are not primarily prohibitive but normativize goals, benchmarks, and action guidance towards a sustainable step-by-step improvement of future livelihoods. This seems useful especially in protracted conflicts where the provision of remedies for violations of the law, for example through the prosecution of war crimes, does not necessarily address the structural root causes of such conflicts, and where future negative impacts of climate change demand sustainable anticipatory action. Also, the HRtW may have more of a prospect of serving as a cross-sectoral legal framework for long-term reconstruction efforts since its content corresponds with the activities of not only humanitarian actors but also, for example, development actors and possibly actors engaged in peacebuilding.

It should not be ignored that the added value of a rights-based approach to water has also been questioned by critics; a central issue here has always been the privatization of water resources and a market-friendly conceptualization of the right more generally.[37] This chapter cannot go into detail here. It should be noted, however, that a critique of a market-based orientation can be considered and addressed within the rights framework: for example, the UN Special Rapporteur became more critical of the issue of privatization over time.[38] Also, the HRtW does not exclude and can be interconnected with other frameworks for water governance informed by differing

emergencies: Müller (n 11) 137ff; Giacca (n 11) 83ff; Manisuli Ssenyonjo, 'Reflections on State Obligations with Respect to Economic, Social and Cultural Rights in International Human Rights Law' (2011) 15(6) The International Journal of Human Rights 969, 991. Likewise, for the African Charter: *Commission Nationale des Droits de l'Homme et des Libertes* v *Chad* (11 October 1995) ACHPR 8, communication no 74/92 para 21.

[35] Sâ Benjamin Traoré and Tiérowé Germain Dabiré, 'The Right to Water for Internally Displaced Persons in the Sahel Region' (2021) 103 International Review of the Red Cross 959, 965–66.

[36] For example, Somalia and Syria are not parties to Protocol II, but are parties to the ICESCR and other human rights treaties relevant for the right to water: OHCHR, 'Status of Ratification Interactive Dashboard' <https://indicators.ohchr.org> accessed 18 May 2023.

[37] Karen Bakker, 'The Commons vs. Commodities—Debating the Human Right to Water' in Farhana Sultana and Alex Loftus (eds), *The Right to Water—Politics, Governance and Social Struggles* (Routledge 2011) 19; generally Malcom Langford, 'Privatization and the Right to Water' in Malcom Langford and Anna Russell (eds), *The Human Right to Water—Theory, Practice, Prospects* (CUP 2017) 463, 470ff.

[38] While earlier statements of the UN Special Rapporteur were rather hesitant to connect the right to water to privatization critique (HRC 'Report of the Independent Expert on the Issue of Human Rights Obligations Related to Access to Safe Drinking Water and Sanitation, Catarina de Albuquerque' (29 June 2010) UN Doc A/HRC/15/31 paras 14ff), a more recent report by the Special Rapporteur clearly acknowledges the risks of privatization (UNGA 'Report of the Special Rapporteur on the Human Rights to Safe Drinking Water and Sanitation, Léo Heller' (21 July 2020) UN Doc A/75/208).

angles, such as Sustainable Development Goal 6.[39] Moreover, arguably, it is precisely individualized, human-centred norms that can help make structural socio-economic suffering seem tangible and addressable, which can give them intrinsic value, especially in protracted conflicts.

2. Complementarity of the Right to Water and IHL during Protracted Conflicts

The HRtW can harmoniously complement the guarantees of water provision in IHL—norm conflicts will not often be found here.[40] The right can clarify their content and interpret them, especially with regard to long-term water needs. For example, the specific guarantees that the HRtW encompasses not only for displaced persons and refugees[41] but also for prisoners and detained persons[42] can be combined with and supplement the guarantees of IHL. The UN Special Rapporteur on the human rights to safe drinking water and sanitation has elaborated the implications of the HRtW in situations of protracted displacement. The report particularly emphasizes long-term solutions for sustainable water access of the displaced, such as strengthening inclusive development approaches as well as the humanitarian-development-peace nexus and creating the conditions for long-term return of displaced persons.[43] Such more detailed standards could support and guide the interpretation of the duty under IHL to provide access to water to displaced persons and to facilitate their voluntary and safe return.

Tensions may nevertheless arise between the norms in some cases. In these cases, interpretive approaches that give appropriate weight to the HRtW should be developed and mainstreamed. An example could be the regulation of starvation in IHL. Severe deprivation of clean water will reach the threshold of starvation under IHL, while also violating minimum core obligations arising from the HRtW.[44] Yet, siege warfare, blockades, embargoes, or other measures that pursue a military objective

[39] Also eg UNGA 'Report of the Independent Expert on the Issue of Human Rights Obligations Related to Access to Safe Drinking Water and Sanitation, Catarina de Albuquerque' (6 August 2010) UN Doc A/65/254; Boisson de Chazournes (n 25) 205ff.

[40] Certainly, this is due to the principle of humanity being in the foreground in these rules, which does not conflict with human rights. The situation may be different regarding rules for the conduct of hostilities in which necessity plays a greater role. For example, while water resources as a part of the environment are protected by IHL only against 'widespread, long term and severe damage' (Protocol I art 35 (3)), the human right to water could provide for a higher protection level. A detailed analysis of all rules is beyond the scope of this chapter.

[41] UNGA 'Report of the Special Rapporteur on the Right to Water' (n 5); CESCR, 'Statement on the Duties of States towards Refugees and Migrants under the International Covenant on Economic, Social and Cultural Rights' (13 March 2017) UN Doc E/C.12/2017/1, para 9; CESCR, 'General Comment No. 15' (n 24) para 16 (f).

[42] CESCR, 'General Comment No. 15' (n 24) para 16 (g), 22.

[43] UNGA 'Report of the Special Rapporteur on the Right to Water' (n 5) paras 39ff.

[44] The CESCR also emphasizes this overlap of the rules by stating that the obligation to respect forbids 'limiting access to . . . water services and infrastructure as a punitive measure, for example, during armed conflicts *in violation of international humanitarian law*' (emphasis added): CESCR, 'General Comment No. 15' (n 24) para 21.

and cause only *incidental* starvation are not prohibited by IHL,[45] while these tactics would often be contrary to the guarantees under the HRtW. If incidental starvation occurs due to an attack, of course IHL already specifically protects water infrastructure.[46] But additionally, the principle of proportionality could be interpreted in light of the HRtW to duly consider long-term impairments of access to safe water for the population in military targeting.[47] Also, if starvation is not caused by an attack, it is most often caused by the obstruction of humanitarian aid to the population by the state concerned. IHL principally conditions humanitarian access on the consent of the state, which may, however, not be arbitrarily withheld.[48] Arguably, a systemic integration of the norms[49] means that the denial of humanitarian assistance is considered arbitrary when the state would thereby violate its obligations under fundamental human rights, including the minimum core of economic, social, and cultural rights.[50] Therefore, if the minimum core content of the HRtW remains unfulfilled without humanitarian assistance, the state's denial of such assistance is unlawful under IHL as well as the HRtW. Notably, the minimum core content of the HRtW demands more than just the provision of basic amounts of water: it also demands, for example, non-discrimination in water access,[51] the realization of which would also require the consideration of special needs of vulnerable and marginalized groups during humanitarian assistance.[52] Thus, if humanitarian relief action ensured water supply in a manner that is non-discriminatory and included special protection for vulnerable groups,[53] a state's denial of consent to such relief could be arbitrary.

The complementary application of the HRtW and IHL is thus sometimes unproblematically feasible, while norm tensions can be manageable. The two fields should thus also increasingly become jointly applied in practice, especially in situations of protracted conflict.

C. The Scope of the Right to Water during Protracted Conflicts

Also, outside of the sphere of overlap with IHL, the state principally retains the whole spectrum of its obligations under the HRtW even during armed conflicts. This would

[45] ICRC Customary IHL Study (n 13) Rule 53, 188ff.

[46] Protocol I art 54 (2), (3); ICRC Customary IHL Study (n 13) Rule 54, 189ff.

[47] This has already been argued with regard to the right to food (Hutter (n 10) 740) and the right to health (Müller (n 11) 156, 179–180).

[48] Generally Dapo Akande and Emanuela-Chiara Gillard, 'Arbitrary Withholding of Consent to Humanitarian Relief Operations in Armed Conflict' (2016) 92 International Law Studies 482.

[49] Vienna Convention on the Law of Treaties (adopted 23 May 1969, entered into force 27 January 1980) 1155 UNTS 331 (VCLT) art 31 (3).

[50] Dapo Akande and Emanuela-Chiara Gillard, 'Oxford Guidance on the Law Relating to Humanitarian Relief Operations in Situations of Armed Conflict' (2016) University of Oxford Guidance Paper, 24, <https://www.unocha.org/sites/unocha/files/Oxford%20Guidance%20pdf.pdf> accessed 18 May 2023. This seems to be an acceptable balance regarding the integration of ESCR in the law of humanitarian assistance: while a consideration of all 'non-core' ESCR guarantees in assessing arbitrariness would make the consent requirement void, minimum core ESCR obligations help clarify further the rather rudimentary regulation of IHL as to which basic needs should be addressed by humanitarian assistance.

[51] CESCR, 'General Comment No. 15' (n 24) para 37.

[52] CESCR, 'General Comment No. 15' (n 24) para 60; CESCR, 'General Comment No. 14' (n 34) para 40.

[53] This could include, for example, the provision of adequate water facilities for persons who menstruate and thus have increased hygienic needs or for disabled persons for whom physical accessibility of water can be problematic.

include, for example, the obligation of the state to provide basic amounts of water by emergency aid, maintain (as far as possible) public water services and infrastructure, (if damaged) ensure their rehabilitation and resilience against future harm, and provide special protection of vulnerable persons concerning water supply.

There might be significant obstacles for the practical enforcement of the HRtW's guarantees in protracted conflicts. Not only might the state's general capabilities have decreased, but it might also have partially or totally lost control over certain areas to armed opposition groups. Nevertheless, at times, it could be too simplistic to assert a lack of resources or capabilities of the state to realize ESCR. In some situations, failures of the water and sanitation system can be traced back to deficient administrative decisions or even the sheer unwillingness of the state to realize any of its ESCR duties, especially when this would contradict its military strategy. It might also be too generalizing to assume that the state cannot assume any duties to realize the HRtW in non-controlled territories. To promote meaningful accountability, it is necessary to look closely at what the actual capacities of the state are and whether and for how long it can justify a failure to fulfil the HRtW.

Accordingly, in the following it is first recalled that IHRL sets clear boundaries regarding the extent to which the HRtW can be limited in times of (protracted) crisis. Second, the protracted nature of a conflict must be considered in the assessment of what is demanded from the state under human rights law. It will be argued in section C.4 that the longer a conflict lasts, the less justification there is for the state to fail to comply with its obligations under the HRtW.

1. Limiting the Right to Water under Article 2(1) and Article 4 ICESCR?

The HRtW in connection with article 2(1) ICESCR postulates for each state party the obligation of progressive realization 'to the maximum of its available resources'. The 'prohibition of retrogression' demands that states do not adopt measures that would deteriorate either the level of enjoyment of rights that prevailed at the time of accession of the state to the Convention, or the current level of enjoyment.[54] Also, the state must reduce factors that could increase the risk of retrogression in the future.[55]

The prohibition of retrogression is, however, not absolute, but context-dependent.[56] The CESCR has not yet issued a General Comment or any specific document on ESCR in the specific situation of (protracted) armed conflicts. The Committee recognizes the possibility to justify retrogressive measures during conflict by stating that it will consider 'serious claims on the State party's limited resources; for example, resulting from ... *recent internal or international armed conflict*'.[57] However, the CESCR does

[54] Aoife Nolan, Nicholas Lusiani and Christian Courtis, 'Two Steps Forward, No Steps Back? Evolving Criteria on the Prohibition of Retrogression in Economic and Social Rights' in Aoife Nolan (ed), *Economic and Social Rights after the Global Financial Crisis* (CUP 2014) 123ff.; also HRC 'Report of the Special Rapporteur on the Human Rights to Safe Drinking Water and Sanitation' (8 July 2020) UN Doc A/HRC/45/10 para 57.

[55] HRC 'Report of the Special Rapporteur' (n 54) para 58.

[56] Nolan, Lusiani, and Courtis (n 54) 124; HRC 'Report of the Special Rapporteur' (n 54) para 60f.

[57] CESCR, 'An Evaluation of the Obligation to Take Steps to the 'Maximum of Available Resources' under an Optional Protocol to the Covenant' (21 September 2007) UN Doc E/C.12/2007/1 para 10 (emphasis added).

not accept the occurrence of such conflict alone as sufficient to justify retrogressive measures.[58] Contrarily, it stated that any 'deliberately retrogressive measures . . . would require the *most careful consideration* and would need to be fully justified *by reference to the totality of the rights* provided for in the Covenant and *in the context of the full use of the maximum available resources*'.[59] In the context of adjustment measures in economic crises, the CESCR has further determined that measures would need to fulfil the criteria of *necessity* and *proportionality*, *temporariness*, and *non-discrimination*.[60] The burden of proof for compliance falls on the state.[61]

It would appear that the general limitation clause of article 4 ICESCR could be another way of justification, given that according to the *travaux préparatoires* it should cover those limitations not related to resources.[62] This could include, for example, security measures such as evacuations that could result in loss of tap water access. However, especially during armed conflicts, it can be difficult to draw a line between state decisions taken because of a lack of resources and such decisions made on other grounds promoting 'general welfare' according to article 4 ICESCR.[63] This is especially so because current doctrine foresees a broad scope of state behaviour covered by article 2(1) ICESCR as well as a wide definition of resources.[64] Amrei Müller has already argued that a unified justification standard should be developed, especially because the requirements of both norms do not actually diverge much.[65] Indeed, the

[58] Müller (n 11) 130ff; also UNGA 'Report of the United Nations High Commissioner for Human Rights: Protection of Economic, Social and Cultural Rights in Conflict' (22 June 2016) UN Doc E/2015/59 para 70f.

[59] CESCR, 'General Comment No. 3: The Nature of States Parties' Obligations (Art. 2, Para. 1, of the Covenant)' (14 December 1990) UN Doc E/1991/23 para 9 (emphasis added). This formula is reiterated in a number of General Comments, eg CESCR, 'General Comment No. 14' (n 34) para 32; CESCR, 'General Comment No. 13: The Right to Education (Art. 13)' (8 December 1999) UN Doc E/C.12/1999/10 para 45. For a detailed interpretation: Nolan, Lusiani, and Courtis (n 54) 134.

[60] CESCR, 'Letter from CESCR Chairperson to States Parties in the Context of the Economic and Financial Crisis' (16 May 2012) UN Doc CESCR/48th/SP/MAB/SW; the CESCR continuously reiterates these criteria in its Concluding Observations, eg CESCR, 'Concluding Observations—Ecuador' (2019) UN Doc E/C.12/ECU/CO/4 para 6 d; CESCR, 'Concluding Observations—Denmark' (2019) UN Doc E/C.12/DNK/CO/6 para 13. Also similarly ACHPR, 'Guidelines on the Right to Water in Africa' (n 26) Guideline 6.3. For a critique: Ben Warwick, 'Socio-Economic Rights during Economic Crises: A Changed Approach to Non-Retrogression' (2015) 65 International and Comparative Law Quarterly 249.

[61] HCR 'Report of the Special Rapporteur' (n 54) para 27 and CESCR, 'General Comment No. 15' (n 24) para 41.

[62] Philip Alston and Gerard Quinn, 'The Nature and Scope of States Parties' Obligations under the International Covenant on Economic, Social and Cultural Rights' (1987) 9 Human Rights Quarterly 156 (194).

[63] Müller (n 11) 136.

[64] The obligation to allocate the 'maximum available resources' refers to states' resource generation and allocation as well as expenditure, eg Olivier de Schutter, 'Public Budget Analysis for the Realization of Economic, Social and Cultural Rights' in Katharine Young (ed) *The Future of Economic and Social Rights* (CUP 2019) 527, 562ff, and the notion of 'resources' has been defined as not only comprising financial but also other (natural, human, technological, institutional) resources, Robert Robertson, 'Measuring State Compliance with the Obligation to Devote the "Maximum Available Resources" to Realizing Economic, Social, and Cultural Rights' (1994) 16 Human Rights Quarterly 693, 695; HRC 'Report of the Special Rapporteur' (n 54) para 19ff. This way, a 'lack of resources' today can often be traced back to a deliberate decision of the state in the past, which could be based also on other grounds than pure resource scarcity.

[65] Müller (n 11) 135ff.

justification in both article 2(1) ICESCR and article 4 ICESCR essentially rests on a proportionality assessment of the measure in question.

Accordingly, the state cannot arbitrarily determine the degree to which the HRtW is realized, even in armed conflict. Retrogressive measures of any kind must pursue a legitimate purpose and be proportionate. At the same time, the obligation to take positive measures to progressively realize the HRtW exists without restriction.

2. The Role of the Minimum Core Content

In addition, the minimum core content of the HRtW can serve to limit the state's decision-making power in conflict by identifying and emphasizing its most fundamental duties. The CESCR essentially has specified that states are obliged (a) to provide a minimum level of water that is adequate at least to prevent diseases, (b) to adopt relatively low-cost targeted programs especially for vulnerable and marginalized groups as well as to ensure that water access is provided in a physically reasonable, equitable, and non-discriminatory manner, and (c) to create a national water strategy and action plan and to monitor progress in the realization of the right.[66]

The CESCR has stated in several General Comments that it principally excludes from justification retrogressive measures that impinge upon the minimum core of each of the ESCR.[67] However, for states affected by protracted conflicts, resource constraints might sometimes be so severe that even the realization of the core HRtW is impossible. Indeed, it has been pointed out that, at least concerning positive obligations to fulfil,[68] even the minimum core must be viewed as resource-dependent.[69] The CESCR also acknowledged this by stating that when a state cannot fulfil minimum core rights, it must prove that '*every effort* has been made to use *all resources that are at its disposition* in an effort to satisfy, *as a matter of priority*, those minimum obligations'.[70]

What is the difference between the thresholds of justification for an impingement on the core content versus the non-core content of the rights? Arguably, the CESCR's language suggests an 'aggravated' justification threshold, which allows for viewing the minimum core content essentially as a means of specifying relative but not absolute priorities[71] within a spectrum of obligations. This means that in a proportionality test for a particular measure, the justification efforts the state must make

[66] CESCR, 'General Comment No. 15' (n 24) para 37.

[67] eg CESCR, 'General Comment No. 15' (n 24) para 42; CESCR, 'General Comment No. 19: The Right to Social Security (Art. 9)' (4 February 2008) UN Doc E/C.12/GC/19 para 64.

[68] Concerning the negative obligation to respect the minimum core right to water, it can be argued that this constitutes an *absolute* duty, since refraining from interfering with basic water access, eg during the conduct of hostilities, does not require significant resources.

[69] Eg de Schutter (n 64) 548f. This idea, of course, results from the fact that an internationally defined minimum core content does not account for differences between national contexts, which makes an alleged resource-independency for all countries too generalized. This could be considered differently in case of a nationally defined minimum core (as it exists in a number of states). For details on the interplay between an internationally and nationally defined minimum core content, Müller (n 11) 78ff, 133f.

[70] CESCR, 'General Comment No. 3' (n 59) para 10.

[71] Also David Bilchitz, *Poverty and Fundamental Rights* (OUP 2008) 208ff.

will be exponentially higher the closer the measure comes to the minimum core content. However, it does not enjoy absolute priority over the non-core content.[72] An ESCR approach to protracted conflicts indeed should contribute to sustainable solutions: measures which pursue a rather long-term reconstructive aim at the expense of a short-term full realization of the minimum core rights (eg spending money on reconstructing large-scale sustainable water infrastructure instead of providing large amounts of bottled water on a day-to-day basis) would not violate the HRtW if the general priority of the minimum core has been given due consideration in the decision.[73] Importantly, this balanced approach could also set limits regarding the modalities of reconstruction, if, for example, privatization would bring short-term benefits but predictably fail to achieve a sustainable water supply in the long term.

3. Limiting the HRtW in Case of Loss of Territorial Control?

These demands imply that the state still has territorial control and thus at least a certain level of capability in terms of the realization of ESCR. However, even if the state has lost control over certain areas, it principally remains bound by its obligations under IHRL, although they might be reduced in their scope according to its capacities.[74] The state retains negative obligations not to interfere with human rights in the non-controlled areas.[75] This might be important regarding sanctions issued by the ousted state regarding these territories but especially regarding the access to humanitarian assistance;[76] in a number of current protracted conflicts, ousted governments have obstructed humanitarian aid to non-controlled areas, such as Ethiopia's Tigray region or north-western Syria.

Other obligations of the state could include the prevention of ESCR violations, for example by adopting measures that mitigate socio-economic impairments caused by non-state entities in control of the territories;[77] or the cooperation with these entities for the benefit of the population in the non-controlled territories.[78] The extent to which the state still retains positive obligations to *provide* for ESCR when it does have some remaining capacities to maintain socio-economic service provision is still an evolving question in international law.[79] It is complicated by the fact that the state might be reluctant to fulfil these obligations due to strategic political considerations: for example, Ukraine blocked all water supply through the North Crimean Canal to Crimea after the commencement of Russian occupation of the peninsula in 2014. Arguably, here, the HRtW must set limits in that at least its minimum core content must be secured for

[72] ibid; Müller (n 11) 96ff.

[73] Also HRC 'Report of the Special Rapporteur' (n 54) para 54ff.

[74] *Ilaşçu and others* v *Moldova and Russia* ECHR 2004-VII para 313; for details Giacca (n 11) 116ff.

[75] Antal Berkes, *International Human Rights Law Beyond State Territorial Control* (CUP 2021) 79; Giacca (n 11) 126.

[76] Also Giacca (n 11) 125.

[77] *Catan and others* v *Moldova and Russia* ECHR 2012-V; Berkes (n 75) 114ff.

[78] Berkes (n 75) 122ff.

[79] Berkes (n 75) 125f; There seems to be no congruent doctrine of the CESCR on this yet either: Giacca (n 11) 124f.

people in the non-controlled areas at any time.[80] Meanwhile, the question of alternative or cumulative obligations of other entities engaging in aspects of socio-economic governance in areas of weak state capacity remains a pressing one. The obligations of non-state armed groups under ESCR, including the HRtW, have been much discussed but not entirely clarified yet in international law;[81] also, the obligations under the HRtW of peacekeeping forces, which might be present in these contexts as well, have been scarcely assessed so far.[82]

4. Integrating the Temporal Factor in the Assessment of Obligations under the Right to Water

After clarifying more generally the possibilities for limiting the HRtW during conflict, a particularly relevant question regarding protracted conflicts is the extent to which the prolonged duration of a situation of violence and insecurity might affect the obligations under the HRtW and other ESCR. A drawn-out conflict could have an effect in particular within the criterion of proportionality. It has already been suggested that varying degrees of intensity of the fighting during protracted conflicts should be observed within the proportionality criterion.[83] It could also be argued that regressive measures as well as the lack of positive measures to fulfil the right must increasingly be seen as disproportionate the longer the conflict continues.

A comparative view of the CESCR's Concluding Observations on states affected by long-term conflict could indicate a certain relevance of the time factor. In its Concluding Observations on Colombia of 1995 as well as 2001, under the section 'Factors and difficulties impeding the implementation of the Covenant', the Committee referred to the persistent armed conflict and simmering violence as a factor impeding the government from fulfilling its obligations under the Covenant.[84] In its Concluding Observations of 2010, under the same section, the CESCR explicitly did not find any circumstances preventing the state from fulfilling its obligations and furthermore stated that it was 'deeply alarmed about the consequences of the long-standing internal armed conflict in the State party'; moreover, it urged the Colombian state to take 'immediate and effective measures . . . to address the ongoing armed violence', reminding that 'it is precisely in situations of crisis, that the Covenant requires the protection and promotion of all economic, social and cultural rights'.[85] In its Concluding Observations on Sudan from 2000, the Committee recognizes that the ongoing armed conflict poses difficulties for the realization of ESCR by the Sudanese

[80] Marco Pertile and Sondra Faccio, 'Access to Water in Donbass and Crimea: Attacks against Water Infrastructures and the Blockade of the North Crimea Canal' (2020) 29 Review of European, Comparative and International Environmental Law 56, 63ff.

[81] For an in-depth account of possible ESCR obligations of armed non-state groups, Giacca (n 11) 230ff.

[82] Mara Tignino and Öykü Irmakkesen, 'Water in Peace Operations: The Case of Haiti' (2020) 29 Review of European, Comparative and International Environmental Law 33.

[83] Müller (n 11) 201–02.

[84] CESCR, 'Concluding Observations—Colombia' (28 December 1995) UN Doc E/C.12/1995/12 para 7; CESCR, 'Concluding Observations—Colombia' (6 December 2001) UN Doc E/C.12/1/Add.74 para 8.

[85] CESCR, 'Concluding Observations—Colombia' (7 June 2010) UN Doc E/C.12/COL/CO/5 para 7.

state.[86] In its Concluding Observations on Sudan from 2015, the CESCR does not mention armed conflict as an impediment but instead denounces the high military and security spending versus socio-economic spending and urges Sudan to 'invest every effort . . . to seek a sustainable settlement of the conflicts in the State party, reduce security and military spending and allocate more resources to the reconstruction of conflict-affected areas'.[87] A comparable shift in the language can be observed in the Concluding Observations on the Democratic Republic of the Congo: while in 2009 the CESCR acknowledged the limited ability of the state to fulfil ESCR due to persistent instability and recurrent conflict,[88] the CESCR in its recent Observations from 2022 urges the state to 'take all effective measures, without delay' to guarantee the enjoyment of ESCR in the regions affected by armed conflict.[89]

One must be cautious to deduce a consciously applied doctrine of the CESCR from statements in the Observations, since they are also contingent upon the informative value of the state reports and civil society contributions, which can fluctuate in terms of quantity and quality, especially in contexts of fragile institutional structures. However, the CESCR has also urged other states affected by longer-term conflict situations to find a quick and peaceful solution to the conflict, while pointing out the negative consequences that the conflict has for ESCR.[90]

That the extended duration of a conflict can make it more difficult to justify the non-fulfilment of ESCR also makes sense regarding the cascading negative effects of longer-term impairments of many socio-economic rights. These are especially evident regarding water access: a short-term restriction to the provision of only a minimum amount of water necessary to secure mere human survival[91] could be justified in exceptional circumstances of conflict. It might also be possible to scale down the requirements in terms of quality to ensure sufficient quantity of water in the short term.[92] However, if such retrogressive measures endure for long periods of time and are not complemented or supplanted by positive (mitigating) measures, they can have grave consequences: insufficient quantity or quality of water can, for example, cause deadly disease outbreaks or disrupt essential medical services. Thus, arguably, with an extending duration of a conflict, the leeway of the state to take retrogressive measures and to fail to progressively realize the HRtW must decrease.

[86] CESCR, 'Concluding Observations—Sudan' (1 September 2000) UN Doc E/C.12/1/Add.48 para 14ff.

[87] CESCR, 'Concluding Observations—Sudan' (27 October 2015) UN Doc E/C.12/SDN/CO/2 para 16.

[88] CESCR, 'Concluding Observations—Democratic Republic of the Congo' (16 December 2009) UN Doc E/C.12/COD/CO/4 para 6.

[89] CESCR, 'Concluding Observations—Democratic Republic of the Congo' (28 March 2022) UN Doc E/C.12/COD/CO/6 para 5.

[90] CESCR, 'Concluding Observations—Sri Lanka' (16 June 1998) UN Doc E/C.12/1/Add.24 para 21; CESCR, 'Concluding Observations—Cameroon' (25 March 2019) UN Doc E/C.12/CMR/CO/4 para 5.

[91] According to the World Health Organisation, 15 litres per person per day 'should be provided as soon as possible', while it might be possible in the 'immediate post-impact period' to limit the supply with (treated) water to a minimum of 7,5 litres, WHO, 'Water Sanitation and Health—Humanitarian Emergencies' <https://www.who.int/teams/environment-climate-change-and-health/water-sanitation-and-health/environmental-health-in-emergencies/humanitarian-emergencies> accessed 18 May 2023.

[92] HRC 'Report of the Special Rapporteur' (n 54) para 52.

D. Strengthening Accountability for a Lack of Clean Water in Protracted Conflicts

This chapter has suggested that the HRtW contributes to finding a sustainable approach to people's water supply in protracted conflicts. To strengthen the effectiveness of the HRtW in practice, it could be fruitful to integrate the HRtW more in investigatory efforts, urge international human rights bodies to focus more on protracted conflicts, and integrate the HRtW in international aid planning.

International investigatory mechanisms established regarding countries affected by protracted conflict could focus more on the state of realization of the HRtW.[93] UN Commissions of Inquiry, for example, generally tend to neglect ESCR (apart from those violations that overlap with international crimes).[94] Similarly, they rarely adopt a forward-looking perspective, which would mean not only stating violations but also commenting on potential progress in the realization of rights.[95] If these two points were addressed, these mechanisms could be helpful in providing an important factual basis for accountability under the HRtW in conflicts. The OSCE report issued on 12 April 2022, examining violations of IHRL and IHL and war crimes and crimes against humanity during the Russian aggression of Ukraine, could serve as a positive example here. The Mission of Experts explicitly addressed the impact of the conflict on the human rights to food and water and emphasized that even in the extreme situation of armed conflict states have not only negative but also positive obligations to prevent impairments on these rights.[96] Notably, the Mission specifically identified 'measures that Ukraine has adopted, or should adopt, to make this enjoyment [of ESCR] possible even in the extreme situation of armed conflict'.[97]

At the same time, long-term awareness and continuous monitoring could be furthered through ESCR enforcement mechanisms. For example, the Special Rapporteur on the rights to safe drinking water and sanitation could issue a thematic report addressing the issue of protracted conflicts. In addition, in-depth interpretive guidance on ESCR, including the HRtW, during protracted conflicts could be provided by a general statement of the CESCR on the issue, similar to the documents it produced regarding economic crises and sanctions. The scrutiny exercised through reporting procedures at the CESCR, but also the African Commission, could then foster long-term responsibility. Here, it would be important that the CESCR proceeds to explicitly consider the duration of conflicts to detect the structural nature of rights violations. To enable a more critical review of states' measures over time during conflict, significant

[93] Some have already addressed the issue of water supply explicitly, such as the Commission of Inquiry on Syria, which has referred to a lack of adequate water supply particularly regarding displaced and detained persons: HRC 'Report of the Independent International Commission of Inquiry on the Syrian Arab Republic' (28 January 2020) UN Doc A/HRC/43/57 paras 17, 64, 83, 96. Tignino (n 9) 87ff.

[94] Hun Joon Kim, 'Are UN Investigations into Human Rights Violations a Viable Solution? An Assessment of UN Commissions of Inquiry' (2019) 11 Journal of Human Rights Practice 96, 107.

[95] ibid.

[96] Wolfgang Benedek, Veronika Bílková, and Marco Sassòli, 'Report on Violations of International Humanitarian and Human Rights Law, War Crimes and Crimes Against Humanity Committed in Ukraine since 24 February 2022' (OSCE 2022) 73–74.

[97] ibid 68–69.

participation of civil society should be specifically promoted through 'shadow reporting' to the Committee.

In parallel, individual complaints mechanisms should be strengthened, which would especially require more state support for the Optional Protocol to the ICESCR.[98] In individual complaints, the structural nature of the violations can possibly be addressed less, but they allow the treaty body to specify in detail the obligations of the state regarding the HRtW in protracted conflicts on the basis of an individual case and to name violations more clearly as such. In comparison to the CESCR, which tends to refrain from clearly identifying violations in its state reports,[99] the African Commission within its individual complaint mechanism has already identified infringements upon the HRtW in conflicts on several occasions. For example, in *Free Legal Assistance v Zaire*, the Commission found that the government of Zaire violated the Convention because it failed to provide safe drinking water to the population during a time of unrest and violence in the country.[100]

Since in protracted conflicts water supply is often supported by international assistance, it is also important to note that for the sustainable fulfilment of the HRtW, short-term humanitarian and long-term development approaches to water provision should be better linked.[101] Here, it could be advantageous to orientate international aid planning towards the interrelation of the minimum core right, securing acute water needs, and the obligation of progressive realization, which brings a longer-term perspective. IHRL already has increasingly been integrated in development cooperation policies and to some extent also in humanitarian policies;[102] thus, singular human rights such as the HRtW could be envisaged as a common legal framework for water governance of these actors.[103] Most importantly, international donors should ensure the continuous provision of financial and other support to realize the HRtW in protracted conflicts. The ICESCR especially obliges those state parties that are in a position to do so to provide international assistance for and cooperation in the realization of ESCR in all countries.[104]

[98] Optional Protocol to the International Covenant on Economic, Social and Cultural Rights (adopted 10 December 2008, entered into force 5 May 2013) UN Doc A/RES/63/117 (Optional Protocol). The Optional Protocol that enables individual complaints to the body has by now only 26 state parties. However, complaints before other treaty bodies could also be considered: for example, a complaint could be issued before CEDAW, since art 14 CEDAW also contains aspects of the right to water.

[99] For details Nolan, Lusiani and Courtis (n 54) 126ff.

[100] *Free Legal Assistance Group and Others v Zaire* (11 October 1995) ACHPR 9, communication no 25/89, 47/90, 56/91, 100/93 para 47. Also, *Centre on Housing Rights and Evictions v The Sudan* (27 May 2009) ACHPR 100 communication no 296/05 para 212.

[101] Guy Jobbins, Steve Commins and Bryn Welham, 'Water Security in the Protracted Crises and Post-conflict Reconstruction of the Middle East' (ODI briefing note, April 2018) <https://cdn.odi.org/media/documents/12157.pdf> accessed 18 May 2023; Edoardo Borgomeo, 'Delivering Water Services during Protracted Armed Conflicts: How Development Agencies Can Overcome Barriers to Collaboration with Humanitarian Actors' (2020) 101 International Review of the Red Cross 1067.

[102] For the humanitarian sector: Sphere Association, *The Sphere Handbook: Humanitarian Charter and Minimum Standards in Humanitarian Response* (4th edn, Practical Action Publishing 2018) 162, 242, 94.

[103] See Ch. 17.

[104] eg CESCR, 'General Comment No. 15' (n 24) para 38.

19

Rights-Based Approaches to Land in Protracted Conflicts

Daniëlla Dam de-Jong

A. Introduction

Land performs key economic, social, cultural, and ecological functions for a wide range of stakeholders. It is therefore not surprising that disputes over the use and allocation of land are among the root causes of and triggers for armed conflicts. Such conflicts can be triggered by grievances over unequal distribution of land, such as shown by the conflicts in Guatemala between 1960 and 1996 and in Colombia between 1946 and 2016, but also by environmental degradation, resulting in communities challenging traditional arrangements on land tenure, such as is currently seen in the Sahel region in Africa.[1] According to a major study, 'land issues played a major role in all but three of the more than thirty intrastate conflicts that occurred between 1990 and 2009'.[2] Many of these conflicts are protracted in nature, in that they are characterized by prolonged periods of political instability and breakdown of public institutions, while the level of violence throughout the conflict is usually more irregular compared to traditional armed conflicts. This implies that there is a sense of normalcy within a highly volatile and unpredictable context.[3]

In such circumstances, resolving land disputes is a difficult task, but ultimately one that is essential for building resilience as a step towards peace.[4] A first complicating factor is that in many countries suffering from protracted armed conflicts, land registers have been destroyed or are not accessible, which makes it difficult for individuals and communities to prove ownership over plots of land when this ownership is challenged.[5] Furthermore, situations of prolonged armed conflict can trigger new land disputes, for instance because internally displaced persons occupy plots of land that

[1] United Nations Interagency Framework Team for Preventive Action, 'Land and Conflict: Toolkit and Guidance for Preventing and Managing Land and Natural Resources Conflict' (United Nations Interagency Framework Team for Preventive Action 2012) (hereafter United Nations Land and Conflict Toolkit). Also Jon Unruh and Rhodri C Williams, 'Lessons Learned in Land Tenure and Natural Resource Management in Post-conflict Societies' in Jon Unruh and Rhodri C Williams (eds), *Land and Post-conflict Peacebuilding* (1st edn, Routledge 2013) 545.

[2] United Nations Land and Conflict Toolkit (n 1) 14.

[3] For an analysis of the notion of protracted conflict: Ch. 1 Section B; further, Ellen Policinski and Jovana Kuzmanovic, 'Protracted Conflicts: The Enduring Legacy of Endless War' (2019) 912 International Review of the Red Cross 965.

[4] United Nations Secretary-General (UNSG) 'Guidance Note on the United Nations and Land and Conflict' (United Nations 2019) 4.

[5] United Nations Land and Conflict Toolkit (n 1).

Daniëlla Dam de-Jong, *Rights-Based Approaches to Land in Protracted Conflicts* In: *From Protracted Conflict to Sustainable Peace?* Edited by: Heike Krieger, Giedre Jokubauskaite, Asli Ozcelik, and Andreas Buser, Oxford University Press.
 DOI: 10.1093/9780198967385.003.0023

belong to local communities or because armed groups drive individuals and communities away from their land.[6] Lastly, due to the institutional vacuum created by years or even decades of conflict, the functions of governmental institutions are often in practice performed by local actors (including warlords), international and regional organizations, and humanitarian agencies. Given the diverging (legal and social) positions of these actors and the various normative frameworks that regulate their activities, there is a considerable risk that the degree and type of protection that is provided to the civilian population will depend on whoever is controlling and/or operating in the relevant region. This creates disparities between communities and enhances instability.

Considering these challenges, this chapter takes the position that there is a need to adopt an approach that places people at its core and that provides guidance to de jure and de facto authorities alike on how to address land disputes for the purpose of relieving tensions between communities and individuals. More specifically, this chapter explores whether and to what extent human rights-based approaches can perform this function. Human rights-based approaches, which can be defined as 'conceptual framework[s] that [are] normatively based on international human rights standards and operationally directed to promoting and protecting human rights',[7] place individuals and communities at the centre of decision-making, which makes them at first face highly suitable for addressing land disputes. It is also precisely for this reason that such approaches have gained considerable traction in international policy in recent years. They constitute the foundation of the 2030 Agenda for Sustainable Development and are one of the principal pillars for United Nations (UN) engagement on land and conflict in fragile settings.[8] Given their prominence in international policy, this chapter aims to assess their merits for addressing disputes over land uses in protracted conflicts. It will argue that rights-based approaches are indeed valuable tools for addressing land disputes in protracted armed conflicts, due to their facilitative nature and the safeguards that such approaches provide to individuals and communities. However, rights-based approaches are mostly 'gap-fillers' for situations in which there are impediments to the direct application of international human rights law (IHRL). For the purpose of developing this argument, section B will first set out the international human rights law framework applied to the protection of land rights. Section C will then critically discuss the characteristics of rights-based approaches. This

[6] ibid.

[7] This definition is based on the UN's definition, as adopted in the context of sustainable development: United Nations Sustainable Development Group, 'United Nations Sustainable Development Cooperation Framework' (June 2019) https://unsdg.un.org/resources/united-nations-sustainable-development-cooperation-framework-guidance accessed 5 November 2024 (thereafter UN Sustainable Development Cooperation Framework) 13.

[8] United Nations General Assembly (UNGA) Res 70/1 'Transforming Our World: the 2030 Agenda for Sustainable Development' (25 September 2015) UN Doc A/RES/70/1. It should be noted that the rights-based approach goes back to the 1990s and therefore considerably predates Agenda 2030. However, the latter is the first sustainable development framework that expressly relies on human rights. See ibid, third preambular paragraph (which states that the Sustainable Development Goals 'seek to realize the human rights of all') and operative paragraph 10 (which states that the Agenda 'is grounded in the Universal Declaration of Human Rights, international human rights treaties'). For the UN's approach to land and conflict in fragile settings, United Nations Secretary-General (UNSG) 'Guidance Note on the United Nations and Land and Conflict' (United Nations 2019).

discussion will set the stage for a more focused analysis of rights-based approaches as applied to selected categories of land disputes in the context of protracted armed conflicts in section D. Finally, section E will offer some final reflections on the merits of a rights-based approach to land in protracted conflicts.

B. Human Rights Pertaining to Land

This section examines the IHRL framework that applies to the protection of land users for the purpose of defining the contours of a rights-based approach to land. As a starting point, it should be noted that there is no autonomous human right to land in international law. Yet, because of the many functions that land performs, access to land is arguably an important precondition for the fulfilment of a wide range of human rights. A first key connection between land and human rights relates to food production. According to the UN's Food and Agriculture Organization (FAO), almost half of the global land surface is used for agriculture, with about one-third used as cropland and two-thirds for grazing livestock.[9] For rural communities, access to land can therefore be regarded as a precondition for the realization of the right to life under Article 6 of the International Covenant on Civil and Political Rights (ICCPR) and of the rights to an adequate standard of living and to health under Articles 11 and 12 of the International Covenant on Economic, Social and Cultural Rights (ICESCR). Second, access to land is crucial for the enjoyment of the right to housing, as protected through Article 11 of the ICESCR on the right to an adequate standard of living and Article 17 of the ICCPR on the right to be free from arbitrary or unlawful interference with privacy, family, home, or correspondence. A third key connection between land and human rights relates to the cultural and spiritual significance of land for particular communities. This connection is particularly pronounced for indigenous peoples. As their ancestral lands are closely connected to their identity and traditional lifestyles, infringements on their lands affect their right to self-determination under Article 1 of the ICCPR and their right to enjoy their culture under Article 27 of the ICCPR.[10]

The connections between land and human rights have furthermore received specific articulation in several important non-binding standard-setting instruments, such as the UN Declarations on the Rights of Indigenous Peoples and on the Rights of Peasants, which both recognize the special bonds that such communities have with land and provide substantive and procedural safeguards to such communities, including protection against forced displacement and a right to participate in

[9] Food and Agriculture Organization of the United Nations (FAO), 'Sustainable Food and Agriculture' (*Food and Agriculture Organization of the United Nations*, 7 May 2020) <https://www.fao.org/sustainability/news/detail/en/c/1274219/> accessed 5 November 2024.

[10] There is a rich case law by the Human Rights Committee connecting Article 27 to Article 1 of the ICCPR on the right to self-determination in relation to indigenous peoples. See for instance the landmark case of *Apirana Mahuika et al. v New Zealand* (15 November 2000) Communication No. 547/1993. For a more thorough analysis of indigenous peoples' land rights, Federico Lenzerini, 'The Land Rights of Indigenous Peoples under International Law' in Michele Graziadei and Lionel Smith (eds), *Comparative Property Law: Global Perspectives* (Elgar 2017) 393; and Jérémie Gilbert, *Indigenous Peoples' Land Rights Under International Law: From Victims to Actors* (2nd ed, Brill 2016).

decision-making.[11] Mention should also be made of the guidelines that the FAO developed in relation to the role of land in food production. Most relevant from a human rights perspective are the 2004 Voluntary Guidelines to Support the Progressive Realization of the Right to Adequate Food in the Context of National Food Security, which call on states to promote and protect the security of land tenure and to establish legal and other policy mechanisms that advance land reform to enhance access for marginalized groups,[12] and the 2012 Voluntary Guidelines on the Responsible Governance of Tenure of Land, Fisheries and Forests in the Context of National Food Security, which contain express provisions addressing land tenure in situations of armed conflict. Most importantly, guideline 25 addresses both States and other parties, requiring them inter alia 'to respect and protect existing legitimate tenure rights and guarantee that these are not extinguished by other parties' in situations of armed conflict, while also containing detailed guidance on the question of land rights of refugees and displaced persons.[13]

Finally, the Committee on Economic, Social and Cultural Rights (CESCR) adopted a General Comment on land in 2023. This General Comment No. 26 addresses the relationship between land and economic, social, and cultural rights in great depth, also building on the land-specific standard-setting instruments mentioned in this section.[14] The General Comment, which is in itself not legally binding, aims to clarify states' obligations that relate to land under relevant provisions of the ICESCR, including the rights to food, water, and housing as integral to the right to an adequate standard of living (Article 11). Relevant obligations identified by the CESCR include both positive and negative obligations.[15] Negative obligations imply a duty to not interfere with the exercise of a right (obligation to respect). In relation to land, such obligations include an obligation to respect the tenure rights of individuals or communities over land, to respect the special connection that indigenous peoples have with their lands, and to refrain from displacing individuals or communities from their lands.[16] Positive obligations on the other hand imply a duty to take action to protect against infringements by third parties, including corporations (obligation to protect)

[11] United Nations Declaration on the Rights of Indigenous Peoples, UNGA Res 61/295 (2 Oct 2017) (adopted by 143 votes to 4, 11 abstentions) and United Nations Declaration on the Rights of Peasants and Other People Working in Rural Areas (UNHRC Res 39/12 (28 September 2018) UN Doc A/HRC/RES/39/12).

[12] FAO Council, *Report by the Intergovernmental Working Group for the Elaboration of a Set of Voluntary Guidelines to Support the Progressive Realization of the Right to Adequate Food in the Context of National Food Security* (23 September 2004) (adopted by the 127th Session of the FAO Council, November 2004) CL 127/10-Sup.1, Guideline 8B.

[13] FAO, *Voluntary Guidelines on the Responsible Governance of Tenure of Land, Fisheries and Forests in the Context of National Food Security* (revised edition, FAO May 2022) Guideline 25.

[14] Committee on Economic, Social and Cultural Rights (CESCR) 'General Comment No. 26 on Land and Economic, Social and Cultural Rights' (24 January 2023) UN Doc E/C.12/GC/26.

[15] On the concept of negative and positive obligations, Dinah Shelton, *The Oxford Handbook of International Human Rights Law* (OUP 2013) 562.

[16] CESCR, 'General Comment No. 26 on Land and Economic, Social and Cultural Rights' (24 January 2023) UN Doc E/C.12/GC/26, paras 16 and 21 for indigenous peoples and paras 22 and 23 more generally. Although not specifically mentioned in the General Comment, as it addresses only the connections between land and economic, social, and cultural rights, it should be noted that similar obligations ensue from Articles 17 and 27 of the ICCPR. In this sense, the Covenants therefore complement and reinforce each other.

and more generally to create appropriate conditions for the exercise of rights (obligation to fulfil).[17] In relation to land, relevant obligations include a duty to recognize existing land rights, for instance by issuing deeds or concessions that prove ownership over land and by protecting land registries, to take measures (including the adoption of legislation) to protect individuals and communities against infringements of their tenure rights by third parties (including corporations), to ensure that members of local communities are properly informed about, and allowed to meaningfully participate in, decision-making processes that affect them, and to remove and prohibit discrimination related to tenure rights.[18]

All these instruments, whether hard or soft law, provide together the foundation for rights-based approaches to land. Before assessing the merits of such approaches in the context of specific land disputes that are prevalent in protracted armed conflicts, the following section will critically discuss the principal characteristics of rights-based approaches and the purposes that they can fulfil in the context of protracted armed conflicts.

C. Defining Rights-Based Approaches to Land in the Context of Protracted Armed Conflicts

While section B has set out relevant obligations stemming from IHRL, the current section elaborates on the function of rights-based approaches in potentially enhancing protection of land rights in the context of protracted armed conflicts. It should first be noted that—even though they are now applied in other contexts as well—rights-based approaches emerged in the context of development cooperation and sustainable development policies.[19] Their primary aim was to strengthen the position of those on the receiving end: they would no longer be seen as mere beneficiaries but as holders of rights which could be claimed.[20] The UN definition set out in the introduction must therefore also be appreciated from this perspective. The current section will examine

[17] Dinah Shelton, *The Oxford Handbook of International Human Rights Law* (OUP 2013) 562.

[18] ibid paras 20, 26–31 and 32–39. Similar obligations apply in the context of the ICCPR. See for instance United Nations Human Rights Committee (HRCttee) 'General Comment No. 23: Article 27 (Rights of Minorities)' (8 April 1994) UN Doc CCPR/C/21/Rev.1/Add.5, para 7, where the Committee observes that 'culture manifests itself in many forms, including a particular way of life associated with the use of land resources, especially in the case of indigenous peoples . . . The enjoyment of those rights may require positive legal measures of protection and measures to ensure the effective participation of members of minority communities in decisions which affect them'. The prohibition of discrimination is especially important in light of widespread gender inequalities, which make it extremely difficult for women to have equal access to land, eg for food production. Furthermore, even if their tenure rights are recognised, they often have difficulties obtaining credit to purchase equipment, which results in significantly lower production rates compared to men. FAO, International Fund for Agricultural Development (IFAD), and International Labour Organization (ILO), *Gender Dimensions of Agricultural and Rural Employment: Differentiated Pathways Out Of Poverty* (FAO, IFAD, ILO 2010).

[19] For an overview, Andrea Cornwall and Celestine Nyamu-Musembi, 'Putting the "Rights-Based Approach" to Development into Perspective' (2004) 25(8) Third World Quarterly 1415; Morten Broberg and Hans-Otto Sano, 'Strengths and Weaknesses in a Human Rights-based Approach to International Development—An Analysis of a Rights-based Approach to Development Assistance based on Practical Experiences' (2018) 22(5) The International Journal of Human Rights 664.

[20] ibid.

this definition, which, as may be recalled, is as follows: 'conceptual framework[s] that [are] normatively based on international human rights standards and operationally directed to promoting and protecting human rights.'[21] The purpose of this discussion is to assess the strengths and weaknesses of using rights-based approaches in the context of protracted armed conflicts compared to legal approaches to human rights proper on the one hand and governance-based approaches on the other. This discussion functions as a preliminary assessment of their suitability for resolving land disputes in the midst of an armed conflict. Whether and to what extent they are indeed suitable frameworks for this purpose will be tested in section D, which provides a more in-depth analysis of the application of rights-based approaches to common land disputes in protracted armed conflicts.

As regards the characteristics of rights-based approaches, it is first of all crucial to distinguish between rights-based approaches and the application of international human rights law (IHRL) as a legal framework. The UN definition clearly sets rights-based approaches apart from legal approaches to human rights, both in terms of their scope and objectives. First, the definition prioritizes an understanding of rights-based approaches as relying on moral or ethical imperatives instead of legal obligations proper. It does so by underlining that rights-based approaches are conceptual frameworks, which are based on standards instead of obligations. Understood in this way, rights-based approaches take relevant standards from international human rights law (IHRL) as a baseline to guide the actions of relevant actors, without inquiring whether such standards represent legally binding obligations for them. They take as their reference that 'plans, policies and processes . . . are anchored in a system of rights and corresponding obligations established by international law',[22] including important principles underlying all human rights, such as equality and non-discrimination, participation, and accountability.[23] In other words, rights-based approaches seek to base policies and regulations on the principles and values underpinning human rights law, without relying directly on IHRL as a normative and institutional framework.[24]

Second, by articulating that rights-based approaches are 'operationally directed to promoting and protecting human rights',[25] the definition underscores on the one hand that human rights protection is the main objective of rights-based approaches while on the other moving away from a discourse of accountability proper. In fact, as also expressed in the UN cooperation framework itself, rights-based approaches primarily 'focus on capacity development of both "duty-bearers" to meet their obligations and "rights-holders" to claim their rights'.[26] Rights-based approaches are therefore primarily facilitative and focus on empowerment of rights-holders and duty-bearers. The use in the UN cooperation framework of inverted commas for the notions duty-bearers and right-holders furthermore confirms a more flexible understanding of these categories, as focusing primarily on power relations instead of legal

[21] UN Sustainable Development Cooperation Framework (n 7) 13.
[22] ibid.
[23] ibid.
[24] Hope Johnson, *International Agricultural Law and Policy: A Rights-Based Approach to Food Security* (Elgar 2018) 47, discussing rights-based approaches in the context of food security.
[25] UN Sustainable Development Cooperation Framework (n 7) 13.
[26] ibid.

relations. In this understanding, the concept of duty-bearer applies to all actors that are in a position of control over territory or individuals, whether or not they are formally bound by IHRL.

For the purposes of this chapter, rights-based approaches are therefore understood to encompass two dimensions: they seek to enhance the capacities of rights-holders to claim rights and of duty-bearers to protect and promote human rights, while also serving as conceptual frameworks to enhance human rights protection as a moral imperative. Compared to legal approaches, rights-based approaches are therefore much more flexible. This can be considered both a strength and a weakness in the context of their application in protracted armed conflicts.

A major strength of the more flexible approach that rights-based approaches bring is that they impose normative expectations on actors that are in a position to exercise control over individuals and communities regardless of the question of whether these actors are formally bound by the underlying obligations. This is of the utmost importance for situations of protracted armed conflict, since IHRL only formally imposes obligations on governmental authorities and not on armed opposition groups.[27] Over the years, UN bodies such as the Security Council, the General Assembly, and the Human Rights Council have developed a rich practice seeking to hold armed groups to account for human rights abuses,[28] without however settling the question of whether such groups are considered legally bound by IHRL. Interestingly, a 2021 Joint Statement by more than forty independent UN human rights experts does not take a clear position either, speaking of responsibilities rather than obligations and stating the importance of the effective implementation of existing international legal protections, 'irrespective of the status or character of the perpetrator(s)'.[29] Rights-based approaches can help to overcome these uncertainties, precisely because they have a more flexible understanding of the notion of duty-bearers, which is based on exercise of control instead of formal criteria.

Another strength of the flexibility of rights-based approaches in the context of protracted armed conflicts is their focus on capacity development, both in relation to right-holders to make their claims, and in relation to duty-bearers to meet their obligations.[30] In relation to right-holders, capacity-building seeks to empower individuals and communities through access to information, participation in decision-making, and access to remedies, whether these are provided by courts or by quasi-judicial bodies such as grievance mechanisms. The focus on capacity development as a

[27] See eg Katharine Fortin *The Accountability of Armed Groups under Human Rights Law* (OUP 2017), who discusses competing theories on the source of human rights obligations for armed groups.

[28] See eg Jessica Burniske, Naz Modirzadeh, and Dustin Lewis, 'Armed Non-State Actors and International Human Rights Law: An Analysis of the Practice of the U.N. Security Council and U.N. General Assembly, Briefing Report with Annexes' (2017) Harvard Public Law Working Paper No. 17-37 <https://papers.ssrn.com/sol3/papers.cfm?abstract_id=2994907> accessed 8 November 2024; and Annyssa Bellal, *Human Rights Obligations of Armed Non-State Actors: An Exploration of the Practice of the UN Human Rights Council* (Geneva Academy of International Humanitarian Law and Human Rights 2016).

[29] Office of the High Commissioner for Human Rights (OHCHR), 'Joint Statement by Independent United Nations Human Rights Experts on Human Rights Responsibilities of Armed Non-State Actors' (Press Release, 25 February 2021) <https://www.ohchr.org/en/press-releases/2021/02/joint-statement-independent-united-nations-human-rights-experts-human-rights#_ftn3> accessed 8 November 2024.

[30] UN Sustainable Development Cooperation Framework (n 7) 13.

facilitative framework instead of applying the law as a set of normative obligations is especially helpful in situations of protracted armed conflict, where capacities are reduced due to governance failures caused by prolonged violence and the dismantling of institutional structures, making it difficult in practice for affected persons to assert their rights against their government as primary duty-bearers under IHRL. In relation to States, the focus on capacity development makes rights-based approaches key tools for international organizations and civil society to support them in upholding their human rights obligations, for instance by providing assistance in setting up land registries. Furthermore, they provide an entry-point to promote other actors, such as armed groups, operating in a human rights-compliant way.

Rights-based approaches also present other strengths in the context of protracted armed conflicts. As already explained in the introduction, protracted armed conflicts are characterized by periods of active hostilities alternated by periods of relative calm. This implies that these conflicts are partly governed by international humanitarian law (IHL) as the primary applicable legal framework governing the conduct of hostilities.[31] In these contexts, rights-based approaches may help to ensure that IHL obligations are applied against the backdrop of relevant human rights standards, thereby ensuring a degree of consistency in the applicable legal framework throughout the conflict. This is especially important as there are important differences between the operation of IHRL and IHL in relation to the protection of persons. Whereas IHL is mostly concerned with protecting groups (notably civilian populations and other persons who do not participate directly in hostilities), IHRL instead primarily provides protection to individuals. Rights-based approaches will therefore ensure that the interests of individuals will be taken into consideration in the application of IHL obligations, most notably through the cross-cutting principle of equality and non-discrimination.

It is precisely for these reasons that rights-based approaches may perform important functions in preventing and resolving land disputes in protracted armed conflicts. However, the flexibility of rights-based approaches also presents weaknesses in the context of protracted armed conflicts compared to the direct application of IHRL. First, as will be shown in the following section, the focus on capacity development falls short when duty-bearers are themselves complicit in human rights violations. In these circumstances, there is a need for the institutional framework of IHRL to step in to promote accountability. Furthermore and related to this concern is the focus of rights-based approaches on standards instead of obligations, which may promote an understanding of IHRL as based on moral imperatives instead of legal obligations. The risk with this understanding is that the actual obligations of actors are obscured, thereby undermining IHRL as a legal framework. It is for these reasons that rights-based approaches are arguably best suited as complementary frameworks to

[31] The relationship between IHL and HRL has been the subject of numerous studies, with scholars taking various positions in relation to their co-applicability. For an overview of the most important streams of the debate, Marko Milanovic, 'The Lost Origins of Lex Specialis: Rethinking the Relationship between Human Rights and International Humanitarian Law' in Jens Ohlin (ed), *Theoretical Boundaries of Armed Conflict and Human Rights* (Cambridge University Press 2016) 78. For a more thorough discussion, Daragh Murray and others, *Practitioners' Guide to Human Rights Law in Armed Conflict* (Oxford University Press 2016).

overcome challenges in the direct application of IHRL. This argument will be developed in section D.

So far, this section has compared rights-based approaches to the direct application of IHRL. However, rights-based approaches were primarily introduced as an alternative to governance-based or 'needs-based' approaches.[32] The principal difference between these approaches is that governance-based approaches seek to enhance emancipation and reduce existing inequalities by relying primarily on quantifiable targets which actors must strive to achieve,[33] while rights-based approaches in contrast are grounded in normative imperatives focused on the protection of human dignity.[34] Criticisms regarding the use of rights-based compared to governance-based approaches or other types of emancipatory processes are wide-ranging, with some being more persuasive than others. The remainder of this section will discuss these, while arguing that they do not affect the inherent value of rights-based approaches.

A first criticism contends that the vocabulary of 'rights' may 'distort the way projects are imagined and framed for international consideration'.[35] In a way, a focus on rights may indeed take attention away from other value systems that are relevant for land governance, such as those underlying customary land tenure systems. For instance, the Tara Bandu system in Timor Leste is largely based on community ownership of land, with areas designated for annual cultivation of food crops.[36] Individual group members are granted rights to farm a specific plot, but only for one cultivation period, after which the land reverts back to communal property.[37] Such a system may be a difficult fit for the traditional human rights framework, which favours the individual over the community. However, it is not irreconcilable with it. Communal land ownership has been recognized in all the major human rights systems and its importance is even articulated in the CESCR's General Comment No 26 on land, where the Committee states that the obligation to fulfil entails an obligation for States to 'recognize the social, cultural, spiritual, economic, environmental and political value of land for communities with customary tenure systems and [to] respect existing forms of

[32] Andrea Cornwall and Celestine Nyamu-Musembi, 'Putting the "Rights-Based Approach" to Development into Perspective' (2004) 25(8) Third World Quarterly 1415; Morten Broberg and Hans-Otto Sano 'Strengths and Weaknesses in a Human Rights-based Approach to International Development – An Analysis of a Rights-based Approach to Development Assistance Based on Practical Experiences' (2018) 22(5) The International Journal of Human Rights 664.

[33] Jaye Ellis and Dylan Edmonds, 'Coming to Terms with the SDGs: A Perspective from Legal Scholarship' (2023) 36 Leiden Journal of International Law 251.

[34] Ginevra Le Moli, *Human Dignity in International* Law (CUP 2021) chapter 5 on the relationship between international human rights law and the notion of human dignity. She argues that one can discern three main levels of relationships between human dignity and human rights, namely human dignity as a foundation of human rights, as the foundation and object of rights, and as the basis of specific obligations.

[35] David Kennedy, *The Dark Sides of Virtue: Reassessing International Humanitarianism* (Princeton University Press 2005) 9. Also Martti Koskenniemi, 'Human Rights Mainstreaming as a Strategy for Institutional Power' (2010) 1(1) Humanity: An International Journal of Human Rights, Humanitarianism, and Development 47; and Robert Dickinson and others (eds) *Examining Critical Perspectives on Human Rights* (CUP 2012).

[36] Naori Miyazawa, 'Customary Law and Community-based Natural Resource Management in Post-conflict Timor-Leste' in Jon Unruh and Rhodri C. Williams (eds), *Land and Post-conflict Peacebuilding* (1st edn, Routledge 2013) 524.

[37] ibid.

self-governance of land'.[38] Likewise, the idea that the rights of individuals sometimes need to give way to the rights of communities is not alien to the traditional human rights framework. By way of example, reference can be made to the *Kitok v Sweden* complaint before the Human Rights Committee, in which the right of individuals of indigenous origin to enjoy their culture by engaging in traditional practices was made subordinate to the right of the community to decide for themselves who had the right to engage in such practices.[39]

However, more fundamentally, one may indeed contend that the human rights vocabulary, which is essentially about formulating entitlements for individuals and communities against designated duty-bearers, does not only emancipate, as human rights advocates argue, but may also pit actors against each other, to the detriment of a broader sense of a shared destiny that spans various communities within a State.[40] This problem is reinforced in situations in which several individuals or communities compete for the same scarce goods, such as land. In these situations, rights need to be balanced against each other, with the 'minimum core obligation' setting the standard.[41] Seeing their 'rights' (partly) unfulfilled may lead to frustration, as the general idea is that rights give rise to entitlements which can be claimed. Other vocabularies, such as those relating to governments' responsibility to provide basic services to the population, do not have such connotations. At the same time, such vocabularies leave much discretion to the government, and they lack essential safeguards that human rights provide, such as equality, non-discrimination, participation, and accountability. Arguably, it is precisely because of these safeguards that rights-based approaches may prevent new grievances. This argument will be further developed in section D.2, when discussing disputes over land between local communities.

A criticism with respect to IHRL more generally is that the State is placed at the core of the emancipatory process.[42] Especially in situations in which the elites that control the State have themselves been complicit in human rights violations, such as dispossession of land, or where the State is at the root of the problem, such as in situations in which a conflict was triggered by inequalities in land distribution policies, this reliance on the State may only entrench existing power structures that are no longer considered legitimate by the individuals and communities that suffered the consequences. This problem is hard to get by, yet it is at the same time not a challenge that is unique to IHRL. Rights-based approaches, in contrast to the use of IHRL as a normative framework, may actually be useful here as they go beyond the traditional duty-bearers in IHRL and may equally be applied with respect to other actors, such as armed groups with effective control over territory or other authorities at the sub-state level.

[38] CESCR, 'General Comment No. 26 on Land and Economic, Social and Cultural Rights' (24 January 2023) UN Doc E/C.12/GC/26, para 35. For a more in-depth analysis of community property rights, Jérémie Gilbert, *Natural Resources and Human Rights: An Appraisal* (OUP 2018) 34–62.

[39] Human Rights Committee, *Ivan Kitok* v *Sweden* (27 July 1988) Communication No. 197/1985.

[40] David Kennedy, *The Dark Sides of Virtue: Reassessing International Humanitarianism* (Princeton University Press 2005) 17.

[41] This minimum core obligation merely seeks 'to ensure the satisfaction of, at the very least, minimum essential levels of each of the rights', which is in itself not sufficient to realise the rights. CESCR 'General Comment No. 3: The Nature of States Parties' Obligations (Art. 2, Para. 1, of the Covenant)' (14 December 1990) UN Doc E/1991/23, para 10.

[42] ibid.

Overall, it therefore seems that rights-based approaches may provide a relatively suitable framework for resolving land disputes in the midst of protracted armed conflicts. The following section will test this assumption within the context of three types of land disputes.

D. Assessing the Merits of Rights-Based Approaches to Land in Protracted Armed Conflicts

This section further explores opportunities, challenges, and limitations of rights-based approaches to land in the context of protracted armed conflicts. It discusses three types of land disputes that are common in protracted armed conflicts and which were already mentioned in the introduction. These are: unequal distribution of land as a root cause of armed conflicts; localized conflicts between tenure holders over the use of land; and forceful removal of communities during armed conflicts.[43] The objective of the discussion is to determine the role that rights-based approaches could play in addressing these disputes, either applied autonomously or in conjunction with other relevant international legal regimes, most importantly IHL. It is argued that rights-based approaches can play a useful role as a secondary framework, to be applied alongside IHRL where possible.

1. Land as a Root Cause of Armed Conflict

A first type of land dispute concerns inequalities in land distribution as one of the root causes of armed conflicts. While such inequalities are never the sole reason explaining the outbreak of an armed conflict, lack of access to land, insecurity of tenure, and weak enforcement of tenure rights by the government can create tensions that, if combined with other social, ethnic, or religious tensions, can easily spark violence. The rise of the Revolutionary Armed Forces of Colombia (FARC), for instance, was connected to widespread inequalities in land distribution and the government's inaction in stopping large landowners from forcefully dispossessing peasants.[44]

What characterizes such situations is that individuals and communities do not have adequate access to the land they need to support their livelihoods, with the State either absent or complicit in these infringements. The connections between the infringements and the ongoing armed conflict are mostly indirect, in the sense that they have

[43] This section will leave out the special case of disputes between displaced persons and secondary occupants. Although highly relevant in practice, such disputes can only be settled once the conflict has been brought to an end.

[44] The role of land as a root cause of armed conflict in Colombia has been recognised in the 2016 peace agreement, which states in the preamble that 'in the opinion of the FARC-EP, [the] transformations [that the agreement should bring] must contribute to solving the historical causes of the conflict, such as the unresolved issue of land ownership, particularly its concentration, the exclusion of campesino populations and the lack of development in rural communities, which affects women and children in particular'. UNSC 'Letter dated 29 March 2017 from the Secretary-General addressed to the President of the Security Council' (21 April 2017) UN Doc S/2017/272, 5 (Annex II, Final Agreement for Ending the Conflict and Building a Stable and Lasting Peace).

contributed to, but are not caused by or part of the hostilities. This implies that IHL—which regulates the conduct of parties to an armed conflict—does not play a role in these disputes. Instead, IHRL is the primary international legal regime for addressing such disputes, with states as primary duty-bearers.

Relevant standards under IHRL include states' obligation to fulfil the right to an adequate standard of living, which requires them to take measures to address existing inequalities in access to land as a productive resource. This is a binding obligation, but only as a matter of progressive realization.[45] According to the CESCR, relevant measures furthermore include a duty to 'support agrarian reform schemes that ensure adequate access to land, particularly for small-scale peasants who depend on access to land for their livelihoods'.[46] For this purpose, states 'should include adequate safeguards [in policies and laws] against land reconcentration following reform, such as land ceiling laws and legal safeguards to protect the collective and customary tenure of land'.[47] Where the duty to support agrarian reforms can be understood as a legally binding obligation, the inclusion of safeguards against land reconcentration is formulated in a more open-ended manner, as can be derived from the use of the word 'should'. This is equally so in relation to compensation, where the CESCR expresses the need for states in post-conflict situations to grant transformative reparations to victims of violence, including 'policies and measures aimed at reducing inequality and improving those persons' standard of living'.[48]

Rights-based approaches can play a helpful role in resolving these disputes, as such approaches provide relevant entry-points and parameters for international organizations and civil society to work with the government on land-related issues as part of efforts towards resolving the conflict or, at the very least, to address persistent inequalities as one of the factors underpinning the armed conflict. However, given the role that governments have played in the infringements underlying the disputes, rights-based approaches are in themselves not sufficient. The institutional framework of IHRL also has an important role to play. The relevant obligations and standards are subject to regular monitoring by the CESCR. Indeed, to return to Colombia as a relevant example, the CESCR repeatedly expressed its concern about the unequal distribution of lands and the absence of a genuine agrarian reform, while consistently calling on the Colombian government to address these issues as part of its obligations pursuant to Article 11 of the ICESCR.[49] Even though the Colombian government

[45] CESCR, 'General Comment No. 26 on Land and Economic, Social and Cultural Rights' (24 January 2023) UN Doc E/C.12/GC/26, para 37 ('States shall use the maximum available resources to progressively realize the rights under the Covenant relating to accessing productive resources').

[46] ibid.

[47] ibid.

[48] ibid para 51.

[49] CESCR, 'Concluding Observations on Colombia' (28 December 1995) UN Doc E/C.12/1995/12, para 7, where the Committee noted that the violence in the country was 'in part brought about by serious inequalities in society, such as enormous disparaties in the distribution of national wealth, including land ownership'; CESCR, 'Concluding Observations on Colombia' (6 December 2001) UN Doc E/C.12/1/Add.74, paras 23 and 44, where the Committee expressed its deep concern about the government's failure to undertake 'genuine agrarian reform in order to address effectively the problems of poverty and economic disparities in the rural areas' and urged 'the State party to adopt the necessary measures to carry out genuine agrarian reform'; and CESCR, 'Concluding Observations on Colombia' (7 June 2010) UN Doc E/C.12/COL/CO/5, para 22, where the Committee repeated its concerns and recommendations.

admitted itself that the results of the agrarian reform programme that it had adopted in the early 2000s were poor, it did report to the CESCR on measures that it had taken in reponse to these concerns.[50] Human rights-based land reform was subsequently included in the 2016 peace agreement between the government and the FARC as an important priority.[51] In this sense, IHRL can provide a useful framework for promoting accountability, by exerting the necessary pressure on States to report on the measures that they have taken to satisfy their human rights obligations, while rights-based approaches can play an important function as a secondary framework in promoting human rights compliance through their focus on capacity development.

2. Localized Conflicts between Legitimate Tenure Holders

Whereas section D.1 focused on situations in which grievances over government policies with respect to land tenure provide a trigger for an armed conflict between the government and armed groups, this section focuses on disputes between communities over land tenure that turn violent within the context of a protracted armed conflict. The armed conflict that raged in Darfur (Sudan) between 2003 and 2020 provides a relevant example. According to Buchanan-Smith and Bromwich, this conflict must be understood as one consisting of three layers:

> At the local level, the conflict is taking place between different ethnic groups or groups with different livelihood strategies, each competing for power and access to natural resources. At the national level, the conflict is between Darfuri rebel groups and the political leadership of the federal government in Khartoum . . . At the wider regional level, the conflict involves Sudan's neighboring countries.[52]

[50] Economic and Social Council, 'Implementation of the International Covenant on Economic, Social and Cultural Rights: Fifth periodic reports submitted by States parties under articles 16 and 17 of the Covenant (Colombia)' (9 January 2009) UN Doc E/C.12/COL/5, particularly paras 730–731. Also Ben McKay, Flavio Bladimir Rodríguez Muñoz, and Darío Fajardo, 'The Voluntary Guidelines on the Responsible Governance of Tenure of Land, Fisheries and Forests in the Context of National Food Security in Colombia: Towards Democratic Land-based Resource Control' International Institute of Social Studies (ISS) Colloquium Paper No. 19, 15–20 <https://www.iss.nl/sites/corporate/files/19-ICAS_CP_McKay_et_al.pdf> accessed 14 March 2025. For a critique of Colombia's legislation, Various Authors, 'Parallel Report to the Fifth Report of the Colombian State to Committee on Economic, Social and Cultural Rights (E./C.12/COL/5)' (March 2010) Colombian Platform for Human Rights, Democracy and Development <https://www.ecoi.net/en/file/local/1313554/1228_1281708777_plataforma-colombia44.pdf>. Land rights are discussed in relation to the rights to food and housing and in separate chapters on peasantry and other marginalised groups.

[51] UNSC 'Letter dated 29 March 2017 from the Secretary-General Addressed to the President of the Security Council' (21 April 2017) UN Doc S/2017/272, 5 (Annex II, Final Agreement for Ending the Conflict and Building a Stable and Lasting Peace) 9 ('Comprehensive rural reform must bring about the great transformation of the rural situation in Colombia by promoting greater inclusion at the regional level, poverty eradication and equality, *and it must guarantee the full enjoyment of citizens' rights*'). Emphasis added.

[52] Margie Buchanan-Smith and Brendan Bromwich, 'Preparing for Peace: An Analysis of Darfur, Sudan' in Carl Bruch, Carroll Muffett and Sandra S. Nichols (eds), *Governance, Natural Resources, and Post-Conflict Peacebuilding* (1st edn, Routledge 2016) 168.

The focus of this section is on the local level. The principal differences between these localized conflicts within the broader context of protracted armed conflicts and those discussed in section D.1 are therefore related to the conflict protagonists and the role of land in the conflict. This also has implications for the role that rights-based approaches play in these situations. Most relevant here is the obligation to protect human rights, most importantly the rights to life, to an adequate standard of living, and to culture (as linked to self-determination). Pursuant to the obligation to protect, States and—based on the more flexible approach that rights-based approaches offer—de facto authorities are required to take measures to protect individuals and communities from infringements of their rights by third parties, including other communities and individuals.

However, where land rights are contested and statutory and customary titles to land overlap or are unclear, the primary role of duty-bearers is—in the words of the CESCR—to 'provide mechanisms for the adequate settlement of those disputes, making every effort to satisfy the right to land of both groups'.[53] In protracted armed conflicts, the capacities of States in providing such mechanisms may have been seriously reduced. Moreover, the role of States in providing constructive solutions may be compromised. Even if the disputes are between local communities *inter se* and not between communities and the government, these disputes often do play out in a broader context. The multi-layered conflict in Darfur is a highly pertinent example. In this context, rights-based approaches to land may be particularly helpful in two respects. First, in situations where capacities are reduced due to the conflict, rights-based approaches may play a role in developing the capacities of the government to provide effective mechanisms for the resolution of land disputes. Second, where the government itself cannot play a constructive role, rights-based approaches may be used to design alternative mechanisms at the sub-state or inter-community level. Since entities operating at these levels (including armed groups in control of territory) are not always formally bound by IHRL, the use of rights-based approaches may help to fill that gap. Arguably, a strength of rights-based approaches compared to governance-based approaches is furthermore that they contain procedural safeguards, most importantly equality and non-discrimination on the one hand and participation of the affected individuals and communities on the other. These safeguards ensure that the process is perceived as fair and that the views of the respective communities are properly taken into consideration in the design of the mechanisms. These aspects are crucial for preventing frustration within communities when they must give up on part of their claims to ensure that the rights of others are respected. In this way, the use of rights-based approaches may therefore help to prevent new grievances among and within communities.

[53] CESCR, 'General Comment No. 26 on Land and Economic, Social and Cultural Rights' (24 January 2023) UN Doc E/C.12/GC/26, para 19.

3. Displacement Caused by the Armed Conflict

A third type of land dispute relates to displacement of civilians caused by the armed conflict. Such displacement can be voluntary or forced. This section will focus on the forced removal of communities and individuals from their lands as a direct consequence of the armed conflict. For instance, many contemporary armed conflicts, such as those in Sierra Leone around the turn of the century and in the Democratic Republic of the Congo from the 1990s onwards, have seen parties to the conflict taking control of territory to access valuable natural resources located therein.[54] Forced removal may however also occur for reasons more directly related to hostilities. For this type of land dispute, the existence of an armed conflict is therefore material for the violence to occur: the displacement is prompted by the armed conflict itself. This also implies that IHL is the primary legal framework governing such violence, with the parties to the armed conflict as duty-bearers both for the purposes of IHL and IHRL.

IHL contains several obligations pertaining to land, including for non-international armed conflicts. The most relevant obligations in this respect are article 49 of Geneva Convention IV (GCIV) and article 17 of Additional Protocol II (APII), which prohibit parties to an armed conflict from ordering the displacement of the civilian population for reasons related to the conflict. This prohibition is subject to the exception that the displacement is demanded by the security of the civilians involved or imperative military reasons and to the condition that all possible measures are taken 'in order that the civilian population may be received under satisfactory conditions of shelter, hygiene, health, safety and nutrition'.[55] These provisions, which are considered to reflect customary international law,[56] therefore provide civilians protection against measures taken by parties to an armed conflict—whether armed groups or State authorities—that would deny them access to their lands, including the safeguard that displaced individuals and communities are received under satisfactory conditions.

The question thus arises whether the use of rights-based approaches to interpret these provisions has additional value compared to the protection that is already provided by IHL. In some respects, IHL arguably provides equally strong or even stronger protection than IHRL. For instance, Article 17 of the ICCPR, which is relevant for displacement as it requires States not to engage in interferences with the right to respect for privacy, family, home, and correspondence, does not contain any safeguards for persons that have been displaced, nor has the Human Rights Committee hinted

[54] See eg. Human Rights Watch, 'Sierra Leone: Sowing Terror: Atrocities against Civilians in Sierra Leone' (29 June 1998) < https://www.hrw.org/report/1998/07/29/sowing-terror/atrocities-against-civilians-sierra-leone>; and Office of the High Commissioner for Human Rights (OHCHR) 'Report of the Mapping Exercise Documenting the Most Serious Violations of Human Rights and International Humanitarian Law Committed Within the Territory of the Democratic Republic of the Democratic Republic of the Congo Between March 1993 and June 2003' (August 2010) <https://www.ohchr.org/sites/default/files/Documents/Countries/CD/DRC_MAPPING_REPORT_FINAL_EN.pdf>.

[55] Protocol Additional to the Geneva Conventions of 12 August 1949, and relating to the Protection of Victims of Non-International Armed Conflicts (adopted 8 June 1977, entered into force December 1978) 1125 UNTS 609 (Protocol II), Art 17.

[56] Rule 129 of the ICRC's customary IHL study. Jean-Marie Henckaerts and Louise Doswald-Beck, *Customary International Humanitarian Law* (Vols I & II, International Committee of the Red Cross, CUP 2005).

at the need to establish such safeguards in its General Comment on the provision. Instead, the Committee consistently refers to the non-binding Guiding Principles on Internal Displacement in its concluding observations, which contain protections that are comparable to those provided by IHL.[57] I nevertheless argue that rights-based approaches can play two important roles in the interpretation and application of the relevant IHL provisions. First, the principle of non-discrimination may provide an additional safeguard for ensuring that a party to an armed conflict does not differentiate between communities based on their affiliation. In the context of land, this implies that a party to an armed conflict cannot deny access to land to communities that are somehow associated with the adversary while providing access to communities that are loyal to them. Second, rights-based approaches can play an important role in relation to the interpretation of the notion of 'satisfactory conditions' in Article 49 of GCIV and Article 17 APII,[58] based on the standards developed in IHRL with respect to the rights to life, an adequate standard of living, and health. As such, humanitarian actors, such as the International Committee of the Red Cross, could rely on rights-based approaches to refine the protection provided by the IHL rules.

E. Assessing the Merits of Rights-Based Approaches to Land in the Context of Protracted Armed Conflicts

This chapter set out to assess the merits of rights-based approaches for addressing disputes over land in protracted armed conflicts, based on the observation that access to land is a precondition for the realization of a wide range of human rights, whether related to subsistence needs, housing, or culture. It presented rights-based approaches as flexible and facilitative frameworks that apply to actors regardless of whether they are formally bound by relevant obligations under IHRL, and that focus on capacity development while firmly rooted in normative expectations based on IHRL. Understood as such, rights-based approaches can play a useful role in addressing root causes of armed conflicts, such as inequalities in land distribution policies, alongside IHRL. By emphasizing that States have actual obligations to reduce inequalities in a non-discriminatory way, rights-based approaches provide a comprehensive framework for international organizations and civil society to work with the State on reforming its policies. Likewise, rights-based approaches provide essential safeguards for setting up institutional mechanisms to mediate between communities over land use rights, ensuring that the process is regarded as fair by those involved. In relation to

[57] See eg. HRCttee, 'Concluding Observations on the Fourth Periodic Report of the Democratic Republic of the Congo' (30 November 2017) UN Doc. CCPR/C/COD/CO/4, para 26. Also United Nations Office for the Coordination of Humanitarian Affairs (OCHA), 'UN Guiding Principles on Internal Displacement' (2004) <https://www.unhcr.org/media/guiding-principles-internal-displacement>.

[58] Protocol Additional to the Geneva Conventions of 12 August 1949, and relating to the Protection of Victims of Non-International Armed Conflicts (adopted 8 June 1977, entered into force December 1978) 1125 UNTS 609 (Protocol II), Art 17 and Geneva Convention relative to the Protection of Civilian Persons in Time of War (adopted 12 August 1949, entered into force 21 October 1950) 75 UNTS 287, Art 49.

displacement caused by armed conflict, the standards provided by IHRL may furthermore provide parameters for the interpretation and application of the relevant IHL obligations.

However, rights-based approaches also come with limitations. When governments are complicit in rights violations, rights-based approaches are too open-ended. In these situations, it is necessary to exert normative pressure on the State through the institutional mechanisms (monitoring bodies, courts) established by IHRL. Likewise, since IHL already contains obligations for parties to an armed conflict in relation to displacement of civilians, the added value of rights-based approaches to the protection provided by IHL against forced removal of communities is minimal. These limitations should however not detract from the significance of rights-based approaches for addressing land disputes. Such approaches may play a crucial role in complementing IHRL when capacities are limited or when the actors that are in the best position to realize the rights of individuals and communities are themselves not formal duty-bearers under IHRL. Both of these factors are prevalent in situations of protracted armed conflict, since these are often characterized by the breakdown of institutions and competing actors exercising control over territory. For these reasons, I argue that it is critical to embed rights-based approaches in the programming, design, and implementation of international interventions.

20

Indigenous Peoples' Land Rights and Peacemaking

The Minoritization of the Lumads in the Bangsamoro Peace Processes

Armi Beatriz E. Bayot

A. Introduction

Long before the separatist armed conflict in the southern Philippine island of Mindanao threw the region into decades of seemingly intractable violence, its inhabitants—the Lumads and the Moros, or the Bangsamoro—had already endured years of government neglect, underdevelopment, and unjust laws and policies dating from the US colonial administration in the early twentieth century. 'Lumad' is the Cebuano term for 'native' or indigenous, used by various indigenous peoples in Mindanao to refer to themselves.[1] Estimates of the number of Lumad groups in Mindanao range from eighteen to thirty.[2] 'Bangsamoro,' on the other hand, means Moro 'nation'.[3] This term encompasses the thirteen native ethnolinguistic groups in Mindanao who converted to Islam,[4] which arrived in the thirteenth and fourteenth centuries in Mindanao through the arrival of Sunni Arab missionaries.[5]

The US colonial government sought to flatten these unique identities and heritages through the establishment of the Bureau of Non-Christian Tribes, which was tasked with 'civilizing' and assimilating the native indigenous peoples across the Philippines

[1] Adopted as a common name by delegates from various ethnolinguistic groups during the Lumad Mindanao People's Federation Assembly in 1986: Arnold P Alamon, *Wars of Extinction: Discrimination and the Lumad Struggle in Mindanao* (Rural Missionaries of the Philippines Northern Mindanao Sub-Region (RMP-NMR), Inc 2017) 9–10; Rudy B Rodil, 'The Tri-People Relationship and the Peace Process in Mindanao' (1997) XII The Mindanao Forum 1, 1.

[2] For instance Oona Paredes, 'Indigenous vs. Native: Negotiating the Place of Lumads in the Bangsamoro Homeland' (2015) 16 Asian Ethnicity 166, 168; Ma Arve B Bañez, 'Poverty, War and Peace: Lumad and Muslim Women's Issues in Mindanao' (*University of the Philippines*, 28 May 2019) <https://up.edu.ph/poverty-war-and-peace-lumad-and-muslim-womens-issues-in-mindanao/> accessed 12 March 2025. Rodil notes that the names of Lumad groups and their numbers is unsettled, and that the census of Lumads is inconsistent due to their very inaccessibility and exclusion: Rudy B Rodil, 'The Lumad and Moro of Mindanao' (Minority Rights Group 1993) 9.

[3] Antonio La Viña, 'The Creation of the Bangsamoro: Issues, Challenges, and Solutions' (2013) 2 Philippine Law and Society Review 3, 12.

[4] ibid 27; Mely Caballero-Anthony, 'Revisiting the Bangsamoro Struggle: Contested Identities and Elusive Peace' (2007) 3 Asian Security 141, 146.

[5] Carmen A Abubakar, 'The Advent and Growth of Islam in the Philippines' in KS Nathan and Mohammad Hashim Kamali (eds), *Islam in Southeast Asia* (ISEAS Publishing 2005) 48.

Armi Beatriz E. Bayot, *Indigenous Peoples' Land Rights and Peacemaking* In: *From Protracted Conflict to Sustainable Peace?*
Edited by: Heike Krieger, Giedre Jokubauskaite, Asli Ozcelik, and Andreas Buser, Oxford University Press.
 DOI: 10.1093/9780198967385.003.0024

to a mainstream Philippine national identity.[6] The US colonial government also instituted land registration laws that did not fully recognize the diverse customary land tenure systems in various parts of the Philippines, which resulted in widespread dispossession among the Lumads and the Moros.[7] A series of government resettlement programmes that brought in settlers from other parts of the Philippines exacerbated this dispossession.[8] The eventual establishment of extractive business ventures such as mining, logging, and agriculture-based businesses took resources out of Mindanao yet did little to improve the welfare of the majority of its inhabitants.[9] Through all this, Mindanao was, and is, underrepresented in central government positions and received less investment in public goods and services than the rest of the Philippines.[10]

These political and economic conditions in Mindanao have contributed to the high incidence of conflict and armed violence in the region,[11] and have fuelled resentment among its Moro inhabitants.[12] This resentment came to a head in 1972 when the Moro National Liberation Front launched an armed campaign for Bangsamoro independence in response to a series of violent attacks by the Philippine military and Christian vigilante groups against Moros and Moro communities.[13] In 1976, the Moro National Liberation Front signed the Tripoli Agreement with the Philippine government, the first major Bangsamoro peace agreement signed after the height of hostilities in the early 1970s.[14] The breakaway Moro Islamic Liberation Front took up the cause of Bangsamoro independence even after the conclusion of this agreement. The armed conflict has since evolved into a series of protracted peace processes which saw the claim for Bangsamoro independence shift to a focus on Bangsamoro autonomy. Peace negotiations lasted almost forty years and were interrupted many times by several major outbreaks of violence, until the signing of the Comprehensive Agreement on the Bangsamoro signalled the formal end of hostilities in 2014.[15]

[6] Philippine Commission Act No. 253, An Act Creating a Bureau of Non-Christian Tribes for the Philippine Islands (2 October 1901).

[7] Owen J Lynch, *Colonial Legacies in a Fragile Republic: A History of Philippine Land Law and State Formation with Emphasis on the Early U.S. Regime, 1898–1913* (University of the Philippines College of Law 2011) 412.

[8] Eric Gutierrez and Saturnino Borras, 'The Moro Conflict: Landlessness and Misdirected State Policies' (East-West Center Washington 2004) Policy Studies 8, 7–13; Miriam Coronel Ferrer, 'The Philippine State and Moro Resistance: Dynamics of a Persistent Conflict' in Miriam Coronel Ferrer, *Costly Wars, Elusive Peace: Collected Articles on the Peace Processes in the Philippines 1990–2007* (University of the Philippines Press 2013) 47.

[9] Gutierrez and Borras (n 8); Patricio N Abinales, 'War and Peace in Muslim Mindanao: Critiquing the Orthodoxy' in Paul D Hutchcroft (ed), *Mindanao: The Long Journey to Peace* (Anvil Publishing, Inc. 2016) 52–54.

[10] Abinales (n 9) 46–59; Coronel Ferrer (n 8) 39–41.

[11] Gutierrez and Borras (n 8) 2–5.

[12] Syed Serajul Islam, 'The Islamic Independence Movements in Patani of Thailand and Mindanao of the Philippines' (1998) 38 Asian Survey 441, 445, 448.

[13] Coronel Ferrer (n 8) 50; Soliman M. Santos, 'War and Peace on the Moro Front: Three Standard Bearers, Three Forms of Struggle, Three Tracks (Overview)' in Diana Rodriguez (ed), *Primed and Purposeful: Armed Groups and Human Security Efforts in the Philippines* (South-South Network for Non-State Armed Group Engagement and the Small Arms Survey 2010) 70.

[14] The Tripoli Agreement dated 23 December 1976.

[15] 21 years of negotiation with the Moro National Liberation Front and 17 years of negotiation with the Moro Islamic Liberation Front: Armi Beatriz E Bayot, 'Elite Bargains and Political Deals Project: Philippines Case Study' (United Kingdom Stabilisation Unit 2018) 5.

Both the Moro National Liberation Front and the Moro Islamic Liberation Front have held on to a foundational claim throughout the long years of peace negotiations: that the Bangsamoro are a people entitled to the right to self-determination *and* to reclaim a Moro homeland or ancestral domain that had been lost to colonial and post-colonial governments. This claim eventually became legitimized in the course of successive peace processes, with various peace negotiation documents and, eventually, laws and Supreme Court decisions reflecting the notion of Bangsamoro self-determination and ancestral domain. The early claims to a Moro homeland formed the basis of the list of provinces over which the Moro autonomous region would be established.[16]

There is a glaring problem with the seemingly uncritical legitimization of this claim—the scope of the territory claimed by the Bangsamoro armed groups as belonging to the Bangsamoro coincides with many of the Lumads' own ancestral domains. Indeed, the Lumads' own narratives have become obscured by the looming shadow of the Bangsamoro armed conflict, and many Lumads have found themselves within the Bangsamoro autonomous region where Bangsamoro goals, aspirations, and way of life take precedence. Lumads have long sought legal recognition of their claims to their own ancestral domains within the Bangsamoro autonomous region. The inaction of both the national government and the regional government on these claims has left many Lumads dispossessed of their lands or otherwise unable to use them meaningfully. Already minoritized in the context of the Philippines' general population, the Lumads are now 'second-order minorities' compared to the dominant Moros in the Bangsamoro autonomous region.

Despite the formal end of hostilities, it is apparent that structural violence persists in the region, particularly with regard to the Lumads. The mere absence of armed violence does not constitute peace, and Johan Galtung's proposition that peace features both a negative component (the absence of personal violence) and a positive component (the absence of structural violence) requires that assertions of a state of peace must be examined, both as to its existence and its quality, with regard to these negative and positive components.

This chapter examines how the same peace processes that facilitated the formal end of armed conflict prevented, and continue to prevent, the establishment of positive peace in Mindanao. Section B demonstrates how exclusionary power-sharing agreements are incompatible with positive peace, especially when positive peace is understood as the existence of governance structures compatible with international human rights law. Section C shows how negotiating power-sharing with the Bangsamoro armed groups entrenched notions of Bangsamoro ancestral domain and self-determination. Section D examines how the Lumads have fared under the Moro-led regional governments that were created as a result of the Bangsamoro peace processes. The chapter ends by linking the elusiveness of positive peace in Mindanao to the lasting legacy of power-sharing in peacemaking.

[16] Tripoli Agreement (n 14).

B. Power-Sharing Agreements as Exclusionary Bargains

Power-sharing is a model of governance usually deployed in deeply divided societies wherein major ethnic, linguistic, and/or religious groups are represented and participate in governance in order to manage potential (or existing) intergroup tension. It is widely used in the negotiated settlement of intrastate armed conflicts[17] (or conflicts between a government and a non-state armed group or groups relating to political incompatibility occurring within a single state jurisdiction).[18] In power-sharing peace agreements, these incompatibilities are addressed through mechanisms such as consociation (power-sharing by communities through proportionality formulas and group autonomy),[19] territorial self-governance (power-sharing by territorially compact communities through federal or territorial autonomy arrangements),[20] and what Wolff refers to as 'complex power-sharing', which combines elements of territorial self-government with other power-sharing methods.[21] Power-sharing has been used in various peacemaking efforts in a wide range of conflict contexts, including Bosnia and Herzegovina, Lebanon, Northern Ireland, Sudan, Macedonia, and the Philippines.[22]

Power-sharing as a peacemaking strategy is exclusionary by design. Because the imperative behind peacemaking efforts is to manage or stabilize conflict, power-sharing arrangements in peace agreements focus on the demands and interests of what are deemed 'politically significant' groups or those communities whose participation in the peace process is deemed crucial to the resolution of the armed conflict,[23] such as the non-state armed groups themselves who are active conflict protagonists. The participation of other 'veto players', or those who have the ability to obstruct a peace agreement if excluded, is also deemed vital to peace processes.[24] On the other hand, the participation of groups that are deemed not politically significant, such as those who have no capacity to destabilize the state through military means or through the mobilization of large popular bases, is not essential to get to the peace deal. Indeed, it has even been argued that the inclusion of more parties than is strictly necessary to conclude a peace deal could be counter-productive to peace processes,[25] and in the logics of peacemaking, getting to the peace deal is paramount.

[17] Chandra Lekha Sriram, *Peace as Governance: Power-Sharing, Armed Groups and Contemporary Peace Negotiations* (2008) 17–26.

[18] Uppsala University Department of Peace and Conflict Research, 'UCDP Definitions—Uppsala University' (29 May 2024) <https://www.uu.se/en/department/peace-and-conflict-research/research/ucdp/ucdp-definitions> accessed 12 June 2025.

[19] Consociational theory as used in comparative politics and peacemaking is primarily associated with Arend Lijphart, see for instance Arend Lijphart, *Democracy in Plural Societies* (Yale University Press 1977).

[20] Sriram (n 17) 23–24.

[21] Stefan Wolff, 'Complex Power-Sharing and the Centrality of Territorial Self-Governance in Contemporary Conflict Settlements' (2009) 8 Ethnopolitics 27, 28–31.

[22] Laura Wise, 'Territorial Power-Sharing and Inclusion in Peace Processes' (University of Edinburgh Political Settlements Research Programme 2018) <https://www.pure.ed.ac.uk/ws/portalfiles/portal/64563830/Territorial_Power_Sharing_Report.pdf> accessed 7 March 2025.

[23] Timofey Agarin and Allison McCulloch, 'How Power-Sharing Includes and Excludes Non-Dominant Communities: Introduction to the Special Issue' (2020) 41 International Political Science Review 3, 12–15.

[24] Nina Caspersen, *Peace Agreements: Finding Solutions to Intra-State Conflicts* (Polity Press 2017) 97.

[25] The exclusion of certain other parties and groups from peace negotiations has also been justified as the appropriate exclusion of so-called peace-process spoilers, defined by Stephen Stedman as those who believe that peace threatens their power, worldview, and interests and who will thus seek to undermine attempts to

Power-sharing peace agreements, however, do more than secure a negative peace—they provide the blueprint for governance in a conflict-affected state for years and decades to come. In securing a negative peace through the deliberate exclusion of many, power-sharing peace agreements fail to reflect the interests of all political stakeholders within a state and infringe on the rights of entire groups of excluded people, ultimately preventing the establishment of positive peace.

1. Framing Positive Peace within International Human Rights Law

The mere cessation of hostilities between conflict protagonists absent broader equitable societal conditions is generally not regarded as constitutive of a comprehensive peace either by peace and conflict scholars or by international instruments pertaining to peace. The 2016 United Nations General Assembly Declaration on the Right to Peace, for instance, enjoins states to 'enhance the principles of freedom from fear and want, equality and non-discrimination and justice and rule of law as a means to build peace within societies'.[26] While the declaration itself seems to conceive of peace as negative peace, with reference to the 'determination of the peoples of the United Nations to live together in peace' 'to save succeeding generations from the scourge of war',[27] it nevertheless refers to the 1999 Declaration and Programme of Action on a Culture of Peace, which states that 'peace is not only the absence of conflict, but also requires a positive, dynamic participatory process where dialogue is encouraged and conflicts are solved in a spirit of mutual understanding and cooperation'.[28] This indicates that the establishment of peace, as envisioned by the UN General Assembly, requires states to undertake measures enhancing equality, justice, and inclusivity.

The thinking that peace requires a community-wide system or structure, such as a well-functioning state government, that ensures equality, inclusivity, and justice is reflected in the work of Galtung, Turan, and other peace scholars as well, particularly in their work on what constitutes positive peace. Galtung has described positive peace as social justice or a system where conflict is addressed without recourse to violence and where power and resources are equitably distributed.[29] Even other scholars' more modest conceptions of positive peace refer to positive peace as the existence of horizontal equality,[30] acceptance of the rights of others, equitable distribution of resources,[31] and harmonious relations among groups.[32] These conditions are

achieve this peace: Patrick Meehan, 'What Are the Key Factors that Affect the Securing and Sustaining of an Initial Deal to Reduce Levels of Armed Conflict?' (UK Stabilisation Unit 2018) 16–17.

[26] UN Doc A/RES/71/189 (19 December 2016) Article 2.

[27] UN Doc A/RES/71/189 (19 December 2016) Preamble.

[28] UNGA Declaration and Programme of Action on a Culture of Peace, UN Doc. A/RES/53/243 (1999) Preamble.

[29] Johan Galtung, 'Violence, Peace, and Peace Research' (1969) 6 Journal of Peace Research 167, 183.

[30] Tuba Turan, 'The 2016 UN General Assembly Declaration on the Right to Peace: A Step towards Sustainable Positive Peace within Societies?' (2023) 23 Human Rights Law Review 1, 2.

[31] As among pillars of positive peace in 'Positive Peace Report 2022: Analysing the Factors That Build, Predict and Sustain Peace' (Institute for Economics & Peace 2022) 8.

[32] Richard Caplan, 'Conceptualizing Peace' in Richard Caplan, *Measuring Peace* (Oxford University Press 2019) 21.

arguably constitutive of the kind of political order made possible when states uphold international human rights norms pertaining to political participation, equality and non-discrimination, and the rights of historically disenfranchised groups such as indigenous peoples and women, among others.

Considering the universality of international human rights law,[33] it can be argued that human rights law is in fact the primary legal and normative framework for positive peace. Hvidsten and Skarstad note that the political practice of peacebuilding, which includes rebuilding national institutions in the wake of armed conflict,[34] entails restoring social contracts between the state and the people. International human rights law contains norms that govern the relationship between governments and people, and the restoration of social contracts between them ought to be guided by confidence-building principles contained in international human rights law such as justice and equality.[35] A comprehensive peace, one characterized by both negative peace and positive peace, can only be realized in human rights-compliant states where effective systems and structures uphold citizens' rights and regulate conflict through non-violent means. When examined against the normative framework of international human rights law, the exclusionary power-sharing governments that are put in place by power-sharing peace agreements fall short.

2. Incompatibility of Power-Sharing with Positive Peace

In granting benefits to dominant groups that are denied to non-dominant ones and in privileging particular non-state armed groups over other would-be political actors, community leaders, and other stakeholders, power-sharing agreements are at odds with international human rights law and, consequently, create obstacles to positive peace. For instance, the creation of state reordering institutions exclusively by political elites and dominant groups without broader public participation is undemocratic on its face. While the existence of a 'right to democracy' continues to be debated,[36] it can be argued that democratic governance is nevertheless the kind of governance envisioned in international human rights law.[37]

Basic democratic principles, that is, the will of the people as the source of government authority, popular sovereignty, and all citizens having the opportunity to participate equally in the political life of their societies, animate both the right of peoples to self-determination and the rights of individuals to political participation

[33] Reading the United Nations Charter (adopted 24 December 1945) 1 UNTS XVI, article 55 and article 56 with the Universal Declaration of Human Rights (adopted 10 December 1948) UNGA Res 217 A(III) (UDHR), see Nigel Rodley, 'International Human Rights Law' in Malcolm D Evans (ed), *International Law* (Oxford University Press 2018) 776; see also Vienna Declaration and Programme of Action (12 July 1993) UN Doc. A/CONF.157/23.

[34] For instance An Agenda for Peace (8 October 1993) UN Doc. A/RES/47120B.

[35] Andreas H Hvidsten and Kjersti Skarstad, 'The Challenge of Human Rights for Peace Research' (2018) 10 International Theory 98, 101.

[36] For instance Susan Marks, 'What Has Become of the Emerging Right to Democratic Governance?' (2011) 22 European Journal of International Law 507.

[37] For instance 'Democracy' in Steven Wheatley, *Democracy, Minorities and International Law* (Cambridge University Press 2005).

and representation in Article 25 of the International Covenant on Civil and Political Rights (ICCPR).[38] Indeed, the right to democratic choice of government is confirmed in Article 21 of the Universal Declaration of Human Rights (UDHR),[39] which states that '[t]he will of the people shall be the basis of the authority of government', which is to be made known through periodic and genuine elections.

The conscious trade-off of a peace deal negotiated by a few to benefit a few is likewise incompatible with norms of equality and non-discrimination. Equality and non-discrimination are among the fundamental principles that animate international human rights law.[40] The UDHR states that individuals are entitled to their rights under the instrument 'without distinction of any kind, such as race, colour, sex, language, religion, political or other opinion, national or social origin, property, birth or other status'.[41] Equality and non-discrimination are not only a requirement in the enjoyment of the rights listed in the UDHR, as article 7 imposes a substantive positive obligation on UN member states with regard to non-discrimination. Equality and non-discrimination are further upheld in the 1966 human rights covenants, particularly in article 2(1) and article 26 of the ICCPR.[42] Similar non-discrimination provisions can be found in regional human rights instruments.[43]

When peace processes exclude non-politically significant or non-dominant groups such as indigenous peoples, their existing, long-standing marginalization is perpetuated and even exacerbated, in violation of their rights to meaningful political participation in international law. The United Nations Declaration on the Rights of Indigenous Peoples (UNDRIP) provides that indigenous peoples' have 'the right to participate in decision-making in matters which would affect their rights'.[44] The UNDRIP further recognizes the right of indigenous peoples to self-determination, and it also requires states to provide effective mechanisms for the prevention of, and redress for, any action which has the aim or effect of dispossessing indigenous peoples of their lands, territories, or resources.[45]

[38] International Covenant on Civil and Political Rights (adopted 16 December 1966, entered into force 23 March 1976) 999 UNTS 171 (ICCPR).

[39] Universal Declaration of Human Rights (adopted 10 December 1948) UNGA Res 217 A(III) (UDHR).

[40] Daniel Moeckli, 'Equality and Non-Discrimination' in Daniel Moeckli and others (eds), *International Human Rights Law* (Oxford University Press 2018) 148.

[41] Universal Declaration of Human Rights (adopted 10 December 1948) UNGA Res 217 A(III) (UDHR) article 2.

[42] International Covenant on Civil and Political Rights (adopted 16 December 1966, entered into force 23 March 1976) 999 UNTS 171 (ICCPR); see also International Covenant on Economic, Social and Cultural Rights (adopted 16 December 1966, entered into force 3 January 1976) 993 UNTS 3, articles 2(1) and 3.

[43] Including African Charter on Human and Peoples' Rights (adopted 27 June 1981, entered into force 21 October 1986) (1982) 21 ILM 58, articles 2, 3, 18(3)–(4) and 28; American Convention on Human Rights (adopted 22 November 1969, entered into force 18 July 1978) 1144 UNTS 123, articles 1 and 24; Arab Charter on Human Rights (adopted 15 September 1994) articles 2, 9, 35; Association of Southeast Asian Nations Human Rights Declaration (adopted 18 November 2012) articles 1, 2, 3, and 9; and European Convention on Human Rights (adopted 4 November 1950, entered into force 3 September 1953) article 14 and Protocol No. 12.

[44] United Nations Declaration on the Rights of Indigenous Peoples (adopted 2 October 2007) UN Doc A/RES/61/295, article 18.

[45] ibid article 3 and article 8 (2)(b).

3. The Exclusionary Legacy of Power-Sharing

Peace agreements are projects in 'societal reconstruction', in the words of Chinkin,[46] given the way that they establish the future political and legal framework of many conflict-affected states. Yet many post-agreement governments are predominantly composed of members of non-state armed groups or the dominant groups they claim to represent, with this preferential access to power translating to the long-term exclusion of many groups from the post-agreement political order.[47] The experiences of non-dominant groups in Bosnia and Herzegovina, Sudan, and Nepal are introduced briefly here as cases in point beyond Mindanao, the Philippines.

The Dayton Peace Agreement, for example, provides for power-sharing in government institutions among three main ethnic groups (Bosniac, Serb, and Croat nations), and this arrangement is institutionalized in the Constitution of Bosnia and Herzegovina.[48] Successive European Court of Human Rights decisions, beginning with the 2009 case of *Sejdic and Finci v Bosnia and Herzegovina*,[49] have ruled that the continued ineligibility of otherwise qualified candidates who did not belong to the main ethnic groups for key government posts, including the Presidency, pursuant to this power-sharing arrangement violates Article 14 of European Convention on Human Rights[50] on the prohibition of discrimination (in conjunction with Article 3 of Protocol No. 1 on the right to free elections for a legislature, as well as Article 1 of Protocol No. 12 on the general prohibition of discrimination). All of these judgments have remained unenforced,[51] and the exclusionary power-sharing institutions remain.

Sudan's contentious peace process did not extend the benefits of the Comprehensive Peace Agreement (CPA) of 2005 to the Nuba indigenous people. Despite the Nuba opposition leadership having allied themselves with the SPLM/A in 1985 in their armed conflict against the Sudanese government,[52] the Nuba people's claims, particularly regarding their identity, traditional lands, and resources, were ultimately sacrificed by the SPLM/A to gain concessions from the Sudanese government in peace negotiations. The CPA left the Nuba people out of a (then) potential independent South Sudan and under the authority of the government against which it had waged armed conflict for years.[53]

[46] Christine M Chinkin, 'Gender, Human Rights, and Peace Agreements' (2003) 18 Ohio State Journal of Dispute Resolution 867, in the context of gender mainstreaming in peace processes.

[47] Sriram (n 17) 27–28.

[48] Annex 4 of the Dayton Peace Agreement, signed 14 December 1995.

[49] *Sejdic and Finci* v *Bosnia and Herzegovina*, No. 27996/06 and 34836/06, EctHR (Grand Chamber), 22 December 2009.

[50] European Convention on Human Rights (adopted 4 November 1950, entered into force 3 September 1953).

[51] Lidia Bonifati, 'Much Ado about Nothing? Ten Years on from the Sejdić and Finci Case' (*IACL-IADC Blog*, 19 December 2019) <https://blog-iacl-aidc.org/2019-posts/2019/12/19/much-ado-about-nothing-ten-years-on-from-the-sejdi-and-finci-case> accessed 13 June 2025.

[52] Guma Kunda Komey, 'Land Factor in Wars and Conflicts in Africa: The Case of the Nuba Struggle in Sudan' [2010] War and Peace in Africa 351, 366–69.

[53] Guma Kunda Komey Kalo, 'The Comprehensive Peace Agreement and the Questions of Identity, Territory and Political Destiny of the Indigenous Nuba of the Sudan' (2010) 5 International Journal of African Renaissance Studies 48, 51- 59; also Aleksi Ylönen, 'Still Caught in the Middle: Nuba Political Struggle and Failure of Comprehensive Peace Agreement in Sudan' in Alexandra Magnólia Dias (ed), *State*

The economically, socially, and politically marginalized Twa[54] are the earliest known inhabitants of Burundi, and while they were not players in the armed conflict from 1994 to 2005, they were nevertheless severely impacted by it. Many of them became victims of killings by both the Hutu and the Tutsi, and they have also been subject to internal displacement because of the conflict.[55] They were left out of negotiations for the 2000 Arusha Peace and Reconciliation Agreement, and while the 2005 post-agreement Constitution required representation for the Hutu, Tutsi, and Twa, only the Hutu and Tutsi had veto power through their guaranteed representation in the legislative and executive branches and the requirement for a qualified majority in decision-making.[56] Minority veto rights are essential in consociational governments such as Burundi's to protect those who lack numerical strength in the face of competing majorities,[57] but the Twa have no veto power even on matters that affect their vital interests.[58]

C. Power-Sharing and Indigenous Peoples' Land Rights in the Bangsamoro Peace Processes

Lumads are not parties to either the peace negotiations or any of the resulting peace agreements dating from the 1976 Tripoli Agreement. While they have been invited as consultants, resource persons, and even peace panel members, the Bangsamoro armed groups' peace negotiation agenda has primarily focused on Bangsamoro self-determination, identity, and heritage, and the Lumad presence on Bangsamoro peace panels has not translated to stronger and more effective advocacy for Lumad concerns, particularly with regard to indigenous peoples' ancestral domains and lands. Lumad efforts at sending a separate panel of Lumad representatives to the formal negotiations were not taken seriously by government.[59]

The Tripoli Agreement does not even mention Lumads or indigenous peoples at all, and they were not present in any of the major peace negotiations with the Moro National Liberation Front (MNLF) in l975, 1976, and 1987, though Lumads eventually participated in negotiating the 1996 Final Peace Agreement.[60] While there

and Societal Challenges in the Horn of Africa: Conflict and Processes of State Formation, Reconfiguration and Disintegration (Centro de Estudos Internacionais 2013) <https://books.openedition.org/cei/288> accessed 14 March 2025.

[54] Plural Batwa, as with Bahutu and Batutsi respectively.

[55] Åshild Falch and Megan Becker, 'Power-Sharing and Peacebuilding in Burundi' (Peace Research Institute Oslo 2008) 12.

[56] Qualified majority requirement for ordinary laws removed in 2018 Constitution, but qualified majority requirement for constitutional amendments retained. Allison McCulloch and Stef Vandeginste, 'Veto Power and Power-Sharing: Insights from Burundi (2000–2018)' (2019) 26 Democratization 1176; 1182,1188.

[57] ibid 1177 citing Arend Lijphart, 'The Power-Sharing Approach' in Joseph Montville (ed), *Conflict and Peacemaking in Multiethnic Societies* (Lexington Books 1990).

[58] ibid 1182; Twa guaranteed representation is 3 seats in legislative 2005 Constitution and 2018 Constitution, still no veto power in 2018 Constitution.

[59] 'The Philippines—Indigenous Rights and the MILF Peace Process' (International Crisis Group 2011) Asia Report No. 213; 6–8, 12.

[60] ibid 4.

has been greater Lumad involvement in the Moro Islamic Liberation Front (MILF) peace process,[61] the negotiation agenda in this process has nevertheless prioritized Bangsamoro self-determination and self-governance, with a focus on 'reclaiming' a Moro homeland/ancestral domain.

1. Negotiating the Issues of 'Ancestral Domain' and Self-Determination

The notion of a unified Bangsamoro identity is the legacy of several Moro leaders' and organizations' efforts to construct a Moro 'nationalist' movement from among various separate ethnolinguistic groups.[62] They appropriated the term 'Moro', which had been used pejoratively by Spanish and American colonizers, to call to mind a mythic anti-colonial historical past, and leaders such as the MNLF's Nur Misuari framed their armed campaign for a Moro independent republic as the reclaiming of a long-lost Moro homeland.[63]

The MNLF styled itself as a national liberation movement during a period when wars of national liberation were being fought around the world in the context of colonial peoples seeking independence from colonial powers. Coronel-Ferrer says that for this reason, the language of self-determination figured prominently in the MNLF's 'resistance discourse', or the discourse which they have developed in opposition to the official accounts of the place of Moros in Philippine society.[64] Misuari asserted, for instance, that the Moros are a separate nation distinct from Filipinos occupying a well-defined territory, and he declared the establishment of an independent 'Bangsa Moro Republik' governing a 'national homeland' in a 1974 Manifesto.[65]

The breakaway MILF led by Salamat Hashim likewise employed self-determination language, but because the MILF mobilized during the rise of indigenous peoples' rights debates in the 1980s, Coronel-Ferrer says that the organization's conception of self-determination is modelled after indigenous peoples' right to self-determination, including their right to their ancestral territories. The MILF successfully pushed for the inclusion of the issue of Bangsamoro ancestral domain in the key areas for peace negotiation in the 2001 Tripoli Agreement.[66]

In employing self-determination language in their resistance discourse, both Bangsamoro armed groups claimed that the Bangsamoro are a 'people' entitled to self-determination as a basis for a right to self-governance and autonomy and as a basis for a claim to a homeland or ancestral domain,[67] but their usage of the term does not align

[61] 'Getting to Peace: GPH-MILF Peace Negotiations Opening Statements 2011–2014' (Office of the Presidential Adviser on the Peace Process 2015) 341–53, members of government and MILF peace panels, as well as technical committees and working groups, from indigenous communities.

[62] Caballero-Anthony (n 4) 151.

[63] ibid. For a critique of the mythologized origins of the Bangsamoro and the Bangsamoro conflict, Abinales, 'War and Peace in Muslim Mindanao: Critiquing the Orthodoxy' (n 9).

[64] Miriam Coronel Ferrer, *Region, Nation and Homeland: Valorization and Adaptation in the Moro and Cordillera Resistance Discourses* (ISEAS–Yusof Ishak Institute 2020) 99, 112.

[65] ibid 100, citing Nur Misuari, 'Appeal to Islamic World for Support of the Moro People in Southern Philippines' Philippine Development Forum (6 no.2 1992) 61, 79–80.

[66] ibid 104–105.

[67] Coronel Ferrer (n 64) 4–8.

with prevailing practice and thinking on self-determination in international law. The Bangsamoro do not appear to be among the groups that international law recognizes as a people entitled to external self-determination.

In the law and practice of self-determination in the context of decolonization, for instance, colonial peoples refer to the peoples of mandate,[68] trust,[69] and non-self-governing territories.[70] The island of Mindanao does not fall under any of these classifications, and it was certainly not under a colonial power in the late 1960s, when Moro independence movements emerged in Mindanao. The Philippine state, a former Spanish and, subsequently, American colony, has been independent since 1946.[71] The Bangsamoro likewise do not seem to fall under the classification of a people under alien subjugation. Outside the colonial context, the term 'peoples under alien subjugation, domination, and exploitation' has been used to refer to the peoples of states under foreign domination in violation of sovereign equality and non-intervention[72] and peoples under racist regimes or regimes founded on racist criteria that ensure the hegemony of a sector of the population (usually white settlers in a former colony) over the rest, such as the apartheid regime in South Africa.[73]

The Bangsamoro could be considered a minority within the state, or a numerically inferior, nondominant group possessing common ethnic, religious, or linguistic characteristics differing from the rest of the population.[74] Minorities, however, are not entitled to self-determination.[75] Minority rights protection in international law pertains to protections designed to ensure that individuals are not denied the full enjoyment and exercise of rights by reason of their belonging to a minority group.[76] Autonomy has been described in the (non-binding) CSCE/OSCE Copenhagen Document 1990 as 'one of the possible means' for securing the rights of minorities.[77] While territorial autonomy has been used to address some self-determination disputes, its employment in these contexts is not an explicit expression of self-determination.[78] While the MILF has claimed that the Bangsamoro are indigenous in the sense of being native to

[68] Colonies of defeated powers after World War I, allocated to Allied powers for tutelage in preparation for self-government, Covenant of the League of Nations (28 April 1919) article 22.

[69] Under the trusteeship system under the UN Charter remaining mandate territories under the League of Nations and territories taken from enemy states after World War II, United Nations Charter (adopted 24 December 1945) 1 UNTS XVI, Chapter XII.

[70] Territories whose peoples have not yet attained a measure of self-government, United Nations Charter (adopted 24 December 1945) 1 UNTS XVI, Chapter XI.

[71] The US government recognized Philippine independence on 4 July 1946, Proclamation 2695 (dated 4 July 1946).

[72] See the situation of the Palestinian people in Legal Consequences of the Construction of a Wall in the Occupied Palestinian Territories (Advisory Opinion) [2004] ICJ Rep 136.

[73] See for instance UNGA Res 37/69 (9 December 1989) UN Doc A/RES/37/69.

[74] See definition in Francesco Capotorti, Special Rapporteur, Study on the Rights of Persons Belonging to Ethnic, Religious and Linguistic Minorities, UN Doc E/CN.4/Sub.2/384/Rev.1 (1977).

[75] Mere minority status in a state does not entitle a group to self-determination, and such a group must demonstrate it is among those groups considered a people entitled to self-determination: Thomas D Musgrave, 'Definitions of the Term "People"' in *Self-Determination and National Minorities* (Oxford University Press 1997).

[76] Declaration on the Rights of Persons Belonging to National or Ethnic, Religious and Linguistic Minorities, UN Doc A/Res/47/135, 3 February 1992.

[77] Document on the Copenhagen Meeting of the Conference on the Human Dimension of the CSCE, 29 June 1990, para. 35.

[78] See discussion in Marc Weller, *Escaping the Self-Determination Trap* (Brill | Nijhoff 2009) 78–90.

Mindanao, it likewise claims that the Bangsamoro are culturally and politically advanced in comparison with the 'tribal' Lumads, tracing their political lineage from Moro sultanates rather than any indigenous political institutions.[79] Their claim to self-determination does not appear to correspond with the right to self-determination of indigenous peoples.

These legal issues notwithstanding, the Bangsamoro armed groups were successful in influencing the official discourse of the peace negotiations with their political rhetoric on self-determination. The MILF's consistent use of indigenous peoples' rights language, in particular, influenced peace negotiations with the government, with the 2001 Tripoli Agreement acknowledging the 'inherent rights' of the Bangsamoro people 'over their ancestral domain'.[80] The 2008 Memorandum of Agreement on Ancestral Domain (MOA-AD),[81] regarded at the time as a milestone agreement between the government and the MILF, uses both the terms 'homeland' and 'ancestral domain' to refer to the territorial basis for Bangsamoro self-governance much in the same way that the MNLF conceptualized a Bangsamoro homeland.[82] The MOA-AD also describes Bangsamoro ancestral territoriality as the root of the Bangsamoro's right to self-governance, arguing that these areas were originally under Moro sultanates (which are claimed to be equivalent to modern-day nation-states[83]). The MOA-AD was declared unconstitutional by the Supreme Court before the government and the MILF could sign it.[84] The centrality of ancestral domain, nevertheless, remained in the negotiating agenda.

2. From Resistance Discourse to Official Discourse: Power-Sharing Agreements and Regional Autonomy for Muslim Mindanao

By the time that the MILF and the Philippine government signed the Comprehensive Agreement on the Bangsamoro in 2014, the Philippine government had already established several successive Moro-majority autonomous regions in Mindanao. The 1976 Tripoli Agreement contained the express agreement for the establishment of autonomy over thirteen provinces that coincided with areas which the MNLF had identified as the Bangsamoro national homeland and over which it had declared a Bangsamoro Republik in 1974.[85] The MNLF, however, disagreed with the government

[79] Paredes (n 2) 168–170.

[80] Agreement on Peace between the Government of the Republic of the Philippines and the Moro Islamic Liberation Front, signed on 22 June 2001 in Tripoli, Libya (also known as the GRP-MILF Tripoli Agreement of Peace of 2001) on the resumption of peace talks following hostilities in 2000.

[81] Memorandum of Agreement on the Ancestral Domain Aspect of the GRP-MILF Tripoli Agreement of Peace 2001 (MOA-AD), initialled by peace panels 5 August 2008 in Kuala Lumpur, Malaysia.

[82] Coronel Ferrer (n 64) 106–108.

[83] MOA-AD (n 81) 2.

[84] The Supreme Court declared the MOA-AD unconstitutional for promising constitutional change, for providing for a central–regional relationship in the form of a compact of free association (which is not contemplated by the Constitution), and the lack of public consultation: *Province of North Cotabato* v *The Government of the Republic of the Philippines Peace Panel on Ancestral Domain (GRP)*, G.R. No. 183591, G.R. No. 183752, G.R. No. 183893, G.R. No. 183951, G.R. No. 183962, 14 October 2008.

[85] The Manifesto of the Moro National Liberation Front: Establishment of the Bangsa Moro Republik, 28 April 1974, reproduced in Patricio N Abinales and Donna J Amoroso, *State and Society in the Philippines* (Rowman & Littlefield Publishers, Inc 2005) 217–19.

of then President Ferdinand E. Marcos's implementation of the autonomy agreement, which was limited to administrative autonomy.[86] This led to a breakdown in the peace talks and the resumption of armed violence between the parties.[87]

After Marcos was deposed in a popular uprising in 1986, the succeeding president Corazon C. Aquino sought to renew peace negotiations with the MNLF.[88] At the same time, a Constitutional Commission was at work in drafting a new Constitution for the Philippines, and it contained several provisions on the grant of autonomy not only to 'Muslim Mindanao' but also to the inhabitants of the Cordilleras.[89] Both regions are inhabited by minoritized ethnic groups, and both regions had been the site of protracted armed conflicts with the government. During the Constitutional Commission deliberations, it was argued that regional autonomy would address the marginalization of these two regions and would hopefully curb the ongoing armed conflicts in these areas.[90]

Because it had no role in its formulation, the MNLF refused to support the creation of an autonomous region as authorized by the 1987 Constitution. The autonomous region contemplated by the 1987 Constitution is granted political autonomy and not just administrative autonomy, with its regional government exercising legislative powers over ancestral domain and natural resources.[91] When a plebiscite was called in 1989 to ratify Republic Act No. 6734, which created the Autonomous Region in Muslim Mindanao (ARMM), both the MNLF and the MILF boycotted the proceedings. In this plebiscite, only four out of thirteen identified provinces voted to join the ARMM. Talks were restarted with the administration of Fidel V. Ramos, resulting in the 1996 Final Peace Agreement,[92] which was meant to contain the terms for the full implementation of the 1976 Tripoli Agreement.[93]

The MILF rejected the 1996 Final Peace Agreement with the MNLF, as well as its implementing organic law Republic Act No. 9054, as it had rejected the previous autonomy arrangements, claiming that none of these were able to address the 'Bangsamoro Problem' or the systemic marginalization suffered by the Bangsamoro under colonial and post-colonial governments.[94] The MILF's negotiations with the Philippine government, which began in 1997 under Ramos, were interrupted by several serious incidents of armed violence,[95] but the talks ultimately led to the signing

[86] Soliman M Santos, 'Evolution of the Armed Conflict on the Moro Front' (Human Development Network Foundation, Inc 2005) 9–10; see discussion in *Limbona* v *Mangelin*, G.R. No. 80391, 28 February 1989.

[87] ibid 14.

[88] ibid.

[89] Now Article X. Local Government, 1987 Philippine Constitution.

[90] Record of the Constitutional Commission No. 53, 11 August 1986.

[91] *Disomangcop* v *Secretary of Public Works and Highways*, G.R. No. 149848, 25 November 2004.

[92] Peace Agreement: The Final Agreement on the Implementation of the 1976 Tripoli Agreement between the Government of the Republic of the Philippines (GRP) and the Moro National Liberation Front (MNLF) with the Participation of the Organization of Islamic Conference Ministerial Committee of the Six and the Secretary General of the Organization of Islamic Conference, Manila, 2 September 1996; also known as the Jakarta Accord.

[93] Santos (n 86) 8.

[94] Soliman M Santos, 'Dynamics and Directions of the GRP-MILF Peace Negotiations' (Alternate Forum for Research in Mindanao, Inc 2005) 3; Soliman M Santos, 'Delays in the Peace Negotiations between the Philippine Government and the Moro Islamic Liberation Front: Causes and Prescriptions' (No. 3, East-West Center Washington Working Papers, January 2005) 6.

[95] Bayot (n 15) 15.

of the Comprehensive Agreement on the Bangsamoro in 2014, paving the way for the current autonomy arrangement in Mindanao. The negotiations for the comprehensive agreement under Aquino involved the explicit acknowledgement of the harms that the government has caused the Bangsamoro, the inefficacy of the ARMM as a 'failed experiment' in autonomy, and the MILF's long-standing aspiration for establishing a system of governance suitable to the Bangsamoro history and culture.[96]

3. The Privileging of the Bangsamoro in the Current Autonomous Region

The Bangsamoro Organic Law's declared purpose is to establish an autonomous region 'in recognition of the justness and legitimacy of the cause of the Bangsamoro people and the aspirations of the Muslim Filipinos and all indigenous cultural communities' in the region 'to secure their identity and posterity, allowing for meaningful self-governance within the framework of the Constitution and the national sovereignty as well as territorial integrity of the Republic of the Philippines'.[97] It also refers to the 'distinct historical identity' of the Bangsamoro people and other inhabitants of the region and their 'birthright to their ancestral homeland'.[98] Notably, there are multiple references to the Bangsamoro people,[99] and any of those who, 'at the advent of the Spanish colonization, were considered natives or native inhabitants of Mindanao and the Sulu archipelago and its adjacent islands, whether of mixed or of full blood' has the right to identify themselves, their spouses, and their descendants as Bangsamoro.[100] Lumads are among those who have the right to self-identify as Bangsamoro, but they are also free to retain their distinctive indigenous identity 'in addition to their Bangsamoro political identity'.[101]

The idea of Bangsamoro self-determination now serves as a shorthand to refer to the right of the Bangsamoro people, as a discrete ethnonationalist group, to political

[96] Speech of President Benigno Simeon Aquino III on the Framework Agreement on the Bangsamoro, 7 October 2012; also The Framework Agreement on the Bangsamoro, signed 15 October 2012.

[97] Republic Act No. 11054, *Organic Law for the Bangsamoro Autonomous Region in Muslim Mindanao*, 26 July 2018, article I, section 3.

[98] Republic Act No. 11054, article I, section 3; preamble; article VII, section 5(a) powers of parliament.

[99] The text of Republic Act No. 11054 appears to distinguish between Bangsamoro people, indigenous peoples, and other inhabitants. For instance, it refers to the preferential fishing rights of the Bangsamoro people, indigenous peoples, and resident marginal fisher folk (article XIII, section 23, agriculture, fisheries, and aquatic resources). Several portions refer to the 'Bangsamoro people and other inhabitants' (preamble; article VII, section 5(a); article ix, section 8), while others just refer to the 'Bangsamoro people' (article IV, section 1; article XIII, section 5, gender and development). Notably, Article IX, section 4 provides that 'the customs, beliefs, and traditions of the Bangsamoro people are hereby recognised, protected and guaranteed', and the parliament is enjoined to adopt measures for the respect and protection of the 'distinct beliefs, customs, and traditions of the Bangsamoro people and the other inhabitants' of the region. The law also refers to the 'legitimate grievances of the Bangsamoro people and the indigenous peoples' (article IX, section 1 transitional justice), but it only provides for reparation to the Bangsamoro people affected by unjust dispossession (article IX, section 2 reparation for unjust dispossession). Among its priority areas is the establishment of 'an educational framework relevant and responsive to the needs, ideals, and aspirations of the Bangsamoro people' (article IX, section 16, integrated system of quality education) and the preservation of 'the rich cultural heritage of the Bangsamoro people and their Sultanates' (article IX, section 24).

[100] Republic Act No. 11054 (n 97), article II, section 1 Bangsamoro people.

[101] ibid article II Bangsamoro identity.

participation and self-governance, as well as to economic, social, and cultural development.[102] It has been recognized by the Philippine Supreme Court, notably in the 2024 case of *Province of Sulu v PAIA, Inc.*, which ruled on the constitutionality of the Bangsamoro Organic Law, among other issues.[103] The term is used by Bangsamoro government officials and in official Bangsamoro communications in relation to governance plans and other projects.[104] Moreover, the early calls for self-determination in the context of the Bangsamoro resistance discourse seem to be echoed in the MILF's continued insistence on a single Bangsamoro ancestral domain in Mindanao, despite the Lumads' claims to their own ancestral domains.

D. The Impact of the Bangsamoro Peace Processes on Lumads' Land Rights

Lumads' access to and use of their lands has been severely impacted by government inaction on their land claims, decades-long campaigns of armed violence by various groups, and the operation of extractive industries. As a result, many Lumad communities have suffered land dispossession and internal displacement. While the autonomous region in Mindanao has been one of the country's poorest regions for decades, the general incidence of poverty is believed to be even higher among Lumads within the region than among its other inhabitants.[105]

A significant proportion of Mindanao's Lumad population live within the territory of successive Bangsamoro autonomous regions (the Autonomous Region in Muslim Mindanao or ARMM created in 1989 and the Bangsamoro Autonomous Region in Muslim Mindanao or BARMM created in 2019), and therefore a large number of Lumads have been under the authority of Moro-centric regional governments for several decades. Many important Lumad sacred sites are now located within Moro-majority provinces, including Batew in the Mt. Firis Complex in Maguindanao province, which is important to the Teduray and Lambangian peoples.[106] It is estimated that the total ancestral domain claim of Lumads in Maguindanao and Lanao del Sur is 309,720 hectares, comprising 215,941 hectares of land and 93,779 hectares of coastal waters.[107]

[102] For instance Priam Nepomuceno, 'BOL Fruit of Bangsamoro's Pursuit for Self-Determination, Governance' (*Philippine News Agency*, 22 January 2025) <https://www.pna.gov.ph/articles/1242371> accessed 12 June 2025.

[103] *Province of Sulu v PAIA, Inc.* GR Nos 242255, 243246, 243693, 9 September 2024; see also *Spouses Maliga v Spouses Tingao,* GR Nos 2110889, 211135, 11 July 2023.

[104] For instance Kasan Usop, 'BTA Ensures Inclusive Decision-Making among Stakeholders for Proposed Local Governance Bill' (7 December 2022) <https://bangsamoro.gov.ph/news/latest-news/bta-ensures-inclusive-decision-making-among-stakeholders-for-proposed-local-governance-bill/> accessed 17 June 2025; 'BARMM Bill Seeks to Make Bangsamoro History a Mandatory Subject in Secondary Schools | Bangsamoro Parliament' (*Bangsamoro Parliament*, 29 May 2025) <https://parliament.bangsamoro.gov.ph/2025/05/29/barmm-bill-seeks-to-make-bangsamoro-history-a-mandatory-subject-in-secondary-schools/> accessed 17 June 2025.

[105] Paredes (n 2) 168–173.

[106] ibid 169.

[107] Carolyn O. Arguillas, 'SPECIAL REPORT (2). From RAG to ARMM to BARMM: The IP's Struggle for Ancestral Domains Continues' (*MIndaNews*, 8 August 2020) <https://mindanews.com/special-reports/

Unlike the Bangsamoro, the Lumads' claim to a right to self-determination and autonomy is supported by an international instrument—the United Nations Declaration on the Rights of Indigenous Peoples (UNDRIP), which the Philippines adopted in 2007. In fact, the Comprehensive Agreement on the Bangsamoro itself provides that the Bangsamoro regional government shall exercise exclusive powers over the protection of the rights of the indigenous peoples in the Bangsamoro in accordance with the UNDRIP.[108] The UNDRIP regards the right of indigenous peoples to their lands as crucial for the meaningful exercise of autonomy and self-determination.[109] Article 26 provides that states must give legal recognition and protection to indigenous peoples' lands, territories, and resources with due respect to their customs and land tenure systems.[110] The UNDRIP also recognizes that indigenous peoples' relationship with their lands goes beyond the ownership of land as property, and Article 25 provides that indigenous peoples have the right to maintain and strengthen their distinctive spiritual relationship with their traditionally owned lands.[111]

The Philippines has enacted domestic legislation, the Indigenous Peoples' Rights Act of 1997, which likewise recognizes indigenous peoples' customary, communal, and inter-generational ownership of their lands and further recognizes the spiritual relationship of indigenous peoples to their lands. The Indigenous Peoples' Rights Act provides that the state recognizes indigenous peoples' right to self-governance and self-determination.[112] It acknowledges that ancestral domains serve as the material basis of indigenous peoples' cultural integrity and that indigenous peoples' relationship to ancestral domains extends beyond their dependence on the land for sustenance. It recognizes indigenous peoples' 'native title' to their ancestral territories or their pre-conquest rights to lands and domains which, as far back as memory reaches, have been held under a claim of private ownership by indigenous peoples.[113] It recognizes the private ownership of these indigenous lands through either the issuance of Certificates of Ancestral Domain Title or Certificates of Ancestral Land Title.[114]

Despite these legal protections, the Lumads in the Moro-majority autonomous region are still fighting for the legal recognition of their ancestral domains. The

2020/08/special-report-2-from-rag-to-armm-to-barmm-the-ips-struggle-for-ancestral-domains-continues/> accessed 8 June 2025.

[108] Annex on Power Sharing, signed 8 December 2013, Part III, section 30 on Bangsamoro government's exclusive powers.

[109] Claire Charters, 'Indigenous Peoples' Rights to Lands, Territories, and Resources in the UNDRIP: Articles 10, 25, 26, and 27' in Jessie Hohmann and Marc Weller (eds), *The UN Declaration on the Rights of Indigenous Peoples* (1st edn, Oxford University Press 2018) 396–407.

[110] United Nations Declaration on the Rights of Indigenous Peoples (adopted 2 October 2007) UN Doc. A/RES/61/295, article 26.

[111] ibid article 25.

[112] Republic Act No. 8371, October 29, 1997, section 13.

[113] ibid section 4, section 5, and section 3(l).

[114] ibid section 3(a) and section 3(b), with ancestral lands referring to land occupied, possessed, and utilized by individuals, families and clans, and ancestral domains being a broader category including ancestral lands.

successive regional governments put in place through the Bangsamoro peace processes failed to help Lumads obtain legal recognition of their lands, and the current regional government has actually blocked and delayed such recognition.

1. Inaction on Lumad Land Claims

Of the 257 approved Certificates of Ancestral Domain Title across the Philippines as of 2022 and since the enactment of the Indigenous Peoples' Rights Act in 1997, 142 cover ancestral domains in Mindanao,[115] but none of these pertain to any Lumad ancestral domain within the territory of successive Bangsamoro autonomous regions. Among the reasons cited for both the national government and ARMM regional government's inaction on Lumads' efforts to seek government recognition of their ancestral domains is the lack of clarity over the devolution of the functions of the National Commission on Indigenous Peoples (the agency tasked with the implementation of the Indigenous Peoples' Rights Act) to the ARMM regional government.[116]

Nevertheless, the ARMM regional government officially adopted the Indigenous Peoples' Rights Act as the legal framework for recognizing the rights of indigenous peoples within the autonomous region in 2003,[117] and the ARMM entered a Memorandum of Understanding with the national commission to create a mechanism to ensure the application of the Indigenous Peoples' Rights Act in the region pending the enactment of relevant regional legislation.[118] In 2008, the regional legislative assembly enacted a regional law for the recognition and protection of indigenous peoples' rights in the region,[119] and pending the creation of a special local body, applications for Certificates of Ancestral Domain Title were to be accepted by the ARMM government as the agent of the national commission.[120] In a 2013 legal opinion, the National Commission on Indigenous Peoples Legal Affairs Office reiterated that the national commission can process Certificates of Ancestral Domain Title[121] within the ARMM, as there are no limitations to this authority in law.[122] The national government and the ARMM regional government formulated ways to overcome the devolution issue, yet no Certificate of Ancestral Domain Title over any Lumad ancestral domain in the ARMM was ever issued during the period that this autonomous region existed.

115 'No Data, No Story: Indigenous Peoples in the Philippines' (World Bank Group 2024) 79–80.
116 'The Philippines - Indigenous Rights and the MILF Peace Process' (n 59) 9–10.
117 ARMM Regional Legislative Assembly Resolution No. 269 dated 15 August 2003.
118 National Commission on Indigenous Peoples (NCIP) Legal Opinion No. 06-10-01-13 dated 10 January 2013, 4.
119 Muslim Mindanao Act No. 241, 11 June 2008.
120 NCIP Legal Opinion (n 118).
121 As well as Certificates of Ancestral Land Title.
122 NCIP Legal Opinion (n 118) 5.

2. Resistance to Lumad Land Claims

The Teduray-Lambangian Lumads' efforts at obtaining a Certificate of Ancestral Domain Title illustrate the difficulties of securing legal protection for ancestral domains in the Moro-dominated autonomous region. The Teduray-Lambangians' ancestral domain straddles the provinces of Maguindanao and Sultan Kudarat. They filed an application for the delineation of their ancestral domain claim and the issuance of a Certificate of Ancestral Domain Title before the National Commission on Indigenous Peoples in 2005, but it was only eleven years later in 2016 that the ancestral domain survey was conducted.[123] The delineation process was halted in 2019 when the MILF-led Bangsamoro Transition Authority (the BARMM's interim government) issued Resolution No. 38 asking the national commission to 'cease and desist' from proceeding with any delineation processes in the BARMM. In the Resolution, the Bangsamoro Transition Authority claims that the national commission 'has no power and authority to conduct delineation process and issue Certificate of Ancestral Domain Title (CADT) in the BARMM' and that it is the BARMM Ministry of Indigenous Peoples' Affairs that has 'exclusive power and authority over Indigenous Peoples' rights and affairs including their ancestral domain in the BARMM'.[124]

These claims by the Bangsamoro Transition Authority are not supported by Philippine law on local government, which provides that the powers of the regional government are subject to the Constitution and national laws.[125] The Bangsamoro Organic Law cannot bar the application of national laws in the region.[126] Thus, while the Bangsamoro Organic Law grants the regional government powers over ancestral domain and natural resources, this is not an absolute grant of power excluding the national government itself, especially considering that the national Indigenous Peoples' Rights Act continues to be in operation. Moreover, in the event that the regional government enacts its own law on indigenous peoples' rights, this law cannot be inconsistent with the Indigenous Peoples' Rights Act.[127]

The MILF, nevertheless, has continuously asserted that there ought to be a single ancestral domain within the autonomous region, corresponding with a historic Moro homeland. Its opposition to the notion of multiple ancestral domains (pertaining to separate claims by various Lumad communities) within the autonomous region is so strong that it refused to change the relevant provision in what was then the draft Bangsamoro organic law from 'ancestral domain' to 'ancestral domains', as proposed

[123] Carolyn O. Arguillas, 'SPECIAL REPORT (3). From RAG to ARMM to BARMM: The IP's Struggle for Ancestral Domains Continues' (*MindaNews*, 9 August 2020) <https://mindanews.com/special-reports/2020/08/special-report-3-from-rag-to-armm-to-barmm-the-ips-struggle-for-ancestral-domains-continues/> accessed 17 June 2025.

[124] Bangsamoro Transition Authority Resolution No. 38, 25 September 2019.

[125] 1987 Philippine Constitution, article X, section 20.

[126] The BARMM cannot limit or restrict the Congress' legislative powers: '(a)fter all, despite the veritable autonomy granted the ARMM, the Constitution and the supporting jurisprudence, as they now stand, reject the notion of *imperium et imperio* in the relationship between the national and the regional governments.' See *Spouses Imbong* v *Ochoa, Jr*, G.R. Nos. 204819, 204934, 204957, 204988, 205003, 205043, 205138, 205478, 205491, 205720, 206355, 207111, 207172 & 207563, 8 April 2014.

[127] See discussion in Dante B Gatmaytan, 'BARMM Jurisdiction Over Ancestral Domains: An Argument for Restraint' (The Legal Rights and Natural Resources Center (LRC) 2021).

by government negotiators.[128] In the run-up to the submission of the first draft organic law to Congress, former MILF peace panel chair Mohagher Iqbal was quoted as saying that indigenous peoples must 'also respect the view and stand of the MILF, clearly contained in all signed documents and in the proposed (Bangsamoro organic law), that there is only one ancestral domain in the Bangsamoro, which is owned by Moros and IPs'.[129] Iqbal, writing as Salah Jubair, has said that the MILF does not deny Lumads the right to their own ancestral domain, but, nevertheless, 'it is the destiny of Lumads to be the "small or young brother" of the Moros, who will protect them.'[130]

The MILF had also previously released an opinion piece on its website *Luwaran* saying:

> As far as the CAB is concerned, there is only one ancestral domain in the Bangsamoro; and this ancestral domain is owned by Moros and indigenous peoples (IPs) particularly the Tidurays, Lambangian, and Dulangan Manobos. (By the way, Moros are also indigenous). If outside of the Bangsamoro, the concept of ancestral domain is more tribal in application, here it is elevated to a more national in character (*sic*), because the term 'Bangsamoro' becomes an identity, similar or at par with 'Filipino'. Both are national identities.[131]

The Constitution does provide for the regional government's legislative powers over 'ancestral domain and natural resources', and not 'ancestral domains' (plural).[132] However, while the constitutional commission deliberations do indicate that the inclusion of 'ancestral domain' in the Constitution's autonomy provisions was inspired by the Bangsamoro armed groups' call for the 'restoration' of a Moro homeland, the deliberations also show that there was no intention to deprive non-Moro indigenous peoples of their ancestral domains.[133]

3. Prospects for Redress of Lumad Land Claims

Despite the unlawfulness of the Bangsamoro Transition Authority's position regarding the Teduray-Lambangian's ancestral domain application before the National

[128] Steven Rood, 'Minorities within the Minority: Indigenous Communities in the Bangsamoro-The Asia Foundation' (2 October 2017) <https://web.archive.org/web/20171002001621/http://asiafoundation.org/2014/08/06/minorities-within-the-minority-indigenous-communities-in-the-bangsamoro/> accessed 5 February 2026.

[129] Carolyn O Arguillas, 'SPECIAL REPORT (1): From RAG to ARMM to BARMM: The IP's Struggle for Ancestral Domains Continues' (*MIndaNews*, 7 August 2020) <https://mindanews.com/special-reports/2020/08/special-report-1-from-rag-to-armm-to-barmm-the-ips-struggle-for-ancestral-domains-continues/> accessed 17 June 2025.

[130] 'The Philippines—Indigenous Rights and the MILF Peace Process' (n 59) 5 citing Salah Jubair, *The Long Road to Peace: Inside the GRP–MILF Peace Process* (Institute of Bangsamoro Studies 2007) 101–112.

[131] 'MILF: Editorial—The Issue of Ancestral Domain in the Bangsamoro' (*Key Philippine Military and Insurgent Events*) <http://retiredanalyst.blogspot.com/search?q=The+Issue+of+Ancestral+Domain+in+the+Bangsamoro> (Repost of editorial originally appearing on Luwaran, the MILF's official website; Original link <http://www.luwaran.com/index.php/editorial/item/900-the-issue-of-ancestral-domain-in-the-bangsamoro> no longer available).

[132] 1987 Philippine Constitution, article X, section 20.3.

[133] Record of the Constitutional Commission No. 53, 11 August 1986.

Commission on Indigenous Peoples, the application was put on hold in 2019 pending negotiations between the regional government and the national commission through the intergovernmental relations mechanism established in the Bangsamoro Organic Law.[134]

In December 2024, the Bangsamoro parliament enacted the Bangsamoro Indigenous Peoples' Act,[135] which not only declares the entire Bangsamoro territory as a shared homeland of all those with precolonial and historic ties to the region, but also acknowledges the distinct and separate ancestral domains of various indigenous communities.[136] However, it provides that ancestral domain applications currently pending with the national commission, including the Teduray-Lambangian claim, shall be turned over to the Bangsamoro's Ministry of Indigenous Peoples' Affairs for immediate action.[137] The regional government and the national commission entered into a Memorandum of Agreement in February 2025 to facilitate collaboration and cooperation on matters relating to indigenous peoples' rights in the Bangsamoro.[138] These talks appear to have been fruitful, and, barring any other setbacks, the Teduray-Lambangian expect their Certificate of Ancestral Domain Title to be issued by June 2026. The regional government also appears to have conceded that the national government retains its jurisdiction over indigenous peoples' rights in the BARMM.[139]

This response to the Teduray-Lambangian claim must be appreciated in the context of the harms that the Lumads have already suffered and continue to suffer, including displacement and the outright loss of ancestral domains. Several parcels of land were awarded in the 1970s to Moros within Teduray-Lambangian ancestral domains in Barangay Kuya, South Upi, which displaced Lumad communities from the area. The Department of Environment and Natural Resources has approved two Integrated Forestry Management Agreements in Rifao, Maguindanao, through which private corporations have been granted the right to develop and utilize forestland and forest resources that straddle Teduray ancestral domains. The logging activities have affected the access of Tedurays to their natural resources, and the corporations have allegedly threatened the Tedurays with violence.[140] From 2002 to 2006, the ARMM regional government created the municipalities of Datu Unsay, Datu Saudi, Guindulugan, Sharif Aguak, Talayan, and Datu Odin Sinsuat from Teduray ancestral domains.[141]

[134] Bangsamoro Organic Law article VI.

[135] Bangsamoro Autonomy Act No. 64, 10 December 2024.

[136] The Bangsamoro Transition Authority's draft bill on indigenous peoples' rights made a reference to 'the entire Bangsamoro Territory as the shared Ancestral Domain of all native inhabitants', which has been removed from the enacted law's declaration of policy.

[137] Section 102 Transitory Provisions.

[138] 'NCIP, MIPA Sign Historic Accord for BARMM IPs, Non-Moro IPs' (*House of Representatives 19th Congress Official Website*, 11 February 2025) <https://www.congress.gov.ph/media/view/?content=5788&title=NCIP%2C+MIPA+SIGN+HISTORIC+ACCORD+FOR+BARMM+IPs%2C+NON-MORO+IPs> accessed 8 June 2025.

[139] Germelina Lacorte, 'Finally, Titled Land for Non-Moro Tribe in Muslim Mindanao' (*INQUIRER.net*, 29 December 2025) <https://newsinfo.inquirer.net/2160297/finally-titled-land-for-non-moro-tribe-in-muslim-mindanao> accessed 3 February 2026.

[140] Jilliane Oria, Rey Palabon, and Ruel Punongbayan, 'In Search of Peaceful Solutions: Land Conflicts and the Plight of the Non-Moro Indigenous Peoples' in Francisco J Lara, Jr and Nikki Philline C de la Rosa (eds), *Conflict's Long Game: A Decade of Violence in the Philippines* (International Alert 2022) 153–155.

[141] Elena Joaquin Damaso, 'Honoring Mamalo: Turning a Paradox into a Paradigm Shift: Recognition of Non-Islamized Indigenous Peoples' Rights in the ARMM' (2011) 7 Autonomy and Peace Review 11, 30.

The ancestral domain claim of the Teduray-Lambangians in Maguindanao is still pending. Nevertheless, plans are currently under way to develop MILF camps Camp Badre and Camp Omar, which are found within the Teduray-Lambangian ancestral domain and which impact the sacred site of Mt. Firis. These camps are among six MILF camps that would benefit from socio-economic development, with the objective of transforming them into peaceful and productive communities, pursuant to the normalization commitments in the Comprehensive Agreement on the Bangsamoro.[142] Once developed, the Teduray-Lambangians fear that the creation of such communities could have the effect of entrenching their displacement.[143] Leaders of Teduray and Lambangian tribes have asked for protection from the government following a series of killings that seem to target Lumad leaders for reasons they believe to be connected with their pending ancestral domain claim. As of 7 December 2024, a total of eighty-three Lumad leaders have been killed since the attacks started in 2018.[144] One Lumad leader lamented that they are being 'displaced by war and killed by peace'.[145]

E. Conclusion

In the context of decades-long protracted armed conflicts, there is a primacy accorded to securing a negative peace. The cost of armed conflict both in terms of resources and human lives can be considerable, and there is a widely held assumption that negative peace is essential if positive peace is to be established. Nevertheless, the assumption that positive peace necessarily follows negative peace seems misplaced. While exclusionary power-sharing peace agreements may persuade armed groups to cease hostilities, the same mechanisms could establish post-agreement governments that prevent the establishment of positive peace.

In the experience of the Lumads, indigenous peoples of Mindanao, in the Bangsamoro peace processes, the post-agreement political order was not only created through exclusionary processes but was also built on exclusionary principles. While the signing of the power-sharing deals has resulted in the cessation of armed hostilities between the government and the Bangsamoro armed groups, it has also helped establish post-agreement government arrangements that privilege the Bangsamoro, the Muslim ethnolinguistic groups of Mindanao, in a Moro-majority autonomous region. The record of successive Bangsamoro governments on the issue of indigenous peoples' rights and their ancestral domain claims is incompatible with the equitable distribution of resources, harmonious relations among groups, or horizontal

[142] Annex on Normalization, signed 25 January 2014, J.1 Confidence-Building Measures.

[143] Germelina Lacorte, 'Non-Moro IP in Bangsamoro Demands Issuance of CADT, Stop to Killings' (*Inquirer.net*, 9 February 2025) <https://newsinfo.inquirer.net/2033113/non-moro-ip-in-bangsamoro-demands-issuance-of-cadt-stop-to-killings> accessed 16 June 2025.

[144] Germelina Lacorte, 'President, Congress Needed to Resolve BARMM Ancestral Land Row' (*INQUIRER.net*, 15 December 2024) <https://newsinfo.inquirer.net/2015765/president-congress-needed-to-resolve-barmm-ancestral-land-issue> accessed 16 June 2025.

[145] Lian Buan, 'Indigenous Peoples Fight for Their Home in Bangsamoro—Some Are Killed Trying' (*Rappler*, 30 January 2025) <https://www.rappler.com/newsbreak/in-depth/non-moro-indigenous-peoples-killing-barmm/> accessed 16 June 2025.

equality—all factors necessary for the establishment of positive peace. The privileging of the Bangsamoro in the power-sharing agreements has translated into the unjust treatment of Lumads, and consequently the absence of positive peace.

Lumads still recount in oral traditions the story of Mamalu and Tabunaway, brothers from whom modern-day Lumads and Moros, respectively, are supposed to have descended. According to the story, when Tabunaway converted to Islam in the fourteenth century, Mamalu chose their ancestral religion and moved to the uplands. The brothers are said to have entered a pact to live in peace with each other and to honour each other's territories.[146] The path towards positive peace lies not in blind reliance on the exclusionary power-sharing bargains of the Bangsamoro peace processes, the operation of which continues to minoritize the Lumads, but in serious attempts at honouring the pact of Mamalu and Tabunaway. Only when the Lumads are able to meaningfully exercise their rights as indigenous peoples in the Bangsamoro region will it be possible to say that genuine steps toward real peace have been made.

[146] Paredes (n 2) 170.

21
Peace Agreements
A Foundation for Sustainable Peace and Development?

Amanda Cahill-Ripley

A. Introduction

This chapter will explore peace agreements as a foundation for sustainable peace and development in the context of protracted conflicts. The nature of such conflicts (the back-and-forth between peace and conflict that is a feature of such violent conflicts) poses particular challenges for peacemaking and peacebuilding.[1] The reality of protracted conflict ensures that there is no linear development from peace agreement to sustainable peace. Rather, the boundaries between conflict, transition, and peace are blurred and messy. Consequently, when considering humanitarian action, sustainable development, and sustainable peace, the relevant actors need to respond in a concurrent and comprehensive manner. Development issues can no longer be deemed a post-conflict activity, nor can humanitarian assistance be limited to an emergency response. The question then is: do peace agreements reflect this nexus approach in their scope and content, and what role can peace agreements play in supporting such a nexus within law, policy, and practice?

The chapter begins by providing an overview of peace agreements and the general challenges they encompass. The subsequent two sections examine how peace agreements have dealt with sustainable development and humanitarian assistance to date. This examination will involve empirical analysis of peace agreements utilizing the PA-X Database[2] and creating new data sets for investigation. The analysis is two-pronged: first, I explore how frequently sustainable development and humanitarian assistance are considered within peace agreements; subsequently, I examine how sustainable development and humanitarian assistance/action[3] are defined in such agreements, investigating the scope and content of such provisions and identifying common themes and significant ideas. The presumed 'neutrality' of humanitarian action is a cornerstone of humanitarian assistance but, once incorporated into a peace agreement, humanitarian action can be immediately politicized. Consequently, the scope and content of humanitarian provisions are important when assessing the effectiveness of peace agreements for sustaining peace and sustainable development.

[1] Introduction to this volume.
[2] Christine Bell and others (2023), PA-X Peace Agreements Database and Dataset, Version 7 at www.peaceagreements.org (hereafter PA-X Peace Agreements Database and Dataset, Version 7).
[3] These terms are used interchangeably in this chapter, although note that possible perceived differences within peace agreements will be discussed.

Amanda Cahill-Ripley, *Peace Agreements* In: *From Protracted Conflict to Sustainable Peace?* Edited by: Heike Krieger, Giedre Jokubauskaite, Asli Ozcelik, and Andreas Buser, Oxford University Press. © Amanda Cahill-Ripley 2026.
DOI: 10.1093/9780198967385.003.0025

Finally, I will consider whether peace agreements currently reflect the nexus of sustainable development, humanitarian assistance, and sustainable peace, and evaluate whether they can support a holistic approach (a triple-nexus approach) in situations of protracted conflict. In conclusion, I contend that peace agreements can act as a firm foundation for sustainable development and sustainable peace.

B. Peace Agreements

A peace agreement in its most basic definition is 'the codification of the terms of settlement between some or all conflict parties for the purpose of ending conflict between them'.[4] Peace agreements are important because they are often the main concrete and formalized outcome of peacemaking efforts and peace negotiations. Depending on the purpose and type, they can be the crucial first step in a cessation of hostilities or a framework for more long-term positive change and compromise to transition from conflict to peace.[5] In protracted conflicts, peace agreements can be even more important: interim agreements can set out temporary measures, which result in improvements to living conditions for those in conflict-affected settings, until consensus can be found on complex fundamental issues.

For the purposes of this chapter, I will focus on whether peace agreements include explicit provisions for sustainable development and humanitarian assistance and subsequently if the nexus between these areas of practice is recognized. However, several key points are worth addressing before proceeding to this analysis. First, the importance of the scope and content of a peace agreement and its role in achieving sustainable peace is disputed: the 'constitutive' approach, in its rudimentary form,

> [v]iews the substance of the peace agreement as key to the overall process, which will reflect its strengths and weaknesses, virtues, and shortcomings. A 'good' agreement will result in durable peace; a 'bad' agreement will result in delays, setbacks, or even the collapse of the peace process.[6]

An alternative view believes a peace agreement to be less important in terms of content—and emphasizes the need to ensure progression in the overall peace process. Such an 'instrumentalist' approach views the peace agreement as one small part of the complex process, in which omissions, revisions, and details can be addressed as the parties progress through the process.[7] Our intuitive response as lawyers is to assume

[4] Robert A. Forster, 'Peace Agreements', *The Palgrave Encyclopaedia of Global Security Studies* (Palgrave 2020) 1.

[5] Broadly defined, peace agreements can be classified as ceasefire agreements; interim agreements, final or framework agreements, and implementation agreements. Varying types of agreements will affect their substantive content, including provisions for humanitarian assistance and sustainable development. Christine Bell, *Peace Agreements and Human Rights* (Oxford University Press 2004) 20–32.

[6] Jean Arnault, 'Good Agreement? Bad Agreement? An Implementation Perspective' (*UN Peacemaker*, 2006) <https://gsdrc.org/document-library/good-agreement-bad-agreement-an-implementation-perspective/> accessed 30 May 2024, 1; Laura Edwards and Jonathan Worboys, 'The Interpretation and Implementation of Peace Agreements' in Marc Weller, Mark Retter, and Andrea Varga (eds), *International Law and Peace Settlements* (Cambridge University Press 2021).

[7] ibid.

that the former position is optimal. However, there is a lack of conclusive empirical evidence to support either position. As Edwards and Worboys note:

> Whether peace agreements have the capacity to effect change depends on a wide range of factors, many of which—such as political will or availability of resources—might not have anything to do with the precise formulation of the text adopted by the parties . . . Nevertheless, to the extent that the formulation can play a role, it is worth examining how it may be approached in drafting.[8]

Second, the legal status of peace agreements is disputed. Debate continues as to whether peace accords constitute legal or quasi-legal agreements or whether they are political and policy agreements with no legal force.[9] A related question is whether legal status matters, that is, does the legal status affect the success of the agreement? Such questions lie beyond the scope of this chapter. However, this chapter takes the position that the substance and content of a peace agreement is a fundamental component to its effectiveness. For example, it will be unquestionably easier for parties to an agreement to press for sustainable development in the post-agreement phase if they have already agreed to it in principle, especially if the agreement includes a clear concept of what sustainable development means and which implementation mechanisms are required. Consequently, it is important to examine the scope and content of a peace agreement while still acknowledging the other factors in play when assessing its success or failure in enabling durable peace.

Third, peace processes are complex. It is often the case that transforming conflict into peace requires not one agreement but several sequenced agreements. This is especially true in protracted conflicts, where initiatives can fail and then require relaunching. Each time this happens, the new agreement will build upon previous provisions and reiterate or repackage key provisions.[10] As Joshi and Quinn note, the longer a war lasts, the more likely a current agreement will be 'followed by a subsequent accord'.[11] Thus, striking a balance between constructive ambiguity to enable a deal and incorporation of key principles that can be meaningfully expanded upon is vital.

[8] Laura Edwards and Jonathan Worboys, 'The Interpretation and Implementation of Peace Agreements' in Marc Weller, Mark Retter, and Andrea Varga (eds), *International Law and Peace Settlements* (Cambridge University Press 2021) 131; also ibid 135.

[9] For example: Christine Bell, *On the Law of Peace: Peace Agreements and the Lex Pacificatoria* (Oxford University Press 2008) and Christine Bell, 'Peace Agreements: Their Nature and Legal Status' (2006) 100 The American Journal of International Law 373; Asli Ozcelik, 'Entrenching Peace in Law: Do Peace Agreements Possess International Legal Status?' (2020) 21 Melbourne Journal of International Law 1; Marc Weller, 'Conclusion: Developments in Peace Settlement Practice and International Law' in Marc Weller, Mark Retter, and Andrea Varga (eds), *International Law and Peace Settlements* (CUP 2021); Laura Edwards and Jonathan Worboys, 'The Interpretation and Implementation of Peace Agreements' in Marc Weller, Mark Retter, and Andrea Varga (eds), *International Law and Peace Settlements* (CUP 2021).

[10] While peace agreements tend not to explicitly recognize the particularity of protracted conflict, references to redouble efforts or recommit to peace deals are often reflected in the titles of accords, eg the 'Revitalised Agreement on the Resolution of the Conflict in the Republic of South Sudan 12/09/2018' (PA-X Peace Agreements Database and Dataset, Version 7).

[11] Madhav Joshi and J Michael Quinn, 'Is the Sum Greater than the Parts: The Terms of Civil War Peace Agreements and the Commitment Problem Revisited' (2015) 31 Negotiation Journal 7, 20.

Finally, timing and the type of agreement—that is, whether a ceasefire or initial agreement; a framework agreement; a specific protocol, for example on development or humanitarian assistance; or a comprehensive agreement (including new constitutions)—will determine to some extent the provisions included and the degree of detail concerning sustainable development and humanitarian assistance. Thus, it is important to recognize that, when considering whether peace agreements are a solid foundation for sustainable development and sustainable peace, we are often considering a suite of agreements with different purposes, which need to be read in their totality and spanning a longer-term timeframe.

C. Empirical Study—Methodology and Overview of Data

To address the key questions of how peace agreements have dealt with sustainable development and humanitarian action to date, a two-pronged approach of large sample data analysis and textual analysis of specific examples has been utilized to gather an overview of how such concepts have been provided for in terms of frequency, scope, and content.

PA-X Version 7 is a database containing 2,003 peace agreements, found in more than 150 peace processes between 1990 and 2023.[12] Analysis of the database using the predetermined coding categories[13] found that from a total 2,003 agreements:

- 254 agreements matched the criteria: category Socio-Economic Reconstruction; issue Development or Socio-Economic Reconstruction; sub-issue Humanitarian Assistance.
- 603 agreements matched the criteria: category Socio-Economic Reconstruction; issue Development or Socio-Economic Reconstruction; sub-issue Socio-Economic Development.
- 207 agreements matched criteria: category Socio-Economic Reconstruction; issue Development or Socio-Economic Reconstruction; sub-issue Infrastructure and Reconstruction.[14]

This means that of the total data set, 53 per cent (1,064) of the peace agreements had some provisions for either sustainable development, humanitarian assistance, or infrastructure and reconstruction. Of course, this figure does not account for any peace agreements which were not included in the coding categories of the original database. Therefore, I also used a free text search of the database to capture any other relevant peace agreements.

[12] University of Edinburgh, Peace Agreements Database, PA-X Version 7 <https://www.peaceagreements.org/search> accessed 1 February 2024.

[13] Christine Bell and others (2022). PA-X Peace Agreements Database and Dataset, Version 6. at <www.peaceagreements.org> accessed 18 May 2022. Updated 1 February 2024 to include entries from Christine Bell and others (2023). PA-X Peace Agreements Database and Dataset, Version 7 at <www.peaceagreements.org>.

[14] Amanda Cahill-Ripley (author), Analysis of the PA-X Database, 1 February 2024.

Due to chapter limitations and feasibility, this large-scale data set was narrowed down further. First, the category of Socio-Economic Reconstruction with the sub-issue 'Infrastructure and Reconstruction' was excluded from this analysis, in preference for a narrower focus on sustainable development and humanitarian assistance (as the central tenants of the triple nexus approach). Thus, the overall percentage of peace agreements with relevant provisions was 43 per cent (857 agreements).

Consequently, the analysis of humanitarian assistance is based on the 254 agreements found coded specifically with the sub-issue 'Humanitarian Assistance'. Moreover, the 'free text' search found that out of the total 2,003 agreements, 26 agreements were found where the agreement document contains free text 'humanitarian action'.[15] These are also included in the analysis of data concerning humanitarian assistance.

When studying the data on sustainable development, it was evident that the coding 'Socio-Economic Development' was very broad in scope and encompassed a wide range of issues. Therefore, due to the high volume of data and the specific aim of the chapter to consider sustainable development, a free text search was undertaken using the terms 'sustainable development' and 'sustainable development goals'. This further analysis found that out of the 2,003 agreements, 63 agreements matched the criteria where the agreement document contained text 'sustainable development' and two agreements were found where the agreement document contained text 'sustainable development goals'.[16] Accordingly, the in-depth analysis of sustainable development is concentrated on this specific subset of data.

D. How Have Peace Agreements Dealt with Sustainable Development?

Within this specified subset of data, textual analysis identified a number of general themes within peace agreements concerning sustainable development: this included connections with the environment, with security and peacebuilding, economic development, growth and privatization, international assistance, and regional assistance (development actors). Other topics included frameworks and funding for sustainable development, equality and the need for special measures, and participation/local development. These themes have been categorized and are explored in the following sections together with examples for illustration.

1. Defining Sustainable Development—Economic, Human, and Environmental Approaches

First, it is important to examine whether the subset of agreements established a common definition or vision of sustainable development. Such normative provisions

[15] Amanda Cahill-Ripley (author), Analysis of the PA-X Database, Free Text search 'humanitarian action', 13 June 2022 (some also included in sub-issue). Updated 1 February 2024 to reflect Version 7 of the PA-X database.

[16] Amanda Cahill-Ripley (author), Analysis of the PA-X Database, free text search, 13 June 2022. Updated 1 February 2024 to reflect Version 7 of the PA-X database (2 agreements within the 63).

are key to understanding how the parties to the peacemaking process understand sustainable development. Although varying interpretations are possible, having a firm normative basis from which to interpret and implement a specific agreement would seem optimal.

While many agreements have no normative definition of sustainable development—leaving it ambiguous or at least open to interpretation through a holistic reading of the agreement—there are also several agreements that develop a normative vision for sustainable development. The findings indicated a number of approaches to sustainable development. For example, the idea of such development as human-centred and dependent on a strong stable state is evident in Yemen:

> Real and effective solutions will be through building a strong state that embodies law and order, provides needed services, and ensures sustainable development for all citizens, guarantees rights and freedoms, builds a strong national army and where religious, political and intellectual rights are protected.[17]

The agreement also embeds provisions stating that development should be 'comprehensive' and 'sustainable', including environmental, economic, and social development.[18] It provides, for example, that water and other natural resources must be protected in order to achieve sustainable development.[19] The theme of conservation and sustainable use of natural resources is found in several peace accords across the sample, demonstrating that parties to conflict and peacemaking recognize the expansion of the idea of development from solely economic and/or human to a holistic model incorporating environmental concerns. This may also reflect the growing number of conflicts around scarcity of resources such as water or situations where conflict has caused harm to the environment.[20]

In the case of Sudan, provisions around environmental protections are also linked to land use and land management. For example, the Doha Document for Peace in Darfur provides eleven conditions for land planning and sustainable development inclusive of environmental protections.[21] Further, it provides that environmental

[17] National Dialogue Conference Outcomes Document 25/01/2014 Yemen, Emancipation from the Past, 230 (PA-X Peace Agreements Database and Dataset, Version 7).

[18] ibid II. Principles, para 8; Social Foundations, para 14 (PA-X Peace Agreements Database and Dataset, Version 7).

[19] ibid, Environment—Legal determinates, article 12.2.2 (7) (PA-X Peace Agreements Database and Dataset, Version 7).

[20] For example, *inter alia*, the Guidelines and Ground Rules for the Implementation and Monitoring of the Agreement on the Cessation of Hostilities between the Government of the Republic of Philippines and the Rebolusyonaryong Partido ng Manggagawa ng Mindanao, 28/10/2005, para 3 (PA-X Peace Agreements Database and Dataset, Version 7), which states: 'The parties jointly affirm and recognize the need to promote and strengthen environment and natural resource protection under the framework of sustainable development.' Framework Agreement on the Bangsamoro 15/10/2012 Philippines/Mindanao Agreement, para 8 (PA-X Peace Agreements Database and Dataset, Version 7); Colombia; Guatemala and Zimbabwe as discussed previously.

[21] Doha Document for Peace in Darfur, 31/05/2011 Sudan/Darfur, Article 37, para 195, 1–11 (PA-X Peace Agreements Database and Dataset, Version 7).

degradation be addressed, with institutions having legal support for such measures as part of sustainable development.[22]

In Guatemala, the Agreement on the Social and Economic Aspects and Agrarian Situation describes sustainable development as:

> a process of change in the life of the human being through economic growth with social equity, involving production methods and consumption patterns that maintain the ecological balance. This process implies respecting ethnic and cultural diversity and guaranteeing the quality of life of future generations.[23]

This agreement is particularly notable given that it was adopted in 1996 and yet it is concerned with the rights and needs of future generations (an idea that is only recently being addressed within development, peace, and human rights fields). Such a concern highlights the 'sustainability' focus of the peace agreement and may be a partial consequence of the agrarian context of the former conflict. Again, the explicit reference to ecological balance indicates a holistic view of development, including the human component but also the environment.

Another unique and notable interpretation of sustainable development is found in the National Peace Accord of South Africa, which provides that:

> Sustainable development implies that all individuals must be assisted and encouraged to accept responsibility for their socio-economic well-being. Each actor must define and accept his/her role and there must be an acceptance of co-responsibility for and co-determination of socio-economic development.[24]

It is significant as it sets out a vision of sustainable development that pertains to the responsibility of 'the people' and every individual, rather than solely interpreting sustainable development as an obligation of the State Parties (and Non-State Parties) to the peace accord. Although one could argue that a cynical interpretation of this provision is that it seeks to diminish the obligations of the government, it is in line with the right to development as provided for in international human rights law.[25]

2. Implementation Frameworks for Sustainable Development

Normative statements, as noted in section D.1, are often followed by substantive provisions, outlining measures to achieve the stated vision of sustainable development. Such

[22] ibid Article 17: Policies of Wealth Sharing, para 125; Declaration of Principles for the Resolution of the Sudanese Conflict in Darfur 05/07/2005 Sudan/Darfur, Article 12 (PA-X Peace Agreements Database and Dataset, Version 7).

[23] Agreement on the Social and Economic Aspects and Agrarian Situation 06/05/1996 Guatemala, para 40 (PA-X Peace Agreements Database and Dataset, Version 7).

[24] National Peace Accord 14/09/1991 South Africa, para 5.4 (PA-X Peace Agreements Database and Dataset, Version 7).

[25] Declaration on the Right to Development, UNGA Res 41/128 (4 Dec 1986); UNHRC (Working Group on the Right to Development), 'Revised Draft Convention on the Right to Development' (6 April 2022) A/HRC/WG.2/23/2.

a pattern is common, that is, moving from general statements or principles, to substance, and sometimes further to outline specific processes and means of implementation. However, such substantive provisions vary in their level of detail, dependent on the type of agreement in question. For example, specific transitional or development-focused agreements, or a new Constitution, will have more details than a ceasefire agreement or interim peacemaking agreement. One example is the Colombian Final Agreement to End the Armed Conflict, where sustainable development is defined as 'development that is environmentally and socially sustainable, requiring protection and promotion of access to water'.[26] The substantive provisions that follow set out how this might be achieved, for example through the establishment of Peasant Enterprise Zones. These zones are defined as 'agrarian initiatives that contribute to the construction of peace, the safeguarding of the political, economic, social and cultural rights of small-scale farmers, to development with socio-environmental and food sustainability and to the reconciliation of Colombian citizens'.[27] Such concrete measures are a positive inclusion that can only aid implementation of the agreement at a later stage.

Peace agreements may also establish an explicit framework for sustainable development, either legally based, policy-based, or a mixture of both. For example, in the case of Yemen, a legal basis is agreed upon to 'provide conditions for comprehensive and sustainable development'.[28] Moreover, paragraph 70 sets out an obligation to formulate

> legal rules and foundations that prevents crises and political conflicts . . . that impede[] the State from performing its obligations and limits the community participation, the private sector and civil society from working in building and comprehensive and sustainable development.[29]

The agreement also provides that '[t]he law shall obligate the government to develop a strategy that would guide the civil society and private sector within the framework of sustainable development'.[30] In this case, the agreement is setting out a legal obligation on the government to establish a policy-orientated strategy.

Other peace agreements are ambiguous as to what form these frameworks will take. For example, the Comprehensive Peace Agreement between South Sudan and Sudan provides for the government 'to meet human needs in accordance with the best-known practices of sustainable development within a transparent and accountable framework'.[31] In this provision, it is not clear whether accountability will be legal

[26] Final Agreement to End the Armed Conflict and Build a Stable and Lasting Peace 24/11/2016, Colombia, 1. Towards a New Colombian Countryside: Comprehensive Rural Reform, Principles, 14 (PA-X Peace Agreements Database and Dataset, Version 7).

[27] ibid 1.1.10. Closure of the agricultural frontier and protection of reserve areas, 21; 4.1.2. Aims, 111.

[28] National Dialogue Conference Outcomes Document 25/01/2014 Yemen, para 4 (PA-X Peace Agreements Database and Dataset, Version 7).

[29] ibid para 70.

[30] ibid para 134.

[31] Comprehensive Peace Agreement between the Government of the Republic of the Sudan and the Sudan People's Liberation Army/Sudan People's Liberation Movement (Naivasha Agreement) 09/01/2005 South Sudan/Sudan, para 5.2 (PA-X Peace Agreements Database and Dataset, Version 7); also previous Protocol between the Government of Sudan and the Sudan People's Liberation Movement on the

or political. However, such terminology speaks to a human rights-based approach to development.[32]

Surprisingly, very few of the peace agreements to date explicitly mention the sustainable development goals (SDGs) as a policy framework for sustainable development, or indeed note the cross-cutting aims of the SDGs in relation to peacebuilding.[33] While it should be noted that many of the peace agreements within the sample predated the SDGs, the predecessor to the SDGs, the Millennium Development Goals, also received very little attention.[34] In fact, only two agreements in the sample specify measures to support the SDGs: in the case of Liberia, the peace agreement provides that the parties will establish a 'Contract and Monopolies Commission' whose mandate will include,'[e]nsuring the formulation and effective implementation of sound macro-economic policies that will support sustainable development goals';[35] in the case of Sudan, the 2020 Juba Agreement details a commitment to tackling environmental challenges as measures to achieve the SDGs:

> The Parties agree that the government shall commit to establishing the necessary foundations, policies, laws, and implementation mechanisms for addressing and coordinating the environmental sector in order to protect the environment and preserve its overall sustainable balance; to end environmental degradation; to mitigate conflict over resources; and to seek to address the socio-economic impacts of environmental degradation, climate change, and all environmental causes of conflict as a key and necessary requirement for peacebuilding, maintaining natural resources, and achieving the sustainable development goals. This requires establishing the principle of sustainable institutional and legal reform and professional reform.[36]

An important and additional concern of frameworks for sustainable development is the key question of monitoring and evaluation of the substantive provisions within a peace agreement. Whom has responsibility for implementing the provisions and

Resolution of Conflict in Southern Kordofan/Nuba Mountains and the Blue Nile States 26/05/2004 South Sudan/Sudan/Southern Kordofan—Blue Nile—Abyei, para 1.3 (PA-X Peace Agreements Database and Dataset, Version 7).

[32] Peter Uvin, 'From the Right to Development to the Rights-based Approach: How "Human Rights" Entered Development' (2007) 17 Development in Practice 597; Wouter Vandenhole and Paul Gready, 'Failures and Successes of Human Rights-Based Approaches to Development: Towards a Change Perspective' (2014) 32 Nordic Journal of Human Rights 291; Annelie De Man, 'The Sustainable Development Goals and the Rights-based Approach to Development: Compatible or Missing the Point?' (2019) 19 African Human Rights Law Journal 445.

[33] In more depth below Sections D.3≠4 and E.

[34] The only example found was the Darfur Peace Agreement 05/05/2006 Sudan/Darfur, 35, Chapter Two: Wealth Sharing, Article 19, para 150: 'The Parties agree to make every effort to bring Darfur states up to the national average level of human development in the shortest possible time with a view to attaining the Millennium Development Goals (MDGs)' (PA-X Peace Agreements Database and Dataset, Version 7).

[35] Peace Agreement between the Government of Liberia, the Liberians United for Reconciliation and Democracy (LURD), the Movement of Democracy in Liberia (MODEL) and the Political Parties (Accra Agreement) 18/08/2003 Liberia Agreement text (excerpts), para 2. Article XVII Contract and Monopolies Commission (PA-X Peace Agreements Database and Dataset, Version 7).

[36] Sudan peace agreement (Juba Agreement) 03/10/2020, para 14.2 The Environment (14.2.1) (PA-X Peace Agreements Database and Dataset, Version 7).

how will the process be monitored, and progress measured? Some peace agreements provide for the establishment of relevant bodies and a process; for example, the Comprehensive Peace Agreement between the Government of the Republic of the Sudan and the Sudan People's Liberation Army/Sudan People's Liberation Movement provides that

> the legislatures of the two States shall each establish a Parliamentary Assessment and Evaluation Commission to assess and evaluate the implementation of the agreement in each State. The two Commissions shall submit their reports to the legislatures of the two States by the end of fourth year of the signing of the comprehensive Peace Agreement.[37]

This provision established a monitoring body for the whole peace accord, but others establish a specific institution and/or a process to implement sustainable development as set out by the agreement. In the case of Yemen (as noted in section C), the National Dialogue Conference Outcomes Document established a legal framework for sustainable development. Additionally, the agreement established a working group on sustainable development and set out their mandate and a monitoring and evaluation process. The plan for their work

> mainly aimed at completing the constitutional and legislative amendments and policies that would achieve sustainable and comprehensive development. In accordance with the plans, the working group interviewed a number of local and international experts in a number of different fields and subjects of development. The groups also held a number of meetings and interviews in the Capital Secretariat, in addition to holding a number of field visits to the related ministries, agencies, and groups to know their methods of work, the obstacles and challenges they face, as well as their vision on sustainable development and what should be included in the new constitution.[38]

This is a positive inclusion, as providing detailed legal frameworks, policies, and institutional structures and processes for implementation of the peace accord can help to avoid poor implementation at a later stage of the process.

3. Funding for Sustainable Development

As noted in section D.2, one of the key challenges for realization of peace agreements is implementation of the agreement's provisions. The success or failure of a peace agreement is reliant on a complex number of factors including *inter alia* the text of the

[37] Comprehensive Peace Agreement between the Government of the Republic of the Sudan and the Sudan People's Liberation Army/Sudan People's Liberation Movement (Naivasha Agreement) 09/01/2005 South Sudan/Sudan, para 5.3 (PA-X Peace Agreements Database and Dataset, Version 7).

[38] National Dialogue Conference Outcomes Document 25/01/2014 Yemen 'Working Group on Development (13 July–13 November 2013: Final report for the second term of the working groups) Introduction (PA-X Peace Agreements Database and Dataset, Version 7).

agreement and political will.[39] However, one of the key variables is that of availability and distribution of resources and funding. As such, provisions for funding within peace agreements are important. These often take the form of establishing mechanisms and institutions for oversight of sustainable development. For example, in Mali's Accord Pour la Paix et la Réconciliation au Mali, details are set out for the

> Establishment of a Development Zone in the Northern Regions, with an Interregional Consultative Council and a specific development strategy based on prevailing socio-cultural geographical and climate conditions. The Strategy shall be funded principally by a sustainable development Fund, financed by national state sources and international contributions.[40]

In the case of Darfur, the Juba Agreement contains detailed provisions setting out concrete measures for development funding, establishing for example a Darfur Peace Support and Development Fund[41] and a national development bank.[42] Additionally, it provides for specific contributions to be paid and time periods for commitments, such as an obligation by the Government of Sudan to pay '750,000,000 (seven hundred fifty million US Dollars) annually for a period of ten years to the Darfur Peace Support and Sustainable Development Fund to fund the implementation of the Peace Agreement in Darfur'.[43] Significantly, this fund is also mandated to support transitional justice and peacebuilding within Darfur including reparations. The agreement provides that the fund will support reparations for a period of ten years[44] and

> [s]hall cooperate and coordinate with other commissions established pursuant to this Agreement, especially the Commission for the Return of IDPs and Refugees, the Development and Reconstruction Commission, the Lands and Hawakeer Commission, the Truth and Reconciliation Committee, the Darfur Special Court for War Crimes, and the mechanisms of traditional justice.[45]

This provision demonstrates that those party to this agreement and involved in the negotiations clearly understood the nexus between sustainable development and peacebuilding (including transitional justice). It is also significant that in the previous Agreement between the Government of the Republic of South Sudan and the South Sudan Democratic Movement/Army, humanitarian assistance is a form of reparations

[39] Laura Edwards and Jonathan Worboys, 'The Interpretation and Implementation of Peace Agreements' in Marc Weller, Mark Retter, and Andrea Varga (eds), *International Law and Peace Settlements* (CUP 2021) 131.

[40] Accord Pour la Paix et la Réconciliation au Mali—Issu du Processus d'Alger 20/06/2015 Mali/Azawad, chapter 2: Foundations for a sustainable resolution of the conflict, article 5; chapter 12: Specific Development Strategy, articles 34 and 37 (PA-X Peace Agreements Database and Dataset, Version 7).

[41] Sudan peace agreement (Juba Agreement) 03/10/2020, para 29.1 (PA-X Peace Agreements Database and Dataset, Version 7).

[42] ibid para 27: Establishing Darfur Development Bank.

[43] ibid chapter 2: Wealth Sharing Protocol, General Principles, para 29.6, paras 29.1-29.8.

[44] ibid para 12.13.

[45] ibid para 12.15.

to be provided by the Government of the Republic of South Sudan.[46] As found in this section in relation to sustainable development, the question of reparations is developing within peace agreements, although it is argued that such developments need to be included with caution, as the nexus between victim reparations and development is yet unclear.[47]

4. Economic Development

While several peace agreements explicitly provided a holistic definition of sustainable development that included ecological/environmental sustainability, human development, and/or social and economic development, other agreements firmly enshrined the notion of economic development based upon growth, the free market, and a neoliberal model of development. On limited occasions, agreements included a clause on targeting vulnerable groups and the issue of economic marginalization. For example, in the case of Guatemala, the agreement includes guarantees of 'social equity' alongside provisions for economic growth.[48] Moreover, it establishes pre-conditions for such development, noting that:

> In the search for growth, economic policy must be directed towards preventing processes of economic exclusion, such as unemployment and impoverishment, and towards optimizing the benefits of economic growth for all Guatemalans. Raising the standard of living and ensuring health care, education, social security and training for Guatemalans are preconditions for achieving sustainable development in Guatemala.[49]

However, the provisions generally indicate a belief that transition to or strengthening of a free market economy, along with privatization and foreign investment, will ensure development and in some cases even social justice. For example, the Tokyo Declaration Partnership for Self-Reliance in Afghanistan states that

> developing a vibrant private sector will be essential for sustainable development of Afghanistan particularly for the long term; and that it requires the firm commitment

[46] Agreement between the Government of the Republic of South Sudan and the South Sudan Democratic Movement/Army, 27/02/2012, para 7. Compensation and Reparations, 'b. Therefore, they have agreed that the GRSS will provide compensation and reparations through social service delivery in the form of, (i) Humanitarian Relief and Assistance.' (PA-X Peace Agreements Database and Dataset, Version 7).

[47] Felix Torres Penagos, 'On Deserving Victims and the Undeserving Poor: Exploring the Scope of Distributive Justice in Transitional Justice Theory and Practice' (2023) 45 Human Rights Quarterly 306; Pubudu Sachithanandan, 'Reparations for Victims and Sustainable Development' in Sébastien Jodoin and Marie-Claire Cordonier Segger (eds), *Sustainable Development, International Criminal Justice, and Treaty Implementation* (CUP 2013); Simeon Gready, 'The Case for Transformative Reparations: In Pursuit of Structural Socio-economic Reform in Post-conflict Societies' (2022) 16 Journal of Intervention and Statebuilding 1.

[48] In the Agreement on the Social and Economic Aspects and Agrarian Situation 06/05/1996 Guatemala, para 40 (PA-X Peace Agreements Database and Dataset, Version 7).

[49] Agreement on a Firm and Lasting Peace 29/12/1996, Guatemala, para 8 (PA-X Peace Agreements Database and Dataset, Version 7).

> of the Afghan Government to taking all steps necessary to achieve an enabling business environment, including establishing regulatory frameworks and building necessary infrastructure. The Participants noted the importance of promoting domestic and foreign investment in Afghanistan.[50]

Another example is the case of Sudan. In the Homeland Call, the parties to the agreement set out a '[c]ommitment to realize sustainable development as a national goal for building infrastructure, social development and free market mechanism to attain social justice'.[51] Finally, in peace agreements relating to Darfur, a clear normative basis is established for economic development based upon the '[c]reation and equitable distribution of wealth in all parts of Sudan consistent with the maintenance of macroeconomic stability and sustainable development'.[52] This is to be achieved through, *inter alia*, equitable tax collection, decentralization of decision making regarding development and '[p]rovision of safe, secure, and open access to markets, goods and services with a view to: . . . a) Securing a conducive environment for foreign investment; . . . e) Implementing sustainable development principles'.[53] Of course, it is not evident from the text who was involved in the negotiations and what power or influence external actors had on the final agreement. What we can say is that the dominance of a neo-liberal approach to development is firmly enshrined in a number of peace agreements across the sample.[54]

5. Equality and Need for 'Special Protections': Provisions for Marginalized or Otherwise Vulnerable Groups

Another key theme which arose in the sample was provision for special protections and the acknowledgement that actions were required to protect and promote the sustainable development of those most marginalized or vulnerable within the conflict-affected society. Some of these provisions were in relation to equality of sex and gender;[55] others were concerning protections for specific groups such as youth or indigenous peoples. For example, in the Arusha Peace and Reconciliation Agreement for Burundi, the agreement states: 'In a country like Burundi where youth under the

[50] Tokyo Declaration Partnership for Self-Reliance in Afghanistan from Transition to Transformation (Tokyo Conference) 08/07/2012, para 20; para 1 (PA-X Peace Agreements Database and Dataset, Version 7).

[51] Homeland Call 25/11/1999 Sudan, para 4.4 (PA-X Peace Agreements Database and Dataset, Version 7).

[52] Doha Document for Peace in Darfur (DDPD) 31/05/2011 Sudan/Darfur, para 1 (PA-X Peace Agreements Database and Dataset, Version 7); Darfur Peace Agreement 05/05/2006 Sudan/Darfur, para 1(a) (PA-X Peace Agreements Database and Dataset, Version 7).

[53] ibid, Doha Agreement, para 2–4; Darfur Peace Agreement para 1 (1–9) (a–i).

[54] Amanda Cahill-Ripley, 'Reclaiming the Peacebuilding Agenda: Economic and Social Rights as a Legal Framework for Building Positive Peace—A Human Security Plus Approach to Peacebuilding' (2016) 16 Human Rights Law Review 223, 240 for a discussion of the role of international actors in peace agreements.

[55] Arusha Peace and Reconciliation Agreement for Burundi 28/08/2000, chapter III Economic and Social Development, para 3.6: The role of women in development, 'Equality between the sexes does much to enhance the well-being of women, men, girls and boys, and is indispensable for achieving people-centred sustainable development' (PA-X Peace Agreements Database and Dataset, Version 7).

age of 15 make up nearly half the population, no sustainable development is possible if the needs and aspirations of youth are not taken into account.'[56] In the case of Mexico, the Agreement Regarding the Joint Proposals between the Federal Government and the EZLN states:

> With regard to sustainable development… There is a need to develop a policy of true sustainability that preserves the lands, territories and natural resources of indigenous peoples, in short, that takes into account the social costs of development projects.[57]

Of particular interest is the Framework agreement between the Transitional Government of Sudan and the Darfur Track, which acknowledges inequality in the specific context of the conflict itself and provides that 'balanced and sustainable development' is required, as is 'positive discrimination to address the effects of war and bridge the development gap between Sudan's regions.'[58]

E. How Have Peace Agreements Dealt with Humanitarian Assistance?

The objective of this strand of analysis is to investigate the attention given to humanitarian assistance within peace agreements; to examine how humanitarian assistance is conceived of within peace agreements; to investigate which humanitarian issues are addressed in peace agreements, and how; and to identify common themes and patterns across and within the data set. Similarly to the analysis of sustainable development in section C, textual analysis of the subset of data 'Humanitarian Assistance' identified a number of general themes that are frequently included within peace agreements. These can be categorized as provisions concerning the definition of humanitarian assistance (including normative statements, scope, and content); access (including prohibitions); frameworks (including process and monitoring); funding and international assistance; equality and special protections. These themes and examples are explored in the following sections.

1. Defining Humanitarian Assistance—Emergency and Long-Term Approaches

Provisions for humanitarian assistance are found in general peace agreements and in separate specific agreements pertaining solely to enabling humanitarian assistance,

[56] Arusha Peace and Reconciliation Agreement for Burundi 28/08/2000, chapter III Economic and Social Development, 3.7: The role of youth (PA-X Peace Agreements Database and Dataset, Version 7).

[57] Agreement Regarding the Joint Proposals between the Federal Government and the EZLN 16/02/1996 Mexico, para 2 (PA-X Peace Agreements Database and Dataset, Version 7).

[58] Framework agreement between the Transitional Government of Sudan and the Darfur Track 28/12/2019, para 8 (PA-X Peace Agreements Database and Dataset, Version 7). Also verbatim in the Juba Agreement 03/10/2020, (B) Framework Agreement between the Transitional Government of Sudan and the Darfur Track, General Principles, para 8 (PA-X Peace Agreements Database and Dataset, Version 7).

such as in Bosnia,[59] Indonesia,[60] and Libya.[61] Due to the sequencing of responses to conflict, provisions for humanitarian assistance are often included within initial or ceasefire agreements. Such agreements enable a suspension of hostilities (sometimes only temporarily) to allow humanitarian actions to take place. For example, the Arsal 24-Hour Ceasefire Agreement between Lebanon/Syria was specifically to 'Permit the delivery of food, medical and humanitarian aid to the town of Arsal'.[62] The Syrian Ceasefire Agreement: Standard Conditions and Procedures Necessary to Ensure the Cessation of Hostilities provided for a 48-hour ceasefire agreement, specifically:

- termination of the application of air strikes, missiles, mortars, and anti-tank guided missiles;
- granting humanitarian organizations access to areas under the operational control RPBD participants, as well as creating conditions for immediate humanitarian aid has been delivered to all in need;[63]

Another example can be seen in Colombia, where:

> With the aim of concrete action relating to humanitarianism, the National Government, and the National Liberation Army, have agreed to develop a bilateral and temporary ceasefire, to reduce the intensity of the armed conflict. Its primary objective is to improve the humanitarian situation of the population.[64]

In the case of Indonesia/Aceh, a specific ceasefire agreement was adopted to enable humanitarian assistance: the Joint Understanding on Humanitarian Pause for Aceh.[65] This utilization of diplomatic language, that is, 'humanitarian pause', could be interpreted as a way for both parties to 'save face' and appear not to have submitted to a ceasefire, but rather to take a high moral stance of humanitarianism for the people affected.

[59] For example, the Agreement on Complete Cessation of Hostilities 31/12/1994, Bosnia and Herzegovina/Yugoslavia (former) 1, para 5 (PA-X Peace Agreements Database and Dataset, Version 7); Agreement between General Smith and General Mladic 19/07/1995, Bosnia and Herzegovina/Yugoslavia (former) 1 para 3 and 6 (PA-X Peace Agreements Database and Dataset, Version 7); Comprehensive Ceasefire Agreement, Pleso 3/12/1994 Bosnia and Herzegovina/Yugoslavia (former) 1 article 3 (PA-X Peace Agreements Database and Dataset, Version 7).

[60] Joint Understanding on Humanitarian Pause for Aceh 12/05/2000 Indonesia/Aceh (PA-X Peace Agreements Database and Dataset, Version 7).

[61] Fezzan Humanitarian Agreement 16/06/2016, Libya p 1; Humanitarian Appeal for Benghazi 16/03/2016, Libya, 1, para 6; p 2, para 3 (PA-X Peace Agreements Database and Dataset, Version 7); Agreement to stop the bloodshed and open the door to dialogue in the Western Region 16/06/2015, Libya, 1, para 1 (PA-X Peace Agreements Database and Dataset, Version 7).

[62] Arsal 24-Hour Ceasefire Agreement, 05/08/2014, Lebanon/Syria, 1, para 5 (PA-X Peace Agreements Database and Dataset, Version 7).

[63] Syrian Ceasefire Agreement: Standard Conditions and Procedures Necessary to Ensure the Cessation of Hostilities 09/09/2016, Reducing the level of violence, restoration of access and the creation of SIG, 4 (PA-X Peace Agreements Database and Dataset, Version 7).

[64] Comunicado Conjunto 4: Acuerdo de Quito 04/09/2017, Columbia, 1 (PA-X Peace Agreements Database and Dataset, Version 7).

[65] Joint Understanding on Humanitarian Pause for Aceh 12/05/2000 Indonesia/Aceh (PA-X Peace Agreements Database and Dataset, Version 7).

As illustrated by these examples, when defining humanitarian assistance, emergency humanitarian responses are clearly a priority and provided for in several peace agreements. In terms of defining such assistance, none of the peace agreements analysed included a definitive characterization of what such humanitarian assistance or humanitarian action constitutes. However, it was clear that agreements appear to differentiate between humanitarian assistance and humanitarian action. While humanitarian action is mainly associated with exchange of prisoners of war, retrieval of bodies, tracing missing persons, and/or mine removal, humanitarian assistance is conceived of more broadly, for example including provision of food, water, clothing, medical supplies, fuel, restoration of power and energy supplies, and other utilities, including the materials necessary for utilities to be repaired/restored.[66] Moreover, there was some limited recognition that humanitarian assistance is not just an issue of immediate emergency response, but can require long-term programming. For example, in the case of Bosnia, the Dayton Agreement recognizes that

> [t]he implementation of the civilian aspects of the peace settlement will entail a wide range of activities including continuation of the humanitarian aid effort for as long as necessary; rehabilitation of infrastructure and economic reconstruction.[67]

Similarly, in the Commitment to a unilateral ceasefire from Youssouf Toloba Mali, it is stated that

> [t]he State of Mali and its partners to work to provide humanitarian assistance commensurate with the needs of all communities in the area affected by the crisis: food aid, medical care, repair, construction, and rehabilitation of basic social infrastructures (health structures, schools, water points, etc.). They also ask for support for economic recovery through the financing of activities such as cattle trade, transport, stock rebuilding, and so on.[68]

Overall, however, examples of humanitarian assistance as a long-term activity were rare within the peace agreements analysed.

In addition to specific content, several agreements include value statements noting the key principles of humanitarian assistance as requiring neutrality, impartiality,[69]

[66] Numerous agreements provided for this content, including *inter alia* agreements pertaining to Bosnia: The Vance-Owen Plan 02/05/1993, 8; Agreement (ICRC Humanitarian Principles) 06/06/1992, pp 3–4; Geneva Agreement on humanitarian principles 22/05/1992, 3 and Ceasefire Agreement 05/05/1992, 1. Also, Syria, Memorandum on the Creation of De-escalation areas in the Syrian Arab Republic 04/05/2017, 1, para 2; Liberia, Final Communique, Economic Community of West African States, First Extraordinary Session of the Authority of Heads of State and Government, Bamako, 27 and 28 November 1990, 28/11/1990, 5, para 16; PA-X Peace Agreements Database and Dataset, Version 7).

[67] General Framework Agreement for Peace in Bosnia and Herzegovina (Dayton Peace Agreement) 21/11/1995, 111, Annex 10: Agreement on Civilian Implementation of the Peace Settlement, Article I (PA-X Peace Agreements Database and Dataset, Version 7).

[68] Commitment to a unilateral ceasefire from Youssouf Toloba and his armed group, Dan Nan Ambassagou, 27/09/2018, Mali, 3, article 3 (PA-X Peace Agreements Database and Dataset, Version 7).

[69] Programme of Action on Humanitarian Issues agreed between the Co-Chairmen to the Conference and the Parties to the Conflict, International Conference on Yugoslavia (The London Conference) 27/08/1992, Bosnia and Herzegovina/Yugoslavia (former) 2, para 3 (PA-X Peace Agreements Database and Dataset, Version 7).

and non-discrimination.[70] For example, the SPLM-United/Operation Lifeline Sudan Agreement on Ground Rules sets out a Statement of humanitarian principles detailing that:

1. [. . .] The right to receive humanitarian assistance and to offer it is a fundamental humanitarian principle;
2. The guiding principle of OLS and FRRA is that of humanitarian neutrality—an independent status for humanitarian work beyond political or military considerations.[71]

Likewise, in the Declaration by the Government of the Republic of Mozambique and RENAMO on the guiding principles for humanitarian assistance, the principle of neutrality is 'recognised and respected' as a guiding norm.[72] Furthermore, reference to standards of international humanitarian law and the rules of the International Committee of the Red Cross (ICRC) and the United Nations (UN) are often linked to such requirements. For example, the Declaration of Principles for the Resolution of the Sudanese Conflict in Darfur requires that '[h]umanitarian assistance will be provided on the basis of humanitarian principles including those enshrined in International Humanitarian Law, UN norms and standards'.[73] Similarly, in the Revitalised Agreement on the Resolution of the Conflict in the Republic of South Sudan, parties agree to 'uphold international law, and shall allow and facilitate unfettered access for people in need to receive humanitarian assistance from the United Nations, and impartial international and national nongovernmental organizations'.[74]

2. Access Including Prohibitions and Guarantees

A second key theme identified within the data is provisions to ensure access for the delivery of humanitarian aid and for humanitarian personnel. Requirements include creation of safe corridors, clearing and repair of roads, and permission for access to specific roads and airports. For example, in Afghanistan, the parties agreed to '[l]ifting

[70] For example, the Additional Protocol to the Memorandum on Stabilization of the Situation in the Idlib De-Escalation Area, 05/03/2020, Russia/Syria/Turkey, 1 (PA-X Peace Agreements Database and Dataset, Version 7); Humanitarian Appeal for Benghazi 16/03/2016, Libya, 1, para 6 (PA-X Peace Agreements Database and Dataset, Version 7).

[71] SPLM-United/Operation Lifeline Sudan Agreement on Ground Rules 01/05/1996 South Sudan/Sudan, A. Statement of humanitarian principles, paras 1 and 2 (PA-X Peace Agreements Database and Dataset, Version 7).

[72] Declaration by the Government of Mozambique and RENAMO on guiding principles for humanitarian assistance 16/07/1992 Mozambique, 1 (I) (c) (PA-X Peace Agreements Database and Dataset, Version 7).

[73] Declaration of Principles for the Resolution of the Sudanese Conflict in Darfur 05/07/2005 p 3, article 8 (PA-X Peace Agreements Database and Dataset, Version 7); Dhahran al-Janoub Agreements on the Cessation of Hostilities in Yemen for Shabwah, al-Dhali', alBaydah, al-Jawf, Ma'rib, Ta'iz and Terms and Conditions, 10/04/2016, Yemen, 1, Preamble (PA-X Peace Agreements Database and Dataset, Version 7); Peace Agreement between the Government of Liberia, the Liberians United for Reconciliation and Democracy (LURD), the Movement of Democracy in Liberia (MODEL) and the Political Parties (Accra Agreement) 18/08/2003 Liberia, 12, para 1(a) (PA-X Peace Agreements Database and Dataset, Version 7).

[74] Revitalised Agreement on the Resolution of the Conflict in the Republic of South Sudan, 12/09/2018, 33, chapter 2, 2.1.10.7.8 (PA-X Peace Agreements Database and Dataset, Version 7).

internal blockades and opening roads for reciprocal trade and delivery of humanitarian assistance in the territories controlled by the various Afghan groups'.[75]

Closely linked to the question of access is the inclusion of provisions prohibiting interference with humanitarian assistance. These can be provisions forbidding physical or economic obstructions. For example, the Agreement on Principles of Settlement of the Georgian–Ossetian Conflict (Sochi Agreement) states that '[t]he Parties deem it inadmissible to apply economic sanctions and blockade, and any other impediments to free movement of commodities, services and people and commit themselves to provide humanitarian assistance to the affected population'.[76]

Access to humanitarian assistance is also facilitated through the inclusion of guarantees, for example that such assistance or aid will be for the use of civilians and not diverted. For example, Bosnia's Joint Declaration declared that the parties must '[e]nsure that all humanitarian assistance reaches its intended civilian beneficiaries and is not diverted to the military or others'.[77]

3. Frameworks for Humanitarian Assistance—Process and Monitoring

In addition to provisions dealing with content and access to humanitarian assistance, some agreements also include clauses on process and institutions for implementing humanitarian actions. This is crucial, as implementation is key if a peace agreement is to be successful. A number of agreements included provisions for the establishment of committees and task forces to oversee humanitarian action,[78] including *inter alia* to undertake inspection of aid at local level with local oversight and representatives. The First Meeting of the Joint Forum, concerning Indonesia/Aceh, notes:

> [w]hile recognising the importance of the role of regional and international humanitarian assistance, the Joint Forum encourages full participation of local community in the implementation of humanitarian programmes, as stated in the Joint Understanding on Humanitarian Pause for Aceh.[79]

[75] Tashkent Declaration on Fundamental Principles for a Peaceful Settlement of the Conflict in Afghanistan 19/07/1999, pp 4 and 5 (PA-X Peace Agreements Database and Dataset, Version 7).

[76] Agreement on Principles of Settlement of the Georgian-Ossetian Conflict (Sochi Agreement) 24/06/1992, Georgia/Russia/(Ossetia) 2, article 4 (PA-X Peace Agreements Database and Dataset, Version 7). Another example can be seen in Libyan Political Agreement (Sukhairat Agreement) 17/12/2015 p 12, article 28 (3) (PA-X Peace Agreements Database and Dataset, Version 7).

[77] Joint Declaration 18/11/1993 Bosnia and Herzegovina/Yugoslavia (former) p 1, para 4, para 3 (PA-X Peace Agreements Database and Dataset, Version 7).

[78] For example, the Joint Monitoring Committee established by the Joint Monitoring Committee guideline for Each Level (Draft) 15/10/2015, Myanmar (PA-X Peace Agreements Database and Dataset, Version 7); the Joint Oversight Committee est. in Agreement between the Government of the Republic of South Sudan and the South Sudan Democratic Movement/Army 27/02/2012, 3, para 9 (PA-X Peace Agreements Database and Dataset, Version 7); the Joint Sub-Committee on Humanitarian and Rehabilitation Needs Declaration in Support of the Peace Process in Sri Lanka (Oslo Declaration) 25/11/2002, 3 (PA-X Peace Agreements Database and Dataset, Version 7).

[79] The First Meeting of the Joint Forum, Switzerland, 23–24 June 2000 24/06/2000, Indonesia/Aceh p 1, II. Directives, A. On Ground Rules of the Joint Committee on Humanitarian Action: chapter IV, article 6.2 (a) (PA-X Peace Agreements Database and Dataset, Version 7).

The importance of local participation is also demonstrated through a commitment to support local capacity building, thus illustrating the nexus with development. For example, the SPLM-United/Operation Lifeline Sudan Agreement on Ground Rules states that:

> All humanitarian actions should be tailored to local circumstances and aim to enhance, not supplant, locally available resources and mechanisms. Strengthening local capacity to prevent future crises and emergencies and to promote greater involvement of Sudanese institutions and individuals in all humanitarian actions is an integral part of OLS's humanitarian mandate.[80]

4. Funding for Humanitarian Assistance Including International Assistance

In parallel to calls for local participation, also significant in the findings is the occurrence of provisions that set out requests to the international community for humanitarian and financial assistance (provisions akin to those requesting donors for development post-conflict). This can be requests for assistance from regional actors or international institutions as well as third states.[81] In addition, these requests are often linked to calls for assistance with development and reconstruction. For example, the Final Communique from the Economic Community of West African States concerning Liberia states in its section 'Appeal for international assistance' that

> [t]he Authority made an urgent appeal to the international community, particularly its humanitarian relief organizations, to step up without further delay humanitarian relief work in Liberia with special emphasis on the provision of food, medical supplies and clothing. It also appealed to the international donor community to contribute generously to the efforts of the Interim Government in the rehabilitation and reconstruction of the damaged economy of Liberia.[82]

In some cases, the assistance offered by third parties can be conditional on meeting certain conditions set out in the peace agreement itself. For example, in the case of Bosnia, it was stipulated that 'Assistance for reconstruction and housing beyond basic

[80] SPLM-United/Operation Lifeline Sudan Agreement on Ground Rules, 01/05/1996 South Sudan/Sudan, A. Statement of humanitarian principles, 2, para 6 (PA-X Peace Agreements Database and Dataset, Version 7).

[81] For example, Libyan Political Agreement (Sukhairat Agreement) 17/12/2015 Libya, 18, International Support Article (57); Humanitarian Appeal for Benghazi 16/03/2016 Libya, 1, para 6; Compte Rendu des Activities du Comité de Suivi de L'Accord de Paix à Bangassou 06/03/2019, Central African Republic, 3; Final Communiqué of International Ministerial Meeting of the Neighbouring Countries of Iraq, the G8 and China 23/11/2004 Iraq, 2, para 11. PA-X Peace Agreements Database and Dataset, Version 7.

[82] Final Communiqué, Economic Community of West African States, First Extraordinary Session of the Authority of Heads of State and Government, Bamako, 27 and 28 November 1990 28/11/1990 Liberia, Appeal for international assistance, 5, para 16 (PA-X Peace Agreements Database and Dataset, Version 7); Declaration in Support of the Peace Process in Sri Lanka (Oslo Declaration) 25/11/2002, Sri Lanka, 3 (PA-X Peace Agreements Database and Dataset, Version 7).

humanitarian requirements will not be channelled to communities that fail to permit the return of displaced people and refugees'.[83] This conditionality highlights a tension between international assistance and local agency. Clearly, there is a balance to be found between international assistance (and therefore international power and decision-making) and the inclusion and active participation and control given to local actors. This balance is reflected in the varying provisions of these peace agreements.

5. Equality and Special Protections

As seen with provisions for sustainable development within peace agreements, the vulnerability of marginalized groups such as refugees, children, and women is also acknowledged and provided for regarding humanitarian assistance. In Libya, the parties state that they will 'work together as one, to facilitate the access of aid, in full, to the whole population, without any discrimination and with justice in distribution, giving priority to the most vulnerable groups, like children, women, and the elderly'.[84] Moreover, the SPLM-United/Operation Lifeline Sudan Agreement on Ground Rules requires that:

> 2 (i) Humanitarian aid must be given according to considerations of human need alone. Its granting or its acceptance must not be made dependent on political factors or upon race, religion, ethnicity, or nationality. It must not seek to advance any political agenda. Where humanitarian assistance is inadequate to meet the needs of all, priority must be given to the most vulnerable.[85]

Similar provisions can be found across the sample, including *inter alia* in the Cotonou Accord regarding Liberia, which notes that special protections are required for children,[86] and in the Makarska Agreement concerning Bosnia, which provides a similar clause to the Sudan agreement on the distribution of aid ensuring non-discrimination.[87]

Overall, when read together, the combination of provisions containing statements of underlying values and principles and provisions setting out specific content can be said to constitute the scope and content of humanitarian assistance within the peace agreements analysed. The findings demonstrate strong inclusion of humanitarian assistance within peace agreements and a number of common themes across the dataset.

[83] Agreement on the Federation of Bosnia and Herzegovina, Sarajevo 30/03/1996 Bosnia and Herzegovina/Yugoslavia (former) 5, Consequences of Non-Implementation, para 10 (PA-X Peace Agreements Database and Dataset, Version 7).

[84] Fezzan Humanitarian Agreement 16/06/2016, Libya, 1 (PA-X Peace Agreements Database and Dataset, Version 7).

[85] SPLM-United/Operation Lifeline Sudan Agreement on Ground Rules 01/05/1996 South Sudan/Sudan, 'A. Statement of humanitarian principles, 1, para 2(i)' (PA-X Peace Agreements Database and Dataset, Version 7).

[86] Cotonou Accord regarding Liberia (Geneva Ceasefire Agreement) 25/07/1993 Liberia, section E, article 17 (PA-X Peace Agreements Database and Dataset, Version 7).

[87] Agreement on the Passage of Humanitarian Convoys (Makarska Agreement) 10/07/1993 Bosnia, 1, para. 2 (PA-X Peace Agreements Database and Dataset, Version 7).

F. Linking Development, Humanitarian Assistance, and Peace: Recognizing Intersections

It is evident from the analysis of peace agreements in section D that both sustainable development and humanitarian assistance are provided for within peace agreements and often in a comprehensive manner. While the explicit intersection between development and humanitarian assistance is limited, the nexus between peace and development is more explicitly recognized. Some agreements focus on security and stability, noting that both are a requirement for development.[88] However, others focus on peacebuilding: both the Acte d'Engagement concerning the Democratic Republic of Congo[89] and the Guidelines and Ground Rules for the Implementation and Monitoring of the Agreement on the Cessation of Hostilities between the Government of the Republic of Philippines and the Rebolusyonaryong Partido ng Manggagawa ng Mindanao[90] state that peace is necessary for sustainable development. The Juba Agreement goes further and acknowledges that sustainable development requires attention to tackling root causes of conflict, stating that '[a]ddressing the root causes of conflicts shall be a key requirement necessary for peacebuilding and sustainable development'.[91]

The in-depth analysis undertaken in section C has demonstrated that specific provisions that reflect the 'triple nexus' between peace, sustainable development, and humanitarian assistance are limited.[92] However, it is perhaps more realistic to read the provisions of a peace agreement as a whole, to understand the overall aim of the agreement—and perhaps this is where the triple-nexus approach is reflected—not within specific provisions but within the holistic interpretation of the objectives of a peace agreement. As Joshi and Quinn argue, parties to the peacemaking should 'view accord content holistically and not just focus on key provisions'.[93] For example, the recent Juba Agreement states within the 'Objectives of this Agreement General Provisions' that:

[88] Accord d'Alger pour la Restauration de la Paix, de la Sécurité et du Développement dans la région de Kidal, 04/07/2006 Mali/Azawad, 'Noting the Interdependence Between Development, Security and Stability' (PA-X Peace Agreements Database and Dataset, Version 7); Protocol of Non-aggression and Mutual Defence in the Great Lakes Region 30/11/2006 Angola/Central African Republic/Democratic Republic of Congo/Kenya/Republic of Congo/Rwanda/Sudan/Tanzania/Uganda/Zambia/(African Great Lakes), para 2 (PA-X Peace Agreements Database and Dataset, Version 7).

[89] Acte d'Engagement, Nord Kivu 23/01/2008 Democratic Republic of Congo, para 6 (PA-X Peace Agreements Database and Dataset, Version 7).

[90] Guidelines and Ground Rules for the Implementation and Monitoring of the Agreement on the Cessation of Hostilities between the Government of the Republic of Philippines and the Rebolusyonaryong Partido ng Manggagawa ng Mindanao, 28/10/2005 Philippines, Preamble (PA-X Peace Agreements Database and Dataset, Version 7).

[91] Sudan Peace Agreement (Juba Agreement) 03/10/2020, chapter 3: Political Issues Agreement Regarding the Issue of Sudan in the Two Areas General Principles, para 6 (PA-X Peace Agreements Database and Dataset, Version 7).

[92] On the 'triple nexus': Paul Howe, 'The Triple Nexus: A Potential Approach to Supporting the Achievement of the Sustainable Development Goals?' (2019) 124 World Development 1. Unsurprisingly, a free text search of the full data set of 2,003 peace agreements found no explicit references to a 'nexus of development and humanitarian action' or 'triple nexus' (Amanda Cahill-Ripley (author), P-AX Database free text search, 28 February 2023).

[93] Madhav Joshi and J Michael Quinn, 'Is the Sum Greater than the Parts: The Terms of Civil War Peace Agreements and the Commitment Problem Revisited' (2015) 31 Negotiation Journal 7, 27.

1. The objective of this Agreement is to serve as a binding framework to which the Parties shall adhere throughout all peace and political negotiations for the Two Areas as part of Sudan during the transitional period, aiming to achieve a *just, comprehensive, and sustainable peace agreement* and a permanent constitution for Sudan.
2. *Realizing peace in the Two Areas in a way that consolidates and complements efforts to achieve a just, comprehensive, and durable peace* in all parts of Sudan and a transition from the oppression of the former regime to a new democratic Sudan.
3. Creating an environment conducive for the safe and voluntary return of refugees and internally displaced persons to their original homes in the Two Areas.
4. Alleviating the continued suffering of the people in the Two Areas through *immediate humanitarian action, reconstruction, and sustainable development, as well as through a process of long-term political, social, and cultural transformation.*[94]

As the ideas of sustaining peace and the SDGs as mutually reinforcing have gathered traction in broader international development and peacebuilding agendas,[95] so too it would seem the idea of the triple-nexus approach is perhaps beginning to be considered in specific peace agreements. Moving forward, one would expect to see further recognition of the mutually reinforcing fields of sustainable development, humanitarian assistance, and peacebuilding.

G. Conclusions

To conclude, this chapter has examined the extent to which sustainable development and humanitarian assistance are entrenched within existing peace agreements, as well as exploring the scope and content of such provisions. Such an assessment of current practice has provided a strong evidential basis from which to assess whether peace agreements provide a foundational basis for sustainable peace and development in the context of protracted conflicts. In sum, the research provides a number of key findings. Concerning scope and content, evidence from the empirical research demonstrates that the idea of a peace agreement as a foundation for sustainable peace and development, including humanitarian assistance, is firmly embedded in practice. A number of common themes have been identified across both sustainable development and humanitarian assistance fields. These core areas include provisions covering definitions and normative statements, frameworks for policy and implementation, funding, international assistance, and involvement and measures for equality

[94] Sudan peace agreement (Juba Agreement) 03/10/2020, 'Objectives of this Agreement General Provisions' paras 1–4 (PA-X Peace Agreements Database and Dataset, Version 7). Emphasis added.

[95] *Inter alia* United Nations Security Council (UNSC) Res 2282 (27 April 2016) UN Doc S/Res/2282 and United Nations General Assembly (UNGA), 'Review of the United Nations Peacebuilding Architecture' 70th sess (27 April 2016), UN Doc A/RES/70/262; UNSC, UNGA, 'Report of the Secretary-General, Peacebuilding and sustaining peace' (30 July 2020) A/74/976–S/2020/773; UNGA, 'Transforming Our World: The 2030 Agenda for Sustainable Development' (21 October 2015) A/RES/70/1, para 35 and overall 18 mentions of 'peace'.

and special protections. This would indicate a common 'blueprint' for sustainable development and humanitarian assistance within peace agreements, at least in terms of structure and broad areas of concern.

On a positive note, of the 43 per cent of peace agreements that include specific provisions for sustainable development and humanitarian assistance, many were comprehensive and surprisingly detailed in terms of both content and process. Sustainable development, particularly in more recent peace agreements, was subject to extensive provisions. While humanitarian assistance provisions were less detailed, they did include a wide range of measures and, significantly, they were not solely focused on emergency aid. However, it should also be noted that nearly half (47%) of peace agreements did not provide for sustainable development or humanitarian assistance. Examining the reasons for this is outside of the scope of this chapter, but it would be useful to undertake further research to assess the reasons for this omission. It could be due to the types of agreement and/or could be due to purposeful omission, for example due to a lack of consensus between parties.

Although the explicit recognition of the nexus between sustainable peace and sustainable development is evident within contemporary peace agreements, explicit recognition of a specific nexus with humanitarian assistance is much less clear. As argued previously, perhaps the best way to acknowledge and support such a triple-nexus approach is to interpret and read the peace accords holistically and across the sequence of agreements.

Finally, it is important to acknowledge that further research is required to examine the implementation of relevant provisions individually and collectively and to evaluate the positive effects of such agreements for long-term sustainable peace and development. Molloy notes that research has shown that the content of a peace accord generally 'and how and the extent to which it is implemented is a particularly strong indicator for durable peace'.[96] However, the reality of a peace agreement 'on paper and positively effecting change from these commitments in practice are two very different things'.[97] Peace agreements can provide a solid foundation for building sustainable peace and development. However, they are not without limitations, and constitute only one element of a complex process that requires not only effective policy and legal frameworks but also adequate resources, political will, and societal and cultural change. As I write this chapter, armed conflict has sadly broken out between warring factions within the capital of Sudan.[98] Thus, the case of Sudan demonstrates the disparity between theoretical transformative provisions within comprehensive peace agreements and the reality of spoilers and resumption of conflict. Crucially, it is important to remember that peace agreements are the starting point (and the re-entry point), not the finale, in transforming a protracted conflict into a situation of positive peace.

[96] Sean Molloy, 'Conceptualising the Transformative Justice Potential of Peace Processes' (2023) 27 The International Journal of Human Rights 307, 320.

[97] ibid 318.

[98] 'As Desperate Sudanese Flee Their Embattled Nation, Security Council Urges Warring Parties to Respect Ceasefire, Reboot Negotiations, Immediately End Fighting' (*United Nations Meetings Coverage and Press Releases*, 25 April 2023) <https://press.un.org/en/2023/sc15265.doc.htm> accessed 17 September 2024.

22

The Challenging Imperative of Ending the War in the Democratic Republic of the Congo (DRC)

Pascal Sundi Mbambi, Patience Kabamba Sindani, and Abhisekh Rodricks

A. Introduction

The war in the DRC has affected Congolese populations in many ways, and people have not remained passive to its dire consequences. In 2005 Nkundabatware's army of the National Congress for the Defence of the People (*Congrès National pour la Défense du Peuple*, CNDP), presently known as the March 23 Movement (*Mouvement du 23-Mars* or M23), attacked Kanyabayonga in the North Kivu province of the DRC. The inhabitants of this town, who were mostly Nande (one of the tribes of the North Kivu), fled to settle temporarily about 60 kilometres further north, in Kayina. The World Food Programme (WFP) came to offer its services, in particular the distribution of biscuits and other food items. The displaced people refused the offer and replied to the WFP agents:

> We know how to produce food. If you really want to help us, go ask Nkunda to leave our land. You are the one arming these militias and you want to feed us? We need to get our land back, not to eat your cookies.[1]

It was the first time in the history of the WFP that displaced people had refused the assistance offered to them. As Stearns puts it,

> Congolese have developed their own, often witty ways to express this sad state of affairs. 'No Nkunda No Job', was a popular saying in Goma around this time, referring to the main rebel commander and suggesting that violence had become a source of employment for foreign aid workers and local militia.[2]

[1] Quote from interviews with civil society activist from Goma (North Kivu, Democratic Republic of the Congo, 27 January–3 February 2022). This point is echoed in Patience Kabamba Sindani, *Business of Civil War: New Forms of Life in the Debris of the Democratic Republic of Congo* (Codesria 2013).

[2] Jason Stearns, *The War that Doesn't Say Its Name: The Unending Conflict in the Congo* (Princeton University Press 2021) 10.

Pascal Sundi Mbambi, Patience Kabamba Sindani, and Abhisekh Rodricks, *The Challenging Imperative of Ending the War in the Democratic Republic of the Congo (DRC)* In: *From Protracted Conflict to Sustainable Peace?* Edited by: Heike Krieger, Giedre Jokubauskaite, Asli Ozcelik, and Andreas Buser, Oxford University Press. © Pascal Sundi Mbambi, Patience Kabamba Sindani, and Abhisekh Rodricks 2026. DOI: 10.1093/9780198967385.003.0026

This incident gives us the opportunity to question the aid narratives in the context of armed conflict, through the following main question: does foreign/international aid hold a potential to end the war in the eastern DRC, especially through its triple-nexus version? In this chapter,[3] we focus on the prospects of the aid narratives in the humanitarian-development-peace nexus approach (hereinafter the HDP nexus, or the triple nexus) in ending or even in fuelling conflicts in the war-torn DRC. The relevance of this analysis stems from the fact that people of eastern Congo, who are the most affected by decades of the ongoing armed conflict, have shown clear signs of 'aid fatigue'.

Our argument is that, unless the DRC becomes a political space, the country will not enjoy peace and stability. A political space implies strong political leadership at all levels of power, and genuine citizen engagement to allow viable functioning of state institutions, followed by smooth power bargaining. This governance setup can be supported not by an 'aid regime' but rather by a shift to a 'right-based regime', or, more precisely, the implementation of the right to development agenda. This would enable the Congo to act as a bearer for its people's rights, thereby placing it in a position within the global platform where it can demand 'reparations' from the international community (actors) for the wrongs endured by the DRC during the past decades.

The research underpinning this chapter is varied as we aim to understand different elements of conflict in the DRC and its proposed 'solutions'. The entire chapter, and the second section in particular, is based on the critical postcolonial literature, and also on the literature in political science that focuses on the drivers of conflict in Africa. The third section focuses on international responses to the DRC conflict, where we also zoom in on the triple-nexus agenda, as the most recent perspective endorsed by the UN towards conflict resolution or settlement. The fourth section discusses the right to development as a way forward for the international policy agenda, an essential approach to reframe the aid narratives and conflict resolution in international law.

B. Perspectives of Global Narratives on the Congolese Conflict

There are a number of narratives which are relevant in order to understand and assess the drivers of conflict in the Congo; these include the interconnections between the global and the local, diverging conceptions of sovereignty, the colonial heritage, and the role of the Congolese society. Each of these will be discussed in more detail in this section.

[3] The chapter has benefited from discussions with DRC government officials and civil society organizations, as well as with development and humanitarian partners in two workshops held in late August 2021 in Kinshasa and in late January 2022 in Bukavu (South Kivu Province), on the relevance of humanitarian and development aid in the post-conflict reconstruction context.

1. Ignoring the Local

In recent decades, young Western scholars have shown a renewed interest in conducting research on the DRC. These researchers entered the Congo as NGO workers or consultants and went on to undertake political science PhD studies on the topic of the Congo. As James Ferguson[4] puts it, NGOs are focused on finding solutions instead of formulating original problems. This model generally constructs a scenario where the problems are internal and the solutions that are suggested and debated upon are external. As Zambakari and Mandani have pointed out,[5] one cannot import solutions. For a solution to be durable, it must be home-grown. Among the most influential and recent international literature on the conflict in the Congo is that by Séverine Autesserre.[6] Her book is a prototype of outside (mis-)understanding of the heart of the conflict in the DRC. By engaging with this author, the current chapter will enlighten the role played by the Congolese and the way it is misunderstood by external actors.

In her book *The Trouble with the Congo*, Autesserre makes a very important remark: many of the conflicts have their roots in local competing legitimacies, and by neglecting these local levels of engagement in favour of national and regional agreements, the international community fails to adequately address the major causes of the conflicts. Autesserre comes to this conclusion after several years of observing and interviewing diplomats, UN personnel, and NGOs in different countries including the Congo[7], Kosovo, Afghanistan, India, and Nicaragua. The book is, indeed, the product of extensive fieldwork in the DRC since 2001.

However, Autesserre's *The Trouble with the Congo* is missing the narrative concerning Congolese efforts to address the conflict. The impression in the book is that the Congolese are powerless to solve this conflict at the local as well as the national levels. Outside intervention seems absolutely needed. This may be the first flaw of this book: an uncritical positing that Congolese fate is in the hands of outside players. For the author, these outside players are critical in bringing sustainable peace and democracy. This is simply wrong. The Congolese are indeed actors from the beginning to the end of the bloody primitive accumulation processes to which their history is taking them. 'Primitive accumulation' refers to the final chapter of Volume I of Karl Marx's *Capital*, where he explains how capitalists gather their first capital by violently confiscating land from peasants.[8] Unless the outside world understands this and plays the role of an external actor without undermining the internal players, it will only unduly

[4] James Ferguson, *The Anti-politics Machine: 'Development', Depoliticization, and Bureaucratic Power in Lesotho* (CUP 1990).

[5] Also Mahmood Mamdani, 'The Invention of the Indigène' (*London Review of Books*, 20 January 2011) <https://www.lrb.co.uk/the-paper/v33/n02/mahmood-mamdani/the-invention-of-the-indigene>; Christopher D Zambakari, 'South Sudan: Institutional Legacy of Colonialism and the Making of a New State' (2012) 17 The Journal of North African Studies 515.

[6] Séverine Autesserre, *The Trouble with the Congo: Local Violence and the Failure of International Peacebuilding* (CUP 2010).

[7] Some observers have drawn a parallel between MONUC's (United Nations Organization Mission in the Democratic Republic of the Congo) intervention and the role the UN played in the 1960s as it was used by some countries as a legal tool to take out Lumumba, soften the heavy-handed tactics used by Belgium, and bar the Soviet Union from 'taking a foothold' in the heart of Africa.

[8] Karl Marx, *Capital: A Critique of Political Economy* (Vintage Books 1977, 1867).

prolong these processes of primitive accumulation, especially in their bloodiest African permutation phases that run deep. There is neither time nor space for the so-called international champions of peacebuilding and state building, which try to impose a rationalizing outsider's dictates on the continent. As Jason Stearns puts it: 'In part, outsiders spent too little time trying to understand the belligerents. This is not surprising; portrayals of the Congo have often dealt in stereotypes.'[9]

Though Autesserre discusses demoralized Congolese who find pride in elections,[10] many Congolese never actually found pride in the 2006 elections, given the violence before and after the voting process. For them, the 2006 elections, characterized by pre-electoral conditions of violence, were designed to satisfy the international community, which needed to justify the billions spent in the Congo with an election. Major Congolese problems were not to be answered by elections but by a new social contract at the local as well as at the national levels. This new deal would have eventually emerged had they been left alone to entirely manage their fate.

Let us now engage with the goal Autesserre sets at the beginning of her book: that '[t]his book is the first scholarly attempt to understand why all of the intense international peacebuilding efforts, including the largest peacekeeping mission in the world, have failed to build a sustainable peace in the Congo.'[11]

This goal, and the whole enterprise of the book, contain a naivety and an idealism which we would like to challenge. A sustainable peace in the Congo could only be built and sustained by the Congolese themselves. It is naïve to think that people who go from one social space to another across the globe without being subjects in any sense to those same social spaces would be the key to building a sustainable peace. It is naïve to think that it is an outside people's burden, especially the UN's, to solve in a sustainable way the instability in the Congo.

Before coming to Kinshasa, the DRC's capital city, many of the UN agents[12] had language training, technical training, but not experience of historical courses—not any reading list where one could find the work of Mudimbe, Mbembe, Mbokolo, Mamdani, or Abdou Maliq, *inter alia*. These critical discourses are not denied, but it is as if such discourses were suspended in the interests of groundwork-type basic rights and amenities-type projects at hand. Troublingly, this sort of brutish commonsensical logic is ridden with problematic assumptions, in particular the tacit sense of the necessity to defer to genealogies of power and the ignorance of complexities involved in local discourse or histories, or urban habitus, among other things.

These external agents arrive with a security-state mentality that must permeate the operations out of Kinshasa, and they bring with them what Povinelli refers to as the 'calling cards of colonizing capital'[13]—representations such as 'freedom' and so

[9] Stearns (n 2) 15.

[10] Autesserre (n 6) 233.

[11] ibid 5.

[12] One UN agent revealed to us that in 2003 they were taken from New York to run the department of the MONUC in the Congo from Kisangani. They did not know many things about that country, except maybe how Lumumba was killed. They were surprised that this was also the case for many of their colleagues in MONUC who were based in Kisangani.

[13] Elizabeth Povinelli, *Economies of Abandonment: Social Belonging and Endurance in Late Liberalism* (Duke University Press 2011).

on. In such a world, the most important thing is now security; even MONUC or MONUSCO is all about security, not an understanding of the genealogy of the conflict, nor even an understanding of the people on the ground. Colonized capitalists pretend to bring freedom and prosperity to justify the civilizing mission. In this view, security is the prerequisite to freedom and prosperity that the colonized people need most. People want first to be understood in their context, or, even better, to be recognized as human beings. Other things, such as freedom and security, should be on their own terms and not imported by outsiders or perceived through outside lenses.

Those who imagine themselves as purveyors of those necessary goods of modernity, such as 'freedom' and 'security' (not disagreeable concepts intrinsically, of course), make the crucial move of imagining themselves (as purveyors) as capable of moving across social spaces without being subject—in any sense—to those same social spaces. They are then a sort of global actor engaged in the elaboration of what may very well be a new or incipient kind of global governmentality, for whom the Congo and the Congolese are purely objects—and never properly historical subjects—upon which various formulations combining 'compassion' (through aid) and international and military policing must be directed in the presumably correct proportions, in order to maintain or reinstitute law and order. What is disturbing about this sort of discourse is that it contains specific political content, while pretending to be only about reportage and universal ethics.

For instance, the land[14] or ethnic issue[15] has been presented by scholars as part of the local reasons why conflict cannot be understood adequately. Unless it is 100 per cent commoditized, land in Africa takes on a level of intimacy and feeling that an outsider could hardly understand. This is not to say that there is no role for an outside actor at the local level; we are rather suggesting that the local arena is generally too complicated to understand, unless one has spent an extensive period of time in the region—a substantial presence with the intention of understanding without superimposing any pre-formulated claim.[16]

[14] For example Koen Vlassenroot, *South Kivu: Identity, Territory, and Power in the Eastern Congo* (Rift Valley Institute 2013); Koen Vlassenroot and Timothy Raeymaekers (eds), *Conflict and Social Transformation in Eastern DR Congo* (Academia Press Scientific Publishers 2004).

[15] Breytenbach and others argue, for instance, that Banyamulenge immigrants (or Tutsis living in the Kivus for 300 years) are considered non-indigenous and are exempted from ethnic citizenship at the independence in 1960; consequently these 'aliens' were denied customary access to land because they had no native authority in colonial days: Willie J Breytenbach and others, 'Conflicts in the Congo: From Kivu to Kabila' (1999) 8 African Security Review 33, 34. Such a claim has been very problematic for indigenous Congolese in the Kivus, for whom the Banyamulenge ethnic group is nonexistent in the colonial ethnic map of the Congo: Léon de Saint Moulin, *Atlas du Jubilé d'or de la RDC* (Centre d'Études Pour l'Action Sociale 2011). Congolese historian Isidore Ndaywel goes further to even deconstruct the myth of the 'Great Rwanda' and the fallacy of the Banyamulenge immigrants' extermination; he argues the Congo does not owe any piece of land to Rwanda, but the Rwanda does to Congo, Isidore Ndaywel è Nziem, 'Les migrations rwandaises dans l'Est de la RDC: histoire d'hier, problèmes d'aujourd'hui et perspectives' (ICREDES, Brussels, 18 November 2020) and Isidore Ndaywel è Nziem, 'Les vérités difficiles de l'histoire contemporaine des Grands Lacs' (2022) 273 Afrique contemporaine 9. This is to say the outside analysis of the land and ethnic issue might be biased as these are issues that need to be approached with a greater understanding of the historical dimensions but also the local complexities of coexistence in the region.

[16] The fact that Autesserre brings Afghanistan or any other countries into her discourse might be said to be sufficient evidence of rushed claims that throughout history have shown little understanding of so-called area Studies.

Generally, while an outside presence can be important to the self-understanding of any local area, the role of the outside player would be to assist internal players by extending their horizons. This could be done sometimes by just being there and lending a hand to build local capacities (further from what they already have and know)—a very difficult request of international community members, as 'purveyors of modernity' and their so-called culture.

2. Diverging Conceptions of Sovereignty

In an era of networks fuelled by interactive decision-making processes that include non-state actors, the idea that power usually flows top-down from a state monopoly is increasingly questioned.[17] Power theoretically understood as *potentia*—the elementary power through which human beings deploy their agency, their productive capacities and creative possibilities—is ontologically prior to power expressed as an obsession with order that is often repressive—here referred to as *potestas*.[18] Granting precedence to *potentia* over *potestas* inevitably leads us to question the conceptual centrality of the state. The DRC, which has long stood—and stands today—as a symbol of the antithesis of social order, offers much material for reflection on this issue. It is critical to consider how people negotiate between the structures inherited from the colonial time, the economic system it embedded, and the elite's responses to this situation in the Congo.

General Africanists limit their research to accurate descriptions and observations. The task for Africans is to incorporate these into a long-term transformative prospective. Quoting Trefon's *Congo Masquerade*,[19] Autesserre states that the 'Congolese state remains a predatory structure, as it has been during most of the Congo's history'.[20] This remark satisfies the Africanist, but leaves the African to wonder why the Congo has always been a predatory state. As Africans, we want to know the root cause in order to transform this structure.

For instance, Timothy Raeymaekers, a UNICEF/Italy consultant doing fieldwork in Butembo in the Eastern DRC in 2005, correctly noticed the struggle by the Nande to keep order and exercise the *de facto* power of protection despite the absence of the state framework.[21] For Raeymaekers, Nande traders were the new power brokers of the new political order on the Congo–Uganda frontier. However, Raeymaekers could

[17] For instance Morten Bøås, 'Returning to Realities: A Building-block Approach to State and Statecraft in Eastern Congo and Somalia' (2010) 10 Conflict, Security & Development 443.

[18] In fact, what international actors (in the DRC) are there for is to keep the very same order and security environment that benefits their countries of origin. Why should the current world order be kept as it is? Because it benefits the so-called international community. So, diplomacy is not about productivity or creativity of people (*potentia*); it is about law and order in the world to let dominant powers continue to impose their logic (*potestas*).

[19] Theodore Trefon, *Congo Masquerade: The Political Culture of Aid Inefficiency and Reform Failure* (African Arguments: Zed Books 2011).

[20] Autesserre (n 6) 18.

[21] Timothy Raeymaekers and Luca Jourdan, 'Economic Opportunities and Local Governance on an African Frontier: Case of the Semliki Basin (Congo-Uganda)' (2009) 3 Journal of Eastern African Studies 317.

not depart from the understanding of power as *potestas*, referenced as an ideal mode of organization. This is partly due to the discipline of political science, for which the state is mostly a given and rarely a questionable constructed entity. As a political scientist, Raeymaerkers remains faithful to a kind of crystallized notion of the state. He continues to see sovereignty as an attribute of the state, instead of viewing it as a social relation for which the state is an objectivized form at a certain point of time. Unlike Raeymaekers, and following Philip Abrams' claim that 'the only plausible alternative . . . to taking the state for granted is to understand it as a historical construct',[22] we understand sovereignty to be that which is inalienable in the human species. This way of apprehending sovereignty is much closer to the anthropological appreciation of power as *potentia*. State power has indeed alienated the sovereign productive power of human beings taken collectively.

In the context of NGO-oriented literature that undermines African knowledge production, the response of African intellectual elites is to find a theoretically sophisticated, empirically grounded, ethnographically and historically rich version of an argument. We need to bring back the complexities and the deferred genealogies of power in order to carve our own 'postcolonial' worlds. This, indeed, is the 'black man's burden'.

3. The Role of Colonialism

One of the debates in the study of Africa opposed two views of the history of the continent. On the one hand, J.F. Ade Ajayi,[23] a Nigerian historian, thinks that African history covers millennia; it is a mistake to reduce it to less than hundreds of years of colonization. For Ajayi, colonialism was only an episode in the long history of Africa. On the other side of the argument, V.Y. Mudimbe[24] points out that while acknowledging Ajayi's argument, one should recognize that the colonial period—even though short—was so intense that Africans see themselves today only as colonial subjects and have forgotten all the years before the colonial subjugation. For Mudimbe, colonial conquest was different from other conquests in the sense that it turned the pre-existing African societies upside down.

Our intention in this chapter is not to take a side, as both views can indeed be sustained. However, what remains true in Mudimbe's position is that the states as we have them today in Africa are the product of colonial coercion. Contemporary African states were colonial creations which passed to new managers at independence. But what did colonialists want to create in Africa?

The British Marxist historian Eric Hobsbawm identifies the search for cheaper raw material as the main reason that pushed Europe and America to occupy the entire

[22] Philip Abrams, 'Notes on the Difficulty of Studying the State (1977)' (1988) 1 Journal of Historical Sociology 58, 80.

[23] Jacob F Ade Ajayi, 'Colonialism: An Episode in African History' in Lewis H Gann and Peter Duignan (eds), *Colonialism in Africa 1870–1960* (CUP 1969).

[24] Valentin-Yves Mudimbe, *The Invention of Africa: Gnosis, Philosophy, and the Order of Knowledge* (Indiana University Press 1988).

planet.[25] The Congo, known as Zaire at one point, was among the most exploited territories during the colonial scramble for Africa. Referring to Hobsbawm, Kabamba points out that the Congo was conceived by King Leopold II of Belgium as an extractive space and never a political space.[26] The colony was organized to ease the extraction of raw material to be sent to Belgium for the technological advancement of King Leopold's population. The network of roads and railways were built from the mines to the seaport for the shipment of raw materials.[27]

The Congo-Belgium colony had one of the best health systems in Africa, but the purpose behind its development was to keep the workforce healthy enough to produce for the colonial masters. Primary schools were also very well organized, as it was important that workers understood orders coming from the colonizers. The entire country was organized in the way an extractive environment would be organized to take the maximum of minerals from the underground. Since Adam Hochschild's *King Leopold the Ghost*, it is well known that King Leopold's Congo Free State was little other but a barbaric looting enterprise.[28]

A country built to serve as a provider of raw materials would never become politically stable after independence because there has never been a political consensus between inhabitants of this space. This is the major problem the Congo is currently facing—how to go from an extractive space to a political one where people can organize their productive lives for their own development and for the development of future generations. This is the major challenge the Congolese have been faced with since independence. This dilemma was already expressed during independence by Crawford Young when he wrote:

> Belgium . . . constructed in Africa a colonial state which stood out by the thoroughness of its organization, the formidable accretion of power through an interlocking alliance of state, church, and capital, and the ambition of its economic and social objectives. The very strength of the system as a colonial structure, and its steadfast refusal to face effectively the problem of political adaptation until it began to disintegrate, made an ordered transfer of power peculiarly difficult. A colonizer who suddenly lost the profound conviction of the righteousness of his policy was confronted with a revolution by the colonized which lacked both structure and ideology. Total colonialism was replaced by total independence virtually overnight, yet the very completeness of the victory of the colonized had as its concomitant an impotence which emptied success of its substance.[29]

The years following independence were characterized by violence due to the trauma emanating from this abrupt change to transform the extractive space into a political one through a certain political consensus. Many parts of the Congo decided to secede

[25] Eric J Hobsbawm, *The Age of Empire: 1875–1914* (George Weidenfeld and Nicolson Ltd 1987).
[26] Patience Kabamba, 'Une Nation Congolaise à Venir' (2015) 492 Congo-Afrique (Kinshasa).
[27] ibid.
[28] Georges Nzongola-Ntalaja, *The Congo From Leopold to Kabila: A People's History* (Zed Books 2002).
[29] Crawford Young, *Politics in the Congo: Decolonization and Independence* (Princeton University Press 1965) 572.

from the extractive space. These regions presented a sort of natural social cohesion. The Katanga and the Kasai, which presented a semblance of political homogeneity, wanted to be independent from the monster King Leopold II had built and maintained for extractive purposes. Thanks to the intervention of the UN, none of these two regions were detached from the Congo. After that time, the Congo should have broken into small and politically coherent pieces, but the Cold War logic imposed itself upon the new leaders. This is why President Mobutu was put in power—to keep the Soviets away from the Congo's minerals, and also to protect Western interests in the region.[30]

For a quarter of a century, Mobutu was the undisputed master of the country; he was the true successor to King Leopold as the owner of the country and its resources.[31] As though to prove that he considered the Congo a personal possession, he unilaterally changed the country's name to 'Zaire' in 1971, and took great pleasure in privatizing the state and its assets for the benefit of his relatives, cronies, and clients.[32]

Indeed, one of the characteristics of the newly independent African countries was that they all maintained the economic structures put in place by the colonial master. As Hobsbawm argues, economies of the colonies were linked to the world market, but only as providers of raw materials.[33] These extractive structures were protected by the colonial administration during the colonial period. At independence, the same structures were protected by African leaders themselves, who have become, in Fred Cooper's words, 'gatekeepers'.[34] Economies of postcolonial Africa were all extroverted economies which continued to exist for the benefit of former colonial powers.

In his book, Jason Stearns seeks to explain why, despite large UN peacekeeping missions and substantial foreign aid, the past two decades have been marked by regular outbreaks of violence in the eastern and north-eastern regions of the Congo; he details the emergence of warlords with ambiguous motivations, the repeated interventions by neighbouring Rwanda[35] and Uganda, and the role of the incompetent and rapacious national army. Stearns makes a convincing case that the violence has been sustained by a 'military bourgeoisie' that benefits from instability by plundering natural resources

[30] Nzongola-Ntalaja (n 28).

[31] ibid 141.

[32] ibid.

[33] Hobsbawm (n 25) 63.

[34] Frederick Cooper, 'From Colonial State to Gatekeeper State in Africa' (working paper, Mario Einaudi Centre for International Studies, Working Paper Series No 04-05, 2005) <https://ecommons.cornell.edu/bitstream/handle/1813/55008/2005_WP4_Cooper.pdf?sequence = 1&isAllowed> accessed 12 September 2023.

[35] Officially, the Rwandan army withdrew from the eastern DRC in 2002, but it has had a clandestine presence since: Stearns (n 2). Security threats, symbolically represented by the FDLR militia responsible for the 1994 genocide, remain the overriding imperative for Rwandan intervention in eastern Congo. But today, the FDLR threat is almost nonexistent as it has been minimized given the repatriation of the majority of its members. And yet, given the central place the genocide still plays in Rwanda's memory and politics, the FDLR remains a powerful symbolic threat: Stearns (n 2). Besides, we know that the Rwandan military doctrine is based on two principles, which recognize the permanent war in neighbouring countries—far from Kigali—as the *sine qua non condition* for the survival of Rwanda. It can be summed up in these terms: 'To defend a house, you have to stand outside.' Thus, can we understand why most of the major rebel groups in eastern DRC, including the Congolese Rally for Democracy (*Rassemblement Congolais pour la Démocratie*, RCD) in 1999, the National Congress for the Defence of the People (*Congrès National pour la Défense du Peuple*, CDNP) in 2007, and the M23 (in 2012 and today) have often had the support of Rwanda.

and foreign aid, while the DRC government has made things worse by shelling out 'fighting bonuses' to military personnel that dwarf their peacetime salaries. Thus, the violence has created a small but influential ruling class that has little motivation to end the bloodshed.[36]

To understand why conflicts last so long in the Congo, it is important to have in mind this backdrop and to place much greater emphasis on local actors, as well as on their interests and interactions, rather than on the variables most commonly invoked by academics, including poverty, state weakness, ethnic tensions, absence of peacekeepers, abundance of natural resources, or ethnic exclusion—even though all are spread relatively evenly across the Eastern Congo.[37] We chose a historical framing of our argument to show that the protracted conflict in the Congo has historical roots and that its seeds were planted at its inception as an economic space. This space called Congo was never envisioned as a political one.

4. The Tasks for the Congolese Society

In addition to turning what was conceived of as an extractive space into a political space, African states have to make their economies work for their people and not for outside powers with the complicity of a handful of locals. However, the Congolese elites have proved incapable of changing the situation. The question is, why are African elites in general, and the Congolese intelligentsia in particular, unable to actively participate in the development of their own countries? Why cannot the country count on the best of its children to take it out of poverty or to end the ongoing bloody conflict?

A glimpse of an answer could be found in the DRC education curricula. The school programmes to which students in the Congo are submitted prepare them to leave their country rather than to invest their intellectual capital within it. After schooling, we become strangers to our own milieu, which makes it difficult to envision a real transformational development. There is indeed a link between the current mode of education and the imbalance of knowledge to which we alluded in the previous paragraph. The only rational option for the Congolese intellectual elite is to emigrate out of the Congo. This has resulted in 10 per cent of the Congolese population living outside the country, which is then run by people allegedly completely immersed in corruption and illegal accumulation. The failure of the elites to invest their intellectual capital to develop their country remains one of the major problems Africans in general, and the Congolese in particular, should solve.

We recall the story of a young Congolese student who graduated with a degree in mathematics in the city of Kikwit (near the capital city, Kinshasa), landing in Paris for the first time to further his studies. On his arrival in the French capital city, he really felt at home, because it seemed that everything he had studied had prepared him to live in Paris. He felt at home because he knew French literature, which was a major part of his training. He knew the geography of France and Europe far better than that of his home country. The Congolese education system had prepared him to live in

[36] Stearns (n 2).
[37] Stearns (n 2) 13.

Paris. When he tried to go to his village in Kasongo-Lunda, he felt like a foreigner; he couldn't understand the lifestyle of his fellows from the same village. The only thing he wanted was to leave the village as soon as possible. His schooling had the consequence of uprooting him from his own roots and his own people.

The tendency of the Congolese elite to gentrify and its failure to build and develop the country remain among the paradoxes of the Congo. It means that education is not adapted to the real needs of the population. This is a challenge that a concerned government of a sovereign nation should solve in order to unleash the *potentia* of its people. However, this nation is still yet to rise from the ashes of the current extractive space protected by the 'gatekeepers' who live off the commissions and kickbacks provided by the old powers.

Problems in the Congo are deep, but they can be captured in the three main elements underlined in this chapter. First, the Congolese would have to build a nation which had never been envisioned by the colonial founder of our country. Indeed, a political consensus could be violent, because it essentially stops the top-down approach imposed on the people by the colonial master and subsequent administration. Second, the effort of nation-building in the Congo should be followed by the effort to turn an economy of raw material destined for outside use into an introverted economy where the primary beneficiaries are local people. Third, to reach this objective, the entire education system inherited from the colonial period should be reviewed, especially as far as the content of the education is concerned. The ways in which the elite are educated, and the teaching materials the students absorb, are very important to the decision to leave or to remain in the country. How could this be changed? Many things will depend on the way the top-down power is negotiated by an elite which is rooted intellectually, physically, and emotionally in its home country.

C. International Responses to the DRC Conflicts

Congo has historically been a land of immense hardships, given its disturbing past. The international community, through the UN or the African Union (AU) mechanisms,[38] has been present all along to assist in finding lasting solutions to the conflict. However, as Autesserre has remarked, the international peacebuilding strategy in Congo has been shaped by the dominant peacebuilding culture of a 'one-size-fits-all' approach, which emphasizes the significance of interventions at regional and national levels, therefore making international responses more top-down, with less consideration for the local dynamics of the conflict.[39]

[38] Expectations were high for the operation through regional mechanisms of effective and realistic solutions; unfortunately even the AU has not lived up to its fullest potential to stem the regional dimensions of the DRC conflict, largely due to the fact that the Organization had neither the power to enforce its decisions nor the financial autonomy to act independently and decisively: Joyce Muraya and John Ahere, 'Perpetuation of Instability in the Democratic Republic of the Congo: When the Kivus Sneeze, Kinshasa Catches a Cold' (Occasional Paper Series Issue 1, African Centre for the Constructive Resolution of Disputes 2014). In situations where the institutions were able to decide, bureaucratic processes and inadequate political will delayed their eventual actions, with grave consequences for lives in the DRC.

[39] Autesserre (n 6) 85.

Indeed, most international interventions have been focused on regional agreements (including the UN or the AU peacekeeping missions) or on national arrangements (eg Sun City dialogue in South Africa, national elections, military and security reforms, etc). And yet, despite all these interventions, the conflict dynamics on the ground have not significantly changed. For instance, despite the Sun City agreement, which led to the first post-conflict elections in 2006, the DRC saw an increased number of armed groups, whereas analysts expected—thanks to the electoral process—a significant de-escalation of conflicts as belligerents agreed to work together. In December 2021, Jason Stearns counted more than 120 armed groups in the eastern Congo, compared to a few dozen in 2006.[40]

Reviewing some of the UN reports on the Congolese conflict, Autesserre points out:

> none of [them] mention action at the local level. Likewise, throughout the transition, the most powerful peacebuilders—diplomats, donors, and international organisations such as MONUC and the World Bank—spent their time mediating and, when necessary, pressuring the main Congolese, Rwandan, and Ugandan political and military leaders, while disregarding grassroots actors.[41]

The reasons for this top-down approach are two-fold. First, peacebuilders understand the continuing violence as a top-down problem. Second, they conceive their role as exclusively concerned with top-down interventions, meaning working at the regional and national levels, rather than working with local warlords, provincial governors, or village and community chiefs[42] (a task that local NGOs in Bukavu have been involved in, with very successful outcomes).[43] The overall perception behind it is that grassroots violence takes place due to the absence of state authority; therefore, state reconstruction would restore peace and order. In Autesserre's words, for many Western diplomats, helping the Congolese to build a state and reconstruct the rule of law was the best way to end violence by armed groups.[44] This is why the political and military components of the crisis interventions remained top-down, geared at high-level elites and only rarely at select provincial elites.[45] The international community, through the Western diplomats, clearly favours *potestas*, order and security, over *potentia*, the productivity and creativity of Congolese grassroots. The global community sees the state as the entity that claims the monopoly over violence instead of seeing it as a form of social relations that creates a space for human productivity, as Hannah Arendt alluded to in her *Human Condition*.[46]

On the other hand, the provision of aid to affected populations stands as one of the pillars of international interventions in the crisis. However, humanitarian and

[40] Stearns (n 2) 20–23.
[41] Autesserre (n 6) 92.
[42] ibid.
[43] Caritas Bukavu has been involved in a mediation process between armed groups and local government representatives in remote areas of the South Kivu Province, whereby warlords have accepted to stop fighting and work hand in hand with the local government.
[44] Autesserre (n 6).
[45] ibid 116.
[46] Hannah Arendt, *La Condition de l'homme moderne* (Paris 1983, 1958).

development aid has been conceived of, and are continually perceived as, an *apolitical solution* to an *apolitical problem* (ie the continuation of violence and poverty on the ground),[47] thus making it possible for international relief workers to deal directly with decentralized authorities and local militia leaders, to negotiate access to the population, and to ensure the security of their staff and beneficiaries. In fact, politicizing development aid or aid relief would hamper efforts to reach the beneficiaries and put development and relief agents at high risk. However, this 'not taking sides' or neutrality approach is perceived by locals as a justification for ignoring the root causes of the conflict, that is, the reasons for the presence of rebel groups or the absence of government authorities in affected areas.

As the presence of armed groups intensifies, this aid neutrality or non-interference has come to increase local perceptions of international aid as a means to entertain (sustain) or even fuel conflicts on the ground,[48] as with aid comes the 'hidden business' of natural resources' control. As a result, affected communities have increasingly developed a sense of aid fatigue and even aid repulsion, as they feel tired of this charity that does not bring an end to their suffering. In fact, in a situation of emergency, the neutrality approach may prove useful; but in times of relative stability, where humanitarian and development agents can focus on more development initiatives (including drilling boreholes, building schools or health centres, offering vocational training, or providing specialized assistance to disabled people), there is a need for an engaged approach that fosters relationships with various stakeholders. To achieve change, local politics must be taken into account and included in the process.[49] Actually, the maintenance of the neutrality paradigm in the eastern Congo context hinders the possibility of any meaningful partnerships with local communities that would enable sustainable effects. Therefore, the provision of humanitarian aid to the areas most affected by conflict, namely in regions controlled by rebel groups, should require reconsideration of issues of sovereignty, the right to intervene, neutrality, and independence.[50]

The aid repudiation in the eastern Congo context is also exacerbated by how the communities have come to perceive the United Nations Organization Stabilization Mission in the Democratic Republic of the Congo (MONUSCO). It is perhaps the world's largest UN peacekeeping mission, with the financial backing of billions of US dollars in international aid, and yet it fails to prevent violence and even to protect civilians and restore state authority, as part of its mandate.[51] MONUSCO has been accused of contributing to challenges faced by local populations in differentiating between military operations and humanitarian activities.[52] Even as they execute their

[47] Autesserre (n 6).

[48] Discussions in a workshop with civil society in Bukavu.

[49] Paul O'Brien, 'Politicized Humanitarianism: A Response to Nicolas de Torrente' (2004) 17 Harvard Human Rights Journal 31.

[50] Elżbieta Drążkiewicz, 'Neutrality in Foreign Aid: Shifting Contexts, Shifting Meanings—Examples from South Sudan' (2017) 77 Journal of Global and Historical Anthropology 90, 92.

[51] Joyce Muraya and John Ahere, 'Perpetuation of Instability in the Democratic Republic of the Congo: When the Kivus Sneeze, Kinshasa Catches a Cold' (Occasional Paper Series Issue 1, African Centre for the Constructive Resolution of Disputes 2014).

[52] Christoph Vogel, 'Congo: Why UN Peacekeepers have a Credibility Problem' *The Guardian* (London, 30 August 2013) <https://www.theguardian.com/world/2013/aug/30/congo-un-peacekeepers-problem> accessed 12 September 2023.

mandate, neither the UN staff involved in peacebuilding, nor the United Nations Security Council (UNSC), have attempted to design a strategy addressing local causes of conflicts in the DRC, either during the war or after ceasefires.[53]

Under the current scenario, there are more and more protests in North Kivu, South Kivu, and Ituri—the three provinces most affected by the conflicts—demanding the immediate withdrawal of MONUSCO. In August 2022, tensions between local populations and MONUSCO peacekeepers led to human losses on both sides,[54] as the UN peacekeeping force—though a very visible presence with its patrols and bases—has been accused of failing to protect civilians from militia violence that has long plagued the region but which had intensified in recent months. In fact, the re-emergence of the Rwandan-backed M23 militia in 2022 is a significant factor in the anger directed at the UN peacekeepers, whose commanders have admitted their lack of resources to confront the rebels.[55]

The narrative has prompted local populations of the eastern Congo to blame the UN peacekeepers for complicity with the M23, and for an appalling record in protecting civilians. For locals, the UN peacekeeping force has shown serious shortcomings in preventing rebel commanders from killing civilians, or in countering threats posed to civilians. This fact has put to the test the mission's credibility, as critics of MONUSCO on X (formerly Twitter) have given it the hashtag #MONUSELESS to emphasize how the UN peacekeeping force is struggling for credibility.[56]

If the UN peacekeeping force is downsizing its mission mandate, with the closure of its various branch offices in the foreseeable future, a popular grassroots demand for MONUSCO to leave the country immediately leads experts to also predict a complete withdrawal of the UN peacekeeping mission in the near future. Unfortunately, by focusing on national and regional responses to conflicts, the peacebuilding and peacekeeping efforts of UN staff have not played very visible roles at the local level, mainly in terms of improving government capacity to protect civilian populations and consolidating state authority throughout the country.[57] For some analysts, the interpretation of the mission's mandate, especially with regard to the protection of civilians, has made it difficult to allow a robust response (with the use of force), as this might prompt the UN peacekeepers to participate in the conflict, thus becoming one of the parties in conflict instead of being the solution.[58]

[53] M H A Menondji, 'Problematic Peacekeeping in the DRC: From MONUC to MONUSCO' (Think Africa Press, 4 February 2013) <https://allafrica.com/stories/201302051114.html> accessed 27 March 2024.

[54] Jason Burke, 'Death Toll Reaches 36 in Eastern Democratic Republic of the Congo as Protesters Turn on UN Peacekeepers' *The Guardian* (London, 5 August 2022) <https://www.theguardian.com/global-development/2022/aug/05/death-toll-reaches-36-in-eastern-drc-as-protesters-turn-on-un-peacekeepers> accessed 12 September 2023.

[55] ibid.

[56] Vogel (n 52).

[57] Menondji (n 53).

[58] Ray Murphy, 'UN Peacekeeping in the Democratic Republic of the Congo and the Protection of Civilians' (2016) 21 Journal of Conflicts and Security Law 209; Landry Ingabire and Yandry Kurniawan, 'The Challenges of UN Peacekeeping Mission in Finding a Solution to Rebel Groups in the East of the Democratic Republic of Congo' (2022) 13 Politica 85; Alberto Barrera, 'The Congo Trap: MONUSCO Islands of Stability in the Sea of Instability' (2015) 4 Stability: International Journal of Security and Development 1.

Against this backdrop, and with the DRC government almost incapable to protect its population, the question thus arises: what added value does the triple nexus perspective bring to the discussions? In what way can the international support contribute to saving the future generations of the Congolese population from the wrath of the proportionally increasing impact of armed conflict?

The HDP nexus approach, or triple nexus, has emerged since 2016 as a new iteration promoting concrete structural shifts across the aid system by not only meeting people's immediate humanitarian needs but also reducing risk and vulnerability[59] through improved collaboration across the humanitarian-development-peace nexus. Since 2018, the DRC has striven to understand the triple nexus as an inclusive and collective process that presents itself as an effective solution in reducing risks, vulnerabilities, and humanitarian needs, thereby addressing underlying causes of conflicts and, with them, widespread poverty and under-development. The process started with a shared risk and vulnerability analysis facilitated by the OECD and its International Network on Conflict and Fragility (INCAF), with various key stakeholders including the DRC government, MONUSCO, bilateral and multilateral agencies, civil society organizations, funding agencies, and others to discuss a concrete development pathway driving the DRC towards capacious development.[60] The review identified the most important areas of vulnerability within the DRC, which included food insecurity and malnutrition, especially among women and children; access to essential social services; gender-based violence; and, most importantly, forced population displacement.[61]

At the national level, these four collective outcomes have been mainstreamed into the 2019–2023 National Strategic Development Plan (NSDP), the Humanitarian Response Plan (HRP), the UN Sustainable Development Cooperation Framework (UNSDCF), the International and Security and Stabilisation Support Strategy (ISSSS), and the renewal of the DRC's eligibility to the United Nations Peacebuilding Fund (PBF). The collective outcomes were also integrated into provincial development plans.[62] Finally, MONUSCO and the UNCT have jointly built a framework of joint interventions based on some of the medium and long-term objectives of the collective outcomes.[63]

The DRC has taken the implementation of the nexus framework seriously and its implementation strategy seems unique when set against most other countries. It has appointed a full-time 'nexus' advisor within its governance structure, thereby allowing a dedicated unit to focus on the current stakeholder schemes and the awareness

[59] Gloria Nguya and Nadia Siddiqui, 'Triple Nexus Implementation and Implications for Durable Solutions for Internal Displacement: On Paper and In Practice' (2020) 39 Refugee Survey Quarterly 466.

[60] Inter-Agency Standing Committee (IASC) Results Group 4, 'Country Brief on the Humanitarian-Development-Peace Nexus: Democratic Republic of the Congo' (IASC 2021).

[61] ibid.

[62] ibid. In 2019, three pilot projects with a clear roadmap to be followed by the nexus Core Team were initiated in three provinces by pairs of UN agencies aiming for a practical learning-by-doing approach. In Kasaï Central, with WFP and UNICEF, the focus was on Sustainable Development Goals (SDGs) 2, 3, 4, 6, 7, and 10; in Tanganyika, with FAO and WHO, the focus was on SDGs 2 and 3; in North Kivu, with UNHCR and UNDP, the focus was on SDGs 3, 4, 6, 7, 10, and 16. The SDGs can be found in UNGA 70/262 (27 April 2016) UN Doc A/Res/70/262 and UNSC Res 2282 (27 April 2016) UN Doc S/Res/2282.

[63] IASC (n 60).

structure. The initiative also involved inputs from the Ministry of Solidarity and Humanitarian Affairs and the Ministry of Planning. The nexus advisor, in consultation with the OECD, conceptualized the humanitarian-development-peace (HDP) strategy. The involvement of MONUSCO in the planning process helped negotiate the inclusion of 'peace' under the nexus, which was a major landmark in the nexus implementation phase of the DRC.[64]

All the government's departments and major stakeholders have shown an effective commitment towards the implementation of the triple-nexus policy, which has seen a considerable shift from a merely programmatic pilot approach to a more concrete structural outlook. The implementation of the policy is, however, at an early stage; a lot of groundwork was hampered due to the Covid-19 pandemic, in spite of the efforts deployed by all the stakeholders to conduct a validity test of the triple-nexus policy in 2019 in different provinces.

Based on our qualitative and participatory research, we have identified three major areas of concern that can potentially affect the operationalization of the triple-nexus policy in the DRC. These include leadership, coordination, and financing. If at national level the approach has proven effective in terms of leadership and coordination (a possible outcome, since collaborating structures have been designed by including all stakeholders), there has been a disconnect with the local level, where there is no reflection of the kind of leadership or the coordination defined at the national level.

The top-down approach that the triple-nexus policy has taken in terms of leadership and coordination may jeopardize the potential for local stakeholders, including local governments and civil society, to be empowered through their own initiatives. As it stands now, the triple nexus narrative happens in Kinshasa with little to no engagement and knowledge of local stakeholders, as we have experienced in our fieldwork in Bukavu. If the triple-nexus approach in the DRC could be more bottom-up oriented, this would allow local initiatives, such as the Caritas-Bukavu peace deal brokering, to be taken into account and recognized, and thus make the nexus process more effective and sustainable. In fact, if the HDP framework does not focus enough on leadership and coordination at the local level, it falls back into the old ways of working (by contrast to the 'new way of working' that it promises) where external assistance is necessary, but at the same time weakens the internal processes. By keeping the top-down perspective, with the HDP nexus programmes being empowering at the national level at the expense of the local level, the operationalization of the approach might lose an opportunity to directly engage with grassroots, thus moving away from the *potestas* understanding of the state, and not allowing the making of norms by those who will be subjected to them.

Looking at financing, it is interesting to refer to the UN Secretary-General's recent statement[65] in the wake of the re-emergence of the Rwandan-backed M23 rebels, where he admitted that the militia had heavy and sophisticated armament and that therefore the UN peacekeepers lack the resources to take on the rebels. This statement raises the issue of how finance can be mobilized in the context of the HDP nexus in order to address not only immediate humanitarian or development needs, but also

[64] ibid.
[65] Burke (n 54).

security priorities, as in the case of the M23 attacks. We believe this remains a challenging task within the current national HDP structures, but it is important to start thinking about some guiding principles that could orient action for resources mobilization amongst the stakeholders. One such principle would be the rights-based approach, as it may constitute a tool to assess how finance and resources should be distributed according to how rights-holders are affected.

Finally, while in the discussions around the HDP nexus implementation almost all actors have been involved, there has not been an effective presence of the regional actors. The key African regional bodies, including the African Union, the Southern African Development Community (SADC), the International Conference on the Great Lakes Region (ICGLR), the East African Community (EAC), and the Economic Community of the Great Lakes Countries (ECGLC), have been absent in the DRC's triple-nexus process. If international involvement is needed, we cannot ignore regional involvement, as almost all peace deals about the DRC crisis are brokered within regional talks; it seems obvious that these organizations should not be left out. Although we emphasize the need to decentralize the nexus process, we cannot talk about international actors and ignore those at the regional level. Their voices should be heard. It is clear that the application of the HDP nexus approach in the DRC will require continued and strengthened cooperation between the UN, multilaterals, and nexus-oriented actors with the African Union and the regional economic communities (RECs), such as SADC, EAC, ICGLR, and so on, as well as the in-country Monitoring Mechanism of the Addis-Ababa agreement framework. Their monitoring mechanisms and analyses, as well as their ongoing peace support and mediation experience, make them natural partners in any HDP nexus initiative in the country.

To sum up, the triple-nexus approach in our opinion does not have the capacity or power within it to bring an end to the long-standing conflict in the DRC, given its external top-down orientation. However, with more leadership and coordination of HDP-oriented interventions, it is possible to make a difference if focus is placed on building capacities from below (unleashing people's *potentia*), thus making people at the grassroots level the actors of their own destiny and development.

D. The Right to Development (RD) as a Way Forward

Our history has made the world feel that we are still standing on the doorstep of our colonizers with an empty bowl in our hands. As we argued in section C, this perception has been embedded in the minds of all the international stakeholders (UN officials, diplomats, INGO workers, researchers) who have or had arrived at the shores of DRC in the name of humanitarian aid or development assistance.

Can the change brought about in 2018, when the Joint Steering Committee of the UN identified the Congo as a pilot nation for the experimental application of the HDP nexus, be an opportunity to change this preconceived notion of a helpless nation? There is a slow but promising shift brought about by the implementation of the triple nexus in the DRC concerning the utilization of international assistance, but in our opinion it does not meet the prerequisites required in order to move from the old practice of development aid to rights-based development, thereby raising the bar of accountability for the governance setup in the Congo. As it stands now, the triple nexus has no potential to empower affected Congolese populations, but rather continues to keep them dependent on foreign charity, despite its pretention to deal with vulnerabilities. To move away from this charity-oriented approach, we suggest the right to development (RTD) as a policy paradigm that can be more empowering, and sustainable.

The term 'right' brings with it the sense of duty, and it indicates a system of accountability towards citizens through the guarantee of those rights. Keeping in mind the application of this right, the DRC state has two major functions to fulfil. The first one is the role of the state as an active participant to protect the rights of the Congolese not only against the internal machinery, but also against external or international influence. The second is to respect their rights through inclusion and equal protection of the dignity of each Congolese citizen, their customs, and their way of life. It is therefore crucial for the state to ensure that every Congolese citizen has their rights fulfilled as a guarantee of human rights provided by the state through various schemes, government grants, and proper implementation mechanisms. Together, these functions of the state build the *potentia* (the *agency*) of each and every single citizen, and enhance government accountability.

To discharge these functions, the state's political machinery should not be restricted only to use of money that is internationally portrayed by donors as philanthropic aid, but in fact is pumped into the Congolese economy by exploitative foreign powers that treat it as a reparative cheque to clear them of all violations that they continue to perform on Congolese soil. From the perspective of international development cooperation, it is important for the sake of Congolese empowerment to slowly shift into the right-to-development regime.[66]

The General Assembly adopted the UN Declaration on the Right to Development in 1986.[67] While the RTD Declaration is not binding, it can further lead to legally binding effects through treaties or the crystallization of state practice and *opinio juris* as customary international law. The Declaration goes on to define that the RTD is the only international document dealing with this right in such depth. The Declaration states that an individual is both subject and participant to their own development, and an individual state has to take an active role to ameliorate the situation in tandem with the State and international community at large. Thus, a prerogative is placed on the equal development of both individuals and states.

The signatories to the African Charter on Human and People's Rights[68] (hereafter the Charter) have gone one step further than the UN General Assembly regarding the RTD, since they are bound to protect, promote, and fulfil the right to development

[66] For instance, Koen De Feyter, 'The Convention on the Right to Development: Drafting a New Global Human Rights Treaty' (2022) 77 Comunità internazionale/Società italiana per l'organizzazione internazionale 413; Koen De Feyter, 'The Right to Development in Africa' in Eva Brems, Christophe Van der Beken, and Solomon Yimer (eds), *Human Rights and Development* (Brill 2015) 23–50.

[67] UN General Assembly Resolution 41/128 (4 December 1986) UN Doc A/RES/41/128; Report of the Secretary-General, 'The International Dimensions of the Right to Development as a Human Right' (1979) UN Doc E/CN.4/1334.

[68] African Charter on Human and Peoples' Rights (concluded 27 June 1981, entered into force 21 October 1986) 1520 UNTS 217.

under Article 22 of the Charter. The Charter is a modern human rights instrument, which recognizes several controversial 'third generation' rights such as the right to development and a clean environment, group rights such as the right to self-determination, and duties such as the duty to promote the achievement of African unity. The African Charter, interestingly, is the very first Charter and the only international human rights instrument that recognizes the right to development as a justiciable right, as now confirmed by the *Endorois* recommendation.[69] The *Endorois* recommendation, which is an example of a balanced negotiation on the RTD vis-à-vis the essential requirement to protect the local identity, is especially relevant in conflict-affected territories.[70] The RTD is also arguably fulfilled through other rights in the Charter, such as the rights to self-determination, property, natural resources, life, and socio-economic rights, as for instance can be ascertained from the recommendation on environmental and socio-economic rights of the Ogoni people in Nigeria.[71]

The concept of the right to development has slowly made its way into the DRC legal structure. The Congolese Constitution refers to the Congo as a state imbedded with communal values, therefore encouraging the state to protect the interests, rights, and welfare of its citizens as a foundational principle.[72] Article 12(2) of the Congolese Constitution of 1994[73] enshrines the right to development as a right that is constitutionally guaranteed to all its citizens; the same is reflected in the 2006 Constitution. This addition was inspired by the dynamic of adopting the African Charter of the 1980s. This constitutional guarantee saw further governmental endorsement in the 2001 National Conference of Human Rights, under the leadership of the Ministry of Human Rights.[74] This right was mainly linked to the management of natural resources and their non-exploitative effective utilization towards the overall development of the DRC and its people.

There are two ways in which the right to development can influence the development of the legal system in the DRC. The first one is legal applicability, which would require judicial intervention in enforcing the effectiveness of this right through the judicial mechanisms. The second would be the legislative perspective, wherein the law and policies drafted by the people's representatives should strive to reflect the right to development at all levels of governance within the DRC.[75]

[69] The 'Endorois case' represents the first legal recognition of an African indigenous peoples' rights over traditionally owned land: *Centre for Minority Rights Development (Kenya) and Minority Rights Group International on behalf of Endorois Welfare Council v Kenya*, African Commission on Human and Peoples' Rights Case 276/2003 (4 February 2010).

[70] In the 'Endorois case', the African Commission on Human and Peoples Rights (ACHPR) grounded its finding of a violation of the right to development in the Kenyan government's failure to guarantee the Endorois community effective participation in development processes regarding their ancestral land and to guarantee them a reasonable share in the profits realized from the land after the government had facilitated their forceful eviction.

[71] *The Social and Economic Rights Action Centre and the Centre for Economic and Social Rights v Nigeria*, African Commission on Human and Peoples' Rights, Case 155/96 (27 May 2002).

[72] Article 1(1) of the DRC Constitution of 18 February 2006 as revised on 20 January 2011.

[73] Article 12(2) of the Constitutional Act of Transition of 4 April 1994.

[74] République Démocratique du Congo (RDC), 'Actes de la Conférence Nationale sur les Droits de l'Homme' (Kinshasa, Ministère des Droits Humains 2001) Vol II, 9–36.

[75] Marcel Wetsh'Okonda Koso Senga, *Les Textes Constitutionnels Congolais Annotés* (Editions de la Campagne pour les Droits de l'Homme au Congo 2010).

Above all, the RTD could increase grassroots participation in the functioning of the government, and thus could foster a decrease in the top-down shift of resources that characterizes the international cooperation, including in its triple-nexus approach. This is because the RTD opens up a concrete path for advocacy by these grassroots organizations to claim constitutionally established rights, and thus leaves little to no window of discretion for the higher governments in the allocation of resources for the impactful realization of these rights, thereby creating a sense of sustainable and justiciable empowerment in the twenty-six provinces of the DRC.[76]

Outside actors have their place in the DRC, to either help with the enforcement of international law or encourage the Congolese to better understand the complexities of a protracted situation of war. This could contribute to empowering the people who have suffered decades (even centuries) of disempowerment through brutal historic violence, including slavery, colonialism or neo-colonialism, and war.[77] However, ultimately, the Congolese people need to bring back the complexities and the deferred genealogies of power in order to carve out their own 'postcolonial' world.

E. Conclusion

After decades of turmoil, the HDP nexus approach may bring hope to the citizens of the DRC. Yet, there is still a lot to be done in the Congo, as the implementation of the triple-nexus policy around developmental cooperation remains top-down and aid-focused. Therefore, the triple-nexus approach in our opinion does not have the capacity or power within it to bring an end to the long-standing conflict in the DRC, given the diversity of actors involved in the conflict and the nature of their claims. In fact, the triple-nexus policy can be perceived as merely a response to the consequences of the conflict, and not a remedy to the root causes of conflicts. On the whole, the HDP nexus approach fails to create a genuine shift from the 'aid paradigm' to a 'paradigm of rights' that has the capacity to politically empower the Congolese citizens, engage their leadership towards their duties, and therefore redevelop the Congolese system of governance into one with the potential to create a visionary change in the fields of peacebuilding and sustainable development. The future of the DRC thus depends on its governance framework and on fulfilling its sovereign functions that nurture the citizens' *potentia*; that is, responding to the requirements of its population, reconfiguring its economic relations within the RECs of the AU, creating an impactful relationship between the government and its citizens by empowering governmental institutions, and providing a different kind of education for the youth who are the future of the country.

[76] Balingene Kahombo, 'The Promises and Realization of the Right to Development in the Democratic Republic of the Congo' (2020) 7 KAS African Law Study Library—Librairie Africaine d'Etudes Juridiques 391.

[77] This is what Pope Francis termed, in his apostolic visit to the DRC, 'economic colonialism': Pope Francis, 'Address of His Holiness: Address to the DRC's Authorities, Civil Society, and the Diplomatic Corps' (Kinshasa, 31 January 2023) <https://www.vatican.va/content/francesco/en/speeches/2023/january/documents/20230131-autorita-repdem-congo.html> accessed 12 September 2023.

23
Conclusion
Towards a Holistic Approach to Armed Conflict

Andreas Buser, Heike Krieger, and Asli Ozcelik

A. Introduction

Protracted conflicts have become a persistent and defining feature of contemporary warfare, shaping the strategic and geopolitical landscape in ways that suggest their enduring presence. Many of the violent conflicts that were active in 2024 erupted decades ago—more than seven decades, in some cases.[1] Likewise, the average duration of armed conflicts has increased, reaching average durations of almost three decades.[2] The conflicts in Chad, Colombia, the Democratic Republic of Congo (DRC), India, Indonesia, Myanmar, Israel/Palestine, and the Philippines are only some examples. Within the relatively short timeframe of the research project underlying this book (2020–2024), the ongoing conflicts in Ukraine and the Sahel region added to the overall picture. Another outstanding case concerns the resurgence of a fully fledged armed conflict in Gaza—leading to International Criminal Court (ICC) investigations on both sides and the International Court of Justice (ICJ) finding it plausible that the situation could amount to genocide.[3] Similarly, while large-scale fighting in Syria has subsided, armed fighting continues to erupt regionally, rendering the country's future precarious, and the protection of human rights of its inhabitants is far from assured. Beyond these 'high-profile conflicts' that overshadow public discourse, numerous other protracted conflicts persist or re-emerge, often receiving less international attention.[4] One such example is the 2025 outbreak of armed violence in Goma, which underscores the broader pattern of sustained instability in various

[1] UCDP/PRIO Armed Conflict Dataset version 25.1.

[2] International Institute for Strategic Studies, *Armed Conflict Survey* (Routledge 2024) 5; UN/World Bank, *Pathways for Peace: Inclusive Approaches to Preventing Violent Conflict* (2018) 18, <http://hdl.handle.net/10986/28337> accessed 29 July 2025.

[3] *Application of the Convention on the Prevention and Punishment of the Crime of Genocide in the Gaza Strip (South Africa* v *Israel)* (Provisional Measures) [2004], I.C.J. Reports 2024, 3 <https://www.icj-cij.org/case/192/provisional-measures> accessed 31 August 2025; *Application of the Convention on the Prevention and Punishment of the Crime of Genocide in the Gaza Strip (South Africa* v *Israel)* (Request for the Modification of the Order Indicating Provisional Measures of 26 January 2024), Order of 28 March 2024, ICJ Reports 2024, 513; *Application of the Convention on the Prevention and Punishment of the Crime of Genocide in the Gaza Strip (South Africa* v *Israel)* (Request for the Modification of the Order of 28 March 2024), Order of 24 May 2024, ICJ Reports 2024, 649.

[4] Jérôme de Hemptinne, 'Why Do Some Wars Matter More Than Others? And Why Must That Change?' Opinio Iuris 24 June 2025, <https://opiniojuris.org/2025/06/24/why-do-some-wars-matter-more-than-others-and-why-must-that-change/> accessed 29 July 2025.

Andreas Buser, Heike Krieger, and Asli Ozcelik, *Conclusion* In: *From Protracted Conflict to Sustainable Peace?*
Edited by: Heike Krieger, Giedre Jokubauskaite, Asli Ozcelik, and Andreas Buser, Oxford University Press.
 DOI: 10.1093/9780198967385.003.0027

regions. If anything, this brief survey of present-day conflicts reinforces the notion that these prolonged hostilities are not mere temporary disruptions but rather an inherent characteristic of modern warfare. They reflect the complexities of asymmetrical warfare, entrenched geopolitical rivalries, and the persistent challenges of achieving durable peace settlements.

Protracted conflicts are not a uniquely contemporary phenomenon, as centuries-long conflicts are not unknown to human history. Yet, their persistence in the contemporary period, despite global legal, political, economic, and social developments that were expected to lead to a decrease in the existence, intensity, or duration of violent conflict, has been striking. With the multilateral system designed 'to save succeeding generations from the scourge of war'[5] currently in turmoil, the intractability of conflicts emerges as an ever-pressing challenge to international peace and security. An often-deadlocked United Nations Security Council that has been unable to act in response to the grave humanitarian consequences of armed conflicts of the past decade, increasing militarization on national and regional levels, and a financially strained global humanitarian system erode the potential of the multilateral system to respond to protracted armed conflicts.

The situation is further aggravated by a deep-seated transformation of the US American approach to humanitarian and development aid. Executive Order 14169 of 20 January 2025 has imposed a '90-day pause in United States foreign development assistance for assessment of programmatic efficiencies and consistency with United States foreign policy' and led to a dismantling of USAID.[6] At the time of writing, legal complaints against this executive order and follow-up decisions were pending,[7] but US foreign assistance has in any case been downsized significantly. According to the Parliamentary Research Services of the European Parliament, in March 2025, 83 per cent of USAID programmes stopped operating. As a consequence, development assistance worldwide is confronted with a funding gap of US$60 billion.[8] Simultaneously, the US commenced a withdrawal procedure from the World Health Organization with Executive Order 14155.[9] With Executive Order 14199 of 4 February 2025, the US (again) stopped funding the UN Relief and Works Agency for Palestine Refugees in the Near East (UNRWA).[10] In the first half of 2025, the US also ended its funding for Gavi—The Vaccine Alliance.[11] While a waiver for emergency humanitarian aid is in place, it 'does not apply to activities that involve abortions, family planning,

[5] UN Charter, preamble.

[6] Federal Register, Vol. 90, No. 19, Thursday, 30 January 2025, Presidential Documents, at 8619.

[7] For an overview of cases <https://www.justsecurity.org/107087/tracker-litigation-legal-challenges-trump-administration/> accessed 29 July 2025.

[8] Members' Research Service of the European Parliament, Cuts in US Development Aid, 25 March 2025, at <https://epthinktank.eu/2025/03/25/cuts-in-us-development-assistance/> accessed 29 July 2025. The information was based on a social media post by Rubio; see Joseph Gedeon, 'Rubio says 83% of USAid programs terminated after six-week purge', *The Guardian* (10 March 2025); <https://www.theguardian.com/us-news/2025/mar/10/marco-rubio-usaid-funding> accessed 29 July 2025.

[9] Federal Register, Vol. 90, No. 18, Wednesday, 29 January 2025, Presidential Documents, at 8361.

[10] Federal Register, Vol. 90, No. 26, Monday, 10 February 2025, Presidential Documents, at 9275.

[11] The New York Times, 'US to End Vaccine Funds for Poor Countries', 26 March 2025; Miriam E. Sunny, Jennifer Rigby, 'US to stop financial support of global vaccine alliance Gavi, health secretary says', *Reuters* (25 June 2025). See also: <https://x.com/SecKennedy/status/1937986463510982869> accessed 29 July 2025.

conferences, . . . gender or DEI ideology programs, transgender surgeries, or other non-life-saving assistance'.[12]

Whereas these efforts to dismantle the development and humanitarian assistance system are unprecedented, severe cuts to financial assistance are also planned elsewhere. By June 2025, eleven member States of the OECD Development Assistance Committee (DAC)—including France, Germany, and the UK—had officially declared reductions in their financial contributions for the next two years.[13] While—for the time being—the World Bank seems not to be affected, all these measures entail long-lasting effects for international humanitarian aid and development cooperation on both a bilateral as well as a multilateral level, given the central role of the US (and Europe) in financing these cooperations.[14]

Against these foundational challenges, this book offers a critical assessment of existing laws, policies, and thinking on how to address protracted conflicts and the hardships they entail for affected communities. These conflicts require new thinking because they share certain characteristics, such as far-reaching civilian harm and vulnerability to international intervention of various forms, that are unique to the contemporary landscape. The contributions to the book demonstrate that the 'protracted conflict' lens helps to understand the legal implications of these conflict dynamics (B). They suggest rethinking international law through a holistic approach (C). While they obviously cannot offer a single definitive solution to overcoming protracted conflicts and securing sustainable peace in view of the vast differences in cultural, economic, environmental, and social contexts, they highlight certain legal, policy, and practical approaches to overcome the significant challenges to the responses of international law and global governance to protracted conflict.

B. Protracted Conflict as a Lens for Research and Application of International Law

While international law involves no distinct category of *protracted* armed conflict, conflict duration merits attention as a multiplying factor of the adverse consequences of armed conflict, as well as due to the shared non-temporal characteristics of such conflicts. In the introduction to this volume, we suggested that 'protracted conflicts' as real-life phenomena are characterized by (i) a certain type of hostilities, which are of a fluid nature over time and space; (ii) root causes such as social inequality, group discrimination, and structural violence; (iii) far-reaching socio-economic and compounded consequences; (iv) resistance to conflict resolution; and (v) vulnerability to and dependence on international intervention. The chapters in this volume provide relevant insights into each of these five characteristics of protracted conflicts,

[12] US Secretary of State, Emergency Humanitarian Waiver to Foreign Assistance Pause, 28 January 2025.

[13] OECD, Policy Brief Cuts in Official Development Assistance, 26 June 2025, 2.

[14] S Haug, A Novoselova, and S Klingebiel (2025) Trump's assault on foreign aid: implications for international development cooperation (IDOS Discussion Paper 4/2025). Bonn: German Institute of Development and Sustainability (IDOS), 13.

demonstrating that the 'protracted conflict' lens is a valuable analytical tool for understanding their legal implications.

Many chapters confirm that protracted conflicts are characterized by intermittent, low-intensity violence that fluctuates over time and geographical areas. The case studies explored in this book, including Colombia, the DRC, Israel–Palestine, the Philippines, and the Sahel, have all seen armed conflicts that persist for decades on end with mutating conflict parties, recurrent violence, and shifting geographical battlefields. This aligns with the normalization of systemic violence in protracted conflicts, where periods of relative normality alternate with active hostilities.

Several authors also identify structural inequality and discrimination as key root causes fuelling protracted conflicts. *Daniëlla Dam-de Jong* highlights how structural economic inequalities and discrimination fuel conflicts over land. *Pablo Kalmanovitz* demonstrates that long-term poverty, marginalization, and institutional fragility fuel not only armed conflicts in the traditional legal sense but also protracted criminal violence that can inflict similarly grave civilian harm. *Patience Kabamba, Pascal Sundi Mbambi*, and *Abhisekh Rodricks* emphasize the postcolonial dimensions of the conflict in the DRC, arguing for a shift from an 'aid regime' to a 'right-based regime' to address systemic inequalities.[15]

Moreover, various chapters discuss the long-term effects of protracted conflicts on livelihoods, infrastructure, the environment, and human development. These conflicts create what *Conrad Schetter* and *Janosch Prinz* call a 'permanent state of complex emergencies' with long-term humanitarian needs. Violent conflicts are often entangled with 'natural disasters, famines, pandemics and food insecurity', not least because fragile statehood leads to infrastructural failure. *Schetter* and *Prinz* note the examples of 'droughts and crop failures (e.g. in Afghanistan, South Sudan, Somalia), floods (e.g. in Afghanistan, Pakistan), tsunamis (in Aceh, Sri Lanka), or earthquakes (in Haiti, Afghanistan, Pakistan)'.[16] Such a nexus of armed conflict, climate change, and long-term environmental degradation is also demonstrated by *Britta Sjöstedt. Sofie Terrey* demonstrates how prolonged conflicts disrupt access to essential services such as water and thereby entail compounded consequences on public health and social stability. Likewise, *Amrei Müller* highlights not only the dire consequences of protracted conflicts for public health and health services but also the challenge of maintaining democratic control of health services and their responsiveness to the actual health needs of local populations in situations of long-term political intractability. *Marc Dubois* refers to these effects as a 'qualitative intensification' of 'the nature of [the] impact on people'.[17]

Protracted conflicts are marked by persistent cycles of violence that defy resolution. Several authors address resistance to conflict resolution as a defining feature of protracted conflicts, and some offer legal pathways to at least facilitate resolution. *Martin Wäehlisch* examines the broad range of approaches at the disposal of the United Nations in responding to protracted conflicts and the limitations and barriers they face. *Amanda Cahill-Ripley* explores the potential of peace agreements as a foundation

[15] Ch. 22 Section A.
[16] Ch. 3 Section C.1.
[17] Ch. 13 Section D.2.

for sustainable peace and development, while *Armi Bayot* demonstrates how social conflict in the broader sense can persist even when an armed conflict formally ends, if peace agreements entrench inequality and discrimination in the pursuit of negative peace.

Finally, several articles address the vulnerability of local populations and dependence on international intervention. Protracted conflicts typically result in heavy reliance on external assistance, creating a cycle of dependency, as *Patience Kabama, Pascal Sundi Mbambi*, and *Abhisekh Rodricks* highlight.[18] A case in point are permanent refugee camps established decades ago to which *Conrad Schetter* and *Janosch Prinz* refer us. These include Dadab and Kakuma in Kenya, Katumba in Tanzania, and Nahr al-Bared in Lebanon.[19] Such dependency frequently marginalizes affected populations further rather than empowering them, an effect often exacerbated by the much-criticized conditionality of international assistance schemes and restructuring programmes.[20] Moreover, the chapter by *Olga Jurasz, Moa Peldán, and Leena Vastapuu* underlines that the effects of protracted conflicts have an even stronger impact on women.

Overall, the chapters predominantly confirm that protracted conflicts exhibit shared characteristics that necessitate tailored legal and policy approaches. Accordingly, the protracted conflict lens is essential for understanding the persistence of these conflicts and their resistance to conventional prevention, regulation, and resolution mechanisms. Aligning with the call of the United Nations Secretary-General to develop 'a more holistic approach to the protection of civilians in armed conflict',[21] these insights raise the question of how to rethink international law through the lens of protracted conflict to account for the compounded nature of physical, social, economic, and environmental issues facing societies entrapped in protracted conflicts in substantive and institutional international legal responses.

C. Rethinking International Law Through a Holistic Approach to Armed Conflict

Overall, the findings of the book are nuanced and sceptical of simple solutions. While they suggest that adopting a holistic perspective on armed conflict may improve legal responses, differing views emerge on how to conceptualize such an approach, and several contributions stress the negative consequences and difficult trade-offs it entails.

In principle, three inter-related ways to conceive of such a holistic approach emerge: one aims to address the compound impact of protracted conflicts by supplementing the protective effects of international humanitarian law (IHL) through other legal frames and to conceive of international law more holistically (C.1); another focuses on the idea of establishing a humanitarian-development-peace (HDP) nexus on

[18] Ch. 22 Section D.

[19] Ch. 3 Section C. 1.

[20] For an overview: Cesare Pinelli, 'Conditionality' in Peters/Wolfrum (eds), *Max Planck Encyclopedia of Public International Law* (OUP 2013).

[21] UNSC, 'Protection of civilians in armed conflict' (Report of the Secretary General) UN Doc S/2024/385 (14 May 2024).

an institutional level to redress the effects of protracted conflicts in a complementary and coherent way, discussing the pitfalls and institutional impediments that remain (C.2); a third relies more explicitly on human rights law to bridge the humanitarian-development-peace divide: the so-called human rights-based approaches that have been adopted by many actors across the different sectors (C.3).

1. Towards a Holistic Reading of the Applicable Legal Frameworks

In order to address the social, economic, and environmental phenomena that often appear both as drivers and consequences of armed conflict, namely in relation to food, health, the environment, and terrorism, many authors in this book suggest a turn from IHL to other bodies of international law, that is, international human rights law (IHRL), international environmental law, or international refugee law, to fill IHL's protection gaps or to complement its protections.

While emphasizing that respect for IHL ensures a significant degree of protection of socio-economic and environmental resources, these analyses reveal the limitations of this body of law. *Antonio Coco* notes that IHL does not contain an absolute prohibition of incidental starvation of civilians and any prohibition of even intentional starvation of enemy fighters. The contribution of *Britta Sjöstedt* shows how environmental harm that is not the direct outcome of hostilities falls outside the scope of IHL's protective remit. To remedy the shortcomings of IHL in addressing the social, economic, and environmental impact of protracted armed conflicts, the suggestion is to turn to IHRL and, in the case of the environment, international environmental law for more comprehensive and holistic protection. However, the application of IHRL, or international environmental law, alongside IHL equally continues to be marked by normative limitations, ambiguities, and contestation. For example, the limitations that naturally flow from the fact that the fulfilment of economic, social, and cultural rights is subject to progressive realization are underlined. Whether non-state armed groups (NSAGs) have obligations under IHRL also remains a significant issue, particularly in the context of protracted conflicts, where populations may live in territories controlled by NSAGs for prolonged periods. On this, *Amrei Müller* explains that 'strong NSAGs/de facto entities may exercise de facto human rights jurisdiction and thus de facto assume the role of human rights duty-bearers' in the context of her exploration of the right to health in protracted conflict.[22]

Mutaz M. Qafisheh and *Jinan Bastaki* demonstrate how a customary law for refugees, derived from human rights law, the laws of nationality, state succession, international humanitarian law, and self-determination, protects the rights of Palestinian refugees, including repatriation and reparation, despite the passage of time and protraction of their refugee status. *Sâ Benjamin Traoré* shows how IHL and IHRL, along with the UN Guiding Principles and the Kampala Convention (African Union Convention for the Protection and Assistance of Internally Displaced Persons in Africa), form a preventive and protective normative framework on IDPs, cautioning,

[22] Ch. 8 Section B.2.g).

however, that this framework is limited to immediate and short-term consequences of displacement and fails to offer transformative and durable solutions. Finally, in the context of terrorism and the overreach of counterterrorism responses, *Ben Saul* emphasizes the need to mainstream human rights across all related areas, including peace and security and development. He explains that although the UN's counterterrorism policy has increasingly aimed for a more 'holistic and balanced approach', human rights and the rule of law remain marginalized and are at times actively undermined.

In addition to a turn to other legal frames, many authors explore the promise of systemic and holistic approaches that are being developed in international law and global governance to address the adverse socio-economic, environmental, and human rights impact of armed conflicts. *Antonio Coco* draws attention to Resolutions 2417 and 2573 of the Security Council that acknowledge the complex relationship between food (in) security and armed conflict and the centrality of both IHL and IHRL in addressing this complex relationship, as well as to the Food and Agriculture Organization's Framework for Action for Food Security and Nutrition in Protracted Crises as a source of helpful guidance for effective preventive and proactive responses to food crises. The Framework approaches food crises not only through the prism of immediate humanitarian needs but also of complex root causes, gender dynamics, and peacebuilding needs. *Britta Sjöstedt* explores the ILC's draft principles on protection of the environment in relation to armed conflicts, which adopt a comprehensive approach in material (drawing not only on IHL but also on other areas and more general principles of international law such as IHRL, international environmental law, and indigenous rights), temporal (considering also pre- and post-conflict phases), and personal (addressing not only the responsibilities of states but also of NSAGs and IOs) terms. *Ben Saul* considers how the UN's 2006 Global Counter-Terrorism Strategy and the Secretary-General's Plan of Action to Prevent Violent Extremism of 2015 aim to address the root causes of terrorism and to ensure respect for human rights and the rule of law in counterterrorism. Finally, in light of the nexus of climate change, conflict, and displacement particularly in the Sahel, *Sâ Benjamin Traoré* points out the emerging recognition of this nexus by the Security Council and the relevance and limitations of the United Nations Framework Convention on Climate Change and the Paris Agreement as the primary international forum for shaping the global response to climate change.

All this is not to suggest that these developments represent ideal blueprints: to the contrary, the authors critically assess the limitations and shortcomings of these developments. Yet, these can nevertheless be read as signs of a growing acknowledgement of the breadth and interconnectedness of drivers and consequences of protracted conflict, however imperfect or perhaps even counterproductive these developments may be in some respects. Overall, within this landscape, there seems to be a growing emphasis on the need for national and/or local empowerment in international responses.

2. The Promises and Pitfalls of the Triple Nexus

While the approaches above aim at a more holistic interpretation of the pertinent legal frameworks, another attempt to meet the challenges of protracted conflicts comes from an institutional perspective via the HDP triple nexus. As elaborated in the Introduction, the triple nexus aims at a 'stronger integration and coordination across the Humanitarian–Development–Peacebuilding spectrum'.[23] *Marc DuBois* argues the nexus could enable common practices that are built on 'intentional . . . complementarity . . . and an understanding of how . . . efforts might undermine, reinforce or explicitly contribute to the efforts of the other sectors'.[24] He offers a critical reappraisal of humanitarianism, challenging the prevailing orthodoxy that views humanitarian principles as impediments to nexus integration. He rejects the argument that the nexus would imperil the neutrality and impartiality of humanitarian actors. Humanitarian institutions fear that a certain dominance of the peace paradigm and the more political nature of the development paradigm might put the compliance with humanitarian principles at risk and thus endanger access to affected communities. In view of the more political goals of the other two branches, there is a concern that they may steer the distribution of humanitarian assistance. However, according to the author, the triple nexus can be conceived in a way that could guarantee compliance with the basic principles of humanitarian relief. He argues for a context-sensitive and compromise-based application of these principles. Thus, he favours an interpretation of the principle of humanity which is rooted in the recognition of shared human dignity, not as a sectoral possession but as a normative anchor capable of guiding all three sectors. This is even more so since most operational obstacles eventually stem from differences in the institutional cultures. This reconceptualization positions humanitarian principles (and international humanitarian law, to the extent that it embeds these principles) not as a constraint but as a potential enabler of inter-sectoral complementarity, particularly in protracted crises where separation of mandates undermines effective response.

Based on case studies in northern Central America, *Pablo Kalmanovitz* highlights the dissolution of established boundaries between peace and war in relation to protracted criminal violence. Although—so far—the ICRC and the World Bank have not cooperated in these cases, the author argues for a nexus approach as a more effective means to get access to affected communities. Eventually, a nexus approach might help to neutralize securitization policies pursued by governmental actors. He emphasizes the parallel challenges arising in situations of protracted violence and protracted armed conflicts for humanitarian support, development aid, and peace processes so that a triple-nexus approach may seem like an adequate response although both constellations still differ in terms of the trade-offs that arise from the different legal classifications. In cases of gang violence, three challenges for humanitarian aid and development cooperation stick out: first, it is the 'unpredictability of violence' that poses specific dangers to humanitarian relief; second, the reluctance of governments to acknowledge the humanitarian consequences of protracted criminal violence hinders effective redress; third, for humanitarian actors, the extent to which they should remain neutral is challenged in situations where only state actors will be able to ensure human rights protection.[25] Similarly, seeing potential benefits in a triple-nexus

[23] Eric Sanchez Garcia, 'Unpacking the Peace Pillar of the Triple Nexus' (2022) 33 Development in Practice 328, 328; Ch. 1 Section E.
[24] Ch. 13 Section D.1.
[25] Ch. 5 Section E.

approach, *Olga Jurasz, Moa Peldán, and Leena Vastapuu* argue that such an approach may facilitate more adequate responses to gendered effects of armed conflicts in the current international institutional architecture. While they claim that implementing the triple nexus was long overdue from a feminist perspective, they fear that the current approach will nonetheless not yield many consequences because of its non-legal nature. However, they still hope that the nexus perspective on international law will help to smother the effects of legal fragmentation.

In contrast, *Schetter* and *Prinz* warn against the risk that the triple nexus is exploited for political purposes. They highlight the crisis that has affected humanitarian relief because the characteristics of protracted armed conflicts impact the principles of humanity, impartiality, and neutrality. Where humanitarian aid is delivered across decades, it risks becoming integrated into the war economy, substituting the state in welfare matters, and thereby eventually contributing to a perpetuation of the conflict. Under such circumstances, humanitarian aid also faces the serious risk of politicization and securitization. *Schetter* and *Prinz* underline, in particular, the risk that the interests of donors or the state government instead of those of the affected populations will be key in the decision on the distribution of humanitarian aid. Against this background, both fear that the triple nexus will get more entangled with war instead of peace, which will ultimately hinder its success. Provocatively, they foreshadow a 'humanitarian aid-development-war nexus' where the nexus is predominantly utilized by security actors.[26]

Adding to the critique of *Schetter* and *Prinz*, others are highly critical of the consequences the nexus entails for the expansion of the mandates of financial institutions, in particular, the World Bank. *Kathryn Greenman* argues that the triple nexus, rather than overcoming institutional silos, fosters a problematic understanding of protracted conflicts because they are seen 'as an ahistorical and technical risk to be managed'.[27] By alleging that protracted conflicts are a new 'risk' phenomenon, policymakers aim to establish practices that would otherwise have met with resistance. She claims that in the case of protracted conflicts, this shift allows for an enlargement, in particular, of the mandates or at least the influence of international financial institutions and a privatization of humanitarian governance. She makes the critique that the turn to risk management as a response to protracted conflicts is used as a pretext to foster market-friendly responses and, as a result, enable further international intervention.

Ansgar Münichsdorfer's analysis of the World Bank reinforces Greenman's findings as he demonstrates how legal interpretation functions as a strategic tool for institutional mandate expansion. The Bank's invocation of the triple nexus and the concept of protracted conflict serves to dissolve the legal binaries underpinning its Articles of Agreement, thereby legitimizing operations in conflict-ridden situations over the past twenty-five years. Previously, the World Bank did not work in conflict-affected situations due to the prohibition in its Articles of Agreement upon interference with political affairs. However, (re-)conceptualizing certain contexts as instances of protracted yet fluid violence allowed the Bank to argumentatively sidestep the restriction limiting its activities to the post-conflict segment. While humanitarian assistance

[26] Ch. 3 Section E.1.
[27] Ch. 2 Section A.

was earlier seen to be 'non-productive' according to the Bank's mandate, the turn to a relief-development continuum allowed for activities in humanitarian crises and for integrating the triple nexus into the World Bank's policies. According to *Münichsdorfer*: 'The notion of protracted conflict has thus helped to frame humanitarian activities as "productive" and "developmental", which is relied upon to legally justify the expansion of operations in humanitarian emergencies.'[28] Yet, the author also highlights the limits of this legal elasticity: the Bank's constant prioritization of economic stabilization and privatization, coupled with its selective engagement with conflict sensitivity, underscores the persistence of a state-centric, risk-averse institutional logic. Thus, the Bank continues to apply its conventional policies in situations of protracted conflict, including its conditionality policies and policy reforms based on a neoliberal agenda. *Münichsdorfer* criticizes that—as a consequence of these approaches—the World Bank on occasions even engages in operations that might contribute to a surge in violence.

In line with these findings, *Johanna del Pilar Cortés-Nieto, Andrés Gómez-Rey, Rafael Alberto Tamayo-Álvarez,* and *Andrés Rodríguez-Morales* also voice harsh criticism of what they perceive as a liberal agenda of some development actors. They explore USAID discourses on liberal peace in Colombia and argue that the asymmetrical impact USAID has exercised in Colombia excludes the possibility of creating different and more suitable approaches for the country and negatively impacts concepts of a territorial peace that were brought forward during the peace negotiations. The idea of territorial peace builds on the approaches and networks of local communities instead of those of donors, and on local and indigenous knowledge and practices. Starting from the idea that an imperialist rationality is imprinted into international law, they warn that the triple nexus will only be effectively implemented if it breaks away from its entanglement with international law's imperial traits and the interests pursued by donors. However, they demonstrate that the HDP nexus is still based on the narrative that the '"backwards" and "uncivilized" [societies in the Global South need to be] subjected to modernization projects'.[29] To overcome this entanglement, they argue in favour of a vision of territorial peace instead of liberal peace, which they deconstruct as an instrument to transfer a certain conception of governance to the Global South.

Martin Wäehlisch turns to the United Nations, examining how the organization's evolving engagement with protracted conflict through peacekeeping, conflict prevention, and SDG implementation intersects with the triple nexus. While international law provides a normative framework for such engagement, the author underscores the practical and structural impediments to its realization. His analysis draws a critical distinction between international law as a body of norms and the multilateral system as its institutional vehicle, suggesting that the latter's limitations often impede the former's effectiveness in complex conflict environments. In this respect, he emphasizes the following key challenges to the meaningful realization of the triple nexus within the UN: coordination between UN agencies and international organizations given the complex and decentralized nature of the UN system; insufficient and imbalanced resource allocation across the humanitarian, development, and peace

[28] Ch. 14 Section B.1.b).
[29] Ch. 6 Section B.

pillars; ensuring local ownership and participation through delicate diplomacy and context sensitivity; and measuring the impact of triple-nexus initiatives and ensuring accountability. *Wäehlisch* also underlines that peace, development, and humanitarian efforts may not always be mutually reinforcing, especially in the unpredictable contexts of deeply rooted conflicts and political instability.

Héloïse Guichardaz interrogates the legal architecture of institutional immunities, focusing on the asymmetries they produce within the nexus. The UN's de facto absolute immunity, she argues, not only undermines accountability but also distorts the institutional ecology of the nexus by privileging the UN over other international organizations that do not benefit from such immunity. While the limitation of immunity is often framed as a pathway to accountability, the author cautions against simplistic solutions, noting that both overreach and underreach in immunity carry risks for inter-sectoral and multi-organization collaboration and presence in situations of protracted conflict.

Taken together, these chapters reveal the ambivalent role of international law in the triple nexus. Rather than treating law as a neutral backdrop to institutional efforts across humanitarian-development-peace sectors to achieve closer collaboration and coherence, the contributions foreground the constitutive role of international law in shaping institutional mandates, operational boundaries, and inadequate accountability structures in contexts of protracted conflict. Law then appears neither as a mere constraint nor a panacea; it is a site of contestation, interpretation, and institutional strategy. A more reflexive and context-sensitive engagement with international law may offer a pathway toward more coherent, accountable, and effective institutional responses to protracted conflicts and their humanitarian consequences.

3. Human Rights-Based Approaches

A third approach relies on a conceptualization of humanitarian, peace, and development objectives in terms of rights-based approaches to overcome siloed thinking. As compared to the turn to IHRL explained in Part C.1, which predominantly concerns the expansion of protections during conflict, the rights-based approaches addressed in this part focus on international assistance in protracted conflict settings and on conflict resolution.

Initiating the discussion within this section, *Andreas Buser* analyses whether a common 'human rights language' in this respect can provide a shared normative foundation for the formulation of overarching objectives in the humanitarian, development, and peace sectors to facilitate cooperation and policy alignment. In particular, his contribution examines the legal framework of rights-based approaches to international assistance across humanitarian, peace, and development sectors, focusing on the UN, the World Bank, and the ICRC. He finds that the rights to development, to peace, and to humanitarian assistance are discussed in isolation from each other and currently fall short of providing a basis for considering recipients of foreign assistance as right-holders or humanitarian, development, and peace actors as duty bearers.

The author also underscores that while sector-specific debates continue over the role of IHRL in guiding humanitarian, development, and peace interventions in legal terms, relevant actors in protracted conflict situations still widely see human rights as a policy commitment focused on improving decision-making rather than a substantive legal duty with mechanisms for implementation and access to judicial review. For example, the World Bank has adopted environmental and social standards requiring its staff and borrowers to assess risks in situations of protracted conflicts but refrained from more wide-ranging reforms, accepting legal accountability, and adopting economic and social rights as a tool to ensure basic needs and services.[30] In other instances, severe shortcomings remain with regard to implementation. *Buser* argues, for example, that the UN increasingly accepts a duty to respect human rights along all its pillars and has adopted due diligence safeguards in line with international law but lacks sufficient (judicial) accountability mechanisms and financial means to compensate for human rights violations of its staff or associated personnel.[31] Thus, despite human rights rhetoric being employed in all three sectors, a common and fully conceptualized human rights-based approach rooted in international law has not emerged. These findings are reinforced by *Patrice Kabamba, Pascal Sundi Mbambi, and Abhisekh Rodricks*, who demonstrate that government officials, international experts, local civil society actors, and academics working on and in the DRC, despite embracing the triple-nexus agenda, have not put people at the centre, and further dialogue is needed to improve implementation.[32]

Shifting the focus from institutional responses to the role of human rights in transforming conflicts, several contributions stress the role of human rights in providing for a longer-term perspective on addressing people's needs in protracted conflicts sustainably, and ultimately in transitioning to peace. *Sofie Terrey* highlights the right to water as a critical but often overlooked aspect of conflict response, advocating for a dual reliance on IHL and human rights law to ensure sustainable access to essential resources. The author underlines that the right to water can function as 'a cross-sectoral legal framework for long-term reconstruction efforts since its content corresponds with the activities of not only humanitarian actors but also, for example, development actors and possibly actors engaged in peacebuilding'.[33] In line with these findings, *Amrei Müller* argues that legal responsibilities and obligations to cooperate, stemming from the right to health, could help in 'overcoming some of the political intractability and thus longevity of protracted conflicts, whilst at the same time promoting processes that address the true local health priorities of the specific local population affected by such conflicts'.[34] *Daniëlla Dam-de Jong* examines the promise of rights-based approaches in addressing land disputes in protracted armed conflicts. While she acknowledges that rights-based approaches may face limitations when concerned governments are complicit in human rights violations, it is nonetheless maintained in this contribution that human rights can provide a facilitative and flexible framework for addressing root causes of armed conflicts, such as inequalities in land distribution

[30] Ch. 17, Section C.2.b).

[31] Ch. 17, Section C.1.; on the UN Human Rights Due Diligence Policy also: Helmut P Aust, 'The UN Human Rights Due Diligence Policy: An Effective Mechanism against Complicity of Peacekeeping Forces?' (2015) 20(1) Journal of Conflict and Security Law 61.

[32] Ch. 22, Section C.

[33] Ch. 18, Section B.1.

[34] Ch. 8 Section D.

policies, and provide safeguards for setting up institutional mediation mechanisms for land disputes.

Two contributions turn the focus to peace agreements—instruments which are concluded in the process of transitioning from protracted conflict to peace but are often limited in what they offer for durable or sustainable peace due to tensions between the requirements of negative and positive peace, limitations of agreement design and content, and the recurrent nature of contemporary conflicts. *Armi Beatriz Bayot's* contribution presents IHRL as a normative framework for positive peace, which requires 'a community-wide system or structure, such as a well-functioning state government, that ensures equality, inclusivity, and justice',[35] and argues that power-sharing arrangements that exclude political minorities, such as indigenous peoples, undermine positive peace and IHRL. The author's account of the Bangsamoro peace processes in the Philippines, which led to a power-sharing agreement and cessation of hostilities but at the expense of 'indigenous peoples' rights and their ancestral domain claims', challenges the assumption that positive peace would follow negative peace. *Amanda Cahill-Ripley* explores whether and how peace agreements can provide a foundation for sustainable peace and development. Her content analysis of some 2,000 peace agreements concluded between 1990 and 2023 reveals that 43 per cent of these agreements included specific provisions for sustainable development and humanitarian assistance. While the author highlights 'the disparity between theoretical transformative provisions within comprehensive peace agreements and the reality of spoilers and resumption of conflict', she holds nonetheless that peace agreements can provide a starting point for building sustainable peace and development should frameworks for policy and implementation, funding, international assistance, and involvement and measures for equality and special protections be included in an agreement.[36]

D. Future Research

Despite increasing recognition of the distinct nature of contemporary protracted conflicts, existing legal frameworks remain ill-equipped to address their complexity. While IHL and IHRL provide general norms applicable to armed conflicts, they hardly account for the protracted nature of many contemporary conflicts, nor the compounded consequences that stem from their persistence. Legal scholarship has to further explore protracted conflicts as a distinct phenomenon and sufficiently address key legal blind spots in relation to the conduct of hostilities, accountability, the role of economic and social rights, or the intersection between protracted conflicts, global challenges such as climate change, and the impact of geopolitical changes on conflict dynamics and consequences. This section identifies persisting research gaps and suggests necessary trajectories for future legal inquiry.

While many contributions in this volume have identified weaknesses and shortcomings of IHL in addressing protracted armed conflicts and their compounded consequences, no contribution casts any doubt that IHL remains the primary legal

[35] Ch. 20, Section B.1.
[36] Ch. 21 Section G (Conclusion).

framework in this respect. In its 2024 Challenges Report, the ICRC highlights the 'cumulative, immediate and long-term, and widespread' consequences of [contemporary] warfare as a key challenge to IHL.[37] There remains a need to investigate fully whether and how existing rules of IHL can respond to distinct characteristics of protracted conflicts identified in this book, such as the prolonged and intermittent nature of violence and far-reaching socio-economic and compounded consequences of conflict. Such investigation can range in focus from the rules governing the conduct of hostilities to special protection regimes (e.g. in situations of prolonged occupation[38]) and from weapons law to accountability for wartime conduct, and beyond. The increasing attention in literature to cumulative civilian harm is a step in this direction.[39] In addition, cases relating to ongoing protracted armed conflicts before international courts will likely bring new questions to the fore.[40]

Second, the future of international humanitarian and development assistance is another line of research that needs to be further deepened. The contributions in this volume are the first to address some of the questions emerging from the process of transformation of international assistance, which has seen humanitarian and development assistance converge. The triple-nexus efforts on the international level have prompted many development and humanitarian organizations to collaborate. For example, the ICRC and the World Bank have entered into a partnership in 2018 and operational collaborations in the DRC, Myanmar, Somalia, South Sudan, and Yemen to date.[41] As these collaborations expand and extend, there will be a need for further empirical and legal studies.

While the humanitarian sector has evolved considerably in the past decades to meet wide-ranging needs with a long-term vision and to collaborate with development organizations, humanitarians are currently unable to address even the most basic needs in dire humanitarian crises such as those in Gaza and Sudan. The fragility of the legal framework that centres on state consent, threats to impartial humanitarian assistance, privatization of humanitarian aid as with the 'Gaza Humanitarian Foundation', and shrinking of assistance budgets will continue to require new thinking and mechanisms.[42] As to development assistance, normalization and protraction of violence in

[37] ICRC, 'International Humanitarian Law and the Challenges of Contemporary Armed Conflicts (ICRC Report)' (2024) 927 IRRC 1357, 1393–94.

[38] See on the right to self-determination and the consequences of prolonged occupation: *Legal Consequences arising from the Policies and Practices of Israel in the Occupied Palestinian Territory, including East Jerusalem* (Advisory Opinion) 2024 <https://www.icj-cij.org/case/186> accessed 31.08.2025, paras 103–120, 243, 257.

[39] See eg Fionnuala Ní Aoláin, 'Cumulative Civilian Harm in Gaza: A Gendered View' (*Just Security*, 25 June 2025) <https://www.justsecurity.org/115407/cumulative-civilian-harm-gaza-gendered-view/> accessed 29 July 2025.

[40] ICC Pre-Trial Chamber II, Situation in Ukraine ICC-01/22 <https://www.icc-cpi.int/situations/ukraine> accessed 31 August 2025; ICC Pre-Trial Chamber II, Situation in Darfur, Sudan ICC-02/05 https://www.icc-cpi.int/darfur accessed 31 August 2025; ICC Pre-Trial Chamber I, Situation in the State of Palestine ICC-01/18 <https://www.icc-cpi.int/palestine> accessed 31 August 2025; *Obligations of Israel in relation to the Presence and Activities of the United Nations, Other International Organizations and Third States in and in relation to the Occupied Palestinian Territory* (Advisory Opinion of 22 October 2025) <https://www.icj-cij.org/case/196> accessed 24 February 2026.

[41] ICRC, 'Sustaining Engagement and Impact in Conflict-Affected Contexts Through the World Bank–ICRC Partnership' (*ICRC*, 2024) <https://www.icrc.org/en/publication/4751-sustaining-engagement-and-impact-conflict-affected-contexts-through-world-bank-icrc> accessed 29 July 2025.

[42] ICRC (n 26) 70–75.

many situations around the world will likely lead to further involvement of development organizations in such settings. Questions around the evolution of mandates and operational legal frameworks, as well as securitization of development assistance, particularly in the current international political climate, are likely to remain significant.

Finally, the dire consequences of climate change and other planetary crises[43] and their legal implications as root causes for protracted conflicts remain underexplored. Many conflicts occur in regions prone to environmental degradation, where climate-induced displacement overlaps with conflict-induced displacement, and populations will increasingly struggle to adapt to changing environmental conditions, or be unable to adapt because of existing vulnerabilities or simply because the climatic conditions become unbearable. Future research could explore in greater depth how legal and policy responses may adequately account for these challenges without necessarily 'securitizing' planetary crises.[44]

E. Concluding Remarks

Contributions to this edited book reveal the Janus-faced nature of the pursuit of the humanitarian, development, and peace nexus in protracted conflict. On one hand, root causes and consequences of protracted conflicts point to an inextricable link between underdevelopment, chronic absence of negative peace, and dire humanitarian consequences of conflict. Contributions on food, water, health, the environment, displacement, and land in particular underline the interconnectedness of drivers, needs, and responses relating to the humanitarian, development, and peace realms as they are experienced in reality. Then, addressing humanitarian needs, investing in sustainable development, and achieving sustainable peace do appear as mutually reinforcing endeavours. On the other hand, critical (realist) perspectives remind us of the ultimately political nature of humanitarian, development, and peace objectives, and how they may clash with each other and become instrumentalized by hegemonic, neoliberal, interventionist, or securitizing agendas. A common theme that is central to many contributions in the book is the need to overcome such approaches, which may appear in the guise of the triple nexus or human-rights-based approaches to development, humanitarian, and peace cooperation, and instead to pursue 'a vision of peacebuilding from the victims' and local rural populations' point of view [that] seeks to overcome the political, economic, and social conditions that have facilitated enduring violence, such as poverty, inequality, marginalization, and exclusion'.[45] In light

[43] UNFCCC Secretariat, 'What is the Triple Planetary Crisis?' <https://unfccc.int/news/what-is-the-triple-planetary-crisis> accessed 29 July 2025.

[44] For a critique of such 'securitization' eg: Cusato, 'Of Violence and (In)visibility: the Securitisation of Climate Change in International Law', London Review of International Law (2022) 10(2) 203–42.

[45] Ch. 6 Section C (text accompanying fn. 50); with reference to Heriberto Cairo and others, '"Territorial Peace": The Emergence of a Concept in Colombia's Peace Negotiations' (2018) 23 Geopolitics 464; María Carolina Olarte-Olarte, 'From Territorial Peace to Territorial Pacification: Anti-Riot Police Powers and Socio-Environmental Dissent in the Implementation of Colombia's Peace Agreement' (2019) 67 Revista de Estudios Sociales 26; Arlene B Tickner, 'Choque Ontológico y Paz Decolonial' *El Espectador* (Bogotá, 24 February 2016) <https://www.elespectador.com/opinion/columnistas/arlene-b-tickner/choque-ontologico-y-paz-decolonial-column-618449/> accessed 19 May 2023; also: Ch. 22.

of these findings, we hope this volume offers readers insights into an alternative vision of (legal) responses to protracted conflict: one that is responsive to the structural drivers of protracted violence and the resultant far-reaching civilian harm, while empowering affected communities to design and implement strategies based on their own experience, knowledge, and practices.

Index

For the benefit of digital users, indexed terms that span two pages (e.g., 52–53) may, on occasion, appear on only one of those pages.